THE
60s
UNPLUGGED

THE
60s
UNPLUGGED

A KALEIDOSCOPIC HISTORY
OF A DISORDERLY DECADE

GERARD DEGROOT

MACMILLAN

First published in the United States 2008 by Harvard University Press

First published in Great Britain 2008 by Macmillan
an imprint of Pan Macmillan Ltd
Pan Macmillan, 20 New Wharf Road, London N1 9RR
Basingstoke and Oxford
Associated companies throughout the world
www.panmacmillan.com

ISBN 978-1-4050-5521-5

A CIP catalogue record for this book is available from
the British Library.

Printed and bound in the UK by
CPI Mackays, Chatham ME5 8TD

To my family—

a fine example of a durable institution

ACKNOWLEDGMENTS

The term "unplugged" began as a reference to concerts involving rock musicians who set aside their electric instruments and used mainly acoustic ones. The term has since come to mean something unprocessed, natural, and raw. That is my aim. This book is the Sixties unplugged, free of the amplifiers, synthesizers, and filters that hide imperfection and distort meaning. No book that I have written has brought as much joy and provoked as much regret. The size of the task at times threatened to overwhelm me, but I got by with a lot of help from my friends. I extend sincere thanks to Michael Fisher and George Morley, my editors, for all their support and encouragement. Maria Ascher was the most agreeable and supportive copyeditor with whom I have worked. Lotte Veldhuis translated sources in Dutch, while Hannah Hurley and David Onkst helped with research. William McKeen read the manuscript and came to the rescue at an opportune moment. Ingo Cornils, Eric Zolov, and Stephen Tyre read various parts, while Natalie DeGroot checked footnotes and found photos (for a fee). For other favors, small and large, I want to thank Katrin Buchmann, Rob Duncan, Sylvia Ellis, Lisa Ford, Bertram Gordon, Peter Hennessy, Chris Hill, Angus Johnston, James Kennedy, Peter Kuznick, Dirk Moses, Tommy Muggleton, Barbara Neeson, Niek Pas, Andrew Pettegree, Marty Sherwin, Will Skjott, Hew Strachan, Barbara Tischler, Nella Van Dyke, and Clare White. Finally, thanks again to my family—Sharon, Natalie, and Josh—this time for allowing a motley collection of Sixties characters into our home.

CONTENTS

THE
60s
UNPLUGGED

INTRODUCTION

"If you remember the Sixties," quipped Robin Williams (and quite a few others), "you weren't there." He was referring, of course, to the haze created by all those mind-expanding drugs the beautiful people popped, mainlined, and smoked. In truth, however, time has proved an equally effective hallucinogen. As years go by, real events have given way to imagined constructs. The decade has been transformed into a morality play, an explanation of how the world went astray or, conversely, how hope was squandered. Problems of the present are blamed on myths of the past.

Memory acts like a filter, yielding a clearer image of the past. The impurities are removed, producing a distillation both logical and meaningful. We forget, for instance, that back then the music business made a lot of money from silly songs like "Yummy, Yummy, Yummy," or that Sergeant Barry Sadler's "Ballad of the Green Berets" outsold "Give Peace a Chance." We remember the Students for a Democratic Society but forget the Young Americans for Freedom. We recall Che Guevara's success in Cuba but not his humiliation in Bolivia. Power, we decide, was exercised by radical students, not right-wing workers. The decade belongs to Kennedy and Dubček, not Reagan and de Gaulle.

This book is the history of a decade, not of an idea. The Sixties is, strictly speaking, a period of 3,653 days sandwiched between the Fifties and the Seventies. It is also, unfortunately, a collection of beliefs zealously guarded by those keen to protect something sacred. Idea has been turned into ideology, with the effect that the Sixties has come to be defined not by time but by faith. Believers object violently to any attempt to redefine the decade, dismissing rebel analysts as reactionary, revisionist, or neoconservative. For forty years, a battle has raged over ownership of the decade, with those who dare to question hallowed truths bombarded with a fusillade of consecrated dogma. In no other period of history has canon been allowed so freely to permeate analysis.

Ownership is often asserted with reference to age. "You weren't there; you can't possibly understand" passes for effective rebuttal, even among those who think themselves serious historians. Apply that logic further and my colleagues in medieval history would be out of a job. In fact, I was there. My earliest memory is the morning after John Kennedy's defeat of Richard Nixon in November 1960. I can vividly recall gazing into the sky, desperately hoping to see Yuri Gagarin's space capsule passing over San Diego. Granted, my age (I was born in 1955) made me an observer of the decade more than a participant in it. But none of this is remotely relevant. The important point is that I have formed my opinions on the basis of recent research rather than on golden memories of a life once lived.

The past is what happened—history the way we view it. For too long, the Sixties has been a sacred zone. The spotlight has been shone upon those people or events we would like to believe were important. But cast aside the rose-tinted spectacles and we see mindless mayhem, shallow commercialism, and unbridled cruelty. China's Cultural Revolution was one of the worst atrocities of the twentieth century. The Six-Day War made victims of every nation in the Middle East. In Indonesia, one million people were slaughtered at the temple of greed. An accurate timeline of the decade is packed with events not normally identified with Sixties iconography. How many people, when considering those times, think about Sharpeville, the Gaza Strip, Vatican II, Tlatelolco, Biafra, Jakarta, Curt Flood, or the cannibals of Guangxi? People remember where they were when Kennedy was shot, but most cannot recall the year Reagan was elected governor of California. Yet that election was far more important in shaping the world we live in today.

Nostalgia for the Sixties is strong precisely because so much did not survive. The decade is important for reasons most people do not understand, or care to admit. Revolution was never on the cards. The door of idealism opened briefly and was then slammed shut, for fear of what might enter. Chauvinism and cynicism got the better of hope and tolerance. The Sixties was the time when the postwar consensus began to disintegrate, when society polarized and liberalism went into steep decline. Perhaps the most enduring bequest of the decade is the convenient gallery of scapegoats it provided. To this day, people have been eager to blame their problems—moral decay, crime, violence, and the plight of the family—on a permissive generation of misfits, delinquents, and revolutionaries more powerful in myth than they ever were in life.

The Sixties was a drama acted out on many stages. The extent to which it has coherence relies in large part on the efforts of subsequent analysts to assign it meaning and structure. The act of writing a book can unfortunately provide the illusion of order; random, chaotic events are linked together in narrative, whose structure implies a continuum that never actually existed. Disparate actions examined under one analytical microscope often suggest a harmony not present at the time. Significance is manufactured through retrospective examination, and connections are easily assumed.

The central point of this book is that most of what happened in the 1960s lacked coherent logic. In order to convey this, I have resisted the temptation to impose order. I have instead presented a tour of the 1960s, an impressionistic wandering through the landscape of a disorderly decade. The tour includes many stops not usually on the Sixties itinerary. Inclusion has been decided on the basis of whether an event happened during the decade, not whether it harmonizes with the idea of the decade. Though there is a vague chronology, causal assumptions are not allowed to intrude upon the journey. This approach might annoy those who like their history linear, who crave a concrete thesis, and who want all the dots connected, all answers provided. But thesis is too often a mask for agenda, a tendency especially noticeable in Sixties scholarship. My thesis is very simple: I feel that too much has been left out of the Sixties portrait, and the omissions have given rise to a misleading, reductive image. What is made of my new revelations, whether they are incorporated into a fresh synthesis or simply ignored, is inevitably up to the reader.

Imagine a kaleidoscope, a brilliantly simple invention capable of conveying complex patterns. It consists of a tube, a lens, some beveled mirrors, and a collection of colored pieces of glass. Look through the lens, and a distinct pattern appears. Twist the end cap and a totally different pattern, a reality equally logical, emerges. That is the effect I have tried to achieve with this book. My short sections, sixty-seven of them in all, were designed to stand alone, and are not linked by continuous narrative. They are the shiny pieces of glass capable of being arranged into myriad realities. How they are arranged depends in large part on the way the reader manipulates the kaleidoscope.

The Sixties Unplugged is not an international history of the decade. I'm not sure such a venture is possible within the confines of a manageable book. Spreading the coverage uniformly across the period and around the globe would result in analysis too thin. My first draft had more than 100 sections and was over 350,000 words, much to the horror of my editors. I removed the equivalent of a good-sized book in order to arrive at this slimmed-down version. It is easy to produce 1,500 pages on the Sixties, as some authors have demonstrated. But legitimacy is not a by-product of length, or of width. While this is not an international history of the decade, it is certainly more global than any book previously produced. It is also, as such, an effective antidote to the hundreds of books so far published which would have us believe that "the Sixties" was a phenomenon confined to the United States. The insularity of so much Sixties scholarship has hindered an understanding of the global implications of the decade.

Books are often judged by what they neglect. I am fully aware of gaps in my chronicle. I could find no room for Angela Davis, Enoch Powell, England '66, the Profumo Affair, the Human Be-In, Andy Warhol, Jean-Paul Sartre, Günter Grass, Stanley Kubrick, or Monterey Pop. I also realize that my ambitious scope occasionally leads to unavoidable generalization. Equivocation and nuance are, I fear, easier with 1,000 pages than with 500. Finally, I am aware that I stand to be criticized for not giving due weight to the subtle achievements of the decade's rebels and movements. For that I plead guilty—I did not feel a need to add to the chorus of praise for individuals whose profile was impressive but whose achievements were frail. Readers will notice that I have my own list of heroes, which includes Rachel Carson, Cesar Chavez, Bob Dylan, Robin Morgan, Peter Coyote, Robert Jasper Grootveld, Mary Quant, Robert Kennedy, and Mario Savio. The eclectic nature of that list will, I hope, convince readers that my analysis is driven by no distinct political agenda.

Louis Menand once wrote that the great problem with Sixties scholarship is that it is written by those who care too much about the decade. He called for a history written by someone who doesn't give a damn. On that score, I'm not sure I qualify, certainly not after spending years with a diverse collection of Sixties personalities who inevitably challenge equanimity. I do give a damn, but in a way that I hope will be seen as refreshing.

1

PRELUDES

Torgau: A Brief Moment of Sanity

In a German town called Torgau, one war ended and another refused to begin. An impressive memorial, in a park bordering the River Elbe, marks the event. Frozen in time are American and Russian soldiers shaking hands, in commemoration of their meeting on April 25, 1945. During the Cold War that memorial was irony cast in bronze, a mocking reminder of shattered alliance.

The early spring of 1945 found Soviet and American armies racing toward the Elbe from opposite directions, squeezing the Wehrmacht in the jaws of a mighty vise. At 11:30 on April 25, a US Army patrol led by Lieutenant Albert Kotzebue came across a lone Soviet cavalryman, near the town of Leckwitz. Kotzebue had been ordered not to proceed further than the Mulde River, but, sensing destiny, he decided to press on to the Elbe. At the village of Strehla, he spotted Soviet soldiers on the east bank.

The air was thick with the odor of lilacs and the anticipation of peace. Shouts of "Americanski!" drifted across the water. The two forces traded friendly greetings and flashed the V-for-victory sign. Searching the bank, Kotzebue found a small sailboat chained to a dock. He broke the chain, then gathered five men for the ceremonial crossing. On reaching the opposite bank, they were greeted by Lieutenant Colonel Alexander Gardiev, commander of the 175th Rifle Regiment.

In Kotzebue's party was rifleman Joseph Polowsky. He and his comrades were fully aware that they had stumbled upon destiny. "[We felt] this exaltation of being alive, after all those days trapped in a trench war. There were even jokes that we were approaching the River Jordan, crossing into

Canaan." Someone remarked on the delightful coincidence that the UN Charter was being signed on the very day they crossed that river of concord.[1]

Near the bank was a scene of carnage. Hundreds of bodies were stacked like cordwood. Polowsky did not know who was responsible and, under the circumstances, did not want to know. He would forever remember a single image: "a little girl clutching a doll in one hand. . . . She couldn't have been more than five or six years old. And her mother's hand in the other."[2]

None of the Americans spoke Russian; none of the Soviets spoke English. Their common language was, ironically, German. Messages of peace and goodwill were fired back and forth between the relay points of two German speakers. "It was very informal," Polowsky recalled, "but it was a solemn moment. There were tears in the eyes of most of us. Perhaps a sense of foreboding that things might not be as perfect in the future as we anticipated. We embraced. We swore never to forget."[3]

After solemn oaths came raucous celebration. Wine, beer, and vodka appeared. "We were real drunk, but not because of the liquor." Accordions and guitars materialized. Girls liberated from nearby labor camps broke into traditional Russian dances. Americans sang "Yankee Doodle." "I was so captivated by the event," Polowsky confessed, "that it took possession of me for the rest of my life."[4]

The world found out about Torgau two days later, when photographs of the historic handshake were emblazoned on newspaper front pages. Writing in *Stars and Stripes*, the journalist Andy Rooney remarked: "The Russian soldiers are the most carefree bunch of screwballs that ever came together in an army. They would best be described as exactly like Americans, only twice as much. . . . You get the feeling of exuberance, a great new world opening up."[5]

In fact, the world was closing. Doors briefly ajar were slammed shut, locked, and bolted. Differences, not similarities, suddenly came to the fore. Alliances, having outlasted their usefulness, were quickly dismantled. Away from the battlefront, politicians carved spheres of influence amid an atmosphere thick with distrust.

The harmony that remained was vaporized in the atomic blast that destroyed Hiroshima on August 6. For President Harry Truman the atom bomb seemed the best way to end the Pacific war, but also a chance to make a point to the Soviets. "It seems to be the most terrible thing ever discovered," he remarked of the Bomb, "but it can be made the most useful."[6]

In 1949, the British physicist Patrick Blackett called Hiroshima "not so much the last military act of the Second World War, as the first major operation of the cold diplomatic war with Russia." Joseph Stalin concurred: "Hiroshima has shaken the world. The balance has been destroyed." That was precisely what Truman intended. His secretary of war, Henry Stimson, saw the Bomb as a "master card" in a great game of international poker. "I called it a royal straight flush and we mustn't be a fool about the way we play it."[7]

Winning at poker depended on the United States' retaining the best cards. American "experts" predicted that decades would pass before the Soviets would develop their own bomb, since, as the joke went, they could hardly build tractors. In the meantime, the United States could use the Bomb, as Stimson suggested, "to bring the world into a pattern in which . . . our civilization can be saved." In fact, the American monopoly was short-lived. Thanks in part to the atomic spy Klaus Fuchs, the USSR exploded a bomb in 1949. Truman reacted by demanding a new, more terrible weapon. The thermonuclear bomb, or Super, was born in 1952, but this time the Soviets matched America atom for atom. Nuclear arsenals became a measure of distrust. Bombs were canisters of virility.[8]

During the war, the American propaganda machine had difficulty working out how to portray the Russian allies and their alien political system. The problem was solved by treating them as ordinary individuals—a people, not a nation. They were drawn as decent, hardworking, God-fearing ordinary folk who loved their country—solid, simple people rather like Midwesterners. The propaganda worked. Polls showed that a majority of Americans felt more in common with the Russians than with the stodgy British. Stalin was *Time* magazine's Man of the Year in 1943.

Then, suddenly, Americans were encouraged to hate their erstwhile allies. The Russians became Commies—an extension of their government, by definition evil. *Time* and *Life* provided a constant stream of stories about the horrors of the Soviet Union, while films like *A Foreign Affair* (1947), *Iron Curtain* (1948), and *I Married a Communist* (1949) encouraged viewers to be vigilant about the Red Menace. The shift of emotion left some people confused. "In 1951 I was going to grade school," Bob Dylan reflected.

One of the things we were trained to do was to hide and take cover under our desks when the air raid sirens blew because the Russians could attack us with bombs. We were also told that the Russians could be parachuting from planes over our town at any time. These were the same Russians that my uncles had fought alongside only a few years earlier. Now they had become monsters who were coming to slit our throats and incinerate us. It seemed peculiar. Living under a cloud of fear like this robs a child of his spirit. It's one thing to be afraid when someone's holding a shotgun on you, but it's another thing to be afraid of something that's just not quite real.

The "duck-and-cover" generation did not have to experience the catastrophic war their parents had witnessed. But they were forced to live with an entirely new type of fear. For the first time in history, humans possessed the capacity to render themselves extinct.[9]

Polowsky never forgot his Russians, never learned to hate. He went to his grave believing that something wonderful had happened on the Elbe, when men met as human beings rather than as representatives of antagonistic systems. "I always felt that American-Russian relations were plagued by bad luck right from the beginning. If we had gotten publicity with the oath of the Elbe, there would have been a certain depth in the feelings. Just think of the millions who died on the Russian side and the tremendous effort on the American side, amidst all those dead women and children and that little girl clutching the doll in her hand." For the rest of his life, Polowsky waged a lonely effort to revive the good feelings felt near Torgau. He remained in contact with his Russians, and occasionally visited them, the trips funded by wealthy benefactors from the American peace movement. Every April 25, he stood on the Michigan Avenue Bridge in Chicago distributing leaflets calling for reconciliation with the Soviet Union. He worked tirelessly for nuclear disarmament. He could never understand the ease with which the Russians were transformed into enemies. In order to keep propaganda at bay, he refused to buy a television. Though an intelligent and skilled man, his political views impeded his gainful employment. "My father was a brilliant man, but his obsession for world peace kept him from being able to keep a normal job," his daughter Melissa thought. "He was haunted by what he saw in the war."[10]

Polowsky, who died in 1983, had always insisted that he wanted to be buried in Torgau. But by that time the town was in East Germany, a place not very welcoming to Americans—dead or alive. His family was nevertheless determined to honor his wish, the cost of which ran to $40,000. The money was raised from sympathetic benefactors in the United States and Germany. Later, a school in Torgau was named in his honor.

"He hoped somehow he would make a difference," said his daughter.[11] In that aim, he failed completely. His attempts to encourage understanding resulted in his being labeled a crank, a traitor, a Commie. While people on both sides of the Iron Curtain obediently indulged in hate, Polowsky refused to march in line. In the history of the Cold War, he is a significant anomaly, symbolic of a road not taken.

AT HOME: THE GENERATION GAP

Toward the end of 1945, millions of men made their way home. In America alone, a soldier returned from the war every five seconds. Many went home to wives they hardly knew and children they had never met. Not surprisingly, the family stumbled navigating the ruins of war. Wives surrendered to men who seemed unfamiliar, while children suddenly had to share their mother's attention with a stranger. Marriages made in haste frequently crumbled.

Pressures increased because women had been changed by war. Those who did important work gained a sense of self-worth, not to mention unaccustomed affluence. Female independence frightened those who worried about social stability. A revival of conventionality seemed imperative. Jobs went to returning soldiers, while women who clung to wartime positions were accused of being unpatriotic. In some countries, "baby bounties" were paid to women who had more than one child. State-run daycare centers closed. Child development experts advised that children in crèches were prone to delinquency; those same experts had, during the war, argued that crèches fostered self-reliance.

Saving the family became the responsibility of women. Salvation would come if wives devoted themselves to the home. "Women have many careers, but one vocation—motherhood," Agnes Meyer argued in the *Atlantic Monthly* in 1950. "It is for women as mother, actual or vicarious, to restore the security in our insecure world." In 1955, Adlai Stevenson advised the highly educated women of Smith College that, in the Cold War struggle, "there is much you can do . . . in the humble role of housewife—which, statistically, is what most of you are going to be whether you like it or not just now—and you'll like it!"[12]

Civil defense literature advised women that surviving an atomic attack was more likely in a clean home than in a filthy one. Women's magazines, which during the war had published quick recipes for wholesome meals that Mother could make after her shift at the factory, were suddenly filled with elaborate dishes taking hours to prepare. Articles warned of a new enemy—the germ—and advised Mother to be ever vigilant. Labor-saving devices like the washing machine and vacuum cleaner did not radically reduce time spent on housework, since minutes saved were reinvested in order to satisfy rising expectations of cleanliness.

Wars are always followed by a surge in the birthrate. No wonder, then, that the biggest war in history was followed by the biggest baby boom. Though feminist historians have seen a patriarchal plot, for many women motherhood seemed an affirmative gesture in harmony with the desire to build a new world. Millions got pregnant immediately after the war for the very simple reason that they wanted to be mothers. Men scattered over the battlefields of Europe and Asia felt similar yearnings. Amid the torn metal, screaming shells, and shredded flesh, soldiers kept sane by imagining a little house, a quiet garden, and a child at play.

Ever since 1947, when its true extent became apparent, the baby boom has been like a piglet slowly passing through a python. At each stage in the life of the postwar generation, its effect has been rudely apparent. More births at first meant more beds in maternity wards, more obstetricians, more midwives. Then came a boom in the toy industry, followed by a demand for more primary schools. Suddenly there had to be more Little League and soccer teams, more Brownie and Scout troops. In the 1960s, more universities were needed. Not long after the boom ended, the boomers started having babies, thus producing another blip. Eventually, there will have to be more pension administrators and assisted-living centers, the halls of which will echo with Dylan's "Forever Young."

A large percentage of baby boomers grew up in suburbia. Between 1950 and 1980, 83 percent of America's growth was absorbed by the suburbs, which gained 60 million people. By the end of the 1960s, more people were living in suburbs than in inner cities. In Europe, also, the suburban migration was striking. "It's like heaven," one English suburbanite remarked.

"People today don't know of the time when we had to live in old broken down houses because we could afford nothing better. . . . Today we are given nice little houses to live in." The *Architectural Review* did not, however, agree, warning in 1955 that "by the end of the century, Great Britain will consist of isolated oases of preserved monuments in a desert of wire, concrete roads, cosy plots and bungalows."[13]

In the suburbs, wrote one cynic, "you too can find . . . people whose age, income, number of children, problems, habits, conversations, dress, possessions, perhaps even blood types are almost precisely like yours." Suburbanites, said the left-wing philosopher C. Wright Mills, had been turned into "cheerful robots." Nor did criticism come exclusively from the left. Fearful of the decline of American individualism, the evangelist Billy Graham warned that "mass-produced machinery has given rise to mass-produced man. We are inclined to think like the Joneses, dress like the Joneses, build houses like the Joneses, and talk like the Joneses." The folksinger Malvina Reynolds put that message to music:

> Little boxes on the hillside, little boxes made of ticky tacky,
> Little boxes on the hillside, little boxes all the same.
> There's a green one and a pink one and a blue one and a yellow
> one,
> And they're all made out of ticky tacky and they all look just the
> same.

Critics shouted loudly, but the weight of opinion was against them. Happy suburbanites, freed from the dark recesses of the city, entered their version of paradise. They wanted uniformity, be it in houses, burgers, or beer. If their houses were all alike, that hardly mattered, since so too were their ambitions. For Sam Gordon, who left New York City, Harbor Isle was "heaven on earth." He told his wife: "It's like everyone who is going to live here is the same. Hundreds of families, it's like we all have the same kind of life."[14]

For women, however, the suburban dream often turned sour. Fathers went off to work, children went to school, but mothers stayed in identical boxes, making instant cakes and burning frozen steaks. Many turned in desperation to "Mother's Little Helpers"—tranquilizers designed to help them cope with the grinding monotony. *Newsweek* remarked on the profound dissatisfaction felt by the typical American housewife. "Her discontent is deep, pervasive and impervious to the superficial remedies which are offered at every hand." The journalist Betty Friedan wrote of the "problem that has no name," the symptoms of which were "a strange stirring, a dissatisfied groping, a yearning search that is going on in the minds of women."[15]

Friedan feared that the baby boom and suburbanization would together erase the progress women had made since 1900. She pointed out that by the end of the 1950s, the typical American woman was married by the age of twenty, while average family size steadily increased. In consequence, the proportion of women in higher education was lower in 1958 than in 1920. Among those who did enter university, a high percentage dropped out after they found a man and got married. "What's college?" an ad for the New York department store Gimbel's asked. "That's where girls who are above cooking and sewing go to meet a man so they can spend their lives cooking and sewing."[16]

Other critics argued that mothers were spending too much time mothering, with the result that children were growing up soft, expecting every wish to be fulfilled. Anger was directed in particular at Dr. Benjamin Spock, whose *Common Sense Book of Baby and Child Care* was first published in 1946. Spock encouraged mothers to feed their babies whenever they cried for food, and to cuddle them when they seemed distressed. His methods militated against the working mother, to him an abomination. Nevertheless, for parents desperate to demonstrate their love, his ideas seemed a benediction. By 1956, one-fourth of American parents were religiously following his advice, and European parents were similarly enthusiastic. Spock's ideas harmonized perfectly with the widespread desire among parents to give their offspring a better childhood than they themselves had enjoyed.[17]

The 1950s witnessed a war for the soul of society in which the main battleground was the home. Sociologists, alarmed by the new strains on the family, provided endless advice on how to survive modernity. According to them, the biggest problem was "atomizing"—a term appropriate to an atomic age. The nuclear family seemed in a state of fission. Experts worried that outside attractions would dissolve the bonds that held families together. While the warnings were probably excessively alarmist, many of the crises they foretold did materialize. The family was indeed atomized by an array of enticements. Children did rebel, without apparent cause. Many left home, some with flowers in their hair. By the end of the 1960s, communes were gaining in popularity as a realistic alternative to the nuclear family. The popularity of marriage declined; that of divorce rose.[18]

In truth, however, there were simply too many variables to take into account when trying to understand why baby boomers rebelled. The simple explanation is probably the best. Children born after 1945 grew up in a world profoundly unlike that of their parents. Theirs was an affluent world, even though not all of them enjoyed its riches. It was also generally peaceful. Conflict usually took the form of small wars fought in distant places. Nor was economic depression a concern. "We had no sense of the Depression," Steve McConnell, born in 1947, recalled. "Parents talked about it, but it had no meaning. . . . I had not been aware that this country had ever suffered economically. I've never had a sense of what people go through when the economy goes to hell."[19]

Work was not, therefore, an all-consuming obsession for the middle-class baby boomer. Peter Roberts, who grew up in Britain, recalled his carefree attitude:

> You could bum around without doing any work and then you'd
> think: "Shit! I'd like to go to Morocco so I'd better get a job for a few
> weeks"—and the job was there to be had. Whenever you wanted to
> work, there was a job there. You could give up a job just like that. . . .
> You'd say, "Oh, God, I don't feel like working any more, I don't like
> the guy, I want to go off, I've got too much heavy enjoying to do, I
> haven't got time for work . . ." Then after a while you'd find yourself
> broke and you'd go and get another one. Like you can buy potatoes
> in a supermarket. You don't need to hoard them, because you know
> there's *always* going to be a bag of potatoes there.

Baby boomers in Europe benefited from a security unknown to their parents. Across the Continent, postwar governments built social welfare systems to cushion the blows of economic hardship. Free medical care, free education, and subsidized housing encouraged a sense of well-being and a belief that opportunities abounded. "We'd the full force of the Attlee administration behind us," Angela Carter recalled. "All that free milk and orange juice and cod-liver oil made us big and strong and glossy-eyed and cocky, and we simply took what was due to us whilst reserving the right to ask questions."[20]

In Britain, Prime Minister Harold Macmillan told his people that they had never had it so good. In the United States, Professor David Potter argued in his book *People of Plenty,* that affluence defined the American experience. "We have, per capita, more automobiles, more telephones, more radios, more vacuum cleaners, more electric lights, more bathtubs, more supermarkets and movie palaces and hospitals, than any other nation. Even at mid-century prices we can afford college educations and T-bone steaks for a far higher proportion of our people than . . . anywhere else on the globe." Abundance did not necessarily spell contentment. Parents who had lived through the 1930s undoubtedly appreciated more affluent times, but their children seldom shared their cozy satisfaction. To the young, the older generation's aspirations seemed prosaic; there was, surely, more to life than wall-to-wall carpets and T-bone steaks. An angry seventeen-year-old German complained in 1963 that "this disgusting economic miracle" had given rise to an older generation unable to recognize its superficiality. Young existentialists had a hard time accepting that their parents were actually happy. "Some would have us believe that Americans feel contentment amidst prosperity," asserted the Port Huron Statement, the manifesto of Students for a Democratic Society. "But might it not better be called a glaze above deeply held anxieties about their role in the new world?" Differences of opinion over the definition of "happiness" defined the generation gap.[21]

"To be young in those days," wrote the novelist Sheila MacLeod, "meant to be idealistic, enthusiastic and full of optimism about a future which was to be so dazzlingly, liberatingly different from the hidebound parental past." Baby boomers, once they reached puberty, began questioning their parents' ethos. Voicing the misgivings of his generation, Tom Hayden derided the "material paradise with all things provided, all choices made, everything laid out neatly." Anne McDermid felt herself revolting against the "stultifying complacency of Christian, white, middle-class and aspiring, suburban family life, two children plus a dog and a cat, squeaky clean housewife/mum, firm but kind breadwinning dad, obedient but cheeky children."[22]

Marsha Rowe felt she was living out the "youthful irresponsibility that our parents, who had grown up knowing only war, thrift and responsibility, had been denied." That might have been true—but for most parents, denial had become habit. The older generation did not feel the desire for freedom and frivolity, because asceticism had been forced upon them by circumstances; it became a way of life preserved long after those circumstances improved. "When I want to go out at night," a young German girl complained in 1962, "[my parents] say: 'We were not allowed to go out when we were young.' Thus, I have to stay at home, too. Or, for instance, I would like to have a record player. Then they say: 'We did not have one.' . . . Thus, I do not get one." Parents knew the exact price of a pint of milk long after its cost became irrelevant. That asceticism made it impossible for them to understand their reckless children. To the young, however, parents seemed self-indulgently Spartan—emissaries of denial who reassured themselves that sacrifice was its own reward. The young revolted against a way of life no longer logical. They were able to revolt because affluence made life more secure and provided the choices essential to the experiment with freedom.[23]

The young fashioned their own identity. They dressed differently from their parents, in clothes calculated to offend. They developed a fondness for weird hairstyles, rock and roll, coffeehouses, skiffle bands, Marlon Brando, and James Dean. In the mid-1950s, there was a sudden explosion in the number of young people applying to art schools or buying guitars. Sex was part of the package—sex for pleasure, not for procreation. It became fashionable to feel alienated, to perfect a scowl and to look back in anger. Almost every teenager understood the angst of Holden Caulfield, even if they hadn't read *Catcher in the Rye*. Those who were lonely, bored, neurotic, self-obsessed, or simply hung over now had a glamorous diagnosis for their malady—namely, alienation—an ailment all the more wonderful because it was so utterly resistant to cure.

The parents of the baby boomers were the "Greatest Generation"—or so they told themselves. They had made the ultimate sacrifice in defending democracy against despotism. The best years of their lives had been spent fighting a horrible war. In time, their sacrifice would, like vintage wine, grow ever more sublime. People would forget that most World War II soldiers had been conscripts, that not all had gone to war willingly, or fought nobly. The Greatest Generation set a standard of conduct their children could never possibly equal. Their children had to live in a different age, with entirely different challenges, yet were judged by the values of the 1930s and 1940s. The fact that the young opposed war and questioned their inheritance rankled with their parents. "My father's generation believed . . . that they had defended democracy against *foreign* despotism," wrote Hayden. "We believed that we were defending democracy from its enemies at home."[24]

Something was happening, Mr. Jones, and it was happening all over the world. Christopher Booker called it a "psychic epidemic"—a mass indulgence in novelty. The young went looking for a new world without much idea of what they hoped to find. The characters in Jack Kerouac's *On the Road* perfectly express that naïve optimism:

> "Sal, we gotta go and never stop going till we get there."
> "Where we going, man?"
> "I don't know but we gotta go."

Unlike their parents, baby boomers did not have to grow up quickly; they could indulge themselves at leisure, safe in a protective cocoon. A "rap session" conducted between German teenagers and their parents perfectly encapsulated the generation gap:

> A number of young men suggested that parents should lazily hang around a whole day with them, dance, have fun, "relax," or debate radical political alternatives. "But this is impossible," a father protested to silent approval of the other parents, "I have to go to the office." Once the students suggested he should skip work, he became agitated. Then he would be dismissed and who would earn the money? That they had such a good life was due to him. . . . By and large all parents present were of the opinion that toil and drudgery were the sacrifice that one had to endure for oneself and one's progeny.

The Sixties was a time when the young were addicted to being different; it was a long, exciting summer between youth and maturity when the lure of fantasy had yet to be conquered and novelty was sacred. The times were a-changin', Dylan warned. Parents should get out of the road. "It is your task to acknowledge the hate of your compatriots and to investigate its real origins," the young Dutch novelist Harry Mulisch advised the older generation. "And you will have to do that with the somber realization that your long-term attempts to prop up Christendom have been undone. You are old people. Your indignation and your hate are too old for us. Even your good qualities, which exist primarily of good intentions, are too old for us. You are too old for us. In twenty-five years, thank god, you will be extinct."[25]

Against this onslaught, the older generation felt besieged, as an editorial in the *Sunday Mail* revealed: "For years now we've been leaning over backwards to accommodate the teenagers. Accepting meekly on the radio and television it is THEIR music which monopolizes the air. That in our shops it is THEIR fads which will dictate our dress styles. . . . We have watched them patiently through the wilder excesses of their ban-the-bomb marches. Smiled indulgently as they've wrecked our cinemas during their rock and roll films." On April 30, 1965, an anguished writer in the *Weekend Telegraph* complained that the young had "captured this ancient island and took command in a country where youth had always before been kept properly in its place. Suddenly, the young own the town." Parents were mystified. How had their comfortable world disappeared so quickly? Philip Roth's character Swede Levov despairs at "the daughter who transports him out of the longed-for American pastoral and into everything that is its antithesis and its enemy, into the fury, the violence, and the desperation of the counter-pastoral—into the indigenous American berserk." The Dutch version of that pastoral was called *kleinburgerlijk* and came with its own smell—*spruitjeslucht*—the odor of cooked Brussels sprouts. To the young, that smell evoked perfectly the "sickening, small-minded virtue of bourgeois Holland."[26]

Ambition was a measure of ego. "We're right at the center of everything," one girl remarked. "It's us, we're right in the center reading about ourselves in the newspaper. It's youth. Everything is youth and us." Through rebellion, baby boomers marked out the boundaries of their milieu. For most, rebellion was short-lived, self-centered, and tame, expressed in growing sideburns, wearing jeans, smoking pot, wearing black eyeliner, or listening to the Rolling Stones. Yet for a small number, revolt became seriously political. Wini Breines believed "we could achieve an egalitarian, free and participatory society. . . . We were going to make a revolution." For that group, disenchantment with the world of their parents fueled an all-consuming desire to create a perfect world of their own.[27]

2

PREMONITIONS

ON THE AIRWAVES: TRANSISTOR RADIOS

"The only regret I have about the transistor is its use for rock and roll," Walter Brattain often remarked. The music was bad enough, but the fact that the radios were made in Japan was a peculiar form of torture.[1]

Brattain worked at Bell Labs in New York. There, in December 1947, he and his colleagues John Bardeen and William Shockley invented the transistor. The tiny piece of germanium crystal with two wires poking out of it had the amplification properties of conventional vacuum tubes, but was much smaller, did not produce heat, did not need to warm up, and used a fraction of the energy. Bell Labs formally unveiled the revolutionary component on June 30, 1948, demonstrating its use in, among other things, a radio.

That was the world's first transistor radio. Logic suggests that the prototype should have been snapped up and mass-produced in time for Christmas 1948. But that didn't happen, due to a number of problems. First, transistors were expensive and no one wanted to pay a lot of money for a radio unless it produced great sound, and transistor radios were hardly high-fidelity. Second, the idea of a small radio was not particularly appealing, since listening had always been a group activity. Most families had one big radio—the central feature of every living room.

As a result, the only transistor radios produced over the next six years were built by amateurs. The transistor was recognized as an important invention (Brattain, Bardeen, and Shockley won the Nobel Prize in 1956), but practical uses were slow to materialize. Then, in 1951, Texas Instruments (TI) of Dallas paid Bell $25,000 for a manufacturing license. TI wanted to sell transistors to IBM but first had to prove that it could mass-produce them. Patrick Haggerty, general manager at TI, decided to invest $2 million in a secret project to develop an all-transistor radio which, the company hoped, would furnish the proof IBM needed. The project was given to the engineer Paul Davis, who came up with a prototype in four days. TI then went looking for a firm to manufacture and market it. The big companies like RCA and Philco all rejected the idea, on the grounds that they were already doing well in the radio and television market and did not see any reason to diversify by making a product that would not actually produce better sound. They failed to grasp that, if the radio could fit inside a shirt pocket, the way it sounded was immaterial.

Some years earlier, John Pies and Joe Weaver had started a new company called Industrial Development Engineering Associates, or IDEA, whose aim was to develop civilian applications for wartime technologies. Eventually, Ed Tudor, originally hired to do marketing, took over, while Pies and Weaver concentrated on development. Tudor hated the name IDEA, which he thought sounded like a building contractor, so he changed it to Regency, the name of his favorite cigarettes.

After TI's rebuff by the big manufacturers, the company knocked on Regency's door. Tudor liked the idea of pocket radios, which he thought would prove useful in a nuclear war. He boasted that he could sell 20 million units to the duck-and-cover generation in just three years. In June 1954, Regency and TI signed an agreement to put the world's first mass-produced transistor radio on the market.

Regency fiddled with Davis' design, cut the number of transistors from six to four, and came up with a radio capable of fitting in a shirt pocket. The TR-1 was five inches tall, three inches wide, one and a quarter inches thick and weighed just twelve ounces. It came in a variety of colors and retailed for a rather steep $49.95—battery not included. The new product hit the shops on November 1, 1954. In keeping with its price, it was marketed as a plaything for the wealthy. As a tie-in with the release of the film *Around the World in Eighty Days,* publicity stills of Trevor Howard and Shirley Maclaine, with radio in hand, were used to advertise the TR-1. In June 1955, *Holiday* magazine carried a similarly targeted ad: "He Drives a 300SL; She Charges at Cartier; He's a Letterman in His Junior Year. They All Have This in Common: A Winter Vacation with a Regency Radio."[2]

Journalists poked fun at the product, remarking that it was not quite as small as the one Dick Tracy wore on his wrist. The most damning critique came in *Consumer Reports:* "Though its transmission of speech was adequate under good conditions, its music transmission was quite unsatisfactory under any conditions. . . . At low volume the sound was thin, tinny, and high-pitched and at higher volume distortion increased."[3] Sales, however, soon demonstrated that the press had grossly underestimated the public's desire to hear distorted music. Regency couldn't produce the radios fast enough to keep up with demand. Stores had long waiting lists. The transistor radio, like the mobile phone and the iPod, was popular because it was private—it did not have to be shared. In that sense, it evoked the exclusivity of the new consumer culture. It was a piece of modern technology which doubled as designer wear and said to those who did not own one: "You like this? Get your own."

Before long, the market was flooded with portable radios—none of them, however, quite as portable as the TR-1. Zenith, RCA, and General Electric entered the fray, though they still didn't grasp that size was more important than quality. New models had combinations of transistors and tubes, making them considerably bigger than the TR-1, though they did sound better. Other manufacturers simply ignored the trend, denied that it was a trend, and concentrated on televisions.

The Japanese, however, had no trouble reading the runes. In 1953, a small tape recorder manufacturer called Tokyo Tsushin Kogyo Ltd., or TOTSUKO, convinced the Japanese minister of trade to allow it to purchase a transistor manufacturing license. In August 1955 they came out with their first radio, a limited edition sold only in Japan. A short time later came the TR-63, a genuinely new compact radio made with specially engineered parts. When it proved slightly too big to fit in a shirt pocket, the Japanese put bigger pockets on the shirts of their salesmen. Improved production techniques and cheap labor meant that TOTSUKO could easily compete with American manufacturers. Around this time, the company began calling itself Sony, a name chosen so that Americans could pronounce it.

By 1958, worldwide sales of portable radios exceeded five million, yet some big American manufacturers still steered clear. Seven years later, in 1965, Americans purchased twenty-one million transistor radios, 94 percent of them made in Japan. The transistor was the first American electronic product to be overwhelmed by foreign competition. When baby boomers were young, "Made in Japan" had been synonymous with "second-rate." Japanese radios changed all that. They came on the market precisely when baby boomers were turning into consumers. "Japanese" began to signify quality, innovation, *and* affordability. After purchasing their transistors, boomers proved steadfastly loyal, buying Japanese stereos, televisions, cameras, and eventually cars.

Before long, Regency quit making transistor radios, citing unfair Japanese competition. They had at least recognized a market and tried to exploit it. More inexplicable is the behavior of the industry giants, who decided not to demean themselves by producing portables. It is difficult to imagine how a technological revolution so profound, and in retrospect so obvious, could have been missed by American manufacturers—to such an extent that some were put out of business by Japanese competition. To be fair, American manufacturers had been tooling up for what they thought would be an even more profound communications revolution, namely color television. In this sense, pocket radios seemed hardly worth the effort, since the profit margin was so small. Unfortunately, by the time color TV really took off, the Japanese had such a firm foothold in the electronics market that it was easy for them to dominate that field as well.

The arrival of transistor radios coincided with the emergence of rock and roll, the two trends reinforcing each other. Bill Haley's "Rock around the Clock," released in 1955, was the first rock single to top the American Billboard charts. Elvis Presley had his first chart topper in 1956. The transistor was perfectly suited to the rock invasion, since it allowed the individual to listen in private. For parents, it provided a solution to the great problem of rock and roll. Teenagers who would insist on listening to Elvis on the family's walnut-cased Motorola could instead be sent to their rooms to listen on their Sony, preferably with headphones. For parents, giving a teenager a transistor was an act of self-preservation. Music that was played out of earshot of parents could in turn be more daring. Transistor radios gave baby boomers the facility and confidence to develop their own musical tastes. "I thought the nice part was that . . . there was music on the radio . . . which made my father say, 'What is *this*?'" one Dutch rock fan recalled. "That was of course what you wanted."[4]

In early 1956, *Scholastic* magazine revealed that thirteen million American teenagers had a disposable income of $7 billion a year, which worked out to an average of $10.35 a week. Meanwhile, the British *Daily Mail* estimated that Britain's five and a half million teenagers were spending £1 billion annually, a good portion of that on fifty million records. "CALL THEM SPENDAGERS!" the paper shouted on October 2, 1963. A billion-dollar industry was built upon the spending power of the young. "There was an arrogance that came along with it," Steve McConnell reflected. "Our music was good, your music was not good. Rock-and-roll was our music, our identity. It was almost good that our parents said, 'How can you listen to that stuff? Turn it down.' It meant that you got bigger speakers and a better stereo and you turned it up."[5]

The fact that teenagers now had their own radios meant that stations no longer had to cater to a diversity of tastes. All-rock stations emerged, funded by advertisements for products teenagers wanted. Live shows like that of Alan Freed, the disc jockey at WINS in New York, showcased new talent. White kids in Memphis were introduced to hip black music by Dewey Phillips who fronted a show called *Red, Hot, and Blue* on WHBQ. Daddy-O Dewey was an irrepressible force in the racial integration of popular music.

In Europe, the diversification of musical tastes was impeded by state-run broadcasting monopolies. The BBC, self-proclaimed arbiter of British culture, decided that too much pop music was harmful to the nation. Broadcasters across Europe took a similar view. Into the breach stepped a London record producer named Allan Crawford, who committed the biggest crime of 1964 by positioning his ship, the *Caroline*, ten miles off the Suffolk coast, from where he bombarded the mainland with the music the young demanded. The Foreign Office, Customs Office, and Post Office all swung into action, as did that righteous mouthpiece of the establishment, *The Times*. "The motive of these operations is profit, cloaked with the assertion that such vessels provide a service which the public wants," the paper complained. "There is not a shred of evidence for this." In fact, there were seven million shreds—the number of regular listeners. Since Radio Caroline was relatively easy to pick up in Holland, young Dutch listeners asserted their independence from their parents not just through rock music but also by speaking English. Interviewed many years later, they recalled how pirate radio had seemed like revolution:

Wil: You had the feeling [the DJ] was part of the conspiracy . . .
John: Against the older people . . .
Karel: Against the government.

When an enterprising Dutchman established Radio Veronica, broadcasting from the North Sea, he insisted that the output mirror Caroline's. English phrases were liberally interspersed with Dutch commentary.

Hardly any Dutch music was played, except when Dutch performers sang in English.[6]

The raw sexuality of the new music, not to mention the influence of black artists, caused tremors in lily-white communities. Disc jockeys were accused of corrupting youth. In the US Senate, witnesses summoned by Estes Kefauver's Juvenile Delinquency Subcommittee made direct connections between rock and the rise in youth crime. One psychiatrist called rock "a communicable disease," while preachers everywhere warned that young people would be permanently scarred. On September 4, 1956, the *Daily Mail* asserted that rock "can make the blood race. It has something of the African tom-tom and voodoo dance." The paper speculated that it might be "the Negro's revenge." Meanwhile, the far-right *American Nationalist*, worried that white girls were "squealing and drooling over Negroidal crooners," called for a boycott of all radio stations playing black music. None of this, however, had the slightest effect on the listening habits of baby boomers. Between 1955 and 1963, the number of top-ten hits by blacks increased by 50 percent. In this sense, the transistor radio made a small but significant contribution in helping the young to develop an immunity against the bigotry of their parents.[7]

In 1968, the radical Czech economist Ota Sik used the transistor radio as a standard of economic health, pointing out that his compatriots had to work 117 hours to buy one, while workers in West Germany needed only 12 hours.[8] To many, the device seemed a revolution in a pocket. Looked at from another angle, however, it was also a rather clever instrument of social control. All that music kept young people content. Like an Orwellian black box, the transistor told them what music to like, what to buy, and ultimately how to think.

SAN FRANCISCO: A COLLECTION OF ANGELS HOWLING AT THE WORLD

In October 1955, Allen Ginsberg was searching for a suitable venue in San Francisco where he and his fellow Beats Neal Cassady and Jack Kerouac could read their poems. Friends spoke to friends, and eventually the Six Gallery at Fillmore and Greenwich was proposed. The venue was both gallery and metaphor: being an old auto-repair shop, it was perfectly suited to the Beats, an artistic movement devoted to dissonance. The podium was an up-ended fruit crate.

Ginsberg took charge of publicity, distributing flyers in the bohemian bars and coffeehouses around the city: "6 poets at 6 Gallery. Philip Lamantia reading mss. of late John Hoffman—Mike McClure, Allen Ginsberg, Gary Snyder and Phil Whalen—all sharp new straightforward writing—remarkable collection of angels on one stage reading their poetry. No charge, small collection for wine and postcards. Charming event." The turnout was larger than expected. More than a hundred people showed up on October 13. The wine was gone in a few minutes, prompting Kerouac to pass around a hat. The atmosphere was not unlike a jazz jam session, with poets offering words instead of music in free-flowing improvisation. The audience occasionally uttered cool words of encouragement, and kept time by clicking fingers or drumming on tables.[9]

Lamantia read the poems of his late friend John Hoffman. Then came McClure and Whalen. After an intermission, Ginsberg took the stage, clutching seven typewritten pages of a poem called "Howl." "I saw the best minds of my generation destroyed by madness, starving hysterical naked, / dragging themselves through the Negro streets at dawn looking for an angry fix." The audience at first cheered him on. Kerouac periodically shouted "Go!" as if there was a risk that Ginsberg might stop. But he couldn't stop; he could hardly pause to take breath. By the end of the first page, the audience sat in stunned silence, letting the words batter them like hailstones in a Midwestern storm. Words were weapons to attack the world—"Moloch whose mind is pure machinery! Moloch whose blood is running money! . . . / . . . Moloch whose love is endless oil and stone!"[10] The end came in orgiastic explosion, leaving listeners bruised, frightened, exhausted. Ginsberg wept.

That was the first public reading of "Howl," the iconic poem of the Beat Generation. The poem still possesses immense power, still shocks and offends. But the energy it emits in print today is nothing compared to the raw force it produced on that night in October 1955. "It was very exciting," Whalen recalled. "Ginsberg getting excited while doing it was sort of scary. You wondered was he wigging out, or what—and he was, but within certain parameters. It was a breakthrough for everybody. The mixture of terrifically inventive and wild language, with what had hitherto been forbidden subject matter, and just general *power*, was quite impressive." After regaining his composure, Kerouac congratulated his friend on both the poem and the performance, which he said would make Ginsberg famous in San Francisco. In fact, his fame would soon stretch from the Golden

Gate to the Brooklyn Bridge and beyond, but that was beside the point. The poem was never about becoming famous; it was an extended howl at a terrible, cruel, ugly world.[11]

Six poets and a hundred listeners do not a revolution make. To pretend that the poetry reading at the Six Gallery was a watershed is to assign far too much power to literature, especially a literature that few people would ever read. But that night was a harbinger; premonitions of much of what happened in the 1960s can be discerned in the atmosphere at the old auto shop. "We had gone beyond a point of no return and we were ready for it," McClure later wrote. "None of us wanted to go back to the gray, chill, militaristic silence, to the intellective void—to the land without poetry—to the spiritual drabness. We wanted to make it new and we wanted to invent it and the process of it as we went into it. We wanted voice and we wanted vision." The pronoun "it" is usually supposed to have an identifiable referent. In McClure's case, what "it" means is unclear. But that hardly matters, since to define it is to contain it. The great power of the Beat message was its elusiveness. It questioned everything and was identifiable as nothing.[12]

Defining the Beat movement is an act of futility leading to vague generalizations and flaccid platitudes. Beat writers lacked direction, whether driving their cars or composing at their typewriters. Comprehensibility was not a priority; rhythm mattered as much as meaning. The conservative critic Norman Podhoretz once called the Beats "Know-Nothing Bohemians"; "spiritually under-privileged" writers who revolted against coherence and destroyed "the distinction between life and literature." The Beats were, he said, "a revolt of all the forces hostile to civilization itself." He was a lover of plot and meaning. Ginsberg responded by defending the "expression of what one feels," however chaotic that might be. The validity of a feeling lies in the simple fact that it is felt. He was not remotely interested in words as diction, preferring instead words as rhythm. Words provided the backbeat to expression.[13]

The term "Beats" was not a musical reference but rather an allusion to the feeling of being roughed up by life—aching souls lost in the wasteland of materialism and conformity. Beats were visionary gypsies on the run from conventional society, which they saw as a smothering monster. They were apolitical for the simple reason that practicing politics implied buying into the system. "In the wildest hipster," wrote poet John Clellon Holmes, "there is no desire to shatter the 'square' society in which he lives, only to elude it. To get on a soapbox or write a manifesto would seem to him absurd." Escape came through aimless wandering "on the road," through mind-expanding drugs, through formless music and art, or through stream-of-consciousness literature. The Beats befriended those on the perilous margins of society—pimps, whores, drug dealers, petty thieves—because, as cultural outlaws, they felt empathy with those who defied rules. The criminal world, likewise, seemed to offer entry into a supreme reality very different from the sheltered middle-class life in which they'd been raised. "The only people for me are the mad ones," wrote Kerouac, "the ones who are mad to live, mad to talk, mad to be saved, desirous of everything at the same time, the ones who never yawn or say a commonplace thing, but burn, burn, burn like fabulous roman candles exploding like spiders across the stars." Theirs was a reckless, risky, and rather naïve quest, but they had little concern for their own physical or emotional safety, since "safety" was a synonym for "conformity." The highways of their exploration became littered with corpses, the casualties of bohemian excess or of criminal friends gone nasty. Yet seldom does one sense that they mourned their dead, since dying constituted the ultimate act of rejection.[14]

The Beats never really saw themselves as a movement; they saw instead a group of like-minded individuals determined to explore the outer reaches of creativity. But the culture of disaffection led inevitably to imitation. Acting like a Beat became cool, which is another way of saying it became a trend. In the Hegelian sense, a trend begins as antithesis and ends as synthesis, an element of conformity and an example of cultural absorption. Around the time the columnist Herb Caen coined the derisive term "beatnik" in the *San Francisco Chronicle* on April 2, 1958, the Beats were dangerously close to becoming a cliché. The beatnik wore a black turtleneck and black beret, grew a goatee, smoked foreign cigarettes, drank strong coffee or rotgut wine, and listened to avant-garde jazz or poetry. Women slithered around in black leotards and let their hair hang long and straight. But behind the mask of nonconformity, beatniks were as normal as 98.6. The Beats resented the hijacking of their motif, but the rest of the world indulged in careless generalization, seeing the two as one. When Beat became beatnik, the jig was up; the cultural edge went blunt. For subsequent generations, living the Beat life became confused with reading Beat literature, which was never what Ginsberg and his friends had in mind.

Tracing the Beat legacy is much easier than identifying what the Beats actually were. That poetry reading at the Six Gallery was thick with premonitions. It was about freedom, the enemy of conformity. "Howl" evokes alienation, but it is also, more specifically, about drugs, homosexuality, and madness. As such, it was a statement of what was to come, plus an act of defiance against those inclined to censor thought. Other harbingers can be found in the rest of the poetry showcased that night. Hints of ecological consciousness are evident in the works of McClure, Snyder, and Kerouac. The outlaws admired by the Beat poets would eventually make their way into songs of Joan Baez, Phil Ochs, and Leonard Cohen. The poems themselves bring Bob Dylan to mind, while the rhythm and ethereality of their delivery would eventually find a place in much Sixties music.

The Beats provided the tempo for a subsequent generation who lacked their seriousness but admired their idiosyncrasy. They were the American cousins of the Existentialists, with whom they shared a disdain for the world and a belief that reason stifled emotion. They lacked the coherence of Camus and Sartre but were much more fun. Their rejection of reason, rules, and logic eventually became a license to do anything at all, especially when it was taken up by their descendents, the hippies. An acceptance that the world is absurd allows every act of lunacy to acquire significance. But that is hardly the fault of the Beats, who cannot be held to account for every fool who walked through the doors they opened. The Beats deserve admiration for asking questions during an era inclined toward nodding compliance. "Nobody knows whether we were catalysts or invented something, or just the froth riding on a wave of its own," Ginsberg later reflected. "We were all three, I suppose."[15]

WORCESTER: THE PILL

"No woman can call herself free who does not own and control her own body," Margaret Sanger wrote in 1922, six years after she established her first birth control clinic. A free spirit, she wanted to divorce sex from procreation. Women could enjoy sex, she argued, only if they were given a reliable form of birth control.[16]

In 1948, Sanger joined forces with Katharine McCormick, heir to the International Harvester fortune. Like Sanger, McCormick was interested in birth control as a way of freeing women from the burden of unwanted pregnancies. She also had a virtually endless supply of money to devote to the search for an effective contraceptive. In 1951, she pledged $2 million to the Worcester Foundation for Experimental Biology, where a team led by the geneticist Gregory Pincus began exploring the possibility that a woman's reproductive capacity might be artificially manipulated with hormones. The right dosage, it was thought, might inhibit the release of eggs for as long as the woman did not want to conceive. Then, if she decided she wanted to become pregnant, she could simply quit taking the hormones and her body would return to its natural equilibrium. That, at least, was the theory. The problem lay in establishing the right dosage.

In December 1954, John Rock of Harvard Medical School started testing a steroid called progestin on fifty women at his clinic. The women were chosen because they were all having problems conceiving. Rock felt that the steroid might stimulate their reproductive system. He was not, in other words, looking for a contraceptive. The test was a modest success—seven of the women got pregnant after coming off the drug. More remarkable, however, was the fact that all fifty women stopped ovulating while on the drug. When Pincus got wind of that result, he invited Rock to join his team.

The Worcester group decided to widen Rock's sample by testing in Puerto Rico—a place conveniently removed from moral inquisitors. In April 1956, tests of the new drug, now called Enovid, began in San Juan. The initial trial, involving 221 women, was astonishingly successful. Not a single woman became pregnant. The tests were then widened to a larger group of Puerto Rican women, and another group in Haiti. While these tests demonstrated that the drug worked, they were too brief to measure its long-term effects.

In the following year, in an interview with TV journalist Mike Wallace, Sanger announced that an oral contraceptive was on its way. Despite having endured decades of abuse, she was astonished at the angry reaction, mainly from the Catholic community. This especially worried her since Senator John Kennedy, a Catholic, was making noises about running for president. "God help America if his father's millions can push him into the White House," she remarked. As it turned out, Sanger overestimated the strength of the Catholic community. In 1957 the Food and Drug Administration approved Enovid for the treatment of menstrual disorders.

Three years later came approval as a contraceptive. By the end of 1963, nearly 2.5 million American women and perhaps half a million British women were taking the drug.[17]

The Pill is often credited with triggering a sexual revolution, but in truth the revolution was already under way. Between 1941 and 1964, illegitimate births in the United States rose by 150 percent. After 1960, Pill usage rose, but so too did the number of unwanted pregnancies, which implies that the rise in promiscuity was not directly linked to the pharmaceutical breakthrough. In any case, the Pill was at first prescribed almost exclusively to married women. For others, the preferred method remained the condom, which perhaps explains all those unwanted pregnancies.

The feminist Judy Wajcman maintains that since the Pill was used to reinforce patriarchal social relations, it is, by implication, an instrument of patriarchy. She believes that the Pill was developed not because it benefited women, but because a greedy pharmaceutical industry recognized the potential for huge profits. The argument is buttressed by claims that potentially deadly side effects were ignored in order to get Enovid on the market. "The devisers of the Pill," Germaine Greer argued, "worried so little about the female psyche that it was years before they discovered that one woman in three who was on the pill was chronically depressed." Granted, the drug was introduced with undue haste, but it seems reckless to assume that this is proof of male conspiracy—rather the opposite. It is difficult to explain away the enthusiasm women felt. To contend that the millions who immediately embraced the Pill were manipulated suggests an implausible level of female submissiveness.[18]

Doubts about the Pill were raised in the late 1960s, even as many people—male and female—were celebrating its merits. By that time, the commonly held opinion was that the woman who took oral contraceptives had a better chance of being alive a year later than one who chose to have a baby. That reasoning, faulty or not, was all the reassurance that most women needed. They desperately sought validation for a method of contraception which, despite its abundant flaws, was life-enhancing.

The Pill gave women the opportunity to enjoy sex without worry of pregnancy and to see themselves as something other than mothers. That said, it also made life easy for men, created new health hazards for women, contributed to the overemphasis upon women as sex objects, and made billions for the pharmaceutical industry. In other words, the issue is far too complicated to permit simple judgments on matters of utility. Benefits and risks were weighed differently by each individual according to the situation in which she found herself and the life she wanted to lead.

"I left home and got on the birth control pill my first semester at college," recalls one baby boomer. "My friends and I considered it very *in*." Another woman confessed: "for the first time in my life I could think about sex just as it was, just as sex and not as a potentially life-destroying event, that you could do something impulsively that would not have consequences for years." A married woman, who had had two children and a miscarriage in quick succession, recalled bursting into tears in front of her doctor over the thought that this might be the pattern of her life. "I . . . just cried and cried and said that I couldn't, I couldn't do it again, I just couldn't bear it and I hated the cap and it didn't work . . . and all those things." Her doctor then told her about the Pill.

> It was completely wonderful. It changed my life. . . . I felt in control, I felt free. If I had known then what we know now about it, how dangerous and so on it is, I don't think I would have cared. . . . I felt so wonderfully clever. Women say now that the Pill was just a man's plot so that women would be more available, but they can't be serious. . . . They would have to be women who can't remember what it was like before: worrying all the time and all that messing about. Sex belonged to me.

Conspiracy theories are the last resort of paranoid groups who consider the construction of society unfair and seek reprobates to blame. The idea that the Pill was a male conspiracy ignores the involvement of women in its development and the fact that it fulfilled an undeniable female need. Emphasizing that it also made life easier for men is to confuse side-effect with motive. "What [the Pill] gave to me was the sense of ownership of myself, which at that point in my life was very, very important," one woman revealed. "The fact that women had a method that allowed them to be free of pregnancy and to make decisions on their own had a profound effect on how we began to think about all sorts of things."[19]

THE CONGO: DEMOCRACY MURDERED

On January 21, 1961, Gerard Soete, a Belgian police commissioner, went with his brother Michel into the Katangan bush, to the site of a fresh grave. They dug up the body, hacked it to bits, and then plunged the pieces into sulfuric acid. Their aim was to erase a hero.

The hero in question was Patrice Lumumba, the first democratically elected leader of the Belgian Congo. Lumumba was doomed from the moment he became prime minister on June 23, 1960. Within days of his inauguration, his enemies were queuing up to kill him. He lasted just ten weeks, leaving behind a country even more chaotic than the one he'd inherited. His heroic status arose from the fact that he died young, before failure could tarnish him. As a result, he achieved more as a martyr than he could ever have accomplished as a leader.

The Belgians were expert exploiters. Untroubled by notions of civilizing the savage, they assumed control of a region with the primary purpose of bleeding it white. Colonies were machines for producing wealth. Belgian Africa was uranium and diamonds; Union Minière, Banque Empain, and Unilever; gonorrhea, rape, mutilation, chain gangs, and floggings—not to mention black bodies floating in the Congo River. Natives were beasts of burden used to extract the natural resources that made whites wealthy. Their abundance made life cheap. Natives did not need to be well educated or well fed, since they were infinitely replaceable.

By the mid-1950s, this kind of imperialism had grown old-fashioned. In the "civilized" nations, sensitivity to exploitation went hand in hand with an acceptance, at least in theory, of self-determination. A change in colonial status, however, did not necessarily mean an end to colonialism. Cynics found ways of adapting old ways in order to allow exploitation to continue, under the guise of democratic reform. This was the sort of transformation the Belgians sought in the Congo. They hoped that, with a few concessions to the natives, the Congo's riches might continue to flow.

The Belgians wanted the Congolese to prove themselves incapable of self-government. That was a reasonable expectation, given that the Congo was an arbitrarily defined country whose boundaries bore no relation to ethnicity. Congolese nationalism was difficult to muster, since the first loyalty of the people was to their ethnic group. The transformation from colony to nation projected clan rivalries onto a national stage, rendering the country ungovernable. Belgium sought a Balkanization of the area in which small regions, defined by ethnicity, would remain dependent upon colonial control to maintain viability. The trappings of power would be transferred to handpicked loyal natives, a ruse that would give the new nation a semblance of self-government yet keep colonial interests intact. In order to increase the likelihood of this scenario, the Belgians intentionally quickened the pace of decolonization, while neglecting to prepare the Congolese for self-rule.

Lumumba stood in the way of this clever plan. He was the only politician who could command anything like a national following, independent of ethnic loyalties. His hero was Kwame Nkrumah, who had achieved a miraculous nationalist transformation in Ghana. Lumumba realized that, while democracy was essential to such a transformation, it also represented the greatest threat. Unrestrained democracy would allow tribal tensions to surface, leading to the erosion of national unity. Like Nkrumah, Lumumba believed that success was dependent upon the establishment of a strong central government in which minority opinion was silenced or eliminated. In time, the loyalty of the people would be won through the progressive improvement of their lives.

Lumumba was a formidable character, which explains why the Belgians feared him. His youth (he was born in 1925) harmonized with a new age and new beginnings. He was also handsome, charismatic, and intelligent, despite his lack of formal education. His life was an allegory: like his country, he had personally suffered exploitation at the hands of the Belgians, but had risen through sheer force of will. The vehicle of his ambition was the Movement National Congolais (MNC), a liberal nationalist organization formed in 1956. The MNC was the only party with any hope of expansion, since others were limited by the size of the ethnic group they represented. As such, the MNC stood to gain from the massive influx of workers to the cities in the years 1940–1955. Urbanization eroded particularist loyalties.

Out of the blue, in March 1959, the Belgians announced plans to quit, setting elections for the following May. This announcement coincided with Lumumba's consolidation of power within the MNC. The party won 33 of 137 seats, a victory that made it the largest parliamentary bloc and gave Lumumba the right to form a coalition government. The fact that his victory was neither decisive nor unifying meant that Lumumba had numerous enemies. From his very first day in office, they worked hard to undermine him. He thought that the answer to this problem was naked strength—a government held together by fear more than by consent. Paraphrasing Nkrumah, he argued: "In a young state, you must have strong and visible powers." Lumumba's power was visible, but never strong.[20]

His Congolese enemies would eventually have disposed of him, if not through assassination then by making it impossible for him to govern. They, however, were not quite as impatient as his external enemies. The Belgians despised Lumumba because he stood between them and the country's wealth of uranium, copper, gold, diamonds, tin, cobalt, manganese, and zinc. Belgian fears were validated when Lumumba used the first Independence Day ceremony on June 30, 1960, as an occasion to criticize colonial rule. The festivities began with a succession of Belgian dignitaries, including King Baudouin, spouting paternalistic platitudes about how the Congolese had been civilized by their European benefactors. Lumumba's speech sent them reeling: "We have known harassing work, exacted in exchange for salaries which did not permit us to eat enough to drive away hunger, or to clothe ourselves, or to house ourselves decently, or to raise our children as creatures dear to us. . . . We have known ironies, insults, blows that we endured morning, noon and evening, because we are Negroes. . . . We have seen our land seized in the name of allegedly legal laws which in fact recognized only that might is right." All this was undoubtedly true, but Lumumba was not very politic to mention it in the presence of the Belgian king, at a time when the new nation was still dependent upon Belgian help and when most businesses remained in Belgian hands. Lumumba's speech, though applauded by his people, was essentially an invitation to murder. The Belgians understood that if their plans were to proceed, the new prime minister would have to go.[21]

The Americans had come to the same conclusion. They balked at Lumumba's frequent use of the word "socialism." "We must adapt socialism to African realities" was in truth a rather tame statement, but not tame enough for American ears. Nor did they appreciate Lumumba's boast that "the Congo's independence is a decisive step toward the liberation of the entire African continent." That kind of talk frightened President Eisenhower, who feared that the Congo was the cutting edge of a socialist revolution in Africa. Privately, he expressed the wish that Lumumba would "fall into a river of crocodiles." American fears were exacerbated by the fact that the Soviets, keen to expand their influence, had cast themselves as champions of Pan-Africanism.[22]

As a gesture of goodwill, Lumumba traveled to New York in late July, hoping to calm American fears. All he wanted, he explained, was to be left alone. "For the Congo, there are no blocs, because we are an African people," he insisted. "We desire no political programs from the US or USSR; we seek only technical assistance." He needn't have bothered, since those words were hardly less frightening to his hosts than an open admission of Communism. Nor did it help that during his visit Lumumba met the black nationalist leader Malcolm X, who sang his praises. The White House feared that Lumumba might become a cause célèbre for militant blacks everywhere.[23]

Meanwhile, at home, Lumumba was powerless to stop his country's descent into anarchy. Within days of the independence ceremony, government troops had mutinied and local despots had begun to assert themselves. Since this deterioration suited Belgium, she refused to intervene, and in fact fomented unrest. The most damaging mutiny occurred in Katanga, the main mining region. Encouraged by Western interests, Moise Tshombe declared Katanga an independent state. Lumumba, unable even to maintain order in his stronghold of Leopoldville, was powerless to stop Tshombe.

The chaos provided Belgium with an excuse to send its troops back into the Congo, on the pretext of protecting Belgian nationals. Desperate for help, Lumumba appealed to the UN, but in doing so sparked a row between the US and USSR, each with a different opinion of how help should be administered. He also found that he could not use UN troops as he pleased—their mission to restore peace conflicted with his need to consolidate power. Eventually he grew exasperated with the UN, but not before the UN lost patience with him.

International distrust fueled misunderstanding. Lumumba never quite understood how his actions fired Western suspicions. The United States, feeling manipulated, decided that his cooperative gestures had been designed to mask Communist objectives. These suspicions seemed to be confirmed when Lumumba, having run out of friends, requested help from the Soviets. CIA director Allen Dulles called Lumumba a "mad dog" who needed to be put down. "In high quarters," he told Eisenhower, "it is the clear-cut conclusion that if [Lumumba] continues to hold high office, the inevitable result will [have] disastrous consequences . . . for the interests of the free world generally. Consequently, we conclude that his removal must be an urgent and prime objective."[24]

Eisenhower agreed that Lumumba had to go. Robert Johnson, a minute-taker at the White House, later recalled a meeting in August 1960 at which the president "said something . . . that came across to me as an order for the assassination of Lumumba." He noted: "There was stunned silence for about fifteen seconds and [then] the meeting continued." Dulles later telegraphed the Congo station to confirm "every possible support in eliminating Lumumba." One such support was CIA agent Sidney Gottlieb, who was sent to Africa with a vial of poison. The lethal dose was supposed to be administered via Lumumba's toothbrush.[25]

Before Gottlieb could get anywhere near the prime ministerial toothbrush, its owner had been arrested. The Belgians, leaders in the race to kill Lumumba, had the advantage of an intimate familiarity with those Congolese who hated him. In September, President Joseph Kasavubu dismissed Lumumba. Though he did not technically have this power, those who objected were helpless to stop him. Real authority now rested in the hands of the defense minister, Joseph Mobutu, who had the backing of the army. Lumumba spent the next two months desperately trying to reassert himself, without success.

In December, Lumumba was sent to Katanga, which, though nominally headed by Tshombe, was in truth under Belgian control. Harold d'Aspremont Lynden, Belgium's minister of African Affairs, had ordered Lumumba's transport, which was in effect a sentence of death. At each stage of the transfer, Lumumba was brutally beaten in an attempt to break the spirit of his movement. Crowds watched as he was led through streets with a rope around his neck. On one occasion, he was beaten outside Mobutu's villa in full view of television cameras. The Americans, now satisfied that an African troublemaker had been brought to heel, took refuge in the assertion that cruelty was culturally defined. "In the Congo what passes as inhumane to US [citizens] is customary among them," an embassy document argued. "Thus, the abuse of Lumumba shocks civilized countries while Congolese themselves consider he is pampered. Fact is he is much better treated than any other prisoner has been, to the best of our knowledge." A Belgian witness noted that pieces of wood had been inserted under Lumumba's fingernails and toenails.[26]

Lynden advised that "the main aim to pursue in the interests of the Congo, Katanga, and Belgium is clearly Lumumba's definitive elimination." That wish was carried out on January 17, 1961, when he was taken into the bush, tied to a tree, and shot. A Belgian commission of inquiry in November 2001 revealed that four Belgian officers were present, though the execution was commanded by Katangans. The Belgian government nevertheless felt moved, the following February, to admit a "moral responsibility . . . in the events that led to the death of Lumumba." CIA documents reveal that the United States was kept informed of Belgian actions but did not actively take part in the execution.[27]

The American and Belgian governments breathed a collective sigh of relief, confident that the Congo was now in trustworthy hands. The Americans, however, did not anticipate the reaction in Africa and the Caribbean, where Lumumba was quickly transformed into a martyr and a symbol of American perfidy. For black nationalists in the US, he became an emotive link between racism at home and neocolonialism abroad. Within the civil rights movement, Pan-Africanism became a shibboleth for militants keen to demonstrate radical credentials. Black leaders would henceforth stumble over one another in their efforts to define their position relative to Lumumba.

In a startlingly honest analysis of the American role in the Congo crisis, former CIA director William Colby remarked in 1984: "The question we faced . . . was whether that country . . . would be run by some toadies of the old Belgian mining companies or by men aided by Che Guevara and supported by the Soviet Union. The CIA found a midpoint between these two extremes—it helped Joseph Mobutu, then a nationalist member of the Congolese forces, become the third alternative." By deft management, Mobutu consolidated his power, eventually establishing a dictatorship which would last thirty-two years. His rule was sadistic and corrupt even by African standards. In contrast to Lumumba, Mobutu was perfectly willing to sell his country to the West, so long as the rewards were substantial. Congo's former UN representative, Thomas Kanga, complained that his country became "an international, and, more specifically, an American colony."[28]

"No brutality, mistreatment, or torture," Lumumba wrote on the eve of his execution, "has ever forced me to ask for grace, for I prefer to die with my head high, my faith steadfast, and my confidence profound in the destiny of my country, rather than to live in submission and scorn of sacred principles." He became the perfect martyr for a decade given to myth and magic. But myths are possible only because he died before he could do much harm. Death rendered him forever young, forever perfect.[29]

The Belgians and Americans undoubtedly acted with cynical criminality, seeking to establish a postcolonial Congo which could be bled of its riches. But the fact that there was evil on one side does not imply that there was perfection on the other. Lumumba's enemies were legion. Had the Americans and Belgians not been so eager to eliminate him, the Congolese would undoubtedly have done so. Lumumba was trying to achieve the impossible: he was attempting to balance the demands of the imperialists with the needs of his oppressed people. The two groups were, however, inevitably antagonistic. If some see him as a democrat, that is only because he died when Congo's experiment with democracy was in its infancy. It is perhaps best to judge him by his heroes—Nkrumah, Julius Nyerere, and Jomo Kenyatta—men who, back then, seemed noble statesmen, but whose reputations have since been tarnished by revelations of the corruption and cruelty they employed to preserve power. They succeeded by accommodating foreign capitalists—to the detriment of their people. Only true romantics can convince themselves that Lumumba would have acted differently.

The Old Bailey: Lady Chatterley on Trial

The seats were hard, the view terrible, the acrid smell of unwashed bodies thoroughly unpleasant. But none of that mattered to the audience, who would not have missed the spectacle for anything in the world. Every day, crowds queued outside the Old Bailey; those who did not arrive ridiculously early were inevitably disappointed in their quest for a seat. In the pubs and on the street, the drama was retold, discussed, disputed, analyzed. For six intense days in the autumn of 1960, the British were gripped by the trial of Constance Chatterley.

Lady Chatterley was not, of course, actually on trial. She is, after all, a fictional character, though that simple fact escaped the prosecutor, Mervyn Griffith-Jones. The trial, conducted under the 1959 Obscene Publications Act, brought suit against Penguin Books for the publication of *Lady Chatterley's Lover,* by D. H. Lawrence. The unexpurgated version had been banned in Britain since its publication in 1928, largely due to the fact that laws against obscenity were so ill-defined that they made no distinction between raw pornography and works of literature. The new act attempted to correct this deficiency by introducing a standard of "literary merit," which the trial was intended to test. Most people had decided beforehand that the prosecution was destined to fail, but that did not stop some tub-thumping moralists from making the most of their time in court.

The act allowed both prosecution and defense witnesses to testify regarding a book's merit. The defense, under the direction of Gerald Gardiner, collected thirty-five such "experts." These included writers, philosophers, theologians, teachers, psychologists, and critics. The prosecution, on the other hand, could find no one of sufficient authority to testify that *Lady Chatterley* was obscene. Many thought the book dull and self-indulgent, but that was hardly sufficient grounds for banning publication.

The trial began on October 20, 1960. Its drama was enhanced by the way the prosecution rose so enthusiastically to its brief. A journalist described Griffith-Jones as "high cheek-boned and poker-backed, a veteran of Eton, Trinity Hall (Cambridge), the Coldstream Guards and many previous obscenity cases; a voice passionate only in disdain, but barbed with a rabid belief in convention and discipline." When judging obscenity, Griffith-Jones applied a simple test: "I put my feet up on the desk and start reading. If I get an erection, we prosecute." On that standard, *Chatterley* seemed a filthy book worthy of a ban. The prosecutor's best line came in the first hour of the trial, when he asked the jury whether this was "a book you would . . . wish your wife or your servants to read." To many, that remark demonstrated that Britain was witnessing a contest between old and new. No wonder, then, that the trial came to be seen as a gateway to modernity, and Griffith-Jones a Praetorian Guard blocking entry. As the critic Bernard Levin later wrote: "The Sixties began with an attempt to stop the decade entirely and replace it with an earlier one."[30]

Griffith-Jones started by addressing not the issue of obscenity, but that of literary merit. He focused on Lawrence's fondness for the words "womb" and "bowels" when describing the effect of Lady Chatterley's sexual arousal, words which seemed inappropriate. "'Another self was alive in her, burning molten and soft in her womb and bowels,'" he read. "I do not want to be unimaginative, believe me, but can one flow and be alive in one's womb and bowels?" When the answer to that question, no matter how often it was posed, proved a resounding yes, Griffith-Jones reluctantly abandoned the argument.[31]

Try as he might, the prosecutor could not break the defense witnesses' conviction that Lawrence had written a work of merit. He therefore changed direction, focusing on the adultery of Constance Chatterley, a crime all the more serious since she was morally obliged to behave in a manner befitting her class. Perhaps better than Lawrence himself, the prosecutor brilliantly brought the characters to life. "There were long periods of the trial," one journalist remarked, "during which an outsider might well have assumed that a divorce case was being heard." Before long, Griffith-Jones, the judge, and the witnesses were talking about Chatterley and her lover Mellors as if they were standing in the dock. So, too, were those beyond the Old Bailey. In the House of Lords, Lord Hailsham explained that, before judging Chatterley and Mellors, he wanted to know "what sort of parents they became. . . . I should have liked to see the kind of house they proposed to set up together; I should have liked to know how Mellors would have survived living on Connie's rentier income of six hundred pounds . . . and . . . whether they acquired a circle of friends." The deputy director of public prosecutions, Maurice Crump, complained that he needed more information about Lady Chatterley's hobbies, "whether she rode, hunted, played tennis or golf."[32]

Not satisfied with damning the morals of a fictional character, Griffith-Jones went on to castigate Lawrence himself. "One doesn't want to talk disrespectfully of the dead, but . . . he had run off with his friend's wife, had he not?" In the end, however, that attack proved fruitless. In desperation, the prosecutor deployed his last weapon. He argued that, leaving everything else aside, Constance and her lover were guilty of buggery. He referred specifically to a passage in which Mellors is allowed to "have his way . . . burning out the shames, the deepest, oldest shames, in the most secret places." Griffith-Jones let the jury ponder a moment on what that might mean. He could not bring himself to explain specifically, since the mere idea was abominable. Instead he feigned confusion, as if to imply that one so morally upright as himself could not possibly have knowledge of the crime in question. Unfortunately, eloquence failed him at a crucial moment. It was, he muttered, "not very easy . . . to know what in fact [Lawrence] was driving at in that passage."[33]

Neither adultery nor buggery could alter the witnesses' conviction that the book had merit and was therefore fundamentally different from the kind of magazines seedy Soho newsagents were selling not far from the Old Bailey. Aware that he was losing the argument, Griffith-Jones in the end reminded the jury that the world seemed to be full of academic experts and for that reason they should resist getting lost in "the higher realms of literature." They should instead think of the factory girls who might read the book during their lunch hour. He went on to argue that the recent rise in crime in Britain was the result of "unbridled sex," a remark which baffled almost everyone in the courtroom.[34]

The jury took just three hours to acquit Penguin. The publisher responded by flooding the bookshops with 200,000 copies of *Chatterley*, which, unsurprisingly, sold out virtually overnight. Over the next two years, 3.3 million copies were sold, though how many were actually read, cover to cover, is unclear.

The event seems so perfectly timed, sitting as it does on the cusp between one age and another. Its momentous nature can, however, be exaggerated. The Obscene Publications Act would, in the course of the 1960s, continue to be used to test literary merit, though never with such fanfare. The trial did not fundamentally alter the moral opinions of the British, the vast majority of whom were oblivious to the implications of what had happened. The chattering classes nevertheless saw the trial as a watershed, for the simple reason that they wanted it to be just that. On questions of culture, their opinions mattered immensely. The critic Kenneth Tynan wrote in the *Observer* that the battle had been "between Lawrence's England and Sir Clifford Chatterley's England; between contact and separation; between freedom and control; between love and death." That was an exaggeration, but legitimate points often demand hyperbole. Many saw greener pastures of tolerance and expression beyond the fence of British prudery. For them, the verdict was indeed the opening of a gate. As an event, the trial was little more than a six-day circus—a carnival of bawdy innuendo. As a symbol, however, it was huge.[35]

WASHINGTON: NEW FRONTIERS

Heavy snow fell in Washington the night before John Kennedy's inauguration. There was talk of postponing the ceremony, but the president-elect insisted it should go ahead. The crowds huddling in the bitter cold were astonished when Kennedy rose to the dais without an overcoat. A hero had arrived.

The speech complemented the man. America's belief in itself was never better expressed than on January 20, 1961. Kennedy's inaugural address embodied both John Winthrop's "City on a Hill" and the confidence inspired by victory in two world wars. "Let every nation know, whether it wishes us well or ill, that we shall pay any price, bear any burden, meet any hardship, support any friend, oppose any foe, in order to assure the survival and the success of liberty." To most Americans, that sounded like an innocent homage to American values. In fact, it was a battle cry. Kennedy, unlike his predecessor, did not want to contain his enemies; he hoped to defeat them.[36]

Kennedy made a career of fooling the American people. If myths surround him, they are largely of his making. To this day, he is carelessly labeled liberal, when in fact he was something else entirely. He is celebrated as a champion of civil rights, yet his actual achievements were motivated more by pragmatism than idealism. His success, such as it was, arose from his extraordinary ability to market himself—he was perfectly suited to a consumer age.

After the 1956 election, liberal Democrats sensed that their turn would soon come. The end of the decade brought social and intellectual ferment—manifested by Elvis Presley, the Beats, J. D. Salinger, Sputnik, James Dean, and the Little Rock Nine. The comfort and security associated with Eisenhower's quiet conservatism suddenly seemed old-fashioned. While liberals sensed that the times were a-changin', they lacked a lead singer.

The logical man was Senator Hubert Humphrey of Minnesota, champion of civil rights, social welfare, and labor reform. But while his politics seemed perfect, his personality did not. Humphrey was a thoroughly decent man, but he reminded one of a weird uncle, the sort of person who, at any moment, could do something totally daft. When excited, his nasal voice turned into an annoying whine. While an undoubtedly distinguished senator, he lacked the stuff to perform on the main stage. So great was liberal desperation that some Democrats still backed Adlai Stevenson, a loser in the previous two elections.

Politics abhors a vacuum. The good politician sees a gap and changes shape to fill it. Starting in 1957, Kennedy turned himself into a liberal in order to gain his party's nomination. Though he had been a senator since 1952, he had never found a natural constituency beyond his native New England. But, in his favor, Kennedy was a hugely ambitious man with a talent for self-promotion and a yachtsman's ability to gauge the political wind. "Kennedy had sensed that subterranean pressures were already beginning to fissure the illusions of the fifties, that national discontent was mounting," wrote his speechwriter Richard Goodwin. With single-minded purpose, Kennedy set out to satisfy the American hunger for something new.[37]

"It is time . . . for a new generation of leadership—new men to cope with new problems and new opportunities," Kennedy argued during the campaign. "New" became the mantra, a substitute for policy. Attaching this adjective to something made that something seem promising and exciting. It also meant that anyone who opposed Kennedy could automatically be dismissed as old hat. Of his Republican opponent Richard Nixon, he said: "His party is the party of the past . . . Their pledge is a pledge to the status quo, and today there can be no status quo." Spoken by Kennedy, that sounded eloquent, dynamic, even meaningful, but in truth it was purely rhetorical. Kennedy had found an effective substitute for policy. He had only to provide a steady drumbeat to the rhythm of the new.[38]

Kennedy's message had a profound effect upon young people who desperately wanted to occupy center stage in a world different from that of their parents. When, during the campaign, he uttered an off-the-cuff remark about establishing a Peace Corps, within two days 700 students had volunteered for an agency that did not yet exist. "For years I have scarcely had a single student asking me about a career in Washington," a Harvard economist remarked just before the inauguration. "But since last November, all my ablest young men have been queuing up as they used to in the New Deal." "All at once you had something exciting," one of Kennedy's campaign workers recalled later. "You had a young guy who had kids, and who liked to play football on his front lawn. . . . Everything they did showed that America was alive and active."[39]

Or so it seemed. In fact, everything relied on smoke and mirrors. Behind the image of youthful vigor walked a man who was in decidedly poor health. His famous suntan, supposedly the result of days spent yachting or skiing, was in fact caused by steroids taken for Addison's Disease. He fostered his reputation as a family man, but was actually a serial womanizer.

He was a Catholic when he needed to be; when surrounded by Protestants or Jews, he argued that religion was irrelevant. He often flaunted his wealth and celebrity, not to mention his famous friends, but also managed to convince the poor and downtrodden that he understood their pain.

The makeover was facilitated by the cooperation of the media. During the campaign for the Democratic nomination, Kennedy got away with murder. He benefited immensely from Irish machine politics, particularly in the crucial state of Illinois, but somehow managed to avoid the stigma that went with that association. Vague noises were heard about his ruthless father and corrupt finances, but none of the allegations stuck. Kennedy also presented himself as a war hero, through clever elaboration of the drama of PT-109. Those who did not quite get the message were encouraged to ask Humphrey what *he* had done during the war.

The relatively new medium of television was the perfect vehicle for a young, handsome, articulate candidate. This advantage was never more apparent than during his first televised debate with Nixon. Kennedy prepared like a movie star readying himself for a starring role; Nixon, like the captain of the high school debating team. Kennedy refused makeup because he didn't need it. That made it impossible for Nixon to ask for the makeup he desperately did need. Kennedy therefore looked healthy and vigorous, while Nixon appeared ghoulish. Nixon, who was never a very good actor, could not keep his inner self from emerging in the form of scowls or cynical grins. He looked scary. Those who watched the debate on television thought Kennedy had won hands down. Those who listened on the radio judged it a draw.

The debate was supposed to be about domestic policy, yet Kennedy began by talking about the dangers of the Cold War, an indicator perhaps of his real priorities. "This is a great country, but I think it could be a greater country, and is a powerful country but I think it should be a more powerful country," he maintained. Echoing Lincoln but extending his rhetoric to a world stage, he argued: "The question is whether the world will exist half slave or half free, whether it will move in the direction of freedom, in the direction of the road we are taking, or whether it will move in the direction of slavery." He questioned whether America was doing as much as it should, and whether it was as strong as duty necessitated. From Lincoln he moved to Roosevelt, talking of a "rendezvous with destiny." The Cold War was neatly brought home: "I think our generation of Americans has the same 'rendezvous.' The question now is: Can freedom be maintained under the most severe attack it has ever known? I think it can be, and I think in the final analysis it depends upon what we do here. I think it's time America started moving again." Spoken by a handsome actor, those words were irresistibly inspiring. Few paused to consider the sacrifices they implied.[40]

Even though he had never shown much interest in civil rights, Kennedy realized he had to address the issue. Thanks to Martin Luther King Jr., the problem was now impossible to ignore. Despite his lack of concern, Kennedy somehow managed to make himself into the black man's champion. His famous claim that discrimination in federal housing could be eliminated "with the stroke of a pen" was as fatuous as it was cynical. Yet instead of revealing the superficiality of Kennedy's understanding, the remark confirmed his reputation as an action man. That reputation was sealed in October with Kennedy's famous phone call to Coretta Scott King after her husband was arrested and denied bail.

In just three years Kennedy transformed himself from a conservative Democrat interested mainly in foreign policy to the logical inheritor of the New Deal. Not everyone, however, found the transformation convincing. Under the circumstances, the Democrats should have won easily in 1960. That they did not do so can be explained in large part by the negatives associated with Kennedy. His money, his aristocratic nature, his father's machinations, but especially his Catholicism turned voters away. Kennedy beat Nixon by the tiniest of margins: just one-tenth of a percent. But margins of victory were misleading, since the number of Americans who voted for Kennedy was tiny in comparison to the number who had high hopes for him. He'd been encouraging Americans to believe that a new frontier beckoned. Now he had to lead them to it.

The Sixties was a decade of consumerism—despite the efforts of all those who tried to make it something else. In the 1960 election, the American people were sold a product named Kennedy. During the course of the long campaign he remained the same person, though his image changed to suit public taste. Image and man were both present on January 20, 1961. Kennedy's inaugural address was a mixture of fancy rhetoric and frighteningly blunt policy, though most people heard only the beautiful words. For baby boomers, one line is remembered above all others: "Ask not what your country can do for you; ask what *you* can do for your country." Those words would be repeated millions of times at school assemblies and debating contests. Yet stirring words seldom lend themselves to deconstruction. They are swallowed whole, enjoyed for their music rather than their meaning. While nearly every American from that generation can recall those words, few understood their implications.[41]

The same holds true for the rest of the speech, in which Kennedy explained what he wanted of America. The message, however, was carefully camouflaged by poetry of exquisite cadence. Read the speech today and it seems frighteningly prophetic—it is littered with clues to the crises in Cuba, Laos, Vietnam, and Berlin, not to mention the billions of dollars shot into space. Listen to a recording of the speech, however, and it still sends shivers down the spine.

Kennedy was an aggressive, manly leader who possessed a quintessentially American belief in the possible. The world's problems were to him opportunities, prime candidates for benevolent American reform. "Let the word go forth from this time and place, to friend and foe alike," he proclaimed, "that the torch has been passed to a new generation of Americans—born in this century, tempered by war, disciplined by a hard and bitter peace, proud of our ancient heritage—and unwilling to witness or permit the slow undoing of those human rights to which this Nation has always been committed, and to which we are committed today at home and around the world." What followed was both a warning to the world and a call to arms. People in "the huts and villages across the globe struggling to break the bonds of mass misery" were put on notice that America would save them. Americans, meanwhile, were warned that they would have to bear the costs—in money and lives—of these rescue missions. America would embark on her new crusade "not because the Communists may be doing it, not because we seek their votes, but because it is right. If a free society cannot help the many who are poor, it cannot save the few who are rich." The Soviets meanwhile were warned that America would arm itself to protect its principles and to implement its plans. "We dare not tempt them with weakness. For only when our arms are sufficient beyond doubt can we be certain beyond doubt that they will never be employed."[42]

The new frontier carried a high price. Two months before the inauguration, Kennedy proclaimed that "men are not afraid to die for a life worth living"—an assertion which, while probably true, had costly implications. On January 20, he told the American people to expect sacrifices.

In your hands, my fellow citizens, more than in mine, will rest the final success or failure of our course. Since this country was founded, each generation of Americans has been summoned to give testimony to its national loyalty. The graves of young Americans who answered the call to service surround the globe.

Now the trumpet summons us again—not as a call to bear arms, though arms we need; not as a call to battle, though embattled we are—but a call to bear the burden of a long twilight struggle, year in and year out, . . . a struggle against the common enemies of man: tyranny, poverty, disease, and war itself.

Like the expert salesman he was, Kennedy swayed the American people with mellifluous rhetoric. They thought they were being sold a shiny new sports car. In fact, they were buying a tank. The message was not, however, misunderstood by the Soviets. As foreign minister Andrei Gromyko warned Khrushchev, Kennedy's victory would mean "a speeding-up of the arms race and, therefore, a further straining of the international situation with all the consequences that result from this."[43]

Kennedy's magnetism, Goodwin argued, arose from the fact that "he was as Americans would like themselves to be." That assessment is only half right, since what Americans saw was not the real Kennedy. It is doubtful that most Americans wanted to be pill-popping womanizers. Nor did they want to fight wars in faraway jungles. Millions would learn to love Kennedy not for what he was but for what he seemed. His promises were handsome, his ideals sublime.[44]

3

HARD RAIN

SHARPEVILLE: APARTHEID IS A WAY OF DEATH

Sharpeville was a model South African township, a place often presented as an example of the efficiency and humanity of the apartheid regime. Strategically situated to serve the large industrial cities of Vanderbijlpark and Vereeniging in southern Gauteng Province, it was established in 1942 when around 5,500 little houses were built for black workers. Eighteen years later, Sharpeville showed the world the horrors of apartheid.

Townships had been built to provide housing for blacks whose labor was welcome, but whose presence was not. They were the outward and visible manifestations of apartheid, providing a convenient (if grossly unjust) way of separating blacks from whites, while maintaining the essential network of dependencies which existed between the two. They were, in effect, colonies within the mother country.

In contrast to American-style segregation, apartheid was planned, systematic, and universally applied. Central to the system were the pass laws requiring blacks to carry pass books, or *dompas,* which allowed them to live in a particular township and to work in the city it serviced. "Of all the apartheid laws none is so pervasive, and few are as perverted," wrote the anti-apartheid activist David Sibeko. "The indignities are legion." No respect was shown for the sanctity of the family—spouses were separated if one of them failed to obtain the dompa for a particular area, and children over sixteen needed a permit to live with their parents. Dompas also depressed the labor market by preventing workers from migrating in search of better jobs.[1]

The ever-tightening apartheid regime, and the worldwide condemnation of it, placed Britain in a difficult position, since South Africa was a member of the Commonwealth. Britain was South Africa's best and, eventually, only friend. This friendship was partly sentimental but mainly pragmatic: nearly two-thirds of overseas investment in South Africa was British. No wonder, then, that Britain steadfastly resisted calls for economic sanctions. Nevertheless, over time, the British position grew increasingly uncomfortable, as Prime Minister Harold Macmillan signaled when he warned the South African parliament on February 3, 1960, that a "wind of change is blowing through this continent." While the speech was mainly intended to signal that Britain would not resist decolonization, its implications for South Africa were difficult to ignore. Politicians in Cape Town had, however, become quite expert at flouting world opinion.[2]

Within South Africa, opposition to apartheid was organized by the African National Congress (ANC), a group committed to a multiracial nation. The ANC sought to work within the system to abolish discrimination. Agitation through the political and legal systems was combined with peaceful protests. This strategy was, however, rendered ineffective by a steady stream of laws buttressing apartheid. As a result, some activists grew disillusioned with the ANC. They dubbed their philosophy "Africanism"—a direct rejoinder to multiracialism. Their policy of "Africa for the Africans" was not simply an assertion of sovereignty, but also an affirmation of racial pride. Africanists believed that only by encouraging black nationalism could the masses be mobilized. Eventually, they split from the ANC and formed the Pan-Africanist Congress (PAC) in April 1959, with Robert Mangaliso Sobukwe as president. "The issues are clear-cut," Sobukwe proclaimed. "In the arena of South African politics, there are today only two adversaries: the oppressor and the oppressed, the master and the slave." He believed that the PAC's militancy would "awaken . . . the imagination of the youth of our land, while giving hope to the aged who for years have lived in the trough of despair."[3]

Extensions to the pass laws served as a catalyst for both the ANC and the PAC. The former was first to announce its plans, outlining a series of protests to begin on March 31, 1960. This alarmed the nascent PAC, still struggling to establish its militant credentials. The PAC decided to steal the ANC's thunder by launching its own demonstration in the Vanderbijlpark/Vereeniging area on March 21. At a press conference on the 18th, Sobukwe affirmed his intention "to make sure that this campaign is conducted in a spirit of absolute nonviolence. . . . If the other side so desires, we will provide them with an opportunity to demonstrate to the world how brutal they can be." Like civil rights campaigners in the United States, the PAC aimed to goad the police into acting violently.[4]

Intent upon a massive demonstration, the PAC left nothing to chance. Activists cut phone lines into Sharpeville, thus restricting residents' exposure to less militant influences. Bus drivers were forcibly detained on the morning of the action, to prevent residents from leaving the township for their jobs in the city. According to Reverend Ambrose Reeves, when residents found that the buses were not running, "many of them set out on bicycles or on foot to their places of work, but some were met by Pan-Africanists who threatened to burn their passes or 'lay hands on them' if they did not turn back." The post-apartheid Truth and Reconciliation Commission (TRC) found "a degree of coercion of nonpoliticised Sharpeville residents who were pressurised into participating in the anti-pass protest."[5]

"The step we are taking is historic, pregnant with untold possibilities," Sobukwe told his followers on the eve of the demonstration. "We must, therefore, . . . appreciate our responsibility. The African people have entrusted their whole future to us. And we have sworn that we are leading them, not to death, but to life abundant. My instructions, therefore, are that our people must be taught NOW and CONTINUOUSLY THAT IN THIS CAMPAIGN we are going to observe ABSOLUTE NONVIOLENCE." In Sharpeville, around 5,000 protesters assembled. Crowds equally large gathered in the townships of Bophelong and Boipatong, while 20,000 assembled at Evaton. According to the plan, demonstrators were to march to the local police station without their pass books and offer themselves for arrest. The mass arrest would, Sobukwe thought, cause jails to overflow and the local economy to grind to a halt. "Industry will come to a standstill and the Government will be forced to accept our terms. And once we score that victory, there will be nothing else we will not be able to tackle."[6]

At first, everything went according to plan. The turnout was impressive and protesters remained entirely peaceful, thanks partly to the presence of large numbers of women and children. Humphrey Tyler, a white journalist, later recalled: "Many people shouted the Pan-Africanist slogan 'Izwe Lethu!' which means 'Our Land!' or gave the thumbs-up 'freedom' salute and shouted 'Afrika!' They were grinning, cheerful, and nobody seemed to be afraid. . . . The crowd seemed perfectly amiable. It certainly never crossed our minds that they would attack us or anybody." When the Sharpeville protesters reached the station, police refused to arrest them. Meanwhile, those at the back continued to advance. Fearing a crush, officers asked PAC officials to disperse the crowd. They complied and the crowd ceased pushing forward. The police, however, were not satisfied. At around 10:00 A.M., a squadron of low-flying jets buzzed the protesters, in an attempt to scare them away. This tactic had worked in Evaton, but the Sharpeville crowd remained steadfast.[7]

About 300 demonstrators remained in the police compound. "While the crowd was noisy and excitable, singing and occasionally shouting slogans, it was not a hostile crowd," Reeves insisted. "Their purpose was not to fight the police but to show by their presence their hostility to the pass system. . . . All through the morning no attack on the police was attempted. Even as late as 1:00 P.M. the Superintendent in charge of the township was able to walk through the crowd, being greeted by them in a friendly manner and chatting with some of them." Perhaps 300 police were present, the vast majority drafted in from outside. They had access to five Saracen armored cars, which were used as platforms from which to observe the crowd. All were armed.[8]

No one quite knows what caused the police to open fire. Some witnesses heard an order, others a single shot, others still the door of a Saracen slamming shut. At any rate, virtually in unison, at precisely 1:15 P.M., between fifty and seventy-five officers started firing. "I heard no warning to the crowd to disperse," Tyler insisted. "There was no warning volley." The police seemed to him intent on mowing down everyone in the compound.

> We heard the chatter of a machine gun, then another, then another. There were hundreds of women, some of them laughing. They must have thought the police were firing blanks. One woman was hit about ten yards from our car. Her companion, a young man, went back when she fell. He thought she had stumbled. Then he turned her over and saw that her chest had been shot away. He looked at the blood on his hand and said: "My God, she's gone!" . . . One little boy had on an old blanket coat, which he held up behind his head, thinking, perhaps, that it might save him from the bullets. Some of the children, hardly as tall as the grass, were leaping like rabbits.

Some were shot, too.... One of the policemen was standing on top of a Saracen, and it looked as though he was firing his gun into the crowd. He was swinging it around in a wide arc from his hip as though he were panning a movie camera.

In the chilly seconds of uncertainty, the crowd stood still. Once they realized that the police were firing live ammunition, they began to stampede. Officers continued to shoot at their backs. In just forty seconds, 705 rounds were fired. When the shooting stopped, sixty-nine people lay dead, including ten children. At least 180 were injured, of which nineteen were children. Around 150 of the injured were shot in the back.[9]

Neither police nor government showed remorse. The official line held that the station had come under attack and, fearing for their lives, officers had defended themselves. Blacks were accused of throwing stones and carrying an array of weapons, though no proof ever surfaced. Justification rested on the premise that the sheer number of protesters by definition represented a threat. "The Native mentality does not allow them to gather for a peaceful demonstration," claimed Lieutenant Colonel D. H. Pienaar, who emerged as spokesman. "For them to gather means violence." He insisted that the police response was not excessive. "If they do these things, they must learn their lessons the hard way." When asked at a Court of Enquiry whether he had learned any useful lessons from Sharpeville, Pienaar remarked "Well, we may get better equipment."[10]

Many years later, the TRC found no evidence of panic among the officers, but rather a "degree of deliberation in the decision to open fire." This indicated "that the shooting was more than the result of inexperienced and frightened police officers losing their nerve." The TRC concluded that

the police deliberately opened fire on an unarmed crowd that had gathered peacefully.... The Commission finds further that the SAP (South African Police) failed to give the crowd an order to disperse before they began firing and that they continued to fire upon the fleeing crowd, resulting in hundreds of people being shot in the back.... The Commission finds ... that many of the people fired upon and injured in the march were not politicised members of any political party, but merely persons opposed to carrying a pass.

The Sharpeville action had precisely the effect the PAC intended. The brutality of the South African government had been clearly exposed, and the anger of the black population overflowed. During the following week, demonstrations, marches, riots, and strikes occurred in every corner of the country, forcing the government to declare a state of emergency. More than 18,000 people were detained.[11]

The reaction abroad was equally dramatic. Most countries simply lost all patience with South Africa, henceforth treating it as a pariah state. On April 1, the UN Security Council condemned the "colonial oppression of the African people." This time, Britain was forced to join the chorus of disapproval, with the result that the UN resolution was virtually unanimous (only South Africa voted against). Ironically, however, in the period after the massacre South African exports to Europe, the United States, and Asia steadily increased—by 300 percent in the case of Asia. This suggests that the Northern Hemisphere's fondness for out-of-season fruit and vegetables and cheap wine outweighed its sense of justice.[12]

Since South Africa's economy continued to boom, the government felt no need to respond to moral outrage. Rather than relaxing apartheid restrictions, it tightened them. Under the Unlawful Organisations Act, passed on April 8, both the ANC and the PAC were formally banned. After a referendum resulted in a majority in favor of republicanism, South Africa withdrew from the Commonwealth in March 1961 and officially became a republic the following May. This policy had the overwhelming support of the white minority population, particularly those of Afrikaans descent.

"Sharpeville was a tragedy showing most plainly that the ideology of apartheid is a way of death and not of life," wrote Ambrose Reeves. The white regime had demonstrated how far it would go to protect its power. It had also graphically revealed its contempt for world opinion. In this context, nonviolent protest was unlikely to succeed. Both the PAC and the ANC reacted to their banning by forming military wings, the latter with Nelson Mandela as chief of staff. Both groups began a campaign of armed resistance.[13]

During the course of the 1960s, protest groups everywhere turned to violence to further their aims, but none with as much justification as the blacks of South Africa. As Mandela pronounced after his capture in 1962: "We have warned repeatedly that the Government, by resorting continually to violence, will breed in this country counter-violence among the people till ultimately, if there is no dawning of sanity on the part of the Government, the dispute . . . will finish up by being settled in violence and by force." Having sown the wind, white South Africans would reap the whirlwind.[14]

BAY OF PIGS: IT SEEMED LIKE A GOOD IDEA

The Bay of Pigs is situated on a desolate stretch of the Cuban coast, far from centers of population. Mosquito-infested swamps border a small beach. The coastal area then turns hilly, making passage into the interior difficult. In other words, it's a terrible place to stage an invasion.

On New Year's Day 1959, rebel forces under Fidel Castro completed the overthrow of the widely reviled Cuban dictator Fulgencio Batista. For those sympathetic to Castro and his sidekick Ernesto Che Guevara, it seemed the perfect example of a peasant-based revolution. Chronicles of the campaign would eventually become required reading for left-wing students around the world. For the American government, however, Castro spelled disaster.

Castro did not at first trumpet his allegiance to Communism, since he still hoped for peaceful coexistence with the United States. He understood precisely how dependent his country was upon America—for aid, investment, and trade. But, like Lumumba, he insisted that the relationship should not compromise the revolution. Before long, the Eisenhower administration decided that Castro's terms were incompatible with the maintenance of American business interests on the island. As the relationship grew frosty, Castro turned toward the Soviets, who were only too happy to gain a foothold in a country just ninety miles from Key West. Meanwhile, wealthy Cubans were leaving in droves, taking their money with them. Facing total economic collapse, Castro began an ambitious program of nationalization, directly threatening American companies. Keen to protect US interests, Eisenhower began plotting.

The task of toppling Castro fell to the CIA. The agency assumed that the raw material for a coup could easily be found, given the number of wealthy Cuban exiles in America who wanted to reclaim their country. On March 17, 1960, Eisenhower approved a CIA memo entitled "A Program of Covert Action against the Castro Regime." The objective, clearly stated, was to "bring about the replacement of the Castro regime with one more devoted to the interests of the Cuban people and more acceptable to the US, in such a manner as to avoid the appearance of US intervention."[15]

For the CIA, Cuba became a sacred vocation; agents displayed the zeal of missionaries. Convinced that Castro was deeply unpopular, they decided that toppling him would be easy. Confidence was buttressed by the successful overthrow of the left-wing government of Jacobo Arbenz in Guatemala in 1954, and his replacement by Carlos Castillo Armas, a man amenable to American interests. The CIA confidently assumed that it could make Cuba a carbon copy of Guatemala.

Preparations gathered pace while Nixon and Kennedy were battling for the presidency. As vice president, Nixon had been one of the main sponsors of the CIA plan. The idea was likewise in harmony with Kennedy's distinctive foreign policy. Kennedy disagreed with Eisenhower's reliance upon nuclear deterrence, preferring instead a strategy of "flexible response" in which military and political options would be carefully tailored to each foreign challenge. That strategy implied cloaks and daggers.

Plans were essentially set in stone by the time of Kennedy's inauguration. The CIA had pulled together a brigade of 1,400 Cuban exiles trained in Guatemala. In Cuba, spies and saboteurs were already preparing the ground. Exile pilots had been taught to fly B-26B light bombers, which would take out Castro's small air force. When CIA agents presented the plan to Kennedy, they brought maps with big, thick arrows extending directly from the Bay of Pigs to Havana. They spoke loudly, puffing out their chests like prize cockerels. Secretary of state Dean Rusk found their confidence infectious. "The CIA told us . . . that elements of the Cuban armed forces would defect and join the brigade, that there would be popular uprisings throughout Cuba when the brigade hit the beach, and that if the exile force got into trouble, its members would simply melt into the countryside." Some officials felt deep misgivings, but could not withstand the tidal wave of confidence. "[I] did not serve President Kennedy very well," Rusk later admitted. "I should have made my opposition clear . . . because he was under pressure from those who wanted to proceed."[16]

The strategists fully accepted that a force of 1,400 soldiers could not defeat Castro's army on its own. But the imbalance in forces did not matter, since the invasion was sure to spark a general uprising. General David Shoup, the Marine commandant, recalled: "The intelligence indicated that there were quite a number of people . . . ready to join in the fight against Castro. . . . My understanding was that the . . . people were just waiting for these arms and equipment." Rusk later admitted that "the uprising was utterly essential to success."[17]

Confidence was not unanimous. The maverick agent E. Howard Hunt had played a prominent part in the Guatemalan operation. A visit to Cuba convinced him that this was an entirely different affair. "All I could find was a lot of enthusiasm for Fidel Castro," he recalled.

> This was . . . a much larger body of land, an entrenched, well-trained, devoted communist group of followers of Castro—and the kind of psychological warfare we were able to run against Castro was insignificant. . . . Castro was secure, and he was beloved by millions in Cuba. . . . So, instead of our having a problem such as we had in Guatemala, of using less than 200 locals to overthrow a government, we were faced with a Cuban army, a Cuban militia, a loyal population—loyal to Castro, that is.

Hunt insisted upon a number of contingencies prior to invasion, one of which was that "Castro would have to be neutralized." Over subsequent months, he was shocked to find that nothing was done to satisfy that requirement. "Is anybody going after Castro?" he kept asking. "'It's in good hands,' was the answer I got, which was a great bureaucratic answer."[18]

Hunt's caution contrasted sharply with the optimism of pre-invasion intelligence reports. "The Castro regime is steadily losing popularity," agents maintained. "Disenchantment of the masses has spread through all the provinces." Resistance was likely to be low: "It is generally believed that the Cuban Army has been successfully penetrated by opposition groups and that it will not fight in the event of a showdown." The agency was confident that "the great mass of Cuban people believe that the hour of decision is at hand and that the survival of the CASTRO regime is in balance."[19]

Meanwhile, the Castro government remained quietly confident. On April 14, Che told the Soviet ambassador to Cuba that "given the presence of large contingents of well-armed people's militia and the revolutionary army, an operation of deploying paratroopers, even numbering several thousand troops, would be doomed to failure. Therefore . . . it is unlikely that the forces of external counterrevolution would undertake such a risk now, knowing that it would be senseless to count on any kind of extensive internal uprisings in Cuba." Che was right about the strength of his forces and the support of his people. He was, however, completely wrong in his assessment of the good sense of the Kennedy administration. Like a teenager buying his first car, Kennedy had bought himself a war without looking under the hood. Yet he was determined to maintain the pretense of detachment. Shortly before the invasion, he openly boasted: "We can be proud that the United States is not using its muscle against a small country." Everyone understood which small country he meant.[20]

On the morning of April 15, B-26B bombers flown by exile pilots from a Nicaraguan airfield and painted with the colors of the Fuerza Aerea Revolucionaria (FAR, the Cuban Air Force) attacked three airbases in Cuba. The planes scored some hits but did not come close to destroying Castro's air power, since he had moved his planes to safety in anticipation of attack. The CIA wanted the world to believe that FAR dissidents had carried out the attacks. The ruse fooled Adlai Stevenson, US ambassador to the United Nations, but almost no one else.

On April 17 the invasion went forward. The CIA had originally wanted an airborne landing, but, according to Hunt, this was vetoed by Rusk, who feared it would be "too obviously American." Planners therefore settled on a seaborne landing at the Bay of Pigs. The surrounding high ground offered Castro's forces plenty of places from which to pour murderous fire onto the tiny beachhead. To make matters worse, Kennedy decided against air strikes on the day of the invasion. That decision might have been motivated by the desire for plausible deniability, even though American involvement was obvious to virtually everyone by this stage. On the other hand, the White House might simply have realized that the plan was doomed and was already cutting its losses.[21]

The lack of air cover made no difference. A small force of 1,400 men landing on a beachhead with light equipment was doomed to fail against 30,000 Cuban soldiers, reinforced by Russian tanks and heavy artillery. Within minutes of landing, the exile force was cut to pieces. Out in the bay, a supply ship was destroyed by air attack, prompting the others to retreat. "We are out of ammo and fighting on the beach," a brigade commander radioed. "Please send help." A short time later came an even more desperate message: "In water. Out of ammo. Enemy closing in. Help must arrive in next hour." The exiles had been led to believe that US Marines would reinforce them, but that was another of the CIA's little fibs. By the time the battlefield went quiet, on the 21st of April, 114 exiles were dead and 1,189 captured. A few dozen managed to escape back to the ships.[22]

"This was a struggle of Cuban patriots against a Cuban dictator," Kennedy insisted on April 20. "While we could not be expected to hide our sympathies, we made it repeatedly clear that the armed forces of this country would not intervene in any way." Rusk called it a minor operation by "a group of courageous men who returned to Cuba determined to do what they could to assist the people in establishing freedom." Hypocritical platitudes, however, provided no shield against justifiable recrimination. Among the immediate casualties were CIA director Allen Dulles and deputy director Charles Cabell. An internal inquiry was commissioned to determine how the agency could have been so hopelessly misguided. Its conclusions were so damning that the report was embargoed and all but one copy destroyed. Efforts to release it were vigorously opposed until 1998.[23]

The report was a catalogue of CIA mistakes, misassumptions, artifice, and incompetence. Few of the agents spoke Spanish, which left them vulnerable to highly biased reports from interpreters. The budget, which started out at $4.4 million, rocketed to $46 million within a year. Agency officials treated exiles "like dirt," leaving the latter "wondering what kind of Cuban future they were fighting for." Members of the Revolutionary Council, a CIA-inspired alternative to the Castro government, were treated like "puppets" by the agency, and given no say in planning the invasion.

"This operation took on a life of its own," the report argued. "The agency was going forward without knowing precisely what it was doing." On the matter of a general uprising, the report revealed that there was "no intelligence evidence that Cubans in significant numbers could or would join the invaders or that there was any kind of an effective and cohesive resistance movement." Finally, "plausible denial was a pathetic illusion." The commission concluded that the invasion "carried death and misery to hundreds, destroyed millions of dollars worth of US property, and seriously damaged US prestige." Analysts could not hide their incredulity over the way the agency had been so hopelessly wrong.[24]

Undaunted, officials immediately began looking for other ways to topple Castro. On 16 March 1962, the counterinsurgency specialist Edward Lansdale advised the administration on possibilities. The mood was upbeat. "I remarked that the thesis of creating a revolution inside Cuba looked just as valid as ever," Lansdale recorded. "CIA professionals were now agreeing more and more that . . . the possibility of fracturing the regime pointed to some real opportunities." General Lyman Lemnitzer, chairman of the Joint Chiefs of Staff, revealed that the military "had plans for creating plausible pretexts to use force, with the pretexts either attacks on US aircraft or a Cuban action in Latin America for which we would re- taliate." One idea involved a rerun of the sinking of the *Maine:* "We could blow up a US warship in Guantanamo Bay and blame Cuba." Another possibility was to "develop a communist Cuban terror campaign in the Miami area, in other Florida cities and even in Washington. . . . The terror campaign could be pointed at Cuban refugees seeking haven in the United States." Someone suggested "sink[ing] a boatload of Cubans enroute to Florida." Another cunning plan, dubbed "Operation Dirty Trick," in- volved blaming the Cubans if the flight of astronaut John Glenn ended in disaster.[25]

A simultaneous study, called "Operation Mongoose," was overseen by attorney general Robert Kennedy. Imagination ran wild. "Operation Good Times" involved faking a picture of a half-naked, obese Castro surrounded by two voluptuous beauties "and a table brimming over with the most de- lectable Cuban food." The photo would carry the caption, "My ration is different." Covert-action specialists suggested, among other things, giving a poisoned scuba suit to Castro, sneaking him a poisoned pen, placing ex- ploding sea shells on the beach where he swam, and providing him with exploding cigars. One of the best ideas was to doctor his shampoo so that his hair and beard would fall out. "This was a bright idea," one CIA agent recalled. "The Cuban people would fall all over laughing at him and he would be ridiculed." According to a Joint Chiefs memo of March 13, 1962, some of these ideas were endorsed as "suitable for planning purposes."[26]

Just three months after Kennedy's rousing inaugural address, the impli- cations of his swashbuckling style had been painfully revealed. Over the years, attempts have been made to deflect blame from Kennedy by arguing that the idiotic Bay of Pigs plan was a legacy from Eisenhower. But Ken- nedy could have canceled the operation at any time up to April 15, with the stroke of a pen. He did not do so, because it harmonized so well with his determination to "pay any price" and "bear any burden" in the fight against Communism. In going ahead, he got the worst of all possible worlds. He had demonstrated that the United States was prepared to scheme in order to remove a leader it did not like, no matter how popular that leader might have been among his people. More important, he had also demonstrated that there were limits to American commitment—in other words, that the United States would not pay *any* price. Kennedy had managed the double feat of alienating his friends and angering his enemies.

America's enemies had long criticized its "imperialist" habits. Until the Bay of Pigs, that criticism was based on debatable evidence. The United States had, after all, championed colonial self-determination at a time when European powers stubbornly clung to colonies. That anti-imperialist reputation was, however, seriously damaged at the Bay of Pigs. America seemed to be embarking on a new wave of colonial adventure under the guise of anti-Communism. For all that Kennedy might have argued that he was only trying to help the poor people "enslaved" by Communism, he could not hide the fact that American tobacco and sugar barons would benefit immensely from his action.

One other result of the fiasco is seldom appreciated. Kennedy gave the emerging student movement a cause and a hero. Throughout the 1960s, students around the world accused the United States of pursuing a cynically imperialist foreign policy. As evidence, they repeatedly cited Cuba, the perfect romantic cause. Thanks to Kennedy, Cuba became defiant David bravely confronting the American Goliath.

BERLIN: THE WALL

Khrushchev called Berlin the testicles of the West. "Every time I want to make the West scream, I squeeze on Berlin."[27]

In truth, Berlin's pain was felt at least as sharply in Moscow as in Washington. For Khrushchev, that pain was caused by rejection. From 1945 to 1950, approximately 1.6 million people left East Germany, turning their backs on Communism. During the subsequent decade, between 100,000 and 200,000 escaped each year, most using West Berlin as a bolt-hole. To make matters worse, a good number were young, highly trained professionals who were desperately needed for the economic development of East Germany.

In November 1958, Khrushchev took action. He felt he could do so because, for the first time since 1945, the United States was genuinely frightened of Soviet military power. Sputnik, the first manmade satellite, seemed proof of Soviet missile prowess. Feeling confident, Khrushchev gave the Western powers six months to quit Berlin, whereupon it would be declared a free city. As fears grew that the border would be sealed, the exodus quickened.

Soviet and American ambitions were remarkably similar: both sought stability in Central Europe, and both saw Berlin as crucial to this need. American ambassador Llewellyn Thompson advised Eisenhower that the Soviets hoped to use Berlin to force "our recognition in some form of the East German regime." Khrushchev desperately wanted the West to acknowledge the validity of East Germany, because stability in Eastern Europe would make the Soviet Union feel safer. Stability was, however, threatened by the fact that West Berlin existed as an easy escape route for East German dissidents.[28]

Khrushchev's fears increased as a result of West Germany's rearmament and its role in NATO plans. In 1955, Eisenhower announced his desire for Western Europe to be a "third great power bloc," to be achieved by helping European powers build their own nuclear arsenals. Bonn's decision in March 1958 to enter into nuclear sharing agreements with the United States understandably worried Khrushchev. He thought rearmament might give West Germany the confidence to undermine East Germany's stability. More fundamentally, given memories of 20 million dead in the last war, the prospect of a revitalized Germany—armed with nuclear weapons—frightened him.[29]

American recognition of East Germany would have eased Soviet fears, but that option was adamantly opposed by West German chancellor Konrad Adenauer, on the grounds that it contradicted the official goal of reunification. The German tail wagged the American dog. Since the Americans could not afford to alienate Adenauer, they had to take a tough line on the question of Berlin and East Germany. Adenauer maintained that any concession would open the door to eventual recognition. The Americans therefore had no option but to reject any change in the status of Berlin and to call Khrushchev's bluff. Secretary of state John Foster Dulles confidently argued that "there is not one chance in a thousand the Soviets will push it to the point of war."[30]

Eisenhower therefore answered Khrushchev's ultimatum with the cold threat of nuclear annihilation. He was optimistic that, if the Soviets were made fully aware of the consequences of aggression, they would be deterred from acting aggressively. His patient determination eventually forced Khrushchev to back down. Instead of enforcing the deadline, Khrushchev agreed to talks. At Camp David, in September 1959, the two leaders agreed that the Berlin problem should be settled by negotiation, not force. There progress halted. Eisenhower seriously considered making Berlin a free city, guaranteed by the United Nations, but Adenauer vetoed the idea. The era of good feelings came to an abrupt end with the shooting down of a U-2 spy plane over the Soviet Union on May 1, 1960. In the aftermath of that incident, Khrushchev announced that he wanted to wait at least six to eight months before resuming talks, meaning that he would start again with a new president.

According to Fyodor Burlatsky, a close aide of Khrushchev's, Berlin offered a genuine opportunity for better US-Soviet relations. "Diplomatic recognition of the GDR [East Germany] could have made a compromise possible and opened up the way for détente," he feels. Interviewed in September 1988, he could not understand why Kennedy had failed to exploit this opportunity. Carl Kaysen, a Kennedy aide, replied: "A one-word answer would be 'Konrad Adenauer.' Kennedy felt . . . responsibility as the leader of the NATO alliance. He felt strongly about the commitment made a long time ago that the Federal Republic [West Germany] was the legitimate government." Kennedy feared that if Adenauer failed, West Germany might be taken over by "dangerous right-wing radicals" bent on aggressive nationalist resurgence.[31]

Khrushchev, Burlatsky argues, "had an inferiority complex and was trying to catch up with the United States. . . . I do not feel that John Kennedy understood this." In fact, the Americans were fully appreciative of Khrushchev's tender ego. "His convictions reflect . . . his nation's persisting range of insecurity and inferiority," a State Department document of May 1961 asserted. "As a result of this, he [is] extremely sensitive to slights real or imagined, direct or inferred, to himself, his political faith, or his nation." Instead of pandering to Khrushchev's insecurity, however, Kennedy tried to exploit it.[32]

Kennedy saw Berlin as more than just a Cold War pawn. As Kaysen argued at the time, American "commitment to the freedom of West Berlin . . . transcends its relation to our ties with Germany or its significance as a forward post in the Cold War. We have repeatedly pledged our word to the two million West Berliners that we would continue to defend their freedom." In other words, beyond issues of Cold War posturing, Kennedy believed in "doing the right thing." He was also convinced that he could achieve more in Berlin than Eisenhower had managed. Believing that his predecessor's strategy of massive retaliation lacked subtlety, Kennedy persuaded himself that a strategy of "flexible response," when combined with a willingness to increase military spending, would yield a better solution. That confidence applied not just to Berlin, but to every foreign-policy problem.[33]

In fact, thanks to Adenauer's intransigence, Kennedy's options were severely limited. Like Eisenhower, he was forced to fall back upon deterrence. He nevertheless insisted that his brand of deterrence was more credible, since it did not depend exclusively on nuclear weapons. He felt that Eisenhower's refusal to consider conventional war had rendered Berlin vulnerable because the Soviets did not believe that the United States, in a crisis, would actually decide that the city was worth a nuclear confrontation. Kennedy therefore set out to persuade the Soviets that he could fight a conventional war. A face-off begun with conventional forces would, in his view, demonstrate American resolve and allow the Soviets time to reconsider their aggression. He and his strategists formulated a ladder of escalation in which the first few rungs did not involve nuclear weapons. The first nuclear rungs, for that matter, entailed purely "symbolic" strikes designed only to demonstrate resolve.

To understand this strategy, we must appreciate Kennedy's credibility problem. Eisenhower, a victorious general, had no problems convincing the Soviets that he meant business. They could not afford to call his bluff, since doing so risked nuclear annihilation. Kennedy, in contrast, seemed weak and unproven—an intellectual, not a leader. The Bay of Pigs fiasco and an egregious settlement in Laos seemed to confirm his weakness. Therefore, unlike Eisenhower, Kennedy could not simply brandish nuclear weapons and expect the Soviets to take him seriously. He had first to prove himself by actually deploying ground troops and forcing a confrontation.

While the administration was reasonably confident that the strategy would work, those at its cutting edge were pessimistic. NATO supreme commander General Lauris Norstad felt that the idea of a non-nuclear battle for Berlin was risky. He questioned whether the Allies would be able to "enforce a . . . controlled development of the battle" and was not confident that they would be able to "dictate the Soviet response." An even more worrying interjection came from Thompson on May 27, 1961:

> [Khrushchev] has so deeply committed his personal prestige and that of Soviet Union to some action on Berlin and German problems that if we take completely negative stand . . . this would probably lead to developments in which chance of war or ignominious Western retreat are close to 50–50. . . . Both sides consider other would not risk war over Berlin. Danger arises from fact that if [Khrushchev] carries out his declared intentions and we carry out ours, situation likely to get out of control and military as well as political prestige would become involved, making retreat for either side even more difficult.

Again, the issue of credibility proved paramount. A fearsome array of weapons was not by itself enough to demonstrate Kennedy's resolve. Khrushchev had been doubtful of Eisenhower's willingness to push the Berlin crisis to the point of thermonuclear war, but never sufficiently so to call the president's bluff. For a variety of reasons, the Soviet premier was even more doubtful about Kennedy's determination, and therefore much more likely to call his bluff.[34]

Despite all the attention paid to Berlin, the Kennedy administration was not adequately prepared for the possibility that the Soviets and East Germans might attempt to solve the refugee problem by building a wall. If the White House considered the possibility at all, it was to accept that little could be done about it, beyond a bit of saber rattling and some complaints to the United Nations. In private, the administration considered a wall a reasonable, if regrettable, solution, in the sense that it would remove the main source of Soviet dismay and perhaps stabilize the situation. That assessment did not, however, take into account the psychological effect upon West Germany.

Burlatsky contends that the decision to build the Wall was more that of the East German leader Walter Ulbricht than of Khrushchev. "You had Adenauer; we had Ulbricht," he maintains. "At least two or three times each month he would . . . harass Khrushchev about his ability and willingness to support East Germany in its quest for . . . the construction of the Berlin Wall." That said, Khrushchev appears to have become convinced of its necessity, after visiting West Berlin in disguise. The stark difference in the standard of living between the two halves of the city made him understand why so many people were leaving. "I spent a great deal of time trying to think of a way out," he later recalled. Since no answers materialized, the simple solution was a wall.[35]

Construction began on August 13, 1961. Khrushchev saw the Wall not just as a barrier, but also as an instrument of foreign policy—a method of testing American resolve. He agreed to its construction on the condition that the first phase would consist only of barbed wire, so that he could see how NATO would react. He was not prepared to push the issue to the point of war, but if the Americans accepted some kind of barrier, it could then be strengthened.

Kennedy expressed anger, but took no serious steps to block construction. As for Adenauer, the Wall itself was less disturbing than the facile response of the Americans. Fearful that the situation would poison America's relationship with West Germany, Kennedy reinforced the Berlin garrison by sending a US Army brigade from West Germany toward the city, with no clear instructions as to what it should do if Russian troops blocked its path. He also sent General Lucius Clay to the city as his personal representative, a man chosen precisely because he was known as a hardliner.

Clay soon had a replica section of the Wall built in a secluded park in West Berlin, for the purpose of practicing assaults and frightening the Russians. American troops also launched probes into East Germany in order to assert their right of passage. These, however, appear to have been misinterpreted by the Soviets, who took them as an intention to break through the Wall. Against everyone's wishes, the situation rapidly escalated. As Norstad had warned, controlling the crisis was easy in theory but difficult in practice. When Clay deployed tanks to reinforce the probes at Checkpoint Charlie on October 27, the Soviets responded in kind. Suddenly, the world stood on the edge of war.

Around this time, Robert McNamara, Kennedy's defense secretary, questioned a senior NATO commander about the likely scenario. "He said the Soviets would probably do *a* and we *b*; they *c* and we *d*; they *e* and we *f*; and then they would be forced to *g*. And when I said, 'What do we do then?' he replied, 'We should use nuclear weapons.' When I asked how I expected the Soviets to respond, he said, 'With nuclear weapons.'" In the end, the superpowers managed to find an escape from alphabetic logic.

While Clay strutted aggressively, Kennedy and Khrushchev engaged in back-channel communications designed to defuse the situation. This exercise of good sense turned out to be much more important than what American and Soviet troops were doing on the ground.[36]

The peaceful resolution is all the more interesting in view of the Soviets' nuclear capability. Kennedy had built his presidential campaign on the "missile gap" which supposedly endangered the United States. Yet surveillance subsequently revealed that the Soviets did not have 1,000 ICBMs, or even 500; they had just four. In a Department of Defense news release of October 21, Roswell Gilpatric, the deputy secretary of defense, warned that the United States has a "nuclear retaliatory force of such lethal power that an enemy move which brought it into play would be an act of self-destruction." He wasn't bluffing. In other words, the United States was perfectly capable of enforcing its will over the issue of Berlin.[37]

The question then arises: If the United States possessed such profound superiority, why didn't it use that power? Surely if ever there was a time for the country to launch a devastating first strike, this was it. Kennedy, however, backed down, perhaps because a RAND study had predicted that an American first strike, no matter how successful, could not prevent some Soviet nuclear weapons from getting through, with the result that two million Americans might die. An even starker prediction came in early June 1961, when Kennedy inquired how many Americans might die in an all-out nuclear exchange with the Soviet Union. The answer came back from the Pentagon: seventy million. Kennedy was visibly shaken. His fears increased when senior strategists admitted on September 20 that they did not know precisely where all the USSR's nuclear weapons were located.[38]

Kennedy also discovered that nuclear weapons did not fit well into his strategy of flexible response. On September 6, General Lemnitzer revealed that the United States had only one Single Integrated Operating Plan (SIOP) for deploying nuclear weapons. The latest version included targets in the Soviet Union, Eastern Europe, North Korea, and China. Lemnitzer admitted that although the plan was woefully short on flexibility, "it is far better than anything previously in existence." Kennedy was not prepared to destroy most of the world in order to achieve victory in Berlin, nor did he believe that his people would consider it worthwhile to sacrifice at least two million American lives in order to enforce a point in Germany. In other words, the United States simply had to learn to live with the Berlin

Wall. As Kennedy candidly admitted, "It's not a very nice solution, but a wall is a hell of a lot better than a war."[39]

The United States hoped that the fait accompli of the Wall would persuade the West Germans to agree to a de facto recognition of East Germany. Adenauer, however, would not budge. As a result, though the scare of nuclear war rendered the Soviets and Americans more inclined to talk, it did not make it easier to find a solution, since any solution involving formal recognition of East Germany remained intolerable to Bonn. Both sides eventually discovered that the only workable system was the one they already had—namely, where the status of Berlin remained unclear and the West continued to pretend that East Germany did not exist. The United States would maintain a massive military presence in Germany in order to reassure the Federal Republic and the rest of Europe of its commitment. For nearly three decades, bitter antagonism would prove more stable than the unpredictability of negotiation.

And what of the Soviets? They apparently did not see Berlin as a crisis to the same extent that the Americans did. "There was no danger of atomic war in Moscow," Burlatsky contends. "Maybe in the American point of view this was a frightening consideration, but for the Soviets there was not the danger." He also argues that, despite all the saber-rattling, neither Eisenhower nor Kennedy managed to convince the Politburo that Berlin was actually a serious crisis. "About 98–99 percent of the Soviets believed Americans would not use nuclear weapons to protect Berlin." Khrushchev, he elaborated, "never thought that the Berlin crisis was fraught with the danger of an armed conflict. He was convinced that the West would swallow the pill." This belief gave Khrushchev the confidence to pursue concessions through the old-fashioned method of bullying and swagger. According to Burlatsky, he wasn't playing a sophisticated game of chess appropriate to the complexities of the nuclear age, but rather a simple game of checkers. "Although he demanded very much, he was satisfied with what he received." In his memoirs, Khrushchev remarked: "The West had tested our resolve by prodding us with the barrels of their cannons and found us ready to accept their challenge. They learned they couldn't frighten us. I think it was a great victory for us, and it was won without firing a single shot." Leaving aside the understandable gloss, this assessment seems rather sound.[40]

On his visit to Berlin in June 1963, Kennedy proclaimed: "All free men, wherever they may live, are citizens of Berlin. Therefore, as a free man, I take pride in the words 'Ich bin ein Berliner.'" They were fine words, even if in this context "ein Berliner" is actually a doughnut. But they were just words. For all that Kennedy feigned contempt for the Wall, he welcomed its existence. Arthur Schlesinger Jr. later confessed that "privately, the Kennedy White House breathed a sigh of relief over each brick Khrushchev put into the wall." On August 15, 1961, the East German paper *Neues Deutschland* carried an editorial with the headline "Fantastic, How Everything Worked Out." That sentiment, it seems, was shared by both sides.[41]

AP BAC: BAD NEWS FROM A PLACE CALLED VIETNAM

Ap Bac was a village of no consequence. Hundreds of hamlets like it existed in South Vietnam—primitive huts clustered around a rice paddy where peasants lived and worked as their ancestors had for centuries. Then, in 1963, Ap Bac suddenly became important because someone decided to hold a battle there. It was chosen at random in this war where place was nothing and killing everything.

In 1961 few Americans could have located Vietnam on a map. Their new president, however, knew the country's precise location and why that location was important. Vietnam, Kennedy had argued in 1956, was "a proving ground for democracy . . . a test of American responsibility and determination." At the time he uttered those words, French imperialists were taking a terrible beating from Viet Minh nationalists at Dien Bien Phu. Vietnam, Kennedy insisted, was "the cornerstone of the Free World in southeast Asia, the keystone in the arch, the finger in the dike."[42]

The defeat of the French in 1956 led to the division of the country between the Communist North (the Democratic Republic of Vietnam, or DRV) and non-Communist South (the Republic of Vietnam, or RVN). This was less than the Communist leader Ho Chi Minh expected, but he was a patient man. Standing in the way of complete unification were the South Vietnamese. Like Ho, they were devout nationalists, but unlike him they were rather fond of commerce. Fearful of Ho's intentions, they looked to the United States for protection, though it galled them to do so. To the United States, the complexities of internal politics were unimportant—Vietnam was crucial because it was a domino that must not fall. In the struggle against Communism, the United States made friends with crooks and tyrants, calling them all patriots. Thus, Kennedy made RVN president Ngo Dinh Diem, a man of dubious virtue, into "one of the true statesmen of the new Asia."[43]

As a Democrat and (supposedly) a liberal, Kennedy was deeply distrusted by the anti-Communist lobby. He had therefore to bark louder than Eisenhower in order to command the same level of respect. To complicate matters further, setbacks in Germany, Cuba, and Laos in the first few months of his administration made decisive action in Vietnam imperative. His strategy of "flexible response" put enormous pressure on the military, which had to prepare for a massive war on the plains of Eastern Europe *and* small guerrilla contests in the jungles of Latin America and Asia. Kennedy also insisted that fighting Communism was not just about winning battles. "Too long," he argued, "we have fixed our eyes on traditional military needs, on armies prepared to cross borders, on missiles posed for flight. Now it should be clear that this is no longer enough—that our security may be lost piece by piece, country by country, without the firing of a single missile or the crossing of a single border." In other words, where Communist insurgency threatened, military action would have to coincide with efforts to win hearts and minds.[44]

By the summer of 1961, Communist insurgents in South Vietnam had so effectively undermined Diem's authority that, according to the CIA, "travel on public roads more than fifteen miles outside of Saigon has become hazardous." Worried that South Vietnam stood on the brink of collapse, Kennedy added $42 million to an aid program already costing $220 million per year. In addition, General Maxwell Taylor and Walt Rostow (Special Assistant for National Security Affairs) were sent to South Vietnam to investigate. On November 1, they suggested a shift to a "limited partnership" and called for the deployment of 8,000 American combat troops to "provide the military presence necessary to produce the desired effect on national morale." Taylor and Rostow also maintained that the DRV was "extremely vulnerable to conventional bombing, a weakness which should be exploited diplomatically in convincing Hanoi to lay off."[45]

Secretary of state Rusk and defense secretary McNamara echoed these sentiments. "The United States should commit itself to the clear objective of preventing the fall of South Viet-Nam to the Communist[s]" they wrote. "We should be prepared to introduce United States combat forces.

. . . It may also be necessary for United States forces to strike at the source of the aggression in North Viet-Nam." The one dissenting voice was under secretary of state George Ball, who warned Kennedy that if he acted on these recommendations, in five years the United States would have 300,000 men in "the paddies and jungles and never find them again." He feared "a protracted conflict far more serious than Korea."[46]

"George, you're just crazier than hell," Kennedy replied. "That just isn't going to happen."[47]

Kennedy nevertheless rejected the recommendations, opting instead for half measures. A changed role for American military advisers was approved, allowing them to work with lower-echelon combat units. Over the following year, an additional 10,000 advisers were deployed, while 120 helicopters and 300 aircraft were also sent. In February 1962, the Military Assistance Command, Vietnam (MACV) was formed to oversee the steadily expanding commitment.

Communist forces meanwhile grew like jungle vines. By the end of 1961, the People's Liberation Armed Forces (PLAF, or Viet Cong), the military arm of the National Liberation Front (NLF), had 20,000 active members—an increase of 12,000 in just six months. Aiding the insurgents was a support system of about 200,000 loyalists infiltrated throughout the country.[48] A big army did not, however, mean incessant fighting, since military violence played a small part in revolutionary strategy. Grassroots political indoctrination was still the preferred way of toppling Diem. In fact, Hanoi feared that military escalation might convince the Americans to commit combat troops. Ho wanted to persuade the United States to accept a compromise in South Vietnam, similar to that achieved in Laos. The NLF would then be allowed a part in governing South Vietnam, a position from which it could gradually usurp power. Ho recognized that this scenario would be less likely to occur if American soldiers were fighting and dying in South Vietnam.

Missing from the American perception was an understanding of the political nature of the revolution, and therefore the realization that a predominantly military response to it was bound to be futile. "The people are the eyes and ears of the army; they feed and keep our soldiers," the great Vietnamese revolutionary Truong Chinh once wrote. "The people are the water and our army the fish." The revolution was utterly dependent upon a dutiful peasantry. Peasants were (according to Ho and Chinh) "unlucky and simpleminded" people who "accept their wretched state because they do not understand the cause of their misery." The revolution would enlighten them, whereupon they would "leap into battle, determined to wage a decisive struggle against their exploiters."[49]

Once enlightened, peasants provided manpower, transport, food, cover, and intelligence for soldiers. Guerrillas protected the people but, more important, impressed upon them the inexorable strength of the revolution—the idea that resistance was futile. A new social code was enforced, facilitating the complete transformation of the peasant's world. Cadres were measured by how completely they transformed village life. Those who failed to meet the revolution's high standards were ruthlessly purged.

Cadres were fanatics wedded to revolution. The NLF was essentially a sophisticated cult in which techniques of mind control were highly refined. Recruits were placed in cells of three to ten individuals and subjected to grueling self-criticism sessions, designed to destroy individuality. "We had no private lives to speak of," a former cadre recalled. "Although we were teenagers, we didn't have any girlfriends. I told myself that I should live as a real Communist lives, the pure life of the revolutionary."[50]

Only a tiny percentage of the population in the South were ever "true believers," devoted to the revolution. Most peasants practiced what the French called *attentisme*—they were opportunistic, their allegiance shifting with the fortunes of the war. Few actually believed in socialism, but instead wanted the parcel of land the NLF offered as a bribe. In many cases, loyalty to the NLF was inversely proportional to the cruelty of the local RVN officials. Peasants who had been alienated by injustice, corruption, and crippling taxes desperately hoped the NLF would provide salvation. As one former NLF cadre admitted, however, there was no sense in rescuing peasants from oppression prematurely, since Saigon's cruelties proved useful. "According to a saying of Mao Tse-tung: 'A firefly can set a field ablaze.' Yet for a firefly to set a whole field ablaze, the field must be extremely dry. 'To make the field dry' in this situation meant that we had to make the people suffer until they could no longer endure it. Only then would they carry out the Party's armed policy."[51]

A strict moral code supposedly governed cadre behavior—they were not supposed to steal, rape, despoil, or murder. That code, however, was another handy myth. When manpower was in short supply or when the war was going badly, moral purity became a luxury. Given the obvious iniquities of the Saigon regime, it is safe to assume that a revolution as righteous as the one Ho advertised would have succeeded much earlier. Though most peasants insisted that the NLF treated them better than the ARVN (South Vietnam's army), thugs existed on both sides.

The revolution was, from the beginning, a brutal, sadistic monster. Its distinguishing feature was not moral purity but naked terror. "Fragment the opposition's . . . leadership, if necessary using assassination and torture," cadres were advised. The process of "liberating" a village involved killing those of influence: village chiefs, landowners, district officials, and schoolteachers. Anyone who could read was particularly at risk, since the revolution depended upon ignorance. According to one study, 36,725 assassinations and 58,499 abductions were carried out in the years 1957 to 1972. Terror, argued the senior commander Vo Nguyen Giap, raised the morale of insurgents, frightened opponents, and kept the masses in line. Honest officials were most at risk, since they posed the greatest threat to NLF influence. Crooks, on the other hand, were kept alive to keep the peasants suffering.[52]

Kennedy's response to political insurgency of this type involved building strategic hamlets. Peasants were herded into fortified compounds, the logic being that anyone outside the fence was automatically an enemy and could be eliminated. Diem began an ambitious program of construction in early 1962, with the goal of 14,000 hamlets in fourteen months. By October, he was claiming that 7,267,517 people were protected. In truth, the scheme provided a golden opportunity for his cronies to sell American construction materials to peasants at extortionate prices. Peasants consequently hated the hamlets, which seemed another form of oppression. Because the hamlet did not protect peasants from exploitation by their own government, they had little incentive to defend it against PLAF incursions. By spring 1963, only 1,500 of the 8,500 hamlets actually constructed were still viable. The debacle revealed the weakness of Kennedy's approach. Good intentions and generous funding had not won over the people, who still associated American policy with the venal Diem.

Progress on the military front was even less impressive. Diem's forces were supposedly better trained, and definitely better equipped, but could not control the war. This was rudely demonstrated on January 2, 1963, when ARVN units went to Ap Bac, in the Mekong Delta, to teach the PLAF a lesson. A short, victorious battle would, it was thought, demonstrate the strength of the Saigon regime and the futility of supporting the NLF. For their part, the NLF welcomed a showdown, since they were keen to demonstrate that American weaponry did not render the ARVN invincible.

PLAF troops were disciplined, well-trained, and deeply committed. Their light weaponry was ideally suited to the type of battle they preferred to fight. By the time the ARVN arrived, they had dug themselves into virtually invisible foxholes on high ground. The plan called for a classic guerrilla ambush: the enemy would be drawn into a trap and dealt a devastating blow, whereupon the guerrillas would escape before ARVN reinforcements arrived.

The ARVN, like their American sponsors, worshiped weaponry. They had a four-to-one advantage in personnel, backed by the best equipment America could provide: helicopters, observation planes, armored personnel carriers (APCs), and fighter-bombers equipped with napalm. What they lacked was leadership—the local commander, Colonel Bui Dinh Dam, was chosen for loyalty rather than competence. He deployed his helicopter-borne troops in the middle of a rice paddy, providing the PLAF with something akin to a carnival shooting gallery. As the helicopters landed, a torrent of fire erupted. Four were destroyed, with seventeen soldiers (including three Americans) killed instantly. At this point, the reserves in the APCs should have been deployed, but their commander was too busy panicking. Skyraiders swooped in with napalm, but with limited effect. When the APCs finally moved in, they were beaten back by ruthlessly precise fire. Troops found themselves pinned down in knee-high water by an enemy they could not even see.

At nightfall the PLAF slipped away, satisfied that a point had been made. The battle was supposed to have demonstrated the invincibility of air mobility—troops in helicopters—but instead confirmed the old values of commitment, discipline, leadership, and training. On the strength of the PLAF's performance, NLF recruitment dramatically increased. Meanwhile, Americans argued about how to interpret the battle. Lieutenant Colonel John Paul Vann, the senior adviser on the scene, and one of the most perceptive commanders to serve in Vietnam, concluded that ARVN troops had no hope of ever defeating the PLAF. The implication was clear: if the United States wanted to destroy Communism in Vietnam, it would have to do the job itself.

Vann was not actually confident that American troops could succeed where the ARVN had failed. Nor was Senate majority leader Mike Mansfield, who toured Vietnam around this time. On his return, he warned legislators that, despite all the time and money spent, the task of establishing a non-Communist Vietnam was "not even at the beginning of a beginning." The implication was painful. The United States would not be able to achieve its aims without "a truly massive commitment of American military personnel . . . and the establishment of some form of neocolonial rule."[53]

In Washington, Mansfield was easily dismissed as a worrywart. Optimism was official policy at the Pentagon. The congenitally cheerful General Paul Harkins, head of MACV, assured Kennedy that "[we] are winning slowly on the present thrust." General Earle Wheeler, Army chief of staff, insisted that "improvement is a daily fact." Analysts magically transformed Ap Bac into a victory, on the grounds that the PLAF had eventually abandoned their positions. It did not occur to them that, in guerrilla warfare, holding ground was immaterial.[54]

America was slipping into a quagmire without remotely understanding its predicament. Each tiny setback implied increased involvement. Yet greater American involvement weakened the ARVN, alienated the peasantry, and, by implication, strengthened the NLF. According to Arthur Schlesinger, at one turbulent Cabinet meeting, Robert Kennedy asked why, if the situation was indeed so dire, the United States did not simply withdraw. The "question hovered for a moment, then died away." It was "a hopelessly alien thought in a field of unexplored assumptions and entrenched convictions."[55]

NOVAYA ZEMLYA AND CUBA: BIG BOMBS

On October 30, 1961, the Soviets tested a new thermonuclear bomb over Novaya Zemlya Island in the Arctic. Observers saw "a huge bright orange ball . . . powerful and arrogant like Jupiter. . . . It seemed to suck the whole earth into it."[56] The mushroom cloud rose to sixty-four kilometers, the flash was seen one thousand kilometers away, and the explosive force leveled houses hundreds of kilometers distant. The bomb, lovingly called Tsar Bomba, had a yield of fifty-seven megatons, or ten times the combined total of all explosives used during World War II. In fact, the device was designed to yield a hundred megatons, but had been intentionally muted.

Tsar Bomba was a huge atomic raspberry blown at the Americans. It was not a weapon, but a political gesture designed to frighten the United States and to underline Soviet disgust with the slow progress in arms control negotiations. Over the years, both sides had made gestures toward limiting proliferation and testing, but progress always stalled in the quagmire of verification. The Paris conference of 1960 had offered real hope but was thrown into disarray with the downing of a U-2 spy plane. A furious Khrushchev walked out, muttering about the impossibility of trusting Americans.

Tensions ratcheted with the Bay of Pigs fiasco and then Berlin. A voluntary moratorium on testing which had begun while Eisenhower was president was ended in August 1961. Seven months after Kennedy took office, relations with the Soviet Union were worse than at any time since Russian and American soldiers shook hands on the banks of the Elbe. Instead of talking, the superpowers were trading insults.

Prior to the Tsar Bomba test, Khrushchev had openly boasted of his new power. "When the enemies of peace threaten us with force," he warned, "they must be and will be countered with force, and more impressive force, too. Anyone who is still unable to understand this today will certainly understand it tomorrow." Washington feigned indifference. The Defense Department proclaimed that American experts had studied the possibility of a huge bomb but had "concluded that the military value was so questionable that it was not worth developing such weapons even though we [have] the . . . capacity to do so."[57]

Immediately after the blast, Kennedy assured the American people that it was not necessary "to explode a fifty-megaton nuclear device to confirm that we have many times more nuclear power than any nation on earth." In fact, the Americans were not as calm as Kennedy suggested. "It became obvious that . . . there was no containing [the Russians]," the nuclear scientist Herbert York recalled. "They were shooting not just this big bomb, but lots and lots of them and we essentially did the same thing. We went and . . . got bombs from wherever we could find 'em and took 'em to Nevada and shot them just in order to respond to these Russian tests. It was a crazy period."[58]

The tests provided a drum roll prior to the great dramatic crescendo of Cuba. On October 14, 1962, the Americans discovered that the Soviets were installing ballistic missiles on the island. "The purpose of these bases can be none other than to provide a nuclear strike capability against the Western Hemisphere," Kennedy warned eight days later. Such a "deliberately provocative" challenge had to be met "if our courage and our commitments are ever to be trusted again by either friend or foe."[59]

For Khrushchev, the missiles were a quick-fix solution to Soviet strategic weakness. According to reliable estimates, the United States had a nine-to-one advantage in deliverable nuclear weapons. In truth, a few missiles in Cuba were inconsequential. Since they were not sufficient to allow the Soviets an effective first strike, to use them would have been suicidal, since the Americans would have responded by leveling the entire Communist world. But that was not the point. Khrushchev must have assumed that Kennedy would not go to war over their removal, since that would mean the certain destruction of a few American cities. The USSR would therefore be allowed to keep the missiles in place, in the process winning a significant propaganda victory that would quiet the Kremlin hawks who were making life difficult for the Russian premier.

Kennedy, however, refused to play ball. He demanded immediate removal, threatening war if the Russians refused. Khrushchev protested that if the United States assumed the right to place missiles in Turkey, why shouldn't his country have them in Cuba? Double standards, however, were part and parcel of international relations. Kennedy simply ignored the protest—for the time being.

The two leaders gambled with the fate of the world. Khrushchev was stubborn and volatile; Kennedy, cautious but resolute. The Air Force commander General Curtis LeMay, irritated by Kennedy's equanimity, demanded immediate air strikes against Cuban sites. If that led to full-scale nuclear war, so be it. "The Russian bear has always been eager to stick his paw in Latin American waters," he argued. "Now we've got him in a trap, let's take his leg off right up to his testicles. On second thought, let's take his testicles off too."[60]

LeMay had devoted the better part of his career to the creation of an invincible nuclear force capable of what he called "killing a nation." As he later confessed, he had repeatedly told Eisenhower in the 1950s that "we could have won a war against Russia. . . . Their defenses were pretty weak."

Yet at the very moment the Soviets provided justification for destruction, the president was reluctant to unleash the dogs of war. It took courage for Kennedy to resist the advice of his generals, who argued that every minute's delay deepened the danger. Robert Kennedy recalled:

> When the President questioned what the response of the Russians might be, General LeMay assured him that there would be no reaction. President Kennedy was skeptical. . . . "They, no more than we, can let these things go by without doing something. They can't, after all their statements, permit us to take out their missiles, kill a lot of Russians and then do nothing. If they don't take action in Cuba, they certainly will in Berlin."

Kennedy instead imposed a blockade, and waited for the Soviets to withdraw their missiles. He understood that Khrushchev did not want war, and had to find a way to allow him to retreat gracefully. "I don't want to put him into a corner from which he cannot escape," Kennedy told his aides.[61]

The world waited. Food was hoarded, survival strategies hastily improvised. At the missile sites, the pace of work doubled, suggesting that the weapons would soon be ready. Then came a single tense moment on October 24, when Soviet ships were prevented from proceeding to Cuba. Triggers were cocked, torpedoes primed. The Soviets, however, turned away. On October 27, Khrushchev sent an anguished note to Kennedy: "If war should break out, it would not be in our power to stop it—war ends when it has rolled through cities and villages, everywhere sowing death and destruction." A subsequent message was less conciliatory, so Kennedy ignored it. He told Khrushchev that he was "very much interested in reducing tensions." Meanwhile, behind the scenes, a deal involving removal of some missiles from Turkey was struck.[62]

We now know that LeMay's confidence was idiotically ill-founded. The Soviets had more missiles in Cuba than American intelligence had estimated, and the possibility of removing all of them with an air strike was remote. Had even one been launched, there is no guarantee that Kennedy would have been able to stop an escalation into full-scale nuclear war. The Americans, it should be recalled, had only one plan: their SIOP involved the release of nearly three thousand weapons, totaling seven thousand megatons. Such an attack would have killed at least 100 million people and would probably have ushered in a catastrophic nuclear winter in the Northern Hemisphere. LeMay, nevertheless, went to his grave believing that an opportunity to destroy Communism forever had been squandered. "We lost the war as a result of the Cuban missile crisis," he insisted.[63]

Chastened by the crisis, Kennedy looked for more secure ways to keep the peace. On June 10, 1963, he argued: "Total war makes no sense in an age when great powers can maintain large and relatively invulnerable nuclear forces and refuse to surrender without resort to those forces. . . . It makes no sense . . . when the deadly poisons produced by a nuclear exchange would be carried by wind and water and soil and seed to the far corners of the globe and to generations yet unborn." He still believed in deterrence, still believed that the United States needed thousands of nuclear weapons. But, he argued, bombs alone were not the best way to assure peace. Solid agreements were essential. As a gesture of goodwill, he announced that the United States would not be the first to resume atmospheric tests. A test ban of sorts followed, on August 5, 1963. It was deeply flawed in that it pertained only to tests in the atmosphere, in space, and underwater. In the years to follow, the number of tests (albeit conducted underground) would actually increase. But that was not the point. What mattered was that Soviets and Americans had met, talked, and agreed on something.[64]

The prominent RAND strategist Thomas Schelling felt that "the Cuban missile crisis was the best thing to happen to us since the Second World War. It helped us avoid further confrontation with the Soviets, it resolved the Berlin issue, and it established some basic understandings about US-Soviet interaction. Sometimes the gambles you take pay off."[65] All that was true, but peaceful coexistence was built upon military security, not political harmony. After Cuba, the Kremlin scrapped the idea of deterrence on the cheap and concentrated instead on amassing an arsenal big enough to prevent an American first strike. The Americans responded in kind. Eventually both sides would have weapons sufficient to destroy the world many times over. By 1969 the superpowers were, between them, spending more than $50 million a day on nuclear armaments. Both sides took refuge in the idea of Mutually Assured Destruction, or MAD. The expense was huge, the waste prodigious, but the sense of security was palpable. Around the world, people learned to stop worrying, even if they did not love the bomb.

4

ALL GONE TO LOOK FOR AMERICA

ALBANY AND BIRMINGHAM: LESSONS OF NONVIOLENCE

Albany, Georgia, was a peaceful place which progress forgot. Surrounded by fields of cotton and peanuts, the town was racially mixed—in 1961, 40 percent of its 56,000 inhabitants were black—but in fact it was two towns, one black, one white, separate and unequal. Blacks had power only within their own community, and then only to a limited extent. The vast majority did not vote; they held the most menial jobs and fatalistically accepted their lowly status. "Most . . . people who had lived in Albany all of their lives had . . . come to expect things as they were," William Anderson, a local civil rights activist, recalled.[1]

The black community drew strength from marginalization. It was down-trodden, but still proud. That pride brought strength, but not success. In an age increasingly dominated by television, a campaign was judged a success if it managed to attract attention. Violence caused viewers to take notice. Good feelings did not.

After the Montgomery bus boycott of 1955-1956, the civil rights struggle shifted from the courts to the marketplace. Battles henceforth took place at lunch counters, on interstate buses, and in public facilities throughout the South. The struggle was conducted by an army of agitators who had experienced the injustices they protested. Direct action offered ordinary blacks an opportunity to assert themselves, in the process fostering empowerment.

On February 1, 1960, four young black men—Joseph McNeil, Franklin McCain, David Richmond, and Ezell Blair—politely took their places at a whites-only lunch counter in Greensboro, North Carolina. They sat passively while they were spat upon, verbally abused, and had food and drinks thrown at them. The tactic soon spread. By October, sit-ins had been staged in 112 Southern cities. Activists, rather than being humiliated by white abuse, were invigorated.

The new spirit was evident in the formation of the Student Nonviolent Coordinating Committee (SNCC) on Easter weekend, 1960. SNCC capitalized on the popularity of the lunch counter protests by providing an outlet for young people—black and white—who were inspired by the possibilities for direct action. While the new group mirrored the adherence to nonviolence common among most civil rights groups, it was uniquely impatient and ambitious. "The pace of social change is too slow," James Lawson, one of the founders, argued. "At this rate it will be at least another generation before the major forms of segregation disappear. All of Africa will be free before the American Negro attains first class citizenship."[2]

A new front was opened the following spring, when activists targeted interstate bus companies. In the 1960 *Boynton versus Virginia* case, the Supreme Court had ruled that segregation of interstate transport facilities was unconstitutional. The Congress of Racial Equality (CORE) decided to test the ruling by staging a "Freedom Ride" across the South. Thirteen volunteers left Washington on May 4, 1961, headed for New Orleans.

When they reached Anniston, Alabama, their bus was met by 200 angry whites, who threw stones and slashed tires. Forced to stop six miles farther on for repairs, the bus encountered another violent mob. During the ensuing melee, a firebomb was thrown through the rear door, enveloping the bus in flames. While the attacks were undoubtedly frightening for the Riders, newspaper photos of the burning bus provided valuable publicity for the movement.

President Kennedy was desperate to avoid having to send troops into the South, but could not ignore a burning bus. He accepted that the Supreme Court ruling had to be enforced, but still hoped that white Southern authorities might see reason and that Freedom Riders might decide their protests were too dangerous. The latter was never likely, given the courage and solidarity the protests fostered. The Nashville Student Movement, with John Lewis at their head, stepped into the breach, vowing to continue to New Orleans.

Another attack occurred at Montgomery on May 20. It later transpired that police commissioner L. B. Sullivan had given white vigilantes ten minutes to use "as they saw fit." On learning of this arrangement, an angry Kennedy ordered federal marshals to protect the Riders and obtained an injunction banning the Ku Klux Klan and other white mobs from harassing them. The Riders meanwhile pushed on to Jackson, Mississippi, where they were attacked and arrested when they attempted to use facilities at the station. Thanks to white intransigence, the Freedom Rides were attracting much more attention than organizers had dared hope. Unable to ignore the steadily swelling protest, Kennedy asked the Interstate Commerce Commission (ICC) to draw up regulations banning segregation on bus routes. These came into effect on November 1, 1961.[3]

The publicity generated by the Rides convinced Martin Luther King Jr., the acknowledged leader of the civil rights movement, that the time was ripe for a new offensive. Beneath the surface, however, dissension was brewing. The young enthusiasts of SNCC, perturbed by King's failure to take an active part in the Rides, accused him of cowardice. Divisions were exacerbated by the concurrent voting rights campaign. Voter registration efforts posed a more direct threat to the edifice of white supremacy than did sit-ins or bus rides. For that reason, they were resisted vigorously. The level of commitment required, and the danger involved, rendered SNCC ideally suited. "When SNCC came, it didn't seem to matter what these white people thought," one black resident remarked. "The only thing . . . that gave courage and determination to the blacks in the South was SNCC." That achievement, however, went largely unnoticed by the Northern press, since small local campaigns did not have the glamour of high profile actions. Yet those actions would not have been possible without the groundwork carried out by SNCC. This caused tension within the movement, since the big protests were often carelessly credited to the Southern Christian Leadership Conference (SCLC) and particularly to King.[4]

In November 1961, SNCC activists in Albany decided to test the ICC ruling on the desegregation of interstate transport by asserting their rights at the local bus terminal. The police cajoled, then harassed, then threatened the demonstrators, who refused to budge. They were finally dragged from the terminal—exactly what SNCC wanted. In the wake of the protest, campaigners gathered to form the Albany Movement, a broad-based coalition intent upon a comprehensive nonviolent campaign against segregation. Despite the local group's enthusiasm, seasoned civil rights leaders feared that Albany was ill-suited to a sustained campaign.

Nonviolent protest is most successful when it is met with violence, for that is when it becomes newsworthy. In Albany, police violence was sorely absent. Black activists were comprehensively outmaneuvered by the local chief, Laurie Pritchett. Using informants from within the black community, he anticipated the campaigners' every move. "I did research," he later explained. "I found [King's] method was nonviolence, that his method was to fill the jails—same as in India. . . . After learning this . . . I started orientation of the police department into nonviolent movement—no violence, no dogs, no show of force. I even took up some of the training the SNCC originated there—like sitting at the counter and being slapped. Spit upon. I said, 'If they do this, you will not use force. We're going to out-nonviolent them.'" By mid-December, more than 500 demonstrators had been arrested, but the campaign had reached a stalemate, thanks mainly to Pritchett. Since the press was unable to produce photos of brutal policemen clubbing protesters, the campaign did not become sufficiently newsworthy to arouse Northern sympathies or provoke the intervention of attorney general Robert Kennedy. Organizers decided to call in King, in order to drum up more publicity. That was not an easy decision. The strength of the Albany Movement had so far been its local character. Calling in help from outside constituted an acknowledgment of defeat and also played into the hands of the white establishment, whose spokesmen invariably described Albany as a peaceful, harmonious community under attack by outside agitators.[5]

King's arrival broke the stalemate. In a rally at City Hall, he urged sympathetic supporters to come to Albany. Around 250 people were arrested, including King. Meanwhile, behind the scenes, negotiations took place between local politicians and the Albany Movement. City commissioners, keen to restore order, offered concessions in exchange for a suspension of the demonstrations. Jailed protesters were also released, thus relieving the pressure on Pritchett's jails. Confident that a victory had been gained, King left Albany. As it turned out, however, the negotiations were a ruse designed to pull the rug from under the movement. Local authorities immediately reneged on their promises.

Albany resumed its war of attrition. Protests were incessant, but progress imperceptible. Pritchett's outsmarting of King and SNCC gave heart to bigots everywhere. Emboldened by their success, city officials grew ever more stubborn. When Kennedy urged mayor Asa Kelly to compromise,

Kelly bluntly refused. Another setback occurred when the Federal District Court issued a restraining order banning further protests. Activists split over whether to obey the order. King, not wanting to alienate the federal government, insisted on compliance. Others, however, argued that an unjust law had to be defied. Demonstrators took to the streets in open defiance of King.

On July 25, Albany's streets were crowded with 2,000 marchers, not all of them committed to nonviolence. When rocks were thrown, town authorities could hardly contain their delight. "Did you see them nonviolent rocks?" Pritchett crowed. King called for a day of penance, but the more intemperate members of SNCC had grown tired of his saintly ways. They began to argue that rigid adherence to nonviolence jeopardized progress. Nonviolence, they decided, might be useful in certain circumstances, but could not be allowed to become an overriding goal.[6]

After ten months of virtually continuous agitation, little had been achieved. More than a thousand protesters had been jailed but the penal system had not collapsed. The campaign ran out of activists before Pritchett ran out of jail space. Organizers struggled to construct positive interpretations of the events. Anderson subsequently insisted that the movement was "an overwhelming success": very simply, people had decided "they would never accept that segregated society as it was anymore." This might have been true, but it was not the sort of success that could be celebrated on the front pages of national newspapers. The civil rights movement had reached the stage where it needed concrete results, not vague notions of empowerment.[7]

King drew his own lessons. "When Martin left Albany he was very depressed," his friend Andrew Young later recalled. "The weakness of the Albany movement was that it was totally unplanned and we were totally unprepared." All that effort had merely revealed deep divisions. The campaign had also demonstrated the limits of what could be expected from the federal government. Washington's first priority was order, not justice. Since Albany had never provided embarrassing scenes of disorder, the government did not feel inclined to intervene. In addition, points of confrontation were poorly chosen. The blanket challenge to segregation in the town confronted local statutes, not national ones, thus rendering the federal government powerless to intervene. "When the movement in Albany moved out of the bus station . . . and into other areas of the city," recalled

Burke Marshall, head of the Civil Rights Division at the Justice Department, "we didn't have the authority we could wave at the city of Albany that we had in the case of the bus stations."[8]

Albany demonstrated that there was great merit in a community movement where local residents joined together to address injustices they themselves suffered. Its strength, however, was also its weakness: a plethora of locally based actions led to disunity and disorganization. Albany also revealed that a balance needed to be struck between the kind of local infiltration that SNCC was so good at and the courting of national attention, which was the expertise of SCLC. Down in the trenches, many activists concluded that SNCC did the work and SCLC got the glory. Feelings like that were inevitably corrosive.

After the disappointment of Albany, civil rights activists were desperate to find a battle they could win. Birmingham, Alabama, seemed just the place. There, an elementary school reader showing black and white bunnies playing together had been banned on the grounds that it endorsed integration. Segregation was enforced by law and by fear. The Ku Klux Klan operated without impediment, staging fifty cross burnings in the years 1960–1963. The same period saw eighteen racially motivated bombings, earning the city the nickname "Bombingham." The city also possessed the one element missing in Albany—namely, a violent, unstable, politically obtuse local lawman. Police commissioner Eugene "Bull" Connor was the perfect caricature of the bigoted sheriff.

In contrast to the Albany efforts, the protests in Birmingham were, from the outset, led by national organizers. The official aim was to attack segregation in public facilities and to end discriminatory employment practices, but the underlying goal was to produce a spectacle that would arouse the nation's conscience. The campaign began in early April 1963, with King's announcement of an economic boycott against segregationist businesses. On the 6th, a small crowd marched on City Hall, prompting police to arrest demonstrators on the flimsiest of charges. Over subsequent days, marches grew, as did the number of arrests.

The first week seemed the perfect model of a civil rights campaign. Protests were carefully orchestrated, an image that suggested unity of purpose. White businesses suffered terribly when the boycott took hold. Above all, the national media paid attention. Images of angry policemen with vicious dogs attacking hymn-singing protesters aroused the nation.

Frustrated at the way they had been comprehensively outmaneuvered, city authorities attempted on April 10 to put a stop to the action by issuing an injunction against street protests. Two days later, King openly challenged the injunction, and was arrested.

While King was in jail, eight prominent Alabama clergymen published a statement criticizing his tactics. While they sympathized with the struggle, they resented outsiders poking their noses into the affairs of Birmingham. Counseling patience, they accused King of provoking violence and jeopardizing the chances for peaceful negotiation. He responded with his famous "Letter from a Birmingham Jail." "I am in Birmingham because injustice is here," he retorted. "Injustice anywhere is a threat to justice everywhere. We are caught in an inescapable network of mutuality, tied in a single garment of destiny. Whatever affects one directly, affects all indirectly. Never again can we afford to live with the narrow, provincial 'outside agitator' idea. Anyone who lives in the United States can never be considered an outsider anywhere within its bounds." King insisted that he wanted negotiation, but maintained that white Southerners would not talk unless forced to do so. "The purpose of our direct-action program is to create a situation so crisis-packed that it will inevitably open the door to negotiation." As for provoking violence, he replied: "Isn't this like condemning a robbed man because his possession of money precipitated the evil act of robbery?" In response to the call for patience, he argued: "For years now I have heard the word 'Wait!' It rings in the ear of every Negro with piercing familiarity. This 'Wait' has almost always meant 'Never.' We must come to see, with one of our distinguished jurists, that 'justice too long delayed is justice denied.'"⁹

On April 23, W. L. Moore of CORE was shot dead during a "freedom walk" through the South. For Birmingham protesters, the murder provided a shot of adrenalin. On May 2, which organizers called D-Day, 6,000 blacks, most of them under the age of sixteen, marched. The young protesters came dressed in their Sunday best, thus underlining their respectability and innocence. Most noticeable were little black girls in freshly ironed dresses with white bobby socks and white gloves—harmless waifs individually weak but symbolically invincible. In stark contrast were Connor's cops, with their billy clubs, snarling dogs, and water cannons. Organizers had set a trap into which Connor obligingly charged. Images of dogs set loose on children instantly changed the temper of the civil rights struggle.

The scenes were repeated the next day. Eventually, more than a thousand children were jailed for daring to confront segregation. Connor prided himself on his toughness, but the rest of the world saw base brutality. America was taught a lesson by a few thousand black schoolchildren. King and his followers had sought not only to expose the injustice of Southern segregation but also to embarrass America, to expose her tolerance of segregation to the world. As a media event it was perfect, but those who cared to look beneath the surface felt unease at the cynicism of putting children in the line of fire. Critics called it the Children's Crusade. "Real men don't put their children on the firing line," a disgusted Malcolm X spat.[10]

Kennedy, though sickened by Birmingham, was still preoccupied with order, not justice. He dreaded a confrontation with the South over states' rights, yet could not see how the crisis could be resolved without federal intervention. Southern hardliners, he feared, would interpret any involvement by him as an attempt to impose a new racial order. Given the narrowness of his victory in 1960, he could not afford to alienate Southern Democrats. Desperate to find a compromise, he appealed to Birmingham officials to negotiate, but they refused. King, realizing he had both the city and the White House on the ropes, was equally intransigent.

Demonstrations continued into May, reaching a peak on the 7th, when thousands of protesters mobilized. Never one for subtlety, Connor deployed a tank. Police wielded fire hoses so powerful they could strip bark from trees. Under the circumstances, demonstrators found it difficult to remain faithful to nonviolence. Instances of rock throwing grew more common with each passing day, much to the chagrin of King. A delighted Southern press was quick to exploit photos of blacks hurling stones.

As King had predicted, unrelenting direct action finally convinced stubborn city officials to see reason. On May 10, a truce was reached, with vague concessions on issues of segregation and the release of prisoners. The truce, however, fired the wrath of hardliners on both sides. White vigilantes responded with a wave of bombings. Meanwhile, disgruntled blacks, disappointed by the concessions, rioted on the 12th.

The campaign was technically over, even though the city remained on a knife-edge. Birmingham was more important for what it achieved across the nation than for what it accomplished within the confines of the city. While local intransigence continued to thwart reform, outside the city significant progress was apparent. From May to September 1963, some fifty cities in the South implemented desegregation measures. White businesses, concerned more with the bottom line than with the racial divide, started making high-profile donations to civil rights organizations. The brutal scenes from Birmingham had also aroused the moral conscience of Northern whites to an unprecedented extent. They donated money, went on marches, wrote to Washington, and, in many cases, journeyed south to join the struggle. The flood of volunteers reached a peak in the Freedom Summer voter registration drive of 1964.

The effect upon blacks was also profound. While Birmingham was largely nonviolent, the protests marked the emergence of a new generation of protesters who were proud, assertive, impatient, and unwilling to compromise. They did not fear going to jail or putting their lives on the line. While most still believed in nonviolence, that belief was pragmatic, not philosophical. Since adherence was not absolute, the possibility of resorting to violence remained open. Meanwhile, a growing number of activists, impatient with the pace of change, were drawn to the militant tactics espoused by black nationalists like Malcolm X. The pace of protest now seemed to be dictated by the rank and file, rather than by their leaders. Gandhi's aphorism, "There go my people—I must catch them, for I am their leader," plagued King.

Southern hardliners answered progress with intransigence. On January 14, 1963, during his inaugural address, the newly elected governor George Wallace told the people of Alabama: "Let us rise to the call of the freedom-loving blood that is in us and send our answer to the tyranny that clanks its chains upon the South. In the name of the greatest people that ever trod the earth, I draw the line in the dust and toss the gauntlet before the feet of tyranny . . . and I say . . . segregation now . . . segregation tomorrow . . . segregation forever." Wallace, who had promised voters that he would "stand in the schoolhouse door" in order to stop integration, did precisely that on June 11, 1963, when he personally prevented two black students from enrolling at the University of Alabama. Prior to Birmingham, Kennedy would have been inclined to negotiate. The rules of engagement had, however, changed. Kennedy instead issued a cease-and-desist order and mobilized the National Guard. After four hours of stubborn posturing, Wallace surrendered.[11]

On that same day, Kennedy addressed the American people on the civil rights issue. Using the confrontation with Wallace as his starting point, he argued:

> It ought to be possible . . . for American students of any color to attend any public institution they select without having to be backed up by troops. It ought to be possible for American consumers of any color to receive equal service in . . . hotels and restaurants and theaters and retail stores, without being forced to resort to demonstrations in the street, and it ought to be possible for American citizens of any color . . . to vote in a free election without interference or fear of reprisal. It ought to be possible, in short, for every American to enjoy the privileges of being American.

A nation which professed to be a defender of freedom abroad could not, Kennedy argued, deny basic freedoms at home. "Now the time has come for this Nation to fulfill its promise." While his appeal was based on morality, Kennedy also warned that if reforms were rejected, chaos would ensue. Rock throwers in Birmingham had clearly had their effect. "The fires of frustration and discord are burning in every city, North and South. . . . Redress is sought in the streets, in demonstrations, parades, and protests which create tensions and threaten violence and threaten lives. We face, therefore, a moral crisis as a country and as a people. It cannot be met by repressive police action. It cannot be left to increased demonstrations in the streets. It cannot be quieted by token moves or talk." The solution, Kennedy had decided, lay in legislation. "Next week I shall ask the Congress . . . to make a commitment . . . to the proposition that race has no place in American life or law." A comprehensive Civil Rights Bill designed to outlaw segregation in all public establishments, integrate public schools, and provide greater protection of the right to vote was put before Congress a week later, on June 19, 1963. "Those who do nothing are inviting shame as well as violence," Kennedy concluded. "Those who act boldly are recognizing right as well as reality."[12]

For the first time, Kennedy had made it patently clear that the civil rights issue was a moral one—"as old as the Scriptures and . . . as clear as the American Constitution." Yet his appeal to the American sense of decency went unheeded in many parts of the South. Just as Birmingham had strengthened the solidarity of the black community, so too it had fired the wrath of those determined to resist. Militant whites, feeling the weight of the nation upon them, developed a bunker mentality. The appeal of violence was growing on both sides. This was patently demonstrated just a few hours after Kennedy's speech, when the white supremacist Byron De La Beckwith gunned down Medgar Evers, director of the NAACP in Mississippi.[13]

Birmingham, an interminably ugly battle, provided a lesson in media management. The campaign demonstrated that violence was a prerequisite to national awakening. The use of young children was cynical but highly effective. Henceforth, organizers chose new battlegrounds on the basis of whether the local sheriff could be relied upon to overreact. Protests were carefully stage-managed in order to provoke the most violent response. Journalists were assiduously nurtured. Andrew Young, unofficial public relations man for King's SCLC, discovered, in the course of his work, what we now call the soundbite—a brief, self-contained, dramatic statement which could be incorporated directly into a news report, without editing. For maximum impact, the soundbite had to be accompanied by striking visual material—and this, in the context of the civil rights movement, inevitably meant shots of brutality and suffering.

"TV does nothing better than spectacle," the journalist and political commentator Theodore White wrote of Birmingham. "The police dogs and the fire hoses . . . have become the symbols of the American Negro revolution—as the knout and the Cossacks were symbols of the Russian Revolution. When television showed dogs snapping at human beings, when the fire hoses thrashed and flailed at the women and children, whipping up skirts and pounding up bodies, . . . the entire nation winced as the demonstrators winced." Birmingham had ramifications beyond the civil rights movement. Henceforth, political agitation became a ritualized dance choreographed for the media. In Berkeley, for instance, student protesters timed actions so that they could be shown live on the late-afternoon news. The media inevitably favored the firebrand. People who had a point to make realized that they could do so more effectively by shouting. Truth was secondary—what counted was drama. Thus, at Selma in 1965, photographers captured shots of the local sheriff clubbing Annie Lee Cooper while she was held down by three officers. They did not, however, show that Cooper had provoked the punishment by first slugging the sheriff.[14]

News had to be extraordinary—a network producer was not likely to devote valuable minutes to the protester or policeman who held his temper, or to the politician who lacked a sense of dramatic timing. The nightly news was sandwiched within a schedule packed with sitcoms, Westerns, and crime dramas. While it is perhaps unfair to argue that it had to be entertaining, it did have to sustain attention. Network executives kept a cold eye on audience figures, aware that a viewer who switched to another channel because of a boring news item might not switch back.

The tyranny of television worried King. His method of protest was noble, but not always newsworthy. Gandhi had not had to worry about the Nielsen ratings, but King did. He realized that he was in danger of losing his movement to militant firebrands who were always ready to satisfy the media's hunger for noise. In a private conversation with the CBS correspondent Daniel Schorr, he pointedly asked: "When Negroes are incited to violence, will you think of your responsibility in helping to produce it?"[15]

PORT HURON: STUDENTS FOR A DEMOCRATIC SOCIETY

Being a student wasn't easy in the 1960s. One study described a "bleak" environment in which the student was "confronted . . . with indifferent advising, endless bureaucratic routines, gigantic lecture courses, and a deadening succession of textbook assignments and bluebook examinations testing his grasp of bits and pieces of knowledge."[16]

A good university did not necessarily provide escape from that desert of boredom and sterility. Prestigious universities were judged not by the quality of their teaching, but by their ability to land lucrative research contracts. During the Cold War, those contracts were often defense-related, a sore point among sensitive students. Research demands rendered the professor less accessible to the student, whose instruction was left largely to postgraduates only slightly older and marginally more mature. Since the mainly middle-class students at prestigious universities sought intellectual fulfillment, not simply a career, they were sensitive to these deficiencies, and inclined to complain. For many, the campus seemed a microcosm of an imperfect world.

Universities confidently assumed that since students were not adults, they needed to be chaperoned as well as educated. The assumption of quasi-parental authority led to the regulation of "adult" pursuits, among them sex and politics. In sexual matters, universities tried diligently but unsuccessfully to curb promiscuity. In political affairs, they proudly defended the ivory tower, discouraging activism. There was, however, a problem with their efforts to act *in loco parentis:* universities aspired to be parents, but managed only to be neglectful ones.

A small core of disgruntled students took seriously C. Wright Mills's advocacy of the intelligentsia as the "radical agency of change." Mills, a sociologist admired in the Soviet Union as a harsh critic of capitalism, was in truth a champion of the individual: he realized that, on both sides of the Iron Curtain, individuality was suppressed. He attacked the oppressive sameness of capitalist culture, which offered limitless abundance but little genuine variety. In doing so, he gave intellectual voice to the alienation that many young people felt—an alienation exacerbated by an oppressively liberal political system offering no outlet for radicalism.

Liberals, argued Mills, had convinced themselves that history ended in 1945. For them, "there are no more real issues or even problems of great seriousness. The mixed economy plus the welfare state plus prosperity—that is the formula. US capitalism will continue to be workable; the welfare state will continue along the road to ever greater justice." The Berkeley activist Mario Savio clearly had Mills in mind when he published his essay "An End to History" (1964), in which he argued that

> America is becoming ever more the utopia of sterilized, automated contentment. The "futures" and "careers" for which American students now prepare are for the most part intellectual and moral wastelands. This chrome-plated consumers' paradise would have us grow up to be well-behaved children. But an important minority of men and women coming to the front today have shown that they will die rather than be standardized, replaceable and irrelevant.

"The Age of Complacency is ending," Mills proclaimed. "We are beginning to move again." He became a mythic figure to a generation of American youths who shared his discontent, or at least thought it fashionable to do so. In time, almost every rebellious act would be justified as a blow struck for individuality, and a tribute to Mills.[17]

Another popular thinker was the German-American philosopher Herbert Marcuse. Unlike Mills, he was a Marxist, but also a devout libertarian, which explains why he had little truck with the Soviets. By the mid-Sixties, hip people were quoting his *Eros and Civilization,* many without ever having read a single page. Daniel Cohn-Bendit, one of the leaders of the French student revolt, remarked: "People wanted to blame Marcuse as our mentor; that was a joke. Not one of us had read Marcuse." It's ironic that a thinker who warned about the superficiality of society should owe his popularity to such a superficial appreciation of his work. "What he does," argued James Jupp in *Political Quarterly,* "is to echo feelings and sentiments which are widespread, but are incoherently expressed by millions." Underneath his mind-numbingly prolix style, Marcuse had some valid things to say about technology and the state. In *One-Dimensional Man,* he argued that "a comfortable, smooth, reasonable, democratic unfreedom prevails in advanced industrial civilization, a token of technological progress." He warned against the careless tendency to confuse change with progress, pointing out that technological developments could close doors as easily as open them. The "communications revolution," for instance, seemed liberating, but was predominantly used for purposes of control. Likewise, the constant flood of new products gave the illusion of choice, when in fact those choices had little significance. The worth of a society, in other words, should not be measured by its ability to produce twenty brands of deodorant.[18]

Marcuse's appeal to activists, not to mention his threat to the status quo, arose from his argument that oppression, in the modern age, came less from poverty than from affluence. While this idea intrigued and occasionally inspired middle-class baby boomers, for the vast majority of people happily stuck on the escalator of ambition it seemed utter nonsense. For them, creature comforts were the outward and visible signs of material success—proof that they had been liberated from the scourge of want. Attempts by radicals to turn alienation into a mass movement failed miserably, for the simple reason that the masses coveted the sort of life that activists despised. It was impossible to convince the working man that the new car he desperately wanted was actually an instrument of his oppression.

Marcuse's solution to the problem of "unfreedom" was revolution; he suggested that only by defying the system could people achieve true liberation. That idea undoubtedly appealed to those in the counterculture who naïvely thought that revolution would be great fun—people who worshiped the word without ever pondering its implications. But while Marcuse espoused revolution, in other ways his philosophy undermined it. His libertarian ideas, though attractive to those who wanted to "do their own thing," were antithetical to unity and organization. As Tom

Hayden later reflected, "Our profound distrust of leadership and structure doomed us to failure on the level of political organization."[19]

Student activism was also encouraged by Old Left radicals only just resurfacing after years of McCarthyite persecution. They saw students as a new proletariat, much more promising than the working class who had failed them. Many Sixties student radicals were "red-diaper babies"—children of parents who had once been active in the Communist party. The repudiation of Joseph McCarthy seemed to them an opportunity: for the first time in a generation, dissenters were not automatically pariahs. Todd Gitlin sensed, among his fellow travelers, "the grand illusion that we, the *New* Left, could solve the problems of the Left by being young."[20]

Among Hayden's fellow students at the University of Michigan were a number of restless souls keen to embrace good causes. One such activist was Robert Haber, who in February 1960 founded Students for a Democratic Society (SDS) from the remnants of the Student League for Industrial Democracy. Haber, inspired by the lunch counter sit-ins, envisaged an organization which could contribute to the civil rights struggle and agitate against other injustices. He originally imagined a national network of activists on campuses around the country, not a mass movement.

Hayden's decision to join came as a result of his travels through America in the summer of 1960, inspired by Kerouac. At the University of California, Berkeley, he witnessed a contagious activism among students and also interviewed the nuclear physicist Edward Teller, a deeply frightening man able to contemplate nuclear Armageddon while he played Chopin on his piano. Later, he attended the Democratic convention in Los Angeles where he met Robert Kennedy, with whom he was hugely impressed. Equally inspiring was Martin Luther King, who told him: "Ultimately, you have to take a stand with your life." Hayden returned home determined to devote himself to a political cause, but he did not want to replicate what he had encountered in the South—a pattern of "beating to beating, jail to jail." SDS seemed the perfect outlet.[21]

After joining, Hayden persuaded the executive committee to transform SDS into a mass movement. Toward that end, around sixty activists converged on Port Huron, Michigan, in 1962. Though the group was politically radical, they hardly looked it. Photos reveal staid-looking, conventionally dressed students who could easily have been mistaken for members of a chess club. This image of geekish industriousness would stick with the group for the rest of its life. Granted, some activists eventually grew their hair long and wore jeans, but their political intensity never waned.

Out of the meeting came the Port Huron Statement, "an agenda for a generation" largely written by Hayden, in homage to Mills. The decade produced few documents more boring, but SDS activists, being dull, loved it. The tedious nature of the statement perhaps explains why the most frequently quoted sentence comes on page 1: "We are the people of this generation, bred in at least modest comfort, housed in universities, looking uncomfortably to the world we inherit." Continuing in that melodramatic strain, the document proclaimed: "We may be the last generation in the experiment with living."[22]

At the heart of the statement was the idea of participatory democracy. SDS called upon the individual to "share in the social decisions determining the quality and direction of his life." Society had to be organized to "encourage independence in men and provide the media for their common participation." This was a utopian idea, but also a quintessentially American one in the importance assigned the individual. It was not enough for people to submit to being governed by representatives of their choice; they had to participate actively in their governance. A logical corollary was the belief that all authority was suspect because it quashed individual expression.[23]

SDS was a religion, and the Port Huron Statement its Scripture. Large parts read like a Sunday sermon. "We regard men as infinitely precious and possessed of unfulfilled capacities for reason, freedom, and love." On the subject of youthful alienation, the document maintained: "Loneliness, estrangement, isolation describe the vast distance between man and man today. These dominant tendencies cannot be overcome by better personnel management, nor by improved gadgets, but only when a love of man overcomes the idolatrous worship of things by man." Hayden sought to redefine the American Dream, replacing material success with spiritual fulfillment, albeit of a secular variety.[24]

Gitlin, another SDS activist, later reflected that "only true believers in the promise of America could have felt so anti-American." The faithful argued that the bureaucracy of government would have to be torn down in order for society to get back to original American ideals. "Political institutions designed to perpetuate a system of power will never become instruments for the transformation of that system," wrote the long-winded Carl Oglesby. "If you want to stop not only the Vietnam war but the system that begot it, if you want not merely to blur the edges of racism but to change the system that needed slaves in the first place and could 'emancipate' them only into ghettoes in the second, if you want not merely to make deals with irrationality but to liberate reason for the conquest of joy, then you will have to go outside the system." SDS sought to sweep away the sterile hypocrisy of the older generation, replacing it with a new, dynamic, people-centered system—an amalgam of European socialism, Jeffersonian democracy, and the participatory politics of the Greek city-state. Politics, being personal, could be practiced anywhere—it need not be confined to the grim bastions where gray men in suits conspired in secretive cabals.[25]

Fueling the movement was the high-octane naïveté of self-important young people who have just discovered "eternal truths." SDS wanted to sweep away the elites—military, business, political—that were controlling America and replace them with a new elite: students. Reflecting on his experiences many years later, Hayden confessed: "I still don't know where this messianic sense, this belief in being right, this confidence that we could speak for a generation, came from." The answer was quite simple: it came from their egos, all of which were extraordinarily large. Their self-proclaimed status as the gifted of their generation convinced them that they had a right and duty to lead the masses back toward the American Dream—as they defined it.[26]

Participatory democracy was fine in theory but difficult in practice. "We [must] . . . reach out to people who are tied to the mythology of American power and make them part of our movement," SDS president Paul Potter proclaimed in 1965. In truth, activists had no idea how to find or communicate with "the people." They spent too much time reading fashionable philosophers, and not enough among the masses. There's little in the Port Huron Statement calculated to appeal to the poor, the workers, minorities, or women. It articulates a young, white, male intellectual's perspective on materialism, democracy, foreign policy, and education, but says hardly anything about class, gender, or ethnicity.[27]

Among the great body of students, SDS activists stood out as an elite, a group who had actually read Sartre and Marcuse, and who took politics and life perhaps too seriously. Oglesby described how, for people like him, the Cold War pre-empted the traditional privileges of youth. . . . By any usual standard, youth never really happened for us. Our high school philosophy was already a well-understood existentialism, whether or not we had heard the word. Our first and abiding god was consciousness. Our first social moves were experiments in freedom. Our first political encounter was with our own world's victims, an encounter in which we found one main source of that superficially serene world's deep discontents.

Oglesby, Hayden, Haber, and the rest made the great mistake of thinking that the alienation they felt was an epidemic. Yet even those who admired the activists did not necessarily feel inclined to follow them. Since fun was such an important element in the youthful rebellion—virtually a prerequisite—the sober politics of SDS had limited appeal. As a formative experience in politicizing students, the civil rights movement had a much greater effect, even if that effect was mere by-product. That campaign appealed because of its simple practicality: pragmatic efforts were devoted to achieving a recognizable goal, without the encumbrance of theory.[28]

SDS, in contrast, was nine-tenths hot air. Its excessive theorizing came under attack by, among others, the historian Howard Zinn, who advocated a more action-oriented radicalism similar to that which he had experienced in the South. "The contributions of the Old Left," he reminded members, "came not out of its ideological fetishism but out of its action. What gave it dynamism was not the classes on surplus value but the organization of the CIO, not the analysis of Stalin's views on the National and Colonial Question, but the fight for the Scottsboro boys, not the labored rationale for dictatorship of the proletariat, but the sacrifices of the Abraham Lincoln Brigade." Zinn attacked the New Left's fondness for "solemn, pretentious argument." Instead of debating "what Marx or Machiavelli or Rousseau really meant," activists needed to take to the streets. "Too much of what passes for theoretical discussion of public issues is really a personal duel for honor or privilege. . . . While we argue, the world moves, while we publish, others perish."[29]

Most SDS members agreed with Zinn, even if their behavior suggested otherwise. They were great believers in the idea that action provided an antidote to apathy. Activists failed to realize, however, that the apparent apathy of the masses was in truth a rejection of the SDS message. The problem was revealed in the SDS approach to the Vietnam War. Members saw the war as a manifestation of the deficiencies of the American political system. "There is no simple way to attack something that is deeply rooted in the society," Paul Potter argued on April 17, 1965. "If the people of this country are to end the war in Vietnam, and to change the institutions which create it, then the people of this country must create a massive social movement." By trying to make opposition to the war into a wider revolutionary struggle, SDS did nothing for their ideals of revolution and weakened their campaign to end the war. The constituency of people who shared Potter's political ideals was tiny. Making their cause predominant alienated the ever-growing group of disenchanted who wanted nothing more ambitious than peace.[30]

Six months later a second demonstration in Washington again heard calls for revolution. Oglesby, the new president of SDS, focused his attack on the American liberal establishment, the nice fellows who espoused progress but only succeeded in killing peasants in Vietnam. Borrowing heavily from Marcuse, he called this approach "corporate liberalism"—the establishment con-trick which made reactionary power appear liberal.

> We are here to protest against a growing war. Since it is a very bad war, we acquire the habit of thinking that it must be caused by very bad men. But we only conceal reality, I think, to denounce on such grounds the menacing coalition of industrial and military power, or the brutality of the blitzkrieg we are waging against Vietnam, or the ominous signs around us that heresy may soon no longer be permitted. We must simply observe, and quite plainly say, that this coalition, this blitzkrieg, and this demand for acquiescence are creatures, all of them, of a government that since 1932 has considered itself to be fundamentally liberal.

Oglesby wanted Americans to get back in touch with the values that had made them great. America, he argued, had lost "that mysterious social desire for human equity that from time to time has given us genuine moral drive." In other words, he wanted Americans to reacquaint themselves with their own revolutionary values. Some people, he admitted, would conclude that he sounded anti-American. "To them I say, don't blame *me* for *that!* Blame those who mouthed my liberal values and broke my American heart."[31]

SDS, which started out as an effort to revitalize liberalism, ended up as a revolt against liberalism. Its favorite enemy was not the reactionary right but those seemingly goodhearted liberals who had given America Cuba, the Congo, and Vietnam. Liberals, as Marcuse argued, were experts at "repressive tolerance"; they had developed a system "capable of containing social change," a system in which traditional forms of protest were "dangerous because they preserve the illusion of popular sovereignty." Mills made a similar point. "Reasoning collapses into reasonableness," he wrote. "By the more naïve and snobbish celebrants of complacency, arguments and facts of a displeasing kind are simply ignored." As they grew increasingly frustrated at their inability to free themselves from the straitjacket of liberalism, SDS radicals came to the conclusion that the system itself had to be destroyed. For many, that implied a descent into violence. When the dust settled, liberalism was indeed vanquished, but in its place came an even more formidable, and much more repressive, authoritarianism.[32]

In 1964, Savio compared the university to a machine and urged his fellow students to throw themselves in its gears. He was not the first to use that metaphor, or the last. The obvious bears mentioning: machines are made of steel and students of flesh. The outcome of their challenge was, therefore, entirely predictable. In 1968, Zbigniew Brzezinski, then a professor at Columbia University, described student radicalism as the death rattle of a group left behind by "technetronic society," an entity he defined as "a society in which technology, especially electronic communications, is prompting basic social changes." Painful as it is to admit, he was probably right. The fact that students—like the nineteenth-century Luddites, who also tried to smash machines—had an admirable cause does not make their quest any less futile.[33]

WASHINGTON: I HAVE A DREAM

The March on Washington began without leaders. The crowd had come from all directions—some walking from places as far away as New York City and the Deep South. At least 250,000 people, perhaps double that number, gathered at the Washington Monument. Impatient to begin their march to the Lincoln Memorial, they ignored stewards and set off well in advance of the official start time of noon. John Lewis, one of the organizers, was surprised to see a great tide of humanity moving away without him, and, like King, remembered Gandhi's words. "I recall thinking, 'There go my people—let me catch up with them.'" Eventually, he and his fellow organizers made it to the front, thus providing a semblance of control. Amid all the drama of the march, the symbolic significance of its leaderless beginning went unnoticed.[34]

The idea had arisen two decades earlier, when A. Philip Randolph, founder of the Brotherhood of Sleeping Car Porters, had threatened President Franklin D. Roosevelt with a march against discrimination. Roosevelt responded by establishing the Fair Employment Practices Committee, prompting Randolph to cancel his march. The proposal was revived in 1962, in response to what Lewis called "an increasing sense of discontent and frustration with the pace of progress on civil rights." The aim was not simply to protest segregation in the South, but rather to draw attention to the economic plight of blacks everywhere. A broad coalition gave the impression of unity. The organizers consisted of the "Big Six" of civil rights leaders—Randolph, Lewis (SNCC), Roy Wilkins (NAACP), James Farmer (CORE), Whitney Young (Urban League), and King (SCLC).[35]

This group approached Kennedy in early June, not to seek permission but to present a fait accompli. "Mr. President, the black masses are restless and we are going to march," Randolph announced. Kennedy, worried about the effect on his Civil Rights Bill, was annoyed at the news. "You could tell by the President's body language that he did not . . . like the idea," Lewis recalled. "We want success in Congress, not just a big show at the Capitol," Kennedy argued. "Some of these people are looking for an excuse to be against us; and I don't want to give . . . them a chance to say, 'Yes, I'm for the bill, but I am damned if I will vote for it at the point of a gun.'" Randolph answered Kennedy's objections: "Mr. President, the Negro people are already in the streets and there will be a march on Washington." Once Kennedy realized that the demonstration would go ahead despite his objections, he reluctantly threw his support behind it.[36]

Bayard Rustin, chief coordinator of the march, sent comprehensive instructions to 2,000 local planners. Publicity agents issued a steady stream of press releases in the weeks preceding the event. News agencies, suitably prepped for drama, mobilized large crews of reporters and arranged for helicopters to provide aerial coverage. Satellite time on the newly launched

Telstar was booked, so that live broadcasts could be beamed around the world. The three major television networks spent over $300,000, more than twice the march committee's budget.

Fearful of a riot, local officials canceled all police leave and brought in forces from surrounding communities. Fifteen thousand paratroopers were put on alert, and seventy different emergency scenarios were assiduously studied. The government cooperated with march organizers in developing a state-of-the-art public address system, which officials suspected might come in handy if the crowd grew unruly. Unbeknownst to the organizers, the police wired the system so that they could take control if trouble arose.

Determined to stop the march, FBI director J. Edgar Hoover tried to convince John and Robert Kennedy that King was influenced by Communists. Hoover ruthlessly exploited Rustin's Communist links and the open secret of his homosexuality. On the eve of the event, he released photos of Rustin talking to King while the latter was in the bath, the suggestion being that the pair were lovers. Hoover also distributed information obtained from wiretaps about King's extramarital affairs. Unable eventually to stop the march, he had his agents pressure celebrities to withdraw support, without success. The "arts contingent" included, among others, Charlton Heston, Ossie Davis, Marlon Brando, Sammy Davis Jr., Sidney Poitier, Lena Horne, Diahann Carroll, Paul Newman, and Harry Belafonte.

Before setting off, the marchers were entertained by Odetta, Josh White, Bob Dylan, the Albany Freedom Singers, and Peter, Paul, and Mary. Joan Baez opened the program with "Oh, Freedom" and also led a rendition of "We Shall Overcome." Dire predictions of disorder were not fulfilled. "From the steps of the Lincoln Memorial, you saw a sea of humanity," Lewis recalled. "You saw Black and White; Protestant, Catholic, and Jewish; old and young; rich and poor. . . . You could feel the great sense of community and family. The March . . . represented America at her best." Surveys indicated that about 15 percent of the participants were students, about 25 percent were white, and a majority of the blacks present were middle-class Northerners. Writing in the *New York Times,* Russell Baker commented: "No one could remember an invading army quite as gentle as the two hundred thousand civil-rights marchers who occupied Washington today. . . . The sweetness and patience of the crowd may have set some sort of national high-water mark in mass decency."[37]

Once the marchers reached the Lincoln Memorial, speeches began. Most speakers, on the urging of organizers, synthesized the prevailing moods of protest and hope, while avoiding the stridency that might alienate those on Capitol Hill. Roy Wilkins politely warned Kennedy not to let his Civil Rights Bill get watered down by cynics in Congress. Whitney Young, focusing on economic themes, emphasized that black suffering was not confined to the South. Blacks, he argued,

> must march from the rat infested, overcrowded ghettos to decent, wholesome, unrestricted residential areas dispersed throughout the cities. They must march from the relief rolls to the established retraining centers. . . . They must march from the cemeteries where our young, our newborn, die three times sooner and our parents die seven years earlier. . . . They must march from the congested, illequipped schools which breed dropouts and which smother motivation. . . . And finally, they must march from a present feeling of despair and hopelessness . . . to renewed faith and confidence.

Lewis' original draft reflected the angry impatience of SNCC, criticizing the Civil Rights Bill as "too little, too late." "We will march through the South, through the Heart of Dixie, the way Sherman did," he wrote. "We will pursue our own 'scorched-earth' policy and burn Jim Crow to the ground—nonviolently. We will fragment the South into a thousand pieces and put them back together in the image of democracy." Fearful of frightening whites and inflaming blacks, Randolph prevailed upon Lewis to think again. His toned-down version delighted most of the crowd, but annoyed black radicals. "I did not think it necessary for [the] speech to be changed," Fred Shuttlesworth complained. "I didn't think we were going up there to be sweet little boys. We were suffering. People were going to jail, people were dying and would be dying. So I didn't think we should . . . act as if everything was pie in the sky."[38]

King came last. "I am happy to join with you today in what will go down in history as the greatest demonstration for freedom in the history of our nation," he began. He urged followers to remain faithful to nonviolence. "In the process of gaining our rightful place, we must not be guilty of wrongful deeds. Let us not seek to satisfy our thirst for freedom by drinking from the cup of bitterness and hatred. . . . We must rise to the majestic heights of meeting physical force with soul force." Then came a rallying cry more inspiring than any King had ever delivered:

> I have a dream that one day this nation will rise up and live out the true meaning of its creed: "We hold these truths to be self-evident: that all men are created equal." I have a dream that one day on the red hills of Georgia the sons of former slaves and the sons of former slaveowners will be able to sit down together at a table of brotherhood. I have a dream that one day even the state of Mississippi, a desert state, sweltering with the heat of injustice and oppression, will be transformed into an oasis of freedom and justice. I have a dream that my four children will one day live in a nation where they will not be judged by the color of their skin but by the content of their character. I have a dream today.

King's closing words were delivered not by a single man, but by a lead singer with a chorus of a quarter million: "When we allow freedom to ring, when we let it ring from every village and every hamlet, from every state and every city, we will be able to speed up that day when all God's children, black men and white men, Jews and Gentiles, Protestants and Catholics, will be able to join hands and sing in the words of the old Negro spiritual: 'Free at last! Free at last! Thank God Almighty, we are free at last!'" Nothing further could be said. After singing "We Shall Overcome," the crowd drifted peacefully away. As marchers withdrew, Rustin noticed Randolph standing alone at the dais. He walked over and put his arm around the old man and said, "It looks like your dream has come true." Randolph, tears streaming down his face, replied that it was "the most beautiful and glorious day of his life."[39]

"The March on Washington established visibility in this nation," King's friend Ralph Abernathy later claimed. "It showed the struggle was nearing a close, that people were coming together, that all the organizations could stand together. It demonstrated that there was a unity in the black community for the cause of freedom and justice. It made it clear that we did not have to use violence to achieve the goals which we were seeking." Nothing could be further from the truth. Unity had been carefully engineered for one day. Underneath the surface, the civil rights movement was a boiling cauldron of discord. Militants complained that the event had been meticulously scripted to project an image of racial harmony in order to satisfy a worried president. Stokely Carmichael of SNCC protested that the march was "only a sanitized, middle-class version of the real black movement." Malcolm X, calling it a "sellout," complained that speeches had been censored and that an act of civil disobedience had been transformed into something altogether more docile. It was, he said, the "Farce on Washington." "Who ever heard of angry revolutionists swinging their bare feet together with their oppressor in lily-pad park pools, with gospels and guitars and 'I Have a Dream' speeches?"[40]

The warm glow of nostalgia obstructs the realities of what actually occurred. King's magnificent speech is remembered for the dreams it evoked rather than warnings it delivered. It is prudent to remind oneself of sentences subsequently forgotten:

> We have . . . come to this hallowed spot to remind America of the fierce urgency of now. This is no time to engage in the luxury of cooling off or to take the tranquilizing drug of gradualism. . . . It would be fatal for the nation to overlook the urgency of the moment and to underestimate the determination of the Negro. This sweltering summer of the Negro's legitimate discontent will not pass until there is an invigorating autumn of freedom and equality. Nineteen sixty-three is not an end, but a beginning. Those who hope that the Negro needed to blow off steam and will now be content will have a rude awakening if the nation returns to business as usual. . . . The whirlwinds of revolt will continue to shake the foundation of our nation until the bright day of justice emerges.

The march seems a triumphant moment, but King did not see it that way. His speech was an expression of worry as much as of hope. Like Malcolm X, he understood that the unity engineered on that day was indeed illusory.[41]

A significant section of black America had given up on the idea of racial harmony and was growing impatient with nonviolence. Lewis, while still prepared to toe the line at the Lincoln Memorial, was already headed in a different direction:

> The shedding of blood is not a part of our framework; it's not part of our philosophy, but I think that when we accept nonviolence, *we don't say that it is the absence of violence.* We say it is the present as-

sumption—much more positive—that there might be the shedding
of blood. You know what Gandhi says: "If I had the personal choice
to make between no movement and a violent movement, I would
choose a violent movement." . . . In SNCC now, there's a growing . . .
trend toward *"aggressive nonviolent action."* You no longer walk quietly
to paddywagons and happily and willingly go to jail.

Compared to his friends in SNCC, Lewis was moderate. The brash young
firebrands who had imparted so much energy to the civil rights movement
had grown openly contemptuous of King. While in Washington, they met
with Malcolm X. King, realizing that his hold over the movement was slipping, warned against the appeal of black nationalism: "The marvelous new
militancy which has engulfed the Negro community must not lead us to
distrust of all white people." Brotherly love was, however, difficult to maintain when white supremacists carried out ever more desperate acts of vengeance. Less than three weeks after the march, a bomb exploded in the Sixteenth Street Baptist Church in Birmingham, killing four young black
girls. On the following day, black youths battled with police. Their reaction was deeply regrettable, but entirely understandable.[42]

Contrary to Kennedy's fears, the March on Washington did not jeopardize the Civil Rights Bill. It passed with relative ease on July 2, 1964. That
was due partly to the fact that it had become a tribute to an assassinated
president, partly also to the expert way it was steered through Congress by
Lyndon Johnson. But it was incomplete, since it did not address the issue
central to the struggle for freedom—namely, the vote. Suffrage provisions
had been omitted in order to secure passage. Lewis was right: the Civil
Rights Act was too little, too late.

James Chaney, Michael Schwerner, and Andrew Goodman, three Freedom Summer volunteers, went to Neshoba County, Mississippi, in order
to further a cause that the federal government would not embrace: the realization of black enfranchisement. On June 21, 1964, they were arrested on
trumped-up charges, imprisoned for several hours, and then released into
the hands of the KKK, who murdered them. A huge outcry ensued, but
black activists rightly concluded that the tumult was due mainly to the
fact that Schwerner and Goodman were white, since the murder of blacks
was hardly news. At Chaney's funeral, David Dennis, the assistant director
of CORE, spoke for a significant proportion of the black community when

he complained: "I'm sick and tired of going to memorials! I'm sick and tired of going to funerals! I've got a bitter vengeance in my heart tonight! And I'm sick and tired and can't help but feel bitter, you see, deep down inside and I'm not going to stand here and ask anybody not to be angry tonight."[43]

At the March on Washington, before the speeches began, two Dylan songs were sung. First came Peter, Paul, and Mary with "Blowin' in the Wind," which evoked perfectly the mood of that day. Then came Dylan himself, who sang "Only a Pawn in Their Game," written in angry response to the murder of Medgar Evers. Few noticed it, but the two songs symbolized the two strands of the civil rights movement which were being unraveled by the pressure of events. One song suggested the patience that King embodied; the other, the frustration that Malcolm X and others would henceforth seek to exploit.

ARLINGTON NATIONAL CEMETERY: KENNEDY AND VIETNAM

For many people, the Sixties ended before they had hardly begun—on November 22, 1963, when John Kennedy was assassinated in Dallas. He had defined the spirit of the decade: the importance of youth, the impression of new beginnings, the lure of new frontiers. His assassination left the nation confused and frightened. The doors he had opened seemed to slam shut.

The assassination ripped something fundamental from the soul of America, leaving a chasm never to be filled. It has often been called the end of American innocence, a statement no less accurate for being trite. Innocence died not just because a promising president had been murdered, but also because, in time, it would become apparent how much the Kennedy myth depended upon the public's gullibility. As years passed, Americans would cling desperately to the hero, while they were battered by evidence of the man. The illusion of greatness could be maintained for the very simple reason that Kennedy died before he had to grapple seriously with the very divisive, costly, and soul-destroying problems of the mid-Sixties: Vietnam, race riots, budget cuts, and student unrest. He was killed before his personal perfidy could surface. As a result, he would forever be given credit for triumphs he supposedly inspired, while escaping blame for problems he bequeathed.

In 1983, *Newsweek* found that Kennedy was the most popular president in American history. While in office, his approval rating hovered around 63 percent, the third-highest rating of all postwar presidents. Yet what is the basis for this massive admiration? Strip away the myths and Kennedy's achievements seem rather thin. But that is the point—it is virtually impossible to separate myth from man. During his presidency, Kennedy was admired more for the dreams he inspired than for the man he actually was. The times required an energetic, dynamic, charismatic leader. Sentimental Americans also wanted a family man, since the good father would also, it was assumed, be good to his country. What Americans wanted they willed: Kennedy became what they craved, an object of worship. Like a warm cloak, hope kept out cold reality.

Kennedy's assassination was so painful because the myth was so perfect. It seemed that something almost divine had been taken from the American people, violently ripped from their grasp in Dealey Plaza. From that day forward, everything that went wrong in America—and so much did— could, it seemed, be traced back to his assassination. Because so much importance had been invested in him while he lived, so much magnitude was assigned his death. It became, inevitably and automatically, a watershed.

On a hill in Arlington Cemetery stands a moving memorial to Kennedy. On one side lies his grave, lit by an eternal flame. Turn around, toward Washington, and one encounters a semicircular granite plinth on which inspirational passages from his inaugural address are carved. They seem designed to remind a cloth-eared capitol of a time when ideals were sacred and presidents articulate.

One tablet reads: "To those peoples in the huts and villages across the globe struggling to break the bonds of mass misery, we pledge our best efforts to help them help themselves, for whatever period is required—not because we seek their votes, but because it is right. If a free society cannot help the many who are poor, it cannot save the few who are rich."[44]

Look up from the stones and far in the distance, across the wide Potomac, one can just barely see crowds gathering around another stone plinth. On black marble are carved the names of 50,000 Americans who died in Vietnam. In a spatial sense, the distance between the two memorials is huge. In a spiritual sense it is tiny. On the Vietnam Memorial one finds the names of people who died acting out Kennedy's illusions.

Oliver Stone, one of the greatest mythmakers to emerge from the Sixties, blames the Vietnam War on Lyndon Johnson. Larry Berman, the consummate Johnsonian scholar, recalls an encounter with his own son after the latter had been to see Stone's film *JFK*. Berman's son, who had never paid much attention to his dad's work, asked: "How come you never told me that Johnson had Kennedy killed in order to fight the war in Vietnam?"[45]

Stone drew his inspiration from John Newman's book *JFK and Vietnam*. In that book, Newman argues that Kennedy's National Security Action Memorandum (NSAM) 263, his last policy document to deal with Vietnam, ordered the immediate withdrawal of 1,000 soldiers, preparatory to complete disengagement by 1965. Then, on November 22, Kennedy was assassinated. Four days later, Johnson issued NSAM 273, canceling the withdrawal. The simple conclusion: Johnson escalated a war Kennedy planned to end.

The paranoiac Oliver Stone turned Newman's skewed reasoning into an enthralling conspiracy: Kennedy was assassinated in order to bring about a war lucrative for the American arms industry. The danger of such a suggestion lies in the fact that it resonates with a public besotted with Kennedy and addicted to conspiracy. For such people, the Vietnam nightmare represents the antithesis of the Kennedy dream. Without the war, they feel, Camelot might have been realized: no war would have meant no defeat, no budget cuts, no Vietnam syndrome, more money, better social programs, better race relations—ergo a more confident and harmonious America. Time, pivoting on a single moment in Dallas, can be imagined to assume a different, more pleasing trajectory. Conspiracy theories are a religion in which the devoted, instead of imagining a better future, pretend a better past.

Kennedy, it seems, did want out of Vietnam. He told Senator Mike Mansfield that "he had changed his mind and wanted to begin withdrawing troops beginning . . . January 1964." Complete withdrawal would be delayed "until 1965—after I'm reelected." Robert McNamara, Kennedy's secretary of defense, claims JFK planned to "close out Vietnam by 'sixty-five, whether it was in good shape or bad."[46]

But then there is the other Kennedy, the one who, in September 1963, told Walter Cronkite that withdrawal would be "a great mistake." On November 22 he was planning to tell a Dallas audience: "We in this country . . . are—by destiny rather than choice—the watchmen on the walls of freedom. . . . Our assistance . . . to nations can be painful, risky, and costly, as is true in Southeast Asia today. But we dare not weary of the task."[47]

With Kennedy, a huge gulf existed between rhetoric and action. "[His] attitude on Vietnam should be derived from what he said and did while president," Rusk maintained, "not what he may have said at tea table conversations or walks around the Rose Garden." His commitment to Vietnam was never half-hearted. During his short presidency, the number of American soldiers increased from 700 to more than 16,000. Strategic hamlets, covert terror, sabotage, and clandestine incursions into North Vietnam were introduced. In other words, he was doing his best to win. He did not, however, possess a very clear idea of how to win, or of what in fact was happening. Military advisers, keen to protect their position, told him what he wanted to hear. Optimism became official policy. The disastrous battle of Ap Bac, it will be recalled, was reported as a victory.[48]

In other words, Kennedy concluded that the war was going well because his advisers told him so. Contrary to what Newman has argued, NSAM 263 was predicated on a belief that victory was in sight. Rusk recalled "a period of optimism in the summer of 1963 when we thought the war was going well and we could begin to think of withdrawing American advisers." The McNamara-Taylor report of October 1963 reinforced this confidence, maintaining that, if trends continued, the situation would stabilize "by the end of 1965." The report concluded: "It should be possible to withdraw the bulk of US personnel by that time."[49]

The one obstacle was the South Vietnamese premier, Ngo Dinh Diem, an expert at alienating his people. While not personally corrupt, he allowed corruption to flourish around him. Peasants were fleeced by his loyal crooks. Meanwhile, Diem's persecution of Buddhists angered his people and embarrassed America. RVN forces broke up Buddhist demonstrations with shocking brutality, killing peaceful protesters. During a demonstration in Saigon on June 11, the Venerable Thich Quang Duc quietly sat down in a public intersection, doused himself with gasoline, and set himself alight. The incident, televised around the world, called into question America's choice of allies. Matters worsened when Madame Nhu, Diem's sister-in-law, referred to the episode as a "barbecue."

Much to the annoyance of Kennedy, Diem was a puppet who pulled his own strings. Though utterly dependent on US support, he pretended to be his own man. His refusal to do as he was told was made worse by the fact that he seemed incapable of holding his country together. In consequence, Kennedy grew convinced that, if the war was to be won, Diem had to go. He could not be allowed to jeopardize progress made on the battlefield.

Kennedy dreamed of a world without Diem. The prime minister could not be removed democratically, since, thanks to the CIA, he'd won election by a landslide. But Vietnam was a dependably violent country. Important people occasionally got murdered. Wish fathered thought. The US ambassador to South Vietnam, Henry Cabot Lodge, contacted a CIA operative named Lucien Conein who had links with Diem's enemies. Conein hinted that the US would not stand in the way of a coup. The only requirement was plausible deniability—that favorite phrase.

On October 25, Lodge confidently assured McGeorge Bundy (special assistant to the president for national security affairs) that "the next government would not bungle and stumble as much as the present one has." With this in mind, Kennedy patiently waited for murder. On November 1, a group of South Vietnamese Air Force officers ambushed Diem and took him away to be shot. The US quietly stood aside. Diem's body was later found in the back of an American armored personnel carrier, a nuance not lost on those sensitive to intrigue.[50]

A few days later, Lodge told Kennedy that the "prospects of victory are much improved." That was grossly optimistic. The US would soon discover that Diem's ruthlessness had been the only thing keeping chaos at bay. In the eighteen months that followed the assassination, Saigon went through five different prime ministers, all of them more corrupt or incompetent than Diem. The US role had, however, changed significantly because of its sponsorship of the coup. It was now committed to supporting each new regime. As Saigon unraveled, American involvement deepened.[51]

Three weeks after Diem's assassination, Kennedy was dead. He bequeathed his successor a problem much more complicated than that which he had inherited from Eisenhower. While a graceful withdrawal might have been possible during Kennedy's presidency, it was never conceivable during Johnson's. Referring to Vietnam, Johnson confessed that he felt like "one of those catfish down in Lady Bird's country. . . . I feel like I just grabbed a big juicy worm with a right sharp hook in it."[52]

Mark Lawson has written an intriguing novel called *Idlewild*, which rests on the premise that Kennedy survived the assassination attempt and won reelection in 1964. Within this counterfactual, the Vietnam War remains a constant, but Johnson becomes the best president America never had. In the novel, Kennedy chats with his former mistress Marilyn Monroe, who, by miraculously surviving her overdose of 1962, is also denied the grace of dying young. Monroe asks: "Do you think Johnson or Nixon—someone else—would have done the same in Vietnam?" Kennedy replies: "I've seen it argued that Lyndon wouldn't. But I have to believe that it would have happened, anyway. Vietnam was more the product of American history than individual whim."[53]

On that score, the fictional Kennedy was probably right. Vietnam was not his war or Johnson's war. It was an American war—an expression of America's self-confidence, of the country's belief in the possibility of re-shaping the world. There was no alternative scenario to futility, disillusionment, and sorrow—no defining moment in Dallas.

By 1968, Johnson was hopelessly stuck in a quagmire. He saw no way out and no way forward. The White House was under virtual siege from protesters, among them hollow-eyed veterans recently returned from Vietnam. From the streets came an endlessly repeated refrain: "Hey, hey, LBJ! / How many kids did you kill today?" In his agony, Johnson must have contemplated the fact that the chant scans equally well if "JFK" is substituted for "LBJ."

5

CALL OUT THE INSTIGATORS

DUXBURY: RACHEL CARSON

The mosquitoes in Duxbury, Massachusetts, in 1957 seemed like a biblical plague. Science, however, came to the rescue. With military precision, the ponds and marshlands around the town were doused with DDT. The mosquitoes disappeared, but so too did the butterflies, birds, and mice.

A frightened Olga Huckins, who ran a bird sanctuary, wrote to her friend Rachel Carson, beseeching her to use her influence to get someone to investigate. Carson, a zoologist by training and a writer by vocation, had become a household name because of her lyrical sea trilogy (1941–1955), which included the bestseller *The Sea around Us*. Her skill lay in her ability to communicate complicated biology in beautiful prose. The problem of pesticides had already begun to worry her; they were, she felt, a gross example of mankind's egotistical attempt to impose its will upon nature. "We still talk in terms of conquest," she argued.

> We still haven't become mature enough to think of ourselves as only a tiny part of a vast and incredible universe. Man's attitude toward nature is today critically important simply because we have now acquired a fateful power to alter and destroy nature.
>
> But man is a part of nature, and his war against nature is inevitably a war against himself. . . . Now I truly believe that we in this generation must come to terms with nature, and I think we're challenged as mankind has never been challenged before to prove our maturity and our mastery, not of nature, but of ourselves.

Carson decided to embark upon her most ambitious project. The shy, soft-spoken lover of nature went to battle against the might of the American chemical industry.[1]

Carson took four years to write *Silent Spring*. She realized that, given the determination and resources of her adversaries in the pesticide business, the science had to be impeccable. Fortunately, she was able to draw help from biologists, pathologists, chemists, and entomologists who shared her concern. She also realized that if the book were to exert maximum impact, it had to read like a novel. She therefore condensed dire scientific forebodings into simple, dramatic homily:

> There was once a town in the heart of America where all life seemed to live in harmony with its surroundings. . . . Then a strange blight crept over the area and everything began to change. . . . There was a strange stillness. . . . The few birds seen anywhere were moribund; they trembled violently and could not fly. It was a spring without voices. On the mornings that had once throbbed with the dawn chorus of scores of bird voices there was now no sound; only silence lay over the fields and woods and marsh.

Serialization began in the *New Yorker* in June 1962, four months before the book's official publication. An industrial toxicologist immediately dismissed Carson's work as "crass commercialism" packaged as "idealistic flag-waving," while the president of the Montrose Chemical Corporation, one of the nation's largest producers of DDT, complained that Carson had written "not as a scientist but rather as a fanatic defender of the cult of the balance of nature." He argued that if nature were allowed to determine its own balance, mankind would be ravaged by starvation and disease.[2]

PR executives worked overtime for the embattled industry. At first the response was temperate; spokesmen welcomed responsible inquiry. "What we have done, we have not done carelessly or without consideration," a Dow Chemical representative pleaded. "The industry is not made up of money grubbers." As Carson's popularity grew, however, the avuncular approach was abandoned in favor of character assassination. Carson was accused of being a Communist and, as a woman, prone to hysteria. "The major claims of Miss Rachel Carson's book," industry spokesman Robert White-Stevens argued, "are gross distortions of the actual facts, com-

pletely unsupported by scientific, experimental evidence and general practical experience in the field." Her credentials as a scientist came under
attack by critics who did not know the difference between a beaker and a
pipette.[3]

The soft-spoken Carson absorbed the attacks with immense dignity—all
the more impressive as she was dying of breast cancer. In response to
claims that she advocated a "return to the Dark Ages," she quietly explained: "I do not favor turning nature over to insects. I favor the sparing,
selective, and intelligent use of chemicals. It is the indiscriminate, blanket
spraying that I oppose." The campaign to discredit her backfired badly,
providing huge publicity for her book. Politicians found that they could
not completely ignore the ecological bandwagon. On June 4, 1963, Carson
addressed a Senate subcommittee investigating pesticides. She used the
occasion to widen her warning:

> Contamination of various kinds has now invaded all of the physical
> environment that supports us—water, soil, air, and vegetation. It has
> even penetrated that internal environment that lies within the bod-
> ies of animals and of men. It comes from many sources: radioactive
> wastes from reactors, laboratories, and hospitals; fallout from nu-
> clear explosions; domestic wastes from cities and towns; chemical
> wastes from factories; detergents from homes and industries.

John Kennedy was not particularly interested in environmental issues, but
he could not ignore the furor Carson had inspired. His Science Advisory
Committee, headed by Jerome Wiesner, reported on May 15, 1963, that the
uncontrolled use of pesticides was "potentially a much greater hazard"
than that of radioactive fallout. Since Kennedy had already expressed concern about that threat, he had to act on this one. A process was set in motion which eventually led to the banning of DDT. More important, Kennedy set a precedent for federal intervention on pollution issues. There
followed a steady stream of environmental legislation: the Clean Air Act
(1963), the Wilderness Act (1964), the Clean Water Act (1965), and the Endangered Species Act (1966). This last was inspired in part by the fact
that the bald eagle, America's cherished symbol, perched on the edge of extinction.[4]

Membership in environmental groups increased tenfold from 1960 to
1972, exceeding one million by the new decade. Carson helped this move-

ment coalesce, but her cause was helped enormously by a steady stream of disasters like the Santa Barbara oil spill and the Cuyahoga River fire. Each pollution problem seemed to reveal a similar source, namely a powerful, wealthy industrial polluter more concerned with amassing profit than with public health, and able to buy support from corrupt politicians.

The environmental movement was, in the main, a middle-class pressure group in which women, as mothers, had huge impact. Mothers provided the perfect voice for future generations—the only special interests they seemed to represent were their own children. Since pollutants had the greatest impact on the young, the old, and the infirm, the concerns voiced were impossible to ignore. This was especially the case after revelations that radioactive Strontium-90 from nuclear tests had been found in breast milk. The environmental cause was, however, weakened by the fact that it seemed a luxury to those on the margins of society. The black activist Vernon Jordan complained that "some people have been too cavalier in proposing policies to preserve the physical environment for themselves while other poor people pay the costs." Labor unions distributed a bumper sticker that read: "IF YOU'RE HUNGRY AND OUT OF WORK, EAT AN ENVIRONMENTALIST."[5]

The movement harmonized perfectly with the hippie counterculture, and received a fillip from it. Flower power was nine-tenths fantasy, but the idea nevertheless focused attention on the beauty and fragility of the natural world. Central to the simple life idealized by hippies was the concept of harmony with the planet and the rejection of artificial, plastic products. While the hippie ideal quickly disintegrated, one lasting by-product was a nascent ecological consciousness. "A lot of us had been [thinking] . . . about the planet," the actor and environmentalist Peter Coyote recalled, "about what the eternal reality was under this thin sheet of asphalt. And we were sensitive to the growing ecological crisis and the fact that a culture that was pissing in its life-support system couldn't continue. And so a lot of people moved out of the city to try to get in touch with the planet and those processes that seemed more long-term and durable and renewable." Macrobiotic restaurants sold "whole food" free of pesticides, synthetic flavors, and preservatives. The word "organic" came to mean something which did not damage the environment and would not endanger health. By the end of the decade, the term "earth" was applied to anything deemed ecologically pure and environmentally innocent. Boutiques sold earth clothes, clubs played earth music, Birkenstock made "earth shoes," and people ate "earth food."[6]

Another tremendous boost was provided, rather ironically, by NASA. The Apollo 8 mission on Christmas Eve 1968 brought back spectacular photographs of Earth, looking like a dappled blue-and-white pearl in a sea of black nothingness. The photos underlined the natural beauty of the planet, but also its vulnerability. Never before had Earth seemed so finite and fragile. Environmentalists loved the photos, even if they condemned the wasteful industry that had produced them. The photos became icons, subsequently used on countless posters encouraging people to recycle waste, clean up rivers, and use public transport. Ecologists spoke of "Spaceship Earth."

Environmentalism was the perfect populist cause; it provided a chance for every would-be David to go into battle against a mean, corporate Goliath. The Earth was something everyone had in common, and its defense was, therefore, a seemingly apolitical act. Even though not everyone could muster the energy to be environmentally responsible, taking a stand on this issue did not annoy one's friends and neighbors the way other political problems inevitably did. It was also a cause which provided something meaningful for everyone to do, be it recycling an aluminum can, cycling to work, or picking up litter. Occasional victories suggested progress was possible.

Progress was, however, illusory. Big industry quickly discovered how easy it was to make small gestures. Soft-drink manufacturers, for instance, made much of their decision to switch to pop tops that did not come loose from the can when the drink was opened. Previously pop tops had been thrown on the ground, where they stayed as indestructible reminders of environmental contempt. Integrated tops cost a bit more, but reaped dividends in positive publicity. They also distracted attention from the fact that the mining of aluminum was raping the environment, and that the massive amounts of sugar in soft drinks distorted agricultural production and contributed to health problems like obesity and diabetes. "Progress," in other words, relied on smoke and mirrors. While the federal government responded to the public demand for environmental controls, those controls were often confidence tricks designed to quiet the outcry while providing renewed opportunity for profit.

Rachel Carson died in 1964. While her books brought her enormous fame, she never acted like a celebrity. Public adulation was never the point, as she explained to a friend: "The beauty of the living world . . . has always been uppermost in my mind—that, and anger at the senseless, brutish things that were being done. I have felt bound by a solemn obligation to do what I could—if I didn't at least try, I could never be happy again in nature. But now I can believe that I have at least helped a little." "We have met the enemy and he is us," said the possum Pogo in a comic strip published on Earth Day, 1971. That was essentially the message Carson tried to convey, but it was not the message most people heard. The destruction of the environment has long been seen as an evil wrought by rapacious megacorporations. Few stop to consider that those corporations make products demanded by us. Toward the end of the decade, the *Whole Earth Catalog* proclaimed: "We are as gods and might as well get good at it." However wise that proclamation might have been, it was never likely to be heeded.[7]

HARLEM: MALCOLM X

The Harlem ghetto made Malcolm X. He saw its terror, its degradation, but also its vibrancy and its strength. "The ghetto people knew that I never left the ghetto in spirit," he claimed, "and I never left it physically more than I had to. I had a ghetto instinct." The ghetto was an instrument of oppression, a place where blacks were kept passive, demoralized, and drugged. For Malcolm, it was all that—and a platform for revolution.[8]

Malcolm Little was born on May 19, 1925, in Omaha, Nebraska. His parents were followers of Marcus Garvey, the Pan-Africanist who dreamed of a separate nation for American blacks. In 1929, the family home in Lansing, Michigan, was firebombed by white supremacists. Two years later, Malcolm's father was run over by a streetcar; police judged it an accident, but the black community decided otherwise. When his mother was institutionalized after a nervous breakdown in 1936, an otherwise stable family was cast to the wind. Though an intelligent boy and a promising student, Malcolm left school and drifted into a life of crime. By the age of twenty-one, he was a professional criminal, with his own burglary ring. His future seemed depressingly predictable, but a spell in prison changed everything. He converted to Islam, turned his back on crime, and emerged in 1952 as Malcolm X.[9]

He joined the Nation of Islam, first established in the 1930s. It offered a spiritual escape from ghetto life; according to its teachings the Muslim faith gave individuals the strength to resist alcohol, tobacco, drugs, sex, and crime. Converts were taught to live within their means, thus avoiding the depredations of the loan shark and the numbers runner. Men were required to dress conservatively in suits and white shirts; women, to keep their hemlines below the knee and to cover their hair. While the ascetic practices of the Nation of Islam restricted its appeal, it nevertheless had nearly seventy congregations in thirty cities by 1960. Converts were drawn almost exclusively from the ghetto. Anyone who doubted the power of the faith had only to look at Malcolm, a walking example of redemption.

Elijah Muhammad, the church's leader, argued that Christianity was a white faith used to delude blacks, a gospel of subservience which taught acceptance of degradation by promising paradise in the afterlife. Whites, those "blue-eyed devils," could never be trusted. In stark contrast to Martin Luther King, who preached racial harmony, Muhammad and Malcolm told their followers that blacks could never live in peace with whites, who were unworthy of their love. "There is nothing in our book, the Koran, that teaches us to suffer peacefully," Malcolm argued in November 1963. "Our religion teaches us to be intelligent. Be peaceful, be courteous, obey the law, respect everyone; but if someone puts his hand on you, send him to the cemetery. That's a good religion."[10]

From his pulpit in Harlem's Mosque Seven, Malcolm urged blacks to separate from white society and establish "a land of our *own*, where we can . . . lift up our moral standards." Integration, he argued, was simply a sop to keep the black man quiescent. "It's just like when you've got some coffee that's too black, which means it's too strong. What do you do? You integrate it with cream, you make it weak. But if you pour too much cream in it, you won't even know you ever had coffee. It used to be hot, it becomes cool. It used to be strong, it becomes weak. It used to wake you up, now it puts you to sleep." Instead of working for integration, "the American black man should be focusing his every effort toward building his *own* businesses, and decent homes for himself." Malcolm accepted that the Black Nation he envisaged could not be achieved peacefully, but would instead have to be wrested violently from the white man's grasp. Violence was neither avoidable nor regrettable. The spilling of blood would lead to the overthrow of white control and would purge black souls. "When a person places the proper value on freedom," he argued, "there is nothing under the sun that he will not do to acquire that freedom. Whenever you hear a man saying he wants freedom, but in the next breath he is going to tell you what he won't do to get it, or what he doesn't believe in doing, . . . he doesn't believe in freedom. A man who believes in freedom will do anything under the sun to acquire . . . his freedom."[11]

"The Negro revolution is controlled by foxy white liberals, by the Government itself," Malcolm argued, with obvious reference to King. "But the Black Revolution is controlled only by God." King's aim was to transform America, so that blacks could live safe and fulfilling lives. Malcolm's aim was to show blacks how to survive America; he wanted to equip them with the moral strength and physical fortitude necessary to live in an irretrievably racist nation. He derided nonviolence and personally questioned the "manhood" of civil rights leaders who stood aside while their followers were beaten and killed. "It is criminal," he argued, "to teach a man not to defend himself when he is the constant victim of brutal attacks."[12]

"Malcolm . . . was simply electric," the writer Alex Haley recalled. "Almost everything he did was dramatic—and it wasn't that he was trying to be, it was just the nature of him." The activist Marian Wright Edelman first encountered Malcolm delivering a speech at Yale Law School: "He was absolutely mesmerizing. He was brilliant. He was funny. He expressed the rage that all of us continued to feel about the slow pace of change in the country, but he did it in the cleverest and funniest way you could imagine. I just remember laughing uncontrollably at some of the ways Malcolm would answer questions and put down whites who were trying to trick him." "The reason why initially we cut off the televisions [when he was on] is that we were scared," claims Sonia Sanchez. "What he did was he said, 'I will now'—in a very calm fashion—'wipe out fear for you.' He expelled fear for African-Americans." She contends that "he made us feel whole. He made us feel loved. And he made us feel that we were worth something, finally, on this planet Earth." He had a particularly profound effect upon women, who previously had felt inferior because of their race *and* their sex. "He made women feel like they were queens of the universe. It was a queen not that set on a throne and did nothing. It was a queen that worked. A queen that talked. A queen that led. . . . So, yeah, you said, 'Hey, I am pretty. Look at here, look at these big lips. Aren't they full? When you been kissed by these lips, you know you been kissed.'"[13]

Malcolm was far too good a preacher and far too charismatic a man to be tolerated for long by Elijah. Finding his popularity threatened, Elijah imposed a gag order. Malcolm respected the order, but grew increasingly resentful: "When a high-powered rifle slug tore through the back of NAACP Field Secretary Medgar Evers in Mississippi, I wanted to say the blunt truths that needed to be said. When a bomb was exploded in a Negro Christian church in Birmingham, Alabama, snuffing out the lives of those four beautiful black girls, I made comments—but not what should have been said about the climate of hate the American white man was generating and nourishing." Silencing Malcolm was like trying to keep a dog from barking. After the assassination of Kennedy, he openly questioned why blacks should mourn the president's death. Kennedy, he reminded listeners, had pursued a course of violence in Asia, Africa, and Latin America; he had supported assassination in the Congo and Vietnam. His murder was a case of "chickens coming home to roost. . . . Being an old farm boy, chickens coming home to roost never did make me sad. They've always made me glad." While the statement was not far removed from the separatist policy of the Nation of Islam, Elijah, who insisted on playing the white man's politics even though he rejected the white man's world, found it unacceptable. Malcolm, recognizing an inevitability, broke with the Nation of Islam.[14]

A break was probably inevitable even if Malcolm had been able to stay silent. He was by this stage developing a more secular philosophy than that espoused by Elijah, one which accepted the possibility of racial coexistence. He regretted having been such an effective promoter of Elijah. "I shall never rest until I have undone the harm I did to so many well-meaning, innocent Negroes who through my own evangelistic zeal now believe in him even more fanatically and more blindly than I did." After a pilgrimage to Mecca and a tour of Africa, his faith became noticeably more cosmopolitan. "I remember him coming back saying he . . . had seen not just black, not just white or yellow or red, but had seen all people and in the eyes of Allah they were one," the singer Harry Belafonte recalled. "It was a major shift . . . and Malcolm knew . . . that a new alliance would have to be forged, that more than ever there was a need for the movements to come together." "Where true brotherhood existed among all colors," Malcolm observed, "where no one felt segregated, where there was no 'superiority' complex, no 'inferiority' complex—then voluntarily, naturally, people . . . felt drawn together by that which they had in common." He wanted this same amalgamation to be achieved in America. This meant modifying his attitude to white people. The actor Ossie Davis recalled Malcolm saying to a white audience: "You know, I do not think all white folks are evil now, but some of you are, and I'm going to keep on at you until you, whoever you are, grant us the respect that we're due as fellow human beings." He also toned down his criticism of civil rights campaigners. He still believed their faith in nonviolence was deluded, but respected their courage.[15]

On March 27, 1964, Malcolm traveled to Washington to hear the Senate debate the Civil Rights Bill. Somewhat coincidentally, King was also present, and the two met for the first and only time in their lives. "I'm here to remind the white man of the alternative to Dr. King," Malcolm announced. A short time later, he founded the Organization of Afro-American Unity, a body reflecting his new cosmopolitanism. He had in mind a worldwide pressure group campaigning for improvements in the lives of blacks everywhere. Included in his list of demands was a call for the US government to establish a "Pentagon-sized department" to address every aspect of black people's plight. At one of his last press conferences, in February 1965, he argued: "It is incorrect to classify the revolt of the Negro as simply a racial conflict of black against white, or as a purely American problem. Rather, we are today seeing a global rebellion of the oppressed against the oppressor, the exploited against the exploiter."[16]

"It is a time for martyrs now," Malcolm remarked on February 19, 1965. "If I am to be one, it will be for the cause of brotherhood. That's the only thing that can save this country." Two days later, he was gunned down at the Audubon Ballroom in Harlem, in front of his OAAU supporters. Elijah called it an "act of divine chastisement," though he denied involvement. A week later, he told a crowd gathered for the Savior's Day rally: "We didn't want to kill Malcolm and didn't try to kill Malcolm. They know I loved him. His foolish teaching brought him to his own end."[17]

Uncertainty about where Malcolm was headed has led to wide variation in the way he has been remembered. Admirers choose the interpretation that pleases them the most. For some, Malcolm was a martyr to black nationalism; to others, he was a champion of world revolution. Some revered him as a separatist, others as a born-again integrationist. While it is tempting to speculate about what he might have become, there is no doubting that he remained just as influential dead as he had been alive.

Malcolm persuaded very few blacks to convert to Islam. But that is not an accurate measure of his impact. Through his example, blacks learned to take pride in their race. Long before the race riots of 1964–1968, he focused attention on how the ghetto destroyed lives. "Malcolm kept snatching our lies away," Ossie Davis said at the funeral. "He kept shouting the painful truths we whites and blacks did not want to hear. . . . And he wouldn't stop for love or money." Davis thought that "Malcolm spoke directly to the emasculation of the black male in particular. He wanted to teach us how, in spite of that, to be men again."[18]

"I felt," Davis reflected, "a determination to say something about who the man was, because at that time the headlines were so full of so many awful things. He was being described as a mad dog whose violence had killed him." Davis, a gentle man, recalled how white liberals later questioned why he had agreed to speak at Malcolm's funeral. "No Negro has yet asked me that question," he invariably replied.[19]

HAVANA: CHE

In November 1967, a photo was released of a Bolivian soldier standing over a half-naked corpse. The Bolivian government was proud of that photo, since the corpse in question was that of Ernesto "Che" Guevara, killed while trying to foment revolution among local peasants.

Two months later came a much more pleasing picture of Che, unveiled as a sixty-foot mural in the Plaza de la Revolución in Havana, in celebration of the ninth anniversary of the Cuban Revolution. The image, captured by Alberto Díaz Korda, showed an achingly beautiful, almost saintly man wearing a black beret and looking upward, as if seeking the truth. Korda's photo would eventually become one of the most widely reproduced images in the history of photography, a modern icon replicated on posters, T-shirts, postcards, matchboxes, table napkins, playing cards, condoms, and tattoos. In the 1990s, Nike replaced the star on his beret with a swoosh in order to advertise athletic shoes made in Third World sweatshops. Billions of dollars have been made peddling the image of a socialist.

Che's appeal can be explained by the fact that, like John Kennedy, Patrice Lumumba, and Jim Morrison, he will always remain young, handsome, and dead. He was killed in the fullness of youth, before age could shatter the ideals and tarnish the image. Though a Marxist, he was a man unencumbered by convoluted theory. The simple, practical nature of his revolutionary style explains his enduring appeal to the young. "Che's writings instilled in me the belief that a revolutionary is motivated by the strongest feelings of love for humanity," one former radical recalled. He seemed genuinely concerned for the suffering of the downtrodden and led by example, sharing the sacrifices he expected of his followers. A man of action more than ideology, he taught peasants to rise up and seize what was theirs.[20]

Thanks in part to the work of the romantic socialist Régis Debray, an idealized account of Che's revolution became the gospel for a generation of radicals in the industrialized West. Debray's book *Revolution in the Revolution,* a title evoking the dynamism craved by the young, was first published in English in 1967. It became an essential accessory for those wishing to establish revolutionary credentials. Love for Cuba became as trendy as a tie-dyed shirt. Castro and Che seemed proof that the revolution could work, and that socialism could deliver justice and equality to the people. While socialists were constantly splintering into tiny factions, they generally managed to agree on the merits of Che, a powerful antidote to disillusionment with Soviet Russia.

Adoration has obscured the questionable aspects of Che's career. His particular contribution to revolutionary theory was his belief that the preconditions necessary for revolution could be created by a small, enlightened cadre which he called a *foco*. In other words, the peasantry could be transformed into a revolutionary mass through inspired leadership. Since Che maintained that leaders would have to come from the educated class, this explains his appeal to middle-class students in the developed world. He implied, to the delight of radicals everywhere, that a few committed activists could change the world. Fired by this thought, the Columbia University firebrand Mark Rudd confessed to a "macho desire to be a great revolutionary hero (and martyr) like Che Guevara."[21]

Che is best judged by his own standards. His experience in the Congo in 1965 demonstrates that enlightened leadership cannot by itself turn a reluctant peasantry into a revolutionary force. "I shall go to the Congo," he announced, "because it is the hottest spot in the world now. . . . I think we can hurt the imperialists at the core of their interests." The plan was launched against the advice of the Egyptian president, Gamal Abdul Nasser, who warned that Africa did not need "another Tarzan, a white man among black men, leading them and protecting them." The idea that Africa was an African problem did not accord with Guevara's internationalism. "I tried to make them understand that it was not just a struggle limited by frontiers, but a war against a common enemy . . . but no one took the point." After nine months of trying to light a fire, Che was forced to conclude that the Congolese made poor revolutionaries. "We cannot pretend that the situation looks good," he wrote. "Organizational work is almost nonexistent, since the middle-rank cadres do not work, do not know how to work, and inspire no confidence in anyone. . . . Indiscipline and the lack of any spirit of sacrifice are the principal characteristics of all these fighters. To win a war with such troops is out of the question."[22]

Similar lessons were driven home in Bolivia, where Che went in early 1967. After nine months, he was forced to admit that "we have not succeeded in developing peasant support. . . . On the contrary, they are becoming informers for the army." His *foco* dwindled from an original forty-five men to just sixteen at the time of his death. Yet this failure occurred in a country specifically chosen because it seemed to offer the best conditions for success. "I feel like a human scrap," he confessed toward the end, "and on some occasions I have lost self-control."[23]

Che's failings were conveniently ignored by those who desperately craved a hero. In February 1968, SDS organized a field trip to Havana, an act of adoration disguised as education. Leftists had been making this pilgrimage for some time; it was an essential item on any radical's curriculum vitae. Cutting cane was one small way they could compensate for the ill-treatment of Cuba by the American government. "I saw in Cuba what I wanted to see," Rudd later admitted. "Factories, farms, and institutions that were owned by the state, socialized. I wanted to see a different way to organize society. But I didn't see the obvious: that you can't have a one-party state, that you have to have elections."[24]

Radicals in the developed world were skilled practitioners of moral relativism. Horrible crimes were perfectly excusable if committed on behalf of a revolution in an oppressed Third World country. Those who reacted with outrage at the execution of the brutal rapist Caryl Chessman in California in 1960 turned a blind eye when Castro executed hundreds of his fellow Cubans for the crime of political infidelity. Susan Sontag, who went to Cuba in 1960, found it "astonishingly free of repression," even though she admitted that it did not have a free press. The fact that 15,000 "counter-revolutionaries" were being held in Cuban prisons by the mid-1960s apparently did not qualify as repression. There is no doubt that American propaganda exaggerated the Cuban threat, but there is also no doubt that student radicals compensated for this propaganda by manufacturing a fairy tale starring Castro and Che.[25]

It is easy to admire a peasant revolution from the safe refuge of an ivory tower. Support comes cheap—merely the cost of a full-sized poster of Che and some Joan Baez albums. There's no need to think about what Che actually accomplished, or the ruthless methods he used. Symbols are a substitute for analysis. Long after Debray's book was forgotten, the power of Che's portrait remained potent. The hero is inseparable from the image: a cult of Che could not have materialized without that photo. He symbolizes an era when images smothered words. As the Russian poet Yevgeny Yevtushenko complained:

> Comandante, your precious name
>   they wish to sell so cheaply.
> With your name industry wants to buy
>   new customers.
> Comandante: in Paris I saw your
>   portrait on little pants called
>   "hot."
> Your pictures, Che,
>   are printed on shirts
> You plunged into the fire.
>   They want to turn you into
>   smoke.
> But you fell,
>   riddled by bullets,
>   by poisonous smiles
> not to become later
>   merchandise for the consumer
>   society.

The image provided rebellion without pain, a fantasy inspired entirely by a face. It was not necessary to examine the grim realities of Castro's revolution, or the real character of Che himself, because that beautiful face said everything. Eventually, the image completely overwhelmed what it was once supposed to represent. Students today still put Che on their walls, but are more likely to eat Cherry Guevara ice cream. Some of them even know that Che once had something to do with Cuba.[26]

MIAMI: THE GREATEST

They called him the Louisville Lip because his voice was directly wired to his ego. Detractors called him the Mouth, for much the same reason. Cassius Clay's talent for bluster was brutally evident on the eve of his first title fight, when he mocked his opponent, Sonny Liston: "The man can't talk. The man can't fight. The man needs talking lessons. The man needs boxing lessons. And since he's gonna fight me, he needs falling lessons. . . . I'm gonna give him to the local zoo after I whup him. . . . He's too ugly to be the world champ. The world champ should be pretty, like me." Vulgar boasts were tolerable because Clay usually delivered what he promised. On February 25, 1964, he combined exquisite grace with vicious brutality, overwhelming the lumbering Liston. "I want everyone to bear witness," Clay shouted. "I am the greatest! . . . I'm the king of the world!" A new hero had arrived, a man everyone talked about but few even remotely understood. "What a strange and uncommon man," Gilbert Rogin remarked in *Sports Illustrated*. "Who can fathom him? We can only watch in wonder as he performs and ponder whether, despite his truly affecting ways, he doesn't scorn us and the world he is champion of."[27]

Clay refused to conform to the image admirers demanded. This was driven home immediately after the Liston fight. Instead of attending the customary parties, complete with champagne and beautiful women, he spent a quiet evening with friends, among them Malcolm X and the singer Sam Cooke. The next morning came an even more unpalatable revelation. Clay announced his conversion to Islam: "I believe in Allah and I believe in peace. . . . I'm not a Christian any more. I know where I'm going, and I know the truth, and I don't have to be what you want me to be."[28]

This declaration of independence was, by itself, shocking. Heroism implies ownership. Sports stars belong to spectators; they sacrifice their private self for public adulation. All this explains why the nation felt betrayed when Clay said, "I don't have to be what you want me to be." The betrayal was compounded when he underlined his independence by adopting a "foreign" religion, essentially saying that America felt foreign to him. This interpretation was confirmed when Clay emphasized that his conversion was not just religious:

> I ain't no Christian. I can't be when I see all the colored people fighting for forced integration get blowed up. They get hit by stones and chewed by dogs and they blow up a Negro church and don't find the killer. . . . I'm the heavyweight champion, but right now there are some neighborhoods I can't move into. . . . I'm no troublemaker. . . . I'm a good boy. I never have done anything wrong. I have never been to jail. I have never been in court. I don't join any integration marches. . . . A rooster crows only when it sees the light. Put him in the dark and he'll never crow. I have seen the light and I'm crowing.

At the time, innocence still reigned in American sports. Fans could not stomach a sporting hero who used his prestige to criticize America. Clay's decision to bring personal grievances into the boxing arena seemed blasphemous. No wonder, then, that he was cast from the temple. Columbia Records, producers of his album *I Am the Greatest,* pulled it from shops. Advertising agencies terminated his product endorsements. Appearances on television were abruptly canceled. "You don't use the heavyweight championship of the world to spout religious diatribe," maintained Harry Markson, the director of Madison Square Garden. "We've made so much progress in eliminating color barriers that it's a pity we're now facing such a problem." The former champion Joe Louis, who knew discrimination, chimed in: "Clay will earn the public's hatred because of his connections with Black Muslims. The things they preach are the opposite of what we believe."[29]

Clay's affiliation with the Nation of Islam was no mere whim. He had essentially been a member since 1962, but had kept his beliefs quiet in order to protect his career. Since Malcolm X and Elijah Muhammad were deeply reviled figures, his association with them was bound to cause disquiet. After Clay announced his conversion, commentators customarily referred to him as a "Black Muslim," as if that was something altogether different from a genuine Muslim. "'Black Muslim' is a press word," he protested. "The real name is 'Islam.' That means 'peace.'" For most white Americans, the "Black Muslim" label fused two already frightening identities. Clay became, overnight, something altogether more threatening and foreign than an ordinary black man. Ed Wassman, president of the World Boxing Association, argued that Clay's behavior was "detrimental to boxing." The conversion was dismissed as a fad, what one reporter called the "Allah routine."[30]

White America's sense of betrayal was exacerbated by the peculiar dynamic of 1960s race relations. The black sports star was given a magic key into the white world. Fans ignored an athlete's color if he was talented. Thus, an inveterate Chicago racist might adore Jim Brown because there was no better running back in football. Acceptance, however, implied duty. In exchange for the keys to the kingdom, the black star was supposed to be grateful, obedient. He was not supposed to present himself as a spokesman for black people. He could not, it was argued, be a spokesman, since his huge income and the admiration he enjoyed separated him from his race. It seemed hypocritical for such a man to complain about racism when he no longer felt its pain.

Clay, however, could not keep quiet. He used the podium of his heavyweight title to lecture on race. "The government should . . . get down on their hands and knees every morning and thank God that 22 million black people have not become anti-American," he argued in January 1965. "You've given us every right to. The whole world would side with us if we became anti-American." Clay's diatribes delighted Malcolm X, who understood just how useful the new champion could be. He wanted a hero exclusively for blacks. "Clay . . . is the finest Negro athlete I have ever known," he remarked, "the man who will mean more to his people than Jackie Robinson, because Robinson is the white man's hero." Malcolm calculated that the annoyance Clay would cause whites would be inversely proportional to the pride he would inspire among blacks.[31]

"This fight is the truth," Malcolm told Clay before the Liston fight. "It's the Cross and the Crescent fighting in a prize ring—for the first time. It's a modern crusades . . . with television to beam it off Telstar for the whole world to see what happens!" This willful divisiveness annoyed white liberal supporters of civil rights. Annoyance increased when Clay told the Louisville *Courier-Journal:* "I'm not going to get killed trying to force myself on people who don't want me. I like my life. Integration is wrong. The white people don't want integration. I don't believe in forcing it, and the Muslims don't believe in it."[32]

Clay's emergence came at an opportune moment, since it allowed Elijah to be much more decisive with Malcolm. The conversion coincided perfectly with the Nation of Islam's annual Savior Day. For the first time in a decade, Malcolm was absent, having been banished by Elijah, who used the occasion to showcase Clay. "I'm so glad that Cassius Clay was brave enough to say that he was a Muslim," Elijah told the crowd. "He was able, by confessing that Allah was his god and by following Muhammad, to whip a much tougher man. They wanted him to get his face torn up, but Allah and myself said 'No!' . . . Clay has confidence in Allah, and in me as his only messenger."[33]

One icon quickly replaced another. Elijah was willing to use Clay as an advertisement for Islam despite the fact that he hated boxing and never attended matches. On March 5, after announcing that Malcolm's suspension would be indefinite, Elijah revealed that Clay would be given the name Muhammad Ali. This came as a surprise, since converts usually had to wait more than ten years for such an honor. While Clay was jubilant, the banishment of his close friend Malcolm at first troubled him. Faith, however, took precedence over friendship. He accepted that he would have to break with Malcolm. "You just don't buck Mr. Muhammad and get away with it," he explained. "I don't want to talk about [Malcolm] anymore."[34]

To whites, the name change was a bitter statement of rejection. As Cassius Clay, he was familiar, containable. As Muhammad Ali, he was foreign, threatening. Those who objected to the change persisted in calling him Clay, as if, by so doing, they could control the man, assert ownership of him, deny him what he wanted to be. The *Los Angeles Times* sportswriter Jim Murray mocked the boxer by calling him "Abdullah Bull Bull" or "Abou Ben Hernia." To confirm that he was entirely serious, Ali made a point of walking out of Madison Square Garden when the announcer introduced him as Cassius Clay. "Clay means dirt," he objected. "My white blood came from slave masters, from raping." "People are always telling me what a good example I could be if I just wasn't a Muslim," he added. "I've heard it over and over, how come I couldn't be like Joe Louis and Sugar Ray. Well, they're gone now, and the black man's condition is just the same, ain't it? We're still catching hell."[35]

The day after Ali announced his conversion, both the FBI and the Defense Department opened inquiries into his draft status. Given the close sequence, it is easy to conclude that Ali was being punished. The issue, however, is much more complicated than Ali worshipers seem to understand. The draft matter predated his title fight and the announcement of his conversion. He was eligible because he was the right age, was unmarried, and was not a full-time student. Fame was not supposed to be a deferment, a point the government occasionally tried to make. While the entire selective service system was undoubtedly iniquitous, it would surely have compounded its iniquities if Ali had escaped the call-up because of his fame.

On January 24, 1964, Ali had failed the military qualification examination, scoring in the sixteenth percentile, well below the threshold for induction. "I tried my hardest," he insisted, but the Selective Service Board suspected otherwise and ordered him to retake the test. When the issue went public in early March, Ali maintained that he would not request exemption as a conscientious objector on grounds of religious faith. "I don't like that name," he said. "It sounds ugly—like I wouldn't want to be called." He instead took the test again on March 13, and failed again. This time, the board accepted the result and classified him as ineligible for service.[36]

Ali's detractors, deeply disappointed that he had escaped the draft, now hoped that another boxer would silence him in the ring. The obvious contender was Floyd Patterson, who had announced that "as a Catholic" he felt obliged to "reclaim the title for America." One suspects he meant "as a Christian," but everyone understood, and most cheered. "Cassius Clay is disgracing himself and the Negro race," Patterson told Sports Illustrated. "The image of a Black Muslim as the world heavyweight champion disgraces the sport and the nation. Cassius Clay must be beaten and the Black Muslim scourge removed from boxing." Ironically, Patterson, the great defender of American values, had only recently been forced to sell his $140,000 home at a considerable loss because of incessant racial abuse from white neighbors.[37]

Ali responded with typical bluster. "Patterson says he's gonna bring the title back to America," he spat. "If you don't believe the title already is in America, just see who I pay my taxes to. I'm American. But he's a deaf dumb so-called Negro who needs a spanking. I plan to punish him for the things he said; cause him pain. . . . The little pork-chop eater don't have a chance." He then shifted to rhyme:

I'm gonna put him flat on his back,
So that he will start acting black,
Because when he was champ he didn't do as he should,
He tried to force himself into an all-white neighborhood.

Ali did not predict a short fight, because he did not want one. On November 22, 1965, he made Patterson suffer, pummeling him with devastating punches, then backing off to allow him to recover, only to resume the punishment. Punches provided percussion to a continuous refrain of abuse. "Come on America!" Ali taunted. "Come on white America!" Fans and critics alike were appalled at his cruelty.[38]

Sublime talent could not mask the stench of hypocrisy. Ali had blamed Patterson for being the victim of racism—it was his fault for moving into a white neighborhood. He subjected his opponent to verbal abuse which, if uttered by a white man, would have been condemned as racist. "No black athlete had ever spoken so disparagingly of another black athlete," the tennis star Arthur Ashe complained. Patterson, not Ali, seemed to recognize the brutal irony of two black men beating each other up for the entertainment of a mainly white audience. "There is so much hate among people," he complained, "so much contempt inside people who'd like to think they're moral, that they have to hire prizefighters to do their hating for them. And we do. We get into a ring and act out other people's hates. We are happy to do it. How else can Negroes like Clay and myself, born in the South, and with little education, make so much money?" On that conundrum, the Mouth was silent.[39]

After the Patterson fight, the draft issue resurfaced. The war was using up America's eligible men at a voracious pace. Desperate to widen the recruiting pool, the Selective Service Board in early 1966 lowered the passing score from 30 percent to 15 percent. Ali suddenly found himself eligible. He was mystified: "For two years the Army told everyone I was a nut and I was ashamed. And now they decide I am a wise man. Now, without ever testing me to see if I am wiser or worser than before, they decide I can get into the Army." "Why me?" he kept asking. "Man, I ain't got no quarrel with them Vietcong."[40]

In truth, not many Americans did. Ali had by this stage been struggling with the draft issue for two years, yet he still had not developed a coherent position on the war, or on where his Islamic faith placed him. He saw himself as different from the thousands of other young black men in his draft cohort, at the same time that he aspired to be their representative. He suggested that he was more valuable to the war effort as a professional boxer than as a GI. "I buy a lot of bullets, at least three jet bombers a year, and pay the salary of fifty thousand fighting men with the money they take from me after my fights." That line of argument was abandoned when he realized how selfish it sounded. He then claimed that his ring career was immaterial to the question of service. "Boxing is nothing, just satisfying some bloodthirsty people. I'm no longer Cassius Clay, a Negro from Kentucky. I belong to the world, the black world. I'll always have a home in Pakistan, in Algeria, in Ethiopia. This is more than money."[41]

Ali claimed he was being victimized, punished for his outspokenness and his conversion to Islam. "I can't understand it. Out of all the baseball players, all of the football players, all of the basketball players—why seek out me, the world's only heavyweight champion?" That argument had some justification. Draft boards were known to call up "troublemakers," like the civil rights leaders John Lewis and Bob Moses, apparently to silence them. Yet there is still something slightly sordid about Ali's line of argument, based as it is on an assumption of exclusivity. His arguments have been accepted with little critical examination because, today, he is universally loved and the Vietnam War seems unjust. From that logic flows the argument that the US government "stole" the career of a gifted boxer. If this is true, however, it must be pointed out that the government also stole the prime years of some nine million other Americans. The issue of Ali's "unfair" treatment is based on the assumption that he was too important to go to war, that those less gifted should have gone in his place. That seems grossly elitist.[42]

Ali's detractors labeled him a coward. He wasn't a coward, but he was an opportunist. Despite at first arguing that it was not right to claim conscientious-objector status, he eventually settled on that as the most promising line of escape. On February 22, he filed for CO status, explaining: "It would be no trouble for me to go into the armed services, boxing exhibitions in Vietnam and traveling the country at the expense of the government or living the easy life, and not having to get out into the mud and fight and shoot. If it wasn't against my conscience to do it, I would easily do it. I wouldn't raise all this court stuff, and I wouldn't go through all this and lose the millions that I gave up and my image with the American public." Rather surprisingly, Justice Lawrence Grauman, on reviewing the case, bought that argument, ruling that Ali was "sincere in his objection on religious grounds to participation in war in any form." This, however, was not the ruling that the government wanted, since it seemed to suggest that the Muslim faith provided legitimate escape from service. As the prosecutor Morton Susman warned, "If [Ali] gets by, all black people who want to be Muslims will get out for the same reasons." The Justice Department, insisting that Ali's refusal was based on racial and political—not religious—grounds, called upon Kentucky's selective service appeal board to ignore the Grauman ruling. They dutifully obliged. The case was referred to the national appeal board, which delivered the decision the government wanted.[43]

In truth, Ali's objections were based as much on politics as on religion. In voicing his opposition to the war, he could seldom resist the opportunity to criticize the government. While touring Louisville, he argued: "Why should they ask me to put on a uniform and go ten thousand miles from home and drop bombs and bullets on brown people in Vietnam while so-called Negro people in Louisville are treated like dogs and denied simple human rights? No, I am not going ten thousand miles from home to help murder and burn another poor nation simply to continue the domination of white slavemasters of the darker people the world over. This is the day when such evils must come to an end." Heartfelt as that objection might have been, it contains a massive flaw. Reversing the logic produces the following possibility: Ali *would* have gone ten thousand miles to drop bombs and bullets if the conditions for black people at home had been better. He confirmed that possibility later in the statement: "The real enemy of my people is right here. . . . If I thought the war was going to bring freedom and equality to twenty-two million of my people, they wouldn't have to draft me—I'd join tomorrow. But I either have to obey the laws of the land or the laws of Allah. I have nothing to lose by standing up for my beliefs. We've been in jail for four hundred years." Only one besotted by Ali can ignore the contradiction in his statement. He'd claimed he had a religious objection to war. Yet that should have applied to all wars, as Judge Grauman suggested it did. Pacifism, as every draft board knows, is supposed to be absolute. His claim that he would join up in a minute if he was convinced that the war was a bona fide freedom struggle merely demonstrates that his objection pertained specifically to this war and was based on politics. There is nothing dishonorable in such an objection, but there is something rather shifty in attempting to pass it off as genuine conscientious objection based on religious opposition to war.[44]

By April 1967, Ali's options for appeal were exhausted. On the 28th he refused to take part in an induction ceremony in Houston. The boxing establishment immediately began their censure of him, suspending his license and stripping him of his title. Then, in June 1967, Ali went on trial before an all-white jury. He was quickly found guilty and sentenced to five years in prison and a $10,000 fine. The severity of the judgment shocked even the prosecutor, given that the usual sentence was eighteen months. Ali, however, remained defiant. "Standing up for my religion made me happy; it wasn't a sacrifice," he later insisted. "When people got drafted and sent to Vietnam and didn't understand what the killing was about and came home with one leg and couldn't get jobs, that was a sacrifice. But I believed in what I was doing, so no matter what the government did to me, it wasn't a loss."[45]

For his crime, Ali spent three years exiled from boxing. That was a significant sacrifice but, as he intimated, it is risky to compare sacrifices when there are nearly 60,000 names on a black-marble memorial in Washington. The system was harsh, but its harshness was felt by thousands of others besides Ali. To single him out as uniquely mistreated denigrates the experiences of those who suffered more. Likewise, to dismiss the system as corrupt demeans those who managed to convince the tribunals that their conscientious objection was genuine, for the simple reason that it was.

CHELSEA: MARY QUANT

In November 1955, a young art student named Mary Quant, along with her boyfriend, the suitably cool jazz trumpeter Alexander Plunket Greene, opened a shop called Bazaar on the King's Road in London's Chelsea district. Like Bob Dylan, Quant anticipated an age; her clothes were fresh, breezy, and bright, at a time when Britain was still gray, boring, and fusty. "Suddenly the King's Road was full with new and unlikely people, all of the magical age in which they were adult but not old," Alexandra Pringle recalled. "The women . . . wore big floppy hats, skinny ribbed sweaters, keyhole dresses, wide hipster belts and, I believed, paper knickers. They had white lipsticked lips and thick black eyeliner, hair cut at alarming angles, op-art earrings and ankle-length white boots. They wore citron-colored trouser suits and skirts that seemed daily shorter. They rode on miniature motorbikes. They had confidence and, it seemed, no parents." Quant loved the adjectives "kooky" and "kinky," words most people still thought pejorative, but which would soon define a decade. "I hated the clothes the way they were," she later explained. "I wanted clothes that were much more for life, much more for real people, much more for being young and alive in." Like the brilliant businesswoman she was, Quant provided a product before people quite realized they wanted it. By the end of her first week of business, it was clear that Bazaar would not only be a huge success, it would also transform fashion around the world.[46]

During World War II, British fashion had been carefully controlled through clothing coupons and utility designs. The latter quashed style by stipulating precisely how many pleats a skirt might have and how long it should be. Dyes were in short supply, since the military had first priority. Fabrics had to be produced at home as much as possible, and this meant that virtually everything was made of wool. The overall effect was that everyone looked the same—something the government encouraged because it strengthened the impression of a people's war.

In 1947 came Christian Dior's New Look, an intentional rebuke to wartime drabness. While undoubtedly modern, it was also assertively nostalgic, a throwback to an imaginary age of plenty. Long dresses and flouncy skirts were conspicuously wasteful of resources; frill attacked asceticism. Most Britons, however, had to admire the New Look from afar, since money was still tight, resources controlled, and austerity still policy. It was not until the mid-1950s that the British could again think of clothes as fashion.

Those who were parents in the 1950s were children of empire, of war, and of economic depression. To them, Britain was an old country and a country which drew strength from its oldness. To their children, however, Britain was postimperial, even though no one used that term. They had heard stories of hard times, but had not felt the pain. No one quite knew what Britain would become in the second half of the twentieth century. What was clear, however, was that it would be something different—something new—and that newness would be defined by the young.

Fashion heralded the triumph of the new. Teds morphed into Mods, a style which defined both clothing and behavior. Those who did not live the Mod life nevertheless coveted the Mod style: sharp lines, simple designs, basic colors—the very antithesis of the New Look. "At first we thought it was just the art-student type that wanted to look like us and buy our clothes," one former Mod reflected. "What we didn't realise at the time . . . was the fact that we were interpreting the mood of a whole generation, not just smart art students. The whole thing caught on in a much bigger way than we expected." That was partly due to Quant, who took an improvised street fashion and turned it into a billion-pound industry. "Suddenly someone had invented a style of dressing which we realised we had been wanting for ages," wrote Brigid Keenan, who covered fashion for the *Daily Express*. "Comfortable, simple, no waists, good colours and simple fabrics. It gave anyone wearing them a sense of identity with youth, and adventure, and brightness."[47]

In November 1965, the model Jean Shrimpton, while visiting Australia, shocked observers at the Melbourne Race Track when she arrived wearing a shift which ended a good four inches above her knees. The event, which was still provoking comment in newspapers a week later, is seen as the official unveiling of the miniskirt, even though hers was not technically a skirt. The revolutionary fashion turned every woman into an exhibitionist. At the same time, the men at the Exchequer tore their hair in frustration. The tax on clothing stipulated that a woman's skirt had to be at least twenty-four inches from waist to hem; anything shorter was a child's skirt, and children's clothing was not taxed. Thanks in part to Shrimpton, the rules of fashion stipulated that a miniskirt was authentic if it measured around twenty inches or less, while the really daring wore microskirts a mere twelve inches in length.

Soon, the controversial style had circled the globe. For Yasmin Alibhai, who grew up in Uganda, the Sixties began when a new girl arrived at her school: "Nadya walked into the school party shimmering in a noisy silver paper foil dress, and hair which reached down three inches below the hemline, much of which she was air-propelling by the deft movement of her head from side to side with extraordinary viciousness. She was also showing a terrifying amount of leg. She cut through the crowd which was paralysed with horrific admiration and put on a Joan Baez tape, belting out some protest song. That too was a first."[48] In the United States, the *Wall Street Journal* discovered that 52 percent of businesses found miniskirts acceptable for office wear, while long hair (on men) was approved by only 5 percent. "It's a functional thing," quipped New York's mayor, John Lindsay. "It enables young ladies to run faster—and because of it they may have to." In the California legislature, however, women were banned from wearing miniskirts. The author of the ruling, Eugene Chappie, explained that he "was getting sick of turning my head when one of them was at a drinking fountain." In San Diego, the Padres baseball team desperately tried to boost attendance by hosting Miniskirt Days, with free admission to women so attired. Management reasoned that if baseball did not bring men to the stadium, short skirts would. Around the same time, Pacific Southwest Airlines enjoyed a brief boost in profits thanks to its reputation for having the stewardesses with the shortest skirts.[49]

What Mary Quant gave to women, John Stephen gave to men. He came from Glasgow in the mid-Fifties to work in London as a tailor's clerk, but before long opened a Carnaby Street boutique called His Clothes. Stephen was not afraid to let street style dictate what was in his shops, instead of the other way around. He would watch what hip Mods were wearing and would put those same clothes on the racks a short time later. So great was his mastery of popular taste that within a few years he had more than fifty shops in Britain, Europe, and the United States.

While Quant and Stephen saw themselves as trendsetters—the instigators of a fashion revolution—they were also astute businesspeople who saw a niche in the market and cleverly filled it. Though most Britons hardly felt affluent, they sensed that better times had arrived. Unemployment was low and so were prices. Young people with a modicum of disposable income spent it on conspicuous finery, in a way that made their ascetic parents cringe. Working-class girls thought nothing of spending half their weekly wage on clothing, cosmetics, and jewelry.

The clothes themselves, like the new music, were designed to be disposable. Because fashion changed so quickly, quality and durability were unimportant. Cathy McGowan, the young presenter of the pop music program *Ready Steady Go!* and one of the foremost exemplars of the "dolly bird" image, was briefly employed as a "teenage consultant" by three large clothing chains. She advised that "kids want clothes to look terrific—and they don't wear them for long, so it doesn't matter if they fall to bits."[50]

Quant, Stephen, and their imitators understood that new fashions required new marketing techniques. Boutiques were not simply clothing stores; they were places where kids went to have fun, to meet people, and to indulge in fantasy. Customers were encouraged to linger. The interior decoration harmonized with the clothing styles. Music was loud and ubiquitous, carefully calculated to raise spirits. Out went the older, professional shop assistant, who made customers feel unwelcome. The new clerks were the same age as their clients, wore the same clothes, and usually managed to give the impression that they, too, were simply having fun. Shops pretended to be democratic, in line with the illusion of a classless society. "Haute couture doesn't have the same meaning anymore, because money, status, and power no longer have the same meaning," the fashion designer Rudi Gernreich proclaimed. "Now fashion starts in the streets. . . . That's why I watch kids."[51] Quant claimed that "snobbery has gone out of fashion, and in our shops you will find duchesses jostling with typists to buy the same dresses."[52] This was rank marketing hype, since her clothes did not come cheap. Fashion perhaps started in the streets, but the retail industry devised a way to sell back to kids (at considerable profit) what they themselves had invented.

With a new look went a new body type: straight lines and simple shifts did not work very well on women shaped like Marilyn Monroe. According to Barbara Hulanicki, the immensely successful founder of the boutique Biba, the perfect look was "square shouldered and quite flat-chested [with] . . . an upturned nose, rose cheeks, . . . a skinny body with long asparagus legs and tiny feet." Big breasts, Quant felt, suggested motherhood, and mothers could never be groovy. Whereas girls had once dressed to look like women, now women were desperate to look like girls.[53]

"The Look" was not confined to clothes. In 1963, Quant asked the young Vidal Sassoon to provide a hairstyle to go with her latest fashion line. He had already been experimenting with "the Shape," a simple bob made revolutionary by the fact that it was long at the sides and short at the back. The line was so clean and the curve so perfect that it looked like it had been cut with precision tools. It had something of the space age about it— the kind of hairstyle an alien might sport. This was no coincidence, given that the outer-space theme was used extensively in fashion to suggest ultramodernity. Manmade fabrics furthered the image; designers took to using PVC and Mylar, or at the very least shiny polyester. Photo shoots were often staged with a backdrop made to look like Mission Control. Designers displayed a fondness for silver, bright white, and fluorescent colors, while geometric patterns and simple stripes suggested functionality. The models themselves, with their flat chests and straight hips, looked and acted like an army of androids.

Fashion is the easiest way to adopt an image: wear the clothes and become the person—at least on the outside. Deconstructing that image is like walking through a minefield. In striving for the youthful look, Quant intentionally mimicked children's clothing, in particular school uniforms. She readily admitted that she wanted women to appear under the age of consent. While that seems a style specifically designed to satisfy warped male fantasies, Quant insisted that her fashions implied strength: "The way girls model clothes, the way they sit, sprawl or stand, is all doing the same thing. It's not 'come hither,' but it's very provocative. She's standing there defiantly with her legs apart saying, 'I'm very sexy. I enjoy sex, I feel provocative, but you're going to have a job to get me. You've got to excite me and you've got to be jolly marvellous to attract me. I can't be bought, but if I want you, I'll have you.'" The novelist Sheila MacLeod disagrees. She wonders in retrospect "how [I] could have been deceived into imagining that the fashions of the Sixties spelled liberation for women." Instead, "their purpose was to imprison women more securely as objects of male attention, male ribaldry, male lust." Germaine Greer, in *The Female Eunuch*, objected vehemently to the way women had been turned into sex objects, as if that were something new. Most miniskirted women, however, saw Greer as a loudmouthed spoilsport. The era witnessed a new version of an old argument: Do women dress for themselves, or merely to please men? The answer is elusive because it differs from woman to woman, depending upon who they were pre-mini and who they became. One woman's flag of surrender was another's weapon of conquest.[54]

Before long, the arbiters of style decided that the only acceptable standard in fashion was unconventionality. At David Bailey's wedding to Catherine Deneuve on August 18, 1965, the bride wore a blue sweater and light-green corduroy trousers and arrived smoking a cigarette. The best man, Mick Jagger, wore blue denim and no tie. In truth, the most unconventional thing a guest could have done would have been to wear a tuxedo. Sartorial nonconformity sent the Look into decline after 1966; its orderliness was out of place in an age devoted to chaos. Quant gave way to the flower children, for whom freedom was paramount. The new trend was to dress as if style was unimportant—to wear whatever one wanted, the more bizarre the better. Hulanicki anticipated this when she opened Biba in

September 1964. Out went the neat lines and precise colors pioneered by Quant; Biba was full of off-tones, flowing fabrics, colors rich instead of bright. As Alexandra Pringle recalled: "A certain lasciviousness, a sort of voluptuousness crept in. . . . I tried on clothes for the sinful and *louche*: slithery gowns in glowing satins, hats with black veils, shoes stacked for sirens. There were shoulder pads huge as American footballers', evening dresses to make Betty Grable sigh, makeup—chocolate and black—for vamps and vampires." While Bazaar catered to the rich, almost anyone could afford Biba. Hulanicki concentrated on volume, packing her stores with cheap clothes guaranteed to fall apart or go out of fashion in a few weeks. By the end of 1967, her main store was reputed to have the highest turnover per square foot of any shop in the world. On any given day, she lost more to shoplifters than most boutique owners made in profit.[55]

"So where does all the Swinging London stuff, pop music, hemlines, where did it all fit in?" the novelist Angela Carter asks. "I'd like to be able to dismiss it all as superficial and irrelevant to what was really going on, people arguing about Hegel and so on, but I'm forced to admit that there was a yeastiness in the air that was due to a great deal of unrestrained and irreverent frivolity. . . . There's no denying that towards the end of the decade everyday life . . . took on the air of a continuous improvisation. . . . *Carpe diem.* Pleasure. It didn't have to cost much, either." The success of boutique-style retail astounded even those at its cutting edge. By 1966, Quant was making £6 million a year and had brokered a deal with J. C. Penney to market her designs in the United States. Stephen, the working-class Glaswegian, had a mansion in the country and a fleet of fancy cars. London, with some 2,000 boutiques, had become the fashion capital of the world. The boutiques, the music, the sheer effervescence of life in the capital had combined to make London the Swinging City. "The city is alive with birds (girls) and Beatles, buzzing with minicars and telly stars, pulsing with half a dozen separate veins of excitement," *Time* magazine proclaimed.[56]

"Britain has lost an empire and has not yet found a role," Dean Acheson remarked in 1962. By 1965, Britannia's role was clear. Whereas once she had prided herself on giving substance to the world, now she gave it style.

6

UNIVERSAL SOLDIERS

THE TONKIN GULF: CARTE BLANCHE

In August 1964 the fog of war proved convenient. On the 2nd, the US destroyer *Maddox*, patrolling in the Tonkin Gulf, was fired upon by North Vietnamese patrol boats. Two days later, another destroyer, the *Turner Joy*, spotted torpedoes approaching, though they might have been dolphins. What seemed murky in the Tonkin Gulf was perfectly clear in Washington: US naval forces had been attacked without provocation.

The war had not been going well. The South Vietnamese government lurched from crisis to crisis, political deterioration exacerbated by military defeat. By early summer 1964, American analysts were predicting that the Saigon regime would not survive to the end of the year. The People's Liberation Armed Forces (PLAF, or Viet Cong) were meanwhile harassing American advisers, hoping to drive them out of the country. President Johnson felt powerless, especially since, with an election in November, he was reluctant to deploy combat troops. His campaign mantra went: "We are not about to send American boys nine or ten thousand miles away from home to do what Asian boys ought to be doing for themselves."[1]

A master manipulator, Johnson realized that, in the event that he needed to go to war, he would need something dramatic to fire the wrath of the American people. This was conveniently provided in the Tonkin Gulf. The fact that the incidents occurred offshore, far from prying reporters, allowed Johnson to manufacture precisely the scenario he required. Though the *Maddox* had indeed been attacked, the second raid was at best an innocent misassumption, at worst an outright fabrication. Johnson privately surmised that "those dumb, stupid sailors were just shooting at flying fish."[2]

Still insisting that "we . . . seek no wider war," Johnson asked Congress on August 4, for the authority "to take all necessary measures to repel any armed attack against the forces of the United States and to prevent further aggression." The subsequent Tonkin Gulf Resolution would remain in force until "the president shall determine that the peace and security of the area is reasonably assured."[3]

The House of Representatives unanimously approved the resolution after a forty-minute debate. In the Senate, only Ernest Gruening of Alaska and Wayne Morse of Oregon disapproved. Gruening was "opposed to sacrificing a single American boy" in "a war in which we have no business." Morse complained that a fundamental check upon presidential power had been squandered. "Within the next century, future generations will look with dismay and great disappointment upon a Congress which . . . [made] such a historic mistake." Most Americans, however, thought that Morse and Gruening were simply whiners. The public, offered a righteous war, bought it enthusiastically. A Harris poll found that 85 percent of respondents supported Johnson's policy.[4]

On August 5, American bombers pounded the port of Vinh, just over the border in North Vietnam. The aim was to punish the North for PLAF sins in the South. Privately, Johnson boasted: "I didn't just screw Ho Chi Minh—I cut his pecker off." The raid and the resolution convinced Hanoi that Johnson was on the verge of deploying combat troops. Firebrands at the Politburo pushed for a general offensive, in order to destroy the RVN before the Americans could mobilize. Driving the strategy was General Nguyen Chi Thanh, recently promoted to senior general, a snub to the more cautious Vo Nguyen Giap. Meanwhile, terror strikes were unleashed upon American targets, including a bombing of the Caravelle Hotel in Saigon—a raid that destroyed the city's illusion of impregnability. On November 1 the American airbase at Bien Hoa was hit, and three servicemen were killed. Johnson, however, refused to be provoked just yet. With an election looming, he did not want Americans worrying about their sons in Vietnam.[5]

By early 1965, Hanoi stood on the verge of victory. A majority of the South was under National Liberation Front (NLF) control, the Saigon regime was steadily weakening, and the ARVN (the South Vietnamese army) was virtually moribund. Johnson, having won in a landslide by promising no wider war, was now free to act as he pleased. His instincts told him to mobilize, but his emotions pulled him back. Johnson's equivocation convinced the North Vietnamese Politburo that the United States would not be able to save the ARVN from complete destruction. Thanh boasted that "the work of twenty years might be achieved in a day."[6]

On February 7, PLAF guerrillas attacked the American camp at Pleiku, killing nine. Johnson, his patience nearly exhausted, moaned: "We have kept our gun over the mantel and our shells in the cupboard for a long time now. . . . And what was the result? They are killing our boys while they sleep in the night." He approved Operation Flaming Dart, a bombing offensive against the North. National security adviser McGeorge Bundy wanted to "ma[k]e clear to our own people" that "at its very best the struggle in Vietnam will be long." Johnson rejected that idea outright. Again came the assurance, "We seek no wider war."[7]

Three days later, an attack at Qhi Nhon that killed twenty-three Americans pushed Johnson over the edge. He approved Operation Rolling Thunder, a program of "measured and limited air action . . . against selected targets" in the North. Instead of tit-for-tat reprisals, the United States would conduct a sustained bombing campaign on the assumption that Hanoi's breaking point would eventually be reached.[8]

Contrary to American assumptions, bombing the North had no effect upon PLAF behavior in the South. Johnson was like King Canute, fighting to hold back a Red tide. He responded as presidents often respond: by sending in the Marines. On March 8, the 9th Marine Expeditionary Brigade hit the beaches northwest of Da Nang, the first combat troops to be deployed. The Marines were sent in to protect the Da Nang airbase from terrorist strikes and thus free ARVN troops for operations against the PLAF. Orders specifically stated: "The US Marine force will not, repeat will not, engage in day-to-day actions against the Viet Cong." Johnson still hoped that bombing alone would do the trick. In other words, the deployment was not supposed to be a change of policy, but this is precisely what it became. Hanoi responded by sending additional PAVN units. An inexorable escalation had begun.[9]

Johnson's political apprenticeship in the 1930s made him a firm believer in the power of government to relieve social hardship. His Great Society was an extension of the New Deal. The Thirties also provided another important lesson—namely, that totalitarian dictators could not be appeased. "The appetite of the aggressor is never satisfied," he declared on April 7, 1965. In the context of the 1960s, those two lessons proved contradictory:

> I knew from the start . . . that I was bound to be crucified either way I moved. If I left the woman I really loved—the Great Society—in order to get involved with that bitch of a war on the other side of the world, then I would lose everything at home. All my programs. All my hopes to feed the hungry and shelter the homeless. All my dreams to provide education and medical care to the browns and the blacks and the lame and the poor. But if I left that war and let the Communists take over South Vietnam, then I would be seen as a coward and my nation would be seen as an appeaser, and we would both find it impossible to accomplish anything for anybody anywhere on the entire globe.

Histrionics aside, that was a fair appraisal. Warnings about the dangers of appeasement were not mere talk, designed for a naïve public. In April 1965, McNamara remarked that failure in Vietnam would result in "a complete shift of world power. Asia goes Red, our prestige and integrity damaged, allies everywhere shaken." Defeat, secretary of state Dean Rusk warned, would cause "the communist world . . . [to] draw conclusions that would lead . . . almost certainly to a catastrophic war."[10]

At a conference in Honolulu in late April 1965, the Joint Chiefs pushed for further escalation. General Maxwell Taylor, who had opposed the deployment of Marines, warned of "ever-increasing commitments until, like the French, we would be occupying an essentially hostile country." His doubts were, however, swamped by a tide of military optimism. The conference recommended increasing troop strength to 82,000 men. The additional troops, when combined with relentless bombing, would "break the will of the DRV/VC." Back in Washington, Johnson, not without qualms, approved the recommendations.[11]

Three months later, the DRV was far from broken. McNamara, after a visit to Vietnam in early July, returned with a sense of foreboding. Now, however, no alternatives remained: having committed to a ground war, the United States could only escalate. On July 21, McNamara backed Pentagon requests for an extra 200,000 troops. George Ball, the loyal pessimist, warned of the "perilous voyage" that lay ahead. "I have great and grave apprehensions. We cannot win, Mr. President. The war will be long and protracted. The best we can hope for is a messy conclusion."[12]

"The tide almost certainly cannot begin to turn in less than a few months," a somewhat chastened McNamara advised, "and may not for a year or more; the war is one of attrition and will be a long one." McNamara's pessimism seems, in retrospect, optimistic. Ball, in contrast, was not sure "that we can beat the Viet Cong or even force them to the conference table on our terms, no matter how many *white, foreign* (US) troops we deploy. No one has demonstrated that a white ground force of whatever size can win a guerrilla war . . . in the midst of a population that refuses cooperation." Failure, he warned, would be catastrophic: "The worst blow would be that the mightiest power on earth is unable to defeat a handful of guerrillas."[13]

Johnson sided with McNamara's view that victory in Vietnam was necessary—but he did so out of fear more than conviction. "This is what I could foresee," he explained in 1971. "From all the evidence available to me it seemed likely that all of Southeast Asia would pass under Communist control, slowly or quickly, but inevitably, at least down to Singapore but almost certainly to Djakarta." He worried about domestic political consequences—specifically, a "mean and destructive debate" over who was responsible for "losing" Vietnam. It would "shatter my presidency." Truman's difficulties after the "loss of China . . . were chickenshit compared to what might happen if we lost Vietnam." Allies around the world "would conclude that our word was worth little or nothing." He feared that "if I don't go in now and they show later I should have gone, then they'll be all over me in Congress. They won't be talking about my civil rights bill, or education, or beautification. No sir, they'll push Vietnam up my ass every time. Vietnam. Vietnam. Vietnam. Right up my ass."[14]

Johnson therefore reluctantly decided that "we should do what was necessary to resist aggression but we should not be provoked into a major war." He would send 50,000 troops immediately, holding an additional 50,000 at the ready. This half-hearted response could not disguise the painful logic of escalation. Sending troops would become an addiction, with ever-larger "fixes" needed to produce the same hopelessly transient high. Johnson escalated sufficiently to suit his political objectives, but not sufficiently to win in Vietnam. He nevertheless hoped it would be enough. "I'm going up her leg an inch at a time," he told Senator George McGovern. "I'll get to the snatch before they know what's happening."[15]

America went to war while pretending otherwise. No declaration of war was issued, no special budget passed, no attempt made to mobilize the American spirit. Johnson feared that war fever would shift attention from his domestic goals, rendering them moot. When he asked McNamara in July 1965 how much war would cost, the latter replied "twelve billion dollars in 1966." In other words, it "would not require wage and price controls." Americans would get guns and butter: a war *and* the Great Society. "We are a nation with the highest GNP, the highest wages, and the most people at work. We can do both. As long as I am president we will do both."[16]

For the moment, the trick worked. Johnson remained popular and, aside from some rumbling on college campuses, Americans supported this strange war. But the demon that Johnson failed to slay in the summer of 1965 grew into a monster within six months. By clinging to the Great Society, he made the war unwinnable. By going to war, he made the Great Society unaffordable. Johnson was a clever politician, but the situation required a statesman. By avoiding difficulty, he sowed disaster.

SINAI: THE SIX-DAY WAR

Wars are started to correct the intolerable. The act of fighting, however, often renders the intolerable a good deal worse, encouraging nostalgia for the status quo ante bellum. Witness what happened in the Middle East in 1967. All of the belligerents—Israel, Egypt, Syria, and Jordan—had logical reason for war. Each sought a more advantageous distribution of land and power. But six days of war turned frying pan into fire. The predicament of Egypt, Syria, and Jordan worsened because they lost. Israel's travails increased because she won.

In February 1966, a moderate regime in Syria was overthrown by radical Baathists. While it was customary for Syrians to despise Israelis, the new government was even more hostile than the old, more inclined to act upon hatred. Bellicosity rendered the Syrians more dependent upon Nasser's Egypt, even though they found his regime distasteful. The Egyptians, in turn, sensed a need to support Syria in order to preserve their status as leaders of the Arab world. A formal defense pact, signed in November 1966, turned inclination into inevitability. Nasser found himself in the worst of all possible worlds: he was committed to defending Syria, but could do nothing to control its belligerence.

Syria, eager to punish Israel, encouraged militant Palestinians to strike against Israeli targets. This inevitably pulled Jordan into the conflagration. King Hussein had assiduously tried to prevent Palestinian fedayeen from using Jordan as a base, but Israel was disinclined to recognize his efforts. When, in November 1966, three Israeli soldiers were killed by a Palestinian mine near the Jordanian border, Israel retaliated by pummeling the West Bank, even though Syria would have been a more appropriate target. Angry West Bank residents turned on Hussein for failing to protect them, a reaction encouraged by Nasser, who had whipped himself into a frenzy.

Nasser had made his reputation through aggression, casting himself as the champion of small states unable to stand up to imperialist bullies. The Congo, Cuba, Vietnam, Indonesia, and the Dominican Republic were interpreted by him as proof of how far the United States would go to extend its power. "The battle we are fighting," he proclaimed, "is not an easy one. . . . We are fighting America, the greatest power in the world." In the Middle East, he concluded, Israel was simply the agent of the Americans. "Israel today is the United States. We challenge you, Israel. No, in fact, we do not address the challenge to you, Israel, because you are unworthy of our challenge. But we challenge you, America."[17]

Nasser sensed a perfect opportunity for a challenge. He presumed that the United States, stuck in the Vietnam quagmire, could not afford another conflict. For that same reason, the Soviet Union encouraged Egypt to foment trouble. A Soviet official confessed: "The USSR wanted to create another trouble spot for the United States, in addition to that already existing in Vietnam. The Soviet aim was to create a situation in which the United States would become seriously involved economically, politically, and possibly even militarily, and would suffer serious political reverses as a result of siding against the Arabs." Soviet advice, however, was dangerously inconsistent. On one occasion, Soviet premier Alexei Kosygin told Egyptian defense minister Shams Badran: "It is better to sit at a negotiating table than to wage a battle by the sword." To confuse matters further, defense minister Andrei Grechko promised that "if America enters the war, we will enter it on your side. . . . If something happens and you need us, just send us a signal. We will come to your aid immediately."[18]

Two minstrels of the changing times: Bob Dylan and Joan Baez, 1964

Democracy murdered:
Patrice Lumumba on the
way to his execution,
December 1960

The aftermath of a
massacre: Sharpeville,
March 1960

John Kennedy: The image
of a family man

top left A rather smug Fidel Castro inspects prisoners captured at the Bay of Pigs, 1961

top right The stability of a wall: German border guards on opposite sides of Berlin

left "I have a dream": Martin Luther King at the March on Washington, 28 August 1963

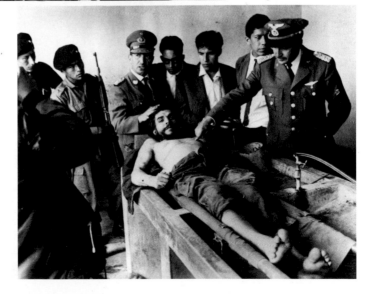

The other photo: Bolivian soldiers proudly display the corpse of Che Guevara, October 1967

Mary Quant plotting a fashion
revolution, 1965

Supposedly the start of it all:
Jean Shrimpton causes outrage
and delight when she shows up at
the Melbourne Races in a
miniskirt—actually a shift

Who's manipulating whom? Cassius Clay and Malcolm X in 1964, just after Clay defeated Sonny Liston for the heavyweight boxing title

Rachel Carson: The silent revolutionary

Losing the hearts and minds: American soldiers with a Vietcong prisoner, 1966

The Hunger War: Biafran women and children at a refugee camp, 1969

The gospel according to Chairman Mao: Chinese peasants recite from the *Little Red Book* before going to work

We do like to be beside the seaside: Mods and Rockers on their way to battle, 1964

Something happening here: Robert Jasper Grootveld performing in front of the Het Lieverdje statue, Amsterdam

Desolation Row: Watts after six days of riots, 1965

Timothy Leary attempting a fusion of the cultural and political revolutions at a meeting of the East Village Motherfuckers in 1968. Lending support are Abbie Hoffman (l) and Jerry Rubin (r); the latter seems more interested in his reefer

Sublime Sixties talent: Cassius Clay meets the Beatles, 1964

The Egyptians felt certain they could defeat Israel, as long as the United States stood aside. They also presumed that the Israelis, fearful of Egypt's power, would do anything to avoid war. "We were confident that our army was ready and that Israel would not attack because . . . we were superior in armored weapons, artillery, and air power," Badran recalled. "It was calculated that Israel would not walk into an open grave."[19]

In fact, Israel welcomed war. Her embattled image was a carefully constructed myth. Attacks by militant Arabs, which appeared unprovoked, were, according to Moshe Dayan, often the result of Israeli manipulation: "It used to go like this. . . . We would send a tractor to plow some place of no value in the Demilitarized Zone, knowing, in advance, that the Syrians would start shooting. If they refrained, we would instruct the tractor to keep advancing, until the Syrians lost their temper and started shooting. Then we would start firing artillery, and, later, also send our air force." The Israelis wanted a showdown. They felt cheated that battles won in the Suez conflict of 1956 had not yielded appropriate reward—they had been forced to surrender territorial gains. The assertiveness of the Palestinians also frightened them. Israeli fears that their enemies wished to destroy the country were given sinister encouragement by Nasser. "The mere existence of Israel is an aggression," he argued. Radio broadcasts on Saut al-Arab, Nasser's propaganda megaphone, proclaimed: "We have nothing for Israel except war. Our aim is to destroy the myth which says Israel is here to stay. . . . Every one of the 100 million Arabs has been living for the past nineteen years on one hope—to live to die on the day Israel is liquidated."[20]

These threats convinced Israel that a quick assertion of power was warranted. An unprovoked attack, however, ran the risk of alienating world (especially American) opinion. Thus, the Israelis could not appear to be aggressors. At the same time, they knew that success depended on speed—in particular, the quick destruction of the Egyptian air force. Israel's dilemma lay in how to appear the victim but still control events.

Nasser solved that problem. He, too, felt a need to assert himself. Though the resolution of the Suez Crisis had been favorable to Egypt, diplomatic victory could not completely hide military humiliation. Egypt needed to demonstrate that it was a true friend of the Palestinians and, more important, needed to restore its authority among Arab nations, who found Israeli dominance intolerable. On May 19, 1967, Amman Radio pointedly remarked: "Will Egypt restore its batteries and guns to close its territorial waters in the Tiran Strait to the enemy? Logic, wisdom, and nationalism make it incumbent on Egypt to do so."[21]

Three days later, in response to this pressure, Nasser ordered UN troops to leave the Sinai and moved his forces into the area. He simultaneously announced that he would blockade the Straits of Tiran, thus cutting off Israel's access to the Red Sea. The waterway, he proclaimed, belonged to Egypt. "Under no circumstances will we allow the Israeli flag to pass through the Gulf of Aqaba." The threat had economic implications, but, more important, suggested to the rest of the world that the Egyptians, whenever they pleased, could strangle Israel.[22]

Nasser, apparently, did not want war. He assumed that the Israelis would not respond aggressively to his challenge, allowing him to derive maximum benefit from their humiliation. Events had, however, spiraled out of control. His army commander, Abd al-Hakim Amer, promised that a surprise attack against Israeli airfields would yield enormous benefit. Amer had personal reason for wanting to attack: a feckless performance in 1956 and, subsequently, during the Yemeni civil war rendered him in need of rehabilitation. Nasser, unwilling to defy Amer, reluctantly approved his plan. The Israelis got wind of it, however, and foreign minister Abba Eban, in Washington on May 26, alerted President Johnson. Johnson in turn warned Kosygin that, in order to avert a global crisis, he'd better restrain Nasser. Kosygin complied, with the result that Amer's attack was canceled.

Nasser, having been warned that he could not expect Russian help if he attacked first, was obliged to wait for an Israeli assault. Despite this setback, he still thought his forces could hold their own at least until the United States and the USSR forced a settlement. Granted, the Soviets and Americans would not have tolerated a prolonged contest, but Nasser failed to appreciate the Israeli capacity to conduct a lightning war and his side's woeful inability to prevent one. Nor did he understand that the United States would welcome an Israeli rout of Egypt. On June 1, Meir Amit, chief of Mossad (Israel's intelligence agency), met with defense secretary Robert McNamara. "He asked me two questions," Amit recalled. "He said, 'How long will it take?' And I said, 'Seven days.' . . . And then, 'How many casualties?'. . . I said less than in 1948, when we had 6,000." Johnson, given similar advice by the CIA, felt confident that the war could go ahead. He told Amit: "Do what you have to. . . . We know that you can hit Nasser, but it all depends on how strong and fast your action will be. Strength, speed, and resolve [will] prevent the intervention of any party you—and we—don't wish to be there." At the same time, for purposes of pretense, he advised prime minister Levi Eshkol: "I must emphasize the necessity for Israel not to make itself responsible for the initiation of hostilities. Israel will not be alone unless it decides to go alone. We cannot imagine that it will make this decision."[23]

Johnson still hoped that the United States, with help from the British, could pressure the Egyptians to reopen the Straits of Tiran. Eshkol was inclined to give the Americans the time they needed, but his generals, led by Ariel Sharon, wanted war. They argued that Eshkol's reticence was humiliating Israel and jeopardizing the chances for a quick victory. "We need to take a deep breath," Eshkol told them on May 28. "We need patience. I don't accept that the fact that the Egyptian army is sitting in Sinai means that we have to go to war. . . . Will we live forever by the sword?" In an attempt to preserve peace, Eshkol sent Nasser secret messages urging calm. Ironically, these had the opposite effect. Nasser interpreted them as evidence of Israeli weakness—Eshkol, he assumed, was frightened of war.[24]

Israel had created a powerful military in order to defend the country's existence in a hostile world. A strong military, however, meant strong generals who assumed the right to bend the government to their will. They had the power to force Eshkol's ouster. The fact that they had that power meant they did not have to use it. In order to keep his generals at bay, Eshkol brought the hardliner Dayan into his cabinet as defense minister on June 1. That was essentially a surrender to those breathing fire. "It haunted him," Miriam Eshkol said of her husband. "He didn't want war. He didn't like war. It was the last thing he wanted in his life." Yet war is what he got. On June 4, he told his wife: "Tomorrow it will start. There will be widows, orphans, bereaved parents. And all this I will have to take on my conscience."[25]

The next day, Brigadier General Mordechai Hod rallied his men: "Soldiers of the air force, the blustering and swashbuckling Egyptian army is moving against us to annihilate our people. . . . Fly on, attack the enemy, pursue him to ruination, draw his fangs, scatter him in the wilderness, so that the people of Israel may live in peace in our land." Hod's pilots then launched a devastating strike against all seventeen Egyptian military airfields. At 10:00 A.M. on that first day, General Ezer Weizman phoned his wife and announced "The war is won." He was not exaggerating. By lunchtime, the Egyptian air force had ceased to exist.[26]

Lacking air cover, Egyptian soldiers in the Sinai were quickly routed. Perhaps 10,000 died acting out Nasser's fantasies on the peninsula; they either fell to Israeli arms or succumbed to thirst in the desert. With Egypt essentially defeated, Israel turned on Jordan. By the end of the third day of war, the West Bank was occupied. Jordan wisely accepted a UN demand for a cease-fire. Next came Syria. On June 10, after Israeli troops had overrun the Golan Heights, Syria accepted a truce. The war was over.

A foreign military attaché asked Hod how his forces had managed such a lightning victory if the war was—as Israel claimed—unexpected. Surely such a well-coordinated assault should have taken at least six months to prepare? "You are right," Hod admitted, "but not quite. We have been preparing for it for eighteen and a half years." Menachem Begin, then minister without portfolio, later confirmed that the war was a calculated act: "We . . . had a choice. The Egyptian army concentrations in the Sinai approaches do not prove that Nasser was really about to attack us. We must be honest with ourselves. We decided to attack them."[27]

The Israelis had prepared for war, but not for peace. Intoxicated by their success, they equated future security with sustained military advance. They pushed across the Sinai, on the assumption that if Israeli soldiers could dip their toes in the Suez Canal, Israel itself would be safer. On the West Bank, the quest for security was reinforced by a perception of historical destiny. Further north, the Israelis pushed through the Golan Heights and would have advanced on Damascus, had not the Soviets and Americans demanded a halt.

The Americans got a glimpse of what could happen when Israel was given a free hand to reshape the Middle East. Though they wanted a withdrawal to the 4 June borders, they were not inclined to force the issue. The consequences were nevertheless clear to Rusk. On June 14, he warned a special committee of the National Security Council that if Israel insisted on holding the West Bank, "it would create a revanchism for the rest of the twentieth century." That was an underestimate. More than forty years after the war, the Palestinian desire to recover lost land remains as fervent as ever.[28]

Territorial gains brought cruel inheritance. The war did not solve Israel's problems; it multiplied them thousand-fold. David Ben-Gurion, first president of Israel and chief architect of its independence, argued immediately after the war that all the conquered lands except Jerusalem should be returned to the Arabs; otherwise, generations of Israelis would suffer terribly in defending them. But Israel had long since raced past Ben-Gurion's good sense. In order to fight the war, ordinary Israelis had been encouraged to believe that they were underdogs. Unfortunately, the propaganda worked too well. Feelings of persecution encouraged a conclusion that territorial expansion was the best response to danger. The desire for well-being transformed Israel from oppressed to oppressor. David became Goliath. As one soldier remarked on his return from the war: "We've lost something terribly precious. We've lost our little country. . . . Our little country seems to get lost in this vast land." Most of his countrymen, however, celebrated the victory, having convinced themselves that land was the same as security.[29]

Biafra: The Problem of Africa

The map of Africa was drawn by imperialists. Borders were lines of convenience, demarcations of greed. Nowhere was this more evident than in Nigeria, which one colonial official called "the most artificial of the many administrative units created in the course of European occupation of Africa." "Nigeria is not a nation," Chief Obafemi Awolowo warned in 1947. "It is a mere geographical expression. There are no 'Nigerians' in the same sense as there are 'English' or 'Welsh' or 'French.' The word 'Nigeria' is merely a distinctive appellation to distinguish those who live within the boundaries of Nigeria from those who do not."[30]

Awolowo's warning was directed at those in the West who believed that African nations could be imagined into existence. Westerners carelessly labeled competing ethnic groups "tribes," a word in harmony with the presumed savagery of Africa. "It is a mistake to designate them 'tribes,'" complained Awolowo. "Each of them is a nation by itself. . . . There is as much difference between them as there is between Germans, English, Russians, and Turks." Many Westerners would eventually grow disenchanted with decolonization because indigenous people stubbornly refused to respect their assigned nationality. To them, scenes of "Nigerians" attacking each other was proof of African savagery.[31]

When Nigeria was still a colony, ethnic divisions were muted by the overarching desire for independence on the part of otherwise contentious groups. Yet once that goal was achieved, in 1960, ethnicity became paramount. Postcolonial Nigeria assumed a dangerously loose federal structure consisting of three regions defined by the principal ethnic groups. In the north, the Muslim Hausa and Fulani held sway. Since that area had been relatively neglected by the British, the people were generally unskilled and often illiterate. In contrast, the southwestern region, dominated by the Yoruba, and the southeastern areas, where the Igbo resided, had been more actively developed, leading to the emergence of a powerful middle class.

The well-educated Igbo had migrated into other areas as merchants, soldiers, and teachers, taking with them their version of modernity. In the context of 1960s Nigeria, education carried dangers. Because the Igbo were quite cosmopolitan, they were the most enthusiastic proponents of Nigerian nationhood. They came to be seen as missionaries for the new Nigeria, an image reinforced by the fact that they secured a disproportionate share of posts in the new government. Rival ethnic groups consequently interpreted the idea of Nigeria as an Igbo plot. Religious, ethnic, and political differences were exacerbated by economic disparities. To make matters worse, the Igbo sector was where Nigeria's rich oilfields were concentrated.

The weak federal structure of the Nigerian government rendered the country prey to corrupt demagogues. Crisis became status quo. Disgusted with perpetual instability, five army majors, led by Chukwuma Nzeogwu, launched a coup in January 1966, ending Nigeria's ill-fated experiment with democracy. "Our enemies are the political profiteers," Nzeogwu proclaimed, "the swindlers, . . . those that seek to keep the country divided permanently so that they can remain in office as ministers and VIPs of waste; the tribalists; the nepotists." Two days later, the five majors were victims of a countercoup, led by Major General John Aguiye-Ironsi. To those suspicious of conspiracy, the only thing that mattered was that four of the five majors were Igbo, as was Aguiye-Ironsi. Rumors spread of an Igbo plot to take over Nigeria and turn other ethnic groups into vassals of the new regime. Responding to the flood of anti-Igbo feeling, Major General Yakubu Gawon toppled Aguiye-Ironsi in July.[32]

The July coup was the opening shot in a nationwide campaign of vengeance. In the north, the discontented Hausa turned on the more prosperous Igbo living in their area, killing some 40,000 and forcing another million to flee to safety. Olu Oguibe watched "whole families set ablaze by their neighbours in the middle of the night, children hacked to death in their sleep, women violated by men who only the previous day would have doffed their hats to them, . . . some men burnt at the stake, some decapitated, others hounded through the streets and stoned, while their adversaries gambled for their clothes." Eventually, perhaps two million Igbo living throughout Nigeria flooded back to their native territory, a region ill-equipped to accommodate the sudden influx. For Western journalists, the massacre seemed proof of African savagery. "There are forces let loose in Africa that white men cannot understand," wrote a smug Frederick Forsyth in the *Sunday Times*. "This is genocide." The fact that the Igbo were well-educated and "civilized," not to mention persecuted, made them a popular cause in the West. They became the "Jews of Africa," a metaphor all the more powerful given the concurrence of the Six-Day War.[33]

"Having been treated like people from another country, and nearly annihilated," wrote Oguibe, "[the Igbo] became another country." On May 30, 1967, Colonel Emeka Ojukwu, the leader of the eastern sector, unilaterally declared independence, setting up the Republic of Biafra. Gawon, unwilling to write off all that oil, immediately mobilized his army. Ojukwu, who quickly promoted himself to general, was not particularly interested in Igbo self-determination, but did fancy becoming an oil-rich African dictator. His status as an underdog made it easy for bleeding hearts to rally to his side. For a brief period in Britain, Biafra was a moral cause more agonizing than Vietnam. In 1969, John Lennon returned his MBE partly as a protest against the government's betrayal of Biafra. Ojukwu kept British passions fired by hiring a very good London PR agency.[34]

The losers in this power struggle were the people of Biafra. They fought with all the fervor of an embattled ethnic minority defending its homeland. After six months of vicious fighting, they had won most of the battles but were nowhere near winning the war. Since fighting had occurred predominantly in Biafra, serious damage was done to a fragile agrarian system. Gawon's troops had also seized the area around the Niger River delta, thus cutting off the major supply routes. He then simply waited for Biafra to starve. "Starvation is a legitimate weapon of war," his finance minister declared, "and we have every intention to use it against the rebels." Gawon, keen to teach the Igbo a lesson, ignored the atrocities of his army. Nor were his soldiers inclined to intervene when rival ethnic groups massacred the Igbo. In December 1968, the Red Cross reported that 14,000 Biafrans were dying every day. The fact that perhaps 80 percent of the casualties were women and children made this a thoroughly modern war. The term "ethnic cleansing" had not yet been invented, but should have been.[35]

Biafra defied solution: the starvation of millions was tragic and reprehensible, but so too was the breakup of Nigeria. If Africa was to modernize, that process implied large nations, not hundreds of competing ethnicities. Balkanization promised only chaos and conflict. "Self-determination pursued to its logical conclusion would not stop at a sovereign Biafra," argued Adepitan Bamisaiye in 1974. "A sovereign Igbo or Yoruba state will most likely not be content until it has been subdivided into sovereign Nnewi and Onitsha Igbo states and sovereign Oyo, Egba, Ekiti, Ijebu states. . . . Self-determination thoroughly carried out in Africa would end in each household or clan having its own separate flag." He concluded that, however regrettable the deaths, bloodletting was necessary in order to ensure the survival of Nigeria.[36]

Western nations seemed fully prepared to let Biafrans suffer, apparently concluding that it was the African nature to do so. "All I really ask is that the outside world look at us as human beings and not as Negroes bashing heads," Ojukwu complained. "If three Russian writers are imprisoned the whole world is outraged, but when thousands of Negroes are massacred . . ." Had the Biafran problem been a simple case of starvation, the West might have been able to act, but the fact that the starvation was wrapped in politics made it messy. The United States, taking refuge in hypocrisy, explained that it was not inclined to intervene in civil wars. The British expressed regret at the enormous loss of life, but argued that they did not want to encourage tribal secession in Africa.[37]

Paper-thin principles camouflaged cynical power politics. The Americans maintained a studied detachment, letting the British carry the can. "We regard Nigeria as part of Britain's sphere of influence," Rusk claimed. The British, who got 10 percent of their oil from Nigeria, were keen to preserve the status quo. Alarmed by the initial success of the Biafrans, they generously supplied Gawon. UK arms exports to Nigeria increased from £70,000 in 1966 to more than £10 million in 1969. This, however, meant that the British found themselves in the embarrassing position of backing the same side as the Soviet Union, who sought a foothold in Africa. Backing the Biafrans were the French, though not for humanitarian reasons. The British argued, with justification, that the French objective "appears to be the breakup of Nigeria, which threatens, by its size and potential, to overshadow France's client Francophone states in West Africa."[38]

Gawon complained that French aid, by prolonging the war, worsened the suffering. That was probably true. Aid without a political solution merely extended the plight of Biafra, which never had a hope of winning. In January 1970, Biafran resistance finally collapsed. At least one million, and probably twice that number, had starved to death. "This war," wrote Auberon Waugh, "will come to epitomize the inhumanity of our age. One day the world will look into the eyes of Biafra and recoil at the reflections of its own image." While his sentiments were admirable, his prediction proved wrong. In retrospect Biafra seems nothing more than mere episode in the long-running tragedy of Africa.[39]

GUANGXI PROVINCE: CANNIBALS FOR MAO

In July 1968, trouble flared in Guangxi Province, in the People's Republic of China, between forces loyal to the Communist party and a rebel faction calling itself the 411 Group. After five months of fierce fighting, the group was completely eradicated, with more than 200,000 rebels and sympathizers killed. "Sympathizer" was loosely defined. Anyone identified as a "class enemy" was liable to beatings, torture, and execution. That included ex-landlords, rich peasants, those deemed bourgeois, and anyone displaying "rightist" characteristics. Guilt could be inherited; those related by family, marriage, or friendship to class enemies were persecuted, including newborn babies. An efficient technique for executing babies evolved: the killer stepped on one of its legs, then pulled the other leg, tearing the baby in half.

In the worst instances of brutality, "class enemies" were viciously murdered, then eaten. Up to 3,000 instances of cannibalism in Guangxi have been documented by the dissident Zheng Yi. He has identified three evolutionary stages. The first was covert and random: an individual would ambush an enemy, cut him open, and crudely remove his heart and liver, which were then cooked and eaten in secret. The next stage was open, public, and highly ritualized, involving refined methods of dissection. The killer would flaunt his expertise before a crowd, after which the body parts were eaten communally. In the final stage, order disintegrated as mobs engaged in frenzied killing, hacking enemies to pieces and fighting over organs in a bacchanalian feast.

The Cultural Revolution was an orgy of violence lasting from 1966 until Mao's death ten years later. In the beginning, it was rooted in coherent revolutionary theory, but the zeal it inspired quickly overwhelmed ideology, not to mention government control. For a decade, China was gripped by unrelenting carnage. Simply killing an enemy was not enough; in order to demonstrate loyalty to Mao, citizens competed with each other in imaginative acts of brutality. In places, this meant eating the enemy, which supposedly fortified revolutionary zeal. At the height of the violence, the cafeteria of the Wuxuan Revolutionary Committee had human flesh on the menu.[40]

The revolution started as an attempt by Mao to reassert authority over his party, and to purge "revisionist" thought. His reputation had been battered by the Great Leap Forward of the 1950s, a disastrous attempt at rapid industrialization. Since progress was measured almost exclusively by the production of steel, service to the party was judged by crude calculations of tonnage. Peasants were persuaded to switch from farming to steel, with primitive backyard smelters appearing everywhere. Production did increase, though the quality was often so poor that the steel had no use other than as propaganda. "Industrialization" came at the cost of a steep decline in agricultural production, partly because farm implements were melted down to meet steel quotas. By the end of the 1950s, the Chinese had plenty of steel, but little food. Probably 40 million died of starvation. "We believe in dialectics," Mao remarked in reference to the famine, "so we can't not be in favor of death." He confessed that he was prepared to sacrifice 300 million people, or half the population, for the victory of the revolution.[41]

In the aftermath of the Great Leap, criticism of Mao reached a crescendo. Revisionists openly advocated more productive ways of managing the economy, at the cost of ideological purity. On December 10, 1958, Mao resigned as chairman of the People's Republic, though he remained head of the Chinese Communist Party (CCP). The change was purportedly voluntary, but in truth he was forced from office, later confessing that he felt like "a dead man at his own funeral." The day-to-day running of the country fell to the new CCP chairman, Liu Shaoqi; the premier, Zhou Enlai; and the general secretary, Deng Xiaoping.[42]

When the Central Committee met at Lushan in 1959, defense minister Peng Dehuai launched an unprecedented attack on Mao's policies. "In the view of some comrades," he argued, "putting politics in command could be a substitute for everything. . . . But putting politics in command is no substitute for economic principles." Though the criticism was justified, Peng made the mistake of consulting Khrushchev beforehand, which automatically rendered him suspect. His outburst was nevertheless indicative of widespread disquiet, even if this was not openly voiced. Whisperers questioned whether Mao still possessed the mental acuity and physical stamina to lead the country. Mao responded by arguing that the Great Leap had been ideologically correct, if flawed in execution. Critics were dismissed as bourgeois revisionists, while Lushan was written off as a minor manifestation of class struggle—an example of "the continuation of the life-or-death struggle between the two great antagonists of the socialist revolution." After Peng was banished for being a Soviet lackey, the new defense minister, Lin Biao, sensing an opportunity, assumed a strategic loyalty. "Chairman Mao is a genius," he later proclaimed. "Every sentence of . . . [his] is a truth. One single sentence of his surpasses ten thousand of ours."[43]

Mao had rid himself of Peng, but now faced an even greater threat from Liu. Backed by Deng, Liu advocated cancellation of the disastrous Great Leap policies and a retreat from collectivism. His sights focused on supreme power, Liu was trying to maneuver Mao into a position of purely symbolic authority. In response, Mao began a campaign to demonstrate his intellectual and physical vigor, which included a claim that he swam ten miles on the Yangtze in just one hour, an extraordinary achievement for a man of seventy-three suffering from Parkinson's disease and apoplexy.

Mao was isolated within his own arrogance. The deep reverence bestowed upon him as a result of his success in the revolution had convinced him that he was indeed superhuman. One CCP official later remarked that Mao "became . . . the source of correct thought; he placed himself above the Central Committee of the Party; he no longer participated in collective political life, and harmed, or even sabotaged, the Party's system of democratic centralism. As he himself said to [Edgar] Snow: 'I am a monk with an umbrella—subject neither to Heaven nor to the Law.'" What began as a struggle for power quickly evolved into a nationwide purification movement. The complaints of Peng, and the reformism of Liu and Deng, seemed to indicate that the country had lost its way. Mao's remedy was continuous revolution. He feared that complacency would lead to the creeping capitalism identified with Khrushchev. In a new offensive, he argued that the original revolution had failed to eradicate the exploiting classes; therefore, a capitalist resurgence threatened. He advocated a new purification struggle—those unwilling to purge automatically identified themselves as worthy of purgation.[44]

The new program was outlined in the "Decision concerning the Great Proletarian Cultural Revolution" (also known as the "Sixteen Points"), adopted on August 8, 1966, by the CCP Central Committee. "Although the bourgeoisie has been overthrown," the document proclaimed, "it is still trying to use the old ideas, culture, customs, and habits of the exploiting classes to corrupt the masses, capture their minds, and endeavor to stage a comeback. The proletariat must do the exact opposite: it must meet head-on every challenge of the bourgeoisie. . . . Our objective is to struggle against and overthrow those persons in authority who are taking the capitalist road." Party functionaries at all levels were urged to "put daring above everything else" and "boldly arouse the masses" in the great struggle. "Don't be afraid of disturbances," the people were advised. "Chairman Mao has often told us that revolution cannot be so very refined, so gentle, so temperate, kind, courteous, restrained, and magnanimous." Around this time, Mao openly complained that "Peking is not chaotic enough. . . . Peking is too civilized." When he met Song Binbin, daughter of the prominent Communist Song Renqiong, he criticized her name, which means "gentle and polite." "We need more violence," he told her. She promptly changed her name to Song Yaowu—meaning "want violence."[45]

Mao had fired a starter's pistol for a monstrous gang of fanatics eager to wreak havoc in the name of purification. The Red Guard was formed to provide shock troops for the Cultural Revolution. Guardists were drawn mainly from the student population, on the assumption that young people were more inclined to zealotry and that they needed to experience firsthand the transforming power of revolution. Students were also the one group free from party control—unlike workers, peasants, and soldiers. Thus, they were perfect for what became an attack upon the party itself.

Students were encouraged to abandon their studies and to roam the nation searching out and crushing all manifestations of revisionism.

The students' first target was, perhaps understandably, their teachers, who were easily labeled capitalist scum. Schoolroom animosities were effortlessly translated into ideological conflicts, thanks to the validation provided by Mao. Esoteric knowledge was automatically equated with middle-class revisionism. The "Sixteen Points" advised students that "the phenomenon of our schools' being dominated by bourgeois intellectuals must be completely changed." This meant, in practice: "The period of schooling should be shortened. Courses should be fewer and better. The teaching material should be thoroughly transformed, in some cases beginning with simplifying complicated material. While their main task is to study, students should also learn other things. That is to say, in addition to their studies they should also learn industrial work, farming, and military affairs, and take part in the struggles of the Cultural Revolution to criticize the bourgeoisie." Instructions specifically stressed that "when there is a debate, it should be conducted by reasoning, not force." In truth, however, that proviso was neither sincere nor realizable. Once students had been invited to join the crusade and had been fired to fever pitch, violence became inevitable.[46]

When Wang Youqin was thirteen, she watched in horror as her female classmates tortured five teachers, pouring boiling water over them, beating them with nail-spiked clubs and forcing them to eat dirt. The vice principal, a fifty-year-old woman, died after three hours of continuous torment. The incident had a profound effect upon Wang, who has since documented more than 700 specific killings of educators, a small fraction of the actual number. "Stalin had show trials," she remarks. "Mao did not even bother with trials. . . . Many teachers and principals were beaten to death by their Red Guard students, in their own schools and without any verdict." Those singled out usually underwent a humiliating and sadistic public persecution, being forced to stand for hours in the "jet liner position" (bent forward at waist, arms outstretched) while reciting the "Oxghosts and Snake-demons" song over and over:

> I am an ox-ghost and a snake-demon.
> I am an ox-ghost and a snake-demon.
> I am guilty. I am guilty.

I committed crimes against the people,

So the people take me as the object of the dictatorship.

I have to lower my head and admit my guilt.

I must be obedient.

I am not allowed to speak or act incorrectly.

If I speak or act incorrectly,

May you beat me and smash me,

Beat me and smash me.

The attacks tore apart schools. If a particular tutor was singled out for condemnation, all students faced a terrible moral dilemma. Since supporting the victim invited similar persecution, many opted to denounce teachers they admired.[47]

The witch-hunt spilled out of the schoolyard, spreading across China. "Learning revolution by making revolution" meant that almost any terrorist act could be passed off as part of the revolutionary education. Attacking the past meant breaking into homes in search of artifacts that might serve as evidence of elitism, traditionalism, or Western sympathy. People wearing traditional clothing were stopped in the street, stripped naked, and forced to repent. Women with long hair were forcibly shorn and frequently raped as punishment. Like a great beast devouring the population, revolutionary mobs grew bolder with each act of brutality. In Daxing County, near Beijing, a group of Red Guards killed 325 people in less than a week. The oldest victim was eighty, the youngest a baby hardly a month old. An old woman was taken into the street and mercilessly beaten by thugs wielding chains and leather belts. When she finally collapsed, a single female Red Guard jumped on her chest and stomach until she died. Another old woman, supposedly a landlord's wife, was killed when her neighbors poured boiling water over her. When a victim died, Red Guards would often write on the ground near the body: "Good riddance, traitor! Even death cannot pay for your sin!" The corpse would be left until it rotted away. Friends and family members were reluctant to claim bodies, or attend funerals, for fear of inheriting persecution.[48]

Those not immediately murdered were sent to detention camps for "re-education," where they encountered unremitting horror. Food was short and disease rife. Sadistic Red Guards felt that they could do anything they wished to the detainees, since their traitorous behavior rendered them beneath contempt. Many were tortured, starved to death, or buried alive. Young girls, whose only crime might be a tenuous connection to an alleged revisionist, were kept as sex toys for guards.

The Cultural Revolution was an officially sanctioned generational conflict in which children were encouraged to question the authority of their elders. Parents were automatically suspect because they had experience of the prerevolution period. The Confucian concept of filial piety was brutally overturned, as children were encouraged to believe that their only essential loyalty was to the revolution and Mao. Liang Heng was astonished at how quickly an orderly society descended into chaos: "Everything was backward, distorted, corrupt, insane. I didn't know if I was dreaming or if my life at home was a dream. . . . I would never trust my perception of reality again."[49]

The attack upon tradition extended to the willful destruction of anything associated with the past. Libraries were ransacked, with ancient texts ceremoniously burned. Artifacts and ancient buildings were destroyed because they encouraged a worship of the past. Much destruction was carried out in self-preservation, as frightened citizens rid themselves of family heirlooms in order to avoid the wrath of the Red Guard. People also changed their names out of fear of retribution; those with "Chiang" in their name were particularly suspect. In desperation, some took the names of Cultural Revolution heroes, only to find that the shifting political climate soon left them with the name of a counterrevolutionary "black dog." Streets, parks, and buildings with names linked to the past were given more politically correct names. In some places, the fact that red meant "stop" on a traffic light was deemed an insult to the revolution. Overnight, green became "stop" and red "go." The resulting chaos in traffic was a perfect metaphor.

Mao's political rehabilitation was more successful than he could ever have hoped. The Cultural Revolution raised him to godlike status—his people trampled one another in their desperate desire to venerate him. Red Guards occasionally demonstrated their devotion by jumping off buildings. The "Sixteen Points" proclaimed: "It is imperative to hold aloft the great red banner of Mao Tse-tung's thought and put proletarian politics in command. The movement for the creative study and application of Chairman Mao Tse-tung's works should be carried forward among the masses of the workers, peasants and soldiers, the cadres and the intellectuals, and Mao Tse-tung's thought should be taken as the guide to action in the Cultural Revolution." Mao's "Little Red Book" became holy scripture. Some people carried two or more copies, the better to demonstrate devotion. Doctors advised patients to chant quotations in order to calm nerves, relieve pain, or assuage political sins. Many gave thanks to Mao before each meal. Houses were filled with Maoist icons, while those who inadvertently posted a photo of the leader in a "disrespectful" place were viciously punished. The cult of Mao, and the simultaneous fall of Liu, posed a terrible dilemma to those who possessed photos containing both men. When one individual, fearful for his life, opted to cut Liu out of the frame, he was publicly beaten for defacing an image of Mao. Another man was brutally attacked for wrapping his wet galoshes in a newspaper that, unbeknownst to him, carried a photo of Mao. A science teacher who casually referred to a principle of electromagnetism as a "universal axiom" was severely beaten because, in China, there was only one universal truth—namely, the teachings of Mao. "We had been brainwashed and deceived," Song Yongyi, an expert on the Cultural Revolution, has written. "We were contaminated beyond redemption." Ba Jin agrees, but nevertheless believes that "They could not have done it, if we had not let ourselves be taken in."[50]

The success of the Cultural Revolution in overturning the party apparatus meant that government nearly ceased to exist. Red Guards efficiently purged officials, but were less effective at finding replacements. The Guard quickly disintegrated into rival factions whose worst excesses were directed at one another. Meanwhile, personal rivalries within the Central Committee were tragically acted out on a national stage. For Mao's wife, Jiang Qing, and her confederates in the "Gang of Four" (Zhang Chunqiao, Yao Wenyuan, and Wang Hongwen), the Red Guard became an instrument of personal ambition. In response to Guardist violence, Liu deployed local militia units to restore stability, but, in doing so, angered Mao. Liu was forced to undergo public self-criticism sessions and was then sent to a detention camp, where he died in 1969. In this period, Deng was repeatedly sent for reeducation and forced to work in a tractor plant. Drunk on power, Jiang openly encouraged Red Guard units to take on Lin Biao's PLA (People's Liberation Army). Open clashes occurred throughout the country. At the same time, armed bands loyal to Deng and Liu occasionally took on Red Guard units.

In December 1968, Mao tried desperately to rein in the monster he had created. Leaders of Red Guard units were summoned to Beijing and subjected to a torrent of criticism, being blamed for "ultra-leftism" and "mad fratricidal combats." With tears in his eyes, Mao accused them of betrayal. "You have let me down," he told one group of faction leaders. "And what is more, you have disappointed the workers, the peasants, and the soldiers of China." Relying on his personal prestige, he launched the "Down to the Countryside" movement, which encouraged young people to share in the life of the peasantry. Urban intellectuals were forced to take up work on farms. While ostensibly designed to put intellectuals in touch with their proletarian masters, it was also an attempt to disperse the power of the Red Guard by scattering them in the hinterlands. Though figures vary greatly, it's estimated that around four million young people were sent into the countryside.[51]

The PLA's gradual reassertion of power contributed to some of the most violent phases of the Cultural Revolution. When stability was finally restored, Lin Biao was able to take credit for the fact that a semblance of government still existed. Of his main rivals, Liu was dead, Deng sidelined, and Zhou severely weakened. Still carefully asserting his loyalty to Mao, Lin became effectively second-in-command. That, however, was a poisoned chalice, since Mao automatically suspected anyone in the number-two spot of plotting a coup. As Lin's ambitions grew, Mao began to undermine him. Frustrated and deeply frightened, Lin railed against his onetime idol: "Today he uses this force to attack that force; tomorrow he uses that force to attack this force. Today he uses sweet words and honeyed talk to those whom he entices, and tomorrow he puts them to death for some fabricated crimes. . . . Looking back at the history of the past few decades, [do you see] anyone he had supported initially who has not finally been handed a political death sentence? . . . He is a paranoid and a sadist." Lin eventually concluded that his only hope was to challenge Mao, while his army remained loyal. His precise role in the abortive coups and assassination attempts of September 1971 is not entirely clear, but he could not convincingly deny involvement. When, having played his last card, he attempted to flee to the Soviet Union on September 13, 1971, his plane crashed over Mongolia, killing all passengers. The whiff of conspiracy still lingers.[52]

The Cultural Revolution is an interesting case study of what happens when a nation systematically suspends its education system for an entire decade. It was by definition anti-intellectual, since intelligence and culture were deemed bourgeois. The educated "played dumb" out of self-protection. Attacks upon teachers and the closing of schools devastated the educational system, making it impossible to control rebellious youths. Later, as a result of the "Down to the Countryside" movement, the cream of China's young intellectuals were sent into the hinterlands. Many did not return to the cities until the late 1970s, becoming in essence a "lost generation," inadequately educated and improperly utilized. The word "lost" connotes not just the fact that they missed a proper education, but also the sense of betrayal which came when they realized that they had sacrificed their youth for a fanatical and destructive cause. Zhai Zhenhua started out as a Red Guard who loyally terrorized her fellow citizens. A few years later she was sent to the countryside to work in the fields alongside peasants; the hard labor ruined her health. Looking back, she feels only betrayal. "No schooling, no university, no future. My hopes were shattered, my dreams perished. It felt like the end of the world."[53]

Song Yongyi cites "secret documents" indicating that 2.8 million people "met with unnatural deaths" during the Cultural Revolution. Others place the death toll much higher. This monstrous brand of revolution was exported abroad, most notably to Cambodia. Khmer Rouge leaders Pol Pot and Khieu Samphan were both trained in China, had audiences with Mao, and were given instruction from Zhang Chunqiao. Similar, but less successful, efforts to export revolution were carried out in Malaysia, Burma, and Vietnam.[54]

At the time, the Cultural Revolution seemed vibrant, dynamic, and forward-looking to those desperate to see it that way. It appealed to Sixties radicals because revolutions always seem so exciting. This one had all the essential elements: great slogans, absolute truths, rousing songs, and righteous violence, not to mention that the shock troops were students. It also produced great posters. For the left, the Cultural Revolution restored a faith battered by Stalin's excesses and Khrushchev's hypocrisy. It seemed a genuine break with history. French Maoists in particular worshiped the idea of the "mass line": in the Cultural Revolution, they assumed, the party was learning from the people, rather than the other way around. For radicals everywhere, Mao seemed to be living the dream of continuous revolution; he demonstrated that political purity was both logical and attainable. "The distinction between intellectual and manual labor is being dissolved," wrote Michael Rossman, in *New Age Blues*. "An intensive anti-Confucianism campaign is in progress; people are motivated by serving the people rather than by private interest; even the schizophrenics in the mental institution . . . are getting well by reading Mao. . . . The Chinese are using dependence on Mao's word to free themselves from dependence on role-defined authority." As radicals saw it, the Communist millennium had been achieved: Mao had shown how class distinctions could be eradicated with one righteous blow. That, at least, was the view of common-room Communists in the West who read about Mao in the cozy warmth of a student flat.[55]

The real story is one of unspeakable cruelty, sadism, genocide, and the betrayal of an entire generation. Jaia Sun-Childers recalls a realization that only truly dawned after the death of Mao:

> We were a haunted people, numb, trapped in lies, made cynical by hypocrisy masquerading as the sacred. . . . Our Great Helmsman incited us to betray and murder one another to prove our loyalty to him. Now he lay, an immortal corpse in a crystal coffin, posing for posterity while we waited in lines stretching across Tiananmen Square to kowtow like fools. . . . Thanks to you, Chairman Mao, to your three million Cultural Revolution deaths, your hundred million exonerated victims, and all the horrors of your decade-long geriatric madness. We close the book on your Little Red Book of fairy tales, where the sublime and the absurd join hands with a nightmare in a convulsive dance. . . . We drank your myth and went mad together, and tore our world apart for your Great Illusion. . . . We don't want to hear one more story that ends singing your praises. And we don't want to spend our future crouching in your shadow, swimming in your abyss, worshiping your sanitized myth.

"Mao's death signifies my release from prison" wrote Pu Ning, "and for many, many more Chinese it meant a release from a long, insufferable period of pain and terror." The condemnation heaped on the Gang of Four after 1976 has allowed Mao to escape blame for the monstrous crimes he inspired. Today, the official line holds that he was guilty of an "erroneous appraisal of the prevailing class relations." That, apparently, is how the Chinese want it. Their determination to ignore their nightmare past is the only thing that has prevented Mao from taking his place among the truly vile dictators of the twentieth century.[56]

7

AND IN THE STREETS . . .

MARGATE: MODS VERSUS ROCKERS

The Battle of Margate began at the railway station on the morning of May 17, 1964. Without provocation, a gang of youths suddenly started breaking the windows of a trackside buffet. "The boy who started it was so good looking and nicely dressed," the manageress subsequently remarked. "You wouldn't have thought he was a nasty type."[1]

The boy was a Mod, a subculture defined by fashion and violence. The Mods might have been just another passing fad in Britain, if not for the fact that they started strutting in seaside towns like Brighton and Clacton. What originated as an innocent bit of fun turned into a style war and then a bona fide social problem—the sort of molehill Britain's tabloids eagerly turn into a mountain.

Youthful rebellion is seldom genuinely political. Disagreements between children and parents are usually fought on the battlefield of culture—in particular, over music and clothes. Every child perceives a generation gap; nearly every one rejects parental advice and seeks to learn life's lessons on his own. "Alienation" is a word few fourteen-year-olds can define and most sixteen-year-olds feel deeply. To establish an independent identity requires doing things differently from the way one's parents did—reject their authority, spurn their moral outlook, scorn their material trappings. The quickest way to demonstrate independence is, ironically, to join a gang and slavishly copy the latest fashion trend.

Youth culture in Britain can be traced by the evolution of sartorial styles—Spivs, Bohemians, Beatniks, Teds, Punks, Skinheads, Casuals, and so on. In the midst of that continuum lie the Mods and their mortal enemies, the Rockers, who frightened polite English society in the early 1960s. The Mods morphed from the Teds, who were themselves descendents of the prewar Dandies. Teds were narcissistic posers who passed their time in small groups standing on sidewalks, chewing gum, smoking fags, causing outrage, and admiring their own reflection in shopwindows. Aside from the occasional harassment of immigrants, they disdained anything requiring physical effort or political commitment. The shallowness of the ethos meant that it quickly grew stale. Standing around looking pretty grew boring, and was uncomfortably cold in winter. In time, most Teds found girlfriends, got married, had kids, and combed out their quiffs.

Into the vacuum strode the Modernists, or Mods, who first appeared around 1958. The trendsetters were a few young men—the sons of tailors in the East End of London—who were sufficiently confident to start a new style and sufficiently wealthy to create one. Their dads whipped together a customized set of clothes that fused Italian and French designs. "I used to knock around with this Jewish guy," one former Mod recalled. "He had a couple of other Jewish friends and one of their fathers was in the rag trade. They started getting into clothes very seriously. It was almost like a religion."[2]

At first, Mods wore suits, but not what most people would call suits. These were tightly tailored, with narrow lapels and sharp lines. Shirts had pointed collars and were invariably buttoned to the neck, whether a tie was worn or not. Jackets were worn with just the top button fastened. Hands were thrust into jacket pockets, thumbs pointed aggressively outward. Trousers, tapered to a narrow ankle, had creases sharp enough to shave with and were hemmed high in order to show off the winkle-pickers: narrow shoes, often of patent leather, with tassels and pointed toes.

In time, the fashion broadened. Mods took to wearing Fred Perry polo shirts with horizontal stripes. Sweaters were V-necked, lightweight, and close-fitting. If a tie was worn, it was narrow and usually black. Eventually, the Mods started wearing Levis, shrunk-to-fit in the bathtub. The defining feature of Mod wear was its minimalism—nothing was baggy, all lines were straight. Clothes were perfectly ironed and impeccably clean. Hair was short, closely cropped, and neat. "Most of us had terrific hair, French style, and you spent a lot of time on it. You had to use sugar water. What you do was wash your hair, then get a bowl of hot water and put sugar in it. Let the water cool and keep stirring it up and then plaster the water on your head and shape your hair. We used to leave it on all night. The longer you left it on the better it was. . . . It was horrible stuff." Mods craved attention, but most of the attention they got was from one another. The only reason to go out was to look good, which meant that the slightest blemish could ruin an evening. "I put on my suit and my shoes were a bit dirty so I got the polish out and—disaster—I looked in the mirror and I'd splashed my shirt. So I . . . didn't go out that evening. . . . I knew guys who'd get on the bus with a sheet of brown paper so they could put it on the seat so they didn't get any dirt on their suit. And they'd sit bolt upright so they were not touching the back of the seat. . . . You had to be immaculate." Styles shifted each week, but changes came from within, not at the instigation of clothes designers or fashion outlets. New designs were part of the ethic of improvisation usually inspired by a self-appointed "Face." Fashion was a stylized ritual of dominance: power expressed through clothes.[3]

Life imitated art, which in turn imitated life. Mod style was quite similar to the costumes worn in James Bond films and in television programs like *The Avengers* and *The Saint*—a cultural stream flowing in both directions. The most popular showcase for Mod style was *Ready, Steady, Go!*—the Friday night pop extravaganza hosted by Cathy McGowan. Aspiring Mods tuned in faithfully, in order to learn the latest dance moves and to absorb fashion trends. The show's popularity inevitably meant that Mod style spread far beyond its East End birthplace. Eventually, not all those who dressed like Mods were Mods.

At first, their music was as clean as their clothes. In the early days, they went for modern jazz—cool and uncluttered. They also liked R&B—artists like Booker T, Fats Domino, the Impressions, and James Brown—an affinity which caused detractors to label them "white niggers." When Mods took up rock after 1960, they went for bands that evoked their image—groups like Herman's Hermits, the Small Faces, the Yardbirds, and the Who. Pete Townshend and Roger Daltrey perfectly embodied the Mod ethos—its fashion, its cynicism, its improvisation, and especially its violence. "My Generation" became a Mod theme song. Their sound filled the room, shook the bones, and rattled the teeth. "The Who are clearly a new form of crime, anti-social and armed against the bourgeoisie," the *Daily Telegraph* warned.[4]

Every Mod lusted after a Jaguar, but few could afford one. They adapted beautifully; in time, sleek scooters like Vespas and Lambrettas became their trademark. These shiny Italian chariots were perfect because, unlike motorbikes, they weren't greasy; riding one didn't dirty one's clothes. Thanks to the liberalization of hire purchase (credit) laws, they could be bought for just £20 down. They could also be personalized in an infinite variety of ways, but always according to a rigid fashion code. An array of lights would be added, as well as ornaments and fancy seat-covers. The most popular accessory was the mirror; sometimes as many as twenty were arrayed in neat lines on either side, like legs on a centipede. These were the perfect accessory for boys obsessed with staring narcissistically at their reflections. Since riding a scooter in the British winter could get chilly, anoraks and army parkas were effortlessly added to the ensemble. Parkas were usually regulation army green, though some Mods dyed them to match their scooters.

Scooters weren't fast, but that hardly mattered since speed was provided chemically. Mods were amphetamine freaks who lived life on fast forward. "Most of us popped a few pills," one confessed. "You could get pills nearly anywhere, from people on the street, in the café you'd buy a cup of tea 'with or without.' . . . It was easy to get hold of drugs, and being Mods, we took loads of them." Uppers called Purple Hearts, black bombers, and French blues were perfect for a group that craved sharp corners and clean lines. In contrast, drugs that deadened the senses, like marijuana, did not harmonize with the rhythm of Mod life.[5]

Amphetamines were essential in order to keep up with a hectic schedule of acting Mod. One former enthusiast described his typical week: "Monday was Tottenham Royal, Tuesday the Lyceum, Wednesday the Scene or maybe stay in and wash your hair, Thursday Tottenham Royal again, then Friday was *Ready, Steady, Go!* . . . Saturday and Sunday was either a party or the Tottenham Royal. Then the next week, you'd start again." A huge amount of energy was invested in sustaining fantasy. Every Mod imagined that he lived in a gangster world of fast cars, beautiful women, expensive clothes, and endless posh parties, even if reality consisted of a secondhand Vespa, fish suppers, and groping Madge in the alley behind the Lyceum. Dressing up provided escape from humdrum lives of limited opportunity.[6]

All those amphetamines deadened the libido. Most Mods were simply too busy admiring themselves to pay much attention to "birds." "The guys were so preoccupied with clothes," one female camp follower remembered. "It got to be a big deal to have a conversation with a guy, and we thought we were lucky if one of those gorgeous creatures actually danced with us." Preening was part of the ritual, but it seldom went further than that. Involvement with a woman implied a tug of loyalties: it wasn't easy to be part of the group *and* be somebody's boyfriend. The emphasis upon looks and style encouraged suspicions of homoeroticism, but in truth the Mods were no more inclined to homosexuality than any other Sixties subculture.[7]

Mods evoked postwar social mobility, or at least the illusion of such. Actually, Britain was a deeply stratified society and the original Mods, despite their dress, were as working class as pork pies and pigeons. Most important, however, was that they didn't seem working class, especially since their style was enthusiastically imitated by the well-heeled who shopped at Bazaar. Even though Mods had to work for a living, they did not usually get their hands dirty; most were shop assistants, minor clerks, and office boys. The postwar boom kept them in jobs and gave them more disposable income than their fathers ever imagined. Extra money was spent sharpening the image.

Since parading was an intrinsic part of Mod culture, it was perhaps inevitable that they should eventually decide to take their show on the road. Trips to the seaside started as a bit of a lark, a sardonic reference to the English obsession with spending bank-holiday weekends in Brighton or Blackpool. "It was the first time most of us had done anything like that since we were kids," Charlie Steele, a former Mod, remembers. "Now we could do what we wanted, go where we wanted, and have it all on our own terms. We ate whelks and ice cream and pissed about on the pier. It was a different buzz to the smoke [London]. To be honest, we downed so many pills and were full on so often that going away was a welcome break. . . . Even getting there was a chuckle."[8]

Heading for the seaside was not originally meant to be confrontational. Unfortunately, the coast was Rocker territory. Rockers were drawn to seaside funfairs like bees to candy floss. "Every rocker . . . dreamt of working on the dodgems, with the sound of Del Shannon echoing past the helter-skelter," recalled Alfredo Marcantonio, a former Mod. "So a lot of us turning up on scooters, it was asking for trouble." He insists, however, that Mods were not itching for a fight. "Real Mods were far too concerned about their clothing. I mean, we're talking about possibly losing buttons—you know, creasing or tearing clothing you'd saved for!"[9]

Rockers were so named for their love of rock and roll. They were Fifties throwbacks, young men frozen in time who still revered Marlon Brando and James Dean, when most of humanity preferred Paul Anka. They listened to Elvis, Eddie Cochrane, and Gene Vincent. Like the Mods, they were descendants of the Teds, but on a different branch of the family tree. They were dirty, loud, vulgar boys for whom motor oil was a fashion accessory. They wore lots of leather, silver studs, and big heavy boots and drove motorcycles—the bigger, louder, and dirtier the better. The Mods, their cultural opposites, they viewed as effeminate dandies. Since violence was an intrinsic part of Rocker culture, they considered it their duty to defend their seaside territory from the Mod invasion. Quiffs met coifs in stylized combat.

Rockers wore their aggression on their sleeves—rolled up with their packet of fags. Even the gentle ones (and they were the majority) looked threatening. The Mods, in contrast, looked polite, but that was simply camouflage. Underneath the surface lurked arrogant, sneering cynics with a taste for menace. Both groups saw a good fistfight or a bit of petty vandalism as a nice way to pass the time on a slow evening. It also provided an opportunity to demonstrate manhood.

If Mods and Rockers had kept apart, they might now be remembered as simply two fashion-and-music trends. When their orbits intersected, however, confrontation became inevitable and so too did moral panic. Rockers came armed with bike chains and bottles. Mods had flick knives and coshes. The real sadists among the latter sewed fishhooks into the cuffs of their jackets, the better to rip an opponent's face. Opportunists on both sides took advantage of the weapons the seaside provided—deck chairs, umbrella poles, and rocks.

The trouble started in Clacton on Easter weekend, 1964, which happened to be the coldest for eighty years. Since most of the regular holiday crowd had stayed home, Mods and Rockers had the town to themselves. They kept warm by running amok. Paul Barker, then a reporter for *New Society*, saw something most observers missed: "What struck me most, as I went up and down the beaches, was the ritual nature of the supposed battle. Mods and Rockers were like flocks of pigeons, clustering, flying up, dispersing. The main point was this: both of them were against the police."[10]

Later, the Clacton paper estimated the damage at about £513. Fleet

Street took that figure and multiplied it by ten. Headlines in the *Daily Mirror* shouted: "WILD ONES INVADE SEASIDE TOWN"—an intentional reference to Brando. In contrast, The *East Essex Gazette* reported: "The troubles . . . were not so horrific as the flood of national press, television and radio publicity suggested. The town was not wrecked, no one, apart from some of the young hooligans themselves, was really hurt and Clacton housewives did not, as one early morning broadcaster said, spend Tuesday 'sweeping up glass from their broken windows.'"[11]

Fifty-one people were arrested in Margate. Dr. George Simpson, chairman of the magistrates, jailed four men and imposed fines totaling £1,900 on thirty-six people. He made himself forever famous by condemning the "long-haired, mentally unstable, petty little hoodlums, these sawdust Caesars who can only find courage like rats hunting in packs." While journalists praised Simpson, most people thought the sentences too lenient. "They all ought to be put in gaol—an old-fashioned gaol," one woman told *The Times*. "They are all a nasty dirty lot."[12]

The press provided the oxygen of publicity for what otherwise might have been an isolated event. Front-page reports, accompanied by shocking photos, were advertisements for future Mod-versus-Rocker prizefights. When Barker wrote a feature about those arrested at Margate, it was picked up by the *Mirror* and given a center spread. "As I went down, by train, to Hastings . . . I saw teenagers reading it. They were checking out how they ought to behave when they got there." "The whole history of Mod was changed after that," Charlie Steele felt. "The publicity was very much a defining moment. All of a sudden . . . we were surrounded by a lot of prats jumping up and down in tacky clothes shouting out they were Mods, they didn't know anything about the Mod ethos, they just bought some clothes and got a haircut." David Cooke, a Mod revivalist and amateur historian of the movement, claims that some famous photographs of the rioting were faked. "The photographer paid the lads a few shillings." The novelist Howard Baker, once a Mod, agrees: "Reporters and photographers were paying a lot of kids. . . . We'd get pissed on it." Public, press, and rebellious youths played in three-part harmony.[13]

After Margate the public expected trouble, as if waiting eagerly for the next episode of *Dixon of Dock Green*. The violence reached a crescendo at the next bank-holiday weekend, on May 17. Since Mods, Rockers, police, and press all expected a confrontation, they willed it to happen. Afterward, came a predictable competition to condemn. David James, MP for Brighton Kemptown, told Parliament that he found "a sense of horror and outrage" in his constituency. "It was almost as if one had been to a city which, at least emotionally, had been recently hit by an earthquake and as if all the conventions and values of life had been completely flouted." "It spreads like a disease," warned W. R. Rees-Davies, MP for Margate. "If we want to stop it, we have to be able to get rid of these children from the school, and quickly. . . . We must immediately get rid of the bad children so that they cannot infect the good."[14]

Violence continued for the rest of the summer, with youths automatically interpreting a bank-holiday weekend as opportunity for aggro. In response to rioting in Hastings on August 3, the *Times* opined:

> The first lesson to be learnt from this weekend is that the popular explanation of Mods and Rockers as the only troublemakers should be ended. The fact is that over three-quarters of the youngsters . . . who descended on this town over the weekend . . . were to outward appearances at least perfectly ordinary. They did not come by scooter or motor cycle, they did not wear fancy clothes, nor did they have long hair. . . . The extraordinary thing is that none of them seems to know why they are doing this. They walk in gloomy silence or sit fully-clothed on the beach waiting for something to happen. Boredom is the likeliest explanation. "We just go with the gang," two young lads said.

Former Rocker Phil Bradley confirms the mindless nature of the violence. "I haven't the foggiest idea why there was any fighting with the mods. I really don't know." In fact, to label it Mods versus Rockers assigns the violence an order and purpose which is misleading. "It really wasn't mods versus rockers, as the press put it," Cooke argued. "Mods were fighting each other. The north London mods hated south London mods. South London mods hated north London mods, and east London mods hated everybody, and everybody hated them."[15]

Perhaps the most ironic aspect of that summer of violence was that it brought Mods and Rockers national attention at a time when both were in decline. By 1964, Mod style had been hijacked and turned into a mass-market phenomenon. The original ethos had been usurped by the beautiful people who shopped at Bazaar. Real Mods, stuck in their nine-to-five jobs, could hardly afford the style they had invented. During its death throes, Mod began to mirror the class divisions of British society—an ironic development, given that the Mod subculture pretended to be classless. At the top were the people who did not have to work and could afford to wear cashmere. No scooters for them—they had cars or took taxis. They went to the right London parties, places where Mary Quant, David Bailey, or Twiggy appeared. They were called, appropriately, the Aces. Below them were the Tickets or Numbers, descendants of the original Mods, who rode around on scooters and were tied to dull jobs. An Ace never had to wear a green parka, yet for a Ticket it was both necessity and shibboleth.

In the midst of the mayhem, a Sussex vicar confidently proclaimed that young people "are as normal and healthy as ever before but they are in revolt. They are in revolt against a society which has lost its values and found no new ones. I believe their revolt to be the healthiest sign." Needless to say, most people did not agree. The *Times* remarked: "Whatever enlightened opinion in the rest of England may think, there is probably not an adult here but would welcome a return to the days when a good thrashing would have discouraged the young people's sheep-like hysteria and a massive display of childishness. In the hotels, cafés, public houses and shops along the seafront, there is complete agreement that this is the solution." Everyone seemed to agree that hooliganism was a new phenomenon, and that permissiveness had destroyed the moral stability of the past. "Law and order" was something the older generation fondly remembered but could not figure out how to restore. Yet "hooligan" is an old word invented to describe an old problem—namely, the propensity of youths toward mindless violence. In the 1890s, a music hall song went:

> Oh, the Hooligans! Oh, the Hooligans!
> Always on the riot,
> Cannot keep them quiet,
> Oh, the Hooligans! Oh, the Hooligans!
> They are the boys
> To make a noise
> In our backyard.

The Mods have been largely ignored by social historians, perhaps because they espoused no coherent political program. There was no body politic underneath the sharp clothes. Yet they were perhaps the most honest of

Sixties subcultures: they were superficial and proud of it. All they wanted was some fun and an occasional bit of aggro. They saw no need to complicate their style with ersatz substance. None of them sought to change the world. As Simpson remarked, they were indeed "Sawdust Caesars"—but in being so, they displayed a characteristic of youth that does not seem unfamiliar.[16]

"It was something to do," one young man confessed rather simply and perfectly in 1965.[17]

WATTS: LONG HOT SUMMER

On Wednesday, August 11, 1965, California highway patrolman Lee Minikus was riding his motorcycle along 122nd Street in south Los Angeles. "It was hotter than hell, maybe 93 or 94 degrees," Minikus recalled. "When it gets that hot, you can smell the heat." The temperature is important to this story.[18]

A passing motorist alerted Minikus to another motorist driving erratically. The officer gave chase and pulled the suspect over at the corner of 116th and Avalon, in a predominantly black neighborhood on the border of Watts. Marquette Frye, age twenty-one, was driving the car, his step-brother Ronald, twenty-two, was a passenger. The spectacle of a white policeman apprehending a black man was painfully familiar to Watts residents. Given the blistering heat, most of them were already outside and inclined to gape at the developing drama. As Minikus put Frye through the standard sobriety test, a crowd gathered. In the meantime, Ronald ran to get his mother, who lived nearby. By the time she arrived, the crowd had swelled to 250 people. Rena Frye scolded Marquette for being drunk, whereupon he lost his temper and vented his wrath on Minikus. In an instant, a simple arrest turned nasty.

Backup arrived, in the form of more white patrolmen. The crowd was growing restless, hurling abuse at uniformed authority. When the patrolmen tried to subdue Frye, his mother lashed out, jumping on Minikus' back and tearing his shirt. Eventually, she and her two sons were thrown into a patrol car, rather too roughly for the watching crowd. As the officers prepared to leave, someone spat on one of them. Holding on to one's temper wasn't easy in that heat. The officer charged into the crowd, billy club swinging, and grabbed the spitter. She was arrested, as was another man standing nearby who seemed intent on provocation. Forty minutes after Frye had been stopped, the patrolmen left the scene with five prisoners. As they drove away, their cars were pelted with rocks.

Frye and Minikus remained friendly for the rest of their lives, able to isolate a petty crime from the conflagration it inspired. Neither thought the arrest worthy of a riot. But that is what occurred. The heat was obviously significant, since rioting is predominantly a summer activity. So too was the spitting incident; had the officers been able to ignore it, there might never have been a Watts riot. And then there was the fact that the woman arrested was wearing a barber's smock that made her look pregnant. Impression turned to fact when relayed along the curbside telegraph. The spectacle of white policemen beating up an innocent, pregnant black woman was reason enough to riot.

After Minikus and his colleagues left, the crowd steadily grew and anger swelled exponentially. An irate mob vented wrath by throwing stones, breaking windows, and overturning cars. White motorists passing through were pulled from their cars and beaten up. Units from the LA Police Department flooded into the area, hoping to restore calm but instead fanning the flames of resentment.

By 1:00 A.M., the crowd had grown tired of mayhem. The neighborhood was a mess of battered cars, broken glass, scattered bricks and stones. Twenty-nine people had been arrested. Few called it a riot, as if not mentioning the word might avert the calamity. The next morning, agents of calm mobilized more quickly than advocates of violence. The Los Angeles County Human Relations Commission was on the streets early, urging everyone to attend a meeting that afternoon. Community leaders, city officials, police representatives, journalists, and ordinary citizens gathered in an auditorium eleven blocks from where Frye had been arrested.

Among those who spoke was Rena Frye, by then feeling a bit sheepish. She implored the crowd to "help me and others calm the situation down so that we will not have a riot tonight." Momentum was moving in the direction of good sense when suddenly a high school boy seized the microphone and shouted that the people of Watts would attack and burn adjacent white neighborhoods that night. TV journalists had the perfect soundbite for the Five O'Clock News. An otherwise calm meeting suddenly became a call to arms.[19]

While those who craved peace far outnumbered those who hungered for violence, there came a point on that Thursday afternoon when passion smothered reason. Even so, the ensuing riot need not have been as bad as it was, but for the fact that around midnight the situation overwhelmed the police. Unfortunately, police commanders, desperate to maintain the pretense of control, failed to admit their own incapacity. The National Guard might at this stage have been mobilized, but approval had to come from the state capital, Sacramento, and governor Edmund Brown was away at a conference in Athens. The lieutenant governor, Glenn Anderson, dithered while Watts burned.

All hell broke loose on Friday the 13th. "It was unbelievable," Betty Pleasant, a journalist, recalled. "There was nothing to restrain anybody. No attempts to quell anything. Nobody to put the fires out." In the absence of an effective countervailing force, rioters and looters did as they pleased. Policeman Jeff Rouzan felt completely helpless when he arrived. "It was total chaos. It was just indiscriminate grabbing people and beating them up. People would see some people doing something and they would all join in. The Fire Department would come in and they'd have to leave because they'd be attacked."[20]

The mayhem seemed random, but in fact was not. Schools, libraries, and civic buildings were not generally attacked, nor were houses. Rioters instead targeted businesses owned by whites—in particular, furniture, clothing, and food stores. First they looted, then they torched. "I asked one of the guys who was throwing the Molotov cocktails why he was doing it, and he said it was to get back at whitey," Pleasant recalled. Pawnshops were attacked because they were a convenient source of weapons and because pawnbrokers made their income from black misfortune. Wrath was directed especially at white-owned grocery stores because they preyed on black residents' lack of mobility by selling substandard food at exorbitant prices. "The food was rotten," Victoria Brown Davis confirmed. "To get better prices and better food, we had to travel to other parts of L.A."[21]

"In the war zone called Watts, whole blocks lay in rubble and ashes," *Newsweek* reported.

> Black men and women—the human debris of war—queued up in bread lines at makeshift relief stations. Jeeploads of heavily armed soldiers prowled the streets, an American army occupying part of

America's third largest city. And outside a pillaged store, a Negro teenager—himself a ruin before he ever reached manhood—surveyed the wreckage without a wisp of remorse. "You jus' take an' run," he said, "an' you burn when they ain't nothin' to take. You burn whitey, man. You burn his tail so he knows what it's all about."

The National Guard, finally mobilized, hit the streets at 10:00 P.M. Their effect was immediate. Protected by troops, firefighters could begin to do their work. Bringing calm to the streets came at great cost, however, since armed confrontations caused the death toll to mount. The police and National Guard, convinced that there were snipers in the streets, responded with maximum force. Subsequent investigations revealed that what seemed like snipers were in fact police and Guardsmen unknowingly shooting at each other.[22]

Not until Tuesday was quiet restored, by which time the death toll had reached 34, with another 1,032 injured. Arrests totaled 3,952. More than 600 buildings were damaged, with over 200 destroyed completely. Property damage eventually exceeded $35 million. Television coverage provided wind for the fire, provoking copycat rioting in San Diego, San Pedro, Long Beach, Pasadena, Monrovia, and other locales.

Watts was not the first such disturbance in the United States during the decade. The previous summer had witnessed seven significant riots, in cities such as New York, Chicago, Rochester, and Philadelphia, resulting in five deaths and nearly a thousand injured. In an attempt to awaken complacent suburbia to the problem of the ghetto, Mayor Robert Wagner of New York had warned: "There are lions in the streets, angry lions, lions who have been caged until the cages crumbled. We had better do something about those lions, and when I speak of lions, I do not mean individuals. I mean the spirit of the people. Those who have been neglected and oppressed and discriminated against and misunderstood and forgotten." Inner-city riots highlighted a dramatic shift in the politics of race. The rhetoric of black protest had changed, partly because of new actors in the drama but more importantly because the definition of oppression had widened. Instead of focusing on issues of liberty, freedom, and franchise, a new generation of activists drew attention to poverty, a problem more complicated and pervasive. Northern blacks might have been able to vote, but that did not make them free or equal. Prejudice and destitution, two sides of the same coin, inhibited freedom. Activists argued that the ability to sit at a lunch counter was immaterial if lunch was unaffordable.[23]

The politics of liberty had given way to the politics of class. The problems highlighted by inner-city riots could not be solved by the passage of a few laws—by the "stroke of a pen," as Kennedy had once boasted. A new word entered the American lexicon: the "ghetto," an iniquity not exclusive to the South. Blacks were confined in relatively small areas of the inner city, where they were prey to unscrupulous landlords and profiteering merchants. Those who could afford to move out found that they were denied access to white neighborhoods. "I own an apartment building in Memphis," the blues singer B. B. King once confessed. "Wouldn't mind moving in, but whites live there, and if I moved in, they'd move out and my property wouldn't be worth a thing."[24]

Fully two-thirds of the 650,000 blacks who lived in Los Angeles in 1965 resided in Watts, which was 90 percent black. The fact that urban black poverty could not be confined to the area below the Mason-Dixon line, and could not be blamed on Southern racism, made it all the more troubling. White America was forced to confront its own prejudices in a way that King's protests had not so far demanded. The McCone Commission investigating the Watts riot remarked: "Caught up in almost a decade of struggle with civil rights and its related problems, most of America focused its attention upon the problems of the South—and only a few turned their attention and thought to the explosive situation of our cities."[25]

Watts was frightening precisely because it seemed an unlikely place for a race riot. A study by the Urban League in 1964 measured ten criteria of city life—including housing, employment, and income—and judged Los Angeles the best place in America for blacks to live. "There is no question about it, this is the best city in the world," one black leader told the McCone Commission. Watts, in other words, was not a slum. There were no filthy tenements or crowded, dirty streets. Most residents lived in detached houses on tree-lined avenues with playgrounds and parks nearby. A third of the houses were owner-occupied. Blacks had access to public facilities—such as schools, shops, restaurants, and cinemas—without restriction on racial grounds. All this meant that if blacks in Los Angeles were angry enough to engage in six days of unrestrained violence, the race problem was much more serious than most Americans appreciated.[26]

Los Angeles reflected a betrayal of expectation. The city's black population had increased nearly tenfold from 1940 to 1965. The vast majority of the residents had come from the South in search of a brighter future. Los Angeles was their Canaan. They assessed their life not against the deprivation left behind, but against the white middle-class standards to which they aspired. High hopes fed deep disappointment. Lacking the skills and education to secure jobs in the highly competitive economy, blacks encountered what the McCone Commission called a "dull, devastating spiral of failure." Many dropped out of school before the age of fifteen; of those who entered high school, only one-third graduated. Unemployment in Watts was three times the county average. "Equality of opportunity, a privilege [blacks] sought and expected, proved more of an illusion than a fact," the McCone Commission admitted. More than 60 percent of the adults arrested for rioting had been born in the South.[27]

The riots were "a symptom of a sickness in the center of our cities," the report continued. Writing of Harlem, Claude Brown expressed the problem more eloquently. Blacks in the South, he said,

> were told that unlimited opportunities for prosperity existed in New York and that there was no "color problem" there. They were told that Negroes lived in houses with bathrooms, electricity, running water, and indoor toilets. To them, this was the "promised land" that Mammy had been singing about in the cotton fields for many years. . . . It seems that cousin Willie, in his lying haste, had neglected to tell the folks down home about one of the most important aspects of the promised land: it was a slum ghetto. There was a tremendous difference in the way life was lived up North. There were too many people full of hate and bitterness crowded into a dirty, stinky, uncared-for closet-sized section of a great city.

Ghetto youths inherited disappointment from their migrant parents. "To add to their misery," wrote Brown, "they had little hope of deliverance. For where does one run to when he's already in the promised land?" No wonder, then, that a sense of fatalism characterized the ghetto mood. "The cops think we are scared of them because they got guns," a young rioter told the McCone Commission. "But you can only die once: if I get a few of them I don't mind dying."[28]

"People keep calling it a riot," Tommy Jacquette remarked on the fortieth anniversary of Watts. He'd thrown rocks at the police in 1965 and has since devoted himself to the rejuvenation of his neighborhood. "We call it a revolt because it had a legitimate purpose. It was a response to police brutality and social exploitation of a community and of a people. . . .We had a revolt in our community against those people who were in here trying to exploit us. . . . Some people want to know if I think it was really worth it. I think anytime people stand up for their rights, it's worth it." Previously, standing up for rights hadn't involved tearing down a neighborhood. Watts was a dramatic manifestation of the new phenomenon of Black Power. Throwing a Molotov cocktail provided a visceral thrill, a momentary feeling of empowerment within a person who had previously felt inconsequential. Rioting implied a new moral code which did not include pleasing whites. One young rioter in Boston told an investigator why the older generation's values were no longer relevant: "All the time my aunt used to say . . . be good, be real good. You know what she meant? She meant to do whatever they tell you, the white teachers and the white police and the white store people. Black people live here, but it's the whites who own us. They'll always own us until we stop them—and that means it'll come to a fight." Black Power was an assertion of sovereignty over the civil rights movement and, as such, a profound statement that blacks no longer needed, or wanted, white help. "We don't need white liberals," argued Stokely Carmichael. Given the slow pace of change and the often vicious white reaction, quite a few blacks were inclined to agree.[29]

For many blacks, the easiest assertion of independence came through throwing stones. "I regret it," twenty-year-old Winston Slaughter said of his participation in the Watts riot. "But deep down inside I know I was feeling some joy while it was going on, simply because I am a Negro." Moderates in the civil rights movement deeply regretted this turn to violence, not just for the grief it caused but for the lack of control it implied. When King visited Watts shortly after quiet was restored, he was heckled by young black men still on a high from the destruction they had caused. As *Newsweek* reported: "Inside a faded, second-story meeting hall, King was quickly ringed by 300 angry Negroes. 'The people don't feel bad about what happened,' one soliloquized. 'They had nothing to lose. They don't have jobs, decent homes. What else could they do?' 'Burn, baby, burn,' someone whooped, to a chorus of laughing applause."

"We won," they boasted, and King cringed. He politely asked how they considered it a victory if their homes were destroyed and their neighbors were dead. "We won," came the reply, "because we made the whole world pay attention to us." King was so shaken by the meeting that he canceled other stops on the tour, "for security reasons." He later decided that the rioting was the forlorn cry of one who was "so fed up with the powerlessness of his cave existence that he asserts that he would rather be dead than ignored."[30]

King always insisted that real equality had to be built on the foundation of law. He was correct, but not in a way downtrodden blacks could appreciate. The law could not right every injustice, especially since so many of those injustices were economic. "They want *recognition,*" Efelka Brown, a Watts community worker, said of the rioters. "The only way they goin' get it is to riot. We don't want to overthrow the country—we just want what we ain't got." It is difficult to call the race riots a success, given the destruction they caused and the hatred they sowed. But they did focus white attention in a way that King's dignified protests never could. When exhortations to seek justice failed to inspire action, appeals to fear sometimes did. Anger and hatred were sometimes more impressive than reason.[31]

On August 18, 1965, President Johnson had a private conversation with John McCone, shortly after the latter had agreed to head the commission to investigate the riots. Johnson made no attempt to hide his frustration. "We are on powder kegs in a dozen places," he said.

> You just have no idea of the depth of feeling of these people. You see . . . these groups, they got absolutely nothing to live for. Forty percent of them are unemployed. These youngsters, they live with rats, and they've got no place to sleep. . . . They [are] all from broken homes and illegitimate families and all the . . . narcotics are circulating around them. And we have isolated them, and they are all in one area, and when they move in, why we move out. . . . We just got to find some way to wipe out these ghettoes . . . and find some . . . housing . . . and put them to work.[32]

The McCone Commission concluded that comprehensive change was essential. "Improving the conditions of Negro life will demand adjustments

on a scale unknown to any great society," the report warned. "We are convinced that the Negro can no longer exist, as he has, with the disad-
vantages which separate him from the rest of society, deprive him of
employment, and cause him to drift aimlessly through life."[33] The recommendations were well meant, but, in truth, the ghetto was a fire raging out
of control. Solving the problem required not just massive expenditure and
commitment, but also time. Blacks, however, were tired of waiting. For the
moment, rioting seemed an appropriate response to years of oppression.
In the years 1964 to 1968 nearly every major city in the United States, and a
good many minor ones, experienced devastating riots.

Like little republics, cities entered an arms race. Police forces underwent
intensive riot training. An increasing proportion of tax revenues went toward the purchase of heavy riot gear. The Detroit police bought five armored vehicles and a half-track—the closest thing to a tank without actually being one. Chicago put its money in helicopters, at the same time
that it was training 11,500 of its personnel in the use of heavy weapons. By
the end of 1968, all that firepower had resulted in 250 dead, 10,000 injured,
and 60,000 arrested—the worst violence occurring in Newark and Detroit
in the summer of 1967. The devastation caused businesses and factories to
hasten their exodus from the inner cities, quickening their decline and
making the ghettoes even worse places to live.

Johnson asked governor Otto Kerner of Illinois to investigate. His conclusions were not altogether different from those of McCone three years
earlier. Americans were warned that their country was "moving toward
two societies, one black, one white—separate and unequal." Comprehensive reforms were urgently needed. "To pursue the present course will involve the continuing polarization of the American community and, ultimately, the destruction of basic democratic values," Kerner emphasized.
"What white Americans have never fully understood—but what the Negro
can never forget—is that white society is deeply implicated in the ghetto.
White institutions created it, white institutions maintain it, and white society condones it." The report was an impressive expression of white liberal guilt, a meticulously prepared and neatly bound *mea culpa*. The great
problem with the riots of 1964–1967, however, was that issues of race distorted their interpretation. Most analysts interpreted them as expressions
of black anger, when in fact they were symptoms of a much wider prob-

lem—namely, the decline of the American city. Class was at least as important as race.[34]

The black migration to Northern and Western cities had reached its
peak during the Second World War, when manufacturing jobs were plentiful. In the same period, and especially after the war, whites who could afford it moved out, partly to distance themselves from blacks, but mainly
because the "good life" was located in the "little boxes" in pastures yon-
der. In that quintessentially American way, whites equated progress with
movement. Moving outward was facilitated by the American love affair
with the car and the belief that land was limitless. Lewis Mumford decried
what he called the "anti-city": "an incoherent and purposeless urbanoid
non-entity, which dribbles over the devastated landscape." This was "the
form that every modern city approaches when it forgets the functions and
purposes of the city itself and uses modern technology only to sink to a
primitive social level." Elaine Brown said the same thing more poetically in
her song "Until We're Free," which tells what it's like to live in a Third
World neighborhood contained within a First World country:

> Yes I remember the yesterdays,
> the poverty that you and me survived.
> We tried living, on streets that weren't giving.
> We laughed and cried; in youth we died.
> We didn't know . . .
> The times we saw, we didn't deserve.
> Hostility, we couldn't see, it was absurd.

Those who stayed in the cities were those who could not afford to leave.
They were blacks, yes, but also Hispanics, Asians, and undereducated
whites. Their existence was made all the more precarious by advanced
technology which eliminated so many unskilled and semiskilled jobs. At
the same time, industrialists moved their factories to the suburbs, where
land was cheap and the workforce better trained. Some moved operations
to underdeveloped countries where labor was plentiful, docile, and inex-
pensive.[35]

In other words, the ghetto was a symptom of neglect, not of overt prejudice. Americans had given up on the cities. Radicals like Tom Hayden liked
to compare the ghetto to a colony—a source of cheap and exploitable la-

bor. Out of that assumption grew the ridiculous hope that ghetto dwellers might liberate themselves the way the Cubans and Vietnamese had. But what Hayden failed to understand was that colonies exist because they are economically viable, while ghettos represent the failure of viability. America's inner cities were in freefall: the exodus to the suburbs deprived them of their lifeblood, and as they declined they also fueled their degeneration by becoming ever more dangerous and rundown. The Puerto Rican author Piri Thomas, a resident of Spanish Harlem, asked the Kerner Commission: "Did you ever stand on street corners and look the other way, at the world of *muchos ricos,* and think, I ain't got a damn? Did you ever count the garbage that flowed down dirty streets, or dig in the back yards who in their glory were a garbage dump's dream? Did you ever stand on rooftops and watch night time cover the bad below? Did you ever put your hand around your throat and feel your pulse beat and say, 'I do belong, and there's not gonna be nobody can tell me I'm wrong'?" The Kerner recommendations were undoubtedly well meant. Some positive reform, such as the integration of urban police forces, did result. But the cities required much more. Americans needed to take on board some painful truths about the way they wanted to live their lives. That did not happen. Liberals praised the report and conservatives attacked it, but both groups agreed that its recommendations were unaffordable. A nation preoccupied with an interminable war and a fantasy in space could not remotely afford to resuscitate its cities.[36]

BERKELEY: FREE SPEECH

Bancroft Avenue borders one edge of the Berkeley campus of the University of California. On one side is the ivory tower; on the other, the real world. Or so it seems. In fact, reality remains elusive in Berkeley. Fantasy and fact tangle like ivy on the walls of stone.

The intersection of Bancroft and Telegraph Avenues is the magnetic center of the Sixties, a place where some of the greatest dramas of that decade were acted out and a place where time has stood still. Forty years later, at that intersection, it's still possible to score some hash, buy a tie-dyed shirt, or plot the overthrow of the capitalist system. Carried on the wind of memory come the sounds of Dylan and the smell of tear gas.

"There is no place in the world where uncomfortable people can feel so comfortable," a visiting academic once remarked.[37]

On October 1, 1964, at that intersection, Mario Savio encountered his epiphany. He had recently returned from the South after a spell on a voter education project. As with so many other white volunteers, Freedom Summer had had a greater effect on Savio than on the disenfranchised blacks he'd gone to help. The life of a student, preparing for a well-paid job and secure adulthood, suddenly seemed trivial in comparison to events in Mississippi. Determined to keep the momentum going, Savio joined the local chapter of SNCC. He was planning on a day of politicizing when he crashed head-on into his own destiny.

While Savio was away, the university had decided to ban political activities on the small parcel of land at Bancroft and Telegraph. For Berkeley politicos, that was like desecrating the Golden Temple. Left-wingers were not alone in expressing indignation; the local chapter of Young Americans for Freedom also revolted at the removal of the right to pontificate. When Savio arrived, he found that Jack Weinberg, a fellow activist, had been arrested and was sitting in a police car in the middle of Sproul Plaza. What the university failed to realize was that it had taken on the television generation. Those like Savio and Weinberg who had been to Mississippi were relatively few, but those who had witnessed protests on television were many. They knew precisely what to do when confronted by authoritarian power: they sat down, immobilizing the squad car for thirty-two hours.

Leadership did not come naturally to Savio. He was not personally ambitious, nor did he crave the spotlight, like so many student leaders who would follow in his footsteps. He was instead driven purely by a belief in justice. Having spent a summer campaigning for freedom in the South, he could not stand aside when University of California authorities trampled freedom in Berkeley. "The same rights are at stake in both places," he argued, "the right to participate as citizens in democratic society and the right to due process of law." He therefore climbed on the police car. But, being a polite young man (unlike later campus rebels), he removed his shoes before doing so.[38]

By climbing onto that police car, Savio became the leader of a movement which had not existed until that moment. Rather like SDS, the Free Speech Movement (FSM) was earnest, liberal, and very American. It wanted not wholesale revolution, but rather a restoration of the traditional political values that had been destroyed by bureaucracy, consumerism, and conformity. "The things we are asking for," Savio proclaimed, "have a deceptively quaint ring. We are asking for the due process of law. We are asking for our actions to be judged by committees of our peers. We are asking that regulations ought to be considered as arrived at legitimately only from the consensus of the governed. These phrases are all pretty old, but they are not being taken seriously in America today, nor are they being taken seriously on the Berkeley campus." Technically speaking, FSM was not supposed to have leaders, being obsessed with democracy to the point of anarchy. "This is not a cult of one personality," Savio told a reporter. "It is a broadly based movement. . . . FSM is not any single individual." He did not want to be its leader. But that is what he became.[39]

Savio had discovered what he yearned for: a righteous cause that he could pursue with relentless energy while still going through the motions of being a student. The university, obsessed with its duties *in loco parentis*, remained convinced that it was doing the right thing in denying free speech. It was, however, fighting a losing battle. The climactic event occurred two months later. Led by Savio, students seized Sproul Hall, determined to occupy it until their demands were met. Prior to the action, Savio fired up the crowd with the best speech delivered by a student in the 1960s: "There's a time when the operation of the machine becomes so odious, makes you so sick at heart, that you can't take part, you can't even tacitly take part, and you've got to put your bodies on the gears and upon the wheels, upon the levers, upon all the apparatus, and you've got to make it stop. And you've got to indicate to the people who run it, to the people who own it, that unless you are free, the machine will be prevented from working at all." Marcuse and Mills had said the same thing, but never with such eloquence. Ironically, Savio was a stutterer; but he never stuttered when speaking to a crowd, or at least no one noticed him doing so. He had the ability to mesmerize a crowd through gut-wrenching sincerity. Suzanne Goldberg, later Savio's wife, remarked that he could "make things ordinary and understandable without using rhetoric. He believed that if people knew all the facts, they couldn't help but do the right thing—which most of us know is not true. He had a naïve faith in people."[40]

The Sproul Hall occupation ended shortly after governor Edmund G.

Brown ordered the arrest of 800 demonstrators on December 3, 1964. By that point, however, the unrest had spread to other California campuses. Brown could arrest hundreds, but he could not arrest thousands. The university eventually realized that unless student demands were satisfied, the ivory tower would come tumbling down. The concession finally granted was ridiculously simple: restrictions on political expression were removed. That concession was, however, less important than the time taken to grant it. The heavy-handed approach fostered a deep distrust among students, not just toward the university, but toward the "Establishment" in general. The university became a microcosm of the real world.

The trouble in Berkeley sent ripples through academia. Savio and his friends became heroes other students enthusiastically emulated. Unfortunately, those who imitate produce imitations: second-rate, often exaggerated versions of the real thing. That is why the student movement produced only one Savio and why the golden moment of revolt came at its very beginning. It also needs to be emphasized that while FSM seems a beginning, it was also an end. It was an outgrowth of the civil rights movement and, as such, an assertion of liberal freedoms that the "system" had quashed. The essentially liberal nature of the movement would seem old-fashioned in just a few short years. Before long, students would direct their anger at liberalism itself. Instead of seeking to improve the system, they would try to demolish it.

With free speech won, students across the country yearned to stretch the limits of their new freedoms. There were causes aplenty and no shortage of emotional fuel to keep the fires of revolt stoked. The curricula seemed irrelevant, professors remote, classes crowded, dormitories shabby, meals inedible, and administrators arbitrarily authoritarian. Mark Rudd, one of the leaders of the Columbia University protests of 1968, later remarked: "I entered the university expecting the Ivory Tower on the Hill—a place where committed scholars would search for truth in a world that desperately needed help. Instead, I found a huge corporation that made money from real estate, government research contracts, and student fees; teachers who cared only for advancement in their narrow areas of study; worst of all, an institution hopelessly mired in the society's racism and militarism." At first, protests were directed inward, toward changing the university environment. Indeed, throughout the 1960s, the most popular issues were not Vietnam or civil rights, but curfews, coed living, cafeteria food, and the structure of classes. Perhaps inevitably, immaturity occasionally overflowed: shortly after the FSM victory, Berkeley's Filthy Speech Movement revolted over the right to shout "FUCK!" on campus.[41]

At the very moment students won the right to protest, Lyndon Johnson gave them an issue: Vietnam. The first major response to Johnson's escalation came at the University of Michigan in March 1965, when students organized a teach-in designed to educate the ignorant about the war. Within weeks, similar events were organized at dozens of universities across the country. Students were protesting not the human cost of the war (American deaths still numbered under 500), but rather the immorality of American action.

The biggest teach-in occurred on May 21, 1965, when more than 10,000 people gathered on the Berkeley campus for Vietnam Day, a twenty-four-hour carnival of protest. The event was the brainchild of Jerry Rubin, later the star of so many Sixties dramas. The self-styled P. T. Barnum of student revolution had an uncanny ability to make things happen—usually by sheer force of personality—and was never so happy as when he was causing annoyance. Though few people liked him, many were in his thrall. A far cry from Savio, he is perhaps the best example of how easily and quickly egotists hijacked the "movement." Whereas Savio was genuinely interested in issues, Rubin wanted mainly to strut on stage.

In late April 1965, Rubin approached mathematics professor Stephen Smale with the idea of a massive teach-in. The latter, a veteran activist, was outraged by the bombing of North Vietnam and therefore agreed to join Rubin. A cadre quickly congregated around the genius and the cockerel. "We didn't spend much time on analysis and theory," Smale recalled. "Our mode was one of continually doing things, all kinds of things, which would make Vietnam Day into a bigger and sharper anti-war protest. . . . It was more like an exciting creative challenge . . . to make Johnson cringe." Having grown up on television, Vietnam Day activists understood the need to manipulate images. Rubin wanted Berkeley to become "a media symbol for the country."[42]

Activists competed with one another in proposing "the biggest, most provocative names" to invite. Bertrand Russell, Fidel Castro, Norman Mailer, and Jean-Paul Sartre were all suggested. "Sometimes it worked and the invitations were accepted," Smale recalled. Morris Hirsch, Smale's friend and colleague, admitted that objectivity was never a concern. This unashamed bias was reason enough for the Johnson administration to turn down an invitation to send a representative. The White House thought a refusal would deprive the event of credibility.[43]

The organizers provided thirty-six hours of nonstop indignation. Speakers included Mailer, Benjamin Spock, the leftist journalist I. F. Stone, the comedian Dick Gregory, Yale history professor Staughton Lynd, and Norman Thomas, perennial socialist candidate for president. Bertrand Russell sent a recorded message. Despite the seriousness, a festive atmosphere prevailed. Comedians, folksingers, and mime artists provided light but relevant relief. The big names drew crowds in excess of 12,000, with perhaps 30,000 attending in all. Police made no arrests and the mood was consistently jolly. The *San Francisco Chronicle*—no friend of the left—praised the "pleasant Chautauqua-like atmosphere."[44]

Over subsequent weeks, the organizers tried to transform the spirit of a single day into a sustained antiwar campaign. "We all had this incredible energy," Rubin recalled. "We believed we could stop the war if we just made enough noise. . . . We were telephoning across the country—two thousand dollars a month in phone bills. We had fifteen different committees—committees to talk to soldiers, committees to plan civil disobedience. Fantastic!" Two conclusions about American politics shaped Vietnam Day policy: first, that "respectable" protest would be ignored by the media; second, that the traditional party system could not accommodate an antiwar movement, since, on the left, liberal Democrats supported Johnson. The organizers consciously shunned liberal America. "We didn't mind alienating liberals," Smale recalled. "We didn't need them."[45]

Over the summer, membership grew to around 400, with perhaps two dozen real activists and ten salaried staff members. Participatory democracy was sacrosanct. Political choices were made in public, rather than imposed from above. This, however, meant that the Vietnam Day Committee was prey to cynics and spies who manipulated the leaderless system. As Morris Hirsch admitted, "We trusted people too much." Often the most enthusiastic campaigners were FBI agents provocateurs. "It remained surprising to me," wrote *Life* reporter Sam Angeloff (who easily infiltrated the group), "that a man could wander off the street and join any VDC decision-making body."[46]

The Vietnam Day Committee, like so many Sixties radical groups, toyed with "expressive politics" in which protest combined with street theater.

The danger of this approach, however, was that style frequently overwhelmed substance. Participation often achieved nothing beyond mere spectacle. The most controversial action began in July 1965, when the escalation of the war brought trainloads of draftees to the Oakland Army Terminal—via nearby Berkeley. The Vietnam Day Committee launched a campaign to stop the trains by blocking the tracks. On only one occasion was a train briefly stopped, but that was not the point. The aim was to attract attention, which the group managed rather well. With no consistent ideology, however, and little centralized direction, the committee behaved like a headless chicken. Members were allowed to pursue idiosyncratic, sometimes contradictory goals. For example, during preparations for a march in November 1965, one faction drew up plans for a nonviolent parade while another advised supporters to bring sticks and other potential weapons.

Actions were designed to "increase the number of people who are opposed to the structure and value system of American society." In other words, an antiwar campaign easily morphed into one that sought to bring down the American system. Since, according to Marcuse, the system depended upon apathy, arousing the consciousness of ordinary people became a rebellious act. Toward this end, the committee sought, "to create controversy where there is apathy." "It was an important policy of the Vietnam Day Committee to make no concessions to respectability," wrote Smale. Or, as Rubin explained more graphically: "We were fucking obnoxious, and we dug every moment of it."[47]

A second teach-in was scheduled for October 15, 1965. The Vietnam Day Committee, burdened by its early success, had to improve upon the May 21 extravaganza in order to show that it was thriving. Aware of this need, the group decided to combine the teach-in with a march on the Oakland Army Terminal. By this stage, however, the committee was no longer unobtrusive: the Establishment took it seriously—perhaps too seriously. Detectives followed Smale and Rubin constantly, while informants worked closely with the FBI and campus police. On October 1, Alameda County district attorney J. F. Coakley warned Governor Brown that the march could cause a "calamity." He demanded that the National Guard and the California Highway Patrol be readied. Coakley, in common with other ambitious Republicans like Ronald Reagan and Senator George Murphy, delighted in using Berkeley unrest to embarrass Brown.[48]

Right-wing vigilantes were also watching with interest. The Minutemen

and Hell's Angels looked forward to the opportunity to give the peace protesters a lesson in civil disobedience. Their threats of violence delighted
Oakland city officials, who welcomed any reason to ban the march. They
waited until the eve of the protest to deny a parade permit, thus leaving in-
sufficient time for a legal challenge. Berkeley officials, however, granted a
permit. The marchers were thus confronted with the prospect of having to
assert their civil rights on the Oakland city line.

The demonstration did not begin well. An impressive list of speakers
failed to excite a community now bored with teach-ins. The entire event
seemed headed for disaster when a larger-than-expected crowd of 10,000
gathered for the march on Oakland. This suggests that many were attracted by the opportunity for mayhem.

A crowd stretching thirteen blocks marched down Telegraph Avenue.
Waiting at the city line were 650 Oakland police, 400 highway patrolmen,
and 250 Alameda County sheriffs—all in a nasty mood. Behind them were
100 Hell's Angels and other right-wing thugs shouting, "America for the
Americans!" In an attempt to outflank the police, the marchers turned
right and traveled parallel to the city line. A few blocks on, march moni-
tors ordered a halt. They were confronted by a choice laden with symbolism: to the left lay Oakland and martyrdom; to the right, Berkeley and ignominy. "LEFT, LEFT, LEFT!!!" cried the crowd. For the first time in the
committee's short life, the organizers abandoned participatory democracy. Nine members of the executive council debated how to proceed.
Smale and Rubin preferred an immediate sitdown—rather like Savio and
FSM. They were in the minority. The council voted five to four to turn
right.[49]

The Vietnam Day Committee subsequently split along the fissures evident on the Oakland city line. Those who had preferred caution turned to
conventional politics. Rubin took his circus act on the road, in search
of adoring crowds. Smale, dismayed at the way participatory democracy
had been trampled on the Oakland city line, entered what he called "a
mathematical phase." What remained of the committee was hijacked by
members of the extreme left, who took it down a steep slope to violence,
futility, and farce. On the first anniversary of Vietnam Day, a teach-in attracted no-name speakers and a tiny crowd. By October 1966, the group
had "shrunken to a dozen Trotskyists with half a dozen letterheads and a
mimeograph machine." The university eventually banned the group, on

the grounds that none of its officers were students. Meanwhile, the Republican right reaped enormous dividends from the committee's stunts. In its death throes, the group caused more damage to the peace movement than it ever caused, during its heyday, to Johnson's war.[50]

The Vietnam Day Committee was just one example of a campus antiwar movement. Its importance lies not in its influence but in its typicality. Its weaknesses—immaturity, sensationalism, insensitivity, naïveté, lack of leadership—plagued the entire movement. Within Berkeley, the committee was influential in combating ignorance and apathy about the Vietnam War. But this was a limited success. When Sartre declined his invitation to the May 1965 teach-in, he provided a clue to the group's ultimate failure:

> The problem is not whether or not I would have helped such Americans more or less by going there. The fact is that I cannot help them at all. Because their political weight, unhappily, is nil. . . . These people are totally impotent. One of them wrote me: "If you do not come to us, if you break off all communication with us, it must be that you regard us as the accursed of the earth!" I do think, in fact, that a man of the American left who has a clear view of the situation, and who sees himself isolated in a land entirely conditioned by the myths of imperialism and anticommunism, such a man, I say, and with all respect, is indeed one of the accursed of the earth. He totally disapproves of the politics carried out in his name and his action is totally ineffective.

The Vietnam Day Committee imagined itself an antidote to radical impotence. But since the moral angst of Berkeley radicals was not widely felt across America, this antidote was not in great demand outside the university community. From 1965 to 1967, the vast majority of Americans, including students, supported the war and condemned the "campus kooks." If a nascent mass movement against the war existed in 1965, it could not be brought to life by shocking media stunts. Triumphant in Berkeley, the committee became the accursed in wider America.[51]

In the middle of his Vietnam Day speech, Paul Krassner, editor of *The Realist*, cautioned the crowd not to get carried away by the energy generated by the teach-in: "Don't let your perspective be disjointed here, because when I speak at a college and then I go away, I fly, and I look out. There's a lot of *them*. You know, who really *like* Ed Sullivan. It's very frightening. I mean they aren't the extremists." The Vietnam Day activists were the extremists, and they reveled in extremism. They had little time for the Ed Sullivan watchers. It might be argued that it was never their intention to break out of Berkeley—though their rhetoric suggests otherwise. But a mass movement confined to Sproul Plaza is a contradiction in terms. No matter how vocal the protest in the university community might have been, so long as it remained quarantined on campus, it could be used by the right as a symbol of moral degradation and extremist excess. The Vietnam Day Committee demonstrated a hugely important Sixties lesson— namely, the futility of trying to build a mass movement by thumbing one's nose at the masses.[52]

AMSTERDAM: PROVO PIONEERS

In the mid-1960s, along the canals of Amsterdam, a movement materialized that aimed to make people laugh. Humor, it was thought, was the best weapon against authority. The movement, called Provo, would eventually inspire a host of imitators, including the Merry Pranksters, the Diggers, and the Yippies. None, however, were quite as funny as the Dutch.

Sixties Holland had its version of Mods and Rockers, called Nozems. These reasonably affluent urban youths rode around on scooters, constantly on the lookout for mischief. A favorite pastime was to throw things into canals—rubbish bins, prams, bicycles, anything would do. Since the Dutch have long looked indulgently on youthful excess, the Nozems were studied more than punished. Sociologists decided that the behavior arose from boredom and alienation; the Nozems seemed lost souls in search of fulfillment. Discontent was expressed in a desire to provoke, a predilection that caused the sociologist Wouter Buikhuisen to call them "Provos."

Roel Van Duyn, a philosophy student at the University of Amsterdam, saw these directionless rebels as a potential revolutionary mass. His personal belief system was an eclectic mix of Dadaism, anarchism, and nihilism seasoned with sprinklings of Marcuse, Marx, and the Marquis de Sade. While Van Duyn never quite succeeded in organizing the Nozems (his anarchism proved an obstacle), he did manage to annex the name Provo.

Van Duyn was Provo's theoretician, the thinker in the background. Much more noticeable was Robert Jasper Grootveld, an irreverent performance artist already famous for his "happenings." The concept, central to the Sixties counterculture, was originally conceived by the New York artist Allan Kaprow, and taken to Holland by the Beat poet Simon Vinkenoog. Grootveld, however, gave happenings their peculiarly Sixties character. The masses, he felt, had been brainwashed into a bland, consumerist way of life that stifled imagination and encouraged the worship of authority. His method of breaking the tyranny of conformity was to awaken people's consciousness by involving them in bizarre demonstrations that combined social protest with street theater. Massive crowds attended his happenings on the certainty of being surprised. To them, Grootveld seemed a cross between a shaman and a magician. "If he is talking you can't do anything but listen," the journalist Wim Zaal confessed. "You . . . wait out of respect till Jasper has finished talking. In one sense . . . he is giving away a show, . . . a revelation of his intense lifestyle. This is his magic."[53]

Grootveld's favorite cause was the promotion of marijuana consumption. In 1962 he single-handedly began a crusade to change Dutch drug laws by exposing their absurdity. In his "Marihuettegames," players got stoned and then competed with one another to get arrested for possessing entirely legal substances. A tip would be called in to the police, who would then raid an address and arrest the occupants. After further investigation, the police would find that the substance seized was something harmless like tea, whereupon the culprits would be released. On one occasion, the police were told that a large hash shipment would be entering Holland from Belgium. Journalists were also alerted. Police and customs officers detained Grootveld and his friends, only to find that the contraband in question was dried dog food. Headlines subsequently read: "Marijuana Is Dog Food." Eventually, the police grew tired of the humiliation and decided to leave Grootveld alone. He responded by opening his Afrikaanse Druk Stoor, where he openly sold marijuana.[54]

A short hospital stay had a profound effect upon Grootveld's political consciousness, turning him into an obsessive campaigner against the tobacco industry. As he saw it, manufacturers and advertisers were amassing huge fortunes by conspiring to encourage a fatal addiction. Grootveld responded by defacing cigarette ads around Amsterdam, daubing them with a single black "K"—for *kancer*. Cigarette machines were broken into, the contents replaced by Day-Glo packs of fake marijuana cigarettes.

1/1T/2/4656757Z-9/027699A

Halifax is a division of Bank of Scotland plc. Registered in Scotland No. SC327000. Registered Office: The Moun...

Where possible we have tried to ensure you only receive one letter. However, there may be instan...
your sole name and held jointly with someone else. If you have a credit card or bank accounts with...
letter, we will write to you no later than 30th September 2009 about the changes that affect those accou...

Colin Walsh
Managing Director, Savings, Investment & Protection

Yours sincerely

We'd like to thank you for saving with Halifax. We...
savings over the years to come.

This leaflet also tells you about new charges that...
with money in a foreign currency. You'll find full o...

Halifax Save4it

We've enclosed a leaflet that will help to put you...
new conditions that apply to the following accou...

will ensure to keep you fully informed.
possible, we have taken this into account in your...
of Business rules (BCOBS). The FSA have not yet f...
regulations and industry guidance that will govern...
the same time, the financial services industry i...

like to tell you about some changes that will...
...ber 2009. **There's no need to do anything as a**
savings account(s) are not affected and the way...

...ean rules, which in the UK are governed by the...
...ed to make Europe's payments system clearer and...
...within the European Economic Area, which includes...
...e standards when making and receiving payments. At...
...ll replace the existing Banking Code with a new set of...
...he way we do business with you, known as Banking Con...
...alised the full details of this industry guidance, but w...
...ew conditions. If there are any substantial chang...

...n the picture, please take some time t...
...t(s) you hold.

...will apply from 1st N...
...etails in our leafl...
...value you...

Ref: PSDUK 08/

August 2009

MISS FREYA BUCHANAN
16 BORNESKITAIG
KILMUIR
SKYE
PORTREE   608
ISLE OF SKYE IV51 9YS   1/0276994

Important information for all our savings cus

Dear Miss Buchanan

We think it's important that you're always fully inf
affect the conditions of your savings account(s) fr
result of these changes, the features and interest
you save or manage your money will not need to

The changes to your conditions are as a result of
Payment Services Regulations. These regulations a
more straightforward. The new law applies to eve
the UK and EU, and means that banks must meet
the same time, the Financial Services Authority (F

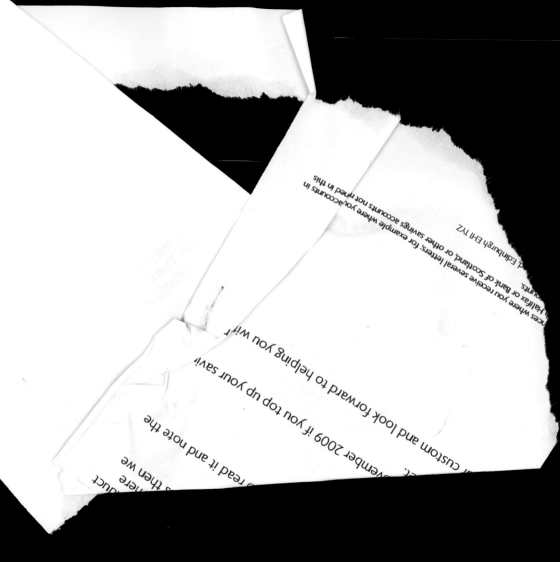

Grootveld occasionally sprayed chloroform in tobacco shops, the idea being that the hospital smell would remind smokers of their ultimate fate.

At his "Antismoking Temple," Grootveld performed weekly Black Masses
with his poet friend, Johnny the Selfkicker. Crowds would gather in anticipation of something outrageous. The ceremony would build to a crescendo, whereupon the crowd would sing the "Ugge, Ugge" song, the official antismoking anthem. Eventually, the masses were moved to Spui
Square, where a small statue of a child called "Het Lievertje" ("The Little
Rascal") had been donated by the Hunter Tobacco Company. As the novelist Harry Mulisch noted, the Dutch version of the generation gap was
acted out every Saturday night: "While their parents, sitting on their re-
frigerators and dishwashers, were watching with their left eye the TV,
with their right eye the auto in front of the house, in one hand the
kitchen mixer, in the other *Die Telegraaf,* their kids went . . . to Spui Square.
. . . And when the clock struck twelve, the high priest appeared, all dressed
up, . . . and started to walk Magic Circles around the nicotinistic demon,
while his disciples cheered, applauded, and sang the 'Ugge Ugge' song."
Grootveld had managed, quite inadvertently, to give Nozems a focus. The
antismoking issue was not particularly important to them, but participating in a spectacle was. Incidentally, throughout his campaign, Grootveld
remained a chain-smoker.[55]

At one happening, Van Duyn began handing out leaflets announcing
the formation of Provo. The choice, he argued, was "between desperate resistance or apathetic perishing. Provo realizes eventually it will be the
loser, but [we] won't let slip away that last chance to annoy and provoke
this society to its depths." While Grootveld normally had little patience
with movements, he found Van Duyn's anarchism deeply attractive. An alliance was struck. For them, anarchism was never really a political philosophy, but rather a romantic approach to life that allowed independence and
self-consciousness to flourish.[56]

In contrast to so many Sixties revolutionary groups, Provo had no grandiose ambitions about politicizing the masses. The vast majority of the
Dutch people were dismissed as *klootjesvolk,* or "people with little balls,"
who lived out humdrum lives and hadn't the guts to be different. Provo
lumped the proletariat and the bourgeoisie into "one big, gray *klootjesvolk*
of enslaved consumers," opposed by a proud, liberated, and determined

provotariat. "We cannot persuade the masses," one document proclaimed. "We hardly want to. How anybody can have any trust in these apathetic, dependent, spiritless bunch of cockroaches, beetles, and ladybugs is incomprehensible." The *klootjesvolk* were useful only as a focus of ridicule. Holland, Van Duyn maintained, was "so easy to provoke, so stupid, so engaged in its old-fashioned moral tradition."[57]

Grootveld was a delightful attention-seeker who needed to be out among the people and grew stronger from their interest in him. The participation of the police was essential to the Provo equation—they were "cohappeners." Everything depended on the police acting like police. "It is obvious that the cops are our best pals," wrote Van Duyn. "The greater their number, the more rude and fascist their performance, the better for us. The police, just like we do, are provoking the masses. . . . They are causing resentment. We are trying to turn that resentment into revolt."[58]

With immense creativity, Provo continually devised new campaigns, usually under the general rubric of "White." The most famous was the White Bike Plan, the inspiration of the industrial designer Luud Schimmelpenninck. Worried that there were too many cars in Amsterdam, he called upon the city to provide free bicycles, which were to be painted white and left permanently unlocked. An individual could then simply pick one up at Point A and leave it at Point B, whereupon another person might ride it to Point C, and so on. In order to kick off the campaign, Provo provided the first fifty bicycles. The idea suited a progressive city like Amsterdam, but was far too logical for the police, who immediately confiscated the bikes on the grounds that they constituted an invitation to theft. Provo responded by stealing some police bikes.

White ideas proliferated like tulips at the Keukenhof. The White Housing campaign attempted to make derelict flats available to low-income families while pointing out the iniquities of real estate speculation. White Chimneys attempted to establish smokeless zones within cities and identified polluters by painting their smokestacks white. The White Wife initiative aimed at increasing access to contraceptives and abortion; the White Kids plan called for free nurseries. The White Chickens Plan was the brainchild of a Provo faction called Friends of the Police. Law enforcement officers, previously known as "blue chickens," would be given a new, gentler image. White chickens would ride around on bicycles, be unarmed, dispense first aid, provide directions, distribute free contraceptives, and, best of all, provide free fried chicken. Unenthusiastic about the idea, the police raided one demonstration and confiscated a dozen white chickens Provo had brought to publicize the scheme.

The first issue of *Provo* magazine came out in July 1965. It contained recipes for making bombs and booby-traps, but no guidance as to what was to be done with them, since Provo was strictly opposed to violence. The aim, as always, was simply to provoke. On this occasion they were successful—police arrested Van Duyn and three others for inciting violence. The magazine worried authorities not just because of the bomb recipes, but also because it suggested that Provo was a great deal more organized than had previously been assumed. "It was very shocking to the establishment," Grootveld recalled. "They realized that we were not mere dopey scum but were quite capable of some sort of organization." The police responded with ever more heavy-handed tactics, playing into Provo's hands. When Provo was banned from distributing literature in Spui Square, campaigners responded with blank banners and blank leaflets. The police arrested them and confiscated empty pieces of paper.[59]

In September 1965, Provo turned its attention to the Vietnam War. Unlike many other antiwar movements (particularly those in Europe), opposition did not inspire them to idolize Ho Chi Minh. They hated war in general, and accepted the fact that thoroughly nasty characters fought on both sides. "Our protests . . . were from a humanistic point of view," Rob Stolk recalled. "We criticized the cruel massacres, but didn't identify with the Viet Cong, like Jane Fonda. That's why later on we didn't end up on aerobics videos." Some Provo sympathizers offered safe houses to American soldiers who deserted their units in Germany.[60]

The sheer fun of Provo helped it to spread across the Netherlands, a country where irony is an industry. Eventually, every town and city had its branch, producing leaflets, staging happenings, and dreaming up White plans. As it spread, Provo tested the tolerance of pluralistic Dutch society. A national poll in 1966 discovered that 71 percent of those surveyed thought the Provos work-shy; while 85 percent saw them as "hooligans." They were summarily dismissed as *snotneuzen* ("snotnoses"), or a more noxious form of Nozems. *Die Telegraaf* called the Provos "an unworthy plague of fleas."[61]

A small but significant minority of Dutch were, however, embarrassed by the image of boring, bourgeois Holland. For them, admiring Provo became symbolic of liberal credibility. "Clergymen, municipal officials, and politicians of every persuasion came to talk and often went away . . . whole-hearted sympathizers," the journalist Aad Nuis reported in 1967. The group's environmental message proved particularly appealing to those worried about traffic congestion and smog. The supermarket tycoon Albert Heijn declared himself a Provo after hearing about the White Bicycle Plan, and Queen Juliana confessed that she was sympathetic to some of Provo's ideas. "The Provos protest against dehumanization, as the socialists once did," wrote Cees Egas, state secretary for culture, recreation, and social work. "The young protest a dehumanized world. They demand re-humanization. They challenge Christians and socialists to shake off their *klootjesvolk* mentality and . . . to be truly human together."[62]

As time passed, the Dutch grew increasingly fond of the Provos, who provided proof of the nation's capacity for whimsy. Their appeal can be explained in part because their campaign to embarrass the police tapped into the public's deeply embedded suspicion of uniformed authority. The reputation of the police plummeted with each desperate attempt to impose order. Increasingly harsh measures succeeded only in provoking ever more imaginative anarchy. The more the police embarrassed themselves, the more the public sided with Provo.

One of the most popular campaigns focused on the Dutch royal family. The Nazi connections of certain members was just the sort of irony Provo liked to exploit. Agitation came to a head in March 1966 over the marriage of Princess Beatrix to the German Claus von Armsberg, a former member of the Hitler Youth. Provo action tapped into a rich vein of anti-German feeling within Amsterdam, a city that had lost 80,000 Jews to the Holocaust. The group launched the White Rumor Plan, designed primarily to encourage an expectation of massive disruption on the wedding day. There was talk of building a giant paint gun to be fired at the royal procession, and of putting LSD in the city water supply. Activists also suggested putting laughing gas in the church organ and drowning out the service with amplified recordings of machine-gun fire. Another rumor held that lion manure would be spread along the intended path of the royal coach. The smell of lions would frighten the horses, causing them to bolt, taking the newlyweds on a wild ride. Finally, Provo promised a concert by a band called "SS and the Gasmaskers."

These plans were never meant to be implemented. The point was instead to poke fun at the monarchy and to alarm the police. Provo was enormously successful at the latter goal, as demonstrated when 25,000 extra troops were brought in to guard the parade route. This necessitated commandeering the Anne Frank House as a temporary police station—precisely the sort of irony Provo enjoyed. On the day of the wedding, Provo was conspicuous by its absence. Thousands of underoccupied police provided the best evidence of the movement's success. Desperately seeking purpose, the police manhandled journalists and roughed up innocent bystanders. The paradox of jackbooted Dutch police protecting the wedding of a former Nazi was not lost on the people of Amsterdam.

Since the Dutch—those in Amsterdam especially—felt profound unease about the wedding, Provo's popularity rose. Likewise, each act of brutality diminished citizens' patience with the police. By the summer, both the mayor and the police chief of Amsterdam were forced to resign, and the Provos had become folk heroes. An admiring public did not, however, suit a group whose raison d'être was to provoke. Since the group had been founded on the idea of resistance to authority, it could not survive a situation in which authority had become tolerant and even respectful. Radical purists saw this accommodation of Provo as an annoying example of Marcusian repressive tolerance. "Fake progressiveness and fake hipness are appearing everywhere," the young comedian Wim de Bie, complained. "We should distrust this like the plague." Some Provotarians on the other hand, rather enjoyed being popular, especially when they were invited on speaking engagements around the country and treated lavishly. While the leadership attended a conference outside Amsterdam, Stolk announced an internal coup by the Revolutionary Terrorist Council. Van Duyn reacted angrily, unaware that he had fallen victim to yet another White Rumor, since the council did not in fact exist.[63]

On May 15, 1967, Provo shocked Amsterdam by announcing that it no longer existed. The end came because the group feared respectability. Like a feral cat, it was in danger of being domesticated. Evidence had come the previous June, when Provo secured 13,000 votes (2.5 percent of the total) in the Amsterdam city council elections—enough for one seat. The Dutch tourist agency had even begun selling tickets to visitors who wanted to be insulted by Provos. "I was totally estranged by all the publicity," Stolk reflected; "it seemed that Provo had become a public relations machine." The breakup, in the end, was remarkably amicable, since most members agreed that their work was done. Those who did not go into politics returned to their studies, while others perfected the art of hedonism.[64]

Grootveld had always been in it solely for the fun, which he found in abundance. As for Van Duyn, he was enough of a pragmatist to realize that his idea of revolution had no hope of success. He came to accept that politicizing the Nozems was a thankless task, since they were only interested in short-term mayhem. He turned his attention instead to the formation of the Kabouters (Gnomes), an anarchist group which by 1970 was the fourth-largest party on the Amsterdam city council. Its greatest success came in pressuring the larger parties to co-opt its environmental and social policies.

For a brief period, Provo gave Holland's disaffected young people a rather harmless focus for their energies—certainly a better one than vandalizing phone booths or terrorizing old ladies. "It was a nice revolution," Kees Hoekert reflected in 1972. "It was not a coup d'état. It was an open revolution which everyone could take part in. . . . Before Provo, Amsterdam was boring. . . . It was as boring as Copenhagen, as boring as Stockholm, as boring as Brussels, as boring as East Berlin, as boring as Moscow. Now it is not so boring." Liberal drug laws, relaxed attitudes toward sexuality, and a general tolerance of diversity transformed Amsterdam into a Mecca for rebellious youth.[65]

Provo was one of the few protest groups of the Sixties to enjoy a steady increase in popularity over time. While that did not harmonize with the group's plans, it did influence its long-term effect. The healthy disrespect for authority which the group encouraged remains a notable characteristic of Dutch politics. Thanks in part to Provo, the Dutch adopted a pragmatic attitude to soft drugs, without giving themselves a serious drug problem. Likewise, versions of the White plans are still evident throughout the country. Even the once-despised Beatrix and Claus eventually mirrored trends set in motion by Provo. She became known as the Bicycling Queen, and both developed an enlightened consciousness of environmental issues.

Grootveld was later in the news for building a raft entirely out of rubbish found floating on Amsterdam's canals. In addition to making an ecological statement, he intended to use the craft to bring marijuana to boring Sweden.

SELMA: BLACK POWER

As time passed, the civil rights struggle grew harder for Martin Luther King. He had to contend not only with angry Southerners, but also with a growing band of black militants who rejected nonviolence. The harmony carefully engineered during the March on Washington was clearly a façade. Though the acknowledged leader of the civil rights movement, he had little control over the direction in which members marched.

King had gambled on the ability of the Democratic party to deliver the comprehensive legislation that would address the manifold problems of blacks in America. The Civil Rights Act of 1964 was a huge step forward, but was also notable for what it did not address—namely, voting rights. Lyndon Johnson openly admitted that electoral reform had been bargained away by cynical deals within Congress. Militant blacks concluded that whites would never willingly surrender power.

Evidence to support that conclusion was provided by Johnson's handling of the Mississippi Freedom Democratic Party. The MFDP had arisen out of SNCC's prolonged efforts to enfranchise black people in the state. These had culminated in Freedom Summer, when students from around the country—black and white—had joined activists already on the ground in Mississippi in a concerted effort to extend voter registration. While the campaign yielded a paltry number of registered black voters, it did inspire solidarity among blacks, as expressed through the MFDP.

The MFDP offered itself as an alternative to the all-white, and therefore illegitimate, Mississippi Democratic Party. Its aims were moderate in that it supported the official platform of the national Democratic party, which the all-white group did not. The MFDP sent sixty-eight delegates (four of them white) to the Democratic Convention in Atlantic City in August 1964. While not expecting to be officially recognized, they did hope to make a point about the inequalities of political representation in the South.

For Johnson, the MFDP was an embarrassment he could do without. He deeply resented being placed in an uncomfortable situation from which he could not gracefully extricate himself. Since becoming president, he had managed to engineer the Civil Rights Act, improvements in urban mass-transit, a food stamp program, new education and health initiatives, and the establishment of the Office of Economic Opportunity. He had more ambitious plans, but insisted that he needed a massive mandate at the election in order to implement them. The actions of the MFDP jeopardized further reform: five Southern delegations threatened to walk out if the MFDP was seated. Johnson feared a mass exodus of white Southern voters to his Republican opponent, Barry Goldwater. He therefore offered the MFDP a compromise of two at-large delegates—the most he felt he could afford.

King recognized Johnson's predicament and was willing to be patient. SNCC, however, attacked Johnson for what seemed a "back of the bus" agreement. Aaron Henry of the MFDP thought the president made "the typical white man's mistake: not only did he say, 'You've got two votes,' which was too little, but he told us to whom the two votes would go. . . . This is typical white man picking black folks' leaders, and that day is just gone." After three days of agonized deliberation, the MFDP decided to reject the offer. For militants, the whole affair demonstrated the futility of King's faith in the Democratic party.[66]

Under enormous pressure from within his own movement, King agreed to another high-profile campaign, this time in Selma, Alabama. The town was chosen in part as a direct challenge to the racist governor of the state, George Wallace, but also because the local sheriff, Jim Clark, seemed a clone of Bull Connor. Since blacks constituted a majority of the population in Selma, but accounted for only 3 percent of registered voters, the town seemed just the right place to pressure the government over voting rights.

The campaign, which began in January 1965, started slowly. Daily marches to the courthouse did not produce the spectacle SCLC needed to attract national attention. Clark, it seems, had been instructed to control his temper. Yet by the end of January, 2,000 protesters had been arrested. A giant demonstration on February 1 resulted in the arrest of another 770, including King. Pressure was maintained over the next two weeks, with arrests mounting and Clark steadily losing his cool. Black activists were nevertheless growing frustrated. Sensitive to their dismay, Malcolm X visited Selma and openly suggested that there were "other ways" to achieve progress.

A turning point came when Jimmy Lee Jackson was killed by police during a nighttime march in neighboring Marion on February 18. Responding to Jackson's death, SCLC scheduled a march from Selma to Montgomery, but Wallace banned it. King urged postponement until the federal government could intervene to quash the ban, but SNCC was intent upon defiance. On March 7, police viciously attacked protesters on the Edmund Pettus Bridge leading into Montgomery. Scenes of police horses stampeding into the crowd provided the images necessary to arouse national attention. It being a Sunday, journalists called it bloody. A flood of volunteers poured into Selma, and scores of sympathy marches took place around the nation. King, already under pressure because of his opposition to the march, was further embarrassed by the failure of the White House to intervene.

Emboldened by the flood of support, protesters decided two days later to make a second attempt to enter Montgomery. In defiance of a federal injunction, they again converged on the bridge. As they approached, they sang "Ain't Gonna Let Nobody Turn Me Around" in order to steel their nerves for confrontation. Fearing another bloodbath, King ignored the lyrics and turned the march around. Bloody Sunday gave way to Turnaround Tuesday.

Many marchers felt betrayed. Turnaround Tuesday might so easily have brought an ignominious end to the Selma campaign, but, not for the first time, the course of events was radically altered by a timely murder. On March 9, J. J. Reeb, a white minister from Boston, was viciously beaten by racist vigilantes in Selma. He died two days later. A renewed sense of outrage gripped the nation, breathing life into the Selma campaign. Sympathizers flocked to the town, the White House was flooded with angry letters, and demonstrations took place around the country. Outside the South, the press was virtually unanimous in its support, thus increasing the pressure upon the White House. On March 15, Johnson announced to the nation that he would be submitting a Voting Rights Bill to Congress. "Every American citizen must have an equal right to vote," he said. "This time, on this issue, there must be no delay, or no hesitation, or no compromise with our purpose. We cannot, we must not, refuse to protect the right of every American to vote."[67]

Johnson followed up that speech with an order lifting the injunction against the march to Montgomery. It took place without serious violence. At its conclusion, King spoke in front of the Alabama State Capitol. "The confrontation of good and evil compressed in the tiny community of

Selma," he maintained, "generated the massive power to turn the whole nation to a new course. A president born in the South had the sensitivity to feel the will of the country, and in an address that will live in history as one of the most passionate pleas for human rights . . . he pledged the might of the federal government to cast off the centuries-old blight."[68]

King was desperately in need of a victory, so it is entirely understandable that he tried to make Selma into one. The Voting Rights Act, passed on August 3, seems fitting tribute to his skillful balancing of antagonistic forces—proof that his pragmatism and caution were appropriate. But sequence should not be confused with consequence; the fact that the Voting Rights Act followed closely on the heels of the Selma campaign does not mean that the former was the product of the latter. Johnson had recognized the need for such an act in the summer of 1964, during negotiations to secure passage of the Civil Rights Bill. Selma might have quickened his hand, but it is difficult to believe that a president so dedicated to reform introduced a voting-rights bill only because his hand was forced.

Selma could easily have been a humiliation for King. His remarkable dexterity, so evident earlier in the civil rights struggle, had deserted him. This was not because King had changed, but rather because "his people" had. Nonviolence no longer inspired them; stirring words no longer brought them into line. To make matters worse, the passage of the Voting Rights Act comprehensively changed the nature of the black struggle in a way that exacerbated King's marginalization.

Arguments over freedom, which had focused on the South, were giving way to campaigns for economic justice pertinent to all parts of the United States. "The more we grapple with the civil rights problem," Johnson told Congress, "the more we realize that the position of minorities in American society is defined not merely by law, but by social, educational, and economic conditions." The new tenor of the struggle rendered it even more difficult for King to hold the movement together, as his attempt to launch a Northern campaign painfully revealed. Blacks in the North were not as tightly knit as those who had endured generations of discrimination in the South, where culture and religion provided powerful social glue. Northern blacks were, therefore, much more difficult to organize, especially since blacks everywhere were growing impatient with the slow rate of change and contemptuous of King's religious adherence to nonviolence. The issues that plagued the ghetto were also much more complicated than simple matters of freedom and segregation. In addition, Northern whites, who had been so sympathetic when the problem was a Southern one, grew less tolerant when it arrived on their doorstep.[69]

On June 5, 1966, almost three years after the March on Washington, James Meredith began his "walk against fear" from Memphis to Jackson. In 1962, he had walked through angry crowds in order to become the first black student to enroll at the University of Mississippi. Aware of the symbolic power of singular protest, on this occasion he walked alone. He did not reach his destination—though he did perhaps make his point, in a manner unintended. On the second day of his march, he was gunned down. Within the civil rights movement, the reaction was one part sadness and nine parts anger. It seemed unbelievable that, after a decade of demonstration, a prominent campaigner could not carry out a peaceful act of protest in safety. As a gesture of defiance, 400 activists from SNCC, CORE, and the SCLC completed Meredith's march. They were harassed along the way by Byron De La Beckwith, the killer of Medgar Evers, who drove menacingly up and down the column. Significant by their absence were representatives of the NAACP and the Urban League, who found it increasingly difficult to share a platform with the firebrands from SNCC.

During the march, Stokely Carmichael was arrested after trying to set up a campground in a black school. After his release, he told his followers: "This is the twenty-seventh time I have been arrested. I ain't going to jail no more. What we gonna start saying now is Black Power." Martin Luther King, who hated the term, found Carmichael's utterance deeply disappointing. He did not, however, blame Carmichael, at least not publicly. If blacks were turning to Black Power, he suggested, it was because the white establishment had made it clear that moderate tactics had little hope of success. "The government has got to give me some victories if I'm going to keep people nonviolent."[70]

Violence was the modern way. When H. Rap Brown replaced Carmichael at the head of Student Nonviolent Coordinating Committee in 1967, the qualifier "nonviolent" was retained, even though it no longer remotely described the group's preferred strategy. At a press conference, Brown advised his followers: "You better get a gun. Violence is necessary—it is as American as cherry pie." King sensed that he had lost the argument. "I'll still preach nonviolence with all my might," he said, "but I'm afraid it will fall on deaf ears."[71]

8

SEX, DRUGS, AND ROCK 'N' ROLL

MILLBROOK: ACID DREAMS

At Millbrook beautiful people gathered to discover their inner selves, helped by a compound consisting of twenty atoms of carbon, twenty-five of hydrogen, three of nitrogen and one of oxygen. According to Timothy Leary, lysergic acid diethylamide, or LSD, would make the world a better place. His psychedelic home, on wooded land in southern New York State, was a lovely place to get high—even the name of the township, Millbrook, suggested tranquillity. From his pastoral laboratory sprang a chemically induced revolution of the psyche.

LSD acts by temporarily dismissing the sentries guarding the gates of consciousness. The unprotected brain is invaded by a mob of unprocessed stimuli on which it is unable to impose logic. "My eyes closed, the impressions became more intense," one tripper wrote. "The colors were brilliant blues, purples, and greens with dashes of red and streaks of yellow-orange. There were no easily identifiable objects, only convolutions, prisms, and continuous movement." Thoughts, reactions, sensations, and emotions collide, sometimes producing bizarre chain reactions and at other times combining in weird amalgams. Visual blends with spiritual: "The dominant impression was that of entering into the very marrow of existence. . . . It was as if each of the billion atoms of experience which under normal circumstances are summarized and averaged into crude, indiscriminate wholesale impressions was now being seen and savored for itself." Since the drug's effect is influenced by emotions and environment, the experience is infinitely varied and unpredictable. LSD provides a trip of unknown destination.[1]

Leary enthusiastically embraced the beneficial attributes of hallucinogens after he first munched some "sacred mushrooms" in Mexico. "I was whirled through an experience which could be described in many extravagant metaphors but which was above all and without question the deepest religious experience of my life." At a meeting sponsored by the Lutheran Church of America in August 1963, he revealed that up to 83 percent of subjects given LSD in controlled tests reported something similarly sacred. The day would come, he predicted, when psychedelic substances would be as widely used as Communion wine in churches around the world. God, he claimed, had created LSD to allow spiritual awakening.[2]

Psychedelics would supposedly unlock the gate to true freedom. Since freedom—be it political, social, or emotional—was the great aspiration of the Sixties, LSD, or "acid," became a sacrament in the decade's liberation theology. By facilitating freedom of thought, the drug was supposed to inspire enlightenment. Chris Rowley recalled signing on to "the powerful psychedelic belief in the goodness of people once they'd been turned on to their inner cortex." It followed that "if . . . everybody could take it together . . . the world would undoubtedly become a much saner and safer place because people would get hold of the problem." Leary taught that psychedelic drugs not only liberated the individual—they were also an effective way to attack conformity. In his *Psychedelic Review,* first published in 1963, he foresaw a comprehensive revolution through their universal use. "Make no mistake," he wrote, "the effect of conscious-expanding drugs will be to transform our concepts of human nature, human potentialities, existence." He dismissed fears of bad trips, blaming them on the insecurities of the "spiritual voyager."[3]

From these ideas came the decree: "Turn on, tune in, drop out"—a directive the Establishment found deeply disturbing and the counterculture consistently misunderstood. Turning on meant activating unused neural processes through drugs. The next step, tuning in, would follow automatically. It involved a harmonious interaction with the world, on levels impossible without drugs. Dropping out was a concept borrowed from Marcuse, who railed against the tyranny of technocratic society. Taking drugs was, in other words, an expression of the Great Refusal. "In a sense, I think, LSD and pot signifies the total end of the Protestant Ethic," argued Rubin. "Fuck work—we want to know ourselves. . . . The goal is to free one's self from American society's sick notions of work, success, reward, and status and to find and establish oneself through one's own discipline, hard work, and introspection." LSD, in other words, was a benign form of revolution which did not necessitate shooting people. Liberation could come entirely through the mind. All this tended to give indulgence the aura of noble purpose, encouraging the assumption that the individual tripper was engaged in self-improvement *and* contributing to social progress.[4]

The Establishment found the "drop out" bit threatening, fearing a drug-induced general strike, with no young people left to fill classrooms, climb the corporate ladder, or kill the Viet Cong. Those who dropped out, it was thought, might not be able to climb back in. On this point, Leary was characteristically vague. While he often presented drugs as a wholesale revolution, at other times he suggested that even a transitory experiment was beneficial. "Take a voyage! Take the adventure!" he urged. "Before you settle down to the tribal game, try out self-exile. Your coming back will be much enriched." In other words, worries about a mass exodus were greatly exaggerated. Advocates argued that LSD could provide a brief spiritual holiday for the part-time rebel, since even those who eventually joined the Establishment would find themselves improved by their sojourn on the other side.[5]

Allen Ginsberg, another drug disciple, saw LSD as a political statement, a spiritual tool, and a "refuge for a person in a plastic world." He wanted all healthy Americans over the age of fourteen to take at least one trip in order to perceive "the New Wilderness of machine America as it really was." "If there be necessary revolution in America," the poet proclaimed, "it will come this way." Rather like Leary, Ginsberg thought that LSD could promote the attainment of good karma by breaking down barriers to inner understanding. In other words, though the trip itself would be enjoyable, much more important was the spiritual destination. He was entirely serious, but, much to his dismay, those who took his advice inevitably simplified his message, lazily assuming that the drug by itself would bring good karma, without any intellectual effort required. For Ginsberg, acid was never simply recreation, yet for the multitude that is all it ever was.[6]

Drugs were part of the official uniform of the counterculture, a badge of belonging. The British radical Robin Blackburn admitted that taking drugs did not add up to "a hefty political statement," but he still felt that they were "among the things that defined a new Left, as against a traditional, rather stuffy old Left." Because they allowed escape from reality, they seemed the perfect elixir for a culture devoted to the abandonment of traditional values. It was easy, therefore, for the user to convince himself that he was engaged in meaningful rebellion. Due to their illegality, drugs were also a delightful way to defy authority—an enjoyable act of insubordination. (Though LSD was not outlawed in the United States until 1966, marijuana had been made illegal in 1937.) Michael Rossman, a Free Speech Movement activist, argued that drugs, by making the user a "youth criminal against the state," politicized a generation.[7]

Achieving personal salvation and social revolution, it seemed, was as easy as swallowing a tab. A simple drug could make one beautiful, creative, kind, committed, intelligent, and perceptive. One devotee argued that LSD

> was one of the best and healthiest tools available. . . . Acid opens your doors, opens the windows, opens your senses. Opens your beam to the vast possibilities of life, to the glorious indescribable beauty of life. . . . Drop down into your consciousness and see the pillars and the roots of the tree which is your personality. . . . You see what your hang-ups are; you might not overcome them but you cope with them, and that's an amazing advance.

"Better living through chemistry" proclaimed a popular psychedelic poster. Though no one overtly admitted it, drugs were an expression of the baby boomers' boundless faith in science—all the ugliness of the world could be made to disappear, thanks to a chemical compound synthesized in a laboratory. Every moment was an epiphany, greeted with wide-eyed stares and surprised exclamations. Druggies convinced themselves that they were improving the world, because their private world of psychedelic fantasy seemed so wonderful. Listening to the Grateful Dead, dropping acid, and staring at a lava lamp for hours could be passed off as both politically vital and personally enriching. LSD transformed utter banalities into pearls of wisdom, making everyone seem clever. "The depths of tedium that can be plumbed by sitting around half stoned, listening to people chatter moonily about reuniting humankind and erasing its aggressive instincts through Love and Dope, are scarcely imaginable to those who have not suffered them," wrote the art critic Robert Hughes. The folk stalwart Dave van Ronk agreed. "Why did people have to build these enormous, rickety, theoretical, bargain-basement, mystical structures to justify getting stoned?" he wondered. "I think that was a very middle-class rationalization. All those kids who were into drugs as a self-awareness trip always struck [me] as silly, just plain silly. And the mystical stuff that went along with it was boring."[8]

Radical politicos had difficulty deciding what to do about the drug culture. Some considered LSD the enemy of revolution—a true opiate of the people. "Flower power can't stop fascist power," one activist complained. "The hippies are making it easy for the fascists. Sniffing daffodils is playing it safe. Chanting isn't going to change anything." The Port Huron Statement, on the other hand, attacked the "hypocrisy of American ideals" and proclaimed a "commitment to social experimentation." To some, that seemed an endorsement of psychedelics. Carl Oglesby, onetime president of SDS, certainly thought so: "The acid experience is so concrete. It draws a line across your life—before and after LSD—in the same way that you felt that your step into radical politics drew a sharp division. . . . It's not necessarily that the actual content of the LSD experience contributed to politically radical or revolutionary consciousness—it was just that the experience shared the structural characteristics of political rebellion." For some radicals, dropping acid was as important as marching. During the Sproul Hall occupation at Berkeley in 1964, protesters openly took drugs as a bold act of defiance against university authority. The ultimate act of rebellion was to get high while sitting at the chancellor's desk rifling through his papers. Drugs became a ritual of rebellion.[9]

For all the hippies' talk of freedom, theirs was a totalitarian movement, ruled by the despotism of drugs. Their Utopia was accessible only to those who indulged and was intimidating to those who, for whatever reason, abstained. Drugs divided the world into hips and squares, with unbelievers ostracized. Like heathens judged by a peculiarly bigoted religion, those who did not indulge were cast from the kingdom. Drug disciples often took it upon themselves to convert the reticent, by trickery if necessary. "We used to have discussions about the ethics of whether it really was a good idea to put LSD in people's drinks, people who needed turning on, like politicians and so forth," John Willcock recalled. Sue Miles lived in constant fear of having her food spiked with a drug she did not welcome. "I never consumed anything in public for years."[10]

The Establishment reacted hysterically to what seemed a drug epidemic.

Government and the media conspired to fuel fear, in the vain hope that the young might be scared away from their chemical paradise. Newspapers competed with one another to produce lurid stories of LSD-inspired tragedy. One of the favorites concerned Stephen Kessler, a boy from New York who killed his mother but claimed to have no memory of doing so because he was tripping at the time. In January 1968, many papers reported that six undergraduates at a college in Pennsylvania were permanently blinded by staring at the sun while on LSD. The story turned out to be a complete fabrication, dreamed up by a Dr. Yoder of the Pennsylvania Institute for the Blind, who explained that he "invented [it] . . . because of my concern about the illegal use of LSD and other drugs."[11]

In 1967 the US Bureau of Narcotics claimed that "the cannabis sativa plant, while having very little medical use, is capable of profoundly disturbing the brain cells and inducing acts of violence, even murder." Two years later, the American Institute of Mental Health spent $100,000 on a TV advertising campaign warning about the dangers of drugs. The ads were narrated, rather appropriately, by Rod Serling of the *Twilight Zone*, whose air of gravitas gave credence to the horror stories. Young people were constantly warned that drugs were an escalator which always went down: the first step (marijuana) led inexorably to heroin and the doom of addiction. "Those who experiment with narcotics can become hopelessly addicted for life, become mindless vegetables, may even die," the wholesome crooner Pat Boone warned in his bestselling book, *A New Song*. "Some authorities claim that *one "trip" on LSD* may affect four generations of children born afterwards!! And, of course, we know that some children born to LSD users have had exposed spines, two heads, and other gruesome physical deformities." Druggies, however, were never likely to listen to an Establishment they were so determined to defy.[12]

Those who believed in the political power of drugs had a favorite mantra: "They have the atomic bomb and we have the acid . . . and we hope to win." If in retrospect the connection between drugs and politics seems illogical, it is well to recall that logic was often seen as an obstacle to enlightenment. Yet the weakness of the drug revolution was revealed whenever political engagement was encouraged. At a 1967 antiwar rally in Berkeley, Rubin found to his consternation that most of the audience had taken seriously his advice that dropping acid or smoking pot was revolutionary. Because they were all tripping, they had no tolerance for what he had to say about the war. They instead shouted at him to shut up and play some music. Rubin grew disgusted with the hippie hero Richard Alpert (also known as Ram Dass), who told followers that social and political transformation was as easy as taking a pill. "He was a sad sack, in my view," Rubin confessed. "Told [everyone] that the truth lies within, that change externally was impossible. . . . I'm getting increasingly bitter as I see the cop-out of youth."[13]

Thanks to Ginsberg, Leary, Alpert, and a host of others, the drug culture had become allied to Eastern religions, which in part explains the popularity of pilgrimages to Marrakech and Kathmandu (not to mention the ready availability of potent hashish). Rubin, however, saw how easy spiritual transformation had become—as easy as chanting "Om." Political commitment had given way to karma and mantra. Some people took these ideas seriously, but most of the time they were bastardized, diluted, and bumperstickered.

The flaw in Leary's revolution lay in the very personal nature of the LSD experience. "Feed your head," proclaimed the Dormouse in Jefferson Airplane's song "White Rabbit." Tuli Kupferberg, the Beat poet and member of the Fugs, proclaimed: "the *first* revolution is in yer own head." For most people who sought rebellion through drugs, the crusade went no further than their own heads. Taking LSD was a selfish act which allowed escape from reality. Politics, in contrast, is a group activity demanding engagement with reality, however discordant that reality might be. Drugs and politics, in other words, do not mix, as the Yippie Paul Krassner found: "The more I laughed, the more I tried to think about depressing things—specifically the atrocities being committed in Vietnam—and the more wild my laughing became." Devoted druggies, for all they might have fantasized about political change, found it difficult to contribute materially to change. Since a colorful and exciting world could so easily be entered through the escape hatch of psychedelics, there was little incentive to work hard to improve the real world.[14]

Many who took LSD thought that the mere act of doing so made them bona fide members of Leary's revolution. They did not understand that changing the world involved something more fundamental than simply turning on, and that dropping out actually required serious thought and effort. In the end, the drug rebellion was defeated by its own excess and by the contradictions inherent in the act of turning on. It is impossible to organize those whose first priority is self-indulgence. In this case, it was doubly difficult because the foot soldiers of this fantasy revolution were usually too high to take directions and the commanders too distracted to give them. Formal organization was exactly the "bad trip" that these revolutionaries were trying to avoid.

In Bed: Sex and Love

During a hippie happening in Central Park in 1969, a rape occurred. That, at least, was what a journalist saw. "A young long-haired girl stripped and danced in the warm rain. . . . Her friends stood by while a dozen young men raped her in an animal frenzy. Of the hundreds who gathered to watch, no one helped her, no one cared. Someone even stole her clothes. As she staggered around dazed and muddy, all she wore was a four letter word painted on her forehead: 'Love.'" Those who carried out the rape, and most of those who witnessed it, saw something different—an innocent, fun-loving "gang bang." "Raped?" Richard Neville asked with an air of incredulity. To him, the incident seemed a harmless example of sexual exuberance. Sex had become play, a group activity carried out in public. Some even called it a political act—an open attack upon repressive monogamy.

Interpretations differed because the Sixties had redefined sex, decoupling it from convention, emotion, and, most important, from love. The generation that convinced itself that "all you need is love" somehow managed to trivialize love's most transcendent expression.[15]

Missing from recollections of the incident in Central Park are the feelings of the person who mattered most: the woman at its center. In that sense, the incident was emblematic—the Sixties sexual revolution was most perplexing and painful for the women it affected most deeply.

Sixties sexual rebels seldom made love. They fucked. The word—vulgar, aggressive, rebellious, unfeeling—was the preferred term of the soldiers in the sexual revolution. It perfectly conveyed an act from which emotion had been excised and which was deliberately intended to offend the "uptight." Meaningless sex became a worthy aspiration. "One of my friends," Neville recalled, "when asked what he remembered most about his days behind the barricades, . . . replied, 'In one afternoon I fucked fifteen girls.'" Neville admired how his generation had completely transformed the dynamic between love and sex:

When boy meets girl, within minutes of drifting off to a comfortable location, boy can be happily splashing about in girl's cunt, both of them up each other's arses, sucking and fucking with compassionate enthusiasm. No more tedious "will she or won't she by Saturday?" but a total tactile information exchange, and an unambiguous foundation upon which to build a temporary or permanent relationship. The pot of gold at the end of the rainbow comes first; later one decides whether the rainbow is worth having for its own sake. If the attraction is only biological, nothing is lost except a few million spermatozoa. . . . If there is a deeper involvement, the relationship becomes richer, and so does the sexual experience. One way to a girl's mind is through her cunt.

Years later, Neville penned his own *mea culpa:* "Steeped in the sexism of the time and thrilled at slamming the citadels of repression, I said stupid things. Making love is still better than making war, but orgies are not the key to social justice."[16]

With monogamy no longer sacred, it was only natural that these pioneers should explore group sex. While far more orgies took place in the imagination than in reality, the phenomenon is deservedly associated with the Sixties. In some cases, group sex was intentionally institutionalized, performed out of duty more than desire. The Weather Underground, for instance, took politicized sex to the point of absurdity with their Smash Monogamy campaign. One member, Gerry Long, recalled a mandatory orgy: "I took the hand of this girl and exchanged a few pleasantries to give it a slightly personal quality, and then we fucked. And there were people fucking and thrashing around all over. They'd sort of roll over on you, and sometimes you found yourself spread over more than one person. The room was like some weird modern sculpture. There'd be all these humps in a row. You'd see a knee and then buttocks and then three knees and four buttocks. They were all moving up and down, rolling around." Awkwardness prevailed the next morning when members scanned the room trying to recall with whom they had coupled. One woman broke the silence: "I'm sure they have to do it this way in Vietnam."[17]

As with drugs, promiscuity constituted rebellion. Those who worshiped "free love" convinced themselves that they were doing their bit to overturn the repressive morality of their parent's generation. With no risk of AIDS, irresponsibility carried little cost—or so it seemed. Granted, there were sexually transmitted diseases, but they were treated with a quick dose of penicillin from a free clinic. Venereal disease became a certificate of service to the sexual revolution. "There was clap, but that was rather a badge, in those happy, far-off days," Nicola Lane recalled. "There was no stigma to having the clap."[18]

The mantra that "the personal is political" meant that heretofore personal acts took on deep political meaning. "[Sex] was part of my growth as a human being, as a woman and as a feminist," Andrea Adam decided. "That's how I justified it. I didn't want a revolution . . . but I wanted women to become equal and I wanted permissiveness. I wanted to have my cake and eat it too. I wanted a license to fuck around and I did fuck around." A respondent to a sexual survey expressed a similar attitude: "I could pick up a guy and take him home with me for one night, and it was my choice. I was in control and I didn't feel he would think I was a 'slut.' My men friends could accept my right and desire to do the same as them." Another woman confessed: "I had no guilt or second thoughts about having sex for sex's sake. If it felt good, I did it, and if someone excited me I'd make sure we ended up in bed."[19]

The great problem with Sixties-style sex was that liberation was so much more unequivocal for men than it ever was for women. The iconic films of the decade—like *Alfie, Room at the Top,* and *Saturday Night and Sunday Morning*—celebrated the sexual adventures of young males at the same time that they sneered at the possessive females who tried to curb their swinging. Women who sought meaning in sexual relationships were often dismissed as frigid. As the feminist Robin Morgan remarked, "A woman could be declared uptight or a poor sport if she didn't want to be raped."[20]

In 1967, Gershon Legman railed against the weekend radicals who, he felt, debased themselves, their partners, and the sexual act by pretending that every lascivious fantasy carried deep political meaning. In *The Fake Revolt,* he argued: "How does the sexual piggery of sharing your girl or your wife with three to six other guys at every end of her pink little anatomy show your rebellion against your parents' bad old world? How does it expose the backside of your parents' ludicrous ideal of 'togetherness' for you to stand in line to gang-bang your own undergraduate wife, with her ass baby-oiled and her teats tattoo-painted like Art Nouveau easter eggs?"

Legman's critique was all the more incisive because it came from a bona fide political radical who promoted sexual openness. A self-proclaimed eroticist, he understood that sex stripped of feeling was a grotesque thing more likely to wound than to please.[21]

"We put out, either because we wanted to be in love or because it was too much trouble to say no," Sue O'Sullivan recalled. "I'm amazed now when I think of the sexual acrobatics I performed back then with no plea-surable outcome—I could move my hips for hours, take it on all fours, fuck fast and furious, be on top, be stimulated by hand or mouth, grudgingly suck someone off and never a glimmer of the pleasure I felt in anticipation or in fantasy." "You had to fill so many roles," commented Nicola Lane. "You had to be pretty and you had to be 'a good fuck'—that seemed to be very important. I think it meant mostly that (a) you would do it with a lot of people, and also (b) that you'd give people blow jobs. . . . It was paradise for men in their late twenties: all these willing girls. But the trouble with the willing girls was that a lot of the time they were willing not because they particularly fancied the people concerned but because they felt they ought to." Lane felt "a huge pressure to conform to non-conformity." "A good many of us," the writer Judith Brown remarked, "are desperately screwing some guy because we think we should and wonder what our friends would think if we didn't."[22]

Reflecting on his experiences, one sexual rebel admitted: "If a sexual rev-olution is fucking a lot, then I did. If it incorporates things like the rights of women, I'm not sure if my involvement meant a damn thing." Rebels succeeded in transforming attitudes toward intercourse, but could not leave behind its emotional baggage. "We grew up with a fairly stultified, Victorian attitude to sexual relationships," Marsha Rowe reflected, "and the only way we had to deal with that was to do what we did; which was to lighten sex, to make it erotic play, to say that sometimes you will just want to sleep with each other. What we didn't see was that this would maybe stretch our emotional or physical resources till they would collapse." "Free love," one veteran of the revolution reflected, "is like a free lunch—there is no such thing." Sex could never be completely separated from love and possession. "There was a lot of misery," Lane recalled. "Relationship miseries: ghastly, ghastly jealousy, although there was supposed to be no jealousy, no possessiveness. What it meant was that men fucked around. You'd cry a lot, and you would scream sometimes, and the man would say,

'Don't bring me down—don't lay your bummers on me, . . . don't hassle me, don't crowd my space.' There were multiple relationships but usually in a very confused way; usually the man wanted it." John Lloyd agreed that it was impossible "to leap out of your own habits and upbringing into this blissful state where there were no hang-ups. . . . All the jealousies and tensions just grew exponentially." What resulted was the worst of all possible worlds: sex still came with a cacophony of guilt and jealousy, but it had lost much of its sublime meaning. Making sex less momentous did not remove its pain. "In spite of all the scientific advances," the novelist Beryl Bainbridge reflected, "there wasn't a pill invented, and we women knew it, that could stop one's heart from being broken."[23]

Like the drug craze, the sexual revolution has often been seen by those who participated as something fun at the time, but in retrospect rather embarrassing, bewildering, and sordid. Self-discovery could be distressing. There was, for instance, nothing more painful than being slapped in the face by one's own double standards. "It is an illusion to suppose that sexual promiscuity helps create personal freedom," Robert Hughes concluded. "There is a huge difference between the condition of freedom and that of accepting no responsibilities to anyone." The Beat poet Tuli Kupferberg agreed: "Politically, the movement was never able to affiliate with the vast majority of people who were not nineteen, who had problems with work and family, education. It said this was the life, when maybe it was just youth."[24]

Reaching a final verdict on the sexual revolution is impossible and pointless. Because sex remained a personal act (despite the best efforts of rebels to render it otherwise), its effect was far too varied to make sweeping conclusions possible. It also seems certain that the carnal Olympics described by some were by no means typical. "There was an awful lot of sex not happening, then being talked about afterwards as if it did happen," Steve Sparks felt. "I suspect that the great sexual freedom of the 60s was not as great as it would appear in retrospect."[25]

Those who look back often do so with binoculars, with the result that everything looks bigger. The tendency to exaggerate experiences, and even to manufacture them, is human. That tendency is most profound when sex is discussed, and especially when it is discussed by men. Measuring the true level of sexual promiscuity is therefore difficult. Studies by Albert Klassen and by the 1994 National Health and Social Life Survey have, however, shed light on the actual extent of promiscuity, mainly by diligently striving to include those who would not ordinarily respond to sex surveys. Klassen discovered that among women born in the 1940s, 37 percent entered marriage as virgins, while a further 31 percent had had sex, but only with their husband-to-be. In all, around half the cases of premarital sex among this cohort involved sex between the woman and her eventual husband. Only 3 percent of women had ten or more sexual partners.

Males were more likely to have sex before marriage. Klassen found that only 11 percent of those born in the 1940s entered marriage as virgins, which suggests that by the 1960s the ideal of premarital chastity was largely abandoned, among men at least. Another 12 percent, however, had had sex only with those women who eventually became their wives. That still leaves a significant 78 percent who were inclined to experiment, compared to just 33 percent of women.

Klassen found that the typical male born in the 1940s had six sexual partners during his life. That constitutes a doubling of experience compared to the generation born before 1900. In other words, the sexual revolution can be reduced to, in reality, an additional three sexual partners per average male. As an indicator of more permissive times, this statistic hardly seems earth-shattering, especially since the generation of men and women born in the 1940s enjoyed better health standards, increased longevity, and greater social mobility, not to mention a reduction in the threat of unwanted pregnancies and sexually transmitted diseases. This cohort also married later and therefore had more time between puberty and marriage to devote to experimentation. Generally speaking, however, experimentation did not usually take the form of rampant orgies and one-night stands—as folklore suggests. While premarital sex and cohabitation did rise during the 1960s, this did not mean the death of monogamy, no matter how hard some tried to smash it. Instead, the most common pattern of behavior was serial monogamy—a sequence of long-term relationships leading eventually to marriage when the right person came along. Sexual restraint remained a respected goal among both sexes, particularly after individuals fell in love.[26]

Something nevertheless had happened. In 1963, 80 percent of American women thought premarital sex was wrong. By 1975, only 30 percent did. In other words, a change had occurred, even if it was not enough to be called a revolution. The change was undoubtedly greatest for women, who could now admit to sexual desires and could openly pursue their fulfillment. "I find it very odd that women who are otherwise perfectly sensible say that the 'sexual revolution' of the sixties only succeeded in putting more women on the sexual market for the pleasure of men," Angela Carter reflected. "What an odd way of looking at it. This seems to deny the possibility of sexual pleasure to women except in situations where it's so hedged around with qualifications." One of the greatest achievements of the decade, she felt, was that "sexual pleasure was suddenly divorced from not only reproduction but also status, security, all the foul traps men lay for women in order to trap them into permanent relationships." In other words, while terrible abuses did occur, the enjoyment of sex was not one-sided. And those abuses were often illuminating, if only in retrospect. When taboos were pulled down, some awful truths were revealed, from which important lessons were learned.[27]

LIVERPOOL: THE BEATLES

In 1960, there were probably 400 pop groups in Liverpool, all competing for stardom. "Every teenager who could tap his foot in rhythm . . . had gathered three mates together, signed an HP [hire purchase] agreement with Frank Hessy's music store, and was rocking away with the requisite set of drums, amp, rhythm and bass guitars," Liverpudlian Maureen Nolan recalled. "I suppose the excitement stemmed from the belief that anything was possible, it was all within reach."[28]

For the Beatles everything was possible. They somehow rose above the fray, eventually becoming the most successful rock group in history. Their success can easily be gauged by record sales, but also by creative versatility—their ability to mold musical tastes. Their catalogue of songs recorded from 1963 to 1969 provides a perfect chronicle of the decade, a collective *Bildungsroman* moving from innocence to excess.

In 1962, however, the Beatles were just a rock-and-roll band singing simple songs. No one would have predicted their enormous success, nor how they would evolve. Granted, their manager, Brian Epstein, claimed they would be "bigger than Elvis," but managers always talk like that. The only ones supremely confident of the Beatles' potential were the Beatles themselves, or, more specifically, John Lennon. "We were smart heads," he explained in March 1966. "We knew from the start we were better." "I'm a genius," he boasted a few years later. "I've been like this all me life."[29]

For quite a long time, genius went unrecognized. John Lennon and Paul McCartney first played together on October 18, 1957, at the Conservative Club in Norris Green. Back then they were the Quarry Men, playing local dances, birthday parties, and church fêtes. What distinguished them was that they performed their own material, but this was hardly sufficient to send them shooting to stardom. For more than six years they played in a succession of dingy clubs, desperate for the big break. During a spell in Hamburg, they performed almost every day, sometimes for six hours at a stretch, to audiences of drunks, soldiers, and prostitutes. John survived the pace by swallowing amphetamines like candy. The artist Klaus Voorman, who first stumbled upon the band in Hamburg, recalled a music "so raw and so fresh, . . . the words of the songs were so simple and so direct and . . . they were so happy, having such a good time on stage. And that was what was missing in all these others I'd seen before. . . . The combination was such magic—unbelievable."[30]

Their break came when they met Epstein in late 1961. "They were fresh and . . . honest," he later recalled, "and they had what I thought was a sort of presence and . . . star quality." He cleaned them up, dressed them in smart clothes, and instilled discipline. "I don't think John particularly liked wearing a suit—nor did I," George Harrison recalled, "but we wanted more work, and we realized that's what we had to do." Being a hot rock band was not, however, a guarantee of success, since it was not yet clear that rock and roll would be the soundtrack for the new decade. The classic rockers—Buddy Holly, Jerry Lee Lewis, Chuck Berry, and the like—had faded away. Elvis had retained his popularity by turning smooth and soulful. Rockers, it seemed, had given way to wholesome crooners and balladeers like the Everly Brothers. In Britain, pop music was dominated by Cliff Richard, who proved that millions could be made from bland songs that couldn't possibly offend one's granny. Some music-industry insiders predicted that jazz would dominate, since it seemed to harmonize so well with the decade's taste for existentialism. "Groups are out; four-piece groups with guitars particularly are finished," Dick Rowe, an executive at Decca, told Epstein when he rejected the Beatles in 1962. Pye, Philips, Columbia, and HMV all decided that the group wasn't worth an audition.[31]

In came George Martin, a producer at Parlophone, an EMI subsidiary. Martin, like Epstein, could hear something special within the loud, rather raucous music. He also had the technical ability to refine the music to make it marketable. The Beatles wisely listened to Martin, at least in the early years. His first significant piece of advice was to drop their much-loved drummer, Pete Best, who had been with them for two years. Lennon, McCartney, and Harrison were sufficiently ruthless to cut Best loose. In came Ringo Starr.

Martin's bosses were not impressed, but he persevered, promising great things. Their first single, "Love Me Do" came out on October 5, 1962, and rose to a respectable seventeenth on the charts. The next song was "Please, Please Me," originally intended as a soulful ballad, in the manner of Roy Orbison. Martin took the song, added a harmonica at the start, upped the tempo, rearranged the vocal harmonies and ended up with something he guaranteed would top the charts. He was right. Released in mid-February 1963, it hit number one on March 2.

After waiting so long for success, the Beatles now found that it came in a torrent. Their next song, "From Me to You" went straight to the top, as did their first album, *Please, Please Me*. The British, most of them at least, fell instantly in love, thanks in part to Fleet Street's conspiracy of adoration. "You *had* to write it that way," one correspondent reflected. "You knew that if you didn't, the *Sketch* would and the *Express* would and the *Mail* and the *Standard* would. You were writing in self-defence." The Beatles had the good fortune to emerge at a time when the papers were full of stories about the scandals and mismanagement of Harold Macmillan's government. Journalists enjoyed contrasting the perfidy of an aristocratic Home Counties Cabinet with the fresh-faced, innocent vitality of the Fab Four from Liverpool. "We were the first working-class heroes in England to ever get anywhere without changing their accents," Lennon claimed, not altogether accurately. For a country eager to pretend that the class system was in decline, the Beatles were welcome folk heroes. "The Beatles are the first people to make rock 'n' roll respectable," wrote the *Evening Standard*. "They have won over the class snob, the intellectual snob, the music snob, the grown-ups and the husbands. . . . They appeal to the family and they appeal to the nation."[32]

Beatlemania gripped Britain. "I Want to Hold Your Hand," released at the end of November 1963, became the biggest-selling British pop record ever released, selling more than ten million copies worldwide. People weren't just buying records—they were also buying a huge variety of merchandise designed to keep the image ubiquitous. Hairdressers were inundated with requests for Beatle haircuts; stores sold out of Beatle wigs. After the group had stormed the citadel of British musical taste, other rock bands—Gerry and the Pacemakers, the Dave Clark Five, the Rolling Stones, the Kinks—swarmed over the ramparts. Those who had predicted the early demise of rock and roll swallowed their words and started moving to the beat. Except, that is, for Cliff Richard, who felt as if a rug had been pulled from under him. "Anyone who can shout can be a Beatle," he told the *Daily Mirror.*[33]

The most conspicuous, and worrying, manifestation of Beatlemania was the horde of screaming girls who went hysterical at the mere mention of the band's name. After a gig in Cambridge on November 26, 1963, the seats and floor were soaked with urine. Psychologists were quick to offer explanation. Some concluded that it was pent-up energy which the girls, had they been boys, would otherwise have released playing football or rugby. One English doctor surmised that "this sort of activity was important for young women because it made the pains of pregnancy easier . . . when they grew up and got married." In the *New Statesman,* Dr. David Holbrook argued that the Beatles were "a masturbation fantasy." Noel Coward, inclined to agree, compared Beatlemania to a "mass masturbation orgy," while the *Daily Telegraph* found disturbing parallels with Hitler's Nuremburg rallies.[34]

Most people, however, simply joined in the hysteria, though rather less loudly than the young female fans. One of the most surprising converts was William Mann, music critic for the *Times.*

> The outstanding English composers of 1963 must seem to have been John Lennon and Paul McCartney. . . . The slow sad song about "That Boy" . . . is expressively unusual for its lugubrious music, but harmonically it is one of their most interesting, with its chains of pandiatonic clusters. . . . But harmonic interest is typical of their quicker songs too, . . . so firmly are the major tonic sevenths and ninths built into their tunes, and the flat sub-mediant key switches, so natural is the Aeolian cadence at the end of "Not a Second Time."

The *Sunday Times* ballet critic, Richard Buckle, joined the chorus, calling the Beatles "the greatest composers since Beethoven." As Buckle and Mann demonstrate, the Beatles had made rock and roll respectable, something further confirmed at the 1963 Royal Variety Show. Lennon delighted the crowd with his introduction to "Twist and Shout": "Those in the cheaper seats, clap your hands, and the rest of you . . . just rattle your jewelry." After the performance, the Queen Mother called it "one of the best shows I've seen. . . . The Beatles are most intriguing." Around this time, the staid *Daily Telegraph* began to publish a weekly listing of the top ten pop records. Politicians eagerly told everyone how much they loved the Beatles. Some even resorted to incorporating lyrics into their speeches.[35]

Next stop America, where music industry executives were contemptuous of the possibility of the Beatles making it big, for the simple reason that no British group ever had. The Beatles bringing rock and roll to America seemed like Rover sending cars to Detroit. But then, on January 17, 1964, came news that "I Want to Hold Your Hand" had reached number one on the US charts, a nice prelude to the American tour, which was to begin on February 7. In no mood to gamble, publicists spent an unprecedented $50,000 on pretour publicity, all to the tune of "The Beatles Are Coming!" This included paying a crowd of teenagers to meet the group on their arrival at Kennedy Airport.

The moneymen needn't have worried. Everywhere the Beatles went, they encountered crowds of young people (mostly girls) desperately indulging in madness. Stores maintained a brisk trade in Beatle memorabilia and concerts were packed. A journalist described the reaction when the Beatles hit Los Angeles:

> For more than twelve hours the crowd has been gathering with quiet anticipation. Now, fifteen minutes before concert time, the Hollywood Bowl is surrounded. People crowding the security guards to get in, while the guards look less than amused and a little apprehensive. . . . Tiny teenage girls, dressed in their finest, wave half-heartedly at each other, not anxious to break the privacy of the mood created by the months of waiting for this day. No matter who they are, each of them feels that SHE is the one who will be seen by the Beatles—SHE is the one who will get backstage and see

them, talk to them. Of course they dress up! No—those aren't early-American night gowns (what kind of nut are you?)—that's the "London look." Don't you even read *Seventeen*?

An appearance on the Ed Sullivan show attracted 78 million viewers, the largest audience ever for any television show. By the beginning of April 1964, the Beatles had the top five spots on the American charts, twelve singles in the top 100, and the top two albums. Bob Dylan, observing the mania, reflected: "I knew they were pointing the direction music had to go. . . . It seemed to me a definite line was being drawn." The rock critic Greil Marcus has written that the arrival of the Beatles in New York "was the moment that took Bob Dylan out of his folksinger's clothes."[36]

By the beginning of 1966, a little over three years after their first hit, the Beatles had published around ninety songs which were recorded in nearly 3,000 different versions by artists famous and forgettable. They themselves had sold close to 200 million records, while sales of cover versions reached half a billion. Most pop bands would have reacted by offering more of the same. Had the Beatles done so, they would have quickly faded away, as most groups do. The shelf life of bands is seldom more than a few years. The Beatles, however, were ambitious, not for money and fame, but for immortality. For them, fame brought freedom, the freedom to let creativity bloom. "We are so well established that we can bring the fans along with us and stretch the limits of pop," McCartney told the *Rolling Stone* journalist Michael Lydon in March 1966. "We don't have to follow what everyone else is doing."[37]

Lennon felt that the Sixties was "a revolution in a whole new way of thinking. . . . We were all on this ship—a ship going to discover the New World. And the Beatles were in the crow's nest." Their artistic whims became international trends. They did not consciously reinvent themselves, nor did they try to anticipate trends. They instead allowed themselves to develop, safe in the knowledge that whatever they produced would sell. As McCartney explained: "We started off first with songs like 'Love Me Do,' with easy, easy, stupid rhymes that didn't mean very much, then we moved to a middle bunch of songs which meant a little bit more. Not an awful lot more, but they were a little deeper. There was no mystery about our growth; it was only as mysterious as a flower is mysterious. . . . We were just growing up." The freedom to improvise was strengthened by the group's conscious decision to retreat into the studio. Playing before a crowd of screaming fans quickly lost its appeal. "We don't progress," Harrison complained in July 1965, "because we play the same things every day, every time we play somewhere." By cutting back on concerts, and eventually stopping them entirely, the group was able to rejuvenate its artistic drive. It also meant that they no longer had to conform to audience expectations. "That's it," George Harrison said after their last concert, "I don't have to pretend to be a Beatle any more."[38]

The Beatles' immense popularity caused many people to endow them with an importance they did not deserve. Their every move was intricately analyzed. Off-the-cuff remarks, like Lennon's assertion that they were more popular than Jesus (which was true), were given far too much weight. As a result of Lennon's statement, thirty-five US radio stations banned their music and some communities staged record burnings. The Beatles were made into role models and then attacked for setting a bad example. Revelations about their drug-taking caused widespread condemnation, when in fact their behavior was no different from that of millions of ordinary young people from a similar background. "One thing that modern philosophy—existentialism and things like that—have taught people," Lennon protested in 1966, "is that you have to live now. You have to feel now. We live in the present, we don't have time to figure out whether we are right or wrong, whether we are immoral or not. We have to be honest, be straight, and then live, enjoying and taking what we can." That said, the Beatles occasionally got carried away with their own celebrity; they began to believe that they might indeed be gods worthy of worship. Lennon, for instance, expected the world to accept without question his credentials as a pacifist, despite the fact that he had a long history of violence, as his first wife, Cynthia, could attest.[39]

The peak was reached in 1967 with the release of *Sergeant Pepper's Lonely Hearts Club Band,* perennially judged the best rock album ever produced. After that came two years of bitter unraveling. The media circus grew unbearable. "If I could be a fucking fisherman, I would," Lennon told *Rolling Stone's* Jann Wenner in 1970. "If I had the capabilities of being something other than I am, I would. It's no fun being an artist. . . . These bastards are just sucking us to death; that's about all that we can do, is do it like circus animals." Their time at the top lasted about seven years—longer than most bands, shorter than some. But bands that stay together for a long time, like the Rolling Stones, do so in part because they don't evolve. Stasis brings stability. The great strength of the Beatles was their versatility, but that was also their greatest weakness. All that improvisation inevitably created conflict, as individual members tried to pull the band in different directions. The breakup left their fans crushed, but to them it seemed logical. "I wouldn't mind being a white-haired old man writing songs," McCartney told Lydon in 1966. "But I'd hate to be a white-haired old Beatle at the Empress Stadium, playing for people." "Always the Beatles were talked about . . . as being four parts of the same person. What's happened to those four parts?" Wenner asked shortly after their demise. "They remembered that they were four individuals," Lennon replied, with perfect simplicity.[40]

"Changing the life-style and the appearance of youth throughout the world didn't just happen," Lennon boasted. "We set out to do it; we knew what we were doing." The Beatles suited their era perfectly. The music industry back then was young, innocent, and open-minded. Improvisation was possible because success had not yet become an algebraic formula. The reason the Beatles phenomenon has not been repeated is perhaps that the industry today could never accommodate a band so creative, autonomous, and progressive. Pop culture in the Sixties, writes Ian MacDonald, was "intrinsically democratic." The Beatles "represented an upsurge of working-class expression into a medium till then mostly handed down to the common man by middle-class professionals with little empathy for street culture." They succeeded in changing so much within the industry, but in the end they could not transform the mechanics of power. "The only significant aspect of pop the Beatles failed to change was the business itself."[41]

Manchester: The Battle for Bob Dylan

The crowd in the Manchester Free Trade Hall on the night of May 17, 1966, confirmed that the times were indeed a-changin'. Half were folkies with rucksacks and sandals who had come to hear their Bob Dylan. The rest were rockers in jeans and black leather eager to hear *their* Dylan. A fair proportion, in other words, were destined to be disappointed. For quite a few, that concert was the Great Betrayal—the day Dylan went electric. In fact, he'd gone electric some time before, but the folk faithful were desperate to deny the truth. For them, seeing Dylan plug in his Stratocaster was like watching Pontius Pilate pass judgment on Christ. The amplified wail felt like nails piercing flesh. The rockers were delighted, but the folkies grew increasingly restless as each song underlined Dylan's treachery. And then came the most famous catcall in the history of rock: "JUDAS!"

Dylan, it seems, was waiting for this moment, this instant of attack in a culture war. He barked to the five members of his band: "Play Fucking Loud!" They responded with a terrifying, ear-splitting fusillade—a seven-minute barrage of "Like a Rolling Stone," played with intent to wound. "It was great," Sue Miles felt. "Half the audience pissed off—all the ones that had rucksacks." Among the angry was Keith Butler, who left in disgust. On the way out, he ran into the filmmaker D. A. Pennebaker. "He's a traitor," Butler muttered. "He wants shooting."[42]

The words "I was there" echo across the ages. The number who recall that seminal event, who felt personally the stab of betrayal, could fill the Free Trade Hall ten times over. That is the nature of rock legends: those who remember an event far exceed those who actually experienced it. Some attended later concerts on the tour; others heard stories from friends; still others saw film clips of the concert. Some even swear the betrayal occurred at London's Albert Hall, not in Manchester. Imagining that one had been present was easy, because the emotional challenge Dylan posed was so profound. With a few wailing notes, he had asked: "Where precisely do you stand?"

In truth, the question was first asked at the Newport Folk Festival on July 25, 1965, the day after "Like a Rolling Stone" had entered the American charts. Dylan came onstage with some members of the Paul Butterfield Blues Band, looking like an extra out of *The Wild Bunch*. He carried his Stratocaster like a Kalashnikov. On that occasion, the crowd was mainly folkies, as befits a folk festival. The new song (played badly) brought forth boos, tears, hysterics. A minuscule few cheered, but most sat in stunned silence. The air was thick with reproach: "Play folk music!" "Sell-out!" "Get rid of that band!" And epithets more abusive. Backstage, Pete Seeger, his face a deep purple, was shaking his head and kicking equipment. "I had never seen any trace of violence in Pete, except at that moment," one witness remarked.[43]

Dylan left the stage, dripping sweat and disgust. Peter Yarrow, of Peter, Paul and Mary, acting as emcee, promised that Dylan would return by himself, accompanied only by an acoustic guitar. The audience was instantly forgiving, urging him back, as if time could be stopped, as if 1963 could be relived. Dylan obliged with "Mr. Tambourine Man," then went straight into "It's All Over Now, Baby Blue." The message of the latter was inescapable. Nevertheless, that strange encore left many Dylan fans confused. Dedicated folkies saw it as a farewell, the end of the end, but those prepared to accept the fact that times might actually be changing felt the encore strangely hypocritical, an act of submission by a man who supposedly knelt to no one.

The Janus-faced concerts continued for a year, incorporating the entire tour of Britain. Dylan, it seems, wasn't actually being hypocritical; he was intentionally trying to stir his listeners, in the process asserting ownership of his music. Audiences mirrored the musical schism. They were, according to Greil Marcus, like "people who had come together to fight a cultural war. . . . Again and again fury coursed through the crowd like a snake, the wails of hate . . . beyond belief." Protests in the United States had been angry and raucous; in Britain, they were all that and political too. British folkies, cultural Stalinists, believed that music was an extension of class and that groups like the Beatles were capitalist—or, worse, fascist—plots. They were Luddites who believed that by shouting loud enough they could smash the machine of pop music. After the Manchester concert, people were recruited from the folk clubs to protest; disgusted departures were carefully choreographed. In Sheffield, someone phoned in a bomb threat. In Scotland, the demonstrations were allegedly organized by the Communist party—allegedly. Whether or not they really were is beside the point, since the allegation demonstrates that some people genuinely believed Dylan had sold out to capitalism. Political oppression, the rules said, could be expressed only in folk harmonies.[44]

Today, Dylan explains his transformation not as an evolution but rather as a conscious change of direction. "The folk music scene had been like a paradise that I had to leave, like Adam had to leave the garden," he wrote in his memoirs. "It was just too perfect. In a few years' time a shit storm would be unleashed. Things would begin to burn. Bras, draft cards, American flags, bridges, too— . . . The national psyche would change and in a lot of ways it would resemble *Night of the Living Dead*. The road out would be treacherous, and I didn't know where it would lead but I followed it anyway. It was a strange world ahead that would unfold, a thunderhead of a world with jagged lightning edges. . . . I went straight into it." That explanation was as obscure as the message in many of Dylan's songs, but understanding Dylan has never been easy. His fans, and indeed his detractors, have perpetually tried to simplify him, assigning him labels that conform to their preconceptions. He, on the other hand, has consciously defied understanding, the message being that to comprehend is to own, and he is not for sale. In this sense, the controversy sparked by his Stratocaster in 1965 is just one skirmish in the battle for Dylan.[45]

Dylan wrote "The Times They Are a-Changin'" in 1962, before most people quite realized that the times were changing. The world was grooving to Elvis, Chubby Checker, and the Everly Brothers, and here came a skinny Jewish kid from Minnesota, raising painful questions about the world and telling people that the answers were blowing in the wind. The world could handle a troubadour, but it was slightly uneasy about one who doubled as soothsayer. The really unsettling thing about Dylan was that he turned out to be right about so much—war, racism, hypocrisy, greed. He seemed to anticipate so eloquently all the problems of a troubled decade. No wonder, then, that people were quick to label him the voice of a generation.

What seemed a determined, perceptive voice back then was in fact a clarion of confusion. If there is inconsistency in Dylan's political message (and quite clearly there is), it is because he had not himself come to any decisions: "As for what time it was, it was always just beginning to be daylight and I knew a little about history, too—the history of a few nations and states—and it was always the same pattern. Some early archaic period where society grows and develops and thrives, then some classical period where the society reaches its maturation point and then a slacking off period where decadence makes things fall apart. I had no idea which one of the three stages America was in." "Dylan is to me the perfect symbol of the anti-artist in our society," the folksinger Ewan MacColl once remarked, wearing his contempt on his sleeve. "He's against everything—the last resort of someone who doesn't really want to change the world." That is the predictable wail of a man enslaved by his own pieties. MacColl sought purity in politics as much as in music. Dylan answered MacColl perfectly in "My Back Pages," his stinging rebuke to those who discovered truth before the age of majority. For that matter, MacColl was also beautifully rebutted when Dylan first picked up his Stratocaster, an act that evoked the elusiveness of certainty, not to mention the certainty of change. Principles, Dylan seemed to be saying, are the last resort of the small-minded. Rules are an obstacle to creativity. We all crave unambiguous truth but are forced to live in a world of nuance.[46]

"He was telling those who were listening a story they already knew," Marcus wrote, "but in a manner that made the story new—that made the familiar unstable, and the comforts of familiarity unsure." Marcus recalled a Joan Baez concert in 1963, when Dylan came onstage to sing a few songs:

> I barely noticed the end of the show. I was transfixed. I was con-fused. . . . This person had stepped onto someone else's stage, and while in some ways he seemed as ordinary as any of the people un-der the tent or the dirt around it, something in his demeanor dared you to pin him down, to sum him up and write him off, and you couldn't do it. From the way he sang and the way he moved, you couldn't tell where he was from, where he'd been, or where he was going—though the way he moved and sang made you want to know all of those things.

The confusion Dylan sowed made listeners all the more eager to label him. This wild force had to be put in a box—otherwise, he might blow apart the world. It seemed that Dylan was an extension of the chaotic times he sang about and that understanding him might bring order to chaos.[47]

"Dylan's talent evoked such an intense degree of personal participation from both his admirers and detractors that he could not be permitted so much as a random action," his friend Paul Nelson reflected. "Hungry for a sign, the world used to follow him around, just waiting for him to drop a cigarette butt. When he did they'd sift through the remains, looking for significance. The scary part is they'd find it." Dylan struggled against the labels and the ever-intrusive analysis of random action. He took refuge in lies—partly to construct an image that suited his aspirations, more to build a barrier behind which to hide. During his first interview at Colum-bia Records, he claimed he'd come to New York on a freight train, because that is what folksingers were supposed to do. Later he lied about his age, his birthday, his hometown, the jobs he'd once had. He claimed he was an orphan, when in fact he had two devoted parents. Sowing confusion was Dylan's way of retaining title to himself. He scattered lies as he walked through life, in order to put off the cultural bloodhounds trying to track him down. "Well I try my best / To be just like I am, / But everybody wants you / To be just like them." Though he sang about the world, he did not feel part of it. Writing meaningful songs was not an act of service, but a personal statement he felt he had to make because of who he was. "I knew that whatever I did had to be something creative, something that was me that did it, something I could do just for me."[48]

His intense desire for privacy caused him to object violently to the labels fans lovingly assigned, even when those labels were accurate. He hated, for instance, being labeled a protest singer: "Topical songs weren't protest songs. The term 'protest singer' didn't exist, any more than the term 'singer-songwriter.' You were a performer or you weren't, that was about it—a folksinger or not one. 'Songs of dissent' was a term people used, but even that was rare. I tried to explain later that I didn't think I was a protest singer, that there'd been a screwup. I didn't think I was protesting anything. . . . Rebellion spoke to me louder. The rebel was alive and well, romantic and honorable." Dylan derided the bona fide protest singer Phil Ochs as a "singing journalist." When asked for his political opinions, he reacted with outrage: "I'll bet Tony Bennett doesn't have to go through this kind of thing." A well-meaning journalist who asked him to name his favorite protest singers got the bitingly sarcastic reply: Eydie Gorme and Robert Goulet. On another occasion, he insisted he was just a "song-and-dance man." Fans of his topical songs wondered why he avoided singing specifically about Vietnam. Tired of being questioned as to whether that was omission or betrayal, he once snapped: "How do you know that I'm not, as you say, *for* the war?"[49]

Dylan deeply resented the fact that fame implied ownership, that fans expected something of him, assumed they were entitled to a piece of him. He recalled a telling incident at the Newport Folk Festival—one that seemed innocent at the time, but foreboding in retrospect:

> Ronnie Gilbert, one of the Weavers, had introduced me, . . . saying, "And here he is . . . take him, you know him, he's yours." I had failed to sense the ominous forebodings in the introduction. Elvis had never even been introduced like that. "Take him, he's yours!" What a crazy thing to say! Screw that. As far as I knew, I didn't belong to anybody then or now. I had a wife and children whom I love more than anything else in the world. I was trying to provide for them, keep out of trouble, but the big bugs in the press kept promoting

me as the mouthpiece, spokesman, or even conscience of a generation. That was funny. All I'd ever done was sing songs that were dead
straight and expressed powerful new realities. I had very little in
common with and knew even less about a generation that I was supposed to be the voice of. . . . I was more a cowpuncher than a pied
piper.

Dylan hated the way his songs became badges of faith, as if by revering
the artist, by listening to his music, one could demonstrate political credibility. "I really was never any more than what I was—a folk musician
who gazed into the gray mist with tear-blinded eyes and made songs that
floated in a luminous haze. Now it had blown up in my face and was hanging over me. I wasn't a preacher performing miracles."[50]

In the years 1962 to 1964, Dylan matured faster than most artists do in a
decade. The good causes he had so eloquently supported seemed not so
simple and clear by 1964; he was, as he announced in "My Back Pages,"
so much older then, so much younger now. He had also become disenchanted with liberalism, a disenchantment rudely and incoherently expressed when he accepted the 1963 Tom Paine Award from the Emergency
Civil Liberties Committee. During his speech, he mentioned that he saw
something of Lee Harvey Oswald in himself, a remark which, however profound, was far too ingenuous to be appreciated or understood at that particular moment. "Here were these people," he later remarked, "who'd been
all involved with the left in the Thirties and now they're supporting civil
rights drives. That's groovy, but they also had minks and jewels, and it was
like they were giving their money out of guilt. . . . These people at that dinner were the same as everybody else. They're doing their time. They're
chained to what they're doing." Dylan, like the black nationalists and student protesters, had become disenchanted with white liberal America's answer to social injustice, the answer that involved changing a few laws but
avoided the much more important, and painful, assumption of guilt.[51]

Dylan had shifted from the political to the personal—or, in a manner
the era would eventually appreciate, had made the personal political. He
was attacking conformity by showing that the movement associated with
change—the liberals—were as conformist as the rest. This was not just an
attack upon the political culture, but also an assertion of independence
from that culture. He was exhausted at having to act out a role America

had assigned him: that of the protest singer and mouthpiece for his generation. His music would henceforth become more introspective and obscure, as if to frustrate those in search of meaning. The songs were carefully constructed labyrinths designed to foil those who sought the artist at their core. Meanwhile, his public utterances took on a tone of absurdity, being calculated to confuse.

In a very personal sense, Dylan resented the way being famous meant that fans assumed they had open access to his life. He found himself imprisoned in his home in Woodstock, New York, having to resort to subterfuge and disguise just to be able to do the kinds of things ordinary people do ordinarily. "It would have driven anybody mad," he reflected years later.

> No place was far enough away. I don't know what everybody else was fantasizing about, but what I was fantasizing about was a nine-to-five existence, a house on a tree-lined block with a white picket fence, pink roses in the backyard. That would have been nice. After a while you learn that privacy is something you can sell, but you can't buy it back. . . . Demonstrators found our house and paraded up and down in front of it chanting and shouting, demanding for me to come out and lead them somewhere—stop shirking my duties as the conscience of a generation.

In retrospect, looking at the soundtrack that Dylan provided for the Sixties, one is struck by its brevity. The songs that most people associate with the era were produced before 1965. By the time the decade laid claim to Dylan, he had already given up on it. "Whatever the counterculture was, I'd seen enough of it," he later reflected. When the news began to conform so vividly to the images he had earlier constructed, he turned away in horror: "The events of the day, all the cultural mumbo jumbo were imprisoning my soul—nauseating me—civil rights and political leaders being gunned down, the mounting of the barricades, the government crackdowns, the student radicals and demonstrators versus the cops and the unions—the streets exploding, fire of anger boiling—the contra communes—the lying, noisy voices—the free love, the anti-money system movement—the whole shebang." Dylan, having entered adulthood, was experiencing the inevitable shrinking of his world that every good parent and husband feels. "I was determined to put myself beyond the reach of it all. I was a family man now, didn't want to be in that group portrait. . . . Outside of my family, nothing held any real interest for me and I was seeing everything through different glasses." However common that experience might be, it was not expected of one so holy as Dylan.[52]

Whether he liked it or not, Dylan was the voice of a generation, though not perhaps in the way people imagined. His admirers wanted him to express an opinion on every political controversy of the day, and treated his utterances as gospel, even when he was only joking. In a wider sense, however, his confusion and alienation, expressed so well in his songs, mirrored that of his generation. He tried to turn the personal into the political, but succeeded only in intertwining the two. Like his generation, he swayed between outrage at the injustices of his age and deep personal hurt at the betrayals felt in love. Like everyone else in the 1960s, and indeed in any age, he could never quite decide which—the personal or the political—was more important. That perhaps explains his longevity: had he kept to politics he would have quickly become a tiresome propagandist stuck in a bygone age.

In the aftermath of that fateful concert at Newport in 1965, Jim Rooney, a musician and critic, wrote:

> It was disturbing to the Old Guard. . . . Bob is no longer a neo-Woody Guthrie. . . . The highway he travels now is unfamiliar to those who bummed around . . . during the Depression. He travels by plane. . . . The mountains and valleys he knows are those of the mind—a mind extremely aware of the violence of the inner and outer world. . . . They seemed to understand that night for the first time what Dylan had been trying to say for over a year—that he is not theirs or anyone else's and they didn't like what they heard and booed. . . . Must a folk song be of mountains, valleys and love between my brother and sister all over this land? . . . The only one who questioned our position was Bob Dylan. Maybe he didn't put it the best way. Maybe he was rude. But he shook us. And that is why we have poets and artists.

Who was, and is, Bob Dylan? It's possible that his recent memoirs are just another attempt at obfuscation, more bricks in the wall of lies he has constructed to protect himself. But, then, perhaps it doesn't really matter who he was, since his importance lies in the effect he had. He unintentionally became what people wanted him to be. Leaving aside his objections, it is the prerogative of any generation to choose its voice. He was a revolutionary, though perhaps a reluctant one. Mouthpiece or not, he was a genius—one who had the good fortune to live in a time when genius could still be recognized, cultivated, and appreciated.[53]

WOODSTOCK: A FESTIVAL, YES; A NATION, NO

Dylan lived in Woodstock, New York. He tried to keep that secret, but failed miserably. The Woodstock Festival of August 15–18, 1969, started out as a pilgrimage to the home of the prophet, yet that idea proved unrealizable, partly because Dylan despised pilgrims but mainly because the locals didn't want half a million hippies destroying their Elysium. The name remained, but the concert actually took place in Bethel, New York, specifically on Max Yasgur's farm.

The idea had originated three years earlier, when investment broker John Roberts met lawyer Joel Rosenman on a golf course. Both were New England preppies; both, bored with their mainstream jobs. While lining up a putt, they started brainstorming about exciting things to do with their trust funds. Over the following year, they considered quite a few hare-brained schemes, but finally settled upon an outdoor rock concert after linking up with Artie Kornfeld, a young, penniless producer at Capitol Records. "It sounds feasible," Roberts said of the idea. "And not really all that risky. After all, how much trouble can you get into putting on a concert?"[54]

Naïveté provided a sturdy umbrella against a storm of trouble. Roberts and Rosenman agreed to put up $150,000 of their own money. Costs were estimated at $200,000. Since a crowd of 75,000 was expected, and admission pegged at $6.00 per day, logic suggested that the promoters would be rolling in money by the end. As it turned out, Kornfeld and his sidekick Michael Lang proved remarkably adept spenders, much of the money going for drugs and beautiful women.

Construction had already begun on a site near Wallkill when suddenly the local council refused a permit. Yasgur came to the rescue, offering his farm for $75,000. Then came a stampede of unanticipated complications. What were guests going to eat? Where would they pee? Where would all the sewage go? Who would provide security? Each answer cost money. In the midst of the planning, Abbie Hoffman summoned Rosenman to his office in New York City and threatened that his Yippie army stood ready to invade. "I don't give a damn about your platform, your agenda," he spat. "We're going to bring this whole thing down around your ears, and if you don't want us to do that you'll write a check." The word "extortion" was not mentioned, but it didn't need to be. Rosenman wrote a check for $10,000.[55]

Shambolic management was completely camouflaged by sublime music, atmosphere, and drugs. Woodstock was turned into a myth long before a single hippie trampled Yasgur's alfalfa. That myth was the creation of the organizers, who cleverly constructed a fantasy world in which a generation could indulge its dreams. That the myth eventually grew larger than the marketers ever intended is testimony to the imagination and sentimentality of the Sixties generation, a generation in thrall to the adolescent verities of rock and roll. Those who lived the fantasy, and those who pretended to do so, made Woodstock into the epiphany they wanted it to be. They saw an opportunity to celebrate the spirit of the Sixties, but also to graft that spirit onto the new decade fast approaching. The myth was deep and meaningful precisely because the Sixties dream was under assault.

By the eve of the event, 186,000 tickets had been sold, meaning that nearly $3.35 million dollars had been collected before a single note was played. That sort of money was enough to finance an impressive list of acts: Crosby, Stills, Nash, and Young; the Who; Jimi Hendrix; Jefferson Airplane; Creedence Clearwater Revival; the Band; the Grateful Dead; Janis Joplin; Santana; and others. Their renown, in turn, ensured success for the concert film, where the real money was made.

Artists were attracted not because it promised to be a magical musical event, but rather because the money was good. The Who, for instance, steadfastly refused to take the stage until they were paid, a wise precaution in an era when producers regularly fleeced musicians. Roger Daltrey, Pete Townshend, et al. took their money, performed their music, and then called it "the worst gig we ever played." It was made worse by the fact that Hoffman invaded the stage in the middle of "Tommy," seized Daltrey's microphone, and started ranting about a friend imprisoned for possession of drugs. Townshend kicked him in the rear and then hit him on the head with his guitar, sending him flying. "[It was] the most political thing I ever did," he later confessed.[56]

The promoters realized that Woodstock's appeal would be enhanced if concertgoers understood beforehand that they would not be prevented from smoking pot or dropping acid. The official attitude to drugs was utterly pragmatic: controlling a crowd of 200,000, some 90 percent of whom probably indulged, was impractical. Harmony, it was decided, would be easier to maintain if drug laws were momentarily ignored. Yet that harmony was quickly incorporated into the Woodstock myth—instead of something engineered by the promoters, it was assumed to have arisen from the assertive will of those who attended.

The organizers had anticipated an audience of 186,000; something closer to half a million showed up. That made it impossible to take entrance fees from everyone, so the managers gave up trying. That, too, was quickly incorporated into myth. The crowd assumed that capitalism had been overturned, that the event had been seized by the people. But the fact remains that the concert was already a financial success long before the capitalist gates were stormed. Gate-crashers pushed at an open door. Ironically, one of the main joists supporting the myth of Woodstock is the eponymous song by Joni Mitchell, who did not actually attend. Her manager feared that, due to the huge crowds on the roads, she would be unable to get out of Bethel in time to make a scheduled TV appearance to promote her latest record.

Mitchell's song suggests a paradise. The reality was something closer to carnage. Torrential rain turned the field into a fetid swamp, made hellishly worse by inadequate toilet facilities. Due to incompetence or greed, there was not enough food or water for a crowd of half a million. The *New York Times* reported: "The dreams of marijuana and rock music that drew 300,000 fans and hippies to the Catskills had little more sanity than the impulses that drive the lemmings to march to their deaths in the sea. They ended in a nightmare of mud and stagnation that paralyzed Sullivan County for a whole weekend. What kind of culture is it that can produce so colossal a mess?" On Sunday morning, the governor of New York State threatened to send in the National Guard. His decision to declare the festival a disaster area has been derided as politically motivated, but was in fact sensible, given the precariousness of the situation at the beginning of the third day. After a hasty meeting with concert organizers, who warned of riot if the site was cleared, the governor decided instead to deploy medical teams, a field hospital, and emergency food supplies, all flown in by US Army helicopters.[57]

Thanks primarily to their own incompetence, Roberts and Rosenman just barely broke even. The big money was made by the swindlers who fleeced them and particularly by those who produced the film. Newly emergent groups like Ten Years After benefited enormously from the publicity. Political radicals at first sensed that that was the whole point: they saw the festival as a clever scheme by the big record companies to sell their products. "Woodstock was absolutely appalling," Townshend reflected. "I hated every minute of it. I thought it was a disgusting, despicable, hypocritical event. The most incredible duplicity everywhere. It was a commercial event."[58]

Eventually, however, even hard-bitten cynics were anesthetized by myth. Dreamers decided that the concert was a brilliant demonstration of youth power. According to the Chicago underground newspaper *The Seed,* "Woodstock was . . . a massive pilgrimage to an electrified holy land where high energy communism replaced capitalism . . . because the immediate negative forces of the outside world, cops, rules, and prices had been removed or destroyed." "With a joyous three-day shriek, the inheritors of the earth came to life in an alfalfa field outside the village of Bethel, New York," *Rolling Stone* proclaimed. Before long, the myth was transformed into Woodstock Nation, a model of a harmonious community that would supposedly resonate around the world. One dreamer recalled: "Woodstock was a time of social change in human freedom and expression. . . . We learned not to be ashamed of our bodies in the nude, we smoked grass to expand our horizons with the music, we spent time with our kids and pets. . . . It was very much focused on a new standard for families. . . . That festival set the standard for peace, music, people, and expression and showed the world that all was not just violence and hatred. . . . It was LIFE!" "I realized I was part of something much bigger than myself, and my life changed," another concertgoer wrote. Woodstock Nation seemed the perfect ending to the Heavenly Decade. It represented the epitome of freedom—free love, free drugs, freedom from repression—even the music seemed free. Belief in a new dawn was reinforced by the guru Swami Satchidananda who arrived by helicopter to bless the crowd. "The future of the whole world is in your hands," he proclaimed. "You can make it or break it. . . . The entire world is going to know what American youth can do for humanity." Believing in Woodstock Nation was an act of faith so transcendent that all the hype miraculously vanished, along with the extortionately expensive hot dogs.[59]

The myth has been sustained by those who want to believe that something special took place in the Sixties, reached its apotheosis at Woodstock, and then was systematically destroyed by the forces of reaction, repression, and greed. Central to the myth is the image of order, politeness, and good humor. In the film *Woodstock,* a local resident remarks: "I was here when the crowd really came in. We expected 50,000 a day, but there must have been a million. And the kids were wonderful. I had no kid that wasn't 'Sir this' and 'Sir that' and 'thank you this' and 'thank you that.' Nobody can complain about the kids. This thing was too big, too big for the world. Nobody had seen a thing like this, and when they see this picture . . . they'll really see something." In fact, that was clever editing. For every local who praised the event there were probably a half dozen who hated it. "Do you want me to explain it in plain English?" one remarked. "A shitty mess—it's a disgraceful mess."[60]

"The older I get," one concertgoer recalls, "I realize I was part of something with . . . far-reaching significance. . . . The whole time reflected something of great almost biblical importance." The Woodstock myth is all the more powerful precisely because the spirit that inspired it dissipated so quickly. Suspended over an abyss of reality, believers cling to vines of sentiment, stubbornly chanting manufactured memory and pop doctrine. "Woodstock was not a concert," one roseate rememberer attested years later. "This was a coming together. . . . The music was just the background music to our lives. We were doing what great men like our High Priest Timothy Leary had led us to do."[61]

However bright the Woodstock myth, it was simply a myth. The festival itself was a flash of emotion confined by time and place. What resonated outward was simply hype. The stage had hardly been dismantled before exploiters invaded. "No sooner was there a Woodstock than there were a million natural-yogurt companies cropping up," John Sebastian, lead singer of the Lovin' Spoonful complained. "I think we are devourers of our own culture and cannibalized a lot of things that could have happened out of Woodstock. A media culture can absorb and regurgitate stuff so fast that it loses meaning almost before it's out of the pot. Somehow every mood that was created was suddenly turned into a marketable item." The dreamers who insisted on seeing the festival as a millennial vision were forced to ignore the fact that a large proportion of the crowd had to leave paradise early on Monday morning, long before Hendrix finished his set, in order to get to work on time. They were nine-to-fivers for whom hippie was hobby, not way of life. Yet their desire to believe was so strong that, many years later, they would be able to recall every note of Hendrix's soul-shattering rendition of the "Star-Spangled Banner," even though, at the time, they were actually caught in an ugly traffic jam headed south.[62]

9

EVERYBODY GET TOGETHER

SHARON: YOUNG AMERICANS FOR FREEDOM

Students for a Democratic Society began, rather appropriately, at a United Auto Workers retreat in the working-class state of Michigan. Its alter ego, the right-wing Young Americans for Freedom, began, equally appropriately, at William F. Buckley's leafy estate in Sharon township, in the gentrified state of Connecticut. Because the staid YAF does not harmonize with the popular image of the 1960s, supposedly a decade of exuberant rebellion, it has often been ignored in studies of the period. Yet on many campuses conservative activism was more widespread and popular than the left-wing variety. YAF also had more identifiable long-term influence, given the direct line from its radicalism to the neoconservatism of today.

In 1961, Medford Stanton Evans, a disciple of Buckley, boasted that "the Conservative element on . . . campus is now on the offensive; it is articulate, resourceful, aggressive. It represents the group which, in fifteen or twenty years, will be assuming the seat of power in the United States. That is why, in my estimation, it authentically represents the future of the country." This was not simply conservative hype; American news magazines confirmed that a tidal wave of conservativism was sweeping across college campuses, largely in reaction to Kennedy's election. *US News and World Report, Newsweek,* and *Time* all reported a right-wing revolt, pointing out that campus conservatives were not merely echoing the political prejudices of their parents. For many, in fact, turning right was rebellion. "My parents thought Franklin D. Roosevelt was one of the greatest heroes who ever lived," Robert Schuchman, chairman of YAF, remarked. "I'm rebelling from that concept." A young conservative at the University of Wisconsin chimed: "You walk around with your Goldwater button, and you feel the thrill of treason."[1]

Buckley wanted YAF to act as a counterweight to the supposedly left-wing bias of universities, which seemed to threaten the American way of life. While at Yale in the late 1940s, he discovered "an extraordinarily irresponsible education attitude that, under the protective label 'academic freedom,' has produced one of the most extraordinary incongruities of our time: the institution that derives its moral and financial support from Christian individualists and then addresses itself to the task of persuading the sons of these supporters to be atheistic socialists." By 1960, Buckley had gathered together a core of conservative purists to whom radical-right students could look for guidance. Students would provide the energy, but their mentors would provide direction. Aware of the dangers of youthful immaturity, Buckley had in mind a highly controlled organization able to impose a consistent political line, with power the predominant objective. Recognizing Buckley's threat, the *Nation* warned in 1961 that while the left was concentrating on issues like civil rights, the right was busily building a movement.[2]

YAF's charter—"The Sharon Statement"—was drafted in Buckley's living room on September 11, 1960, by Evans. "In time of moral and political crises, it is the responsibility of the youth of America to affirm certain moral truths," the statement proclaimed. Foremost among these truths was free will. In the emphasis placed upon freedom, YAF and SDS had much in common, but while SDS also promoted equality, YAF never did. YAF maintained that "political freedom cannot long exist without economic freedom." The free market was endorsed as "the single economic system compatible with the requirements of personal freedom . . . and . . . the most productive supplier of human needs."[3]

Big government threatened freedom. "When government interferes with the work of the market economy, it tends to reduce the moral and physical strength of the nation," the statement declared. "When it takes from one man to bestow upon another, it diminishes the incentive of the first, the integrity of the second, and the moral autonomy of both." The biggest threat to freedom was, however, "the forces of international Communism." The protection of liberty at home required the defeat of, "rather than coexistence with," the Communist menace. Thus, foreign policy became an extension of domestic affairs. "American foreign policy must be judged by this criterion: Does it serve the just interests of the United States?"⁴

"What is so striking in the students who met at Sharon is their appetite for power," Buckley later confessed. For them, politics was not a game but an intensely serious crusade. They equated conservatism with maturity and therefore saw themselves as "older" than their fellow leftist students, whose cultural rebellion seemed trivial. The generation gap hardly bothered them; materialism and conformity seemed worthy ideals. As a result, YAF did not waste its time on parochial issues relating to university life. Dissent was expressed in exclusively national and international terms. Nor did they court publicity, since publicity invited attack. In stark contrast to Hoffman and Rubin, YAF organized in secret and zealously preserved anonymity. "We never got the publicity and we weren't interested in that," one activist maintained. While the left sought immediate solutions to distinct social problems, the right concentrated on a gradual assumption of power which would eventually allow them to exercise authority in all realms. Some activists formulated five-year plans; others, more realistically, thought in terms of a conservative millennium decades ahead.⁵

Buckley provided the iconic inspiration, but much more important was the practical guidance provided by *National Review* publisher William Rusher and the conservative fundraiser Marvin Liebman. Since age was no barrier to trust, YAF members venerated "old fogeys" like Arizona senator Barry Goldwater and the novelist John Dos Passos. Rather predictably, the Establishment loved YAF, generously providing financial and moral backing. Benefactors like Charles Edison and the manufacturer Herbert Kohler opened their wallets, so much so that Rusher was eventually driven to criticize the "rich-uncle" tendencies which seemed to encourage profligacy. Friends in high places also ensured that YAF never had difficulty finding venues for rallies. While SDS struggled to get a parade permit in Ann Arbor, YAF was booking (and filling) Madison Square Garden.⁶

At its inception, YAF espoused an instinctual conservatism, untainted by pragmatism. For this reason, members revered Barry Goldwater. His proclamation at the Republican convention in 1964 that "extremism in the defense of liberty is no vice" seemed written for YAF. Besotted with Goldwater's purity, they assumed that the rest of the nation would be equally smitten. For that reason, his landslide defeat left them heartbroken. Lessons were nevertheless learned. Most members concluded that fundamentalist crusades do not harmonize well with electoral politics. They also learned that an ideology, no matter how perfect, still needs an attractive voice. Goldwater's problem, they decided, was not so much his ideas but his personality.[7]

The lessons of 1964 explain the enthusiasm with which YAF embraced Ronald Reagan, first in the 1966 California gubernatorial campaign and then, two years later, during the Republican presidential campaign. On the surface, Reagan was not a natural YAF standard bearer, since his populism contradicted the intellectual elitism of the movement. But while Reagan lacked ideological purity, he was indisputably a formidable candidate. YAF's enthusiasm demonstrates that, in contrast to students on the left, the group understood the importance of winning elections and was not irresistibly attracted to the purity of lost causes.

That said, the right had its share of ideological purists. The belief in minimal government and the worship of liberty encouraged some YAF members to espouse a rarefied form of libertarianism, opposing not only welfare and the income tax, but also drug laws and the draft. The "Tranquil Statement," produced by one such faction, might easily have been mistaken for an SDS document:

> Whenever any form of government becomes destructive of . . . life, liberty, and the pursuit of happiness, . . . it is the Right of the people to alter or abolish it, and to institute new government. . . . When a long train of abuses and usurpations (draft, drug laws, military industrial complex, police terror, taxation, imperialism, sex laws, and government), pursuing invariably the same object, evinces a design to reduce [the people] under absolute despotism, it is their right, their duty, to throw off such government, and to provide *New Guards* to their future security.

YAF, like every other Sixties political movement, had its share of renegades. Holding a party line was the great challenge of the decade. At the 1969 YAF convention, banners like "Fuck the Draft," "Kill the Commies," "Fuck the State," and "Sock it to the Left" reveal the leadership's difficulty in maintaining conformity. In contrast to SDS, the strength of YAF lay in its ruthless willingness to oust those who jeopardized the quest for power. After that convention, libertarians were purged.[8]

College campuses provided fertile ground for right-wing politics. According to a poll conducted by *Newsweek* in 1967, the most popular student political group was the Young Republicans, which had four times as many members as SDS. During that year, 49 percent of college students surveyed considered themselves "hawks," while only 35 percent were "doves." At the 1968 election, Americans in their twenties preferred Nixon to Humphrey by a margin of 39 percent to 30 percent. Twenty-five percent supported George Wallace, the most enthusiastic response he received from any age group. All this suggests that YAF might easily have been even more successful than it was, if not for the fact that student apathy (the same demon encountered by the left) prevented political inclinations from being converted to activism.[9]

"The left battled for the campus; the right won politics," one YAF member reflected on his years of student activism. Despite its conservatism, YAF was not a collection of squares. They demonstrated that one could not automatically guess a person's beliefs by what he wore, the length of his hair, or the music and drugs he enjoyed. Many wore the uniform of the counterculture, tasted its pleasures, and shared its craving for freedom. What distinguished them was that they saw no need to indulge in left-wing politics in order to be part of the Sixties ethos and did not confuse the personal with the political. They accepted sex and drugs as simple pleasures, instead of investing them with profound political meaning. Ironically, they occupied a political position, as students, to which a good many of their campus adversaries would eventually gravitate, after their brief flirtation with socialism. As one activist who later served in the Reagan administration remarked: "My political views are no different than they [once were], but there has been a change [in] the mainstream—not that I went to the mainstream, but the mainstream came to where we were. . . . Before, I was on the outside; now I'm in the middle." As Evans rather perceptively remarked in 1961, "Historians may well record the decade of the 1960s as the era in which conservatism, as a viable political force, finally came into its own."[10]

LONDON: LOVE IS ALL YOU NEED

At some point in 1967, a gang of drugged-up anarchists from the London Street Commune, backed by some really frightening Hell's Angels, raided the offices of *IT* (*International Times*), hallowed journal of the British counterculture, intent upon seizing control. Chanting "Property is theft!" they ran amok for most of an afternoon. The invasion plunged the *IT* staff into a deep moral dilemma. Many believed that property was indeed theft, and had argued as much in their paper. After frenetic debate, staff members decided that the principle did not apply to one's own property. Unfortunately, they lacked the muscle to eject the invaders. An agonizing argument ensued over whether the police—hated agents of oppression—should be summoned. Eventually, principles gave way to pragmatism and the cops were called. Order was restored.

The dilemma encapsulates the nebulous nature of the British counterculture, a reactive movement based more on feeling than on logic. If the counterculture seems riddled with contradictions, that is because its "sacred" principles varied widely, according to time and circumstance. "The political character of the underground is . . . amorphous," wrote Germaine Greer in 1969, "because it is principally a clamor for freedom to move, to test alternative forms of existence to find if they were practicable, and if they were more gratifying, more creative, more positive, than mere endurance under the system." To call this amorphous body a movement suggests order, purpose, and organization. It was simply an alternative way of living.[11]

British hippies discussed "ideology," and occasionally quoted Marx, Sartre, or Camus, but the talk was like clouds of smoke from a well-rolled spliff, endlessly spiraling in the air. The one unanimous ideal was "a better quality of life," which did not involve gainful employment. "I think it was probably the first time the children went to college without any idea of getting a job at the end of it," said Sue Miles. "It had never occurred to me what I was going to do, never." The fellow traveler Richard Trench remembers wanting the world "to be sort of left-wing socialist, but I didn't want to work. . . . Everybody would work less, everybody would become middle-class like us, everybody would read poetry like us."[12]

Indolence made for an uneasy relationship with genuine politicos who worked hard for revolution. The radical historian E. P. Thompson, for instance, derided the counterculture as "psychic self-mutilation, . . . self-absorbed, self-inflating and self-dramatising." Hippies replied that true liberation could only come through forsaking politics. "Politics is pig-shit," John Hopkins argued. "What we were doing was political, but it was not party politics. It was alternative politics." The movement was defined by what it was not, Rosie Boycott felt. "There would be no taxes, there would be no Conservative party, there would be no forcing people into doing what they didn't want to do, there would be no discrepancy between rich and poor." Simply by doing whatever they wanted, hippies hoped to "prove that there was a different way of running the world."[13]

Logic was oppression, seriousness a disease. Hippies sincerely believed that what was sordid or soul-destroying could be willed out of existence—ugliness could be made to disappear simply by wishing for a better world. Nicola Lane imagined "a sort of Tolkienesque landscape where industry and nuclear weapons and nasty politicians would somehow fade away under the powerful vibes of the good people." A vague millenarian philosophy was constructed from romantic myth—an airy concoction which had as much historical foundation as a fairy castle. The vision started from the assumption that, in simpler times, people had been happier and work had not been oppressive. Jeff Nuttall envisaged "some kind of a Stone Age village. . . . People would build their own houses imaginatively and live there sophisticatedly and in a literate way and with a total permissiveness and . . . they would live with their hands and with their minds and they would not be dictated to by anybody selling them anything and they would not welcome anybody preaching to them." A storybook world was built from the bricks of desire and the mortar of innocent imagination. "We are born into a world where work is considered ennobling, unlike the lucky ancient Greeks, for whom a life of leisure was essential for a man of wisdom," wrote Richard Neville in his hippie manifesto *Playpower*. "It was during his full-time leisure that man could cultivate his mind and seek the truth. Work was considered degrading. It was something done by slaves. As the centuries rolled by, we *all* became slaves." Neville never quite explained who would clean the toilets and remove the rubbish in his world free of work.[14]

Hippies espoused an alternative culture, but in reality created a parallel universe in which power, though differently distributed, was still crucially important. Labels changed but human nature did not. Middle-class values proved difficult to jettison. Thus, in common with the "straight" world, the counterculture had its own restaurants, bookshops, record stores, newspapers, art galleries, clothing stores, theaters, concert halls, cinemas, travel agencies, and people ripping each other off. Ambitious entrepreneurs did precisely what they might have done in the straight world, while convincing themselves they were rebelling. No surprise, then, that when the party ended, the elite had little difficulty rejoining reality.

Only the middle class could pretend to ignore money. "We weren't really living in Edge City," Jerome Burne thought. "We all had parents and backup systems, which the working-class people didn't have." Pretense was sometimes difficult, however, since pleasure carried a price. Hippies who eschewed government and politics happily lived off the welfare state, convincing themselves that accepting the dole was a bona fide act of rebellion against capitalism. When funds ran short, they resorted to shady practices to keep reality at bay. They stole, dealt drugs, and fleeced their fellow travelers.[15]

One of the most disappointing aspects of the underground, for those who sought a perfect world, was the way it mirrored British class divisions. "There were stars, there were walk-ons and there were cannon-fodder," Peter Roberts recalled. Andrew Bailey found that those at the top of the hippie heap freely exploited their celebrity:

> I was slightly in awe of the underground heavies like Richard Neville and Germaine Greer. You'd meet them, you'd be in the same room in parties, but they were stars. The underground had a star system exactly as did pop music and films and everything else. The stars knew what they were doing: they were as fundamentally insincere as everybody else. They knew what people wanted them to be, to look like, and to say and they dutifully went ahead and performed that task for the pleasure of television and the rest of the media.

"There were rich people and there were poor people and there were people in the middle," Cheryll Park recalled. "Elitism took the whole movement over. . . . If you were an ordinary person who lived in some suburb, you had no chance at all." Jonathan Park found the cynicism demoralizing. "The elitism meant that I was always an outsider, I had no starry nature, no wild wit or gift of the gab, lots of money or leather trousers." Another camp follower recalled: "The prevailing memory I have of the 60s is the fear of being uncool."[16]

While cynicism lurked beneath the surface, innocence was official policy. Hippies tried to ignore capitalism, even though they still had to buy goods and exchange money. Their naïveté rendered them easy prey. Crooks camped out on their perfect island, entrepreneurial sharks swam offshore and vultures circled overhead. "Movement people steal from each other more than from Harrods," Neville reluctantly discovered. Craig Sams tried to run a macrobiotic cafeteria on an honesty system, but found that hardly anyone voluntarily paid. Miles tried to run an alternative bookshop, but was plagued by hippies who would run off with handfuls of books, shouting "Books should be free!"[17]

The underground eventually fell victim to its own success. The quest for more outrageous and magnificent happenings catapulted countercultural impresarios back into the real world. "You had to get record company support, you had to build stages, you had to pay for security, you had to pay for police," Peter Jenner recalled. Principles gave way to profit. "That's when they started doing things with Richard Branson, loathsome people like that who started living off the underground, pretending to be hip." Clever entrepreneurs like Branson and Felix Dennis spotted opportunities and moved in for the kill. Sue Miles recalled Tony Elliott coming into the *IT* office one day and announcing that he wanted to do a listings magazine. The general reaction was "Hey, cool"—everyone instantly agreed that he could have what had previously been a neglected section of the magazine. What they failed to realize was that Elliott was a corporate raider dressed in a kaftan. He stripped a loss-making magazine of its one marketable product, renamed it *Time Out*, and made millions. "What was important was that we weren't exclusively dedicated to the alternative society," Elliott later confessed with admirable honesty.[18]

A movement founded on novelty discovered it could not keep pace with the constant need to renew itself. Before long, the alternative became orthodox. What started as a carefree adventure in cultural exploration deteriorated into mindless hedonism: mind-numbing drugs and meaningless sex. More fundamentally, hippies found that politics could not simply be ignored, especially not in the highly charged political year of 1968. Ignoring politics was not the same as abolishing it; changing the world was a bit more difficult than lighting a bong.

The idea that "all you need is love" heightened the appeal of the counterculture but also ensured its demise. It seemed so simple, beautiful, and true that the sordid, cruel world could be purified by an innocent outpouring of love. The light-show impresario Mark Boyle saw how flimsy faith doomed the movement: "I was angry with them for not defining what they meant by 'peace' and 'love.' I said, 'Everyone through all time has been for peace and love—you've got to define what you mean.' But of course they couldn't define what they meant, because that would have split the whole thing apart. And the whole consensus among that group of people was entirely based on the fact that everyone was in favour of peace and love." The counterculture was eventually crushed by its own contradictions. The world simply refused to conform to hippie naïveté. "Were society to be organised according to the rules that we were . . . mapping out, we might have been horrified," the journalist John Lloyd reflected. "Only afterwards [did] you realise how exploitative it was, how far you were following your own games, your own pursuit of your own desires."[19]

The greatest success (and most serious harm) of the underground was that it convinced so many young people that flowers and love could indeed change the world. "She's leaving home," the Beatles sang. Parents who had given their children everything watched helplessly as they left home in search of the holy hippie grail. "The people who suffered," wrote David Widgery, "were . . . those who hung on to the myths and ended up in the squalid rat-infested squat shooting up. If people as a result of reading *Oz* decided to leave their parents, hitchhike to London and then ended up a mess, the underground, despite its occasional pretensions, couldn't provide a welfare state. And if you're going to have a new society based on new values, you need new social institutions." A lot of people had a lot of fun and emerged in one piece at the end of their brief period of indulgence. For them, no harm was done. But some never returned home; others never returned to sanity.[20]

Some people lived the Sixties; others merely lived through the decade. In London, where the beautiful people congregated, it was easy to feel part of something. But the hip crowd was a small group from whom fantasy radiated outward and flattery inward. In 1969, a reader from the wilderness wrote an achingly accurate letter to *Oz:*

> Reading your mag makes me feel very small. It's all right for the Living Theatre to take off their clothes, but I've got a few nasty spots which I'm very embarrassed about. The fucking scene out here is nonexistent, we have to do it with our hands. . . . The smoking scene? One of the most efficient drug squads in the country. Then there was the time that I turned up at the Arts Lab to see the Dylan

film [*Don't Look Back*] and couldn't afford it. Fifteen bob for a fucking film. I was thrown out by some irate trendy who kept muttering about royalties. I thought the idea of doing your own thing would be cheap and for everybody, not just cliques. I can't play guitar, write poetry, act or sing, and my understanding of politics and economics is very limited. So what happens to me in the great cultural revolution? In my nineteen years I've had three women, a nervous breakdown and some bad education.

Can't you people realise that twenty miles north of *Oz*, *IT*, Arts Labs, etc., NOTHING HAS CHANGED. What's the fuss about? Do I hear smug laughter?

As a cultural revolution, the Sixties was predominantly white, middle-class, and urban. Miles from the epicenter, the great seismic shifts were felt as tiny tremors. An awareness of what was happening came only from reading newspapers and watching television, not from taking part. "Apparently all hell was breaking loose," Terri Quaye, a member of Britain's black community, recalled, "but it made little difference. . . . The release from society's constraints only applied to the young whites, and as with most phenomena, those enjoying it would find it hard to believe that it was of little consequence to those only permitted to be onlookers." In 1959, the novelist Beryl Bainbridge was a twenty-five-year-old mother of two living in Liverpool. Motherhood kept her from taking part in the cultural upheaval. "The music and the Purple Hearts passed me by, and it wasn't until I came to London and Churchill had died and the Kennedys had both been butchered that I woke up to the years I was living through."[21]

San Francisco: It's Free Because It's Yours!

In 1966, thousands of young people went to San Francisco with flowers in their hair. The city could accommodate a small community of harmless nonconformists congregating around the intersection of Haight and Ashbury. It could not, however, adjust to hordes of wannabe hippies—penniless runaways armed only with their fantasies. The "invasion" occurred because of the publicity given to the hippie phenomenon in songs and in the media. Old-timers joked about "bead-wearing *Look* reporters interviewing bead-wearing *Life* reporters." "The media was publishing all these articles about the Haight," Peter Coyote recalled, "seducing and attracting young people to come out there. . . . The city was capitalizing on it and taking no responsibility for it; telling all these kids . . . to get lost."[22]

Coyote helped found the Diggers, self-appointed guardians of the hippie generation. "Our feeling was that they were our kids. . . . This was America . . . We started feeding them and sheltering them and setting up medical clinics, just because it needed to be done." Charity was not the objective but the by-product; Diggers were trying to create a new society in which suffering would not occur. Like the Provos, they adhered to a philosophy centering on the concept of "free," which had two intertwined meanings. "Free" meant free of charge, but also free of restraint. That which was free cost nothing but was also liberated and therefore liberating. The word provided description and it implied obligation. The aim was to place the adjective before almost any aspect of human existence and then attempt to bring that imaginary construct into being.

The Digger philosophy was deeply rooted in liberal individualism—the American dream amplified through the prism of LSD. Diggers maintained that individuals should be free to be whatever they wanted to be. Nothing should be predetermined. Freedom could be discovered only through action—by "doing it"—"it" being whatever inspired the individual. Everything the Diggers did, from their free stores to their anarchic street happenings, was designed to expose the tension between freedom and conformity.

The Diggers emerged from the San Francisco Mime Troupe, a radical group of actors devoted to "guerrilla theater." The troupe's aim, according to the founder, R. G. Davis, was to present "moral plays and to confront hypocrisy in society." "This is our society," he argued. "If we don't like it, it's our duty to change it; if we can't change it, we must destroy it." Action-orientated radicalism appealed to Coyote, who had become disenchanted with traditional protest. "It came home to me indelibly that I was never going to change anything in America by walking around carrying a sign. It was a great revelation. It saved me a lot of anxiety and a lot of wasted energy."[23]

Through the SF Mime Troupe, Coyote met Peter Berg and Emmett Grogan, both of whom shared his radical politics and restless energy. He developed a "comprehensive world view" which was essentially Marxist, though without the dogma. "Not necessarily doctrinaire, but analysis: class, capital, who owned what, who did what, who worked for what. . . . It was like speed for the imagination. You suddenly started looking at the world in this whole new way. . . . Suddenly, everything came together." Eventually, working for a theater company, no matter how radical its politics, seemed hypocritical. Coyote, Berg, and Grogan decided that "theater was no longer an adequate vehicle for change, because the fact of paying at the door told you that it was a business." Receiving reward for an action, putting a value on an achievement, destroyed autonomy. In that sense, fame, praise, and admiration were essentially money. "Free means not copping credit," one Digger leaflet proclaimed. All action had therefore to be anonymous. "If you received recompense for what you were doing, [in the form of] fame, then it wasn't Free. . . . You had to be doing it just for the fuck of it."[24]

During a 1967 SDS conference, a Digger staged an unusual protest when he suddenly stripped off his clothes. Asked to explain, he replied: "Somebody has to be naked around here." Ideologies, in other words, were protective clothing which prevented the individual from emerging. Political labels violated autonomy and were therefore "bullshit." Communists were "creeps," Grogan felt, while the New Left was "as full of puritanical shit as the country's right wing was cowardly absurd." "From our perspective," Coyote wrote, "all ideological solutions, left and right, all undervalued the individual, and were quick to sacrifice them to the expediencies of their particular mental empires." Instead of allowing individuality to flourish, radicals clothed themselves in political "truths," while ritually attacking the intellectual garb of their opponents.[25]

Along with a distrust of ideologies went a deep suspicion of ideologues. Individuality as espoused by the Diggers was deeply threatening to those who used ideology as a method of control. "I . . . used to joke that Jerry Rubin and Abbie Hoffman would be the people to shoot me," Coyote reflected. "The Communist party would be the people to shoot me. Not the FBI. All those architects of the revolution, the Tom Haydens of the world, would have blown my brains out, because we stood for the sanctity of the individual." The Diggers developed a profound suspicion of anyone who sought power. "You scratch a revolutionary," Coyote said, "[and] I'll show you a guy who thinks that he should be in charge."[26]

Diggers also had no time for the counterculture's heroes, those who pretended that hedonism had political meaning and escaped commitment in the getaway car of drugs. Timothy Leary was dismissed as naïve and irresponsible, a dangerous and self-indulgent publicity seeker. Grogan derided "the absolute bullshit implicit in the psychedelic transcendentalism" promoted by the "tune-in, turn-on, drop-out, jerk-off ideology." Diggers "were more social-oriented than revelatory," Berg explained. "If someone took LSD to find out the inner truth and mystery of life, that kind of individual was disregarded or derided. . . . [We] . . . saw drugs in terms of individual personal fulfillment within a social context."[27]

Diggers provided "alternatives to society's skimpy menu of life choices." They opened "stores" that offered free food and clothing, set up a free medical clinic, and ran a free bank. The bank consisted of a box full of cash from which an individual could take what he needed. He could take, but he must not steal. The oft-repeated slogan went: "It's free because it's yours." Every day, they provided Digger Stew and Digger Bread, sometimes feeding a thousand people. Those who partook had first to pass through a huge wooden frame, brightly painted yellow, called the "Free Frame of Reference." The frame was intended as a doorway between the actual and the possible. By stepping through it, individuals would change the way they viewed their world.[28]

Diggers believed fervently that changing the world started with changing oneself. The free stores, Coyote explained, were intended to show "customers" that one's "life was one's own, and if you could leap the hurdles of programmed expectations and self-imposed limits, the future promised boundless possibilities." "One day, on my shift as 'manager,'" he recalled,

> I noticed an obviously poor black woman, furtively stuffing clothing into a large paper bag. When I approached her she turned away from the bag coolly, pretending that it wasn't hers. In a conventional store, her ruse would have made sense because she knew she was stealing. Smiling pleasantly, I returned the bag to her. "You can't steal here," I said. She got indignant and said, "I wasn't stealing!" "I know," I said amiably, "But you thought you were stealing. You can't steal here because it's a Free Store. Read the sign, everything is free! You can have the whole fucking store if you feel like it."

Berg was certain that once everything became free, "theories of economics [would] follow social facts. . . . Human wanting and giving, needing and taking, [would] become wide open to improvisation. . . . No owner, no manager, no employees and no cash register. . . . When materials are free, imagination becomes currency for spirit. . . . The question of a free store is simple: What would you have?"[29]

Rather like the Provos, Diggers engineered gigantic street happenings. One action, which started as a protest against traffic and pollution, had the public participate in a play called "Fool on the Street" by literally taking over the streets and blocking traffic. The police arrived and, in appropriately surreal fashion, began arguing with two huge puppets over the definition of "public" and "free." Another demonstration, called "Death of Hippie," was designed as an attack upon the media's role in publicizing, sensationalizing, and inevitably cheapening the counterculture. A huge coffin was carried through the streets, into which bystanders ceremoniously tossed the paraphernalia of hippie culture, thus registering their disgust with media hype.

Money to fund this great adventure often came from drug dealers who had an interest in keeping the hippie community fed. The Haight Independent Proprietors (HIP) also contributed from profits made selling souvenirs to tourists. Donations proved problematic, however, because, if everything was free, there should technically be no charity. On occasion, when hip philanthropists tried to donate cash, a Digger would burn the money in front of the startled benefactor. When Allen Ginsberg, Gary Snyder, and other Beat writers organized a fundraiser at a North Beach bar, Diggers rejected the benevolence, explaining that charity was simply a salve to the conscience and an escape from commitment. In truth, however, moral standards were little more than self-righteous posturing. Diggers could not have survived without help from friends. In order to satisfy their own conscience, they convinced themselves that goods and cash donated had in fact been "liberated." In some cases this was literally true, as stealing was not unknown. But since property was not acknowledged, neither was theft.[30]

The Diggers were products of affluence. The economic system they derided was in fact their lifeblood. Great Society welfare programs cushioned the blows of self-imposed poverty. Strictures against charity did not apply to welfare checks and food stamps. More fundamentally, a buoyant economy provided a surplus which could be redistributed as if it were free. "There's already enough stuff for everybody," Coyote maintained. "Money is a way of creating scarcity. There's machinery that can create a television set for every man and woman and child on the planet. . . . The money is a valve that's been put between you and the TV."[31]

At the heart of this philosophy was a rather traditional faith in American technology as the Great Provider. Capitalist enterprise was usually seen as a monster, but sometimes as a savior, since it had the potential to provide for everyone, while at the same time setting the masses free. "Give up jobs so computers can do them," a Digger leaflet instructed. The group sincerely believed that within ten years "machines and computers will do most of the work," giving the people more time to pursue their dreams. Out of this belief grew the conviction that money would soon become obsolete. In one street pageant celebrating the "Death of Money," a giant coffin was carried through the streets, into which spectators threw bills and coins.[32]

The attack upon conformity did not extend to a destruction of patriarchy. "Our men are tough," a pamphlet proclaimed. "They have style, guile, balls, imagination, and autonomy. Our women are soft, skilled, fuck like angels; radiate children scent and colors like the crazy bells that mark our time." Coyote admitted that "[women] were the real backbone of the whole deal," because they could use their charm to liberate supplies from local merchants and wholesalers. A skimpy blouse worn with no bra could buy a lot of free food. Digger women also had to deal with pregnancies and childrearing in what was a frontier existence. Coyote recalled fierce arguments between women who needed money for their babies, and men "who wanted truck parts or . . . a bag of smack." A strict hierarchy existed in which the men were "creating mythologies, dreaming, scoring dope. . . . The guys held down a lot of the visionary, metaphysical end of things. You know, like in an orthodox Hebrew community. The men are studying Talmud and they're looking at heaven. The women are taking care of the household and paying the bills and cooking the food." Men's work was important because men did it, women's work trivial because women did it. "The women were literally kept barefoot and pregnant and in the kitchen making herb tea for the guys," the singer Tracy Nelson recalled. "Either that, or they were this bizarre kind of whore . . . just the total earthy sexual persona." Inequities could be excused by reference to the absolute certainty that everyone was free to do as he or she pleased. "Basically, in an autonomous system, you're on your own," Coyote insisted.[33]

Diggers had a pathological aversion to organization, structure, and leadership. "There must not be a Plan," one leaflet proclaimed. "We have always been defeated by our Plan." This aversion to management eventually spelled the end of the free food program. "Well, man, it took a lot of organization to get that done. We had to scuffle to get the food. Then the chicks or somebody had to prepare it. Then we got to serve it. A lot of people got to do a lot of things at the right time or it doesn't come off. Well, it got so that people weren't doing it. . . . Now you hate to get into a power bag and start telling people what to do, but without that, man, well." "There was no leader," one anonymous Digger complained in April 1967. "Whoever happened to come in and sit behind the desk assumed control until someone else happened in to sit. No one knew what anyone else was doing and no one would assume . . . responsibility." The "O'Donnell Plan," the brainchild of Tommy O'Donnell, called for the setting up of a six-man committee to direct the various Digger enterprises. Unfortunately, that idea contained too many words ("plan," "committee," "direct," etc.) abhorrent to the true Digger. The old guard reacted by running away.[34]

The Diggers were victims of their own success. Admirers took them more seriously than they themselves ever intended. Perhaps inevitably, they spawned imitations. Digger groups started popping up around America, with "free" stores especially prevalent in the hippie community of New York City. This led to factionalism, envy, and conflict. Apparently the only thing that wasn't free was the Digger identity, which the founders hoarded jealously. They were especially perturbed at their inability to prevent the corruption of the hippie ethic by the media. "Death of Hippie," their last great demonstration, was more a pained acceptance of defeat than an act of defiance.

Most of the original Diggers escaped to the hills, taking with them those parts of the philosophy they found holy. Grogan decided to walk back to his New York home, in symbolic counterpoint to the traditional American tendency to equate western migration with renewal. Several years later, he was found dead on a New York subway, the victim of a heroin overdose. When Coyote recalls the short history of the Diggers, he remembers the enormous creativity and vitality, but also those who did not survive.

Coyote once described the Diggers as "social safe-crackers, sandpapering our nervous systems and searching for the right combinations that would spring the doors and let everyone out of the box." That quest was ultimately unsuccessful, in some cases disastrously so. Diggers never quite appreciated the subtle interplay between individual fulfillment and social responsibility. Nor did they understand the sense of security that lies in structure and ownership: boxes feel safe. Their version of freedom might have been essentially American, but for most Americans it was completely alien. A beautifully symbolic act of rejection came during the Summer of Love, when the free store in San Francisco was burglarized.[35]

For Coyote, the lessons were personal and social. The personal lesson had to do with the limits of freedom, and probably saved his life:

> There were real prices to pay—and sometimes the body, sometimes your life itself, was the coin. . . . My investigation of limits began when I was bedridden for fifteen weeks with my second case of serum hepatitis. And I was on a ranch, by myself, with no electricity, and I couldn't walk. I lay in bed and I thought: How did I get here? And it started me rethinking about what was healthy. What was health? What did it mean? And once you accept anything as tacked down, then you begin to build a structure, to accept limits. Then you have to make a choice as to whether or not you're going to accept that structure. If you do, you give up the notion of total freedom. Your freedom only becomes meaningful within that structure.

From that lesson came a realization that undiluted freedom was, ironically, tyrannical. "I sat in rooms and listened to people oppressing everyone . . . in the name of freedom," he recalled. "It restricted you from participating in anything which the majority culture endorsed." In his case, this meant that he was not allowed to pursue his passion for acting through conventional theater or films. "We adhered to a one-sided vision. We excluded people who didn't see it our way. We created a dichotomous universe: us and them, good guys and bad guys. And to some degree, you define yourself, or one defines oneself, by what one's not."[36]

Structure, Coyote came to realize, was absolutely essential to human fulfillment: "Any structure is mutable, but once you've chosen it, then you have to accept it—if you're ever going to get any depth. Because depth only comes in the struggle with limits. If there are no limits, you're like a water strider skimming over the surface of the water. It's only struggling against the geometry of a piano that you really find out what it can do. If you had a piano with unlimited keys . . . what's it mean? . . . It means you write songs that nobody sings and nobody remembers." "I no longer see anything as free," he concluded. "Because 'free' to me means 'without limits.' And free means not interdependent." "Autonomy," that great Digger shibboleth, was ultimately recognized for the danger it posed and the harm it caused.

GREENWICH VILLAGE: YIPPIE!

Yippie started out as an exclamation, uttered in a Greenwich Village flat on New Year's Eve, 1967. Jerry Rubin, Paul Krassner, and Abbie Hoffman were gathered in semi-serious discussion. Out of the smoky haze emerged an idea, in a manner symptomatic of pot. Why not transform a lifestyle into an ideology? Or, better yet, a political party? The word "party" had delightful double meaning. "We realized that we couldn't build things around just a youth festival," Rubin explained. "We had to build it around a new person. Let's create a new figure, we said, a long-haired, crazy revolutionary. I said it had to have youth in it because we definitely believed it was a generational thing. And it had to be international because we envisioned youth festivals in Russia, in Latin America." Krassner shouted "Yippie!" and a movement was born. Exclamation eventually became acronym—"Yippie" would stand for Youth International Party. "What's a Yippie?," Hoffman was asked. "A hippie who has been hit over the head by a cop."[37]

Rubin and Hoffman defined four specific objectives to guide their new movement:

1. The blending of pot and politics into a political grass-leaves movement—a cross-fertilization of the hippie and New Left philosophy.
2. A connecting link that would tie as much of the underground together as was willing into some gigantic national get-together.
3. The development of a model for an alternative society.
4. The need to make some statement, especially in revolutionary action-theater terms, about LBJ, the Democratic party, electoral politics, and the state of the nation.

For Rubin, the Yippie movement offered the chance to fuse the counterculture and political protest, which had previously been antagonistic. He was enchanted by the drug scene, but still attracted to politics. Hoffman provided the solution. "In Abbie Hoffman he found a man who had developed a style of action which would liberate the person . . . as well as changing society," Rubin's friend Stew Albert recalled. "If it was Hippie which gave Jerry a sense of his own liberation, it was Abbie and Yippie which gave him a way of carrying it out." Or, as Timothy Leary recounted: "The dogmatic leftist activist chapter had been written, and here was Merry Jerry the Lysergic Lenin, the grass Guevara, the mescaline Marx."[38]

Yippies originally saw themselves as a sort of East Coast branch of the Diggers, much to the Diggers' dismay. While the Yippies mirrored Digger theatricality, they could not match their social conscience. That deficiency was important, since ethics gave Digger mayhem meaning. The Yippies, in contrast, were percussion without melody and lyrics. A telling distinction can be made between how the two groups looked upon the thousands of runaways who flocked to hippie havens. The Diggers saw tragedy and desperately tried to help them. The Yippies, in contrast, saw cannon fodder. "Runaways are the backbone of the youth revolution," Hoffman claimed. "A fifteen-year-old kid who takes off from middle-class American life is an escaped slave crossing the Mason-Dixon line." As one Yippie pamphlet boasted: "We tear through the streets. Kids love it. They understand it on an internal level. We are living TV ads, movies. Yippie!" Hoffman and Rubin envisaged a Children's Crusade, ignoring the tragedy this implied.[39]

While Diggers cultivated anonymity, Yippies craved celebrity. They were pathologically self-obsessed; self-promotion became both method and objective. "Jerry was always a media junky," Coyote reflected. "Abbie, who was a friend of mine, was always a media junky. We explained everything to those guys, and they violated everything we taught them." Coyote was especially incensed by Hoffman's decision to publish *Steal This Book*, a guide to the scams which would allow the would-be hippie to live on the street without having to get a job. According to Coyote, that book "blew the hustle of every poor person on the Lower East Side by describing every free scam then current in New York—which were then sucked dry by disaffected kids from Scarsdale."[40]

Cleverly turning selfish gratification into ideology, Hoffman articulated a political and cultural vision based solely on the fulfillment of desire. "I don't like the concept of a movement built on sacrifice, dedication, responsibility, anger, frustration, and guilt. All those down things. I would say, Look, you want to have more fun, you want to get laid more, you want to turn on with your friends, you want an outlet for your creativity, then get out of school, quit your job. Come on out and help build the society you want. Stop trying to organize everybody but yourself. Begin to live your vision." In Hoffman's view, it was entirely possible to smoke, dance, and fuck for the revolution. Marijuana, LSD, free love, long hair, and psychedelic music were chisels for chipping away at the Establishment. "I consider the yippies to be an acid movement," Rubin once remarked, "in that the attempt is to wipe out a person's total frame of reference, and to establish a new frame of reference. We are trying to put the country on an acid trip."[41]

Simply being a hippie was not, however, enough; Yippies believed that the Establishment would crumble under the weight of nonconformity. They insisted upon action; "Just do it" was Rubin's mantra. "Act first. Analyze later. Impulse—not theory—makes the great leaps forward." Borrowing from the Diggers, they staged their own version of guerrilla theater, which Hoffman called "media-freaking." Not much thought was given to the message, since action was the point. "Once you get the right image, the details aren't that important," Hoffman explained. "Over-analyzing reduced the myth. A big insight we learned during this period was that you didn't have to explain why. That's what advertising was all about. 'Why' was for critics." Everything was geared to generating maximum publicity. "The trick to manipulating the media is to get them to promote an event before it happens," Hoffman explained. "In other words, . . . get them to make an advertisement for . . . revolution—the same way you would advertise soap."[42]

Politics became theater, an arena to act out fantasies. Taking drugs and wearing silly costumes were imagined to be profound political statements. Having fun was a way of thumbing one's nose at the Establishment. On one occasion Yippies talked their way into the New York Stock Exchange and dropped dollar bills from the gallery to the trading floor below. The point was to watch the traders in imaginary money trample over each other in order to grab real money. The stunt worked, but it was just a stunt—the message was lost on all but the perpetrators.

"We believe that people should fuck all the time, anytime, whomever they wish," another Yippie manifesto proclaimed. "This is not a program demand but a simple recognition of the reality around us." What precisely that meant was not clear, but, then, it wasn't supposed to be. Words were chosen for the outrage they inspired rather than the meaning they conveyed. "Outrageous talk was cheap," Todd Gitlin argued, with the Yippies in mind. Rubin dreamt of "the Marxist acidhead, the psychedelic Bolshevik," without really contemplating the implications. He saw himself as the model of the "dope-taking, freedom-loving, politically committed activist." The Yippie recipe for revolution was effortless and simple: having fun, dressing up, and getting high would somehow create a better world. Oppression and conformity would be defeated by color and fantasy. Ideology, in other words, wasn't necessary as long as the spirit was powerful. "Ideology," Rubin argued, "is a brain disease." In reply to that statement, an angry Fred Halstead of the Socialist Workers party wrote: "I have to plead guilty. I read books and I try to learn from the past. . . . And in order to get the masses you have to achieve unity of diverse forces, and that takes some careful detailed work, some boring, yes, some boring things."[43]

The 1968 Democratic Convention in Chicago was supposed to bring the great transformation from hippie to Yippie. The plan called for hippies to converge upon Chicago for a festival of youth, where they would be politicized by the experience of sharing center stage with the earnest members of the antiwar movement and the brutal forces of the Establishment. Chicago would be not just an act of protest against the war or the government, but the start of a concerted offensive against American culture. Rubin explained:

> Our idea is to create a cultural, living alternative to the Convention.
> . . . We want all the rock bands, all the underground papers, all the
> free spirits, all the theater groups—all the energies that have con-
> tributed to the new youth culture—all the tribes—to come to Chi-
> cago, and for six days we will live together in the park, sharing,
> learning, free food, free music, a regeneration of spirit and energy.
> . . . The . . . Convention . . . gives us a stage, a platform, an opportu-
> nity to do our own thing, to go beyond protest into creative cultural
> alternative.

The purpose, said Rubin, was to "put people through tremendous, radicalizing changes." He wanted to stimulate a "massive white revolutionary movement which, working in . . . cooperation with the rebellions in the black communities, could seriously disrupt this country, and thus be an internal catalyst for a breakdown of the American ability to fight guerrillas overseas." Among the left, quite a few people were bothered at the way Yippies turned naïve youths into cannon fodder. "When [Rubin] tells us he supports 'everything which puts people into motion, which creates disruption and controversy, which creates chaos and rebirth,' he might easily be one of the Fascist intellectuals explaining the merits of German National Socialism," argued David McReynolds of the War Resistance League. *Rolling Stone* warned that the "media gamesmanship" risked "serious injury and possible Death." "You radicals are all alike," Phil Ochs told Rubin; "lashing out at the approaching armed tractor with Yo-Yos."[44]

"In Chicago in August, every media [outlet] in the world is going to be here," Rubin told the faithful. "We're going to be the news, and everything we do is going to be sent out to living rooms from India to the Soviet Union to every small town in America. It is a real opportunity to make clear the two Americas. . . . At the same time we're *confronting* them, we're offering our alternative and it's not just a narrow, political alternative—it's an alternative way of life." Copious quantities of drugs encouraged outrageous fantasies of infinite possibility. Yippies convinced themselves that they could attract hordes to Chicago and that those hordes could, in one dramatic act, bring a nation to its knees. In fact, protesters were vastly outnumbered by police. Not given to introspection, Yippies blamed everyone but themselves. "We looked around Lincoln Park and counted noses—maybe 2,000 to 3,000 freaks—and we organizers looked at each other sadly," Rubin reflected. "We once dreamed 500,000 people would come to Czechago. We expected 50,000. But [Mayor] Daley huffed and puffed, and scared the people away."[45]

Rubin nevertheless found reason for pride. "Although we were few, we were hard core," he later wrote. "And we *were* motherfucking bad. We were dirty, smelly, grimy, foul, loud, dope-crazed, hell-bent and leather-jacketed. We were a public display of filth and shabbiness, living in-the-flesh rejects of middle-class standards. We pissed and shit and fucked in public; we crossed streets on red lights; and we opened Coke bottles with our teeth. We were constantly stoned or tripping on every drug known to man." By every sane standard, Chicago was an abject failure. The crowd of protesters was tiny. No great countercultural conflagration started. The Establishment did not come tumbling down. But, like the spindoctor he would become, Rubin turned failure into success. "Everybody played out their karma," he claimed. "It was all perfect. We wanted to show that America wasn't a democracy, that the convention wasn't politics. The message of the week was of an America ruled by force. That was a big victory." Hoffman, however, wasn't so sure. By the end of convention week, he'd had enough of Rubin. "Jerry's a tough son of a bitch," he later wrote. "He's got a hell of a fuckin' ego. . . . Jerry wants to show the clenched fist. I want to show the clenched fist and the smile."[46]

"They were trapped in a media loop, dependent on media standards, media sufferance, and goodwill," argued Gitlin. "These apostles of freedom couldn't grasp that they were destined to become clichés." Clichés, yes, but dangerous ones nonetheless. Yippies were dangerous not just for the way they manipulated confused kids, or for the violence they inspired, but also for the damage they caused to political protest in general. Because they came at the end of the decade of protest, critics saw them as a logical conclusion rather than as an aberration. It was easy to dismiss the entire political culture on the basis of this single, warped offspring. A movement without ideology is a balloon without a string. Action has to seem to have a point—otherwise, it appears self-indulgently nihilistic. While they tried to inspire outrage, in the end Yippies aroused mainly scorn.[47]

OAKLAND: THE BLACK PANTHERS

Huey Newton was a beautiful man, the perfect image of black pride. He could easily have passed for a running back for the San Francisco 49ers, or a model straight out of *Ebony*. In fact, he was minister of defense of the Black Panther party, a revolutionary who loved to quote Mao: "Power grows out of the barrel of a gun." In the late 1960s, one could often find, in the dorm rooms of white students, a poster of Huey, looking suitably bad, with a rifle in one hand and a spear in the other. Fantasists put that poster next to the one of Che.[48]

Newton and Bobby Seale formed the Black Panther Party for Self-Defense in Oakland, California, in late 1966. They were socialists, though they did not have much truck with Marx. They disagreed with his contention that it was impossible to form a revolution out of the raw material of the peasant class, preferring instead the ideas of Franz Fanon and Che. Peasants, they believed, responded not to words, but to action. In 1968, Newton declared:

> The large majority of black people are either illiterate or semi-literate. They don't read. They need activity to follow. . . . The same thing happened in Cuba, where it was necessary for twelve men with a leadership of Che and Fidel to take to the hills and then attack the corrupt administration. . . . They could have leafleted the community and they could have written books, but the people would not respond. They had to act and the people could see and hear about it and therefore become educated on how to respond to oppression.

Panthers believed that a revolutionary mass could be formed from the human detritus of the ghetto, from the "brothers off the block—brothers who had been . . . robbing banks . . . pimping . . . peddling dope . . . brothers who had been fighting pigs—because . . . once you organize those brothers . . . you get niggers . . . you get revolutionaries who are too much." In line with Fanon's philosophy, violence was presented as an effective way to empower the oppressed: through fighting came liberation.[49]

The Panthers were part social workers, part ghetto army. They set up schools for black children, political education classes, free health clinics, and free breakfast clubs. Most of the demands outlined in their party platform were entirely reasonable, encompassing education, housing, full employment, human rights, and an end to police brutality. Others, however, betrayed the militant nature of their politics. They wanted blacks to be exempt from military service and those in prison to be freed immediately, since they could not, by definition, have received a fair trial. Finally, they demanded "a United Nations–supervised plebiscite to be held throughout the black colony in which only black colonial subjects will be allowed to participate for the purpose of determining the will of black people as to their national destiny."[50]

The Panthers were an outgrowth of the intensifying black consciousness in the 1960s, expressed as Black Power. Neither the party itself, nor the name chosen, was entirely original. After the disappointments of the 1964 Democratic convention, Stokely Carmichael went back to Mississippi intent on forming a black political party in Lowndes County, which was 80 percent black. The state Democratic party, which excluded blacks, had a provocative white rooster as its official symbol. Carmichael chose as his symbol a black panther, which would make short work of a rooster.

Carmichael became the most outspoken advocate of Black Power. Martin Luther King found Carmichael's enthusiasm for "Black Power" disruptive and the phrase itself too aggressive. He tried to persuade Carmichael to substitute "Black Equality," but had no success. King's misgivings merely underlined the fact that he could no longer claim authority over the militant wing of the civil rights movement. To militants, the threatening nature of the phrase "Black Power" defined its perfection. As Julius Lester wrote in *Look Out, Whitey! Black Power's Gon' Get Your Mama!*:

> Everybody wanted to know what this Black Power meant. If SNCC had said Negro Power or Colored Power, white folks would have continued sleeping easy every night. But BLACK POWER! Black. That word. BLACK! And the visions came of alligator infested swamps arched by primordial trees and moss dripping from the limbs and out of the depths of the swamp, the mire oozing from his skin, came the black monster, and fathers told their daughters to be in by nine instead of nine-thirty. . . . BLACK POWER! My god, the niggers were gon' start paying white folk back. . . . The nation was hysterical.

Black Power went hand in hand with the decision to extend agitation into the North. Northern whites would come under attack, and they would henceforth be unable to pretend that racism was a contagion quarantined in the South. The problem, Carmichael argued, was not Southerners but white people in general. For white liberals who had devoted themselves to the civil rights cause, this seemed a cruel rebuff.[51]

After Carmichael took over the Student Nonviolent Coordinating Committee in 1966, replacing the moderate John Lewis, he turned it into a movement synonymous with Black Power and violence, rendering its name a contradiction. Within months, a ruling was proposed to ban white people. It narrowly passed (19 to 18, with twenty-four abstentions). This left white liberals understandably confused as to where to devote their energy. They were not, however, the only ones ostracized as a result of the new fashion for separation. Since whites were defined as oppressors and blacks as victims, the black who succeeded in the white man's world was clearly a traitor—an Uncle Tom.

That argument was put forward most vehemently by Eldridge Cleaver, a highly talented writer who used his gift to peddle hatred. In his book *Soul on Ice,* which he wrote while imprisoned on a rape charge, Cleaver savaged those who had previously been role models, including James Baldwin, Louis Armstrong, Lena Horne, Jackie Robinson, Joe Louis, and of course Martin Luther King. King's "award of a Nobel prize . . . and the inflation of his image to that of an international hero, bear witness to the historical fact that the only Negro Americans allowed to attain national or international fame have been the puppets and the lackeys of the power structure." For militant blacks, it became fashionable to disparage King. After 1966, the angriest reaction King received was often from his own people, who shouted him down with chants of "Black Power!" King took to reminding his listeners that "whenever Pharaoh wanted to keep the slaves in slavery, he kept them fighting among themselves."[52]

Huey Newton and Bobby Seale disagreed with Carmichael on the matter of soliciting white help. Since they believed that the class struggle transcended race, they were willing to form alliances with anyone eager "to move against the power structure." Rejecting black nationalism as too negative, they railed against the "racism" inspired by Malcolm X. In any case, whites had money, and Panthers liked to spend it. But while they did not reject white help, neither did they trim their sails to attract it. They were, in the nomenclature of the time, bad dudes who reveled in badness. Loving the Panthers became radical chic, an acquired taste rather like smoking filterless cigarettes and drinking Mezcal. At a fundraiser in New York hosted by Leonard Bernstein, rich whites and militant blacks shared champagne and canapés. One Panther promised a white woman "that she would not be killed even if she is a rich member of the middle class with a self-avowed capitalist for a husband." For those hoping to induce *mea culpa,* the Panthers were a potent purgative. They were also fashionable among those who thought it cool to talk of killing. White middle-class kids who dreamed of "offing pigs" (killing policemen) derived vicarious pleasure from the fact that some Panthers were actually doing this.[53]

The "self-defense" part of the group's official title came from the fact that the members were dedicated to combating police brutality. They took to following police patrols through the Oakland ghetto, proudly brandishing their weapons. Black youths who had never seen anyone stand up to white authority so assertively were understandably impressed. Occasional gunfights enhanced the image of ghetto Robin Hoods. "Ninety percent of the reason we carried guns in the first place was educational," New-

ton proclaimed. "To set an example, . . . to establish that we had the right."
When the California legislature responded by proposing a bill barring the
carrying of firearms in public, thirty Panthers burst into the Sacramento
statehouse on May 2, 1967, brandishing weapons and proclaiming that the
legislation "aim[s] at keeping Black people disarmed and powerless while
racist police agencies throughout the country intensify the terror, brutality, murder, and repression of Black people." Newspapers reported a surreal scene: "grimfaced, silent young men armed with guns roaming the
Capitol surrounded by reporters, television cameramen, and stunned policemen and watched by incredulous groups of visiting schoolchildren."
Five Panthers, including Seale, ended up in jail, but, as a gesture calculated
to impress, their action was brilliant. Fully aware of the white community's deep-seated fear of "niggers with guns," the Panthers intentionally
sowed panic.[54]

For black male youths rendered impotent by poverty and prejudice,
there was something understandably appealing about these exemplars of
indignant machismo. They offered the opportunity to belong to a group
that was built on bravery and pride, and that, far from being cowed by
white authority, could make whitey tremble. Panther pride was reinforced
by their uniform: black trousers, light-blue shirts, and black leather jackets, complemented by black berets, dark sunglasses, and unconcealed
weapons. For a brief period, their allure was contagious; by 1968, they had
perhaps 5,000 members, with branches in at least thirty cities. Nor was the
attraction confined to males. Regina Jennings was one of a significant
number of women attracted to the machismo. "As a runaway since the age
of fifteen, a witness to vulgar police brutality, and a victim of racism on
my first job, I was ready to become a Panther. Their mystique—the black
pants, leather jackets, berets, guns, and their talk—aggressive and direct—
attracted me."[55]

While Newton was serving time for shooting a police officer, a new generation of leaders emerged, Cleaver the most prominent among them. His
obvious intelligence, not to mention the critical success of *Soul on Ice*,
made him a *cause célèbre* among leftist intellectuals. Clever syntax was, apparently, sufficient compensation for moral failings. Underneath the artistic veneer lurked a racist, psychopathic, misogynist thug who labeled his
raping of a white woman "an insurrectionary act." "It delighted me that I

was defying and trampling upon the white man's law, upon his system of values, and that I was defiling his woman."[56]

While his discourse on politics was often sophisticated, Cleaver's appeal to the black masses was cynically shallow:

> There are enough people in Babylon to kick pig ass from the Atlantic to the Pacific and back again. We can kick pig ass for days, if we all start doing it. So why not? . . .
>
> In times of revolution, just wars, and wars of liberation, I love the angels of destruction and disorder as opposed to the devils of conservation and law-and-order. Fuck all those who block the revolution with rhetoric—revolutionary rhetoric or counter-revolutionary rhetoric.
>
> We are either pig-killers or pig-feeders. Let the pigs oink for themselves, till their last oink. When we finally pull all of the American people out of their pads, out into the streets, out into the night, into the jungles of our cities, then we will hear some farewell oinking.

Thanks to Cleaver, self-defense gave way to self-promotion. The Panthers' genuine program of social reform became submerged beneath nihilistic destruction and egotistical attention-seeking. In 1968, cashing in on his enormous popularity among radical intellectuals, he negotiated an alliance with the New Left in California, forming the Peace and Freedom party, which selected him as its candidate for president. Efforts to make the alliance of hippies, Yippies, and ghetto blacks sound logical were thwarted by anarchic gags and puerile vulgarity. His running mate, Jerry Rubin, promised to put LSD in the drinking water, and Cleaver, at a rally dubbed "Pre-Erection Day," mobilized what he called "pussy power." He later challenged Ronald Reagan to a duel, offering the governor a choice of weapons: a gun, a knife, a baseball bat, or a marshmallow.[57]

The Panthers were victims of their own hype. The violent image quickly overwhelmed the pastoral role. Writing from prison, Afeni Shakur remarked: "There is a great need for the sisters and brothers to know the true meaning of 'Power to the People.' Very few of our young brothers and sisters have ever read the ten-point program. They are unfamiliar with the party's purpose. We are looked upon as an all-black gang dedicated to destruction. When the brothers in Oakland sat down and put the ten points together, that is not what they had in mind." Panthers wanted white America to fear them, and white America did precisely that. J. Edgar Hoover called them "the greatest threat to the internal security of the country." The fear they encouraged became justification for extermination. Few protested if a Panther was shot in the back, or, in the case of Fred Hampton, killed by police while sound asleep in his bed. Millions of dollars were spent on espionage and infiltration. Agents provocateurs exacerbated internal tensions and skillfully maneuvered Panthers into violent confrontations with the police.[58]

The Panthers were also very good at killing one another. Chapters competed in vicious turf wars, made more complicated by the extortion and drug dealing necessary for fundraising. The party was too small to accommodate so many huge egos. Violent arguments also erupted over political issues, in particular the reliance upon white support. Richard Moore, a New York Panther, accused the Oakland group of selling out. Newton and his sidekick David Hilliard were condemned for "destroying the desire in comrades to wage resolute struggle by confining the party to mass rallies and 'fundraising benefits.'" They were, he argued, encouraging "dependency upon the very class enemies of our people." Moore especially objected to the way Newton and Hilliard lined their pockets with money collected for the movement. "Outlaws cannot enjoy penthouses and imported furniture," he argued. Newton and Hilliard had "betrayed . . . young black men and women who came out of the depths of despair that are the ghetto streets and who transformed themselves for an idea that gave meaning to their existence." While that criticism was justified, in truth there was very little virtue within the Black Panther movement against which to measure its abundant vice.[59]

The Panthers proved much more adept at impressing middle-class whites than recruiting ghetto blacks. The blacks they did attract proved poor revolutionaries, their pride already polluted by alcohol, drugs, and poverty. Cleaver called them "jackanapes"—an undisciplined mob unable to focus on politics. The problem might, however, have arisen because the Panthers did not offer a sufficiently clear alternative to ghetto culture. The black lumpenproletariat failed to make an effective revolutionary mass, for the simple reason that they could not grasp the distinction between the crimes they were accustomed to committing (drug-dealing, theft, murder) and the political crimes their leaders committed (drug-dealing, theft, murder).

Delano: Boycott Grapes

In the Sixties, white Californians were stubbornly disdainful of the Hispanic culture that surrounded them. They lived in houses designed to look like haciendas on streets with Spanish names, dined out at Mexican restaurants, and listened to pasteurized versions of mariachi, courtesy of groups like Herb Alpert and the Tijuana Brass. (No one in Alpert's band was actually Hispanic. He used to joke that the band consisted of "three pastramis, two bagels, and an American cheese.") The Chicanos themselves were ignored. They cleaned houses, mowed lawns, and picked fruit, but where they came from and where they went at night, no one seemed to care. They were not a problem, since, unlike blacks, they didn't protest, even though unemployment among Chicanos was higher than in any other ethnic group. The McCone Commission investigating the Watts riot drew attention to the fact that the Hispanic community in Los Angeles was almost equal in size to the black community, and suffered more. "That the Mexican-American community did not riot is to its credit," the commission concluded. "It should not be to its disadvantage."[60]

Many of the Mexicans were braceros—farm workers from south of the border who, under the terms of a bilateral agreement, were recruited to work in US fields. The first such agreement lasted from 1917 to 1921 and was terminated when the Mexican government protested that the workers were little short of slaves, their pitifully low wages wiped out by their indebtedness to the company store. The system was revived in 1942 as a solution to wartime labor shortages. Technically, braceros could be used only if a farmer could demonstrate that no local workers were available and if the employment of braceros did not depress the domestic wage rate. In truth, however, these regulations were easily ignored.

Braceros were often outnumbered by "wetbacks"—Mexicans who crossed the border illegally. Occasionally, in order to tidy the records, wetbacks were rounded up, returned to Mexico, and then taken back across the border, where they were issued legal documents that made them braceros. A symbiosis existed: farms in the United States needed cheap labor in order to keep food prices low, and entire communities in Mexico depended on the income from the farm labor system. A circular migration existed in rhythm with the agricultural cycle. The arrangement artificially depressed wage rates on farms, mainly in California and Texas. The typical farm worker in the early 1960s made around $10 per day, and (since work was seasonal) around $1,200 annually. Domestic workers (a large percentage of whom were Hispanic) understood that they could be undercut by braceros, who in turn could be undercut by wetbacks. Both braceros and wetbacks were used as strikebreakers when domestic workers tried to protest their low wages and long hours.

In the years 1942 to 1964, some 4.6 million braceros crossed the border. The arrangement was brought to an end because of growing disquiet among the American people, fueled in part by the 1960 documentary *Harvest of Shame*. Embarrassment centered not on the braceros, but rather on the domestic farm workers who were kept in poverty because of cheap Mexican labor. Under pressure from President Kennedy the Department of Labor tightened the regulations, and in late 1963 Congress voted to end the system entirely, despite the vociferous opposition of farmers. Legislation did not affect the illegal traffic of wetbacks, though large farms grew wary of flouting the law.

The cessation of the bracero system was a boon to those who had struggled to unionize farm labor, since strikebreakers became less easy to recruit. It benefited in particular Cesar Chavez, a saintlike figure who came to symbolize not just the campaign for better conditions in the fields, but also the struggle for Hispanic civil rights.

Chavez had been born in 1927 on a small farm near Yuma, Arizona. His entire family became migrant workers ten years later, after losing their farm in the Depression. As a boy, Chavez attended more than thirty schools around the American West. He was forced to give up his education entirely after the eighth grade in order to help his family make ends meet. His experience as a migrant worker gave his subsequent struggle on behalf of farm laborers resounding moral force.

After a short spell in the Navy, Chavez settled in the poor San Jose barrio known to locals as Sal Si Puedes ("Get Out If You Can"). There he met two people who would profoundly influence his development as a campaigner for social justice. The first was Father Donald McDonnell, who introduced Chavez to the writings of Saint Francis and Mahatma

Gandhi, instilling in him an absolute faith in nonviolence. The teachings of McDonnell were given practical application through Chavez's association with Fred Ross, of the Community Service Organization. For Chavez, the CSO provided the logical outlet for his crusading zeal. From 1953 onward he worked tirelessly in the San Jose area on voter registration, immigration, discrimination, and tax issues, thus helping poor Hispanic immigrants adjust to life in the United States.

Chavez could not, however, forget his past as a migrant farm worker, nor could he ignore the fact that the people most in need of help were those least able to draw attention to themselves. When, in 1962, the CSO refused permission to organize farm workers, he struck out on his own, forming the National Farm Workers Association (NFWA), which later became the United Farm Workers (UFW). He hesitated to call it a union because of the tragic history of unionization in the fields. "The revolt . . . is more than a labor struggle," one member insisted. It was instead "the desire of a New World race to reconcile the conflicts of its 500-year-old history." The preamble to the NFWA constitution, drawn from Pope Leo XIII's encyclical *Rerum Novarum* (1891), demonstrated that the struggle was as much for social justice as for material benefit: "Rich men and masters should remember this—that to exercise pressure for the sake of gain upon the indigent and destitute, and to make one's profit out of the need of another, is condemned by laws, human and divine. To defraud anyone of wages that are his due is a crime which cries to the avenging anger of heaven."[61]

The NFWA reflected Chavez's personal philosophy. A humble man, he never developed the ego that usually went with leadership of a large campaign, despite the fact that reverence for him was deep and widespread. Drawing from the teachings of Gandhi and Saint Francis, he turned the humility and poverty of the farm worker into a powerful propaganda tool. In their struggle against farm owners, he urged followers to "resist with every ounce of human endurance and spirit. . . . Resist not with retaliation in kind but to overcome with love and compassion, with ingenuity and creativity, with hard work and longer hours, with stamina and patient tenacity, with truth and public appeal, with friends and allies, with mobility and discipline, with politics and law, and with prayer and fasting." Eliseo Medina was an eighteen-year-old farm worker when he first came across Chavez at a rally. "I didn't know what the hell he looked like," he recalled.

A friend introduced him. "He's a little pipsqueak. That's Cesar Chavez? He wasn't a great speaker, but he started talking and made a lot of sense. We deserved to be paid a fair wage. Because we're poor we shouldn't be taken advantage of. We had rights too in this country. We deserve more. The strike wouldn't be easy. The more he said how tough it would be, the more people wanted to do it. By the time the meeting ended, . . . that was it for me." NFWA organizers were expected to live like the people they represented and were continually reminded of their duty to serve the powerless. The NFWA gave them room and board and just $5 a week pocket money, in order to ensure that they were not attracted to the job for reasons of pay. Intense training ensured that organizers were "fit not only physically but spiritually." Woven through every action was an uncompromising faith in nonviolence. "We do not need to destroy to win," Chavez stressed. "We are a movement that builds and does not destroy." In what could have served as a direct rejoinder to Malcolm X, Chavez proclaimed: "It is how we use our lives that determines what kind of men we are. . . . I am convinced that the truest act of manliness is to sacrifice ourselves for others in a totally nonviolent struggle for justice. To be a man is to suffer for others." "Participation and self-determination remain the best experience of freedom," he argued. "Only the enslaved in despair have need of violent overthrow."[62]

Chavez perceived a big opportunity in 1965, when the Agricultural Workers Organizing Committee (AWOC), a predominantly Filipino organization centered in Delano, California, went on strike after farm owners cut wages in the middle of the grape harvest. As a gesture of solidarity, the NFWA joined the action, and before long Chavez emerged as leader. A conventional strike was linked to a high-profile campaign to persuade consumers to boycott grapes. This involved acquainting them with the hardships behind the fruit on their table. "The consumer boycott," Chavez explained, "is the only open door in the dark corridor of nothingness down which farm workers have had to walk for many years. It is a gate of hope through which they expect to find the sunlight of a better life for themselves and their families." At the peak of the boycott, more than 13 million Americans refused to buy grapes.[63]

The NFWA was not simply a union, and the strike was not simply a strike. Chavez called his campaign "La Causa." He wanted something permanent—a movement. This would come when there are enough people with one idea so that their actions are together like the huge wave of water which nothing can stop. It is when a group of people begins to care enough so that they are willing to make sacrifices. The movement of the Negro began in the hot summer of Alabama ten years ago, when a Negro woman refused to be pushed to the back of the bus. . . . Sometime in the future, they will say that in the hot summer of California in 1965 the movement of the farm workers began. It began with a small series of strikes. It started so slowly that at first it was only one man, then five, then one hundred. This is how a movement begins.

While the wage cut was the trigger, Chavez was not interested exclusively in bread-and-butter issues. He wanted to give farm workers dignity. Their humility in the face of extreme poverty was used to inspire public sympathy; they did not stridently demand a raise but instead appealed to the American sense of justice. Because it was not a one-issue struggle, La Causa could not be broken by strikebreakers or by simple concessions on matters of pay.[64]

Organizing a group of itinerant workers who had little education posed unique problems. The nature of their work—unskilled, low-pay, temporary, and grueling—rendered farm workers notoriously lacking in self-esteem and gave them a fatalistic attitude toward oppression. The conventional methods of mobilization—meetings, speeches, pamphlets, and so on—were ineffective. Organizing had to be personal, based upon a gradual establishment of trust between worker and representative. Art, music, and theater were used to communicate potent messages. Since modes of expression were rooted in Latino culture, they simultaneously helped to encourage the development of cultural pride. Plays by the touring company El Teatro Campesino were first performed in the mid-1960s on the back of a flatbed truck. Luis Valdez explained that humor proved the best weapon against oppression:

> Humor is our major asset . . . not only from a satirical point of view, but from the fact that humor can stand up on its own and is a much more healthy child of the theater than, let's say, tragedy or realism. You can't do that on the flatbed of a truck. . . . We use comedy because it stems from a necessary situation—the necessity of lifting the morale of our strikers. . . . We try to make social points, not in

spite of the comedy, but through it. This leads us into satire and slapstick, and sometimes very close to the underlying tragedy of it all—the fact that human beings have been wasted in farm labor for generations.

El Teatro Campesino has since become synonymous with Latino culture, performing in theaters around the world. Likewise, Latino artists such as Antonio Bernal, Malaquías Montoya, and Ester Hernández, whose work is now shown in galleries in New York, Paris, and London, started out making murals and posters for La Causa.[65]

Farmers responded by trying to besmirch the reputation of Chavez, portraying him as an untrustworthy foreign subversive who exploited the lowly farm worker to satisfy a craving for power. When E. L. Barr, president of the California Grape and Tree Fruit League, accused Chavez of using terror tactics, the latter responded with his "Letter from Delano," an intentional echo of Martin Luther King's "Letter from a Birmingham Jail." "We have," he argued, "seized upon every tactic consistent with the morality of our cause to expose . . . injustice and thus to heighten the sensitivity of the American conscience." He further insisted that "if to build our union required the deliberate taking of life, either the life of a grower or of his child, or the life of a farm worker or of his child, then I choose not to see the union built."[66]

Chavez was never as articulate as King, but the dignity of his message made up for his lack of eloquence.

> You must understand . . . that our membership . . . are, above all, human beings, no better and no worse than any other cross-section of human society; we are not saints because we are poor, but by the same measure neither are we immoral. We are men and women who have suffered and endured much, and not only because of our abject poverty but because we have been kept poor. . . . God knows that we are not beasts of burden, agricultural implements, or rented slaves; we are men. And mark this well, Mr. Barr, we are men locked in a death struggle against man's inhumanity to man in the industry that you represent. And this struggle itself gives meaning to our life and ennobles our dying.

"Time," argued Chavez, "accomplishes for the poor what money does for the rich." Because he had absolute faith in the justice of his cause, he could be patient; because he was patient, he did not need violence. "We know that our cause is just, that history is a story of social revolution, and that the poor shall inherit the land."[67]

Chavez demonstrated his own commitment with a twenty-five-day fast in 1968, during which he consumed only water. As he explained: "A fast is first and foremost personal. It is a fast for the purification of my own body, mind, and soul. The fast is also a heartfelt prayer for purification and strengthening for all those who work beside me in the farm worker movement. The fast is also an act of penance for those in positions of moral authority and for all men and women activists who know what is right and just, who know that they could and should do more." Those who might not have been sympathetic to La Causa could not help being impressed by Chavez. The fast inevitably raised his profile across the nation and, by implication, that of the farm worker. Politicians desperate to attract the Hispanic vote threw their weight behind La Causa. Robert Kennedy, during his 1968 presidential campaign, came to Delano to break bread with Chavez at the end of his fast. Chavez in turn promised to help mobilize the Latino vote in the California Democratic primary.[68]

If Chavez was the Latino Martin Luther King, Reies Tijerina was the Latino Malcolm X. Tijerina rejected assimilation, emphasizing instead ethnic nationalism, expressed through an attempt to reclaim ancestral land. Like Malcolm, he condemned Chicanos who had "sold out" to white America, calling them traitors—or "Tio Tomases" (Uncle Toms). He was not averse to violence. His militancy left him vulnerable to allegations that he was a Communist stooge or a dangerous demagogue; newspapers delighted in characterizing him as a monster. To Chicanos, his most profound effect came in the way he encouraged ethnic pride. For those who had already assimilated, however, his message rankled. "You know what that bastard . . . has done to me?" one Chicano complained. "He has questioned my whole life. All my life has been based on my denying I am a Mexican to myself. Now there are two sides of me and I have to decide which one I am. . . . I hate that bastard. Who appointed him my conscience?"[69]

Chavez had a similar effect, achieved more quietly. In 1969, he signed a historic agreement with California growers recognizing the UFW as the official union. In that year also, a march to the Mexican border poured scorn on the growers' practice of using wetbacks as strikebreakers. While these demonstrations brought some improvements to the farm labor system, gains were eventually neutralized by increased mechanization and the easy availability of nonunion labor. By 1980, less than 10 percent of the Delano grape harvest was picked by UFW members. That, however, should not detract from Chavez's success in raising Latino consciousness. The deep ethnic solidarity he helped to tap would eventually make Latinos a formidable force in the politics of the Southwest.[70]

Robert Kennedy felt that Chavez was one of the true American heroes of the 1960s. Luis Valdez, who founded El Teatro Campesino, agreed: "What amazed me was that he could completely absorb everything around him. He was brilliant, a genius. He didn't just read about Gandhi; he became a living late-twentieth-century version of him transposed to the American Southwest. He didn't just read about labor movements; he started one. He didn't just read about the arts; he became them." A grower who finally had to accept the power of La Causa put it more bluntly: "Our biggest mistake was to think that Chavez was just another 'dumb Mex.'"[71]

10

TURN, TURN, TURN

SAIGON: TET

Up until December 1967, American soldiers had difficulty finding their Vietnamese enemy. "It was a sheer physical impossibility to keep the enemy from slipping away whenever he wished it," a general reflected. Then, suddenly, during the Lunar New Year called Tet, the enemy was everywhere, most worryingly in the grounds of the American Embassy in Saigon. In an instant, the war changed completely.[1]

From the moment American combat troops had first been deployed, in 1965, the United States had followed a simple strategy of attrition: kill enough of the enemy, and eventually they'll surrender. The body count became the main measure of progress. That strategy, however, worked against the complex task of achieving a politically viable South Vietnam. Americans were destroying Vietnam in order to save it. "At the end of the day the villagers would be turned loose," William Erhart, a young Marine officer, recalled. "Their homes had been wrecked, their chickens killed, their rice confiscated—and if they weren't pro-Vietcong before we got there, they sure as hell were by the time we left."[2]

The war was stuck in stalemate, yet the only logical response was escalation. This, however, put enormous strain on the American economy, especially given Johnson's commitment to the Great Society and NASA. His limited war was not sufficiently limited. Americans had constraints—of time and money. Hanoi, however, had none. Ho Chi Minh understood that Americans would not tolerate a long war, so a long war was what he provided.

The American commander, William Westmoreland, remained stubbornly optimistic. "I am absolutely certain that, whereas in 1965 the enemy was winning, today he is certainly losing," he announced on November 21, 1967. He pledged that "within two years or less, it will be possible . . . to phase down our level of commitment and turn more of the burden . . . over to the Vietnamese armed forces." The Johnson administration sang in harmony. On November 26, vice president Hubert Humphrey claimed "there has been progress on every front in Vietnam. . . . There is no military stalemate."[3]

Optimism was a dish cooked for public consumption. Behind closed doors, anxiety festered. Defense secretary Robert McNamara was utterly disillusioned. "Ho Chi Minh is a tough old S.O.B.," he confessed in private. "He won't quit, no matter how much bombing we do." The sense of futility drove him to tears. "He does it all the time now," McNamara's secretary revealed. Meanwhile, the other members of the administration tried desperately to maintain their composure. Nearly everyone could find evidence of progress when called upon to do so. That, however, was a far cry from believing in victory.[4]

Hanoi, ironically, was also worried. Losses were atrocious. The collapse of the Saigon regime seemed further away in late 1967 than it had three years earlier. According to the Maoist formula, the revolution was supposed to climax in *khoi ngia*—a popular uprising triggered by a general offensive. Politics and war would converge at a single point when the enemy was fatally weakened and the people were absolutely confident in the revolution. In 1967, this conjunction seemed more elusive than ever. The only consolation lay in the fact that Hanoi was better equipped than the United States to endure protracted war. The Communists were winning, but not in the way Mao had prescribed. Guerrilla action, by itself, was not supposed to bring victory. Yet through hundreds of small battles the Communists were gradually eroding American will, bleeding America to death.

The strength of the revolution had been its patience, yet in April 1967 patience wore thin. The Politburo decided to push for a "spontaneous uprising in order to win a decisive victory in the shortest possible time." The decision was not unanimous. A group around Nguyen Chi Thanh argued that the time for *khoi ngia* was fast approaching, while those loyal to Giap steadfastly adhered to protracted war, with its emphasis upon political struggle. Ho Chi Minh was ultimately persuaded to push for quick victory. An official document proclaimed: "We need to inflict a decisive blow, to win a great victory, creating a great leap forward in the strategic situation."[5]

The offensive would begin with an all-embracing attack, planned to coincide with the Tet holiday, traditionally a time of raucous celebration. Ubiquity of action was supposed to demonstrate the strength of the revolution and thus trigger a general uprising. Party officials carefully emphasized that the general offensive would still involve "extremely arduous and complicated military combats and protracted political struggles." Complete victory was nevertheless expected by the end of 1968.[6]

Viet Cong troops were told that the offensive "will be the greatest battle ever fought throughout the history of our country." With that rallying call ringing in their ears, 84,000 soldiers attacked at midnight on January 31, hitting thirty-six provincial capitals, sixty-four district capitals, and a number of military bases. The most conspicuous assault occurred when twenty insurgents penetrated the American Embassy compound and held off a counterattack for six hours, in full view of television cameras. That action was doomed from the outset, but the suffering of American soldiers made unpleasant viewing on the nightly news. Johnson's friend Jack Valenti recalled a common reaction in Washington: "My God, if they can get that close to the embassy, the war is over!"[7]

After order was restored in Saigon, the photographer Eddie Adams was roaming the streets in search of a story. Ahead of him he saw an emaciated man—a Viet Cong guerrilla—being dragged along by Vietnamese marines, his hands tied behind his back. Adams had never found himself so close to the elusive enemy. He quickly aimed his camera. Suddenly, into the frame stepped the chief of the national police, General Nguyen Ngoc Loan, who drew his revolver, put it to the man's head, and fired. Adams captured the moment of execution perfectly, and in so doing produced the most famous image to emerge from the Vietnam War. The New York Times, recognizing its monumental nature, printed the photo prominently on the front page. (Large photos on the front page were unusual back then.) Readers saw an image of utter brutality, made worse by the fact that the perpetrator was an ally. What the photo did not show was that the victim had earlier murdered one of Loan's aides, the aide's wife, and all of his children. (A photo on the same page showed an RVN officer holding the body of his daughter, recently executed by the Viet Cong. That photo was quickly forgotten.)

In Hué, a place of huge symbolic importance, Communist units swept aside the Americans and held the city for a number of weeks. During this period, the revolution's real cruelty was revealed. "Hué was the place where reactionary spirit had existed for over ten years," a party report remarked with clinical detachment. "It took us only a short time to drain it to its root." Translated, this meant that hundreds, perhaps thousands, were executed for the vague crime of being "reactionary."[8]

Elsewhere, Tet was little more than a brief disturbance. It did, however, decimate the Viet Cong (or PLAF). Suddenly conspicuous, insurgents were rounded up and executed. A movement that had taken years to build was ripped to shreds in a moment. Meanwhile, peasants stubbornly refused to throw their weight behind the revolution. No general uprising occurred. The people remained confident that the Communists would eventually win, but until that happened they stayed firmly on the fence.

The offensive continued for the next eighteen months—the bloodiest period of the war. In some places, genuine success was achieved. But the revolution paid bitterly. By the end of 1970, victory was more remote than it had been on the eve of Tet. The Politburo concluded that "although Tet had been a great victory and a turning point in the war, further military successes might be delayed for years." Only a fool could fail to notice the contradiction in that statement.[9]

Westmoreland boasted that Tet was a "colossal military defeat" for the enemy. The United States, he said, had "never been in a better position." Eager to exploit this "great opportunity," he asked for 206,000 additional men, which implied the mobilization of reserves. Many Americans, even those who still supported the war, wondered why, if Communist forces had been so decisively beaten, Westmoreland needed more troops.[10]

Johnson feigned tenacity. "I do not believe we will ever buckle," he told reporters. "There will be blood, sweat, and tears shed. The weak will drop from the lines, their feet sore and their voices loud. Persevere in Vietnam we will and we must." His brave face was, however, purely cosmetic. Johnson faced a classic dilemma: if he rejected Westmoreland's request, he might lose the war; yet if he granted it, he might lose the election. Tet had destroyed the illusion of limited war: there was no "middle way" between escalation and withdrawal.[11]

Public support melted like ice cream in summer. Gallup found that one person in five shifted from hawk to dove between early February and mid-

March. Before Tet, approval of Johnson's handling of the war had stood at 39 percent; afterward it fell to 26 percent. On February 27 the CBS anchorman Walter Cronkite, reporting from Vietnam, vividly expressed American unease: "We have been too often disappointed by the optimism of the American leaders, both in Vietnam and Washington, to have faith any longer in the silver linings they find in the darkest clouds. . . . For it seems now more certain than ever that the bloody experience of Vietnam is to end in stalemate." Listening to the broadcast, Johnson remarked: "If I've lost Cronkite, I've lost the war."[12]

Johnson consulted Clark Clifford, who would shortly replace McNamara as secretary of defense. "We can no longer rely just on the field commander," he warned. "He can want troops and want troops and want troops. We must look at the overall impact on us, including the situation here in the United States. We must look at our economic stability, our other problems in the world, our other problems at home; we must consider whether or not this thing is tying us down so that we cannot do some of the other things we should be doing." "I was convinced that the military course we were pursuing was not only endless, but hopeless," Clifford reflected. He recommended that Westmoreland's request be denied and that the military burden should be shifted toward the ARVN. Accepting the thrust of Clifford's recommendations, Johnson approved only a token troop increase of 22,000.[13]

"Tet . . . shook the enemy's aggressive will to its foundation and put an end to the US dream of achieving 'victory' by escalating the war," the North Vietnamese general Tran Van Tra boasted. "It awakened the United States to the fact that might, resources, and money have their limits." That is a fair assessment. Tet *was* a psychological defeat for the Americans. Those inclined to praise Hanoi's handling of the war assume that that must have been the plan all along. Giap encouraged this interpretation: "We wanted to project the war into the homes of America's families, because we knew that most of them had nothing against us." That, however, is tripe, all the more indigestible coming from a man who originally considered the offensive insane. Granted, the Communists were expert propagandists acutely aware of the war's effect upon the American people. But no government is so stupid as to sacrifice 40,000 soldiers in the elusive hope of psychological victory. Tet was supposed to lead to a decisive *military* victory, not something that could be packaged as psychological triumph. The commander Tran Do was more honest: "We didn't achieve our main objective, which was to spur uprisings throughout the South. . . . As for making an impact in the United States, it had not been our intention—but it turned out to be a fortunate result."[14]

Tet is often carelessly labeled a turning point. Occasionally, however, events turn in the wrong direction. The Communists had been winning the war before the offensive; they were shattered after it. As for the United States, it fought for two and a half years before Tet, and five years afterward. Nearly as many Americans died after the battle as before. Johnson was a demoralized commander-in-chief whose direction of the war was deeply flawed. His defense secretary, McNamara, was a broken man, while Clifford (McNamara's replacement) could not muster enthusiasm for futility. Tet, however, opened the door for Richard Nixon, Henry Kissinger, Melvin Laird, and a number of other hardliners who were determined to make North Vietnam pay dearly for every inch of gain. In other words, Tet hardly seems a clever psychological victory. It was in fact a colossal blunder which prolonged the war, causing unnecessary suffering on both sides. The true nature of the calamity can be gauged by Ho's reaction. According to the historian Thai Van Kiem, Ho "silently regretted not having listened to Vo Nguyen Giap. . . . Following this burning debacle, Ho's health declined day by day. He never got over this defeat. Unable even to sleep, he died the next year, in 1969."[15]

ATLANTIC CITY: FROM MISS AMERICA TO MS. WORLD

Wherever lovely women gathered, Bert Parks was often nearby. In the Sixties, he was often master of ceremonies at beauty pageants. Few people knew why he was a celebrity; fewer still could recall him doing anything other than hosting beauty contests. Parks believed sincerely in his role. Judging the female form was only natural, he insisted, since a beautiful woman was like a sublime work of art. His opening monologue always celebrated the fact that the contest brought lovely women together in an arena free of politics. Afterward, the winner was sent on a goodwill tour to Vietnam.

Since pageants were highly ritualized, Parks had no reason to expect that the 1968 event in Atlantic City would be any different from previous ones. His jokes were canned, the contestants predictably pretty. But then came weird noises from the wings, puffs of smoke, loud bangs, and a clutch of women who did not remotely resemble Miss Nevada. Looking decidedly shaken, Parks was hustled from the scene by burly men in black suits. His face showed utter bewilderment: Why would anyone want to disrupt something so beautiful as a beauty pageant? After about twenty minutes of shouting, two dozen protesters from the New York Radical Women collective (NYRW) were hustled from the scene and unreality was restored.

Prior to the action, the protesters had picketed outside the venue, where they had crowned a sheep Miss America. They had also grabbed a rubbish bin, dubbed it the Freedom Trash Can, and proceeded to fill it with symbols of women's enslavement—girdles, bras, makeup, curlers, mascara, high-heeled shoes. City authorities denied permission to ignite the contents, for fear the fire would spread to the wooden boardwalk. No one present recalls the bin being ignited, but that is how the event was subsequently reported. "It was a time of draft card burning," Susan Brownmiller recalls, "and some smart headline writer decided to call it a 'bra-burning' because it sounded insulting to the . . . women's movement. We only threw a bra symbolically in a trash can." From that day forward, feminists were called "bra-burners" by those disinclined to understand. In truth, more bras were burned in off-color jokes told by men than ever were burned in protest by women.[16]

The women who took part in the Atlantic City action were almost all veterans of the civil rights movement or other New Left protests. They had been the support troops and camp followers, the good little girls who did precisely what their men asked. This, however, was *their* action. "We . . . all felt, well, grown up," their leader Robin Morgan confessed. "We were doing this one for ourselves, not for our men." Respecting themselves was, however, much easier than earning the respect of others. At the time, "feminist" was essentially synonymous with "spinster," "lesbian," or "witch." In the *Washington Post*, Harriet Van Horne described the NYRW as an army of women who were "unstroked, uncaressed, and emotionally undernourished."[17]

The scene was reenacted two years later at the Miss World pageant in London. This time the master of ceremonies was Bob Hope, a man who, like Parks, believed in the therapeutic properties of feminine beauty. Again, some loud bangs interrupted the proceedings, whereupon female invaders started shouting, "We're not beautiful! We're not ugly! We're angry!" For perhaps the first time in history, the public saw the nasty side of Hope. On returning to the stage after order was restored, he sneered: "Anyone who wants to disrupt something as beautiful as this must be on some kind of dope. The perpetrators will pay for this. Upstairs will see to that."[18]

For Laura Mulvey, one of the demonstrators, the event was an epiphany—an attack upon sexism but also a personal liberation. "It was enormously exciting, the adrenalin, a feeling that it was a gesture that came out of political commitment but was very contrary to any kind of actions I might have expected of myself." The protest was important because it was entirely free of male interference. Women had not submitted to male direction, nor had they been forced to subsume their gender-based goals into a wider social revolution, as had customarily been the case within the "movement." They had used the tools of the revolution for themselves.[19]

Earlier in the decade, Betty Friedan's *Feminine Mystique* (1963) had exposed the discontent of women in a world of limited opportunities. Housewives trapped in suburbia were, Friedan argued, slowly driven to despair by drudgery. Friedan's work provided a foundation for the later feminist movement, but not an entirely appropriate one. She wrote about white, middle-class, suburban women who lived the "good life" but still felt unfulfilled. "As she made the beds, shopped for groceries, matched slipcover material, ate peanut butter sandwiches with her children, chauffeured Cub Scouts and Brownies, lay beside her husband at night—she was afraid to ask even of herself the silent question—'Is this all?'" Women of the Sixties generation, because they rejected that suburban ethos, assumed that they could also sidestep the discontent it implied. Radical baby boomers were certain that the world they would create would have limitless opportunities for both sexes and that enlightenment would render sexism obsolete.[20]

As it turned out, change did not spell liberation. "From a girl's point of view, the important thing to remember about the 60s is that it was totally male-dominated," Nicola Lane recalled. "You were not really encouraged to be a thinker. You were there really for fucks and domesticity. . . . It was a difficult time." The alternative society, built on freedom, in truth meant the freedom to exploit women. "The treatment [women] got was so offhand and casual, verging on the contemptuous," Charles Shaar Murray felt. "It was all 'Yay! Freedom! Let everyone do what they want,' but the little woman is still over in the corner. She may be wearing a flowered dress and a headband, but she's still the one who rolls the joints . . . and generally does . . . 'the chick work.' A lot of the girls were trying to be good hippies, doing whatever good hippies did, which meant that a lot of them would literally fuck anybody, do all the washing up, and so on." "What finally knackered the underground was its complete inability to deal with women's liberation," David Widgery wrote in Oz. "Men defined themselves as rebels against society in ways limited to their own sex, excluding women except as loyal companions or mother figures." Morgan felt that the "Hip Culture and the so-called Sexual Revolution . . . functioned towards women's freedom as did the Reconstruction toward former slaves—reinstituted oppression by another name."[21]

For many women, sex was their way into the movement, but also the method of their debasement. Since many joined as girlfriends of activist men, it was difficult to discard that sense of belonging to a man and be taken seriously as a comrade. Rather too typical was the advice Dieter Kunzelmann of the German radical group Kommune 1 gave to his male colleagues on the process of indoctrinating female members: "It's like training a horse. One guy has to break her in; then she's available for everyone." A movement that placed such heavy emphasis upon sex, and particularly sex without emotional commitment, perhaps understandably ended up treating women like sex objects. The novelist Sheila MacLeod feels that the "revolution" allowed men to "indulge their preferences for irresponsibility and lack of emotional commitment." Women who objected were invariably banished from the temple and told to take their "hangups" elsewhere.[22]

For all the talk of participatory democracy, the Sixties generation was rather keen on male heroes. Movement leaders enjoyed both political and sexual status. Robert Haber's wife, Barbara, noted that "there were a few dozen men who stood out as incarnations of the Revolution, so that to sleep with them was the equivalent of taking political communion." Like the dominant male in a pride of lions, they easily attracted women desperate to service them. Marjory Tabankin, an activist at the University of Wisconsin and the first female president of the National Student Association, recalls her eager anticipation of a visit by Tom Hayden. "The first thing he handed me was his dirty laundry and asked if I would do it for him. I said, 'I'll have it for you by tonight.'" Inevitably, women who had entered the movement with millennial visions of an equitable society grew disappointed at the stubborn survival of patriarchy. "The point about the underground was that this was not the way things were supposed to happen," observes Rosie Boycott. "They were meant to be equally beneficial to everybody. But for a long time even the communes felt that it was right that Sue bakes bread and Bill brings in the cows."[23]

Suzanne Goldberg, wife of Mario Savio, recalls the irony of struggling to express herself at Free Speech Movement meetings. "I was on the executive committee and the steering committee. . . . I would make a suggestion and no one would react. Thirty minutes later Mario or Jack Weinberg would make the same suggestion and everyone would react." Subservience, being familiar, impeded enlightenment. Old patterns were hard to break. Sue Miles, a hugely intelligent and creative woman who helped found *IT,* recalled that "as the only woman there my job was to make the tea and the sandwiches, and whenever they were going to actually make decisions I was asked to go out of the room. And I did." Cassandra Wedd, who worked for the British underground weekly *INK,* recalled: "I was treated badly but I didn't realise it at that stage—I was used to being treated badly. I'd been a secretary and I didn't expect to be treated any better." Richard Neville admitted that he could never have produced *Oz* without a few women who managed to make sure that the important things got done while the "creative" males indulged in drugs and sex. But those women were never mentioned on the masthead. It did not occur to him to do things differently. "It was the culture of the time."[24]

Male SDS activists saw nothing remotely wrong with a document arguing that "the system is like a woman—you've got to fuck it to make it change." White Panthers went further, calling upon members to "fuck your woman so hard till she can't stand up." New Left women gradually came to realize that their male comrades' behavior in bed was a good indication of the level of their enlightenment. In Germany, the Frankfurt Broads collective launched a particularly furious attack upon male activists:

> We won't open our mouth! If we open it, nothing comes out! If we leave it open, it gets stuffed for us: with petty-bourgeois dicks, socialist screw pressure, socialist children, love, socialist flotsam and jetsam, turgidity, socialist potent horniness, socialist intellectual pathos, . . . revolutionary fumbling about, sexual-revolutionary argu-

ments . . . BLAH BLAH BLAH! . . . Let's vomit it out: we have penis envy, we are frustrated, hysterical, uptight, asexual, lesbian, frigid, shortchanged, irrational. . . . We compensate, we overcompensate. . . . We have penis envy, penis envy, penis envy.

The attack came with a political cartoon showing a proud, naked woman holding an axe. On the wall are the mounted penises of prominent members of the German New Left. The message ended: "Liberate the socialist pricks from their bourgeois dicks!"[25]

Casey Hayden and Mary King, both members of SNCC, found that male colleagues reacted with derision when they tried to compare the plight of women to that of blacks. "If the question is raised, they respond: 'That's the way it's supposed to be. There are biological differences.'" Wini Breines felt that "the main reason that [we] relied so heavily on the comparisons between sexism and racism is that white male politicos recognized the race issue as morally legitimate, while dismissing feminism as 'a bunch of chicks with personal problems.'" When Marilyn Webb tried to inject a feminist point of view into a political rally in 1969, men in the audience shouted: "Take her off the stage and fuck her!"[26] Misogyny was deepest in militant movements with a heavy emphasis upon masculinity. Within the Black Panthers, for instance, the cherished image of a bad dude was enhanced through sadistic exploitation of women. Elaine Brown recalled "slave-like beatings and other sexist power plays." Black power obviously did not extend to black women. "A woman," says Brown, "was considered, at best, irrelevant. A woman asserting herself was a pariah. A woman attempting a role of leadership was, to my proud black Brothers, making an alliance with the counter-revolutionary, man-hating, lesbian, feminist white bitches."[27]

In contrast to the later feminist movement, which trumpeted the slogan "The personal is political," female activists found that thinking personally was actively discouraged. Women were instead supposed to submerge their interests within those of the movement, always reassured (by men) that, since patriarchy was a product of capitalism, the revolution would bring sexual equality. Meanwhile, by doing the dishes, they would hasten the advent of the socialist millennium. For a very long time, women bought this radical cant. For instance, as late as 1969, an SDS women's group placed a resolution before the annual convention to the effect that "as long as the material base for male chauvinism exists, it cannot be completely defeated. Therefore, the primary fight must be against this capitalist system of exploitation." Those who complained about subservience were criticized for placing selfish concerns before those of society. Ellen Willis recalled: "It's hard to convey to people who didn't go through that experience how radical, how unpopular and difficult it was just to get up and say, 'Men oppress women. Men have oppressed *me*. Men must take responsibility for their actions instead of blaming them on capitalism. And, yes, that means *you*.' We were laughed at, patronized, called frigid, emotionally disturbed man-haters, and—worst insult of all on the left!—apolitical."[28]

All these experiences were folded into a batter of consciousness. Female activists learned that individual liberation had to be pursued distinct from the broader social transformation which radical groups advocated. "As we analyze the position of women in capitalist society," one SDS women's group resolved in 1967, "we recognize ourselves as part of the Third World. Women, because of their colonial relationship to men, have to fight for their own independence." A male-dominated organization could not be trusted to deliver emancipation, since men were never likely to appreciate that they were the problem. That resolution heralded an eventual break from the movement, since the problems it outlined were irresolvable within the mechanism of a male-dominated group.[29]

The transformation often occurred as a result of practical experiences of protest. "We fought shoulder to shoulder [with the men] and we couldn't see any difference between what were our roles and battles and what were theirs," a Mexican female protester argued. "We were all androgynous. We were brave fighters, the same as any man." Demonstrations were democratic in the distribution of pain. Police swung billy clubs with no consideration for gender. Tear gas floated everywhere. For women, most of whom were unfamiliar with violence, this was their first opportunity to show bravery. Direct action also provided a very effective way to sidestep traditional bureaucratic obstacles to women's participation. Women got noticed at demonstrations, even if for the wrong reasons. All this meant that protests often brought epiphany. One female Harvard graduate commented that they "changed my life—in the way I questioned everything, in the sense of involvement in something greater than myself, and in the sense of my outrage."[30]

The emergence of a new feminist movement came at the end of the decade because it took time for otherwise patient women to realize they were being short-changed. "If the fool persist in his folly he becomes wise," Angela Carter reflected, alluding to William Blake. "I suppose that was how I came to feminism, in the end, because . . . all the time I thought things were going well I was in reality a second-class citizen." Sheila MacLeod feels that feminism's "time had come because the sixties were over, and eyes which had been clouded with 'peace and love' . . . were now wearily cold and clear." Looking back, she recalls a transformation in her assessment of the Sixties. At first, the blatant sexism so appalled her that she found it difficult to discern anything of worth. "The sixties looked very much like a male invention based in power, promiscuity and self-abuse," she once thought. But, as time passed, she began to see that hypocrisy and betrayal were necessary to the development of consciousness. "It is not mistakes as such which are reprehensible but the inability to learn from them," she now feels. A German feminist expressed that coming-of-age more graphically, declaring that she no longer wanted to be "just a . . . shapely mass of flesh with a hole."[31]

The endless talk about freedom eventually convinced some women to exercise it. "In the midst of sexist movements, women were having experiences that transformed their consciousness and changed their lives," asserts Breines. "When women acquired the experience and skills that enabled them to feel strong enough to move out on their own, it was with political ideas that they had inherited from the sixties." For those women who called themselves feminists by 1970, the decade had been a hard but necessary apprenticeship. Because of what they had learned, better days lay ahead. They'd come to realize that protest was more powerful if it had an identifiable goal, such as affordable childcare or the legalization of abortion, and not simply the wholesale transformation of society. "Certainly for me, it's the seventies which signal change, growth and understanding of things," Sue O'Sullivan concluded. "It was in the seventies that I became part of a movement which made sense of the world in a way which also gave me agency."[32]

"There is a tendency to underplay, even devalue completely, the experience of the 1960s, especially for women," Carter has observed. "But towards the end of the decade there was a brief period of public philosophical awareness that occurs only very occasionally in human history; when, truly, it felt like Year One, when all that was holy was in the process of be-

ing profaned, and we were attempting to grapple with the real relations between human beings."[33]

GREENWICH VILLAGE: STONEWALL

The Stonewall Inn was a squalid dump of a bar in the West Village. For
that reason, New York City's gay community loved it. "It was a dive," Eric
Marcus admitted. "It was shabby and the glasses they served the watered-
down drinks in weren't particularly clean. . . . Patrons included every type
of person: some transvestites, a lot of students, young people, older people, businessmen." "The Stonewall . . . had become, in the late sixties, my
own bar of choice," Martin Duberman recalls. "I loved its cruisy, non-
vanilla mix of people, its steamy dancing." Its appeal derived in part from
the fact that, at any moment, the police might raid the place.[34]

Raids were an accepted part of gay life in New York, and usually took
a ritualized, benign form. Police would phone in a tip beforehand and arrive in the early part of the evening, so that business could return to normal in time for the after-midnight crowds. "The lights suddenly went on
(announcing the arrival of somebody suspect)," Duberman remembers.
"Dancing and touching of any kind instantly stopped, and the police
stalked arrogantly through, glaring from side to side, demanding IDs, terrifying those not having them with threats of arrest." After a brief flutter
of excitement, the bar would return to normal.[35]

The night of June 27, 1969, was different. Eight officers from the First
Precinct arrived at 1:20 A.M. The mere sight of men in uniforms sent shock-
waves through the crowd, even before the lights went up. Doors were then
locked and no one was allowed to leave. Fifteen minutes later, the police
announced that patrons were to line up and proceed single-file out of the
bar. At the door, IDs were checked and all staff, all transvestites, and any
other "undesirables" were detained. They were herded into the coatroom—
put into the closet.

Those allowed to leave congregated on the pavement, waiting to see
what would happen. After a short while, prisoners were escorted to a
paddy wagon. The crowd grew restless, shouting and gesticulating at the
police. The exact sequence of events is confused, due to differing perspectives. Eric Marcus thought that the police deliberately turned their back
on the prisoners, allowing them to escape. Others witnessed a scuffle as a

prisoner was bundled into a patrol car. The first sign of trouble occurred when people started throwing pennies at the police. A light shower quickly turned into a downpour. Then someone threw a rock. Then another. The windows on the second floor were smashed, showering glass on the police. Feeling dangerously outnumbered, they retreated into the bar.

At one point the front door opened and someone from inside pointed a gun at the crowd, ordering people to stay back. A few retreated, but a solid angry core advanced. Someone uprooted a parking meter and proceeded to use it as a battering ram, breaking the bottom-floor windows. Someone else set fire to a trashcan and threw the burning material through the broken window. The police put out the fire from inside with a hose, and then trained it on the crowd. Instead of causing people to disperse, the water had the opposite effect. A full-scale riot broke out.

A fire engine arrived, followed closely by the serried ranks of the Tactical Police Force (TPF), a special unit trained to respond to violent demonstrations. Showing up in full riot gear, they seemed in no mood for dialogue. Meanwhile the storm of projectiles continued, occasionally punctuated by shouts of "Gay Power!" At first the police tried to herd the crowd away, but, outnumbered, they had little success. They occasionally charged, grabbing one or two protesters to beat mercilessly. "Seventh Avenue . . . looked like a battlefield in Vietnam," one witness recalled. "Young people, many of them queens, were lying on the sidewalk, bleeding from the head, face, mouth, and even the eyes. Others were nursing bruised and often bleeding arms, legs, backs, and necks."[36]

After about forty-five minutes of mayhem, the crowd dispersed, calm was restored, and the police left. "HOMO NEST RAIDED," the *Daily News* shouted the next day. "Queen Bees Are Stinging Mad!" New York gays had experienced firsthand the cohesive power of violence. On the following night, an angry crowd returned to Stonewall, to drink again from solidarity fountain. Lucien Truscott was there:

> Friday night's crowd had returned and was being led in "gay power" cheers by a group of gay cheerleaders. "We are the Stonewall girls / We wear our hair in curls / We have no underwear / We show our pubic hairs!" . . . If Friday night had been pick-up night, Saturday was date night. Hand-holding, kissing, and posing accented each of the cheers with a homosexual liberation that had appeared only

fleetingly on the street before. One-liners were as practiced as if they had been used for years. "I just want you to all know," quipped a platinum blond with obvious glee, "that sometimes being a homo-sexual is a big pain in the ass."

Irreverence was an expression of assertiveness. "Older boys had strained looks on their faces," wrote Truscott, "and talked in concerned whispers as they watched the up-and-coming generation take being gay and flaunt . . . it before the masses."[37]

The streets were quiet for the next two days, but then, on the fifth day, another riot broke out, again notable for its solidarity. In riot terms, what had happened was hardly remarkable. Inner-city disturbances were ten a penny in the late 1960s. What distinguished Stonewall was the constitu-ency from which the rioters arose. To many people, a militant gay seemed an oxymoron, which explains why the protesters' viciousness took police by surprise. Gays had previously responded to discrimination by turn-ing the other cheek. They felt isolated, in part because they could not call upon a reliable phalanx of sympathetic supporters from the straight world. Straights might not have objected to homosexuality, but they were unlikely to campaign actively on gays' behalf. "The result," wrote Truscott, "was a kind of liberation, as the gay brigade emerged from the bars, back rooms, and bedrooms of the Village and became street people."[38]

Up until 1965, police in American cities had felt free to harass gays, liber-ally interpreting indecency laws in order to make arrests on the flimsiest of grounds. The names of those present at gay hangouts were frequently published in the press even when no crime had been committed. In re-sponse to gentle protests by the Homophile Movement and the Matta-chine Society, these practices had moderated somewhat by the latter half of the decade. Nevertheless, in New York, it remained possible for the Li-quor Control Board to revoke the license of a bar if the staff knowingly served homosexuals. In 1966 Dick Leitch challenged this ruling by holding a "sip-in" with his gay friends. When they were refused a drink, they com-plained to the Human Rights Commission, causing the Liquor Control Board to relax its policy. Nevertheless, bars remained reluctant to serve gays, for fear of attracting police attention, or out of reluctance to become known as a homosexual hangout. As a result, most openly gay bars were owned by members of the Mafia, who sensed a financial opportunity and who already had a secure relationship with the police.

The Stonewall raid seems to have run counter to an increasing liberality on the part of police and city officials. The fact that New York was embroiled in a tight mayoral race might explain the show of force. The police and the city failed to realize, however, the extent to which feelings within the gay community had changed since the mid-Sixties. Tolerance of gays may have been increasing, but not as fast as gay anger. "We don't give a damn whether people like us or not," James Owles of the Gay Activists' Alliance argued. "We want the rights we're entitled to." If gays at Stonewall had seemed to act with uncanny unanimity, it is because they had in common a deep sense of oppression. No one would have predicted an event of this magnitude on that particular night, but at the same time no one familiar with the gay community would have been surprised. For gays, throwing things at police or shouting slogans was empowering. As Marcus has written: "I watched. I wasn't looking for a fight. I can't claim credit for the small acts of violence that took place. I didn't break any windows. I wasn't the one who had a knife and cut the tires on the paddy wagon. I didn't hit a cop and I didn't get hit by a cop. But it was a very emotional turning point for me. It was the first time I had seen anything like that. . . . For me, this festering wound, the anger from oppression and discrimination, was coming out very fast at the point of Stonewall." "Sheridan Square this weekend looked like something from a William Burroughs novel," wrote Truscott. "The sudden specter of 'gay power' raised its brazen head and spat out a fairy tale the likes of which the area has never seen." For Allen Ginsberg, the effect was immediately apparent on the faces of gays in New York. "They've lost that wounded look that fags all had ten years ago."[39]

Instead of feeling alone and defeated, gays suddenly felt united and powerful. Stonewall was a turning point in the history of gay politics in America and the world. But however appropriate that description might be, it cannot be denied that the moment of epiphany had a long gestation. Gay solidarity was expressed with such intensity in 1969 for the simple reason that it was the product of a culture of protest that had been gathering strength since the beginning of the decade. Gay liberation was built on the intersection of New Left radicalism and countercultural revolt. Gays borrowed their tactics and dialectic from the politicos, but learned confidence in their own sexuality and a belief in sexual freedom from the hippies. The gay movement was also typical of late-Sixties separatist groups such as the radical feminists, black nationalists, and Chicanos. Like them, gays had lost faith in the potential for a comprehensive political revolution and had instead decided to fight for their own distinct cause, with violence if necessary.

The sense of liberation borrowed from the counterculture made gays more inclined to come out of the closet. This was more likely to occur in big cities, which provided anonymity and also allowed gays to hook up with similarly oppressed soul fellows. In San Francisco and New York, the gay communities reached critical mass, achieving a culture within a culture. As Carl Wittman explained: "San Francisco is a refugee camp for homosexuals. We have fled here from every part of the nation, and, like refugees elsewhere, we came not because it is so great here, but because it was so bad there. By the tens of thousands, we fled small towns where to be ourselves would endanger our jobs and any hope of a decent life; we have fled from blackmailing cops, from families who disowned or 'tolerated' us; we have been drummed out of the armed services, thrown out of schools, fired from jobs, beaten by punks and policemen." Greater confidence led to greater openness. This made gays more visible, but at the same time more vulnerable. Most straights preferred homosexuality to remain out of sight. "Straights . . . prefer to think it doesn't exist, but if it does, at least keep quiet about it," one gay man complained. Once in the open, gays became easy targets for homophobic abuse. That explains why violence against homosexuals increased at the same time that tolerance rose. It also explains the Stonewall raid.[40]

Stonewall turned gays from an affinity group into a movement. The riots led directly to the formation of the Gay Liberation Front (GLF) in the United States, with similar radical separatist groups forming across Europe in the early 1970s. The appropriation of the label "gay" was a deliberate affront to polite society and, as such, symbolic of newfound pride. Calling the movement a liberation front implied a parallel with the Viet Cong, another group fighting American oppression. The GLF was dedicated to eradicating the "dirty, vile, fucked-up capitalist conspiracy," a somewhat strange mission, given that most gays were dyed-in-the-wool capitalists and the socialist countries were hardly notable for their tolerance of homosexuality. None of that seemed to matter, however, since the important thing was to feel part of a worldwide community of oppressed. Thus, radical gays often supported the black, Chicano, Vietnamese, Third World, and female-liberation struggles, and felt certain that their struggle was as valid as any other. "Negroes, Spanish Americans, hippies, [and] homosexuals . . . represent minority elements of society," one gay man reasoned. "They are also the public. Who, then, will defend the public from the public defenders?" As Wittman argued: "There is no future in arguing about degrees of oppression. A lot of 'movement' types come on with a line of shit about homosexuals not being oppressed as much as blacks or Vietnamese or workers or women. We don't happen to fit into their ideas of class or caste. Bull! When people feel oppressed, they act on that feeling. We feel oppressed. Talk about the priority of black liberation or ending imperialism over and above gay liberation is just anti-gay propaganda." The obvious deserves mention: blacks, Chicanos, and women did not first have to come out of the closet before asserting their rights. For gays, the first step toward liberation was to invite even more oppression.[41]

The strength of the gay movement lay in the way a spectrum of sexual preferences was turned into something akin to ethnic identity. Sexual practices were less important than political freedom. As Duncan Fallowell explains, "Gay Lib started about '69. The wonderful thing about it was that it had nothing whatsoever to do with sex. Politicized gay life is not a sexual thing. . . . Gay Lib was nothing to do with sex, it was to do with political banners. It's even more true about the lesbian thing, which has nothing to do with the hunger of women to satisfy each other's lusts with each other's bodies—much more to do with trying to live a life in which they're not going to be eaten up by men." The strengthening of "gay" as a political label weakened it as a social label. In order to achieve solidarity and strength, a plethora of disparate groups—homosexuals, bisexuals, lesbians, transsexuals, transvestites, sadomasochists, and so on—marched under a single banner of gay pride. "Our first job is to free ourselves," argued Wittman. "That means clearing our heads of the garbage that's been poured into them." The sense of pride was based on three incontrovertible assumptions: first, that there was nothing abnormal or distasteful about homosexuality; second, that gays could realize power only by coming out; and third, that nothing could be achieved without solidarity. Gay strength was based not on ideology (which can be compromised or discarded), but on identity, which in this case could not easily be denied. Gays lived politics in their everyday life, but especially after they decided to come out. "If we are liberated, we are open about our sexuality," argued Wittman. "Closet queenery must end." A gay person automatically became a radical simply by admitting to being gay.[42]

"Laws discriminating against homosexuals will almost surely be changed," Merle Miller predicted in the *New York Times Magazine* in 1971. But, he argued, "private acceptance of homosexuals and homosexuality will take somewhat longer. Most of the psychiatric establishment will continue to insist that homosexuality is a disease, and homosexuals, unlike the blacks, will not benefit from any guilt feelings on the part of liberals. So far as I can make out, there simply aren't any such feelings. . . . Most people of every political persuasion seem to be too uncertain of their own sexual identification to be anything but defensive. Fearful." New pride nevertheless encouraged new assertiveness. Gays suddenly felt strong enough to adopt the tactics of earlier protest movements: they marched, they demonstrated, they occasionally fought. In time, they would demand rights and use their considerable purchasing power as a political weapon. Gay pride was a product of Sixties radicalism, but the political progress of the gay movement was a phenomenon of subsequent decades. The success of gays in integrating themselves into mainstream society speaks volumes for the long-term effects of the Sixties sexual revolution. That revolution has been widely criticized for being the root cause of many social problems, from the AIDS epidemic to the rise in divorce, the ubiquity of pornography, and the decline of the family. But the most impressive achievement of that revolution was the way sexual relations were accepted as the business of the individual, rather than of the state. While the speed of change varied from area to area, the state gradually came to the conclusion that it had no right to interfere in what occurred between consenting adults. Henceforth, the law was instead used to punish sexual behavior which the vast majority of people deemed unacceptable—rape, polygamy, pedophilia, and so on. Gays, emboldened by Stonewall, argued for "the right to make love with anyone, any way, anytime." Most people still found that goal distasteful, but the vast majority no longer wanted to translate their displeasure into law. In time, the concept of sexual normality would cease to become a central preoccupation of the police and the courts. Both would eventually be called upon to protect the rights of those once considered abnormal.[43]

SAN FRANCISCO: SUMMER OF RAPE

For hippies, San Francisco was the perfect place to build Jerusalem. The mild climate suited the pursuit of hipness, a predominantly public, and sometimes naked, pastime. The Bay Area also had a stable economy, the result, ironically, of the huge influx of Vietnam-era defense spending. Unemployment was low and rent still relatively cheap. Dropping out was easy in an age of affluence.

Hippies parked their wagons in the Haight-Ashbury district around the same time that the Beats were fading into obscurity. The city's tolerance of nonconformity—the result, perhaps, of its multiculturalism—meant that hippies were at first accepted, if not exactly welcomed. Residents were not normally offended by bizarre behavior. In that sense, hippies were simply a new version of the old: a sybaritic group given to flamboyance, attracted to pleasures of the flesh, and dedicated to intoxication.

At first, they seemed harmless. The shenanigans of Ken Kesey and his Merry Pranksters led seamlessly to the joyous hedonism of the Trips Festival and the Human Be-In, all of it played to the soundtrack of the Grateful Dead, Jefferson Airplane, and Buffalo Springfield. The great thing about being a hippie was that it did not require much thought; hipness was a visceral pursuit enjoyed with the brain in neutral. Ideological commitment was not essential, other than the commitment to have fun. While the Beat life had required some intellectual effort, being a hippie was much more superficial—identity could be achieved with a kaftan, a psychedelic poster, a black light, a range of drugs, a few hip phrases, some incense, and a handful of lentils. Granted, there were those like Leary, Ginsberg, and the Diggers who tried to graft ideology onto escapism, but their preaching was largely ignored. In any case, the prevailing philosophy was to let everyone do their own thing. To impose rules was against the rules. It seemed genuinely possible to create the perfect world in California, as long as the acid was pure and the music loud. Gentle people found love everywhere. "Haight is love" went the mantra.

Back when brothers Ron and Jay Thelin opened the first psychedelic shop in Haight-Ashbury on January 1, 1966, hippies were rare. Eighteen months later, they could have filled Candlestick Park. Tour buses took bewildered sightseers to "the largest hippie colony in the world." It was, one company boasted, "the only foreign tour within the continental limits of the United States." Publicity encouraged wannabe hippies to go west in search of flower power. A 1967 CBS documentary entitled "The Hippie Temptation," though intended as a stern warning about the dangers of hip life, acted instead like advertisement. The somber advice of sociologists and psychologists was, for many viewers, completely negated by delightful background shots of hippies having fun. The Bay Area came to be seen as a hippie Lourdes. *Time* estimated 50,000, while *Newsweek* predicted that 100,000 would gather by the summer of 1967—the Summer of Love. "Kids thought, 'Wow, I can just get stoned and all this wonderful stuff will come out,'" Travis Rivers, owner of the Print Mint, recalled. "So we ended up with all these mental cripples. . . . You had a lot of people talking to posts."[44]

"Today is the first day of the rest of your life," the Diggers said. Back then, the phrase, which has since been appropriated by manufacturers of cheesy greeting cards, actually meant something to those who wanted it to mean something. Going to San Francisco was supposed to be a spiritual migration, the start of a new life. When the journalist Nicholas von Hoffman interviewed residents of the Haight in 1967, he found that those who had arrived in 1965 and 1966 were mostly college-educated and upper middle class. For them, the hippie life implied both an intellectual commitment and a spiritual transformation. They went to San Francisco because the city harmonized with the way they wanted to live.

Not so the class of '67. The second wave included a lot of tortured souls escaping abusive families, dead-end schools, or chronic depression. They were also younger—some as young as fourteen. The journalist Leonard Wolf observed in late 1967:

> The new look of the Haight may be encapsulated in one word: tougher. The kids are tougher, the kicks are tougher, and the problems are tougher. . . . Young people come and go, but what now brings them to the Haight is not so much an intuition of a better world to come as, rather, a personal unwillingness or incapacity to deal with the world they have left. . . . LSD, which was the key to the hippie experience, is being replaced in popularity by Methedrine, thereby signaling a shift from a vision- to a kick-seeking community. . . . The hippie experience is becoming increasingly the experience of the very young who are impatient with visions and the rhet-

oric that was invented to go with them. For distressed teenagers, kicks, hard kicks, are their own justification, and Methedrine more than fulfills their expectations.

They were refugees in America, all escaping something, all looking for something, all hopelessly ill-equipped to care for themselves. "The people that I knew on the street," recalled one disheartened hippie, "were running around with the Everything-Is-Perfect viewpoint. Real *Candide* nonsense about how living is groovy, and the fact that somebody was starving or a kid was freaking out on Methedrine was not a reflection of evilness or discomfort or something being wrong at all. It meant he wasn't in tune with his karma." She added, with deep regret: "It's one thing to turn away from an institution, because maybe it's no longer feasible to change something. . . . But you can't turn away from human beings and abandon them, and that's what a lot of these people are doing."[45]

The hordes arrived for the Summer of Love, but, in truth, love was in short supply. Haight-Ashbury was a poor black neighborhood before the hippies invaded. Hippies talked of sharing and togetherness. They didn't believe in property, but blacks did. When a middle-class white kid plays at being poor, it causes offense to those for whom poverty does not involve choice and is not fun. Resentment spilled over into violence. For the police, a turf war between blacks and freaks made life easy—there was no reason to show leniency to either side.

"All of a sudden, the game got real hard and real gritty and the city was overrun," recalled Peter Coyote, a Digger who tried to pick up the pieces. The Haight was overrun not just with hippies, but with those keen to exploit them. A pack of nasty hyenas had followed the migrating herd, ready to pounce on the weak, the sick, and the vulnerable. Exploiting a newly arrived hippie was not terribly difficult, since their dependencies were great and their faith in humanity boundless. "It was ugly to watch the efficiency with which that scene was dismantled," Robert Hunter of the Grateful Dead remarked. "The Abyssinians came down like wolves upon the fold. There was no bone worth picking that wasn't stripped clean and the marrow sucked."[46]

Young girls who quickly ran through their meager horde of cash soon found the city short on charity. Aside from the pimps, no one seemed to care. Turning tricks was sometimes the only way to get food. Drug dealers had a peculiar talent for turning wide-eyed adventurers into hopeless junkies in a matter of weeks. There was not much money in pot or acid, which were often given away free. The real profits came from addictive drugs: speed, codeine, Quaaludes, heroin. Barbiturates—"downers"—were particularly suited to a dream gone bad. Getting a hippie hooked was a form of ownership; the junkie, enslaved by the drug, belonged to the dealer. Flower children often turned to petty theft in order to feed their dependency. Some discovered that the most lucrative profession open to them was to become a dealer. The murder rate consequently rose as pushers fought vicious turf wars.

Rape was popular in the Summer of Love. Rape was easy because there were so many naïve young girls separated from parental protection. A group called the Communication Company drew attention to a common scenario:

> Pretty little sixteen-year-old middle-class chick comes to the Haight to see what it's all about & gets picked up by a seventeen-year-old street dealer who spends all day shooting her full of speed again & again, then feeds her 3,000 mikes [micrograms of LSD, twelve times the standard dose] & raffles off her temporarily unemployed body for the biggest Haight Street gang bang since the night before last . . .
>
> Rape is as common as bullshit on Haight Street. Kids are starving on The Street. Minds & bodies are being maimed as we watch, a scale model of Vietnam. . . . Are you aware that Haight Street is as bad as the squares say it is?

Often it was not even called rape—merely an expression of sexual freedom by a man or men unconcerned about issues of consent. Nor was assault essential for sex to be dangerous. Rampant promiscuity fired an epidemic of venereal disease.[47]

The sordidness was not exclusively Californian. In October 1967 came news of the double murder of Linda Fitzpatrick and James "Groovy" Hutchinson, two flower children who had sought tranquillity in Greenwich Village. They were killed while high on LSD. Fitzpatrick, two months pregnant, was also raped. The rock critic J. Marks felt the murders "irrefutably demonstrat[ed] the innocent stupidity of our belief that you could build a good life in society's dead cities: the slums." Desperate parents took out ads in underground newspapers calling their children home. *Newsweek* reported: "Almost overnight, the East Village seemed aswarm with parents searching for some of the 9,000 runaway children believed to be living the hippie life in New York." Fitzpatrick's parents confessed that while their daughter was busily learning to be hip, they thought she was studying art. For too many parents, that sounded eerily familiar. "I wonder if I'm really getting through to my daughter," one mother confessed to *Newsweek*. "How can anyone be certain? For all I know, she could be leading a double life too. I die a little every day."[48]

The Summer of Love was supposed to have been a celebration of hipness. In fact, it turned out to be a bizarre funeral—"Death of Hippie," as the Diggers proclaimed. The original hippies had already begun abandoning ship when the streets of the Haight grew crowded with imitators, manipulators, impostors, and tour buses. Quite a few migrated north and set up communes, where they hoped to recreate the hip ethos in microcosm. Those who stayed behind fell mainly into two camps: the hardcore fantasists who refused to abandon the dream (some are still there), and the frightened souls desperate to escape their personal nightmare but unable to do so. What remained of the vision was what hippies called "shuck," the transformation of dream into dollars. "Hip is saleable," Leonard Wolf observed. "The market is flooded with hippie clothing, jewelry, school supplies, hardware. The Haight-Ashbury is well on its way to becoming one of the gewgaw centers of the world: posters, marijuana pipes, roach holders, buttons, and light-show equipment are items in the new marketplace. Street signs reading Haight/Ashbury are for sale at thirty dollars a pair."[49]

"Linda and Groovy were sacrifices, the movement's first real martyrs," one demoralized hippie told *Newsweek*. "But they showed us something, man. They showed us you can't find God and love in Sodom and Gomorrah. So it's time to split." Hippies had rebelled against their parents by going to San Francisco, and had rebelled against conformity by adopting the look—beads, sandals, tie-dyed shirts, flowers in their hair. That look had gained them entry to a community, but it had also earned them the disdain of the straight world. Nonconformity was a self-fulfilling prophecy. Public disapproval and police persecution merely confirmed that rebellion had been justified. But then it all went horribly wrong, and, to make matters worse, the nastiest evil came not from the Establishment, but from inside the hippie haven. "The world of the young, with all its fervent belief in man and myth, was . . . heading rapidly toward extinction," J. Marks concluded. Parents' warnings, once so easily ignored, took on a worrying ring of truth. There was, however, no clear direction home. To return was difficult because it constituted an admission of defeat—acceptance of the fact that hippies could not in fact make a better world.[50]

11

GONE TO GRAVEYARDS

Memphis: The Death of King

During the Montgomery bus boycott, Bayard Rustin told Martin Luther King: "You had better prepare yourself for martyrdom, because I don't see how you can make the challenge that you are making without a very real possibility of your being murdered, and I wonder if you have made peace with that."[1]

By 1968, Martin Luther King had come to resemble a museum exhibit. Sermons on nonviolence seemed rather quaint after three successive summers of inner-city riots. King was tired, depressed, and demoralized. His people, it seemed, had given up on Gandhi. Eldridge Cleaver, Huey Newton, and H. Rap Brown had no trouble getting attention, since throwing a Molotov cocktail guaranteed coverage on the nightly news. A violent movement and a sensationalist media were feeding on each other. "Maybe we just have to admit that the day of violence is here," a tired King told Ralph Abernathy in 1968. "Maybe we just have to give up and let violence take its course. The nation won't listen to our voice. Maybe it will heed the voice of violence."[2]

Death became a frequent theme in his speeches. "Well I don't know what will happen now," he told the congregation of the Mason Temple in Memphis on April 3, 1968. "We've got some difficult days ahead. But it doesn't matter with me now. Because I've been to the mountaintop. And I don't mind. Like anybody, I would like to live a long life. Longevity has its place. But I'm not concerned about that now. I just want to do God's will. And He's allowed me to go up to the mountain. And I've looked over. And I've seen the promised land. I may not get there with you. But I want you to know tonight that we, as a people, will get to the promised land."

On the following day, King was resting in his hotel room when he was shot dead by James Earl Ray, an escaped convict. The movement which had grown tired of King now embraced him as a martyred hero. Allegations that he had sold out, that he was a stooge or an Uncle Tom, suddenly stopped. "Now that they've taken Dr. King off," Carmichael shouted, "it's time to end this nonviolence bullshit." He was apparently unaware of the irony of that statement. In 120 cities across America, blacks rioted in King's honor. "We know that we cannot change violent people by nonviolence," a statement by the Black Student Union proclaimed, with depressing finality. "We must build mass armed self-defense groups. We must unite to get rid of the government and people that oppress and murder Black People."[3]

King, it seems, had plagiarized his Ph.D. thesis at Boston University. In addition to being a cheat, he was also a sex addict. "Fucking's a form of anxiety reduction," he once confessed. His lasciviousness was not unusual; a lot of prominent people at that time freely indulged their sexual hunger and delighted in the uninhibited nature of the permissive society. What perhaps set him apart was his hypocrisy: others indulged openly, but he did so in secret, all the time trying to maintain the image of an upright, moral, Christian husband and father. His womanizing at times put his movement in danger, so much so that colleagues urged him to behave. J. Edgar Hoover leaked evidence to journalists in an attempt to destroy King, but they decided that his misbehavior was not really relevant to the larger civil rights cause. (These were old-fashioned times.) Frustrated, Hoover had evidence sent directly to King and his wife, Coretta, with the advice that the wisest course was to commit suicide.[4]

Does any of this matter to the judgment of a man? Heroes habitually go through a process of being worshiped, then mourned, then pilloried. Journalists and historians struggle to decide what behavior is relevant to the assessment of an individual and what is not. Hypocrisy is distasteful but, under the circumstances, pretense was probably essential for the larger good of the civil rights movement. King was not the man he pretended to be, but that pretense was itself a response to what the public demanded. Americans wanted King to be saintly and convinced themselves that he was so. A bit of make-believe strengthened the movement.

"People are often surprised to learn that I am an optimist," King confessed shortly before his death. "Man has the capacity to do right as well as wrong, and his history is a path upward, not downward." That sentiment seems surprising coming from a man who had seen very little of man's goodness. The evil of those who opposed him was at times overwhelming. But it was the shortcomings of those supposedly on his side that was most difficult to bear. When King died, his movement was inherited by a collection of charlatans who exploited the cause in order to give legitimacy to self-promotion and thuggery.[5]

Birds shit on statues. Heroes are defenseless against Time's erosion. Every great accomplishment is susceptible to the ravages of revisionists. In the end, King should be judged on his talents and his achievements. The world has seen few heroes like him. He, more than anyone, managed to fire the conscience of America—white and black. He made the injustice blacks were suffering impossible to ignore. His talents and achievements render him a great deal more admirable than many other Sixties heroes who also had feet of clay.

PRAGUE: SHORT SPRING

The people of Czechoslovakia were finding it increasingly difficult to maintain the pretense of Iron Curtain animosity. Polls in the 1960s showed that many Czechs actually liked the Americans and, even if they did not like them, grudgingly admired them. (Though the populace consisted of Czechs and Slovaks, the former term will be used here to describe the totality.) The West was symbolic of modernity, the USSR of stasis. Quite a few Czechs had a yearning to be modern. Leading the way were the young, insatiably hungry for everything Western. Blue jeans and rock 'n' roll were not just cultural commodities in Czechoslovakia; they were political statements. While Czechs wanted the fruits of Western capitalism, however, most did not want to be capitalists. A poll in the summer of 1968 revealed that 89 percent wanted to remain Communist.

Czechoslovakia was not immune to the Sixties' contagion of rebellion. East of the Iron Curtain, yearnings for freedom actually had meaning; when Czechs complained of oppression, they spoke with authority. Writers demanded relief from rigid censorship, and students took to the streets in their quest for a more open society. Mirroring protests in the West, the first student demonstrations, in November 1967, were protests over inadequate heating and lighting in dormitories. The police, unsympathetic to dissidence of any kind, reacted more harshly than was warranted, a reaction which backfired when word of the unrest leaked out.

The party secretary and president, Antonín Novotný, was a dyed-in-the-wool Stalinist. His government reacted to unrest in a manner typical of the Eastern bloc: it initially ignored the trouble, and then, when pretense crumbled, blamed it on the West. To his credit, Novotný did try to placate dissidents with promises of reform. These, he maintained, would not be confined to politics and the economy, but would apply to culture also. While politically well intentioned, Novotný was moving a bit too slowly to suit members of the Central Committee, who, fearing a repeat of Hungary 1956, removed him from the post of first secretary. In his place came Alexander Dubček, a Slovakian mystery man unknown to most Czechs. Meanwhile the Soviet premier, Leonid Brezhnev, kept a cold eye on the events occurring in Russia's satellite state. Novotný had tried to win the Soviet leader's favor with slavish loyalty, but Brezhnev wanted only a leader who could keep Czechoslovakia quiet.

Dubček was an unlikely hero. Though a tall man, he managed, for most of his political life, to go virtually unnoticed. This might have been because he was a painfully boring speaker in an age when presentation was so important—even in the Soviet bloc. Like Kennedy, he was young, but, unlike Kennedy, he was too gray to seem young. Nor was he particularly ambitious; when he took over from Novotný, it was more out of duty than desire. His people, desperate for a hero, happily threw themselves behind Dubček, while his family bemoaned their miserable luck. He inherited an impossible situation: he had to convince the increasingly dissatisfied populace that he could deliver reforms, while at the same time convincing Moscow that he could keep control. A less brave man might simply have retired from politics and let events take their course.

When the Central Committee toppled Novotný, it also proclaimed that "there must be far greater encouragement of an open exchange of views, and all officials must create the conditions for such an exchange. The qualities of a Communist include a sincere, comradely attitude toward human beings and an awareness of and respect for the needs of fellow workers." Since the populace was inclined to agree, this made life immensely difficult for Dubček. The sudden relaxation of controls meant that the papers started carrying real stories which the people actually read. They told of widespread corruption within the official bureaucracy, including the perfidy of the Novotný family. Much more worrying, for both Dubček and Brezhnev, were the increasingly strident editorials attacking the USSR. Criticism published in the papers, Dubček complained, sometimes displayed "an impulsive character."[6]

Dubček was no revolutionary. When he told Brezhnev in January that "friendship and alliance with the Soviet Union are the cornerstone of all our activities," he was actually being honest. He believed sincerely in Communism. A one-party state made sense to him because "we don't know of any better party than the Communist party." Dubček nevertheless accepted that serious problems affected the governance of Czechoslovakia and therefore the continued viability of Communism. His program of reform was based on the assumption that authority had to be earned through good example and trustworthy leadership; it must not be imposed. "We must remove, along both state and party lines, all the injustices being done to the people, and we must do so consistently and without reservation," he announced on February 22. In practice, this meant that, "while retaining the essential centralism, we should place the emphasis on developing more and, above all, deep democratic foundations."[7]

The Communist system's faults were most apparent in the management of the economy. Centralism, Dubček argued, had brought about "slow increases in wages, . . . stagnation of living standards, . . . the present state of the transport system, poor-quality goods, and [inadequate] public services." He even questioned the sanctity of egalitarianism, arguing that it promoted "careless workers, idlers, and irresponsible people." Remuneration, he argued, should be linked to productivity—a proposal that fired the fears of the working class.[8]

Dubček wanted to create what he called "socialism with a human face." That seemed enormously appealing to his people, not just because it promised better living standards and more political freedoms, but also because it was an assertion of independence from Moscow. The difficult part, however, lay in sustaining a harmonious relationship with the Kremlin at a time when the Czechs were determined to follow an independent road. Equally risky was the way Dubček inadvertently provided inspiration to nascent student movements across Eastern Europe. Polish students brave enough to demonstrate carried signs which read "Polska Czeka na Dubčzeka!"—"Poland Awaits Its Dubček!" Those signs were like a signal to the Soviets that the beast of rebellion had to be put down. The minute it seemed that insurgence might spread, Dubček was doomed. On March 23, he was summoned to Dresden for a tongue-lashing from his Eastern bloc colleagues. At that meeting, Brezhnev told Dubček: "No situation in Czechoslovakia justifies attacks on the party and government, because such difficulties would arise that demand the abandonment of cooperation with the socialist countries, and above all with the Soviet Union, which allegedly has been 'robbing' Czechoslovakia. That's exactly the phrase used in your country. I do not know if you have enough time to read your own press. But we are obliged to read it, and we are very concerned." Brezhnev concluded by warning Dubček "to change the course of events and stop these very dangerous developments. . . . If you disagree, we cannot remain indifferent."[9]

As spring turned to summer, Dubček showed no evidence of being able to rein in his people. He realized he was walking a thin line, but thought that Czechoslovakia's special relationship with the Soviet Union would stand the country in good stead. The Czechs had always been cooperative allies who did not make trouble. Most were loyal Communists. None of that, however, mattered to Brezhnev. On August 11, 1968, the Soviets made clear their impatience. "Authoritarian power" was a favorite phrase of Sixties radicals, most of whom had no idea what they were talking about. This was the real thing. At 11:00 P.M., 165,000 soldiers and 4,600 tanks entered Czechoslovakia at twenty crossing points situated on the borders of its four Warsaw Pact neighbors. Those neighbors—Hungary, East Germany, Poland, the Soviet Union—along with Bulgaria, contributed to the invasion force, as if to suggest that the entire Warsaw Pact was unanimously condemning the actions of an errant member. The operation was essentially over the minute the troops mobilized, since resistance was futile. Dubček was quickly "taken into protective custody."

World leaders defined themselves by their reaction. Romania's Nicolai Ceauşescu and Yugoslavia's Josip Broz Tito condemned the invasion, in order to underline their cherished autonomy. Władysław Gomułka of Poland, keen to ingratiate himself with the Soviets, enthusiastically praised it, blaming Czechoslovakian behavior on Zionist influence. Harold Wilson of Britain roundly condemned the Soviet action, as did Charles de Gaulle, but the latter, in the same breath, compared the action to the American invasion of the Dominican Republic in 1965. This was all part of the French fantasy of nonalignment.

Dubček was a man of principle. He was not playing a power game, nor was he trying to play East off against West. While he was admired in the West because he had attempted to defy Moscow, that was a highly superficial judgment. Most Westerners would not have cared for Dubček had they bothered to notice his commitment to Communism. His dream was to bring about an improved form of the ideology—the ideals without the naked authoritarian power and the abuse of human rights. Brezhnev intervened not because he was a despot, but because he genuinely believed that Czechoslovakia posed a threat to the entire Communist bloc. In that assessment, he was probably right. By the summer, Dubček had lost control of the movement identified with him. The people were miles ahead of the party, demanding ever more radical reforms. They had developed a taste for policy making and were disinclined to relinquish their newfound freedoms. Dubček had tried to control the pace of reform, but by July seemed like a passenger in a runaway car without brakes or steering. That said, his failure presaged the end of Communism, since it suggested that Moscow would never allow significant deviation from its version of the ideology. In that sense, Dubček's defeat also signaled the beginning of the end for the USSR.

LOS ANGELES: THE DEATH OF HOPE

For many Americans, hope died not on the streets of Dallas in 1963, but on the floor of a hotel kitchen in Los Angeles in 1968. John Kennedy's assassination was a tragedy; his brother Robert's a disaster. "I bottomed out and went nuts when he died," one baby boomer recalled. Another confessed: "When they killed him, a little of my zeal and sense of hope died with him."[10]

For liberals, the 1968 election was a voyage between Scylla and Charybdis. Johnson still offered the best hope for domestic reform, but, like some devilish bargain, his Great Society came with war attached. If the war continued, the acrimony it engendered would deepen. The only alternative, however, was Richard Nixon—the liberals' devil incarnate. While LBJ offered war and welfare, Nixon seemed to offer only war.

Into the breach strode Eugene McCarthy, a senator hardly known out-side his Minnesota constituency. He declared his candidacy on November 30, 1967. That a Democrat should challenge Johnson, who had won so re-soundingly in 1964, reveals just how deep were the wounds of war. McCarthy offered himself as healer: "I am hopeful that this challenge . . . may al-leviate . . . [the] sense of political helplessness and restore to many people a belief in the processes of American government." He was gentle, urbane, introspective, articulate, innocent—in every way the polar opposite of LBJ. He didn't run for president; he walked, smelling flowers along the way. Antiwar liberals grabbed McCarthy the way a shipwrecked man lunges desperately for flotsam. Those on the far left, however, were distinctly unimpressed. Carl Oglesby thought McCarthy a bargain-basement Adlai Stevenson. He saw the same culture, urbanity, and wit, but the "edges have grown soft, . . . [the] center has grown murky."[11]

The Democratic party has long had a weakness for smooth-talking Northern liberals, even though they are as dangerous as a double whiskey to an alcoholic. The party was (and remains) a collection of warring tribes. McCarthy gave expression to white, middle-class anxiety, but offered little to urban workers and poor blacks, the other tribes in Democrat Nation. In healing some wounds, he opened others. In other words, his candidacy was always doomed. No wonder, then, that Johnson at first refused to take him seriously.

Then came Tet, which changed everything. The humiliation called into question the war's continuance. As Walter Cronkite afterward told the na-tion, defeat did not seem possible, but neither did victory. On March 12, 1968, came the New Hampshire primary, the first formal expression of popular opinion after Tet, and Act One in a long campaign drama. McCarthy drew 41.9 percent. Johnson was not on the ballot, but a write-in effort yielded 49.6 percent. Heavy snow on the day of the poll might have kept Johnson supporters indoors—safe in the assumption that the president did not really need their help. In truth, it was probably a meaningless re-sult, but Americans desperately sought meaning. Johnson, pundits de-cided, had been dealt a severe blow. More important, the result seemed an indictment of the war. Only later was it discovered that, among McCarthy supporters, hawks outnumbered doves by three to two.

Lurking menacingly was New York senator Robert F. Kennedy, acknowl-edged heir to Camelot. Since entering the Senate in 1966, RFK had courted liberals by defending the Great Society and attacking the war. "We've got to get out of Vietnam," he said repeatedly. "It's destroying the country." By early 1967, polls on university campuses revealed that Kennedy was the students' choice. Echoing his brother John, he told Berkeley students that they had "the opportunity and the responsibility to help make the choices which will determine the greatness of this nation. . . . If you shrink from this struggle . . . you will betray the trust which your own position forces upon you."[12]

At first, Kennedy ignored his own entreaties and shrank from the struggle for the White House. While he dreaded Johnson's reelection, he refused to challenge him, fearing the damage it might cause. To enter the race would, he worried, encourage allegations "that I was splitting the party out of ambition and envy. No one would believe that I was doing it because of how I felt about Vietnam and poor people." Kennedy must have realized that, before Tet, he had no hope of winning. He had more at stake than McCarthy, who could make his point and then return to the wilderness. New Hampshire, however, suggested that Johnson was beatable. An emboldened RFK officially entered the fray on March 16, 1968, explaining: "These are not ordinary times, and this is not an ordinary election."[13]

In public, Johnson pretended to be unperturbed. In private, he promised to destroy "that grandstanding little runt." As for the war, bluster was sold as leadership. "Let's get one thing clear!" LBJ bellowed. "I am not going to stop the bombing!" "Make no mistake about it, we are going to win!" Shouting did not, however, frighten away the demons lurking in the bamboo of Vietnam. On March 26, a more chastened Johnson summoned his "Wise Men"—the same men who had, four months earlier, overwhelmingly endorsed the war effort. On this occasion, they struggled to find good omens. "The issue is, can we do what we are trying to do in Vietnam," Dean Acheson summarized. "I do not think we can." Johnson had desperately hoped for different advice, but in truth was not surprised by what he heard.[14]

On March 31, Johnson addressed the nation. Bruised by Tet and battered by protest, he announced a halt to the bombing offensive and invited Hanoi to the conference table. Then came the most dramatic and unexpected ending to any presidential speech in American history: "I shall not seek, and I will not accept, the nomination of my party for another term as your president."[15]

Two days later, Jack Valenti, the president's close friend, found Johnson "calm, almost serene, as if whatever plague had been visited upon him was now exiled from his mind and heart." Valenti could not hide his dismay. "Why would you do this?" he asked. "You can beat Nixon." The president sighed, the weariness of four years condensed in that sigh. "Yes, I think I would beat him," he replied. "But [the race] would be too close for me to be able to govern. The nation would be polarized. Besides, the presidency isn't fun anymore. Everything has turned mean. No matter what I accomplish, the damn war infects everything."[16]

Johnson was not a coward. Bruising electoral campaigns were his forte; he was not the sort to run from a challenge. Though honesty was not his most conspicuous quality, one is inclined to believe his reasons for dropping out. He recognized that the nation's welfare and the cause of peace would be better served if he did not run. Country was placed before ego, a priority few politicians ever manage. "I never was surer of any decision I ever made in my life," he confessed. "I have 525,000 men whose very lives depend on what I do, and I must not be worried about primaries."[17]

Johnson was out of the race, but still determined to control it through his puppet, vice president Hubert Humphrey. Humphrey declared his candidacy in late April. He was Johnson neutered and lobotomized, a decent man who lacked the ruthlessness of his mentor. "With the smell of the White House so close to him, [Humphrey] turned into ectoplasm," the journalist Jimmy Breslin remarked. "Most people say he was rice pudding. I don't have that much against rice pudding." Humphrey would have made a great president in the land of make-believe where everyone was destined to live happily ever after. Homilies about restoring the "politics of happiness, the politics of purpose, and the politics of joy" were as useful to an embattled nation as a Band-Aid to a patient in cardiac arrest. Humphrey nevertheless had at his disposal those who still supported Johnson, a significant constituency. He also had behind him the Democratic city machines, particularly that of Mayor Richard Daley of Chicago, where the convention would be held. Simply by existing, he became the frontrunner.[18]

Robert Kennedy, in contrast to McCarthy, was not simply an antiwar candidate. He recognized the necessity of a wide constituency. Yet the more he tried to widen his appeal, the more his contradictions were exposed. His support for the Great Society alienated workers fearful of higher taxes. His criticism of the war annoyed those who still supported it. Voters had every reason to be confused, but the confusion was not Kennedy's fault. The country had changed radically since his brother's narrow victory in 1960. The once solidly Democratic South had become alienated by civil rights legislation and Great Society programs. Yet, in the North, a plethora of interest groups, often operating at cross-purposes, pushed for big government and increased spending. Kennedy had somehow to appeal both to the future of the party and to those stuck in its past. For a liberal from New England, that feat of political alchemy was nearly impossible. "In one corner of his very complicated mind," Tom Hayden wrote, "[Kennedy] believed he could use the structure and then destroy it. Use Mayor Daley to become president and, at the same time, encourage the ghetto to rise up against Mayor Daley. . . . It doesn't work."[19]

For a brief period, magic seemed possible. Victories in the Indiana, Nebraska, and District of Columbia primaries suggested that Kennedy might indeed have been able to turn the party's base elements into solid gold. Then, on June 4, came the California primary, which he won with 46 percent to McCarthy's 42. At his victory address, Kennedy called upon McCarthy supporters to cast aside their differences and join his campaign. He sensed that the momentum was his, and that he had the strength even to overwhelm Humphrey. "On to Chicago and let's win there," he told the cheering crowd in Los Angeles. And then he was dead.[20]

A few weeks before he was shot, Kennedy had confessed that he expected an attempt on his life—"Not so much for political reasons, but through contagion, through emulation." That prediction proved eerily correct. The name of his assassin, Sirhan Bishara Sirhan, suggested a Middle Eastern connection, but no real link to the politics of Palestine has been discovered. Sirhan was just a mentally disturbed man who managed to get too close to Kennedy. In that sense, he had much in common with Lee Harvey Oswald.[21]

Kennedy's quest for unity might have failed. What is certain, however, is that, after his assassination, there was no one left in the race who had even a remote chance of succeeding. Democratic disunity was agonizingly uncovered in Chicago. Though McCarthy inherited some of Kennedy's support, Humphrey was in truth unstoppable. Victory, however, proved a far cry from unity. In Chicago, the party flailed itself while the whole world watched. Inside the convention hall, delegates used words as weapons in the bitter struggle for political hegemony. Outside, the weapons were rocks, chains, billy clubs, and tear gas.[22]

Leading the mayhem were the circus performers: Rubin, Hoffman, and their Yippie army. This, it seemed, would be their finest hour. The plans, such as they were, called for a virtually continuous street party—more theater than demonstration. Yippies performed for the cameras, which were ubiquitous. Outrageous plans did not actually need to be carried out in order to make the nightly news, as was demonstrated by the Yippie boast that they would put LSD in the Chicago water supply, rape the wives of convention delegates, and have a mass copulation in Lincoln Park. The main event was the nomination of a pig for president. That stunt was briefly thrown into disarray when Rubin and Hoffman both brought a pig—the former's ugly, the latter's cute. Rubin's won the nomination, much to Hoffman's disgust. Shortly after the nomination, police arrested President Pigasus.

Present in Chicago were some committed protesters armed with legitimate points. Unfortunately, their message was completely smothered by Yippie clowns whose politics had been distilled to hurling obscenities and throwing stones. A week before the convention, Rubin told his starry-eyed admirers: "Thousands of us will burn draft cards at the same time . . . and the paranoia and guilt of the government will force them to bring thousands of troops. . . . Our long hair alone will freak them out. . . . And remember—the more troops, the better the theater." The goal, it seems, was to create a spectacle. "Like typical Americans," one organizer proclaimed, "we got our biggest kicks from contemplating our image in the media."[23]

The Yippies should have been nothing more than a nuisance. Rubin and Hoffman had failed miserably in mobilizing the force they had fantasized. But television cameras and omnipresent police made the demonstration into something altogether terrifying. Twelve thousand Chicago police were backed by 5,000 army troops and 6,000 members of the Illinois National Guard. The British journalist Max Hastings, usually a dutiful respecter of authority, reported: "Police smashed their clubs into the human mass, aiming between their legs, at their heads, shoulders—anything. They used chemical spray to disable them and were still hitting them as they lay on the floor. . . . After the events of the last few hours, it will never again be possible to think of either the city or Mayor Daley without feeling slightly sick."[24]

Daley's police behaved the way the Yippies wanted. Jimmy Breslin recalled a telling confession from Dick Fernandez, one of the protest heavyweights: "We say we want to march to the Amphitheatre. I hope they tell us no. If they tell us it's all right for us to march, that's the worst thing that can happen. Hell, we're dead if they say we can march. Five or six miles of a march. The whole thing will fall apart." Breslin concluded: "Stupidity made the night possible. A permit to march, an escorted guide to an Amphitheatre they could not have reached, would have ended it all. But we were dealing with such deep stupidity and unawareness and so many hardened brain arteries and dying brain cells in Chicago that the trouble was insured." The apocalyptic fantasies of Rubin and Hoffman combined with the paranoia of Daley to create one of the most shameful episodes in American political history. "We want[ed] to fuck up their image on TV," Hoffman later explained to the Walker Commission investigating the riot. "It's all in terms of disrupting the image, the image of a democratic society being run very peacefully and orderly and everything according to business." If that was indeed the goal, the Yippies succeeded brilliantly.[25]

Many protesters came itching for a fight. Richard Goldstein, a reporter for the *Village Voice,* observed a group in Lincoln Park preparing for a night of violence. "Not all their accoutrements were defensive," he remarked. "I saw saps and smoke bombs, steel-tipped boots and fistfuls of tacks. My friend pulled out a small canister from his pocket. 'Liquid pepper,' he explained." Goldstein struggled to understand: "Watching these kids gather sticks and stones, I realized how far we have come from that mythical summer when everyone dropped acid, sat under a tree, and communed. If there were any flower children left in America, they had heeded the underground press and stayed home. Those who came fully anticipated confrontation. There were few virgins to violence in the crowd. . . . Most had seen—if not shed—blood, and that baptism had given them a determination of sorts." "I wish that there had been a greater turnout of people experienced in militant nonviolence," activist David Dellinger reflected. "More, for example, who do not think it is revolutionary to taunt the police by screaming 'oink, oink' or 'pig' at them." For Tom Hayden, on the other hand, Chicago provided a rite of passage. "It was a good test of who is serious about being in the streets and who is not, and that probably will lead to possibilities for consolidation of the movement," he remarked with obvious pride. "In terms of American public opinion, we raised some very provocative and important questions in the best possible way."[26]

The Yippies, like so many other activists of 1968, believed it was possible to expose the authoritarian nature of government by provoking violent confrontation. But violence has a way of smothering subtle political points and of making the otherwise uncommitted side with authority. Instead of opening eyes, the radicals caused ordinary people to turn away in horror. The National Commission on Violence concluded that the Chicago police had been "unrestrained and indiscriminate" in dealing with demonstrators. Yet, when polled, only one in five Americans agreed with that judgment. Within this dichotomy lay a promising political constituency. The country might have been turning against the war, but it still despised those who protested it. Two years earlier, Ronald Reagan had capitalized on this revulsion in his brilliantly successful gubernatorial campaign in California. Of the candidates who remained in the presidential race in 1968, only Nixon was able to emulate Reagan on a national scale. Only Nixon could exploit the somewhat contrary feelings of the American people—their desire for peace abroad and order at home. He built a constituency from what he called the "forgotten Americans": "They are black and they are white. They are native-born and foreign-born. They are young and they are old. They work in America's factories. They run America's businesses. They serve in the government. They provide most of the soldiers who died to keep us free. They give drive to the spirit of America. They give life to the American dream." He would later call them the Silent Majority.[27]

Opinion polls suggested that support for the war was hemorrhaging. But polls are easily misinterpreted. Throughout the war, pollsters asked: "Do you support continued American action in Vietnam?" Those who answered no were carelessly labeled "doves"; those who said yes were crudely termed "hawks." But the no's were a broad church. Some were pacifists. Others were bothered by the war's immorality, or by its apparent futility. Others had pragmatically decided that, even if victory could be achieved, it would not be worth the cost. When a voter crossed the line from hawk to dove, he took his bedrock political principles with him, discarding only his unquestioning support for the war. The new doves, in other words, still believed in the good of their country, still cherished its institutions. They wanted an end to the war, but did not want to sacrifice American honor. This explains why the 1968 election did not produce a genuine peace candidate, despite loud demands for peace. It also explains Nixon's appeal: he promised to withdraw the troops but would not compromise America's reputation.

Nixon at first seemed unbeatable. He boasted of a "secret plan" to end the war, a possibility that appealed to those inclined to optimism and trust. He promised "fresh ideas" and railed against the "tired men around the president." His campaign was aided by the independent candidacy of George Wallace, whose bigoted conservatism appealed to many working-class Democrats. In imitation of Wallace, Nixon chose as his running mate Spiro Agnew, the pit-bull governor of Maryland whose populist tirades made him an instant hero among those who liked their politics loud, crude, and simple.[28]

Since Americans had grown disenchanted with Johnson, they were hardly likely to get inspired by Humphrey, a pale imitation. His cozy platitudes were completely inappropriate to a country mired in confusion and torn by discord. "Put aside recrimination and disunion," he urged. "Turn away from violence and hatred." Had he been orbiting the Moon in an Apollo spacecraft, he could not have been more out of touch with grassroots America. Then, late in the campaign, Humphrey started to gather steam, helped in part by a slump in the Wallace vote. He began to construct an identity separate from Johnson. On September 30, he told a crowd in Salt Lake City that he would stop the bombing of North Vietnam and would call upon the South Vietnamese to "meet the responsibilities" for "their own self-defense." While this was hardly different from what Johnson had already advocated, Americans were desperate to find difference. Humphrey's "conversion" appealed to those wavering voters whose support for Nixon had always been heavily laden with fear.[29]

A sudden breakthrough in the peace negotiations, cleverly engineered by Johnson, also inspired a surge in Humphrey's support. Under pressure from party leaders, Johnson asked Averell Harriman, the American representative at the peace talks in Paris, to indicate to his North Vietnamese counterparts that the United States would halt the bombing in exchange for concessions from them. Hanoi responded by agreeing to negotiations involving both the South Vietnamese government and the National Liberation Front. President Thieu of South Vietnam, until then an obstacle to progress, seemed amenable. Sensing a breakthrough, Johnson announced a bombing halt on October 31. But Thieu then backtracked. Anna Chan Chennault, co-chair of Republican Women for Nixon, used her Asian contacts to foment opposition to the plan in Saigon, in the process encouraging Thieu to believe that he would get a better deal from Nixon.

On November 5, 1968, Nixon secured 43.4 percent of the vote, Humphrey 42.7 percent, and Wallace 13.5 percent. Given the tiny margin of victory, it is tempting to conclude that Humphrey was defeated by Chennault's scheming. Speculation of this sort seems all the more credible given the corrupt character of Nixon. But the Democrats lost the election; it was not stolen from them. Circumstances had caused them to lose the support that had been so loyal to the party for over a century. Humphrey lost because blue-collar workers had been alienated by the attention given to "fringe" groups, because the Southern Democrat had become an endangered species, and because many blacks and antiwar liberals were not sufficiently inspired to venture out on election day.

According to Valenti, Johnson had decided not to run because he feared the election would polarize the nation. Johnson was right, but his absence did not bring about a restoration of unity. Instead of uniting the country around a single candidate, the campaign tore open wounds and poured salt on them. In that sense, Nixon suited the times: instead of healing discord, he found ways to profit from it.

MEXICO CITY: SHOOTING STUDENTS

On October 2, 1968, in the Plaza of the Three Cultures in Mexico City, protesters learned that bullets have no respect for political legitimacy. Of all the student movements which erupted around the world in that terrible year, the Mexican one was the most moderate, well-organized, and serious. Mexicans did not blindly idolize Mao, nor did they allow puerile sexual fantasies to obscure political goals. Drugs were not a problem, and the "counterculture"—such as it was—was decidedly tame. Mexican activists were revolutionary only in the sense that they demanded the implementation of democratic principles clearly set out in their nation's constitution. None of this, however, rendered them immune to tragedy.

Martyrdom was deeply imbedded in Mexican student culture. In 1929, protests over university governance and exam procedures had been viciously quashed when the government sent troops onto the campuses of the National University. The students were defeated, but they claimed victory: a subsequent reform created the National *Autonomous* University (Universidad Nacional Autónoma de México, or UNAM), which theoretically meant that the government could not intervene in campus disputes. From martyrdom sprang myth. Students henceforth saw themselves as the moral conscience of the nation, the ones to steer Mexico back to virtue whenever she strayed from the ideals of the 1910 revolution.

When Mexican students in the 1960s complained about authoritarianism, they did so with credibility. Mexico was essentially a one-party, corporate state. The Partido Revolucionario Institucional (PRI) had in effect governed since the revolution, in the process creating the ultimate oxymoron: a revolutionary party of the status quo. The language of revolution was used constantly, but was mainly rhetorical. The PRI referred frequently to the "Revolutionary Family," but this family had an authoritarian father. Complaint was, however, muted. In contrast to most of Latin America, Mexico was stable and prosperous. A 6 percent annual growth rate and a stable exchange rate kept the middle class happy and workers relatively quiet. Economists praised the "Mexican Miracle." When the president, Gustavo Díaz Ordaz, predicted that there would be no serious student unrest in Mexico, he came to that conclusion because he could not conceive of anything worthy of student complaint.

Mexico's progress was validated by its selection to host the 1968 Olympic Games, the first time a developing country had been chosen. For the government, the honor implied admission to the First World. Critics, however, saw things differently. To them, the games seemed emblematic of the PRI's distorted priorities and dictatorial rule. At the same time, however, dissidents perceived an opportunity. The PRI had, throughout its forty-year rule, been able to govern virtually free of foreign attention. The games, however, would focus awareness on Mexico. The summer of 1968 might, in other words, provide an opportunity to expose social and political inequalities, while the whole world watched.

Conscious of 1929, radical students decided to exercise their legendary role as guardians of the Mexican conscience. Events in Paris, Prague, and Berkeley also convinced them that they were part of a worldwide student revolution. "We are conscious of our historical vision: to transform reality, to transform society," one protest document proclaimed. "And in this task we are not alone. For the first time, youth from around the world are identifying with one another in this common task." In comparison to industrialized countries, however, Mexico severely restricted freedom of action. In Mexican society, long hair and short skirts were seen as dangerously subversive; any act of nonconformity was bound to provoke repression.[30]

The catalyst for unrest came on July 22, 1968, when two rival gangs of youths clashed in the Ciudadela neighborhood of Mexico City. The gang problem had been cause for concern for some time, a fact that explains why the police response was so brutal. Riot police pursued the gangs into university buildings, where innocent bystanders were sucked into an orgy of violence. On campuses, the behavior of the police caused a dam to burst. Students, who had grown increasingly restless over previous months, now had cause to unite. On July 26, a protest march by Polytechnic students linked up with a pro-Castro rally in Alameda Park. Unruly behavior on the fringes of the demonstration gave the police reason to attack. Later, a bus was burned and the first barricades appeared. The students were eventually forced to flee, but sporadic outbursts of violence continued over the following week.

Since the mayhem was occurring in the city center, where international journalists were gathering, a worried government quickly mobilized the army. Students, assuming that the autonomy of the university would provide safe refuge, holed up in campus precincts. Autonomy, however, was a thin shield. On the morning of July 30, troops armed with a bazooka smashed the heavy wooden door of the National Preparatory School No. 1, a shrine of student movements past. After gaining entry, the soldiers, in a nasty temper, went on a rampage. Anyone who strayed into their path was clubbed with a rifle butt.

The bazooka was a starter's pistol—students and faculty at UNAM who had heretofore refused to join the protests suddenly felt an irresistible pull. Nearly 90,000 members of the campus community took to the streets. Sympathy strikes spread across the nation, with high school students joining the cause. Within a week, a National Strike Committee (Consejo Nacional de Huelga, or CNH) emerged, representing more than 150 educational institutions.

The larger the movement grew, the more unwieldy it became. A decentralized structure was purposefully forged, partly because of a fear of demagogues, partly to protect the movement from decapitation by the government, and partly as an overt reaction to Mexico's authoritarian political culture. The effect, however, was a movement so democratic that it was incapable of coordinated action. Some activists wanted a change in government; others wanted attention paid to social inequalities; still others wanted the autonomy of the university restored.

The CNH program, as it existed on paper, was moderate and reformist, in stark contrast to the revolutionary wet dreams of activists in France and the United States. "We insist on the principle that all discussion must be made in public," one rather tame document proclaimed. "We want to end the corrupt practice of smoke-filled rooms or little groups, where the give-and-take excludes the masses from any participation." The group carefully distanced itself from existing Communist and pro-Castro movements, concentrating instead on practical reforms to government. The CNH did not advocate the overthrow of Díaz Ordaz, nor did it campaign for the cancellation of the Olympics. The students were also highly nationalistic, arguing that they were the true inheritors of the revolutionary spirit of 1917. The constitution of that year, it was argued, already guaranteed basic human liberties; what was necessary was a government committed to honoring them. This, in itself, threatened a government which laid sole claim to the revolutionary mantle. One student leader remarked: "Here in our country, anything that represents a spontaneous movement on the part of the people and of students, an independent popular organization that forthrightly criticizes the despotic regime that unfortunately rules our lives, is considered dangerously militant."[31]

Perhaps the most striking feature of student protest in Mexico was its respectability. Activists were not remotely interested in lifestyle revolution, therefore issues of sex and drugs did not intrude. Nor were they bent on mayhem. In this sense, the protests had more in common with the Albany Movement than with the Chicago confrontations. Men in suits and women in sober dresses were as common as those in jeans or miniskirts.

A counterculture of sorts nevertheless did exist and influenced the way the student revolt was perceived. Called "La Onda" ("The Wave"), it was a fusion of international youth culture and indigenous Mexican elements. Though the primary goal of the political movement was not a style revolution, worried parents stubbornly perceived themselves threatened by a style war—a worldwide countercultural rebellion. Students were identified as a threat not because their political demands were dangerous, but because their hair was long. Linking the political movement with La Onda made it easy for critics to dismiss the former as juvenile delinquency.

In a pathetic attempt at appeasement, Díaz Ordaz tried to appear liberal toward La Onda. "Everyone is free to let his beard, hair, or sideburns grow if he wants to, to dress well or badly as he sees fit," he announced. On August 1, he appealed for calm. "Public peace and tranquillity must be restored," he said. "A hand is stretched out; Mexicans will say whether that hand will find a response. I have been deeply grieved by these deplorable and shameful events. Let us not further accentuate our differences." Demonstrators, however, made clear their lack of trust. Signs reading "The outstretched hand has a pistol in it" appeared almost immediately on the streets. Another showed a bayonet with the simple caption, "Dialogue?"[32]

The students had reason to be suspicious. Díaz Ordaz had only one priority—namely, to make sure that the Olympics went ahead in an atmosphere of quiet. Student demonstrators could not be allowed to stand in the way. He realized that any compromise would be interpreted by students as a victory, leading to even greater demands. To negotiate in public would undermine his authority. His job was made easier by the knowledge that the vast bulk of the Mexican population supported him. Most people credited the government with the country's dramatic economic growth. It represented stability, which the students seemed to threaten. Since higher-education students enjoyed privileges denied most citizens, jealousy encouraged intolerance. Confident of public support, Díaz Ordaz went through the motions of encouraging dialogue while preparing for a showdown. He had a timetable: the unrest had to be silenced before the world's press arrived to cover the Olympics. The students were therefore given a few months to prepare the noose by which they would hang. Every act of protest increased the impatience of the people and strengthened the president's mandate to take action.

During August and September, students tried desperately to forge links with local communities in order to demonstrate their legitimacy. Tactics were highly imaginative. Instead of simply marching, they used street theater to create public debates designed to encourage the people to examine the government they blindly supported. They also staged takeovers of symbolic national sites, in an effort to redefine their meaning. Carefully scripted demonstrations at the Angel of Independence statue and in Mexico City's Zócalo (central plaza), for instance, sought to underline how the government had distorted their meaning. Inevitably, the government and loyal journalists accused students of desecrating Mexico's past.

During one action at the Zócalo, the Maoist flag was raised and the Mexican flag torn down. This undoubtedly delighted the government, since it provided proof that the students were traitors. While the action was undoubtedly unwise and immature, the students at least had the ability to learn from their mistakes. Shortly afterward, the CNH issued a decree prohibiting the use of imagery borrowed from foreign revolutionaries. Henceforth, only Mexican heroes and symbols were to be used, a further attempt to reappropriate patriotic iconography. An official directive read: "Let's have no more vituperative slogans, no more insults, no more violence. Don't carry red flags. Don't carry placards of Che or Mao! From now on, we're going to carry placards with portraits of Hidalgo, Morelos, and Zapata, to shut them up. They're our heroes. *Viva Zapata! Viva!*"[33]

Efforts were made to undermine the image of Díaz Ordaz as the benevolent father of the Revolutionary Family, most elementally by directly connecting him to corruption and police brutality. This shocked most Mexicans, since never before had the president been drawn into such a dispute. He was supposed to be the wise patriarch who mediated between squabbling family members. That was of course a myth, but a hugely powerful one. The students mocked the president with graffiti, jokes, and rude caricatures. "Ordaz, get your teeth pulled," the students chanted, in a reference to his prominent overbite. In cartoons, he was frequently caricatured as a monkey. Students would steal buses, paint them with slogans, and then race them around the city with horns blazing. "Suddenly the old rules no longer applied," recalled Evelyn Stevens. "I saw buses speeding down the avenues, their sides painted with the slogan 'Death to Díaz Ordaz.'" Stevens was impressed by the way the CNH turned protest into carnival. At one particular event, when the police chief was burned in effigy and protesters carried aloft a coffin labeled "Dead Government," there was raucousness but "no violence; the crowd was in excellent humor, in a mood to find each incident hilariously funny, as at a circus."[34]

Alarmed by the coverage given the unrest by the world's press, Díaz Ordaz decided to get tough. In his State of the Union address *(Informe)* on September 1, he warned students that "there is a limit to everything, and the irremediable violations of law and order that have occurred recently before the very eyes of the entire nation cannot be allowed to continue." Then came the ominous bit: "We will do what we have to." Unfortunately, after openly mocking the president for so many months, the students had difficulty taking him seriously.[35]

Had Mexican students been as ineffectual at broadening the base of their revolution as their colleagues in the United States or Europe, the government might have been able to ignore them. As the Olympics approached, however, militancy spread. Díaz Ordaz became convinced that an international Communist conspiracy had infiltrated his peaceful country and polluted the minds of Mexican students. In mid-September, the army raided the UNAM campus and the Polytechnic, in an attempt to decapitate the movement. Autonomy was trampled under the soldiers' boots. For two weeks the army occupied the campus, in what was clearly intended to be a war of attrition. Each wave of arrests deprived the movement of its core activists. Others were forced underground. The students' will began to crumble.

On October 1, the army withdrew from the UNAM campus, while remaining at the Polytechnic. Meanwhile, meetings between CNH representatives and the government stalled, for the simple reason that the government had no intention of negotiating with a movement it planned to erase. On the following day a march to the Polytechnic was canceled when rumors floated that the army was blocking the proposed route. In an attempt to avoid confrontation, the CNH decided instead to rally at the Plaza of the Three Cultures, located in the middle of a hideous public-housing project called Tlatelolco. The CNH intended to use the occasion to announce plans for protests over the ten days remaining before the start of the Olympics.

Some say that 5,000 people were present in the square; others claim double that number. Many were simply spectators—local residents who had wandered outside on a warm evening to see what was going on. At the main podium, leaders exchanged worried whispers about government forces having infiltrated the crowd. These fears were well-founded: the Olympic Battalion, specially trained for security during the games, had been sent to the scene to demonstrate its expertise in crowd control. They came wearing one white glove—the better to identify one another when all hell broke loose.

A helicopter suddenly appeared from nowhere, circled the plaza in a wide arc, and then dropped two flares—the signal for the deadly exercise to begin. Scores of troops converged on the square, in the process blocking the only avenues of escape. Then the firing began. Soldiers had placed themselves on the balconies overlooking the plaza and on the domed roof of the nearby church. They did not need to take aim, since targets were everywhere. The crowd ran wildly for the walkways between the buildings, but found escape routes blocked. Those who sought sanctuary in the church encountered bolted doors.

The soldiers conducted a clinically perfect operation—also known as a massacre. According to some witnesses, the firing continued for more than two hours. The slaughter was so horrendous that, forty years later, the Mexican government remains protective of its secrets. In a knee-jerk response, the government claimed that the students had fired first and the soldiers were merely defending themselves. Initially, it declared that just four protesters had been killed. The official death toll was eventually placed at forty-nine, but foreign journalists estimated around two hundred, with hundreds more injured.

After the massacre came the mopping up. The army hunted down protesters with the determination of bloodhounds. Arrests were indiscriminate, and so numerous that prison space was quickly exhausted. Meanwhile, troops sealed off hospitals and morgues to keep prying journalists and grieving relatives at bay. Weeks passed before all the dead were identified and all the injured found. Many of those present at the rally simply evaporated, never to be heard from again. Parents who persisted in their inquiries about a missing child were threatened with further violence.

Like nodding donkeys, the Mexican legislature, on the day after the massacre, overwhelmingly approved the use of force, which was easily blamed on Communists and foreign agitators. A short time later, the Olympics opened in a blaze of conservative glory, with the dove of peace the official symbol of the games. Everyone sang to the prescribed script—everyone pretended there was nothing rotten in the state of Mexico. Díaz Ordaz went to his grave believing that one of his most impressive achievements was the way the student movement had been defeated so that the Olympics could proceed.

"All of us were reborn on October 2," remarked the activist Álvarez Garín. "On that day we also decided how we are going to die: fighting for genuine justice and democracy." While that statement was suitably romantic, befitting a martyred movement, in truth it was fantasy. Tlatelolco was not a rebirth; it was, as Díaz Ordaz intended, eradication. The massacre and subsequent arrests broke the back of the movement. Members who had not been captured went underground, left the country, or simply retired from activism. Recognizing that there was no point in going on, the CNH officially disbanded in early December.[36]

The students' grievance had been legitimate: Mexico *was* a genuine autocracy. But their failure reveals the strength of the PRI's grip on the Mexican polity. Students made some inroads into the community, but the vast majority of people saw the movement the way the government wanted them to see it. A very successful propaganda campaign transformed the students' movement into a rejection of parental authority—a generational conflict. Too many adults saw the attack upon the government as an attack upon them. "This is about a challenge of adults' capacity for comprehension, a defiance of their imagination and of their experience at governing," one journalist remarked on the eve of the massacre, calling the movement "The Parricides." Students were easily dismissed as immature, rebellious kids. "It's the miniskirt that's to blame," one public employee remarked.[37]

After the massacre, the dissidents became what their critics had always accused them of being: a counterculture. La Onda evolved into a form of symbolic protest, as long hair and loud music seemed the next best way to register objection to the PRI. Symbols provided solace, but, in truth, a government which had proved impervious to the most formidable and righteous student movement of the 1960s was never likely to get too rattled by three guitars and a set of drums.

12

YOU SAY YOU WANT A REVOLUTION?

BERLIN: RUDI THE RED

On December 11, 1967, *Der Spiegel* carried on its cover a photo of an angry, unkempt young man, his mouth wide open in a shout, his piercing eyes evoking menace. The accompanying article began: "The revolution wears a sweater, coarsely knitted, with a violent pattern. Colored stripes over chest and biceps signal the contrariness of the rebel. The sleeves are pushed up in a 'let's do it' manner. The upper body moves back and forth, in time with his speech. His fist, with thumb held up, lies clenched on the table; his forearms seem to grasp space, a gesture fit for accompanying a workers' song." The magazine intentionally identified the student revolution with a single, dangerous individual, thus providing a focus for fear. The Germans, for good reason, are suspicious of demagogues.[1]

Hitler aspired to demagoguery. Rudi Dutschke—the radical in striped sweater—did not. He was made into a hero by those who worshiped him and those who despised him. Prominence, however, was an indication of failure, since he was never supposed to become "Red Rudi"—the icon of a movement that was not meant to have leaders.

West German baby boomers dressed in jeans, listened to rock music, and revolted against parental mores. They worshiped Dylan, Che, Lenin, and Lennon, rather indiscriminately. In other words, they were not unlike young people in Britain, France, and the United States. Peculiarities did, however, exist. German students who attended university in the 1960s were the first generation raised in the post-Hitler era; for them, democracy carried special resonance, particularly in contrast to the Fascist past and to their Communist neighbors. The "liberal democracy" they experienced, however, had been seriously distorted by Cold War expediency. The United States, leader of the supposedly "free" world, was an occupying power—the overseer of West Germany's postwar reeducation. America's support for nasty dictators, and her oppressive behavior in Cuba and Vietnam, caused young Germans to question the liberal dream. West Germany, argued Dutschke, was a "colony of the United States" and therefore, like Vietnam, obliged to support the worldwide struggle against imperialism. "Comrades, anti-authoritarians, human beings!" he shouted. "We do not have much more time. We, too, are being destroyed daily in Vietnam. . . . We have a historical opportunity. It is our will that shall largely determine how this period of history ends. If the Viet Cong is not joined by an American, European, and Asiatic Cong, the Vietnam revolution will fail, like all others before it."[2]

The political system seemed to offer little opportunity for change, due to the decision by the Social Democratic Party (Sozialdemokratische Partei Deutschlands, or SPD) in 1959 to abandon Marxism in favor of a social market economy. This "de-ideologization" meant that there was little difference between the SPD and the Christian Democrats, a fact confirmed by the Große Koalition established between the two parties in 1966 in order to combat recession. As in the United States, students grew suspicious of the "corporate liberalism" identified by Marcuse.

Young people in Germany were also forced to come to terms with their country's Nazi past. "You can't talk to people who created Auschwitz," the future Red Army Faction terrorist Gudrun Ensslin complained. Reflecting on her radical days, the feminist Barbara Köster recalled

> a horrible moral conformism, against which we naturally rebelled. We wanted to flee from the white Sunday gloves, to run away from the way one had to hide the fingernails behind the back if they weren't above reproach. . . . For a long time I had severe altercations with my parents and fought against the fascist heritage they forced on me. At first I rejected their authoritarian and puritanical conception of childrearing, but soon we came into conflict over a more serious topic: the persecution of Jews. I identified with the Jews, because I felt myself to be persecuted by my family.

Because the young valued freedom and democracy, truth and justice, they found the presence of former Nazis in positions of power (including the federal president Heinrich Lübke and Grand Coalition chancellor Kurt-Georg Kiesinger) especially galling. Hypocrisy, that favorite Sixties demon, seemed rife.[3]

West Berlin had an unusually large student population, due in part to the fact that young residents were exempt from military service. Until the mid-1960s, students mirrored the virulent anti-Communism of the city, but a new generation, born after the war, were more inclined to think independently. The contrast between the democracy they read about in books and that which they experienced in daily life led to a feeling of alienation which they eagerly expressed in public. Prior to 1968, students in West Berlin were more rebellious than any others in Europe.

Dutschke experienced in microcosm all the political turmoil of his generation. Raised in Luckenfelde in West Germany, he witnessed firsthand the shortcomings of Moscow-inspired socialism. He saw workers exploited in a system that was supposed to be a workers' paradise. Disturbed by these contradictions, he moved to West Berlin shortly before the Wall blocked escape. He soon found, however, that the supposedly free West was, like the East, addicted to authoritarianism and riddled with contradictions.

Studying sociology at the Free University, he immersed himself in socialist theory, convinced that Utopia could be built on the ruins of capitalism. He became expert in the rhetoric of revolution—words like "oppression," "confrontation," "class," and "struggle" peppered his everyday speech. The state, he decided, could be brought down, crushed under the weight of its own contradictions. A free people could then create a truly democratic system that would enhance their lives. Like many Sixties revolutionaries, Dutschke had enormous faith in the people. But he believed that, weighed down by toil, they were incapable or unwilling to recognize oppression and lacked the confidence to revolt. Like Tom Hayden, he decided it was the duty of students, the gifted of their generation, to lead the masses to the promised land.

In January 1965, Dutschke and a few like-minded friends joined the Sozialistischer Deutscher Studentenbund (SDS), which, before its expulsion in 1961, had been the official youth wing of the Social Democratic Party. SDS adhered to the Marxist faith in the working class as agents of change. Dutschke, who disagreed with that fundamental point, was determined to steer SDS toward the idea of a student-led revolution. Students, he believed, would be radicalized through demonstrations designed to provoke a violent, authoritarian response. Borrowing from Che, he envisaged a system of "action centers" that would be located at universities and that would resemble the revolutionary cells established in peasant villages. They would spread the word but also provide safe havens for urban guerrillas who would take on the government, exposing its cruelty and further politicizing the masses.

Dutschke admired Marcuse, who, along with other members of the Frankfurt School, highlighted the ideological suasion of the "administered society." Marcuse argued that the modern industrial state was a sophisticated system of control devised by technocratic elites who found popular will inconvenient and had therefore constructed a comprehensive apparatus for neutralizing democratic power. Institutions of the establishment—the government, the military, the media, big business, and so on—colluded to enfeeble ordinary people. The Establishment not only stifled political expression; it also controlled the dissemination of information, so that most people were kept blissfully ignorant of their oppression.

Dutschke read widely but did not tie himself to any ideological mast. "No abstract theory holds us together," he insisted. "Instead, it is the existential disgust with a society which chatters about freedom while subtly and brutally oppressing the immediate interests and needs of individuals and the people fighting for their socioeconomic emancipation." His Utopia was big on dreams but short on structure. He spent little time thinking about practical economics and the machinery of government, preferring instead to dream of an Elysian paradise in which people would have the time and inclination to be beautiful. It would be a classless society because he said so. It would be based on participatory democracy because he assumed that people wanted to participate. Their apparent apathy was really just the effect of a suffocating government and a manipulative media. Once freed, the people would rediscover their creativity and take control of their lives. Work would become more fulfilling because people would do what they wanted to do. After their spiritual rebirth, these people would set about establishing the practical institutions to buttress their perfect world.[4]

Being students, German activists had profound belief in the power of learning. Left-wing bookstores and publishing houses sprouted like crocuses in spring. Marxist study groups and debating circles provided the

illusion of action. Copying the American example, Dutschke and his colleagues organized teach-ins, where arcane argument was translated to theater. As in America, issues ranged from personal concerns (overcrowded
universities, inattentive teachers, vague alienation) to external matters like
the Vietnam War. Demonstrations were highly ritualized, lacking the creative energy evident in Paris or Berkeley. Dutschke, who cherished discipline, found that some students were attracted more to juvenile mayhem
than to genuine reform. The sybaritic attractions of the counterculture
worried him. He could not, for instance, prevent the clowns of Kommune I
from marching with signs that read, "What do I care about Vietnam? I'm
having problems achieving an orgasm." Referring to their blatant sexism
and puerile shenanigans, Dutschke complained: "This is not what I imagine a commune should be. The exchange of women . . . is nothing but
the application of the bourgeois principle of exchange under the sign of
pseudo-revolutionism." As Hayden had already discovered, commitment
was often paper-thin. Most students simply wanted a bit of anarchic fun
before embracing conformity.[5]

The Establishment reacted predictably, given the deep apprehension of
anything remotely Marxist. The university took disciplinary action against
Dutschke, exactly the aggressive response he wanted. While this action
suggested that Dutschke was a leader, in theory leadership was inimical
to an anti-authoritarian movement wedded to participatory democracy.
Dutschke preferred instead to see himself as "chief ideologist." His prominent role nevertheless encouraged friends and foes alike to call him leader.
The contradiction was partly his fault. Though he believed in mass participation, he knew precisely which direction the mass should go, and did not
hesitate to point the way. He wrote articles and gave interviews designed to
inspire the people, but these merely confirmed his status as the one in
charge—the spokesman ready to offer opinions. Dutschke struggled with
this contradiction but never resolved it. Nor did he work out the dilemma
of needing the media, but also despising it.

On June 2, 1967, during a demonstration in West Berlin against a visit by
the shah of Iran, a student activist named Benno Ohnesorg was shot dead
by police. The authorities immediately claimed it was an accident, with
mayor Heinrich Albertz blaming the students. He was supported by the
right-wing publishing house Springer Verlag, which had been conducting
a virulent campaign against the student movement. Ohnesorg's death gal-

vanized the movement, with protests spreading to otherwise conservative universities. Nor was outrage confined to students. "Everybody knows that it was not a single mishap, but a deliberate campaign of terror against dissenters," the historian Karl Dietrich Bracher argued. "It has to do with the rights of critical opposition and free speech, which are important for the success or failure of our . . . German democracy."[6]

Albertz used the emergency to push through stringent laws banning demonstrations. For many Germans, this was a painful echo of the Emergency Laws passed by Paul von Hindenburg during the Weimar period. Dutschke was delighted, since overt demonstrations of authoritarian power helped to politicize the masses. Taking the initiative, he, along with a few hundred other students, challenged the government by turning Ohnesorg's funeral into a political demonstration. They gave speeches accusing the government of sanctioning political murder. Dutschke also signaled a new phase in the struggle, one in which violence would play a part. "The established rules of the game in this irrational democracy are not our rules," he proclaimed. "The starting point for the politicization of the students must be our conscious breaking of these established rules." The demonstrations showed that Dutschke had a remarkable talent for focusing people's outrage and transforming it into a willingness to take to the streets. But, like hundreds of would-be revolutionaries, he made the mistake of confusing a mass march with a mass movement. He was absolutely right about the power of provocative acts to arouse emotion, but did not understand the feelings he inspired. He failed to appreciate that demonstrations are fun; people like to march. The difficulty lay in converting a momentary fondness for protest into a commitment to protracted struggle.[7]

Dutschke's actions after the death of Ohnesorg attracted the unwelcome attention of the prominent sociologist Jürgen Habermas. Though sympathetic to the need for reform, Habermas accused Dutschke of encouraging mob violence and called him a "left-wing fascist," a remark which left the public queasy. The criticism was all the more damaging because it came from an independent thinker on the left, not the nodding donkeys of Springer Verlag. Dutschke countered that, after the formation of the Große Koalition (a move fully supported by the unions), there was no longer any opportunity for leftists to voice their views within the existing political system. In the absence of pressure, the authoritarian state would simply become more authoritarian. It had to be confronted, he argued, and the streets were the only appropriate arena.[8]

Dutschke felt that since violence was intrinsic to authoritarian rule, the revolution had no choice but to respond with "counterviolence." Thanks in part to Dutschke, violence was discussed all too casually by rebellious youths; it became as fashionable as long hair and jeans. "A gun in your right hand—a joint in your left," went the popular slogan. When students rioted in November 1968, one underground newspaper remarked: "One hundred and thirty cops now have a hole in their head. Few can complain about that." Helmut Gollwitzer, a professor of theology, called Dutschke's flirtation with violence "the most lunatic piece of advice possible at this moment." Rebels, in turn, dismissed Gollwitzer as a "liberal shit."[9]

The refusal to condemn violence rendered Dutschke Public Enemy Number One, or, as Springer Verlag dubbed him, Roter Rädelsführer Rudi (Red Rabble-Rouser Rudi). For all the talk of taking on the right-wing press, Dutschke was actually its best friend. Monsters, real or imagined, sold newspapers. Springer had more success mobilizing the masses than Dutschke. In February 1968, 50,000 Berliners marched in opposition to a student antiwar demonstration. Police had to intervene when the crowd attacked an unfortunate student who looked like Dutschke.

Aware that he was being manipulated, Dutschke tried desperately to improve his image. His efforts included granting a television interview to the journalist Günter Gaus on December 3, 1967. Gaus, fancying a bit of provocation, introduced Dutschke as the leader of a minuscule band of "young revolutionaries at a time when one cannot believe in revolutions anymore." Dutschke rejected this idea, and countered with a distillation of the Marcuse line that capitalism kept the people in a state of permanent somnolence. "We aren't hopeless idiots of history, unable to take our fate into our own hands," he calmly explained. "We can create a world such as has never been seen before. This world would not know war or hunger anymore, anywhere on this planet. . . . For this we will fight, and have begun to fight." Viewers undoubtedly found it unsettling to witness the demon Rudi speaking with serene eloquence about revolution. The image was certainly far removed from that constructed by Springer Verlag, even though the message was rather disturbing to those sleeping comfortably in the status quo. Gaus, in perfect evocation of the gap between the young and the old, replied: "The difference between *your* generation and the generation of the today's forty- to fifty-year-olds seems to be that you, the younger people, do not possess the understanding gained during recent decades—namely, that ideologies are used up. You are capable of believing in ideologies [*ideologiefähig*]."[10]

The public was understandably confused about the real Rudi. His gentlemanly appearance on television contrasted sharply with his behavior at an SDS conference in February 1968, itself a harbinger of the terrorist violence that would plague Europe in the 1970s. Dutschke drew from Che's "Mensaje a la Tricontinental" calling for a protracted struggle against the "imperialist" United States. Urban guerrillas, he explained, would bring war onto the streets of the United States and its allies. The demands of fighting the internal war would make it impossible to wage external war in places like Vietnam. A short film on how to assemble Molotov cocktails was shown. While Dutschke argued that he was merely providing the means for the masses to be politicized, the emphasis upon violent provocation seemed to confirm Springer's warnings. Dutschke may have complained that the media had made him into a demon, but every once in a while he behaved like one.

Dutschke became the leader he supposedly did not want to be. His protestations that no one was indispensable sounded increasingly hollow. Aware of this contradiction, he told the television journalist Wolfgang Venohr that the "system" was to blame. He understood that the media had to personalize the struggle, but protested that in this case it was misguided. He warned that attention paid to him would attract authoritarians keen to strut on Springer's stage. Aware that he had become the greatest obstacle to his own ideals, he announced that he would withdraw from the limelight. He hoped that by removing himself from power he could encourage a free discussion of the movement's future, or what Marxists called self-criticism. He wanted to demonstrate—to his followers and to the Establishment—that the movement could survive without Rudi.

Whether one takes seriously Dutschke's announcement depends to a large extent on one's fondness for the man. Granted, he had long complained about the media's excessive emphasis upon leadership, and might genuinely have felt that his identification as a leader was causing harm. He had also recently become a father, in the process discovering pursuits more important than violent revolution. For nearly a year, he had been constantly in the spotlight, demonized by the press and adored by followers. This sort of thing appealed to Hitler, but not to Dutschke. Threats upon his life came regularly. Then again, he might have been plotting a re-structuring of internal SDS administration in a way that would allow him to have his *Kuchen* and eat it too. He may have fancied a quiet spell away from the internecine struggles of SDS administration, while still enjoying the status of an elder statesman to whom the media could turn for revolu-tionary wisdom. Whatever the motivation, it is clear that the manner in which he announced his retirement merely confirmed his prominence.

On April 11, 1968, Joseph Bachman, an unemployed house painter from Munich, walked up to Dutschke on a Berlin street and fired three bul-lets. One hit him in the face, another in the chest, and the third lodged in his brain. While Dutschke lay bleeding on the pavement, the gathering crowd was more inclined to heckle than to help. Judging by letters written to *Der Spiegel,* many Germans celebrated the assassination. "It was the most beautiful Easter gift imaginable to hear that Dutschke had been put out of action," one correspondent wrote. News of his miraculous sur-vival brought disappointment: "When will this Communist pig Dutschke finally croak?"[11]

After being apprehended by police, the assassin explained: "I heard of the death of Martin Luther King, and since I hate Communists I felt I must kill Dutschke." It later transpired that Bachman worshiped Hitler (a fellow Munich painter) and was an avid reader of *Bild Zeitung,* a sensation-alist tabloid owned by Springer Verlag. German radicals responded by la-beling Springer an accomplice to murder. Five days of riots followed. By the end, two people lay dead, hundreds were injured, and hundreds more had been arrested. Since street violence and political assassinations evoked painful memories, German fears rose exponentially. Ordinary people re-acted by blaming the students. One poll found that 92 percent of Germans were opposed to student violence. Even more significantly, 78 percent of working-class Germans under the age of thirty expressed disapproval. While the shooting of Dutschke might have fired the anger of radical students, it also unified opposition to them.[12]

Dutschke survived the attempt on his life, though he never fully recov-ered and his death ten years later was attributable to the long-term effects of the shooting. Since assassins do not usually shoot nonentities, the at-tack confirmed what was known all along: Dutschke was the leader of the German student movement. The attack also made moot his plan to retire, since retirement was now inevitable. The decline of his movement soon after his departure seemed to confirm just how important he was, though student organizations were admittedly in decline everywhere.

The assassination attempt bequeathed the worldwide student movement a convenient martyr. Fallen heroes encourage speculation as to what might have been. The martyr is assigned an importance and nobility he never earned in life. So it went with Dutschke. The impracticalities of his utopian dream, and the violence it implied, were quickly forgotten. The myth subsumed the man. Dutschke became a symbol of the Sixties, a time when heroes had the guts to dream and were shot for doing so. Though the student movement had clearly failed, he escaped blame. Fallen heroes like Dutschke continue to block the path to understanding the decade.

"Our life is more than money," Dutschke announced in 1971. "Our life is thinking and living. It's about us, and what we could do in this world. . . . My question in life is always how we can destroy things that are against the human being, and how we can find a way of life in which the human being is independent of a world of trouble, a world of anxiety, a world of destruction." Spoken by any other student radical, such a shallow statement would have received the harsh critique it deserved. Spoken by a martyr, however, it sounded like the Sermon on the Mount. The Sixties is a basket of brilliant myths, and Dutschke one of the shiniest.[13]

NEW YORK: UP AGAINST THE WALL, MOTHERFUCKER!

Grayson Kirk was a typical Ivy League president, a well-mannered patrician of liberal temperament who saw himself as a guardian of the best traditions of American higher education. To manage Columbia University well, to allow it to grow and to prosper, was his vocation. In any other era, Kirk might not have been noticed outside the academic community. Unfortunately, he served as Columbia's president at a time of rampant student unrest and had to confront a group of militants who considered his liberal philosophy complacent and the university itself a bastion of authoritarian power.

Kirk was bewildered by the anger he encountered. In a speech at the University of Virginia, he remarked: "Our young people, in disturbing numbers, appear to reject all forms of authority from whatever source derived, and they have taken refuge in the turbulent and inchoate nihilism whose sole objectives are destructive. I know of no time in our history when the gap between generations has been wider or more potentially dangerous." The gap was not simply one of generations; it was also one of understanding. Rebel students would not have considered their behavior nihilistic or inchoate. Kirk clearly did not understand them—a fatal fault for a university president in 1968. But they, in turn, did not understand Kirk.[14]

Trouble started when Columbia scheduled a memorial service for Martin Luther King. For politically aware students, the plan smacked of hypocrisy. At that very moment, the university, located on the edge of Harlem, was demolishing slum housing it owned in order to build a fancy new gymnasium. At the same time, the university was blocking the unionization of ancillary staff, the vast majority of whom were black or Puerto Rican. Alleged links with the Institute for Defense Analysis (IDA), a military think tank, caused further disquiet. Kirk apparently failed to see a contradiction between these issues and the ceremony in honor of King. His students did. When they protested that the gymnasium plan smacked of American racist imperialism, the university compromised by suggesting that local residents might occasionally be allowed access through a rear door—an astonishingly insensitive response which students labeled "Gym Crow." It seemed that the university was actively trying to emulate the US government.

During the memorial service, a student named Mark Rudd jumped onstage and seized the podium, pushing aside the university vice president, David Truman, who was eulogizing King. Rudd shouted: "Dr. Truman and President Kirk are committing a moral outrage against the memory of Dr. King!" The microphone was cut off, causing Rudd to shout louder, railing against the university for stealing land from the people of Harlem.[15]

An angry and impatient young man, Rudd had long been looking for a cause to which to devote his brains and fists. Having just returned from a pilgrimage to Cuba organized by Students for a Democratic Society, he was utterly convinced of the necessity for violence in order to carry out a Cuban-style revolution in the United States. In that sense, he was at least as hypocritical as Kirk, since he had clearly rejected the nonviolent teachings of King. "Rudd continually accused people of cowardice," one rebel recalled. "That was a big word back then. . . . [He] said . . . you had to get a gun, and stop being afraid, and be a man, and all that." In common with the civil rights movement, a split was developing in SDS between those who wanted to march and those who preferred throwing stones. Rudd, disenchanted with the excessive intellectualizing of SDS, had begun to hang out with the East Village Motherfuckers, who took their name from a line in a LeRoi Jones poem: "Up against the wall, motherfuckers, this is a stick-up." The Motherfuckers proudly asserted their intention to "defy law and order with . . . bricks, bottles, garbage, long hair, filth, obscenity, drugs, games, guns, bikes, fire, fun, and fucking." Their tendency to mix politics with mayhem was rather too provocative for most SDS members, who took to calling Rudd's group the "Action Faction," a name the group rather liked. For the Action Faction, loyalty would be measured by one's willingness to mix Molotov cocktails.[16]

The university responded exactly the way Rudd hoped it would. "Authoritarian" power behaved in authoritarian fashion, banning certain types of demonstrations. When Rudd subsequently led 150 students on a march protesting the university's participation in defense research, the administration reacted, again predictably, by disciplining him and six other students. On April 23, he sent Kirk an open letter which referred specifically to the president's complaints about the generation gap. The gap was "a real conflict between those who run things now—you, Grayson Kirk—and those who feel oppressed by and disgusted with the society you rule—we the young people. . . . We can point, in short, to our meaningless studies, our identity crisis, and our repulsion with being cogs in your corporate machines. . . . We will take control of your world, your corporation, your university, and attempt to mold a world in which we and other people can live as human beings." The first part of the letter was reasonably logical and sane, if rather melodramatic. Rudd's childish fantasies, however, surfaced in the last paragraph. "There is only one thing left to say," he concluded. "It may sound nihilistic to you, since it is the opening shot in a war of liberation. I'll use the words of LeRoi Jones, whom I'm sure you don't like a whole lot: 'Up against the wall, motherfucker, this is a stick-up.'"[17]

On that same day, Rudd launched another demonstration, whose purpose was unclear. "I had only the vaguest idea about what we were doing," he later confessed. That did not appear to matter, since action was all-important. Rudd's mob resembled a worm on a pavement, squirming without purpose or direction. Its first target, the Low Library, was locked.

They then turned in the direction of the gymnasium site, but were stopped by a sturdy fence, a cordon of police, and a counterdemonstration of 150 right-wingers. Rudd's group grew increasingly frustrated at the lack of a building to occupy. He was losing control. Someone then suggested seizing nearby Hamilton Hall. The dean, Henry Coleman, blocked their way. In the heat of the moment, it seemed logical to take him hostage.[18]

To say that events quickly spiraled out of control would be inaccurate, since control had never existed. Those who crave action frequently forget to plan. Rudd and his followers held meetings about what to do next, but these quickly descended into arcane discussions about the proletariat, Marx, Lenin, and dialectical materialism. Meanwhile, a group of blacks from Harlem joined the occupation. Since they were even more action-oriented than the students, they eschewed intellectual debate and instead simply seized the building. The students wanted it to remain open for classes; the blacks didn't. Since the latter had guns, they won the argument. They then suggested that perhaps the students should find another building to occupy.

Rudd's group moved to the library, which they managed to force open. Since it was the site of Kirk's office, it at least had symbolic importance. Students took the opportunity to look through the president's secret files and smoke his cigars. Tom Hayden, who was working on an SDS-sponsored inner-city project in nearby Newark, was impressed when he paid a visit:

> I had never seen anything quite like this. Students, at last, had taken power in their own hands, but they were still very much students. Polite, neatly attired, holding their notebooks and texts, gathering in intense knots of discussion, here and there doubting their morality; then recommitting themselves to remain, wondering if their academic and personal careers might be ruined, ashamed of the thought of holding an administrator in his office but wanting a productive dialogue with him, they expressed in every way the torment of their campus generation.

As time passed, the sit-in grew more popular, with the result that more buildings were occupied—a total of five by the end of the week. There was still, however, no plan or purpose. Each occupied building was like a free republic, pursuing its own agenda and producing its own propaganda. On

Friday, April 26, the administration finally admitted that it had lost control and closed down the university. On the following Monday, Truman attempted to hold negotiations with Rudd and other student leaders, but these went nowhere. It proved impossible to negotiate with a group that had no idea what it wanted.[19]

Early Tuesday morning, the New York police provided the students with a lesson in violence, efficiency, and organization. At 2:30 A.M., the university was sealed off and 1,000 heavily armed officers descended on seven targets, sweeping aside some well-meaning students desperately appealing for calm. Police violence was indiscriminate; no attempt was made to distinguish between perpetrators and bystanders. The university resembled a war zone and, in the aftermath, 120 charges of brutality were brought against the force. The Columbia revolt had nevertheless been crushed and order restored—at least for the moment. Rudd, still believing in his cause, decided to replay the sorry episode by again occupying Hamilton Hall, with the same disastrous effect.

No one emerged with honor. Rudd and his friends convinced themselves that, despite their defeat, they had demonstrated "that the administration was more willing to have students arrested and beat up . . . than to stop its policies of exploitation, racism, and support for imperialism." They called this "maximizing the contradictions." In the process, however, they had also shown that they were hardly capable of organizing a bunfight in a cafeteria. That said, the administration had provided useful lessons in how not to handle militant students. An official inquiry later criticized the university for allowing a rather simple crisis to escalate out of control. Kirk, singled out for blame, wisely retired. No longer inclined to preach eloquently on the dilemma of the generation gap, he now simply blamed his troubles on "the permissive doctrines of Dr. Spock." The behavior of the police was roundly condemned, even by those usually inclined toward knee-jerk opposition to student radicalism. But most of all, the revolution was revealed as hollow and superficial. What had started as legitimate grievance deteriorated into childish tantrum. A year after the revolt, Rudd admitted: "We manufactured the issues. The Institute for Defense Analysis is nothing at Columbia. And the gym issue is bull. It doesn't mean anything to anybody. I had never been to the gym site before the demonstration began. I didn't even know how to get there." Since the politics of the demonstration were always difficult to discern, it is probably safe to conclude that most of the protesters were drawn by the lure of mayhem. "The issue is not the issue," Rudd shouted at one point during the action. At the time, quite a few people praised his profundity. In retrospect, that inane sentence seems a suitable explanation for the descent into anarchy.[20]

Hayden, intoxicated by drama, afterward called for "two, three, many Columbias." "A crisis is foreseeable that would be too massive for police to handle," he argued. "It can happen; whether or not it will . . . is a question which only time will answer. What is certain is that we are moving toward power—the power to stop the machine if it cannot be made to serve humane ends." He later added: "I think the problem in the movement is not so much the tendency toward adventurism, to running out in the streets, as it is the tendency in the opposite direction—to look for ways to achieve social change without pain, without loss of life, without prison sentences. America, I think, is no different from any other country in this respect— someone will have to pay dues in order to make the system move." Rudd agreed. "At a time when the radical movement was the most disheartened and dispirited," he later claimed, "the Columbia student rebellion broke through the gloom as an example of the power a radical movement could attain." For him, that meant a divorce from SDS—a group too obsessed with theory. He grew enamored with a French idea called "exemplary action." This was simply a posh way of arguing that a small demonstration could inspire a big revolution. In June 1969, Rudd helped to found a new organization devoted to exemplary action. Paying homage to a line from Bob Dylan, he and his friends called themselves Weathermen.[21]

PARIS: ABSURDISTS REVOLT

Paris in the spring of 1968 was not quite what Cole Porter had in mind. "The streets . . . looked dismal," Anne McDermid, a British student drawn to the "events," recalled. "Smouldering hulks of cars still left in the middle of the road, other cars which had not been destroyed, but whose owners had been too nervous to come back to reclaim them, . . . many street signs torn down to add to the barricades, most of the trees along the Champs Elysées cut down for similar reasons; piles of garbage bags torn by cats and dogs during the night, with their contents rotting." Despite the ugliness, Paris of 1968 still evokes romance. Sentimental interpretations dominate recollection. Screen out the rosy glow of burning barricades, however, and the picture that emerges is one of anarchy, egotism, and emptiness. The revolutionaries achieved nothing but a very big mess. Instead of a blossoming, May inspired spring-cleaning.[22]

France in the early 1960s was an anachronism, a country where national pride impeded modernization. Pride was chiefly expressed in the person of General Charles de Gaulle, president of the Fifth Republic, a man whose vocation was to uphold France's status as a great power. Since the Second World War, two futile imperial wars had been fought in order to maintain that illusion. France had also become a nuclear power, because the Bomb, the government maintained, was essential if "France is to remain a great modern country."[23]

While desperately clinging to past glory, France underwent rapid economic modernization. Real wages rose by 3.6 percent in the years 1963 to 1969, an improvement manifested in a consumer boom focused on automobiles and electrical goods. The benefits were not, however, shared equally. Manual workers justifiably argued that modernization was achieved at their expense, since their wages remained low. Official statistics revealed that, at the beginning of 1968, 40 percent of workers earned less than $1,800 per year. Only one household in four could boast a refrigerator, a washing machine, *and* a television, while only one in five laid claim to all those *and* a car. Rural laborers had migrated to the cities in search of more stable and better-paid employment, not always finding their holy grail. This put enormous pressure upon urban areas, resulting in appalling slums. De Gaulle remained popular among nationalist elements in the hinterlands, but in the cities he seemed an old-fashioned autocrat.[24]

Baby boomers who entered university in the mid-Sixties found conditions worse in France than in any other Western country. The student population had trebled in a decade, yet facilities had not kept pace. There were not enough student rooms for everyone, and residence halls were often indistinguishable from slum housing. Students accustomed to a more permissive society than that of their parents wanted a university responsive to their needs, but encountered instead a very traditional authoritarian culture which demanded reverence for teachers. France had twice as many university students as Britain, but granted only half as many degrees, a statistic that convinced de Gaulle that students were lazy and therefore incapable of sustained political action.

Disgruntled students sampled new ideologies with great enthusiasm—there were more factions than cheeses in the market. Radicals easily claimed to be victims of "oppression," in the process manufacturing commonality with other genuinely subjugated peoples around the world. Jacques Sauvageot of the National Union of French Students (Union Nationale des Etudiants Français, or UNEF) argued that "we can think of the present movement as a consequence of the anti-imperialist struggle. Our solidarity with struggles in the Third World cannot be overemphasized."[25]

The Chinese Cultural Revolution seemed like a beacon of hope. Maoism was embraced without concrete knowledge of Mao. Fantasies of Che also proliferated. Meanwhile, the war in Vietnam provided a convenient focus for anger. American efforts were interpreted as merely a continuation of what French imperialists had failed to achieve. In France, the market for American flags rose as fast as the demand for matches. "The stars and stripes have been lit up all over Europe and we may not see them go out again in our lifetime," Richard Neville remarked rather cleverly.[26]

At the beginning of 1968, unrest broke out at Nanterre, a new university built in the bleak working-class suburbs of Paris. During a visit on January 8, the minister of youth and sports, François Misoffe, was challenged by a student named Daniel Cohn-Bendit over the government's refusal to allow men to visit women in their residence halls—a regulation that was causing "sexual misery." "I read your white paper on youth," Cohn-Bendit interjected. "In three hundred pages, there is not one word on the sexual issues of youth." Misoffe insisted that he was there to promote sports and suggested that if Cohn-Bendit was having problems with sex he should perhaps get more exercise. The latter retorted: "Now, there's an answer worthy of Hitler's youth minister." The exchange left Misoffe flummoxed and made Cohn-Bendit a star. Thereafter, he was known as Dany le Rouge. His willingness to take on Misoffe greatly enhanced his revolutionary credibility. Likewise, the minister's facile response reinforced the impression that the government had ears of cloth.[27]

French students were a class apart and behaved as such. While they professed an interest in wider social revolution, they concentrated upon improvement of their own lives. They demanded a restructuring of the ivory tower, mainly by removing aspects they found unpleasant. The criteria by which degrees would be awarded should, they insisted, be changed, with tests replaced by nondiscriminatory group discussions, and self-assessment. Their version of Student Power in practice meant the right to veto rules they hated. "A thoroughgoing analysis never truly evolved," McDermid says. "In fact it seems ironic now how humble were the aspirations, how unambitious the demands. . . . The expressed demands were always for reforms perfectly consistent with capitalism."[28]

Feeling emboldened, activists occupied the "Tower," one of the main Nanterre buildings. As in Germany and the United States, the government overreacted, immediately suspending classes. "If the government had not thought they had to crush the movement," Cohn-Bendit later reflected, "we never would have reached this point of a fight for liberation. There would have been a few demonstrations and that would have been it." Sympathy strikes followed at universities around the city. Before long, it seemed that everyone aspired to revolution. The Parti Communiste Français at first wanted nothing to do with the students, but then decided that the government's difficulties presented an opportunity. The same could be said of labor organizations—on May 1, workers marched from the Place de la République to the Bastille. Events were spiraling out of control. On the 3rd, police broke up a meeting of activists at the Sorbonne, again providing evidence of authoritarian power. A week later, demonstrators occupied the Latin Quarter, in response to the government's refusal to allow the broadcast of a television program on the student movement. On the 13th, students and workers for the first time marched together, to the great dismay of de Gaulle.[29]

Lacking a coherent strategy, the movement resorted to violence as the simplest expression of Marcusian refusal. "Violent revolt is in the French culture," Cohn-Bendit claimed with too much fatalism. Dreaming of the Revolution of 1848, students quickly learned to build barricades and improvise weapons. With battles raging on the streets of Paris, the government mobilized the Compagnies Républicaines de Sécurité (CRS), who resembled a fiendish army of Daleks. "It's a moment I shall never forget," recalled one protester. "Suddenly, spontaneously, barricades were being thrown up in the streets. People were piling up cobblestones because they wanted—many of them for the first time—to throw themselves into a collective spontaneous activity. People were releasing all their repressed feelings, expressing them in a new festive spirit. Thousands felt the need to communicate with one another, to love one another." McDermid was surprised at how easily violence erased a culture of restraint. "I threw my *pave* with all the force I could muster, and the shriek of triumph in my ears was probably my own. I had broken a fundamental taboo against civil disobedience which lies very deep." Violence validated participation. The government's heavy-handed response convinced the students that they deserved to be taken seriously as a revolutionary force. "The possibility of being shot," McDermid reflected, "not hit over the head, dragged by the hair, kicked in the stomach, not suspended from classes or ostracised by relatives—but wounded by an actual bullet fired from a real gun—made those snide comments about middle-class revolutionaries somehow lacking in point."[30]

In truth, there were few real bullets fired from real guns. The riots had a distinctly avant-garde, symbolist nature, as if the whole affair had been scripted by André Gide and filmed by Jean-Luc Godard. The barricades were constructed not for strategic purpose but for symbolic value. Their strength lay in their existence, not in the fact that they prevented the passage of Authority. Demonstrators hurled more gestures than Molotov cocktails. The same could be said of the authorities: the CRS achieved a great deal more by suggesting oppression than through actual oppressive force. Even the actual violence seemed choreographed and symbolic. A police spokesman admitted that "violence was the price we paid for the refusal, on both sides, to kill."[31]

"I was completely surprised by 1968," Francois Cerruti, who ran a radical bookstore, confessed. "I had an idea of the revolutionary process, and it was nothing like this. I saw students building barricades, but these were people who knew nothing of revolution. They were high school kids. They were not even political. There was no organization, no planning." Nadja Tesich later decided that 1968 was a "bourgeois revolution"—an uprising of wealthy children bent on wrecking their parents' cars.[32]

Having previously been reluctant to join the fray, the Confédération Générale du Travail (CGT), France's largest trade union, eventually found it irresistible. In conjunction with the French Communist Party, the CGT fomented demonstrations around the country. Strikes spread like a plague, with factories shut down and public services paralyzed. By May 18, perhaps six million workers had downed tools, the biggest strike in French history.

Students and workers made strange bedfellows. While the situation suggested an organized uprising, in fact it was nothing of the sort. Dissident groups acted opportunistically, in pursuit of their own aims. There were no attempts at coordination, no long-term goals. Visiting the Sorbonne in the midst of the crisis, Ian Dengler found that the students there "really don't understand what they are after." A proclamation pinned to the entrance of the Sorbonne stated: "The revolution which is beginning will call in question not only capitalist society but industrial society. The consumer society must die a violent death. The society of alienation must disappear from history." When it came to describing what would replace the old, however, the proclamation was studiously vague: "We are inventing a new and original world. Imagination is seizing power." The students fantasized about revolution, while the workers simply sought better pay and shorter hours. A poll taken in 1967 found that only 19 percent of workers were dissatisfied with their circumstances, while 81 percent were "generally" or "frankly" satisfied.[33]

French Maoists insisted that mass participation was the only way to achieve liberation. They camouflaged their insignificance by shouting loudly. Traditional forms of political expression were derided as boring or—shades of Marcuse—part of an elaborate plot to silence dissent by providing an illusion of consent. While the students were supposed to be fomenting a revolution, in truth micro-communities emerged which were remarkably similar to the society the students supposedly sought to overturn. There were leaders, social classes, in-groups, out-groups, and virulent prejudice toward those accused of deviation. Anti-authoritarians reveled in the exercise of authority. For all the talk of democracy and free speech, anyone deemed "moderate" or "bourgeois" was automatically purged. One anarchist periodical claimed that the only thing forbidden was to be on the right. Occupiers of the Odéon Theater refused admission to anyone deemed bourgeois.

In theory, the students idolized the working class and demanded workers' control. Some insisted that the percentage of working-class students at the universities be increased. Others openly advocated the demystification of "proper" speech and defiantly adopted the idiom of the workers. In practice, however, students were rudely contemptuous of their "comrades." The two groups were determined to exploit each other. Workers considered students elitist snobs, and students considered workers stupid sheep. Mutual incomprehension fueled disdain. Because the students had never had to worry about their daily bread, they could indulge in esoteric politics. Because bread (both the paper kind and that made from wheat) mattered deeply to the workers, they had no time for fancy ideologies.

According to Ian Dengler, only those workers who had already proven their credentials by being members of approved political groups were accepted. "The worker who just drifts in for a look is treated with all the intellectual disdain and scientific detachment a technician would have for his children: surprised to find that they have anything to say to him, after he has arranged things so well for them." When Dengler found the toilets at the Sorbonne blocked and the whole place a stinking mess, he wondered to himself who would take care of the plumbing after the revolution.[34]

Actually, there was no such thing as a French student movement. There were instead myriad movements espousing contradictory aims. In the absence of leadership, factions flourished. As the narrator reflects in Jean-François Vilar's novel *Nous cheminons entourés de fantômes aux fronts troués* (We Walk On Surrounded by Ghosts with Faces Full of Holes; 1993), Paris was a three-ring circus: "We like one another, we detest one another with that inexpiable hatred that links those who are not building the same identical embryo of the future and necessary revolutionary party. The 'Italians,' the Trots [Trotskyites], the Maoists, the anarchists, the spontaneists, the Bordighists, the archeo-situationists, the Posadists, the ones who are against all tendencies, and a few others besides." Every attention-seeking rebel laid claim to the revolution by making himself a poster and shouting from a soapbox. Most people joined for the excitement, sampling ideologies like tarts from a bakery. The entire affair was a gigantic exercise in political masturbation, as thousands of activists feverishly sought individual fulfillment. "In this revolution we are trying to reinvent the concept of life, of language, and of political expression," Jean-Jacques Lebel claimed. In attempting to explain the ideology of the movement, he managed only to convey its self-indulgence. "We are for the total destruction of categories. We want everyone to use the university for whatever they want. Not only for education, but to eat, sleep, fuck, and get high. . . . We want to demolish the structure of the consumer society—and that includes culture."[35]

McDermid initially thought French students much more intensely politicized than those in America or Britain. She was impressed by the fact that "our debates contained Marxists, Trotskyites, libertarian anarchists,

Maoists, but no American-style hippies with their emphasis upon life-style instead of theory." She gradually realized, however, that "it was . . . life-style that the students were really interested in, but their manner and their language was so formal and stylised I was quite misled." Most French revolutionaries were nothing more than hippies able to quote from Mao's Little Red Book. Posters on the walls of the Sorbonne proclaimed: "The more I make revolution, the more I want to make love." "Imagination has seized power" was another favorite. One anarchist at the Sorbonne demanded the "right to urinate where I like," a demand which would have delighted Jerry Rubin. Like the kids they were, the group occupying the Odéon Theater broke into the costume closets and then went out to face the police dressed as centurions, princesses, jesters, and pirates. "I never believed, from Day One, that they would take power—because they were too chaotic and disorganized," Nadja Tesich reflected. As Baudelaire wrote of 1848: "The revolution was charming only because of the very excess of its ridiculousness."[36]

The leaders in the self-indulgence stakes were the Strasbourg-based Situationists, who turned the pursuit of sensual gratification into a political creed. "We do not want a world in which the guarantee of no longer dying of hunger is exchanged for the risk of dying of boredom," they argued. It was their aim "to live instead of devising a lingering death, and to indulge untrammeled desire." They took their name from the belief in the need to create "situations" which would provoke authority to demonstrate its repressiveness—something Provo did better and with a lot less pretense. The revolution, they argued, had to be fun, or it was no use having it at all. Cut through the verbiage and one found a basically antidemocratic, elitist movement dominated by the desire for orgasms on demand. To postpubescent men still in the process of discovering the joys of sex (though yet to learn the beauty of loving), the Situationists had enormous appeal. The puerile had suddenly become political.[37]

Conditions in Paris were approaching a crisis, with work stoppages causing food shortages and general chaos. The government seemed clueless; its helplessness exacerbated public panic and made the demonstrators more daring. Then, on May 27, prime minister Georges Pompidou struck a deal with the CGT by granting higher wages and shorter hours. Hopes of a breakthrough, however, were dashed when workers at Renault unilaterally refused to ratify the deal. Meanwhile, the head of the French Socialist Party, François Mitterrand, announced that he would be prepared to form a new government of the left, with himself as president and Pierre Mendès-France as prime minister.

De Gaulle responded by leaving the country, to the considerable alarm of his people. No one quite knew the reason for his departure, or indeed if he remained in control. He turned up in Baden-Baden, where he held discussions with General Jacques Massu, commander of French military forces in that sector. Having apparently secured the reassurance he sought from Massu, he returned to Paris reinvigorated. On May 30, he announced that elections would take place the following month. The tide had turned. On that same day, a pro-government demonstration marched along the Champs-Elysées. An estimated one million people took part, some of them chanting slogans like "Send Cohn-Bendit to Dachau"—a demand all the more frightening given that he was half-Jewish. Since students had depended on the support of the workers, when that support evaporated their threat disintegrated. Elections on June 23 and 30 gave a landslide victory to the Gaullists. De Gaulle, who had seemed so old-fashioned at the start of the crisis, was suddenly in vogue again. He played a part he knew well—that of France's hero in its hour of need. Never mind that the crisis was largely his creation.[38]

In that remarkable French way, humiliation was transformed into *triomphe*. "Last May we took to speaking up," the cultural theorist Michel de Certeau argued, "just as in 1789 we took the Bastille." Certeau unwittingly summarized the attitude of a new generation of revolutionaries whose ambitions could be satisfied with mere display. According to Cohn-Bendit, what mattered was that the students had launched a spontaneous experiment designed to make a complete break with society. The fact that the experiment failed was unimportant, since the revolutionaries had done "enough to prove that something could exist." Competing with Cohn-Bendit in vague justifications, Jacques Rémy claimed that 1968 had "no goals, no plans—only sensations and good feelings and a desire to see to a conclusion what had been begun." Those with romantic recollections of the episode are hard-pressed to prove that it was anything more than a rollicking good time—a month of juvenile mayhem free of parental supervision. Alain Peyrefitte, the French minister of education, dismissed the uprising by claiming that "certain French students, having found out that students in other countries have shaken up and smashed everything, want to do the same." In retrospect, that sounds about right.[39]

The uprising is best known for the clever slogans painted on walls throughout the city. The wittiest of the lot was probably "I have something to say, but I'm not sure what," a simple sentence which perfectly encapsulates those directionless days. Meaningless futility does not, however, sit well with the French. Many insist that their society was more open and democratic after May 1968, and credit students for this change. There seems to be, within France, a conspiracy to paint the past in bright colors. The official version holds that youthful rebellion, though at times ferocious, smoothed France's transition to modernity. Commenting upon this convenient myth, a disgusted Régis Debray has written: "The France of stone and rye, of the apéritif and the institute, of *oui papa, oui patron, oui chérie*, was ordered out of the way so that the France of software and supermarkets, of news and planning, of knowhow and brainstorming, could show off its viability to the full, home at last. This spring-cleaning felt like a liberation and, *in effect*, it was one."[40]

"Our generation was generous, the bearers of very strong moral values that were perverted by politics," wrote Jean-Paul Ribes. Positivists desperately connect the May events to everything good that happened after 1968. They lay claim to the emergence of feminist and green movements in the 1970s, even though there was little feminist or environmental consciousness evident on the barricades. Educational reforms after 1968 seem no more impressive than the normal pace of change would have produced. In truth, the May events seem to be the manifestation of a freer, more permissive society, rather than the progenitor of such a society. Though the uprising grew from a youthful sense of exuberance, it left the French public frightened and suspicious. Playful students encouraged authoritarian backlash, as evidenced by the success of the Gaullists at the June election. The dream of social change wilted around the same time as the narcissi.[41]

"In 1968, the planet embraced itself," wrote Cohn-Bendit in 1986. "In Paris, as in Berlin, Rome, or Turin, the paving stone became a symbol of a generation in revolt." One of de Gaulle's first acts after the crisis was to order the paving of the Latin Quarter with asphalt. For nearly 800 years, cobblestones had provided a ready source of ammunition for disgruntled citizens. Never again.[42]

Bad Dudes: Some New York Black Panthers posing in May 1969

La Causa: César Chávez telling a California crowd about the suffering that lies within a bunch of grapes

far left 1968: Alexander Dubček looking rather miserable about the role he has inherited

left 1968: Rudi Dutschke, the leader who was not leader

1968: Paris in the springtime

1968: Tariq Ali preparing to tell the English how to riot

1968: three Chicago conspirators—(l to r) Jerry Rubin, Abbie Hoffman and Rennie Davis

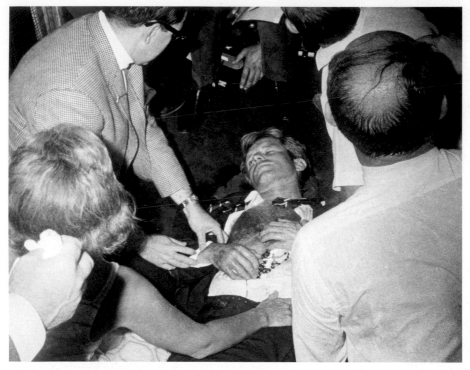

The death of hope—Robert Kennedy dying on a kitchen floor in Los Angeles

above left Happier days: President Achmed Sukarno of Indonesia laughing with Nikita Khrushchev

above Revolution in a vacant lot: Protestors confront police in People's Park, Berkeley, 1969

Ronald Reagan looking tough (and presidential) in 1970

"Farewell to the joy of Jimi"—Hendrix playing his last concert, at the Isle of Wight on 18 September 1970

From the sublime: The Beatles at the start of their stardom in 1964

. . . to the ridiculous: The Monkees, a band made in Hollywood

The business of baseball:
Curt Flood at bat

The day the music died:
Altamont after the carnage

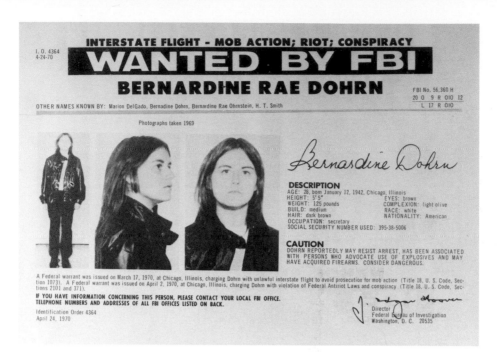

Radical chic: Bernardine Dohrn's wanted poster

Innocent schoolboys: (l to r) Richard Neville, Jim Anderson and Felix Dennis on the way to the Old Bailey in 1970

LONDON: A VERY BRITISH REVOLUTION

In 1968, outside the American Embassy in Grosvenor Square, the British momentarily dispensed with civility. If the antinuclear Aldermaston marches of the previous decade seemed scripted by the Ealing Studios, Grosvenor Square was a film by Kubrick. "[We] were really having a go," Nina Fishman recalled. "That took everyone by surprise, because it wasn't good manners." Though she had witnessed violence firsthand in the American South during Freedom Summer, she had never seen that sort of thing in civilized Britain. The past, it seemed, had been left behind.[43]

The British may have been the stars in the Sixties cultural revolution, but in the political upheaval they were bit players. For most of the decade, the pursuit of happiness kept British youths too occupied to get excited about serious issues of life and liberty. British police kept reserves of tear gas, but never used it. Students, for the most part, went to classes and took exams.

History books seldom pay attention to the mundane—to the dogs that refuse to bark. Riots and demonstrations make interesting reading, but the tendency to concentrate on them encourages the assumption that the Sixties was a decade of incessant turbulence. In fact, even in America, where student protest was supposedly rife, mass demonstrations occurred at only 10 percent of campuses and, on those campuses, only 10 percent of students took part. In other words, protesters were a tiny minority of an otherwise apathetic student body. Apathy was even more the norm in Britain, where politics seemed too much like hard work. One Leicester University student complained that "virtually all intelligent and worthwhile debate . . . still takes place among relatively small groups in an atmosphere of comparative privacy. The subject of greatest concern has been the apathy that most of us display."[44]

British students lived in a stable society in which protest of any kind was rare. The welfare state provided a safety net and encouraged the impression of a caring society. The government was not involved in costly wars abroad; it had refused Lyndon Johnson's invitation to fight in Vietnam. Of all the developed countries, Britain was least bothered by the generation gap. One poll of adults across Europe found that a whopping 59 percent of Britons had a generally positive opinion of the younger generation. All this meant that it was rather difficult to foment unrest. "It was pretty quiet," one frustrated activist admitted. "It was very hard to struggle against the nanny state. . . . London was a huge party and everyone was having a good time."[45]

Craving seriousness, some students occasionally laid claim to the problems of the world. The Radical Student Alliance argued:

> The path from the examination-room to the paddy-fields of Vietnam may appear to be a rather long and devious trek; this is because of our neat habit of separating issues into their "well-defined" compartments. . . . But the path of Student Power rejects this segmentation of our thought-processes. . . . There is a social pattern to these events which can be traced back to the social and economic organisation of societies—in other words, examinations and support for the American policy in Vietnam—both emanate from a certain type of society, from the same social set-up known as monopoly capitalism.[46]

That was, of course, a load of tripe, but the British are fond of tripe. This sort of reasoning allowed some students to convince themselves that seemingly trivial campus issues were deeply important, because they symbolized the oppressive power of the state. Presto, the ivory tower became part of the real world.

At most British universities, however, protests were infrequent, small, and invariably peaceful. The one exception was the London School of Economics (LSE), where students were much more agitated about issues, and much more inclined to protest. This fervor had historical precedent. The LSE had been founded in 1898 by Fabian socialists and had retained its radical reputation. It was also an institution that was dedicated to the social sciences and that tended to attract politically aware middle-class students. In addition, the university had a rather strange tradition of hiring reactionary administrators who reveled in righteous authority.

The LSE was the unofficial headquarters of the British New Left, a group less new and more left than its American counterpart. At least in theory, the British were much more willing to embrace the communal at the expense of the individual. Theory was, however, usually as far as it went. The British New Left consisted of political junkies who could spend days arguing the finer points of Marxist dialectic without ever descending to practicalities. Though they dreamed of taking revolution out into the streets, they hardly ever managed to get up from their desks. "I knew the *New Left Review* people but always felt distanced from their politics," Michael Horovitz recalled. "They seemed such literal-minded disciples of Sartre and purveyors of long words. Talking a lot but not getting that much done, beyond all their publishing." The Marxist historian Eric Hobsbawm dismissed them as "negligible," since they produced "neither new parties of the left . . . nor lasting new organizations of significance . . . nor even individual national leaders."[47]

Alan Marcuson agreed in retrospect that so much of what he witnessed at the LSE was just political playacting. The very fact that the revolutionaries were still going to classes and still interested in getting degrees seemed to confirm that politics was just a hobby.

> All those revolutionary arseholes, when it really came down to it, had to finish their courses and get their jobs and secure their careers. And that's the reason, I believe, that the LSE failed—the revolutionaries wouldn't give up their goddamn careers.
>
> It was very interesting and exciting but it was a complete fuckaround. Just a load of talk, endless, endless meetings and arguments and bad feeling and factions of the Left.

The battles were fierce, but the weapons just words. "People would come to my flat and have discussions about, 'Could Bukharin be resurrected? Could Bukharin be made a hero?'" Nina Fishman recalled. "It was an intellectual fashion, really." Chris Rowley witnessed "Troskyists [fighting] each other with venom and vituperation beyond anything I could recall from school debating classes. . . . There was no right wing, and the Socialists were the centrists." The Socialist Society wanted nothing to do with members of the Labour party, who were revisionist scum. Socialism implied revolution, which in turn implied worship of the Vietnamese and hatred of the Russians. Debates usually took place in the Union Bar, perhaps the whole point of the exercise. Bitter political enemies bought each other pints. Argument, like the beer, was lukewarm and flat.[48]

A change came in February 1966, when David Adelstein, self-proclaimed activist and believer in participatory democracy, became union president. He had no intention of confining agitation to the price of a pint in the Union Bar. Nor was he particularly interested in purely theoretical debate. Quite fortuitously, a few months after his election, the LSE appointed Dr.

Walter Adams its new director. Adams had previously been principal of University College in Rhodesia and, much to the dismay of leftist students, had not sufficiently distanced himself from the racist policies of that country.

Adelstein's outspoken criticism of the appointment prompted university authorities to discipline him. This rather stupid move gave Adelstein exactly what he wanted—namely, proof that the university had no respect for free speech. The university had obviously not been paying much attention to events in the United States, or perhaps felt confident they could be ignored.

In February 1967, during a demonstration against the appointment, an altercation between protesters and a university porter resulted in the latter's suffering a fatal heart attack. Since the demonstration had been banned, the university felt that it could take stringent action against the organizers, two of whom, Adelstein and Marshall Bloom, were "rusticated" until the following academic year. Radical students reacted by organizing a boycott of lectures and a sit-in lasting eight days. This time, the university took notice. The involvement of otherwise apolitical students convinced authorities that the protest had to be taken seriously. In response, the board of governors suspended the rustications. A new staff/student committee was set up to hear grievances. Students felt emboldened by their victory, but hadn't a clue what to do next.

The war in Vietnam provided an answer. British students had protested against American policy in Vietnam from as early as 1962, but always politely. After ground troops were deployed in 1965, Vietnam became a prominent issue on campus—virtually every university staged some sort of protest. "The Vietnamese were demonstrating in the most concrete fashion imaginable that it was possible to fight and win," the radical leader Tariq Ali later reflected. "This fact was critical in shaping the consciousness of our generation. We believed that change was not only necessary, but possible." "So much seemed at stake in Vietnam," Angela Carter thought. "The very nature of our futures." Nevertheless, until 1968 protests remained consistently quiet.[49]

The war, which seemed to reveal in microcosm the worst aspects of American neo-imperialism, provided the perfect romantic cause. David was taking on Goliath. Poorly armed peasants were using Maoist tactics to defend their country against the American bully, and seemed to be winning. British youths found it easy to support the Viet Cong because they were untroubled by moral dilemma. Protesting the war was not unpatriotic, since no British boys were fighting. Furthermore, since the British had already disposed of most of their colonies, they could freely lay claim to moral superiority. Vietnam provided the perfect gut issue: hating America taxed neither the conscience nor the wallet.

The British antiwar movement reached its climax in Grosvenor Square. The demonstrations were organized by the Vietnam Solidarity Campaign (VSC), a group founded in January 1966 by Ali and Pat Jordan, two Trotskyites. The group, Ali boasted, was "committed to the victory of the Vietnamese people against the war of aggression and atrocity waged by the United States." Not strictly speaking a student group, the VSC was dominated by young people and, as such, was a marked departure from the older pacifist groups, which had originally protested nuclear weapons. The old tactics of nonviolent moral protest by respectable men smoking pipes and women pushing prams were rudely discarded. Quite suddenly, political protest in Britain was hijacked by a band of desperados intent on mayhem, or what the *Observer* called "a highbrow version of football hooliganism." Johnny Byrne, who lived in a proto-commune in London, recalls the arrival of a young American woman named Nadia, a veteran of Berkeley. She "radicalised everybody. . . . She was the one who got them all down to Grosvenor Square during the big demonstration in '68. I remember endless weeks and weeks of people talking about using their banners as lances, spears, unhorsing policemen and charging them—the tactics of confrontation."[50]

This aggression violated the sensitivities of the British Council for Peace in Vietnam (BCPV), a traditional pacifist group. The BCPV accused the VSC of being more interested in drama than message. The VSC defended itself by arguing that stridency was essential: "By adopting a decisive and clear-cut position, it is much easier to mobilize effective support. By watering down one's aims, one merely becomes so diffuse that one is totally ineffective."[51]

The VSC was not simply interested in ending the war in Vietnam. Like SDS, the group also wanted a total transformation of society, and believed wholeheartedly in the necessity of violence to achieve that end. According to the widely accepted dialectic, violence provoked an aggressive response from the authoritarian state, thus radicalizing the people. Jo Durden-

Smith experienced this effect firsthand: "You went on a demonstration tentatively: you didn't know whether you were a radical or not—and one of the things that happened was that it radicalised you. Because it didn't matter whether or not you were actually a radical—you still got beaten up. It was a collective rite of passage." That said, commitment based on emotion, rather than belief, meant that loyalty to the cause was often fickle.[52]

What Ali and his friends did not understand (or perhaps ignored) is that violence provides its own attraction; politically apathetic people join in because mayhem is alluring. Writing in *Political Quarterly* in 1969, the political scientist James Jupp observed:

> [The] Marcusean tactic of "ripping the mask from violence" satisfies the youthful desire to fight. It gives intellectual justification for the kind of behaviour long found among adolescents at football matches and on Glasgow housing estates. The battles between mods and rockers have been replaced by those between "the fuzz" and the forces of good. In so far as violence is directed against the sort of forces which strafe American campuses from helicopters, then Marcuse has opened a window on truth. But where, as so often in Britain, the fight is deliberately provoked to prove a point, then he has simply licensed the creation of a public nuisance.

John Hopkins found the VSC all too transparent and cynical—history provided too many examples, he felt, of demagogues taking advantage of the forbidden allure of mob violence. After the first Grosvenor Square demonstration, in October 1967, he railed against Ali in *IT.* "Who's cannon-foddering these people?" he asked. "From that day I took no part in that kind of demonstration."[53]

The first march on the American Embassy took place on October 22, 1967, and involved perhaps 10,000 people. "What we felt was that if we were able to smash up a bit of the Embassy it would be a way of demonstrating solidarity with the Vietnamese," Robin Blackburn later explained. "We were partly hoping that the media might report it and generally add to the view of an American president under siege, even from loyal allies like the British with their tame Labour government." The demonstration was considerably angrier than anything the English had recently seen. Marchers reached the doors of the US Embassy before police forced them back. Forty-four demonstrators were arrested.[54]

The next demonstration came on March 17, 1968. Referring to Tet, Ali boasted that the aim was to occupy the building "for just as long as the Vietcong held the American Embassy in Saigon seven weeks ago." A crowd of between 10,000 and 25,000 took part, depending on who was counting. More important than the size was the way the demonstration revealed an addictive attraction to violence. Durden-Smith, who covered the demonstrations for ITV's *World in Action,* felt that the media provided encouragement: "[Television] was the mirror . . . in which our gestures became grandiose." He saw students prodded from two directions. "The media played a sort of pushing, forcing role: 'Be like that only more so. Do more, be more extreme.' At the same time there was this pressure from the radical Left of exactly the same kind, towards more and more revolutionary purity, towards final exorcism of the bourgeois elements buried deep within." Melodramatic reaction by the Establishment provided further validation: the *Daily Mail, Sun,* and *Telegraph* called for demonstrations of this sort to be banned, while in the House of Commons, the MP Tom Iremonger called for the deportation of "foreign scum"—a clear reference to Ali.[55]

The final demonstration came on October 27, 1968. Given the May events in Paris, the media dwelt on the possibility of similar occurrences in London, thus providing even more publicity for the VSC. Alarmists warned of full-scale revolution. The turnout was huge, with perhaps 100,000 taking part. Scuffles between police and protesters provided an interesting manifestation of the class war, as working-class bobbies vigorously defended the Establishment against middle-class troublemakers. On the whole, however, good sense prevailed. The demonstration did not produce the orgy of violence widely expected.

For every individual radicalized by action, many more, it seems, were alienated by it. Prior to the October 1968 demonstration, Geoff Martin, president of the National Union of Students (NUS), issued a statement to the *Times* in which he urged students not to take part. "The trend to violence must be halted. Ignore the demonstration, it won't help the Vietnamese people. . . . NUS defends the right to peaceful demonstrations. But we see student political involvement as a matter of brain, not brawn. Many groups planning violence on Sunday are conning the students and the general public into believing their main concern is Vietnam. It is not; their purpose is confrontation with the police. . . . These political hooligans, many of whom are not students, admit they want a 'weekend revolution.'"

Honesty of this sort attracted howls of protest from the NUS rank and file. At a subsequent conference, the leadership was censured for "blatant abuse of their position." Meanwhile, the Radical Student Alliance and the Revolutionary Socialist Students Federation labeled Martin a reactionary stooge.[56]

John Lennon agreed with Martin. His "Revolution," released as a single in August 1968, was a reaction to the mindless violence of that year—the shooting of Kennedy and King, Tet, the riots in Chicago and Paris, and the increasing fondness among youths for Maoist tactics. Lennon's message is crystal clear: if the revolution wished to emulate Mao, count him out. He wanted nothing to do with "minds that hate," and his demand to be shown the "plan" seems a pointed reference to the fact that "leaders" like Ali did not have one. "Don't expect me to be on the barricades unless it's with flowers," Lennon announced.[57]

Lennon's forthright advocacy of nonviolence earned him few friends. McCartney was opposed to releasing the song as a single, fearing it would alienate a significant portion of the Beatles' fan base. In America, radicals lambasted Lennon for his "betrayal," calling the song "a lamentable petty-bourgeois cry of fear." His cozy assurances that everything was going to be "alright" were, according to his critics, no less than could be expected from a millionaire. The jazz singer Nina Simone released a musical rebuttal, and the filmmaker Jean-Luc Godard, a self-confessed fan of Mao, accused Lennon of apathy. Right-wingers in America, on the other hand, argued that Lennon was simply being clever: his real message was that Maoists risked jeopardizing the revolution by pushing too hard.[58]

Lennon's behavior stands in sharp contrast to that of Mick Jagger, who joined the crowd outside Grosvenor Square and took delight in throwing stones. He then went home, wrote "Street-Fighting Man," and made millions off the revolution. That sort of behavior might have been what Martin had in mind when he railed against "weekend revolutionaries."

According to the home secretary, James Callaghan, the Grosvenor Square protests were "a demonstration of British good sense." He praised the "self-control" shown by the vast majority of protesters and complimented the "discipline and restraint" shown by police. The latter, he maintained, "remained completely calm even under the provocation of the disorderly charging and shoving. . . . I doubt if this kind of demonstration could have taken place so peacefully in any other part of the world." Callaghan was probably right. Remarking on the March demonstration, the *Manchester Guardian,* a traditionally leftist paper, commented that "it was only after considerable provocation that police tempers began to fray and truncheons were used, and then only for a short time. The demonstrators seemed determined to stay until they had provoked a violent response of some sort from the police." In other words, the demonstrations are notable for what did not happen. No one was killed. Neither tear gas nor water cannons were used. A Commons bill calling for the imprisonment of the organizers and the deportation of foreign agitators garnered just 62 votes out of more than 600 MPs. The attorney general, Sir Elwyn Jones, briefly threatened to use the 1936 Public Order Act (which prohibited the formation of paramilitary organizations) as a weapon against the VSC, but that turned out to be nothing more than bombast.[59]

Those who participated in the demonstrations are certain they did their bit to chip away at the American edifice of war. In truth, however, Grosvenor Square was more important for what it revealed than for what it achieved. Britain was and remains a stable society not given to expressing emotions in the street. "Hanging on in quiet desperation is the English way," Pink Floyd would later contend. There always exists in Britain a small core of committed politicos who feel a genuine need to protest, as well as another group of hooligans who love the sound of breaking glass. Occasionally, the two groups form a brief and uneasy alliance, in the process exaggerating each other's importance.[60]

13

WILTED FLOWERS

THE VATICAN: HUMANAE VITAE

Less than three months after his election in 1959, Pope John XXIII announced his intention to convene the Second Vatican Council. "I want to open the windows of the Church," he declared, "so that we can see out and the people can see in." Its purpose, he proclaimed, would be *aggiornamento*, or modernization.

Just how much fresh air would be allowed in through the open windows was unclear. Prior to the council, the pope sent out mixed signals, maintaining that "the present situation in the world makes it all the more urgent for Christianity, if it is not to perish, to proclaim its ancient principles with vigor." That did not suggest an enthusiasm for reform. But then, in his opening speech to the council on October 11, 1962, he seemed to welcome the winds of change. "The Church should never depart from the sacred treasure of truth," he proclaimed, "but at the same time, she must ever look to the present, to the new conditions and the new forms of life introduced into the modern world."[1]

The Second Vatican Council met in four sessions during the years 1962 to 1965. In all, 2,908 men (and no women) were entitled to attend. As many as 2,500 took part in the general sessions, making it the largest ecumenical council in the history of the church. At times, the atmosphere was not unlike a political convention. Debates were sometimes acrimonious, secret cabals abounded, and plots were hatched in the smoky cafés surrounding the Vatican. While the council was technically democratic and votes were frequently taken, final decisions rested with the pope.

The first session ended on December 8, 1962, and the next was due to begin the following autumn. During the intervening period, on June 3, 1963, Pope John died. Eighteen days later, Pope Paul VI was elected and immediately confirmed that the council would proceed. In the remaining sessions, the council covered much ground and pronounced upon numerous controversial issues concerning church governance. Most of the pronouncements were, however, far too arcane for lay Catholics, who had difficulty perceiving the impact upon their own lives.

The one issue on which Catholics most desired clarification was birth control. Early in the third session (1964), the pope withdrew that issue from the jurisdiction of the council and informed bishops that the topic would be referred to a special commission appointed by him. Frightened by the potential consequences of an entrenched papacy, the Patriarch of Antioch warned his fellow cardinals: "I beg of you my brothers; let us avoid a new Galileo case: one is enough for the church."[2]

The pope bluntly disregarded that warning. He seemed to signal his position on October 4, 1964, when he addressed the United Nations and suggested that the solution to the problem of overpopulation lay in the reduction of poverty and the expansion of food production, not in limiting the birthrate. As he put it, the aim should be "to multiply the bread on the table, not to diminish the eaters." On the other hand, he suggested to the journalist Alberto Cavallari of *Corriere della Sera* that he had no firm opinions: "The world asks us what we think about [birth control] and we must give an answer. We cannot remain silent. It is difficult to know what to say. For centuries the church has not had to face such problems. And this matter is a little strange for churchmen to be handling, and even embarrassing from the human point of view. . . . Deciding is not as easy as studying. But we have to say something. What can we say? God must enlighten us." Subsequent events demonstrated just how complicated this issue was for the church. The need for a new doctrine was widely recognized, but the Catholic church is not adept at changing direction.[3]

The papal commission was two-tiered, consisting, first, of fifteen cardinals and bishops and, second, of sixty-four lay experts. According to Thomas Burch, a professor at Georgetown University and member of the lay committee, the pope suggested that he wanted to find a way to change the church's position, but was worried that to do so would challenge papal authority. After two years of deliberation, the lay members voted 60 to 4 in favor of a change, while the clergy voted 9 to 6. The majority opinion expressed in both cases was that reform was appropriate even though it would undermine the doctrine of papal infallibility.

Among the minority group, the issue of papal authority was more important than the rights or wrongs of birth control. Dissenters argued: "If it should be declared that contraception is not evil in itself . . . this would mean that the leaders of the church, acting with extreme imprudence, had condemned thousands of innocent human acts, forbidding, under pain of eternal damnation, a practice which would now be sanctioned. The fact can neither be denied nor ignored that these same acts would now be declared licit on the grounds of principles cited by the Protestants, which popes and bishops have either condemned or at least not approved." The author of that opinion was the Polish archbishop Karol Wojtyla, who would later become Pope John Paul II. His views mirrored precisely those of Pope Paul. As the Roman Catholic historian and theologian August Hasler has concluded, "The core of the problem was not the Pill, but the authority, continuity, and infallibility of the church's magisterium."[4]

Whatever the real rationale behind the church's subsequent ban on contraception, the pope took steps to root that ban firmly within Christian doctrine. The long-awaited papal encyclical *Humanae Vitae*, issued on July 25, 1968, recognized the problems of overpopulation and gave lip service to the desire of parents to limit family size, but stressed without equivocation that any means of artificial birth control constituted a violation of natural law. A husband and wife "are not free to act as they choose in the service of transmitting of life, as if it were wholly up to them to decide what is the right course to follow. On the contrary, they are bound to ensure that what they do corresponds to the will of God the Creator. The very nature of marriage and its use makes His will clear, while the constant teaching of the Church spells it out." According to the encyclical, "God has wisely ordered the laws of nature and the incidence of fertility in such a way that successive births are already naturally spaced." The important point, however, was that the conjugal act could not and should not be separated from the act of procreation. "An act of mutual love which impairs the capacity to transmit life which God the Creator, through specific laws, has built into it, frustrates His design which constitutes the norm of marriage, and contradicts the will of the Author of life. Hence, to use this divine gift while depriving it, even if only partially, of its meaning and purpose, is equally repugnant to the nature of man and of woman, and is consequently in opposition to the plan of God and His holy will." The encyclical went on to condemn, specifically, abortion ("even for therapeutic reasons"), sterilization, the Pill, the IUD, condoms, and every other method of artificial contraception, whether used by the individual or promoted by the state as a method of population control. The only approved means was the rhythm method.[5]

The encyclical constituted not simply a ruling against birth control but also an attack on the promiscuity which easy access to the Pill had supposedly inspired. Following more closely the rules of God would, it was hoped, turn back the clock to an age when sex was sacred. "The right and lawful ordering of birth demands, first of all, that spouses fully recognize and value the true blessings of family life and that they acquire complete mastery over themselves and their emotions," it was proclaimed. "Self-discipline . . . is a shining witness to the chastity of husband and wife and, far from being a hindrance to their love of one another, transforms it by giving it a more truly human character." Further to this end, the pope addressed the issue of permissiveness in the media. "Everything . . . in the modern means of social communication which arouses men's baser passions and encourages low moral standards, as well as every obscenity in the written word and every form of indecency on the stage and screen, should be condemned publicly and unanimously." It was no use, he argued, to "defend this kind of depravity in the name of art or culture," or to hide behind arguments based on individual liberty.[6]

The reaction to *Humanae Vitae* varied from person to person, country to country. In some quarters in Latin America, the encyclical was seen as a bold challenge to American neo-imperialism. Concern had been raised by recent American emphasis upon the need to slow population growth in the developing world. Latin Americans reacted angrily when Lyndon Johnson remarked that "five dollars spent for birth control are rather more profitable than a hundred dollars to favor development." American-sponsored birth control was condemned as "genocide"; Marxist students in Colombia and Ecuador openly attacked family planning clinics. Catholic clerics, arguing that the "population explosion" was an American invention, maintained that resources were sufficient to feed an additional five or six billion people and that starvation was simply a problem of distribution. "The solution to the demographic problem is not to corrupt mankind in his moral foundations," the rector of the Roman Catholic

University in Santo Domingo argued, "but to educate him so that he may make more rational use of his resources." At the same time, opinion polls across Latin America consistently showed a majority of women in favor of small families and artificial birth control.[7]

In the developed world, outrage was mixed with disdain. The British journalist Bernard Hollowood argued that "those who will suffer most from this philosophical nonsense will be the poor and underprivileged, those who lack the strength of mind and body to resist religious enslavement. Many of them will obey out of fear and ignorance, and as they do so they will bring increasing hardship upon themselves, increasing misery, and hopelessness. Religion is a terrible and terrifying force when it can be so abused." The *New Scientist* argued that "bigotry, pedantry and fanaticism can kill, mutilate and torment their victims just as well as bombs, pogroms and gas chambers." A group of 2,600 American scientists signed a petition vehemently condemning the encyclical. "Each action to prevent the efforts to stop numerical development of world population sanctions the misery in which millions . . . are living today," they warned. "The world should be aware as quickly as possible that Paul VI has sanctioned the death of endless numbers of human beings with his wrongly inspired and immoral encyclical." The biologist Jeffrey Baker pointed out that during the five years from Paul's accession to the release of the encyclical, the population of the world had increased by 300 million and 20 million had died of malnutrition.[8]

Individual Catholics were presented with a stark choice: either use birth control and run the risk of damnation, or follow the dictates of the church and surrender to the tyranny of unrestrained procreation. In the industrialized world, the choice commonly made was defiance. Polls consistently showed at least 80 percent of American Catholic women were determined to ignore the ban. That was, nevertheless, not a choice made easily. The encyclical placed a heavy burden on the consciences of Catholics, and drove many from the church. "I stopped going," one woman confessed. "I have thirteen children, and I can't really afford to have any more, so I had to make my choice." The most noticeable effect, however, was observable in the poorer countries, particularly in Latin America. The countries least able to deal with the pressures of overpopulation were also those most reluctant to disobey. As the theologian Hans Kung has written, "for the people in many under-developed countries, . . . [*Humanae Vitae*] constitutes a source of incalculable harm, a crime in which the Church has implicated itself."[9]

MAYFAIR: CASUALTIES OF THE CULTURAL REVOLUTION

In early January 1969, Jimi Hendrix entertained the reporter Don Short from the *Daily Mirror* at his new house in Mayfair, next door to the former home of George Frideric Handel. "To tell you the God's honest truth, I haven't heard much of the fella's stuff," he confessed. "But I dig a bit of Bach now and again." In spite of himself, Short was charmed by Hendrix. Like so many others who first encountered the wild man of rock, he was surprised to find a polite, soft-spoken gentleman. Short asked him about his outrageous image. It wasn't an image, he insisted. "No, I'm just natural all the time. What others think or say doesn't worry me."[10]

Hendrix embodied everything the counterculture held sacred—the exuberance, the excess, the fun, the music, the drugs. Yet those attributes competed with one another; they could not long coexist. Exuberance was difficult to maintain while consuming copious quantities of drugs. Perhaps more fundamentally, style threatened to smother substance. Hendrix made his reputation as a wild man, even though that image did not do justice to his complex sensitivity. Drugs masked his suffering: the more success he achieved, the more exploited he became, and the more he craved escape. His manager, the vile Michael Jeffrey, treated Hendrix like a mother lode to be stripped of ore as quickly as possible, until only a pile of poisonous slag remained. If Hendrix seemed destructive, it was perhaps because he was being destroyed.

Music brought him "some kind of peace of mind or satisfaction," in direct contrast to politics, which was "really an ego scene—it's the art of words, which means nothing." His wild antics were cathartic. "When you bring your girlfriend . . . and watch us play," he told Dick Cavett, "you can get it out of your system by watching us do it. Make it into theatrics instead of putting it in the streets. So that when you get home . . . you have all this tension out of the way. It's nothing but a release, I guess."[11]

The contradictions in Hendrix's life were brutally apparent during a long European tour in the winter of 1968–1969 when he was criticized as "listless and tired."[12] His bass player blamed the poor performances on the scarcity of amphetamines. That said, a concert at the Albert Hall at the end of that tour was ruined because he was too stoned to play. At the Isle of Wight on August 31, 1970, Hendrix played brilliantly, but was too exhausted to provide the outrageous behavior everyone expected. Richard Neville thought the event cruelly foreboding: "Farewell to the joy of Jimi, farewell to the fun at the funfair. . . . Jimi failed because we all failed. . . . We've created nothing, nothing." On this occasion, melodrama was appropriate, since it turned out to be Jimi's last concert. Eighteen days later he was found dead at the Samarkand Hotel in London. He'd choked on his own vomit.[13]

"The 60s ended for me in 1970 when they announced on the radio that Jimi Hendrix was dead," John Marsh recalled. "My first reaction was I knew the 1970s were going to fuck it all. And by God they did." Marsh's reaction was not uncommon; quite a few people saw the death of Hendrix as the end of the party. The clues had long been there. "By 1969 it all broke apart and some went to money and others to total insanity," Spike Hawkins felt. "I saw the end coming with overdoses. It turned very nasty. . . . Deaths came left, right and centre. . . . The energy went." Hendrix himself told Short that death did not frighten him—a rather short-sighted view for a man supposedly in love and planning a family. "People still mourn when people die," he said. "That's self-sympathy. The person who is dead ain't cryin'. . . . When I die I want people to play my music, go wild and freak out an' do anything they wanna do." That sounds like the feelings of a man who expects to live forever. Unfortunately, neither the artist nor his spirit was immortal.[14]

"Hope I die before I get old," the Who sang in their iconic "My Generation." While the band did not perhaps mean that literally, far too many of their generation realized that wish. The ability to stay young and to live in the moment was the greatest strength of baby boomers, but also their greatest weakness. "What are you doing with life?" a reporter asked Janis Joplin in 1969. "Getting stoned, staying happy, and having a good time," she replied. "I'm doing just what I want with my life, enjoying it. I don't think you can ask more of life than that. . . . When I get scared and worried, I tell myself, 'Janis, just have a good time.' So I juice up real good and that's just what I have." Her doctor had warned her that excessive drinking was doing irreparable damage to her liver. "I don't go back to him anymore. Man, I'd rather have ten years of super-hyper-most than live to be seventy by sitting in some goddamn chair watching TV. Right now is where you are. How can you wait?" Joplin didn't get her ten years. A few months later she was dead, the victim of a heroin overdose. For a very brief moment, she provided inspiration to young people determined to resist the prudence of their parents. But by living in the moment, she denied herself a future.[15]

Among those who survived, the drug experience seemed in retrospect fun, colorful, and relatively harmless, something to be remembered nostalgically but (in most cases) to be stored securely in the past. "Sometimes being stoned helped you to perceive the things that were hidden from you by all the advertising," the actress Julie Christie reflected. "Perhaps getting stoned was the only way to overthrow the sort of mind-fucking that had been going on, this brainwashing. Although there were a lot of casualties, it wasn't such a bad thing—trying to get on another plane." Quite a few musicians convinced themselves that LSD improved their creativity, allowing them to discover harmonies otherwise elusive. "When you stop exploring with drugs, now that's a bad scene," Steve Winwood of Traffic argued. "I never want to stop exploring."[16]

Explorers sometimes got swallowed by the jungle. Among the casualties, history remembers a few famous faces, immensely talented individuals like Hendrix, Joplin, and Jim Morrison, who died far too young. Behind them rank thousands of faceless dead remembered only by their families. And then there are the living dead, those whose minds were ravaged by drugs but whose bodies somehow survived to torment those who knew them when. The producer Joe Boyd recalled seeing guitarist and songwriter Syd Barrett in the spring of 1967. "He was charming, impish and witty." A couple of months and many tabs of acid later, "he had gone through a dramatic deterioration and he was almost monosyllabic and very blank-faced." June Bolan was offstage at the last gig Barrett played with Pink Floyd: "He was so . . . gone. I kept saying, 'Syd, it's June, it's me, look at me . . .' Roger Waters and I . . . got him out to the stage. He had a white Stratocaster and we put it round his neck and he walked on stage and of course the audience went spare because they loved them. The band started to play and Syd stood there. He had his guitar round his neck and his arms just hanging down and . . . he stood there, tripping out of his mind." Barrett went mad. Susan Lydon, on the other hand, retained her sanity but became a junkie. In the late 1960s Lydon was one of the most promising journalists of her generation. A decade later she was selling her body for a fix. Her mental faculties remained intact, but she could no longer use them productively. Like a ruthless overseer, drugs usurped her mind. For her, heroin started as something beautiful: "Beyond its jazzy status, [it] gave you an incredible high. . . . It made you feel lovingly buffered and protected, like someone peering at the world through a private one-way mirror. Heroin laid down a sensuous sound track under a vision of a world melting into peace. . . . A heroin high came with its own voice. The heroin voice whispered in a way that made your eyes roll back, 'Everything will be fine.'" Everything was not fine. Like so many talented people, Lydon convinced herself that addiction was a calamity suffered only by the poor or the stupid. Though she eventually kicked her habit, drugs claimed what should have been the best years of her life, and brought immense misery to those who loved her.[17]

"The competition to 'de-school' yourself, to continually transcend limits when you discover them, was an unending strain on the imagination," thought Peter Coyote. His quest was "fueled by drugs. A lot of speed, a lot of acid, a lot of smack." Coyote eventually discovered that there were limits to everything. "The problem is, the body is an inviolable limit. And you have to really hurt it before you know that." Fortunately, he made the discovery before irreparable damage was done:

> I didn't want to die—and I was going to die. And furthermore, I didn't want to live and be ugly. I was skinny, and yellow, and fetid, and nicotine stained, and burned, and chipped. I wasn't even a beautiful mammal. You know, I had these two coyote puppies on the porch of my place, and I was looking at them one day, and they were laying in the sun, and their hair shone, and their eyes shone, and their teeth were white, and they were illuminated beings. And I realized that health was beautiful. It's just physically beautiful. And I thought: "What is it about my friends and me, all these charismatic geniuses, who are all sallow and sickly? We're smart, but are we healthy? We don't look healthy and beautiful. We don't look like vigorous, lusty, energetic mammals." And that startled me, I thought: "That's how I want to look. That's how I want to be."

The irony, Coyote concluded, was that "many of us were championing the environment and other species and . . . at the same time . . . we were degrading our bodies." By the end of the great drugs experiment, the landscape was littered with casualties. "A lot of my friends are dead," Coyote admitted. "And some of the carnage was not death—some of it was just dissolution."[18]

"People didn't care about themselves," observed Sue Miles, who managed to avoid getting sucked into the vortex of madness. "I used to think I wouldn't do this—I had more regard for myself. I also always thought: I'm going to live beyond my twenties. I am not about to expire here and now, thank you very much. I'd like two lungs, two arms, two legs and a brain."[19]

People's Park: The Future in a Vacant Lot

Up until 1967, the San Francisco Bay Area neatly reflected the divisions in Sixties rebellion. On one side of the bay was Haight-Ashbury, the epicenter of the lifestyle revolution. On the other side was Berkeley, a battleground in the political revolution. The two communities shared the paraphernalia of the counterculture but were otherwise distinct and often mutually suspicious. Hippies thought the politicos a bad trip, while the New Left feared that the freaks would tarnish their image.

In 1967, the Human Be-In, billed as a "gathering of the tribes," attempted a synthesis of the two strands of rebellion. An even more significant blending, however, occurred when hippies began to put down roots in the shabby streets where Berkeley borders Oakland. The Haight had begun to crumble under the combined weight of curious tourists, unscrupulous drug dealers, repressive police, and gouging landlords, causing hippies to flee to the cheap housing and tolerance of Berkeley. The Haight's sordidness soon followed them. Berkeley's crime rate soared.

East Bay tolerance had limits. Conservative Republicans, always a force in the area, demanded that the university, which owned the slum housing where many hippies lived, take action. They were supported by William Knowland's *Oakland Tribune*, always proficient at firing up public wrath. Under immense pressure, the university decided in late 1967 to demolish an entire block bordering Telegraph Avenue, thus forcing out the undesirables under the guise of urban renewal and university expansion—two good liberal causes.

Berkeley radicals suspected a sinister design—namely, the goal of "eliminating the culture of protest by denying it its turf." In *Ramparts*, Robert Scheer argued:

> South Campus expansion was based on the presumed need to sanitize and control the University environment. . . . Students would literally be forced to dwell within an ivory tower of concrete and glass dormitories which—along with other official buildings, churches, and a few spanking-new store fronts properly up to code—would be the only structures permitted in the central South Campus area. All others would be pushed out by the University Regents exercising their power of eminent domain. . . . If the [university] was to be a knowledge factory, South Campus Berkeley would be a company town.

In other words, the issue was not simply a matter of what to do with a plot of land. It became instead an argument over rights, a struggle for authority, and a battle for the soul of the Sixties.[20]

As it turned out, the university had funds for demolishing but none for building. Ronald Reagan, elected governor of California in 1966, had brought to an end the period of relentless expansion. He also used the budget as a stick with which to punish Berkeley for its leftist behavior. As a result, a year after the housing had been demolished, the six-acre site was nothing more than a makeshift parking lot.

Michael Delacour, boutique owner and hippie impresario, decided to seize the lot for "the people." The Berkeley left, always game to confront authority, rallied behind him. On April 20, 1969, hundreds of activists invaded the lot armed with picks and shovels. A tractor materialized from nowhere. Those who were not helplessly stoned worked hard to create something. A radical newspaper celebrated the seizure: "The Telegraph Avenue community which has long been in the forefront of the nation's youth revolt, built a park, People's Park, on land the University said it owned because it had a piece of paper. Land in this society is owned by men rich enough to afford such pieces of paper. Either the land belongs to the University or the land belongs to the people." Over subsequent weeks, a park of sorts took shape, but its inspiration was also its weakness: it grew out of innocent anarchism, lacking plan, purpose, or future.[21]

For radicals, the park symbolized the best of Sixties values: people

power and ecological harmony. It was, argued Michael Lerner, an important lesson for the revolution. "The great significance of People's Park"
was that "everyone could see a vision of the new society being realized
through the collective work of the people, and they could also see that
[that] new society would come only by rejecting the capitalist principle of
private property." The park became an important point of conflict with
the ruling class. Hayden, overcome with revolutionary ambition, had recently called for "two, three, many Columbias." People's Park fit the bill,
given that it seemed another case of a university using its authoritarian
power to ride roughshod over the poor and defenseless. The possibility of
meaningful confrontation also seemed all the more likely given Reagan's
penchant for dramatic demonstrations of power.[22]

The left saw the park as Shangri-La; the right, as Sodom and Gomorrah. Caught between these two views was the university chancellor, Roger
Heyns, a thoroughly decent man despised by both sides because he kow-
towed to neither. While the left rallied and the right fumed, Heyns desperately sought compromise, without success. On May 15, 1969, at the request
of the Republican mayor, 250 police officers from various forces took over
the park, evicted the squatters, and erected a fence. Word spread through
the radical community, and within hours 4,000 demonstrators had mobilized. Neither side was in the mood for restraint. Demonstrators tossed
bricks and rocks from the rooftops. The police, increasingly frustrated,
used tear gas, then birdshot, then buckshot. As time passed, their aim
grew more random, their range shorter. By the end of the day, more than
a hundred demonstrators had been injured, thirteen of them requiring
hospital treatment. A rioter named James Rector was killed when buckshot ripped open his stomach; another was blinded after being hit with
birdshot. The police later claimed they had fired in self-defense, yet not a
single police officer was seriously injured. "The indiscriminate use of shot-
guns [was] sheer insanity," Dr. Harry Brean, chief radiologist at Berkeley's
Herrick Hospital later remarked.[23]

That night, Reagan sent in the National Guard. For the next seventeen
days, Berkeley was a war zone. On one occasion, guardsmen threw tear gas
canisters into a lecture hall for no apparent reason. On May 20, a National
Guard helicopter sprayed tear gas on a bewildered crowd of staff and students. The outcry was tremendous, but Reagan remained unrepentant:

"There was no alternative. Whether that was a tactical mistake or not, once the dogs of war are unleashed, you must expect that things will happen and that people, being human, will make mistakes on both sides."[24]

Reagan's brutality caused Lerner to qualify his praise. "It is useless to say we need more People's Parks," he wrote, "for that struggle showed that the ruling class is willing to use its entire army, if necessary, to prevent us from building the new society." He nevertheless insisted, "People's Park did show that putting forward positive visions gives us the greatest chance of building a large revolutionary youth movement." Others were not so sure. Jerry Rosenfeld, a veteran Berkeley radical, sensed manipulation: "The Park Struggle was used for ulterior motives, of both the personal, subconscious kind, and the consciously political kind. . . . If the unknown policeman who killed James Rector was only a pawn, . . . by the same token . . . the blood of James Rector lies also on the hands of my brothers Frank Bardacke, Mike Delacour, Stew Albert, and numerous others. I believe that the death of the next James Rector will be a murder, and whoever writes the leaflet that helps send him to his death will be an accomplice to that murder." Stephen Smale, a stalwart of the Vietnam Day Committee four years earlier, was bewildered by People's Park and saw no reason to join the protests. His colleague Morris Hirsch wondered if the entire university had gone mad. Classes had been canceled and the campus had been turned into a war zone, all for the sake of a place for hippies to smoke pot. Hirsch felt that real political issues had been removed from the debate and that the conflict between right and left had been transformed into ritualized combat.[25]

The battle for the park produced, ironically, two winners. Governor Reagan won his war with the hippies, but they won the park. The university subsequently decided that the wisest course was to leave the site alone—a decision fiscally suited to the lean 1970s. Official policy was to pretend that the park did not exist. The city mowed the pitiful patches of grass, but landscaping was otherwise left to the free spirits who congregated on Telegraph Avenue and called the park their own. A makeshift children's play area was built, along with a speakers' platform and a recycled clothing bin. Hippies grew vegetables and little clumps of flowers as and where they pleased. The vegetables were stolen before they ripened and the flowers were never very pretty, but none of that mattered, since both had been made into important symbols of the people's power.

San Diego: A Burning Desire to End the War

On a warm spring day in May 1970, on the campus of the University of California, San Diego, George Winne walked to the center of Revelle Plaza and sat down, cross-legged. He paused, drew a breath, and looked as if he planned to meditate. Since meditating on campus was hardly unusual back then, few students paid any notice. Then, in a movement so swift it seemed choreographed, he produced a bottle of gasoline, twisted the cap, and poured it over himself. A match was lit. Before anyone could react, an ordinary student was transformed into an inferno.

Few people remember Winne's name. His face does not spring to mind when the casualties of those strange times are recalled. He is, at best, a statistic: one of eight sad souls in the United States who set themselves on fire to protest the Vietnam War. His anonymity makes him an appropriate symbol for the wretched end to the heavenly decade.

In 1965, when American combat troops were first sent to Vietnam, the preferred method of protest was the teach-in, as seen at Michigan and Berkeley. The concept was wonderfully idealistic: students weren't just complaining about the war—they were also, in theory, learning. In truth, however, teach-ins were simply platforms for proselytizing radicals. Students were exposed to the stalwarts of the American intellectual left—the "corpse evangelists" for whom the events offered a temporary ladder out of obscurity (see Dylan, "My Back Pages"). Beyond the ivory tower, however, teach-ins were nothing more than a nuisance—living proof of the marginality of the student peace movement. The Johnson administration simply ignored them.

Even though most students were protected from the draft, they felt the war personally. It seemed close and, as it escalated, it drew closer. Male students realized that, but for the accident of intelligence, they might be facing the horrors of a jungle patrol. In other words, the war provided the perfect Sixties cause: personal *and* political. It was individually threatening and, in a wider sense, seemed to embody everything wrong with America. Student radicals wanted not just an end to the war, but also an end to the mentality that produced it.

Student opposition arose from the belief "that the war is immoral at its root, that it is fought alongside a regime with no claim to represent its people, and that it is foreclosing the hope of making America a decent and truly democratic society." That argument might have seemed logical to those in Political Science 101 at Berkeley or Columbia, but was never likely to strike a chord with the American people, who did not appreciate accusations of immorality. "It was a time of intense certainty," the student activist Sam Brown recalled. "We were young, smart, intellectual (so we thought), and committed to a moral cause. We believed ourselves patriots defending America's ideals. They (and by that time 'they' were almost always older) were, as far as we were concerned, narrow-minded, intolerant, and unwilling to accept our patriotism. . . . The ideas espoused by either group were almost automatically opposed by the other. Each side held to its half-thoughts and unfounded assumptions. Each side hurt the other." Out of incomprehension grew contempt, which inhibited a united effort to end the war. In working-class bars across America, the peacenik and the Communist guerrilla were reviled equally. Workers applauded when Spiro Agnew called student protesters "an effete corps of impudent snobs who consider themselves intellectuals."[26]

Protesting the war was hugely enjoyable. "It was a social thing," Mark Rudd admitted. "People hang out. And the subculture is fun. There were drugs and girls." Campus protesters like Jerry Rubin derived enormous fun from being "psychic terrorists" who sought to jolt Americans out of conformist apathy. Demonstrations were devised not for the message they conveyed but for the controversy they created. Robert Nisbet, a Berkeley professor of sociology who opposed the war, felt that "the actions of the student rebels . . . resembled nothing so much as the jack-boot authoritarianism of Hitler Youth in the 1920s: complete with shouted obscenities, humiliation of teachers and scholars, desecration of buildings, and instigation of various forms of terror." Even though opposition to the war steadily grew, so too did disgust with students. "I was thoughtless, arrogant, horrible, hysterical, and unbelievably selfish," one former protester confessed. "I still will not forgive myself for the pain and agony I caused."[27]

In time, the unpopularity of the Vietnam War was translated into love for the Viet Cong. As early as 1965, Berkeley students donated blood and collected money for the Viet Cong, though whether the revolution ever benefited is doubtful. While this sort of behavior was more prevalent in Europe, where admiring Ho Chi Minh became a popular way to express hatred for America, it was sufficiently prevalent in the United States to cause damage to the image of the peace movement. The Progressive Labor faction of SDS, for instance, judged the Viet Cong a perfect example of the righteousness of Maoist revolution. In some circles, kind Uncle Ho and his band of virtuous guerrillas became chic heroes. They were the ultimate romantic warriors: peasants who fought the Yankee imperialist on a bowl of rice per day.

An entirely separate movement arose among ordinary people in towns and cities across America. It grew gradually, each agonizing month adding to the chorus of discontent. Middle American unease was rooted not in the immorality of the war, but in its futility. As casualty lists lengthened, doubts grew. Student protesters never quite understood that most Americans were concerned only about the fate of their sons and the significance of their sacrifice. Quite typical was Clem Labine, former star pitcher for the Brooklyn Dodgers, whose son Jay lost a leg in Vietnam: "First I guess I was a hawk. Then I was a dove. Then Jay went over and I went superhawk. Atom-bomb those Northern bastards for my kid. Now that he's back . . . what do you think? I'm superdove."[28]

Eugene McCarthy, during his presidential campaign, tried to establish a common ground between the campus and the heartland. Central to this effort was the "Clean for Gene" campaign, which attempted to persuade young radicals to jettison hedonism for the greater good. "I fought hard against associating lifestyle issues—drugs, rock music, sex—with the peace movement," Stephen Cohen, a young McCarthy activist, recalled. He did not succeed. "[The behavior of students] so alienated and turned off people who would have been genuinely against the war. Students generally made a fundamental strategic error." SDS activist Todd Gitlin recalls how his friends, certain of their moral virtue, had no time for McCarthy's good sense. "Strategy-minded antiwar liberals rudely reminded us that we were forfeiting the respect of Americans who were turning against the war. . . . But to hell with them! Which side were they on, anyway?"[29]

The National Mobilization Committee to End the War (known as Mobe) was, as its name suggests, an effort to knit together the disparate anxiety. Students were present, but not dominant. Mobe was instead a coalition of the Old Left and New Left, liberal pacifists, young men worried about the draft, parents, and students. Unity was preserved because of a single-minded focus on the war. Talk of overturning the government was discouraged. Organizers tried desperately to create a movement that would seem antiwar, not pro–Viet Cong.

In October 1967 came Mobe's first great March on Washington, with some 100,000 protesters taking part. The demonstration lacked cohesion, but that hardly seemed important, given the weight of numbers. That said, the weakness of the coalition was painfully evident. The veteran pacifist David Dellinger called it a mix of "Gandhi and guerrilla"—the former admirable, the latter not. Hippies, perhaps unfortunately, had decided to join in. As they freely admitted, participation of this sort was unusual, given that they seldom had time for anything so serious as politics. Some decided it would be fun to levitate the Pentagon. "There are seven million laws in this country," Abbie Hoffman proclaimed, "and we aim to break every single one of them, including the law of gravity." Quite a few hippies were sufficiently stoned to convince themselves that America's biggest building actually did rise. Rubin convinced himself that theatrics of this sort could end a war. "It made me see that we could build a movement by knocking off American symbols. We had symbolically destroyed the Pentagon, the symbol of the war machine, by throwing blood on it, pissing on it, dancing on it, painting 'Che lives' on it. It was a total cultural attack on the Pentagon. The media had communicated this all over the country, and lots of people identified with us, the besiegers." In truth, self-indulgence undermined otherwise impressive commitment.[30]

Three months later came the Tet Offensive. The slow erosion in support for the war turned into avalanche. After Tet, a peace movement of substance, rooted in the anxieties of ordinary Americans, gained dominion. Egocentric campus activists could not bring themselves to merge with this deluge of popular protest, which eventually overwhelmed them. Polls showed that, while support for the war fell, so too did support for student protesters. In 1968, a poll rated them 28.4 on a scale from zero (very unfavorable) to 100 (very favorable).[31]

In the presidential election of 1968, Americans turned not to avowed peace candidates like McCarthy or McGovern, but to Nixon, who promised that he could end the war *and* salvage American credibility. Nixon's victory is probably the best indication of how little the campus peace movement had achieved in three turbulent years. The American people wanted the war over, but they did not buy the fundamental reconstruction of their society that students espoused. After his election, Nixon arranged for troops to trickle home, thus suggesting that an end was near. For most

Americans, that was enough; they were still sufficiently patient to allow Nixon the time he needed to deliver peace with honor.

The peace movement's finest hour was also its grand goodbye. Vietnam Moratorium Day, October 15, 1969, was marked by rallies in 500 towns and cities across America. Then, on November 15, came a huge demonstration that brought 250,000 protesters to Washington. The crowd was peaceful, orderly, and fundamentally ordinary. Student radicals drowned in a sea of conformity. Reacting to the spectacle of protesting stockbrokers, lawyers, and tennis-shoed moms, Rubin sneered: "Peace has become respectable!"[32]

The demonstration was impressive, but Nixon cleverly manipulated it to his advantage. In his famous "silent majority" speech nine days later, he warned that "the more divided we are at home, the less likely the enemy is to negotiate in Paris." He continued: "And so . . . to you, the great silent majority of my fellow Americans—I ask for your support. . . . Let us be united for peace. Let us also be united against defeat. Because let us understand: North Vietnam cannot defeat or humiliate the United States. Only Americans can do that." The gambit worked. After the speech, Gallup found that 75 percent of those polled thought that the term "silent majority" referred to those people who believed that "protesters have gone too far."[33]

"One of the reasons the president can get away with such nonsense is that many of us in the peace movement failed to dissociate ourselves strongly enough from violence on the left," wrote a dejected Sam Brown, one of the moratorium's organizers. Nixon's subsequent policy epitomized Middle-American sentiment: a gradual withdrawal of troops was combined with virulent attacks upon campus dissenters. Students were the new enemy—a handy distraction from the disappointment of Southeast Asia. Despite the popularity of the November demonstration, Gallup found a 6 percent *rise* in public approval "of the way President Nixon is handling the situation in Vietnam."[34]

In the spring of 1970, Mobe shut its offices in Washington. Nixon had silenced dissent, even if he had not ended the war. But then came Cambodia. The war that was supposed to be ending was instead widened. The invasion launched on May 1, 1970, sparked a torrential resurgence of campus unrest. Within four days, more than a hundred campuses erupted. "The overflow of emotion seemed barely containable," wrote the *Washington Post*.

"The nation was witnessing what amounted to a virtual general strike by its college youth." The new protests lacked the radical bombast of earlier campus activism, when students wanted to end the war *and* change the world.[35]

Kent State University was typical of the post-Cambodia protests and atypical of Sixties activism. A second-tier university, it catered mostly to students who were intent on earning a degree, getting a job, and buying a house in the suburbs. Since 1965 the campus had been comparatively quiet, with small bands of SDS activists trying desperately to drum up alienation. But even the mild-mannered Kent State students would not tolerate war in Cambodia. As tension rose, Ohio governor James Rhodes warned that he would "employ every weapon possible" in confronting protesters. "No one is safe in Portage County," he added for dramatic effect. Faced with a tough battle to win the Republican nomination for the Senate, he was trying to duplicate what Reagan had achieved in California—namely, a populist campaign fired by hatred of students. Campus demonstrators, he argued, were the "worst type of people we harbor in America," and he promised that "we are going to eradicate this problem in Ohio."[36]

On May 4, students came out en masse. Rhodes had mobilized the Ohio National Guard, made up of kids not all that different from the protesters. The guard carried live ammunition, even though none of the students were armed or particularly bellicose. Someone panicked and pulled a trigger. Others followed. Thirteen seconds later, four students were dead and nine others lay wounded. Sandy Scheuer was walking to class, 300 feet from the line of soldiers, when she was cut down. "She was everything we lived for, and now our lives are an empty shell," her father later wrote. "Sandy represented everything good in this world. She was a gentle girl blessed with a fine sense of humor, a love for life tempered with compassionate concern for the misfortunes of others—qualities which made her warm personality so appealing to all who knew her. What greater anguish is there than the thought that Sandy's devotion to her studies, her desire to help people, . . . should lead her into the path of a bullet, shot through her lovely neck." A spokesman later claimed that the National Guard had responded to a "grave threat." Yet at the time weapons were fired, no student was closer than sixty feet from the line of soldiers.[37]

Ten days later, a repeat performance took place at Jackson State University in Mississippi, where two students were killed. The outcry on campuses across the country dwarfed any previous period of activism. More than four million students came out in protest. Over 1,300 colleges and universities were affected, with 536 temporarily closed, 51 for the rest of the academic year. For most students, this was their first (and last) taste of activism. Kent State inspired what had previously proved elusive—namely, a unified student movement of monumental power. But solidarity born of anger could not be sustained; fissures quickly developed between true pacifists, anarchists, hippie pranksters, proto-revolutionaries, and the habitually apathetic. Nixon found it easy to manipulate these divisions. His promise of a withdrawal from Cambodia by June 30 (not, strictly speaking, a departure from his original plans) cooled tempers. Most students returned to their books, while a few psychopaths indulged in destruction. Almost two years later, the last combat troops left Vietnam.[38]

Shortly after the killings, one Kent State student—frightened, bewildered, and dismayed—went home to seek solace with his parents. "My mother said, 'It would have been a good thing if all those students had been shot.' I cried, 'Hey, Mom! That's me you're talking about,' and she said, 'It would have been better for the country if you all had been mowed down.'" A similar sentiment was expressed by Dr. Paul Williamson, a physician living in McComb, Mississippi. When his son entered Tulane University in the autumn of 1970, Williamson warned him not to confront authority. "If you choose . . . revolution, expect to get shot. Mother and I will grieve but we will gladly buy dinner for the National Guardsman who shot you." He urged his son to use his energies for more practical purposes. "Have you ever considered how many coeds there are to be kissed?"[39]

These incidents were not perhaps typical, but they are revelatory. A deep gulf had always existed between the baby boomers who went to university and their "Greatest Generation" parents who put them there. That gulf was widened by the war, but especially by the inclination of students to doubt the honesty and morality of their country. "I am tired of being blamed, maimed, and contrite," wrote K. Ross Toole, a forty-nine-year-old professor of history at the University of Montana, and father of seven.

> My generation has made America the most affluent country on earth; it has tackled, head-on, a racial problem which no nation on earth in the history of mankind had dared to do. It has publicly declared war on poverty and it has gone to the moon; it has

desegregated schools and abolished polio; it has presided over the beginning of what is probably the greatest social and economic revolution in man's history. . . . It has declared itself, and committed itself, and damn near run itself into the ground in the cause of social justice and reform.

By attacking America, the protesters attacked their parents. No wonder, then, that when parents felt torn between family and nation, many sided with the latter. The escalation of violent protest at the end of the decade caused the older generation to become distinctly less liberal. Support for the right of students to protest (even peacefully) steadily declined, to less than 40 percent in 1969. A Gallup poll in March 1969 found 82 percent of respondents in favor of expelling militant students and 84 percent in favor of withdrawing their federal student loans.[40]

Neither the campus protests of the mid-1960s nor the massive reaction to the Kent State killings had any measurable effect upon the way Middle America ended its war. Sixties romantics often view the antiwar movement as a continuum which began on the campuses of Berkeley and Michigan, gained strength from Walter Cronkite's post-Tet commentary, coalesced in the March on Washington, and triumphed when the troops came home. If such a scenario were accurate, the student protesters would emerge as heroes—true martyrs who endured scorn in order to right a wrong. But it is difficult to assign credit to student activists for shaping the opinions of Middle America, since each regarded the other with deep contempt. In any case, courage seems a prerequisite for martyrdom. Civil rights protesters in the South went into the lion's den, risking severe injury and death. In contrast, student antiwar protesters operated within the closed, protected, and tolerant world of academia. They protested to one another more than to their enemies. In November 1965, the civil rights activist Bayard Rustin challenged a Berkeley crowd to "go out into the community instead of spending so much time talking to yourselves. . . . Then when people read in the newspapers that you've been arrested, they'll know why." That challenge went unheeded.[41]

"However much they rewrite that war and whatever else the United States does," the novelist Angela Carter has remarked, "it was the first war in the history of the world where the boys were brought back from the front due to popular demand from their own side." While that might be true, it is not true in the way Carter imagines. The various antiwar movements did affect the outcome of the war. Johnson and Nixon, two paranoid presidents, formulated military strategy with the public's reaction in mind. Protest convinced Hanoi that it could win a protracted war and Washington that it could not. But two points deserve emphasis. First, Americans would have supported a war which was being won; therefore, defeat had to become apparent before dissension could turn critical. Had American forces really been winning, as Westmoreland and Johnson repeatedly insisted, the protesters would never have been more than a noisy nuisance. Second, no one group should claim credit for mobilizing Americans against the war—certainly not the students. Success came because diverse and antagonistic groups eventually attained critical mass. In fact, with a bit less egotism on the part of some protesters, and a bit more political finesse, success might have come sooner.[42]

14

MEET THE NEW BOSS

JAKARTA: A PERFECT LITTLE COUP

On a lonely hill in the Krawang region of Java, in an area surrounded by rice farms, one finds an irregular hump of ground overgrown with wild mustard. Just beneath the surface lie the bodies of perhaps twelve victims—a tiny fraction of what the CIA called "one of the worst mass murders of the twentieth century." Perhaps 500,000 were killed, or maybe a million—no one bothered to count. Relatives would like to give those twelve a proper grave, but they are still too frightened.[1]

The trouble began on September 30, 1965, when six of Indonesia's senior generals, including the army commander General Ahmad Yani, were murdered and thrown down a well. A seventh, Major General A. H. Nasution, somehow survived the plot, but his daughter and an aide were murdered. The fact that the seven generals were all outspoken anti-Communists led immediately to assumptions that the murders were the work of the Indonesian Communist Party (Partai Komunis Indonesia, or PKI).

Allegations against the PKI have survived to this day, while the real perpetrators have escaped blame. In fact, the six dead generals, while definitely rightists, were all members of the Yani faction, a group loyal to President Achmed Sukarno. The most likely scenario is that a separate group of right-wingers who wanted to get rid of Sukarno decided that they first had to liquidate his most senior supporters. Their leader was General Suharto, who eventually ousted Sukarno and ruled Indonesia until 1998.

The coup was fostered by the intelligence services of the United States, Great Britain, and Australia, all of whom wanted to oust the troublesome Sukarno. The president had made a nuisance of himself in 1955 when he had hosted the Bandung Conference, from which the Nonaligned Movement was born. Sukarno promoted himself as a leader in the resistance against neocolonialism, behavior which did not endear him to those nations eager to extend Western capitalist interests. He had angered the British by complaining in 1963 that the Malaysian Federation, consisting of Malaysia and Singapore, was a "neocolonial plot" designed to weaken the Indonesian economy and promote British commercial interests in the area. His reputation plummeted further when he told the US ambassador, "Go to hell with your aid," after learning of the strings attached.[2]

Heru Atmojo, an air force officer imprisoned for fifteen years because of his loyalty to Sukarno, later reflected on the impossible position in which his country found itself in the early 1960s:

> The pressure on Indonesia to do what the Americans wanted was intense. Sukarno wanted good relations with them, but he didn't want their economic system. With America, that is never possible. So he became an enemy. All of us who wanted an independent country, free to make our own mistakes, were made the enemy. They didn't call it globalization then; but it was the same thing. If you accepted it, you were America's friend. If you chose another way, you were given warnings. And if you didn't comply, hell was visited on you.

The West might have been able to stomach Sukarno's neutralism, but his growing friendliness toward the Communists was unacceptable. Sukarno argued that this tolerance was motivated by self-preservation, since the PKI, with three million members, was the largest Communist party outside China and the USSR. That argument did not, however, convince his Western critics, who considered the Communist problem to be of his own making. Nor did it matter that the PKI's popularity within Indonesia arose not because of its status as a revolutionary party, but because it was widely seen as a trusted friend of the poor. Nuance did not move the hard-bitten men at the US State Department or the British Foreign Office.[3]

As early as 1953, a US National Security Council resolution recognized the need for "appropriate action, in collaboration with other friendly countries, to prevent permanent Communist control in Indonesia." Millions were spent arming and training insurgent groups willing to challenge Sukarno. According to a CIA memorandum, by 1962 Harold Macmillan and John F. Kennedy had agreed on the need to "liquidate President Sukarno, depending on the situation and available opportunities."[4]

Kennedy's wish was father to Lyndon Johnson's action. While JFK's policies in Indonesia were ad hoc and opportunistic, those of his successor were programmed and purposeful. America's actions in Indonesia, however, contrasted sharply with its behavior in Vietnam, probably for the simple reason that the Johnson administration could not afford two wars in East Asia. While some advisers urged an assertive approach, the administration instead settled upon a "low posture," or what William Bundy likened to playing an "eight-high hand." The administration understood that active US intervention might encourage nationalist reaction in Indonesia and prove counterproductive to American interests. Johnson's advisers concluded that the situation could be resolved by a showdown between the PKI and forces on the right, so the sensible policy was to maintain a low profile and let nature take its course. As the ambassador to Indonesia, Ellsworth Bunker, advised, "US visibility should be reduced so that those opposed to the Communists and extremists may be free to handle a confrontation, which they believe will come, without the incubus of being attacked as defenders of the neocolonialists and imperialists." The United States simply made sure that, when the confrontation came, the right held all the cards.[5]

To this end, unbridled American speculation contributed to a collapse in the value of Indonesian currency and a general destabilization of the economy. The price of rice quadrupled in the four months preceding the coup. At the same time, all official aid ceased, while unofficial funding was channeled to anti-Sukarno elements. Military support included 200 Aero-Commanders, light aircraft ideally suited to counterinsurgency. Senior Indonesian air force personnel were trained in the use of the planes at bases in the United States. Meanwhile, the CIA routed hefty payoffs to soldiers known to be sympathetic to Suharto. In other words, the United States had decided which side to back long before the coup was actually launched.

Suharto used the September 30 murders as an excuse to move against the PKI. The men who might have stopped him had, of course, already been dropped down a well. Since Sukarno had no loyal forces capable of countering Suharto's army, the latter had free rein. Suharto's campaign was not just an effort to defeat the Communists but a comprehensive program of liquidation. Lending help were his CIA friends, who kept the Indonesian people well fed with black propaganda. "Media fabrications played a key role in stirring up popular resentment against the PKI," Ralph McGehee, a CIA senior operations officer, later admitted. "Photographs of the bodies of the dead generals—badly decomposed—were featured in all the newspapers and on television. Stories accompanying the pictures falsely claimed that the generals had been castrated and their eyes gouged out by Communist women. This cynically manufactured campaign was designed to . . . set the stage for a massacre."[6]

The efficiency and brutality of Suharto's purge defies description. In less than a year, between 500,000 and one million Indonesians were murdered. The comprehensiveness of the slaughter is testimony to how well American and British intelligence agencies had supplied and trained dissident groups opposed to Sukarno. The United States, by its own admission, had focused on "religious and cultural organizations, youth groups, veterans, trade unions, peasant organizations, political parties, and groups at regional and local levels." Granted, the PKI and Sukarno were not entirely innocent victims. On occasion, they responded in kind. The intensity of the crisis meant that, for nearly a year, Indonesia was torn by civil war, with killings sparking reprisals and counterreprisals.[7]

The mere suspicion of Communist sympathy was sufficient to warrant a death sentence, usually carried out on the spot. Survivors of the slaughter describe rivers "jammed with bodies like logs." One popular tactic among pro-Suharto vigilante groups was to enter a village, round up the young men, brutally murder them, and leave a row of severed penises behind as a reminder to the rest. One survivor recalls seeing the headmaster of his school dragged into the playground and beaten to death in front of a crowd of terrified children. "He was a wonderful man: gentle and kind. . . . I can hear his screams now, but for a long time, years in fact, all I could remember was running from the classroom, and running and running through the streets, not stopping. When they found me that evening, I was dumbstruck. For a whole year I couldn't speak."[8]

On December 1, 1965, a delegation from Suharto's headquarters visited the US embassy and told the new ambassador, Marshall Green, that "the right horse was now winning and the US should bet heavily on it." The Americans did precisely that. They kept close tabs on the progress of Suharto's operation, the aim being to "shape developments to our advantage." This meant supplying Suharto with a state-of-the-art field communications system in order to speed the liquidation of Communists. One tactic was to encourage Islamic vigilante groups to attack the PKI, so that subsequent atrocities could be blamed on sectarianism, allowing the army to distance itself from the bloodshed. At the height of the purge, Green, known within the State Department as the "coupmaster," assured Suharto: "The US is generally sympathetic with and admiring of what the army is doing."[9]

The CIA, having studied Communist activity in Indonesia, provided Suharto with a hit list of some 5,000 prominent names. These were crossed off as they were liquidated. "We were getting a good account in Jakarta of who was being picked up," Joseph Lazarsky, deputy CIA station chief in Jakarta, recalled. "The army had a 'shooting list' of about 4,000 or 5,000 people. . . . The infrastructure [of the PKI] was zapped almost immediately. We knew what they were doing. . . . Suharto and his advisers said, if you keep them alive you have to feed them." Howard Federspiel, the Indonesia expert at the State Department's Bureau of Intelligence and Research, reflected: "No one cared, as long as they were Communists, that they were being butchered. No one was getting very worked up about it."[10]

News of the massacre was carefully controlled by Western intelligence agencies. Journalists, prevented from entering the country, relied unquestioningly on official word emanating from embassies. The British Foreign Office's Information Research Department, headed by the professional deceiver Norman Reddaway, made sure the media were given the kind of story that would suit the furtherance of Britain's interests. Not long after the shooting started, the British embassy in Jakarta advised intelligence headquarters in Singapore on how the news should be presented: "Suitable propaganda themes might be: PKI brutality in murdering Generals and Nasution's daughter . . . PKI subverting Indonesia as agents of foreign Communists. . . . But treatment will need to be subtle, e.g. (a) all activities should be strictly unattributable, (b) British participation or cooperation should be carefully concealed." "It was a triumph for Western propaganda," Roland Challis, the BBC's reporter in the area, later reflected. While journalists were undoubtedly deceived, it has to be said that they colluded in their own deception. Too often, the official story was relayed without analysis. In a confidential note, Reddaway praised a Fleet

Street journalist who had promised to give the government's "angle on events"—"i.e., that this was a kid glove coup without butchery." While journalists sipped champagne in the British Embassy, bodies were washing up on the riverfront outside.[11]

On March 11, 1966, Suharto felt strong enough to push Sukarno aside. Sukarno spent the next four years in virtual house arrest, and died in 1970. British and American papers welcomed the transfer of power. "The West's best news for years in Asia," remarked *Time,* praising a "scrupulously constitutional" new regime supposedly "based on law, not on mere power." Echoing the praise, *US News and World Report* saw reasons for "hope . . . where there was once none." The highly respected journalist James Reston called it "a gleam of light in Asia," while skipping over the butchery. Leading the cheers was Rupert Murdoch and his paper the *Australian.* As recently as 1998, its editor was still insisting that Suharto's cruelties were a figment of the left's imagination, while eyewitness accounts of atrocities were dismissed as Communist propaganda.[12]

On August 8, 1967, Walt Rostow, the new national security adviser, told President Johnson that "Suharto . . . is making a hard try at making something of Indonesia which could be very good for us and the world." Johnson concurred: "Here is a country which has rejected communism and is pulling itself up by its bootstraps. . . . We can make it a showcase for all the world." In Britain, foreign secretary Michael Stewart praised the new dictator's "laudable economic policies" and rejected any suggestion that his was an aggressive regime. In November 1967 Time-Life sponsored a conference on the future of Indonesia. The prime mover was the Ford Foundation, working in cahoots with the CIA and a gaggle of sympathetic economists from America's most prestigious universities. James Linen, president of Time, Inc., opened the conference by outlining its aims: "We are trying to create a new climate in which private enterprise and developing countries work together . . . for the greater profit of the free world. This world of international enterprise is more than government. . . . It is the seamless web of enterprise, which has been shaping the global environment at revolutionary speed." In truth, the conference was little more than a deliberate effort by Western interests to feast on the choicest dishes from the Indonesian rijstaffel. A glittering array of corporations attended, including General Motors, Siemens, ICI, British Leyland, British-American Tobacco, American Express, Goodyear, and US Steel. They negotiated with Suharto's economic team to dole out concessions. Afterward, LBJ congratulated Linen on "a magnificent story of opportunity seen and promise awakened." The Copley Corporation was equally effusive: "It is [in Indonesia] that the deep-rooted American concepts of free enterprise and Yankee ingenuity are finding new forms of expression. Moreover, the profit potential fairly staggers the imagination."[13]

Everything had worked out brilliantly. William Bundy later remarked that the secret to success lay "in the cooking, not in the recipe." Indonesia was now ruled by a pro-Western dictator, its economy had been made safe for capitalist exploitation, and at least a half million Communists were dead. In stark contrast to Vietnam, the Communists had been defeated without American soldiers dying. The operation had proceeded so smoothly that the CIA was able to construct a credible alibi. The official line, widely believed, was that of the head of the agency's Far Eastern Division, William Colby, who later claimed that "Indonesia exploded, with a bid for power by the largest Communist Party in the world outside the Curtain, which killed the leadership of the army with Sukarno's tacit approval and then was decimated in reprisal. [The] CIA . . . did not have any role in the course of events themselves." In contrast, Ralph McGehee admitted privately that "the Agency was extremely proud of its success . . . and recommended it as a model for future operations." Also impressed was Richard Nixon, who, according to Marshall Green, "was very interested in that whole experience as pointing to the way we should handle our relationships on a wider basis in Southeast Asia generally, and maybe in the world." McGehee admitted that Indonesia was a "model" for later operations, like the one that ousted Salvador Allende in Chile. "You can trace back all the major, bloody events run from Washington to the way Suharto came to power. The success of that meant that it would be repeated, again and again."[14]

Indonesia also became a model for globalization, though that term was hardly used in the 1960s. Suharto made himself a billionaire by selling his people to General Motors, Goodyear, Siemens, and ICI, and later to Gap, Nike, and Starbucks. "We are the people, the nation, that the world forgot," lamented Adon Sutrisna, a political prisoner during the Suharto years. "If you know the truth about what happened in Indonesia, you can understand clearly where the world is being led today."[15]

HOLLYWOOD: TAKIN' CARE OF BUSINESS

On April 10, 1957, at the age of sixteen, Ricky Nelson performed the Fats Domino song "I'm Walkin'" on national television during an episode of *Ozzie and Harriet*. He sounded awful, but that was hardly his fault, since he was not a singer. Theoretically, that did not matter, since *Ozzie* was a situation comedy, not a musical variety show. Television, however, has a way of making people famous even when they hardly deserve it. As a result of singing one song badly on national TV, Ricky was suddenly a star. In 1958, he was the top-selling pop artist in the country.

Hollywood invented Ricky Nelson. His success reveals how show business had taken over rock music, turning it into an industry. Ricky was the perfect commodity: an artist who did not upset milktoast America. He was Elvis without grease, without swinging hips. His nice, sanitized West coast accent was perfectly middle class—devoid of ethnicity. Though time would eventually reveal that he actually had talent, this was never the reason for his popularity. He sold records because he was marketable; industry executives understood the profit potential of wholesome rock.

One of Ricky's fans was the young Bob Dylan. "He was different than the rest of the teen idols," Dylan later reflected. "Ricky had a smooth touch, the way he crooned in fast rhythm, the tonation of his voice. . . . He didn't sing desperately, do a lot of damage, and you'd never mistake him for a shaman. . . . He sang his songs calm and steady like he was in the middle of a storm, men hurling past him. His voice was sort of mysterious and made you fall into a certain mood." Dylan and Nelson are seldom juxtaposed when Sixties music is discussed. One was a media creation, the other an artist. Yet both are important to understanding the decade and its music. Nelson is symptomatic of the industry's ability to create marketable stars with planned obsolescence—rather like washing machines. After a brief run in the charts, they are quickly forgotten, and immediately replaced by equally anodyne assembly-line singers designed solely to make money. Dylan, on the other hand, provided the soundtrack for a generation—his songs evoke the events of those days and will never be forgotten. If importance is measured by meaningfulness, then Dylan is deservedly remembered. But if sales are a measure of significance, then Nelson also deserves attention. He was a harbinger of a brand-new force: a billion-dollar industry which turned music into a commodity.[16]

When Dylan was starting out, in the early Sixties, all the folk labels he approached rejected him on the grounds that his music would never sell. "What I was playing at the time were hard-lipped folk songs with fire and brimstone servings, and you didn't need to take polls to know that they didn't match up with anything on the radio, didn't lend themselves to commercialism." He was, however, lucky enough to find a producer with an ear for meaningful music. At Columbia Records, he stumbled upon John Hammond, "a music man through and through." Dylan was charmed. "He talked the same language as me. . . . Money didn't make much of an impression on him. . . . [He] didn't give a damn about record trends or musical currents." That might be true, but Hammond was also astute enough to hear the tunes behind Dylan's sandpaper voice. He knew that even if Dylan didn't sell, his songs would. To date, "Blowin' in the Wind" has been covered around 375 times, each time with a nice check to the copyright holder.[17]

Folk provided Dylan shelter from the storm—the rapid and bewildering developments in music. "Practically speaking, the '50s culture was like a judge in his last days on the bench," he recalled. "It was about to go. . . . With folk songs embedded in my mind like a religion, it wouldn't matter. Folk songs transcended the immediate culture." This transcendence gave Dylan's songs an importance far beyond their position in the charts. He did not have to produce number-one hits to be important.[18]

That transcendence can also confuse. Politics played in stereo is easily absorbed. Music fuels myth. Play a few bars of "Blowin' in the Wind" and suddenly the most apathetic listeners imagine that they, too, manned the barricades in 1968. The "meaningful" music of the Sixties smothers rational assessment of that confusing decade. It is easy to forget that while Dylan, Joan Baez, and Phil Ochs alerted listeners to injustice, militarism, and hypocrisy, the Ohio Express made a great deal of money singing "Yummy, yummy, yummy, I got love in my tummy." The political songs of the Sixties may be widely remembered, but they were seldom among the "greatest hits." In the United States, the top ten artists over the course of the decade, measured in sales of singles, were: the Beatles, Elvis, the Supremes, Brenda Lee, the Beach Boys, the Four Seasons, the Temptations, Connie Francis, Ray Charles, and Marvin Gaye. The biggest-selling single of 1969, "Sugar, Sugar," was sung by a band called the Archies, which did not actually exist. A group of studio musicians was pulled together and given some songs to sing; sound engineers then enhanced the tapes. Perhaps appropriately, the lead vocalist, Ron Dante, later made a fortune recording "You Deserve a Break Today" for McDonalds.[19]

The counterculture thought it could use music to defeat the conservative mentality of the Fifties, typified by saccharine love songs. A battle raged for the soul of the consumer, or so it seemed to those in the trenches. In fact, baby boomers could not be bothered; they simply wanted good tunes. As one perceptive student observed, "You don't have to be radical to love rock music. . . . Most of the record-buying kids of today are about as aware as eggplants." When the Beatles occasionally sang about politics, their songs still sold—for the simple reason that the music sounded nice, and because they were the Beatles. The one constant of this period was that young people had money to spend on music. They bought for enjoyment, not because they sought political enlightenment. "I don't find [Vietnam] a thing to sing songs about," Mick Jagger once confessed. "It's music for us and it's supposed to be fun. We want you to get up and dance, not sit back and be worried about what you're supposed to do." Even those who sang about politics often had paper-thin commitment. The Byrds seemed politically aware, but Roger McGuinn, their lead singer, confessed: "I was political in that I didn't like inhumanity to man. But I really didn't get involved. I didn't vote either. I didn't do anything. I was tied up in my own little world. . . . And staying stoned a lot. That was my life. I mean, we were hedonists."[20]

Fun sold better than politics. The great irony of the 1960s was that radicals—New Left, student protesters, hippies—thought they were conducting a social revolution. In fact, the most profound revolution that occurred was the emergence of a consumer society. Ordinary people spending money were the shock troops of an economic revolution. "The rock revolution failed because it was corrupted," Germaine Greer argued in 1969. "It was incorporated in the capitalist system, which has power to absorb and exploit all tendencies, including the tendencies towards its own overthrow." While the young attacked the materialism of their parents, they spent billions on conspicuous consumption. "We've bought the values of our parents' generation more than we thought we would," Steve McConnell admitted. Baby boomers had their cake while gorging themselves on Hostess Twinkies.[21]

The greatest success of the music business during this period lay in its ability to take a packaged product and sell it as something new. The industry created an illusion of daring, but in truth few risks were taken. Rock and roll, according to Jeff Nuttall, one-time happening artist, "is the most unchanging, conservative popular music that there has ever been, and continues to be so, under the banner of perpetual revolution." He was briefly under the impression that the counterculture could determine its own tastes, but eventually discovered that clever music industry executives were pulling strings like puppeteers. "I thought we had to invade the media, but what we misjudged was the power and complexity of the media. The media dismantled the whole thing. It bought it up."[22]

In the 1960s the profit motive allowed only a tiny bit of room for songs challenging the political status quo. Granted, a lot of Sixties music was socially rebellious—it flouted conventions, especially those pertaining to sex and drugs. It provided the theme music for a generation bent on defying parental authority. But it did so because that's what young consumers wanted. It wasn't shaping trends; it was mirroring them. In any case, the charts frequently found room for blatantly counterrevolutionary songs like Guy Drake's "Welfare Cadillac" and Merle Haggard's "Okie from Muskogee."

As for politics, before 1968 only one protest song—Barry McGuire's "Eve of Destruction"—was sufficiently successful to be termed a hit in the United States. At that time, Vietnam and student unrest were minority issues, and music was produced for a mass market. Since fewer than 29 percent of those younger than twenty-nine opposed the war in 1966, a large market for antiwar music did not exist. In that year, Sergeant Barry Sadler made a small fortune with his rousingly patriotic "Ballad of the Green Berets," which ended up the most popular war-related song ever produced, selling seven million copies. Country artists produced more prowar songs, with greater success, than rock artists produced antiwar songs. No issue was too controversial for patriotic songwriters, as demonstrated by the success of "Battle Hymn of William Calley," which celebrated the massacre at My Lai and instantly became a gold record.

After the Tet Offensive, support for the war dipped below 50 percent for the first time. The shift in public opinion was reflected in the success of John Lennon's "Give Peace a Chance," which rose to number 11 on the American charts. From 1969 to 1974, the industry produced thirty-four identifiably antiwar songs, of which twenty-six made it onto the charts.

Even Motown, usually preoccupied with love and romance, got into the act, most notably with Edwin Starr's "War" and Marvin Gaye's "What's Going On?" "The music business is a whore," one BMI executive admitted. "It will make and market anything that it thinks will sell." Protest songs had become commodities manufactured for profit. Reacting to the sudden popularity of his "I Feel Like I'm Fixin to Die Rag," Country Joe MacDonald admitted that he felt like he was "selling peace . . . for $3.98."[23]

Protest songs did not inspire opposition to the war; they simply reflected that opposition. In any case, the protest message was often lost on listeners. The lyrics of McGuire's "Eve of Destruction" should leave little room for confusion, since they cover racism, militarism, hatred, and greed. Yet a poll of American students in 1965 revealed that only 14 percent correctly understood the song. A greater proportion actually misinterpreted it, while by far the majority had no idea what it was about. Around 70 percent confessed to being attracted by the beat rather than the message.[24]

Record producers may have considered themselves hip, but sideburns and shades could not hide a capitalist mind. "The rock business was full of the same sharks as it always has been full of, except they were wearing kaftans and smoking dope instead of sinking pints of beer and wearing suits," Mark Williams, the first music editor at *IT*, discovered. When asked why the Beatles never produced an identifiably anti–Vietnam War song, John Lennon claimed that their manager, Brian Epstein, would not let them. (Paul McCartney gave perhaps a more honest answer when he explained: "We're not the preaching sort. . . . We leave it to others to deliver messages of that kind.") No producer wanted to annoy a significant proportion of the record-buying public.[25]

At the beginning of the rock revolution, Ricky Nelson picked up a guitar and became a pop star overnight, simply because of the power of television. Eight years later, a bunch of ordinary young men were transformed into a pop sensation, again simply because of television. The Monkees were an industry invention, a cynical attempt to mate two media: pop music and the situation comedy. Instead of fab, they were prefab. The aim was to produce a moneymaking show which would emulate, on a weekly basis, the success of the Beatles' film *A Hard Day's Night*. An ad was placed in *Variety* asking for applications from "folk and rock" musicians who wanted to appear in a TV series. A flood of replies and a long selection process produced two musicians who wanted to act (Mike Nesmith and Peter Tork) and two actors who wanted to sing (Micky Dolenz and Davy Jones). Stephen Stills (later of Buffalo Springfield and Crosby, Stills, Nash, and Young) made the short list, but the producers were put off by his stringy hair and bad teeth. They asked him if he knew anyone who looked just like him, but with better teeth and hair. Stills recommended his friend Tork, until that time a respectable member of the Greenwich Village folk scene.

"The Monkees wasn't a pop group—it was a TV show," Dolenz admits. "We weren't family like the Beach Boys, or childhood friends like the Beatles. The producers picked us and then introduced us on a stage set. . . . We were members of a cast." They were four separate elements combined like chemicals in a laboratory beaker. The amalgam that emerged was hugely successful. The songs were provided by a stable of talented artists which included Tommy Boyce, Bobby Hart, and Neil Diamond. The experiment underlined just how powerful the industry was, how easily executives could manipulate the medium. In 1967, the Monkees outsold the Beatles and the Rolling Stones combined. The top-selling song that year was "I'm a Believer"—a delightful irony, since they believed in nothing. In perhaps the best example of what Greer wrote about the power of the industry to absorb, one of the most memorable Monkees episodes was "The Frodis Caper," in which the group saves the world from an alien force bent on controlling earthlings' minds through television.[26]

The creation lasted only two seasons and began to unravel when the Monkees started behaving like rock stars. "It was a unique phenomenon, to be a member of a group that wasn't really a group and yet was a group," Tork feels. "If we'd been a group, we would have fought to be a group or we would have broken up as a group. But we were a project, a TV show, a record-making machine." Eventually, they developed pretensions, started arguing with each other and, even more significantly, demanded creative control. That, however, hardly mattered to the producers, who had already moved on to the next big idea.[27]

The great names of Sixties pop music—Dylan, Lennon, McCartney, Jagger, Joplin, Diana Ross—were loved by the music-buying public, but were nightmares for the industry. True artists had an unfortunate habit of thinking for themselves. They decided what kind of music they wanted to make and had the clout to get their way. They haggled over contracts and sued over copyright. Much easier were the hundreds of poor players who strutted their hour on stage and then were heard no more. The music industry depended upon the fact that bands, like clothes, went out of fashion.

As Ricky Nelson and the Monkees demonstrated, stars need not be born, since they could so easily be made. Creativity was a quality more important in the producer than in the musician. A pop star needed a nice face and a bit of charisma, perhaps some sex appeal. He or she didn't need to be able to write music, since the tunes could be supplied by people like Gerry Goffin and Carole King who turned out songs like toys from a factory. Most Sixties music has been long forgotten, but that is exactly what the industry intended. When music became an industry, songs became commodities—something to be enjoyed for a short period and then thrown away.

We remember the songs of the Beatles and Dylan because they seem to evoke the mood of an age and because they ooze talent. But if we look at the industry today, and understand the importance of synthesizers, drum machines, sequencers, managers, makeup artists, stylists, publicists, marketers, and the like, we begin to appreciate the implications of music as a business. The Monkees were a band carefully made for television, the creation of a marketing mind. We are plagued by such bands today. Dylan might have written great music, but the Monkees were the real harbinger of where we are now.

LOS ANGELES: A GODDAMNED ELECTABLE PERSON

Shortly after Lyndon Johnson's landslide victory in the 1964 election, Vernon Christina, linchpin of Barry Goldwater's electoral team in California, ran into two other campaign staffers, Walter Knott and John Gromala, in a Los Angeles parking garage. "We were talking about, 'What shall we do now?'" Christina recalled. They all agreed on the need to continue. "So we lost an election, we lost a candidate, but we didn't think our cause was that bad."[28]

Quite by chance, along came Ronald Reagan, who had delivered the best speech of Goldwater's campaign. "A Time for Choosing," broadcast on national television, had summarized perfectly every aspect of the Republican platform, but in a manner that did not frighten voters. The central issue in the election, Reagan had argued, was "whether we believe in our capacity for self-government or whether we abandon the American Revolution and confess that a little intellectual elite in a far-distant capital can plan our lives for us better than we can plan them ourselves."[29]

That speech was a bright spot in an otherwise dismal campaign. "The idea hit each of us about the same time," Christina recalled. "Why doesn't he . . . run . . . for governor? He's got all the ingredients to make a god-damned electable person. I don't give a damn how smart you are—if you're not electable, forget it. You know. You've got to have that charisma to get elected."[30]

The Republican nomination was supposed to have gone to George Christopher, the urbane mayor of San Francisco and darling of party pa-tricians in the north of the state. He was widely favored to defeat the in-cumbent Democrat, Edmund G. (Pat) Brown, who, after two terms, had outlived his welcome. Republicans from Southern California, however, had other ideas. They espoused a new conservatism: a brash, populist, chauvinistic sort attractive to blue-collar workers in the new industries of San Diego and Los Angeles. All that was missing was an inspiring person-ality who could humanize Goldwater conservatism and take it out of its Southern enclave.

The selection of Reagan laid the foundation for a political movement that would dominate American politics for the next forty years. Republi-cans tapped into a rich conservative vein among white workers of low to moderate income and low educational attainment. This group had once loyally supported the Democrats but had been alienated by Great Society programs, which, to them, meant tax increases and blacks moving in next door. In order to persuade workers to shift allegiance, Republicans had to address their alienation. Television provided the perfect vehicle for doing so. Working-class disaffection was exacerbated by nightly images of inner-city race riots, student unrest, and countercultural excess. Television also provided salvation in the form of Reagan, a candidate with an instinctive gift for communicating with the common man.

Reagan's candidacy at first provoked ridicule. The *San Francisco Chronicle* called it "a flagrant example of miscasting" and predicted that, after an initial wave of bemused interest, his campaign would "bottom out." "If Reagan wins the Republican nomination in June," another analyst warned, "the Democrats, in all likelihood, will smash the GOP in Novem-ber—a loss that could set back the Republican Party for many years." The Brown team shared these preconceptions. "A Republican can't win in November unless he gets the votes of Democrats," one staff member pre-dicted, "and they won't go for Reagan." Richard Kline, who served on Brown's staff, later admitted that "we were conventional thinkers: the peo-ple want to elect to high office those politicians who are qualified for high office. . . . Ronald Reagan was a movie actor with no public experience, and a right-winger to boot."[31]

While Reagan often seems an embarrassingly simple man, his simplicity lies in his paper-thin ideology and his "aw shucks" image. His presenta-tion, on the other hand, was highly sophisticated, requiring skills for which he is seldom credited—namely, shrewdness, sensitivity, perfect tim-ing, and an extraordinary memory for detail. He was also cleverly mar-keted by a thoroughly modern campaign team. Critics who claim that he was merely a media creation ignore the fact that in modern politics *every* candidate is.

The Reagan team was one of the first to recognize and exploit this inevi-tability. After selecting their candidate, Vernon Christina and his friends took the unusual step of hiring the advertising and public-relations firm Spencer-Roberts to manage the campaign. They turned Reagan's lack of experience to advantage by playing upon the public's disenchantment with politics. Thus, when announcing his candidacy on January 4, 1966, Reagan stressed: "I am not a politician in the sense of ever having held public office, but I think I can lay claim to being a 'citizen politician.'" According to Stuart Spencer, the "citizen-politician" label arose "some-where out of our long brainstorming sessions. . . . We felt it was a strength to have somebody that had been out of the system. . . . We felt that that's what people wanted, for a change." At the same time, Reagan repeatedly emphasized that Brown *was* a politician, one who had lost touch with the people. He was, Reagan claimed, "aided by his well-oiled and heav-ily financed machine"—a somewhat ironic charge. The Brown camp had not prepared for a campaign of this sort. "We were surprised," Richard Kline admitted. "We didn't understand that the public wanted non-politicians."[32]

"This is my campaign," Reagan insisted. "Goldwater is not running it. I want the voters to listen to what I have to say and how I stand on the is-sues and then make up their own minds what is the Reagan image." The word "image" was ironically apropos. Reagan did not change his beliefs; he merely changed his makeup: he did his best to *appear* different from

Goldwater. As the *Sacramento Bee* reluctantly admitted on the eve of the election, packaging had become all-important: "Ronald Reagan ... resembles a carefully designed, elaborately 'customerized' supermarket package, complete with the glossiest wrapping and the slickest sort of eye appeal."[33]

The makeover was successful in part because Reagan's conservatism was entirely natural—unfettered by dogma. More a populist than a conservative, he was able to tune into voters' feelings, in a way the inflexible Goldwater never could. Reagan's warmth and optimism also made his conservatism less frightening. After his primary victory over George Christopher, the *San Diego Union* concluded: "Ronald Reagan proved that ... the people have not rejected conservatism, when it is constructive and there is an opportunity to properly present it and make it understandable."[34]

Those who disparage Reagan's B-movie background ignore the fact that modern politics is a form of acting. Reagan knew precisely how to command attention, charm a crowd, and feign deep emotion. His timing was impeccable. "Ron was a man trained ... in the movie business, where you have a director and a producer and everybody carries their load," Spencer maintained. "And because of that ... background, he was a very easy candidate to work with." He was, however, woefully ignorant on issues. Spencer therefore hired the Behavioral Science Corporation (BASICO), a firm of public-opinion consultants run by Stanley Plog and Kenneth Holden, both professors of psychology. Experts in voter profiling, Plog and Holden sought to discover what really mattered to California voters in the summer of 1966. "These vile-sounding fellows," Pat Brown complained, "are digging into the minds of people and finding out how to exploit their anxieties." That was precisely what they did, and what virtually every campaign team has done since.[35]

The Reagan team quickly discovered that student unrest was an effective anxiety trigger. "We jumped on it," Spencer admitted. "I think Reagan escalated it into an issue and it started showing up in the polls." The campaign was supposed to be about big government, welfare, and high taxation, but, as Reagan recalled: "After several weeks of the campaign I had to come back and say, 'Look, I don't care if I'm in the mountains, the desert, the biggest cities of the state, the first question is: "What are you going to do about Berkeley?"' and each time the question itself would get applause."[36]

Student unrest brilliantly highlighted the populist themes of Reagan's campaign: morality, law and order, strong leadership, traditional values, and, it must be said, anti-intellectualism. California higher education had, he argued, failed the heavily burdened taxpayer who financed the system and the parents who entrusted their children to it. By adroit manipulation of this issue, Reagan won comfortably in 1966. Time and again he told the voters that "a small minority of beatniks, radicals, and filthy-speech advocates have brought shame to . . . a great University. . . . This has been allowed to go on in the name of academic freedom. What in heaven's name does 'academic freedom' have to do with rioting, with anarchy, with attempts to destroy the primary purpose of the University, which is to educate our young people?" Reagan's supporters cared little about the nuances of higher-education policy; what they wanted was a governor who could bring order to the universities, by force if necessary. Brown's mistake was that he cast himself as the benevolent uncle of the university. Reagan convinced the voters that an authoritarian father was needed.[37]

At the beginning of the campaign, Reagan tended to overanswer questions, and often got himself into trouble as a result. Under the tutelage of Plog and Holden, he learned the art of the soundbite. Issues were distilled into epigrammatic statements, which were then typed onto small cards and collected into little notebooks. These were then memorized by Reagan, rather like a script. The technique was entirely familiar to those who worked in sales and advertising, but was relatively new to politics. Brown ridiculed Reagan as a man who knew nothing of California problems other than that which could be crammed into his notebooks. Hostile journalists described how his carefully crafted one-liners sounded like "a broom sweeping up broken glass." "Evasive, photogenic, given to generalities and angelic-sounding platitudes," one journalist remarked, "Reagan has left his public almost completely in the dark as to how he will accomplish the things he says he will." What critics failed to understand was that that was precisely his intent.[38]

Reagan's soundbites annoyed seasoned veterans of the political circuit, but they delighted ordinary voters, as a correspondent from the *New Republic* found: "'One of the great problems of economics,' he explained, 'is unemployment.' The crowd cheered. 'For every ounce of federal help we get, we surrender an ounce of personal freedom.' 'There's no such thing as left or right any more; it's up or down.' Steady cheers right along. . . . We knew that pretty soon he was going to say, 'I am not a politician' (he did), and add, 'Ordinary citizens created this country of ours' (Flourish, Cheers)." Reagan's simple conservatism fit perfectly with the superficial coverage television provided. He carried into the campaign some basic beliefs about the relationship between citizen and state. These were culled from a mythical past when politics was supposedly simple. Since the myths in question were close to American hearts, Reagan's platform had enormous appeal. For example, every American cherished the Bill of Rights—in particular, freedom of speech. But while most people worshiped freedom in the abstract, few understood its implications. Those who revered the image of Patrick Henry asserting his rights in Boston in 1776 had no time for Jerry Rubin asserting his in Sproul Plaza. Reagan capitalized on this dichotomy: "Freedom of speech stops short of vulgarity and obscenity forced upon those that don't want to hear it, and certainly freedom of speech, when some Americans are fighting and dying for their country, must stop short of lending comfort and aid to the enemy." "Mr. Reagan spoke down-to-earth American language, about down-to-earth United States of America constitutional Americanism," a correspondent to the *San Diego Union* wrote. "To me, it is the fresh breeze of realism that has been absent from the political scene for thirty-five years."[39]

Since registered Democrats in California outnumbered Republicans by approximately 1.3 million, in order to win by even a whisker Reagan had to attract, according to one estimate, 90 percent of the traditional Republicans and 25 percent of the traditional Democrats. Since, in fact, he defeated Brown by over a million votes, he obviously managed to impress an enormous number of Democrats. "We lost votes with the conservative Democrats," Donald Bradley, a Brown campaign manager, confirmed. "I'd say the backbone of the party, the blue-collar majority worker. That's who we lost." According to Caspar Weinberger, then a San Francisco lawyer and former state Republican chairman, Reagan "got something in excess of 40 percent of the union labor, and he did that because he was talking about things they were very interested in. . . . When he talked about low taxes and keeping government small and less intrusive . . . he was striking a very strong chord."[40]

In 1970, Reagan easily won a second term. During his eight years in Sacramento, he was one of the most popular governors in the history of the state. He was able to maintain his support not by delivering practical policies which improved the lives of his constituents, but rather by keeping their anger and fear stoked. In this regard, unruly students helped enormously. During his first term, Reagan's approval rating on higher education was always comfortably over 50 percent—no other aspect received a score as high. His popularity was at its lowest in spring 1968, when campuses were quiet. It surged again in 1969, after prolonged confrontations with militant students at San Francisco State and Berkeley. As governor, Reagan's reaction to campus unrest was identical to that revealed during his campaign. He stressed the same populist messages, promised the same dynamic action. Reagan, like his supporters, did not really understand the disorder, but he did understand voters' fears. Supposedly off-the-cuff remarks allowed him to communicate directly with the people by echoing their chauvinism. On one occasion he described a bunch of protesters who "were carrying signs that said 'Make Love Not War.' The only trouble was they didn't look like they were capable of doing either. His hair was cut like Tarzan, and he acted like Jane, and he smelled like Cheetah." He also promised that he would protect the rights of those 'who are legitimately trying to get an education, . . . at the point of a bayonet if necessary." The conflict with campus militants was, according to him, a war. He referred to "moment[s] of confrontation" and the need "to make a stand." The universities were presented as a battlefront in the Cold War—in Vietnam and in Berkeley, the dominoes would not be allowed to fall. "This is guerrilla warfare," he argued, adding: "The only thing that can win in campus guerrilla warfare is . . . you eliminate them by firing the faculty members and expelling the students."[41]

Firebrands like Reagan who defied dissidents with ersatz bravado were like the war heroes of a previous generation: they benefited from the public's desire for strong leadership. As an actor, Reagan was ideally poised to exploit the voters' taste for heroes: he knew how to look courageous. His warnings, though often paper thin, sounded ominous. The voters believed that he meant business. Those most impressed were the "middle Americans" who resented the activities of the privileged elites on campus. Once Reagan attracted this group to his side, they never left him. Their unswerving support allowed him to be as conservative as he wished. As one disgruntled moderate California Republican remarked: "For the first time, the Republicans don't see the rainbow ending in the middle of the spectrum. In the past, Republican conservatives, to survive, had to move toward the middle. But the law-and-order issue and the Reagan phenomenon have created a view that it is dangerous to occupy the middle."[42]

Reagan had clearly discovered a potent formula for success. After his first campaign tour, his press secretary, Lyn Nofziger, remarked to Stuart Spencer's partner William Roberts, "Hey, this guy could be president someday!" Outside the campaign team, observers took only slightly longer to come to the same conclusion. The *Daily Oklahoman* was sufficiently impressed by his defeat of George Christopher in the primary to consider Reagan a firm contender in the 1968 presidential election. As early as June 16 (in other words, *before* Reagan had defeated Brown), seventy-four Republican county chairmen across the nation, polled by Gallup, supported Reagan for the Republican presidential nomination. *New York Times* correspondent David Broder, reporting on Reagan's visit to Washington in August, remarked on what seemed, "in the eyes of many of those present, the Washington debut of a potential presidential candidate."[43]

The most successful political revolution of the 1960s was not conducted by students, nor was it left-wing. It was instead a populist revolution from the right, which had Ronald Reagan as its standard bearer. Some analysts, frightened by the implications of the Reagan phenomenon, insisted that California had taken leave of its senses. They assumed that if the people supported Ronald Reagan, something must be wrong with the people. That refrain would reverberate through subsequent decades as liberals struggled to come to terms with the Reagan revolution. "Perhaps only the capricious California electorate could stage such a political jest," Emmet John Hughes remarked in *Newsweek*. Reagan's victory, he decided, "dramatizes the virtual bankruptcy, politically and intellectually, of a national party. . . . The political point should not be more sharp. Some men learn from history. Some men run from it. And the GOP has chosen feckless flight." To an extent, Hughes was right. The GOP, with Reagan in front, *was* running from history. What many failed to realize, however, was that the voters were running in the same direction. Unique among the revolutionaries of the Sixties, Reagan did not need a weatherman to know which way the wind was blowing.[44]

St. Louis: Curt Flood versus Baseball

In 1969, the sporting world was stunned by the success of the New York Mets, the team that, prior to that year, had deservedly been dubbed the worst team ever to play major-league baseball. The underdog image was carefully nurtured by coaches and management, while, behind the scenes, the Mets underwent a careful process of development. This suddenly bore fruit in 1969 and provided the team with some of the most gifted ballplayers of their generation. In sports, however, fairy tales make the action on the field much more meaningful, and so fans are only too willing to believe them. The sportswriter George Vecsey wrote:

> On October 17, the miracle happened. The Mets had stormed through an unbelievable season to capture the World Series, and the people were piling into the street to celebrate. . . . People were dancing in the streets, holding hands with strangers, reaching back to their childhood for ways to express their joy. . . . It was like the closing minutes of some old Bing Crosby movie, the kind of ending that had become impossible in our world of war and ghettoes. . . . The Mets reminded people of love and hope, sentiments that were not very stylish nor realistic in 1969. If the Mets could win the World Series, people said, anything was possible.

To people around the country, the Mets seemed to embody the best about sports: the idea that a mere game can embody profound moral truths. Most of all, the victory seemed to suggest the importance of the Team— the principle that a theoretically weak group of players can emerge victorious if they believe in one another.[45]

Forty years later, American sports fans—many of whom weren't even born by 1969—nostalgically recall the heroics of Tom Seaver and his fellow Mets. Few remember another athlete from that remarkable year, Curt Flood—yet he had a much greater impact on the future of professional sports than any of the Mets. Flood was the star centerfielder for the St. Louis Cardinals, a gifted player who had been an All Star three times and had won the Gold Glove seven times for his defensive prowess. At the end of the 1969 season, the Cardinals decided to trade him to the Philadelphia Phillies. Since they owned the rights to Flood, they were fully entitled to send him where they wanted. Under the terms of baseball's "reserve clause"—written into every player's contract—a player was bound in perpetuity to the club owning his contract.

Philadelphia was America's "northernmost Southern city," a hotbed of racism. For that reason, Flood, a black man, had no desire to join the Phillies. His reluctance was not based exclusively on an aversion to the City of Brotherly Love. He also objected to the fact that he had had absolutely no say in the decision. "After twelve years in the Major Leagues," he wrote in a letter to baseball commissioner Bowie Kuhn, "I do not feel I am a piece of property to be bought and sold irrespective of my wishes. I believe that any system which produces that result violates my basic rights as a citizen." Aside from professional sportsmen, no other workers, he argued, operated in such a restricted market. To baseball, however, the idea of challenging the reserve clause was as preposterous as questioning the fact that the game was played on a diamond. The sanctity of the clause was validated by no less an authority than the US Supreme Court, which, a half-century before, had ruled that since baseball was not a form of commerce, usual practices did not apply.[46]

Flood felt that the issue went beyond mere matters of baseball and law. He saw it as a question of freedom. The reserve clause, he felt, rendered him chattel—a slave—albeit a highly paid one. He considered his challenge of the reserve clause as significant as Jackie Robinson's breaking of the color barrier in baseball in 1947. A fight for freedom harmonized well with the mood of the Sixties, as he explained years later:

> I'm a child of the sixties, I'm a man of the sixties. During that period of time, this country was coming apart at the seams. We were in Southeast Asia. Good men were dying for America and for the Constitution. In the southern part of the United States we were marching for civil rights and Dr. King had been assassinated, and we lost the Kennedys. And to think that merely because I was a professional baseball player, I could ignore what was going on outside the walls of Busch Stadium was truly hypocrisy. . . . All of those rights that these great Americans were dying for, I didn't have in my own profession.

Flood knew all about racism. He had worked his way up through the minor leagues in the Deep South, everywhere encountering the sharp edge of segregation. While his white teammates ate at restaurants, he was handed food through the back door. When the team bus stopped at a public toilet, he peed in the bushes. But the freedom he fought for in 1969 was not racially determined. He struggled for the right of all players—black, white, Hispanic, or Asian—to control their own destiny. Nevertheless, his crusade was made all the more powerful by the fact that it was fought by a black man.[47]

Flood decided to challenge the trade, even though he knew that this would almost certainly mean the end of his career. The Players Association backed his challenge and former US Supreme Court justice Arthur Goldberg provided legal representation. From January 1970 to June 1972, Flood meandered his way through the American legal system, encountering failure at every stage. Eventually, the Supreme Court rejected his argument, maintaining that the integrity of baseball depended upon exemption from antitrust statutes.

Flood had lost, but so too had baseball. The protracted legal battle had revealed that the reserve clause, though technically legal, was untenable. Realizing that a new system was required, in 1975 the sport brought in the Messersmith-McNally rulings, which instituted the system of free agency. Under the new regime, a player was bound to a team only during the term of his contract, rather like any other contracted employee. After the contract expired, he became a free agent and could sell his services to the highest bidder.

Flood died in 1997. At his memorial service in Los Angeles, he was acclaimed not just as a hero but also as a martyr, a man who had sacrificed his career in order to right an injustice. Among the mourners were dozens of former ballplayers, most of them millionaires, who had benefited enormously from his crusade. One mourner compared Flood's effect to that of Rosa Parks, whose challenge to segregation on public buses in Montgomery, Alabama, ushered in the modern civil rights movement. The conservative columnist George Will, a baseball fanatic, called Flood the Dred Scott of baseball.

Flood felt that his cause harmonized perfectly with the spirit of the Sixties. He was right in a way he probably never realized. The Sixties was the selfish decade, a time of fragmentation when social harmony was abandoned in favor of factionalized goals. Nothing was sacred in the pursuit of self-interest, not even America's national pastime. Free agency became the norm not just in baseball but in other professional sports in the United States, and around the world. Sportsmen, even rather average ones, became enormously wealthy, and teams were built on the strength of an owner's checkbook. Players became free agents not just in terms of negotiating their contracts but in a much wider sense. Free agents belong to no one. They represent only themselves. The individual had won, but the Team was never the same.

Today, it is difficult to decide whether Flood's crusade was a victory for justice or for greed. The reserve clause was undoubtedly iniquitous, but the law is notoriously unsubtle, unable to take account of the nuances of the sporting world. At the time of his trade to the Phillies, Flood was earning $100,000 a year, making him one of the highest-paid employees in the United States. A few decades later, Alex Rodriguez signed a $252 million contract with the Texas Rangers, a figure that made baseball fans cringe. Flood, in other words, had opened the floodgates. When teams become mere collections of selfish stars, and players earn more per game than the average person's yearly salary, it is difficult to find real heroes in baseball. The reason few people remember Flood is that, to the ordinary fan, his victory was not very glorious.

Or so it seems. Back before the Civil War, one of the first organized baseball games was played at Elysian Fields in Hoboken, New Jersey. Baseball fans, lovers of romantic myth, drool over that historical tidbit. The place sounds heavenly, but in fact the infield produced vicious bad bouncers, and the outfield was riddled with gopher holes. The past, in other words, is never as lovely as we like to imagine. Critics argued that Flood's victory would mean the end of competitive baseball, that a handful of rich teams would share the titles. Yet in the immediate aftermath of the demise of the reserve clause, from 1978 to 1987, ten different teams won the World Series. Compare that to the period 1936–1964, when the New York Yankees won twenty-two American League pennants. Furthermore, though ticket prices rose steadily after 1976, so too did attendance figures. Ordinary people somehow found money to watch baseball.

The romance of baseball is nine-tenths illusion—a myth made durable by the fans' eagerness to believe. The Team was in large part an artificial creation, a group of self-centered individuals held together by an invidious law which restricted their freedom. If the Team had been holy, it would have survived the death of the reserve clause. Curt Flood's campaign was simply an unpleasant dose of reality which demonstrated that all sportsmen, contrary to what we want to believe, are simply mercenaries who fight for their paymaster.

NO DIRECTION HOME

ALTAMONT: THE DAY THE MUSIC DIED

The Woodstock Festival of August 1969 was supposed to have been a beginning, the green shoots of the cooperative commonwealth in which everyone would be nice to one another and leaders would conform to the popular will. In fact it was the end—or, rather, a false dawn. Reality was revealed in gory Technicolor four months later at a dusty racetrack called Altamont.

The runes were already there for anyone inclined to read them. In the month before Woodstock, the Rolling Stones gave a free concert in Hyde Park, London, with the Hell's Angels providing unofficial security. Sixties peddlers of peace and love were smitten with the black-leathered brutes, a gang so bad they were good. They guarded the fenced-off area near the stage, where VIPs gathered and sipped champagne. That should have been a clue to something amiss, since the communal paradise of Hippie Nation was not supposed to have Very Important People. Far from the radiant center, the peasants could hardly see the stage or hear the music. Their enjoyment was ruined by the early appearance of a Seventies phenomenon: blue-overalled skinheads, or bovverboys, with swastikas tattooed on their foreheads. They lurked in the trees and pissed on the peaceful hippies below.

If Hyde Park was mildly unsettling, the Isle of Wight later in the summer was undiluted nightmare. Far from being a love-in, it was a cash-in. Greedy entrepreneurs capitalized on the hippies' failure to bring food by selling disgusting hot dogs at exorbitant prices. Immense symbolism was packed into each slimy sausage. "The festivals destroyed the underground:

everyone trying to make a buck out of it," Jeff Dexter complained. "After Woodstock the music industry said, 'Hey, there's a mass audience out there'—it was still wide open and everyone wanted a piece." Richard Neville, who somehow endured the whole thing, remembered: "The nights were freezing, all the blankets sold, the food ran out and the latrines stank. For the last hot dogs, the queue was three hundred yards long. . . . Huddled around huge bonfires of rubbish . . . 200,000 fans tried not to feel anticlimactic." "This was when my first wave of disillusionment with hippies set in," Charles Shaar Murray confessed. "People would be standing up to get a better view, then go down because a full can of Coke caught them in the back of the head. . . . For me, that was the beginning of the end of hippie. . . . I'd been to the Woodstock movie, read all the stupid books and I thought life could be an endless free rock festival. At the Isle of Wight I realised that it couldn't be and that it was dishonest to carry on claiming that it was feasible. I had bought the whole package, as much as I could swallow." The final indignity came when demoralized fans found no direction home. British Rail had neglected to realize that if hordes of people went to the Isle of Wight, they might eventually want to get back.[1]

Given the portents of doom, it is perhaps surprising that so many people thought Altamont was going to be like Woodstock, even though Woodstock was not really like Woodstock. As the rock journalist Michael Lydon found, the festival momentum was driven by the hippies' irrepressible ability to hope: "[Altamont] was the biggest gathering in California since the Human Be-In three years before, not only in numbers but in expectation. . . . It would, all believed, advance the trip, reveal some important lesson intrinsic to and yet beyond its physical fact. The 300,000, all in unspoken social contract, came not only to hear music, but to bear living testimony to their own lives." Altamont came at the end of a long and highly profitable Rolling Stones tour of America. It was, in essence, their way of saying thank you. In line with that sentiment, it was supposed to be a free concert and, as such, homage to a golden idea.[2]

Agents representing the Stones met informally in San Francisco with some people from the Grateful Dead. The latter were experts at staging big, free outdoor events—or at least they claimed to be. Ambition, fueled by drugs, went unrestrained. The manager of the Sears Point raceway, in a generous mood, offered his grounds for free. Everything seemed to be go-

ing smoothly, but leaving organization to the Dead was like entrusting nu-
trition to Cap'n Crunch.

"An essential element of free concerts is simplicity," Lydon wrote. Unfortunately, nothing about the Stones could ever be simple. "Everybody
wanted a piece of the action. Hustlers of every stripe swarmed to the new
scene like piranhas to the scent of blood." After sleeping on it, that nice
man at Sears Point started getting greedy. He asked for $6,000, plus an-
other $5,000 deposit to cover possible damage. That was a hitch, but not
an obstacle. In order to cover the steadily mounting costs, the Stones sold
the film rights. It then turned out that the Filmways Corporation was the
actual owner of Sears Point, and when their people got wind of a concert
movie, they demanded distribution rights. The Stones told them to get
lost, at which point the rent was raised to $100,000. This was on Thursday.
The concert was scheduled for Saturday. Crowds were already gathering,
and the stage was being built.[3]

Enter the lawyers. In San Francisco, no lawyer was bigger than Melvin
Belli. A lover of things huge and sordid, he offered to help the Stones in
their tussle with Filmways. The Dead were elbowed aside as Belli's office
became Concert Central. The hippies, who had originally seen the concert
as a celebration of their culture, got sick at the sight of so many men in
suits.

Out of the blue came Altamont, a stock-car track fifty miles east of
Berkeley, whose manager, Dick Carter, could hardly contain his delight at
the prospect of hosting the Stones. The stage was dismantled and moved,
volunteers migrated eastward, and radio stations frantically advised listeners about the new venue. From all directions, the faithful converged. "At 7
A.M. the gates are opened. Over the hill and down into the hollow by the
stage comes a whooping, running, raggle-taggle mob. . . . In minutes the
meadow is a crush of bodies pressed so close that it takes ten minutes to
walk fifty yards. Only the bravest blades of grass still peep up through the
floor of wadded bedding. On and on comes the crowd; by 10 A.M. it spreads
a quarter-mile back from the stage, fanning out like lichen clinging to a
rock." Astrologers warned that it was not a good day for a concert. Something indeed seemed amiss. The crowd, encouraged after Woodstock to expect something truly magnificent, grew impatient when paradise failed to
materialize. Everyone was supposed to feel love for one another, but it was

hard to muster affection with someone's elbow poking into your ribs, when drunken hippies stepped on your toes, and when it rained rubbish. The air was thick with the stench of cheap wine, sweaty bodies, pot, shit, and vomit. Instead of paradise, Altamont seemed more like a dream of Hieronymus Bosch. Lydon saw not the usual concert crowd, but "weirdos, . . . speed freaks with hollow eyes and missing teeth, dead-faced acid heads burned out by countless flashes, old beatniks clutching gallons of red wine." The music might have distracted attention from the squalor, but not many could hear the music. Todd Gitlin left in the afternoon, long before the Stones started to play. "Altamont already felt like death. . . . Behind the stage, hordes of Aquarians were interfering with doctors trying to help people climb down from bad acid trips. On the remote hillside where I sat, stoned fans were crawling over one another to get a bit closer to the groovy music." A friend told him that, after dropping acid, he'd had a vision that "everyone was dead." Gitlin was not usually tuned to mystical visions, but this one seemed painfully portentous.[4]

The presence of the Hell's Angels didn't help—they brought an air of menace to a gathering supposedly founded on love. The Stones had hired the Angels to provide unofficial security. The idea might have come from the Hyde Park experience, when the bikers looked menacing but generally behaved better than the crowd itself. Unfortunately, British Angels came from a more pacific branch of the family tree than their Californian cousins. They were promised free beer, but the real attraction seems to have been the opportunity to run riot on such a large stage.

That opportunity did not go wasted. While Jefferson Airplane was in the middle of a furiously exuberant version of "Three-Fifths of a Mile in Ten Seconds," a fight broke out below the stage. Marty Balin, the lead singer, intervened, whereupon a Hell's Angel started beating him with a pool cue. The crowd, paralyzed in confusion and terror, could not decide whether this was a bad trip or, worse, reality. The band stopped playing; the stage now filled with menacing bikers looking like sentries at the gates of Hell. The crowd called for peace and love, but the pleas were about as effective as an umbrella in a tsunami. Everyone wanted the Angels to leave the scene, but they refused to surrender territory conquered. "In the awesome presence of the Angels we gleaned something of that deep, silent terror we had of brutes when we were kids on the playground," wrote the rock critic J. Marks. "And in the scuffles and glares of anger we began to recognize the sheer helplessness of our great pop superstars and prick-deities who could not turn back the sea with a single command so that we might safely stride uninterrupted toward the magic milieu of their music as we had at Woodstock and Monterey."[5]

Worse was to follow. In the middle of the Stones' set, carnage erupted. Four Angels jumped from behind the amps. One, Alan Passaro, leaped down and, brandishing a knife, charged into the frightened crowd. The music faltered, recovered, then stopped completely. More Angels appeared from nowhere, jostling the band members, who were not about to yield. Jagger, taking seriously his role as leader, politely asked the Angels to clear the stage. No one was quite sure what was going on below. The music started again, then stopped.

The focus of the Angels' violence was Meredith Hunter, an eighteen-year-old from Oakland. The exact sequence of events remains a matter of dispute. Some claim that the Angels attacked first, perhaps because Hunter, a black man, had a white girlfriend. Others contend that, without provocation, Hunter pointed a gun at Jagger. No one disputes that he did brandish a gun, though whether he or the Angels were acting in self-defense remains unclear. Once that gun appeared, the result was inevitable. A witness later described an execution:

> They hit him . . . I couldn't tell whether it was a knife or not . . . but on the side of the head. And then . . . he came running towards me, and then fell down on his knees and the Hell's Angel . . . grabbed onto both of his shoulders and started kicking him in the face about five times or so, and then he fell down on his face . . . and then one of them kicked him off the side and rolled over and he muttered some words. He said, "I wasn't going to shoot you."
>
> We rubbed his back up and down to get the blood off so we could see, and there was this big hole on his spine and a big hole on the side and there was a big hole on his temple. A big open slice. You could see all the way in. You could see inside. You could see at least an inch down and stuff, you know.

The audience seemed ready to stampede. Those more than fifty feet away (which included 99 percent of the crowd) had no idea what was going on or why the music had stopped. Boos were heard as impatience grew.[6]

Rather bizarrely, given the circumstances, the Stones eventually resumed their set. By this stage, however, the spirit had evaporated. Most people wanted to go home. The Grateful Dead never did play. "Looking back, I don't think it was a good idea to have Hell's Angels there," Keith Richards admitted. "It was a complete mess and we were partly to blame," Jagger confessed in 1989. "You expected everyone in San Francisco—because they were so mellow, nice, and organized—that it was going to be all those things. But of course, it wasn't."[7]

According to subsequent reports, there were three births and four deaths at Altamont. The former might be a myth; the latter, sadly, is not. Two friends, Mark Feiger and Richard Savlov, were killed by an out-of-control car during the stampede from the concert. Another man, his faculties impaired by drugs, wandered into an irrigation canal and drowned. Finally, there was Meredith Hunter, beyond hope even before a doctor reached him. In May 2005 Alameda County sheriffs closed the case on Altamont, concluding that "Passaro acted [alone] to stop . . . Hunter from shooting."[8]

"We knew it was all over," wrote J. Marks. "We were dying. . . . Dying of our own massive appetite for humanity: the act of faith which had directed us not only to imbibe mysterious potions which changed our heads, but also directed us to engulf and absorb huge, fatal doses of derelict humanity." He saw a direct line from the Haight, to the murder of Linda and Groovy, to Altamont, and ultimately to Charles Manson and his "Family." "The huge ranks of alienated, anti-social psychopaths were being naively absorbed into the generation's main flank, where they were then turning into mad dogs and destroying those who had welcomed them."[9]

The Stones, apparently, were brilliant, as brilliant as the crowd had dared hope. So was the play at Ford's Theatre on a certain night in 1865. Brilliance was irrelevant amid the deaths—of concertgoers and of a dream.

CHAPPAQUIDDICK: A CAREER DROWNED

Martha's Vineyard, off the coast of Massachusetts, had long been the playground of the Kennedy family. Everyone in the extended clan was familiar with its little roads and bridges. All that knowledge went for naught on the night of July 17, 1969, when Ted Kennedy inexplicably lost his way. A wrong turn, excessive speed, and impaired reactions resulted in his car plunging off a small wooden bridge on the Vineyard's companion island,

Chappaquiddick, and landing upside down in eight feet of water. He escaped, but his passenger, Mary Jo Kopechne, did not.

The Sixties began with one Kennedy, and ended with another. Ted, the youngest of the brothers, seemed destined to take up the mantle left by Jack and Bobby and thus satisfy those who still believed that only a Kennedy could save America. Fans of the clan (and they were many) wanted Ted, senator from Massachusetts since 1962, to run for president in 1972. Those hopes, however, died with Kopechne in Poucha Pond. When considering the end of the Sixties, it is difficult to resist the metaphoric possibilities of a car upside down and underwater, an innocent young woman dead inside, and a wealthy middle-aged man swimming away.

Kopechne was one of the guests of honor at a small party at Lawrence Cottage after the Edgartown Regatta. The party was a gesture of thanks to six "Boiler Room Girls" who had worked on RFK's 1968 presidential campaign. All the young women were single. All the men attending—Kennedy and five cronies—were married. All their wives were absent.

Kopechne left the party at 11:15 P.M. Kennedy offered to drive her back to her hotel in Edgartown. Though she had her own car and supposedly did not drink, she accepted Kennedy's offer. The senator might have asked his driver, John Crimmins, to take them to Edgartown, but for some reason he insisted on driving himself. They left in time to catch the last ferry, due to depart at midnight. On the way, Kennedy inexplicably took a sharp right turn onto Dike Road—a dirt track—instead of bearing left onto Main Street, the more natural route. After about a half mile, he descended a hill going far too fast and overshot a small wooden bridge set at an oblique angle to the road. According to the accident report, the car "somersaulted through the air for about 10 meters . . . and landed upside down."[10]

"I attempted to open the door and window of the car but have no recollection of how I got out of the car," Kennedy later stated. "I came to the surface and then repeatedly dove down to the car in an attempt to see if the passenger was still in the car. I was unsuccessful in the attempt. I was exhausted and in a state of shock." He then lay on the bank for a short time, catching his breath. Even though houses were nearby, he did not call for help, choosing instead to walk back to the party. Though he passed a pay phone on the way, he did not call the police.[11]

On reaching the party, Kennedy summoned Paul Markham and Joseph Gargan; the latter was his cousin. They decided not to call the police but instead raced back to the scene, supposedly to see if Kopechne could still be rescued. Efforts to reach the car failed. According to Gargan, who kept quiet about the incident for twenty years, Kennedy immediately started constructing a scenario which would absolve him of blame. He allegedly suggested he would claim that Mary Jo had been driving, that she had dropped him off, driven to the ferry herself, and taken a wrong turn. Gargan vigorously rejected the idea. "You told me *you* were driving!" he shouted. Apparently intent on going ahead with that plan, Kennedy returned to his hotel in Edgartown, without contacting police. Finding that the last ferry had already left, he chose to swim the narrow channel. He slipped into his hotel unseen, put on dry clothes and then established his presence by asking a hotel employee the time. His actions suggest that he was trying to construct an alibi, but the idea was abandoned when Markham and Gargan arrived the next morning and refused to follow the script. The three men then reported the accident to police, by which time a passing fisherman had already alerted authorities to the car in the water.[12]

John Farrar, the police diver who recovered the body, believed that Kopechne did not drown, but rather died of asphyxiation. He thinks she found an air pocket in the car, from which she breathed until the oxygen ran out. If so, she could have lived up to two hours after the accident, in other words, more than enough time to save her, had Kennedy summoned police immediately. George Killen, the detective who conducted the investigation, came to the conclusion that Kennedy "killed that girl the same as if he put a gun to her head and pulled the trigger."[13]

A week later, Kennedy attempted to explain. By this time, the air was thick with rumor. In a formal statement, he steadfastly maintained his innocence. "There is no truth, no truth whatsoever, to the widely circulated suspicions of immoral conduct that have been leveled at my behavior and hers regarding that evening. There has never been a private relationship between us of any kind. I know of nothing in Mary Jo's conduct on that or any other occasion . . . that would lend any substance to such ugly speculation about [her] character. Nor was I driving under the influence of liquor." Since Kennedy could not blame his behavior on drink, he had to blame it on a lapse of judgment. "My conduct and conversations . . . make no sense to me at all." He suggested that he might have been suffering the effects of concussion, or that he might have been in shock. Nevertheless, "I regard it as indefensible the fact that I did not report the accident to the police immediately." He claimed that he had turned down Dike Road in error, yet he was intimately familiar with the area, having driven that route on two previous occasions that same day.[14]

The police handled Kennedy like the crown prince of an absolute monarchy, charging him only with leaving the scene of an accident. For that, he received a suspended two-month jail sentence and a one-year driving ban. On no occasion was he pressed to provide credible answers to the hundreds of questions arising from the case.

To this day, questions outnumber facts. Holes in the story have been obligingly filled by eager conspiracy theorists. Some have argued that Kennedy was drunk and was having an affair with Kopechne, or was about to consummate one. Others claim Kopechne was pregnant and that Kennedy murdered her. Still others have asserted that the CIA or other dark forces engineered the entire incident in order to scupper a Kennedy bid for the White House. Perhaps inevitably, there are those who suggest that Chappaquiddick is simply part of one giant conspiracy whose tentacles stretch to the assassinations of Jack and Bobby.

Chappaquiddick was swept under a rug in a way that, post-Watergate, seems quaint. But though the Kennedy family successfully contained the scandal, they could not suppress the stink it emitted. Though Ted continued to harbor dreams of the White House, Chappaquiddick was in truth the last act of the Kennedy presidential drama. The public did not need all the answers to know that something was amiss. They did not need conspiracy theorists to tell them that the events of July 18 were scandalous. No possible explanation for Kopechne's death could be imagined which did not reveal Kennedy in a bad light. He was either cynical or foolish or stupid. Any one of those characteristics was enough to disqualify him from the presidency.

Camelot, and all the innocence it implied, was over. In time, Americans would discover that the moral deficiencies Chappaquiddick rudely exposed were not unique to Ted, but were shared by his brothers. They all seemed to possess an errant gene which caused them to misbehave in the presence of beautiful women. The people of Massachusetts remained loyal to Ted, but most Americans considered him a liability. How things had changed in the course of a decade. In 1960, Massachusetts gave the nation a president. After 1969, the voting behavior of that state would seem an anomaly.

THE MOON: MAGNIFICENT DESOLATION

The terrible year 1968 ended with the crew of Apollo 8—Frank Borman, James Lovell, and William Anders—becoming the first human beings to orbit another celestial body. In a live broadcast from the Moon, they read from the Book of Genesis and wished the people of Earth a merry Christmas. Most Americans judged it a sublimely beautiful event even while they agonized over its enormous cost. "Thank you for saving 1968," one woman wrote to NASA.[15]

The journey to the Moon seemed long at the time, but was incredibly short in retrospect. In seven years, the Americans had gone from brief, suborbital flights involving chimpanzees to a voyage around the Moon with three astronauts. The journey had been marked by tragedy, but astronaut deaths had not caused Americans to question the need to beat the Russians. Debate about the real worth of space travel was smothered by the need to make a political point.

The drama of the Moon race overshadowed entirely the genuinely important developments in space. In August 1960, the Soviets launched into orbit a large capsule containing two dogs named Strelka and Belka. The American public was plunged into despair, as had happened after every Soviet space feat since Sputnik. What few Americans realized, however, was that their country had so far achieved the genuinely important advances in space. Four months earlier, on April 1, the United States had launched Tiros 1, the world's first weather satellite, which instantly transformed meteorological forecasting. Twelve days later came Transit 1B, the world's first navigation satellite, which allowed ships to calculate their position with pinpoint accuracy.

These feats inspired little pride among Americans for the simple reason that the Soviets had defined the terms of the space race. Ever since the launch of Laika, the first space dog, the standard of achievement became the ability to put a living being into space, even though doing so had about as much importance as shooting a scantily clad woman from a circus cannon. The logical extension of this paradigm was the meaningless race to the Moon. Because the United States was behind in that race, it had to endure a long crisis of confidence. Meanwhile, away from the anguish, American satellite engineers laid the foundations of a communications revolution which would rival the invention of the printing press.

That, however, was hardly noticed amid all the barking about Strelka and Belka.

Tiros and Transit were appetizers before the main meal. The entrée came on July 10, 1962, when a Delta rocket placed in orbit a satellite called Telstar, belonging to AT&T. A short time later, Telstar was used to relay the first satellite TV pictures—showing an American flag outside a ground station in Andover, Maine. Thirteen days later came the first live broadcasts. The plan had been to relay to Britain and France a presidential press conference, but the satellite went live before Kennedy was ready, so technicians inserted a few plays from a baseball game at Chicago's Wrigley Field. Later that day, the satellite was used to transmit overseas a phone call and a facsimile transmission—what would later be called a fax.

"The achievement of the communications satellite, while only a prelude, throws open to us the vision of an era of international communications," said Kennedy with less drama than the event deserved. Kennedy understood that space travel, though enormously exciting, was a rather shallow matter of Cold War prestige which in the long run would have very little effect upon ordinary people. Satellites, on the other hand, had potential beyond the wildest dreams. In the same speech in which he pledged to land a man on the Moon, he asked Congress to approve an additional $50 million for communications satellites. While that sort of money would hardly buy a space toilet for an astronaut, it would make a huge difference in satellite development.[16]

Aside from the simple and innocent potential of instant communication across vast distances, the satellite had huge political importance, especially in the Cold War, where battles were won with words. Satellites offered the opportunity to beam messages into areas where communication was previously blocked and to places heretofore inaccessible due to their remoteness or technological backwardness. They made it possible to tell the people in "huts and villages" around the world about the beneficence of American capitalism.

Satellites meant that the world was suddenly much smaller; and it was a place in which those who spoke English would increasingly do so with an American accent. In April 1965, Senator John Pastore of Rhode Island described the first Intelsat satellite as "the shop window through which America can and will be seen throughout the world." Before long, people everywhere—the young in particular—would strive to look and act like

Americans. Satellites provided the ability to market American products into every dark corner; modernity would be defined by the consumption of Levis, Cokes, and Big Macs. The entertainment industry, after a decade in which individuality and creativity seemed to blossom, would suddenly be smothered by the homogenizing imperative of a worldwide communications network. American culture, beamed via Intelsat, would achieve far more victories in the Cold War than the US Army ever did. A few countries would grumble (the French, for instance, would set up new ministries dedicated to the preservation of Gallic identity), but most would simply surrender to the tidal wave of American culture. "Space for the benefit of all mankind," as Kennedy benevolently called it, would benefit America most of all.[17]

Satellites were, however, bit players in the space drama. American attention was focused almost exclusively on astronauts who might carry Old Glory to the Moon. While the Moon race attracted enormous attention, underneath the surface lurked profound unease. Rather like parents at Disneyland, Americans could not avoid thinking about how much the adventure was costing.

On the eve of the Apollo 11 launch, two dominating issues of the 1960s, space and civil rights, collided. Leading a protest at Cape Kennedy, Ralph Abernathy complained about the "bizarre social values" which motivated America to spend $35 billion on an adventure in space, while back on Earth one-fifth of the nation lacked adequate food, clothing, shelter, and medical care. Given such deep poverty, the lunar mission seemed obscene.[18]

Abernathy was not a lone wolf howling in the wilderness. After the Watts riots in 1965, the McCone Commission had warned: "Of what shall it avail our nation if we can place a man on the moon but cannot cure the sickness in our cities?" Apollo was a great deal less popular than is commonly assumed. The poor, the unemployed, most blacks, and most women were unenthusiastic. On only one occasion during the 1960s did a poll show a clear majority of Americans agreeing that the space program was worth the cost. Difficult as it is to imagine, throughout the 1960s the Vietnam War was more popular than Apollo.[19]

Virtually every NASA publicist had mentioned "man's need to discover" when justifying the huge budget. In 1969, the theologian Daniel Migliore questioned this justification. "Americans are accustomed to transcending the old and the oppressive by spatial movement," he noted. Simply stated, they equated progress with movement. Migliore, like Abernathy, advocated a different conception of moral progress. "We must make up our minds. Is freedom primarily to be found in spatial migration (to outer or inner space)? Or is freedom to be sought first in shaping a new future for men here on the good earth?"[20]

Neil Armstrong did not agree that a choice had to be made. According to him, man's first step on the Moon would be a giant leap for mankind. His famous eleven words uttered when he first stepped on the Moon ("That's one small step for man, one giant leap for mankind") were undoubtedly enormously popular, but few stopped to contemplate their logic. Few paused to consider how walking on the lunar surface would help starving children in Biafra or blacks in Alabama.

Some highly influential people agreed with Armstrong. In an article in *TV Guide* prior to the launch, Walter Cronkite remarked: "When Apollo 11 reaches the moon, when we reach that unreachable star, we will have shown that the possibility of world peace exists . . . if we put our skill, intelligence, and money to it." Wernher von Braun, the ex-Nazi engineer who sold space to the Americans, called the lunar landing "equal in importance to that moment in evolution when aquatic life came crawling up on the land." Nixon, eager to get in on the act, called it "the greatest week in history since the beginning of the world, the creation. Nothing has changed the world more than this mission."[21]

"It is the spirit of Apollo that America can now help to bring to our relations with other nations," Nixon remarked with a quiver in his voice. "The spirit of Apollo transcends geographical barriers and political differences. It can bring the people of the world together in peace." How precisely that would happen was not explained. At the very moment that Armstrong stepped on the lunar surface, Americans and Vietnamese were killing each other with ruthless efficiency. They continued doing so after Armstrong left the lunar surface. Nixon apparently forgot that Cold War mistrust was the single most important motivation for the journey to the Moon.[22]

The best of American technology and billions of American dollars had been devoted to a project whose real benefit was illusory. One year after his return to earth, even Armstrong had lost hope in the giant leap. Asked whether he still believed that the conquest of space would render war obsolete, he replied: "I certainly had hoped that point of view would be correct . . . [but] I haven't seen a great deal of interest, or evidence of that being the truth, in the past year."[23]

The Moon was not a beginning but an end. NASA suggested as much when, shortly after the landing, they flashed on the big screen at Mission Control Kennedy's famous words: "Before this decade is out . . ." Below was a simple message: "TASK ACCOMPLISHED, July 1969." The message was deeply symbolic of NASA's greatest difficulty—namely, the desire to graft grandiose dreams of limitless space exploration onto the much more finite ambition of the American people to kick lunar dust in Soviet faces.[24]

Nixon, despite the rhetoric, was eager to wrap up the space adventure, in order to reduce the federal budget. "We must . . . realize that space expenditures must take their proper place within a rigorous system of national priorities," he told the American people. His budget office had produced a devastating critique of manned space travel. "No defined manned project can compete on a cost-return basis with unmanned space flight systems," the report argued. "Missions that are designed around man's unique capabilities appear to have little demonstrable economic or social return to atone for their high cost. Their principal contribution is that each manned flight paves the way for more manned flight." The memo, written just one month after the Moon landing, constituted an astonishing outbreak of realism after a decade of somnolent lunar fantasy.[25]

Congress agreed with Nixon. Even before the Apollo 11 launch, legislators had been circling like a pack of wolves. Senate majority leader Mike Mansfield announced that he would oppose any further space adventures "until problems here on earth are solved." Congressman Ed Koch, the future mayor of New York, confessed: "I just can't for the life of me see voting for monies to find out whether or not there is some microbe on Mars, when in fact I know there are rats in . . . Harlem apartments."[26]

The American people agreed. Shortly after the Moon landing, Gallup found that 53 percent of those polled were opposed to a Mars program; only 39 percent were in favor. A *Newsweek* poll showed 56 percent wanted Nixon to spend less on space, while only 10 percent thought he should spend more. A live broadcast from Apollo 13 was canceled by CBS due to lack of viewer interest. In its place came the *Doris Day Show*. During the Apollo 17 mission, instead of showing what would be the last steps of man on the Moon, NBC aired a repeat of the *Tonight Show*.[27]

Cronkite, who watched the space race at close quarters, from Sputnik to the last lunar journey, felt that the adventure was worth every penny. "The . . . space program . . . in that terrible decade of the 60's, played an important part in maintaining a semblance of morale in a country that was very, very depressed in everything else that was happening." He was a staunch supporter of new space goals, no matter what the cost. "How much is it worth," he asked in 1974, "to prove in an era of cynicism and gloom that man can do anything he wants to do as long as he has the will to do it and the money to spend." In the Sixties, that sort of remark sounded uplifting. In the lean 1970s, it sounded insensitive and arrogant.[28]

Those, like Cronkite, who fondly remember Apollo struggle to provide justification beyond the fact that it made Americans feel good. What was the cost of this happy pill? The combined effect of the Vietnam War and the Moon mission nearly sent the American economy into crisis. At various times during his presidency, Johnson was urged to make drastic cuts in NASA's budget. But he refused, because he could not betray John Kennedy's pledge to land on the Moon by the end of the decade. At one point, Americans were urged to forgo foreign holidays due to an escalating balance-of-payments crisis. Americans could go to the Moon, but they should not go to Mexico.

Sputnik had inspired a complete overhaul of American education. Billions were injected into the teaching of science. Yet when Armstrong walked on the Moon, hundreds of scientists with Ph.D.s were driving taxis or collecting unemployment checks. By the end of the decade the United States had thousands of underutilized space engineers, but was short of plumbers and electricians. The lunar module was a beautiful thing to behold, but the Pinto, the pride of Ford Motor Company, had a tendency to explode. While Armstrong rode in a craft made by Americans, an increasing number of Americans rode in cars made by the Japanese.

Armstrong's first words from the Moon will be remembered forever. Buzz Aldrin's were instantly forgotten. He looked around the lunar surface and muttered, "Magnificent desolation!"—unwittingly providing the perfect two-word synopsis of the lunar race. The achievement was magnificent, combining the best of American imagination, courage, and technological prowess. Its meaning, however, was desolate—as dry and worthless as lunar dust.

The Moon was a Cold War battlefield, just like Korea and Vietnam. It was the finishing line in a race for supremacy—not because it was important, but because it was there. It didn't make sense financially, as the voyages of Columbus and Magellan had; but during the Cold War, money didn't matter. Scoring points against the Russians was priceless. Just after Sputnik, Eisenhower had tried to keep the American people focused on what was really important. He had tried to persuade them that they did not need meaningless space stunts to demonstrate their worth. But he had failed. In 1964, he returned to the theme, reminding Americans of the money they were wasting. One day, Eisenhower feared, historians would judge that "here was where the US, like Rome, went wrong—here at the peak of its power and prosperity . . . it forgot those ideals which made it great."[29]

Greenwich Village: You Don't Need a Weatherman

Travel up Fifth Avenue in New York, turn onto 11th Street, and you come to a legendary block. Number 48 is the house where Oscar Wilde rested for several months in 1882 after conquering America, armed only with his genius. A short distance away is the home of actress Cynthia Harris, whose windowboxes are celebrated in the *New York Times Magazine*. The street has, at various times, been home to Dustin Hoffman, Mel Brooks, Anne Bancroft, and Angela Lansbury. Gerald and Sara Murphy, the real-life inspirations for F. Scott Fitzgerald's Nicole and Dick Diver, once lived at Number 50. The poet James Merrill was born at Number 18, a house bought by his father, Charles, one of the founders of Merrill Lynch. That's also the house that blew up in 1970.[30]

The explosion occurred on March 6, when Terry Robbins, busily constructing a nail bomb, wrongly connected a wire. At that time, the house belonged to James Wilkerson, a wealthy ad executive who had no idea that his daughter Cathy had turned it into a bomb factory. Bits of Robbins and his friend Diana Oughton were found by neighbors in unlikely places over the following weeks. Ted Gold, another friend, had just returned from an errand when the house collapsed around him. He was crushed by a heavy beam.

Cathy Wilkerson and Kathy Boudin were also present, but miraculously survived. Near-naked and dazed, they were taken to Dustin Hoffman's house next door. A neighbor provided clothes. In the confusion that followed, they simply melted away, and didn't surface again for more than ten years.

Robbins, Wilkerson, Gold, Boudin, and Oughton were members of Weatherman, the terrorist group at war with "Amerika." At the very moment when Weatherman became famous because of the bombing, the group also began its ignominious decline. That decline was not, however, apparent to diehard members, who existed in a state of deep delusion even when not tripping on LSD. According to the Weather forecast, Oughton, Gold, and Robbins—martyrs of the revolution—would inspire American youths to topple the Establishment.

> How does it feel
> To be inside
> An explosion?
>
> Was there time
> To flash upon
> The way we came?
>
> Came from childhood
> of horror and hope
> To black awakening
> petition and protest
> Massed in resistance
> to their whip and wars
> Came youth on fire
> fighting for freedom
> Naming the enemy
> embracing our friends
> Learning war through war
> in the world revolution.[31]

Weatherman emerged from the frustration that infected radical politics in 1968. Peaceful protest had not ended the war or liberated blacks or toppled the Establishment. A group of firebrands within SDS argued that violence would shake America and "show young people that we *can* make a difference . . . and also that life within the radical movement *can* be liberated, fulfilling, and meaningful." Violence, by provoking repression, would reveal the true evil of the state. "We felt that doing nothing in a period of repressive violence was itself a form of violence," Naomi Jaffe later explained.[32]

Rejecting Marxist class theory, these militants focused instead upon race, lumping American blacks and Third World peasants together as victims of American imperialism. Bernardine Dohrn, a young radical lawyer who had provided legal counsel to Mark Rudd's Columbia cabal, explained: "The best thing that we can be doing for ourselves, as well as for the Panthers and the revolutionary black liberation struggle, is to build a fucking white revolutionary movement."[33]

Whites, because of their skin color, were automatically evil unless they switched sides. "Virtually all of the white working class," it was argued, "has short-range privileges from imperialism . . . which give them . . . [a] vested interest and tie them . . . to the imperialists." Differences of opinion about how to politicize the white masses led to fatal splits in SDS in 1969. The showdown came at the SDS national convention in Chicago on June 18. On that day, an article in *New Left Notes* entitled "You Don't Need a Weatherman to Know Which Way the Wind Blows" outlined a new direction. The title was taken from Dylan's "Subterranean Homesick Blues," a tribute that did not please him. The statement was coauthored by Dohrn, Rudd, Billy Ayers, John Jacobs (JJ), Terry Robbins, and Jeff Jones, a group already calling themselves Weatherman.[34]

Their position clashed fundamentally with the Maoism of Progressive Labor (PL), the dominant faction within SDS. PL opposed all forms of nationalism, including the black nationalism espoused by SNCC. Weatherman, on the other hand, saw nationalist self-determination as the best way to combat American imperialism at home and abroad. They saw blacks in America as a colony and insisted that the black liberation struggle could, by itself, trigger world revolution.[35]

While delegates were debating the Weatherman statement, a group of Panthers burst into the hall, shouting slogans. They focused their attack on PL, branding them "white supremacists" whose "egocentric policies and revisionist behavior" were "counterrevolutionary." Those in the SDS mainstream were confronted by an uncomfortable dilemma. While most regretted the disruption, no self-respecting student radical could afford to alienate those at the vanguard of the black liberation struggle.[36]

With the convention descending into chaos, Dohrn sensed an opportunity. Over the next two days she carefully engineered a coup. On June 21, she called upon the convention to expel PL. "We are not a caucus!" she shouted. "We are SDS!" Without waiting for a vote, she marched her troops out of the hall, fists raised defiantly. The action implied that only those who knew the weather could still consider themselves part of SDS.[37]

Weatherman claimed to be democratic, but preferred mob rule. In 1969, SDS had around 100,000 members. The number who supported Weatherman never exceeded 1,000; active members could hardly fill a bus. Among the rank and file, profound disappointment was felt at the way SDS had been hijacked by an authoritarian gang. "You don't need a rectal thermometer to know who the assholes are," one delegate remarked. The bulk of self-respecting radicals, appalled at the showmanship, immaturity, and violence of Weatherman, took their political commitment elsewhere.[38]

Weatherman worshiped the NLF revolution in Vietnam, but had neither the patience nor the sensitivity to copy that model. Instead of education and indoctrination of the masses, they had in mind an instantaneous miraculous conversion based on the realization that "imperialism sucks." Those who did not immediately convert were automatically labeled reactionary. "Either we push on to become soldiers in the world revolutionary war," a manifesto argued, "or we completely slide back to our respective bourgeois holes and become anti-Communist pigs." The left-wing journalist I. F. Stone saw this as "a typically American idea that revolution could be 'instant' like coffee or iced tea."[39]

After their coup, the members of Weatherman went searching for a revolutionary mass. Adroit logical contortions allowed them to identify young whites like themselves as the most promising raw material. As they saw it, they were oppressed by the expectations capitalism imposed upon them, not to mention the shame of their "white-skin privilege." Youthful alienation would stoke the fires of revolution. In practice, this meant building a revolution from the raw material of the counterculture—in other words, Woodstock Nation. This, however, rested on the assumption that hippies had a political consciousness not already deadened by drugs. In fact, those clear-headed enough to understand their world sensed that Weatherman was just one more group of exploiters. As Tibor Kalman, an underground writer, complained: "Weatherman attempt[ed] to suck off the youth culture in a way that's not qualitatively different from . . . Woodstock moneyfuckers."[40]

Weatherman unashamedly appealed to white youths through the visceral thrill of violence. Instead of "All you need is love," happiness would thereafter come from a warm gun. Rudd and Robbins wanted "a movement that fights, not just talks about fighting." Violence would, they predicted, "attract vast numbers of working-class youths." That was undoubtedly true, but Weatherman ignored the way violence provides its own attraction, regardless of the dialectic in which it is expressed. Before long, bikers and inner-city toughs were joining demonstrations, completely oblivious to the cause they were ostensibly supporting.[41]

Unlike the Panthers, who saw themselves as a self-defense force, Weatherman took on the role of revolutionary shock troops—the advance guard of a future rebel army. The aim was to create "strategic armed chaos"—a nice name for mayhem. According to the accepted theory, demonstrated in Cuba and Vietnam, violence was supposed to go hand in hand with political indoctrination. With Weatherman, however, violence was like a medicine man's potion: a cure for every ill. "Armed struggle starts when someone starts it," one hopelessly simplistic Weatherman paper proclaimed. "International revolutionary war is reality, and to debate about the 'correct time and conditions' to begin the fight or about a phase of work necessary to prepare people for the revolution is reactionary."[42]

Violent actions became a rite of passage—or what the faithful called a "gut-check." Violence did not need specific purpose; mindless brutality was useful in creating chaos, building confidence, and sowing fear. "Kill all the rich people," Billy Ayers told the faithful. "Break up their cars and apartments. Bring the revolution home, kill your parents—that's where it's really at." On one occasion, Dohrn and JJ terrorized passengers on a plane for no discernible motive. "They didn't know we were Weathermen," she later boasted. "They just knew we were crazy. That's what we're about—being crazy motherfuckers and scaring the shit out of honky America."[43]

Revolutionary purity meant that enemies were easy to find. In the autumn of 1969, Weatherman raided Mobe offices in Boston and terrorized staff because of their "counterrevolutionary" behavior. Weatherman's quarrel with Mobe arose in part because suburban parents were joining the antiwar movement, rendering it disgustingly respectable. Likewise, young draftees in Vietnam were condemned for "serving their pig role as counterrevolutionary gendarmes." They were told: "Turn your gun around, or you are the enemy."[44]

Instead of spreading revolution, the Weather egoists spent hours in collective naval gazing, intent upon self-purification. They sought "inner strength," which would come from "digging ourselves." To become "self-reliant Communist revolutionaries" meant "smashing the pig inside ourselves, destroying our own honkiness." Central to this process was the criticism session, an idea loosely borrowed from Che but punctuated with drugs. Because love and affection were deemed destructive of loyalty, relationships were systematically destroyed. The Smash Monogamy campaign started from the premise that monogamy was a form of "dependency . . . in which people held on to each other rather than pushed each other." A person afflicted by love could not be trusted to take the risks expected of the street fighter. Monogamy was smashed by forcing members to have sex with partners not of their choice. "People literally hid from each other to avoid having sex with comrades for whom they had no sexual desire," one former member complained. "Could anything be more absurd?"[45]

The first major battle with "pig Amerika" took place in Chicago. Keen to settle old scores, Weatherman mobilized members for the Days of Rage, to begin on October 8, 1969. "Chicago is the site. It is here that thousands of young people faced the blind terror of the military state; where dreams of grandeur and new life turned into the slaughter of innocence. . . . We are coming back to turn pig city into the people's city." The faithful were urged to "Bring the War Home." "We're not just saying bring the troops home," Ayers explained. "We're saying bring the war home. We're . . . going to create class war in the streets and institutions of this country." Drunk on their own enthusiasm, organizers predicted that 10,000 discontented young people would attack the edifice of imperialism.[46]

The tiny crowd that assembled in Lincoln Park was testimony to the purity of the movement. Estimates differ, but it would be generous to say that four hundred were present, which meant that police outnumbered protesters by about five to one. Despite the low turnout, the leadership refused to call off the action. Instead, its purpose was cleverly changed to reflect its smaller size. Mass confrontation became instead "exemplary action."[47]

Into the breach charged the four hundred. "This is it baby, tear the fucker down!" they shouted. "Smash the state!" Wearing padded clothing, goggles, and motorcycle helmets, and armed with makeshift weapons, they made for the Gold Coast, Chicago's wealthy district. The police, though fully prepared, were nevertheless astonished by the suicidal fanaticism of the mob. By the end of the first night, seventy-five had been arrested, untold numbers were injured, and three rioters had been hospitalized with gunshot wounds.[48]

"Within a minute or two, right in front of my eyes, I saw and felt the transformation of the mob into a battalion of . . . revolutionary fighters," Shin'ya Ono wrote. "All of us lost whatever fear and doubts we had before. . . . Each one of us felt the soldier in us." Violence inspired rebirth. The ritual was repeated over subsequent days, conclusively proving the law of diminishing returns. By the time quiet was restored, nearly three hundred arrests had been made and property damage exceeded $1 million. That alone was reason for Weather pride, but what really pleased the group was that fifty-seven police officers had to be hospitalized. "Offing a pig is more than just hate," one female member remarked. "It's love. Love for the revolution, love for the oppressed people."[49]

As passions cooled, unease grew. Some foot soldiers complained that they had been used as cannon fodder for the maniacal fantasies of the leadership. The Panther Fred Hampton called the action "anarchistic, opportunistic, adventuristic, and Custeristic." The leadership ignored these complaints, preferring instead to wallow in righteous martyrdom. The Days of Rage constituted their Tet Offensive—a military defeat but a psychological victory. "Chicago was an unqualified success," wrote Ono. "We . . . establish[ed] our presence as a fighting force in a dramatic way. . . . As a result, millions of kids are grappling for the first time with the existence of a pro-black, pro-VC, white fighting force that understands that this social order can be, and is going to be, brought down."[50]

The Days of Rage widened the gap between the New Left and Weatherman. Even Tom Hayden struggled to understand: "there was something deeply wrong with what happened in Chicago. . . . Trashing Volkswagens was not 'materially aiding the Vietnamese,' it was just plain random violence. . . . To ourselves, revolution was like birth: blood is inevitable, but the purpose of the act is to generate life, not to glorify blood. Yet to the Weathermen bloodshed as such was 'great.' They were striking terror into Pig Amerika, Volkswagens and all, and their tiny numbers would be unimportant, they claimed, in the vast myth they were creating." Those who dreamed of a popular front to end the war deeply regretted the antics displayed in Chicago. "Nothing could have served the interests of the ruling class more," Michael Lerner complained. He and others openly wondered if perhaps Weatherman had been taken over by FBI agents provocateurs "intent on discrediting the whole left."[51]

The next manifestation of Weather madness occurred at a war council held in Flint, Michigan, in early December 1969. The hall was decked with huge banners depicting revolutionary heroes—Che, Ho, Castro, Malcolm X, and Eldridge Cleaver. A cardboard cutout of a machine gun hung from the ceiling—a harbinger of violent weather. In an atmosphere reminiscent of a revival meeting, members whipped themselves into a murderous frenzy. Among the items for debate was the question of whether it was acceptable to murder white babies in furtherance of the revolution. "All white babies are pigs," some members argued. "We're against everything that's 'good and decent' in honky America," JJ told the crowd. "We will loot and burn and destroy. We are the incubation of your mothers' nightmares."[52]

Flint brought Bernardine Dohrn to the pinnacle of her power. She was the human embodiment of a Molotov cocktail—a volatile combination of anger, egotism, malice, and raw sexual power. Jumping onstage wearing an obscenely short jumpsuit and thigh-high boots, she used her voice like an acetylene torch, ranting against materialism, racism, love, and beauty. "She was prancing up there like Mick Jagger," one observer recalled. "Boys and girls both were panting." Included in her performance was an extended eulogy to Charles Manson, admired for the simple reason that he killed whites and spread fear. "Dig it! Manson killed those pigs, then they ate dinner in the same room with them, then they shoved a fork into a victim's stomach." Before long, the Weather faithful had developed a new salute, which consisted of imitating a fork with four fingers slightly separated and the thumb tucked in.[53]

"[Dohrn] possessed a splendor all her own," Susan Stern thought, "like a queen . . . a high priestess, a mythological silhouette." Within the organization, status was determined by access to her bed. To have sex with her was to be anointed. "She used sex to explore and cement political alliances," Jim Mellen felt. "Sex was for her a form of ideological activity." It was also a tool of humiliation, as Steve Tappis recalled: "Bernardine [was] . . . arguing political points at the table with blouse open to the navel, sort of leering at JJ. It wasn't a moral thing, just sort of disconcerting. I couldn't concentrate on the arguments. Finally, I said: 'Bernardine! Would you please button your blouse!' She just pulled out one of her breasts and, in that cold way of hers, said, 'You like this tit? Take it.' Since relationships were useful to her, Dohrn unilaterally ignored strictures against them. Rudd, disgruntled at his inability to play the power game according to Dohrn's impossible rules, once complained: "Power doesn't flow out of the barrel of a gun. Power flows out of Bernardine's cunt."[54]

Flint revealed that the elite were intent upon taking Weatherman underground—isolating it in its own dreamworld. The decision was perhaps inevitable for a group drunk on drama. It was also a self-fulfilling prophecy: those who could not abide the masses decided instead to hide from them. Toward this end, the last public office of SDS was closed in February 1970, thus completing Weatherman's destruction of the organization. In the interests of secrecy, the group purged two-thirds of its members. The remainder broke into tiny cells and kept communication to a minimum. Going underground was like a neverending game of hide-and-seek. Instead of directing their energies to furthering the revolution, members could now devote their imaginations to the challenge of staying hidden.

Due to the decentralized nature of the organization, most members were surprised to hear of the Greenwich Village explosion that killed Gold, Robbins, and Oughton. That cell, which called itself the Fork in homage to Dohrn's homage to Manson, had earlier firebombed the house of Justice John Murtagh, the presiding judge in a trial of Black Panthers. The nail bomb Robbins was making was intended for a noncommissioned officers' dance at Fort Dix. The attack was, according to Dohrn, supposed to be the start of a "large-scale, almost random bombing offensive." In the rubble, police found fifty-seven unexploded sticks of dynamite, thirty blasting caps, and a number of timing devices.[55]

The Greenwich Village explosion demonstrated that the theory of dying was altogether different from the reality. Ayers calls it a turning point. "It was a terrible tragedy . . . but also a . . . moment to stop and think and pull back from what might have been a . . . really disastrous course." His sister-in-law Melody agrees: "It had always been a question of who would die first. We didn't say it aloud, but we all understood it quite well. If we hadn't killed ourselves, we would have killed others. Deep down, we knew that the townhouse saved us."[56]

On May 21, 1970, Dohrn signaled a new direction in a formal declaration of war:

> This is the first communication from the Weatherman underground.
>
> All over the world, people fighting Amerikan imperialism look to Amerika's youth to use our strategic position behind enemy lines to join forces in the destruction of the empire.
>
> . . . Revolution is touching all of our lives. Tens of thousands have learned that protest and marches don't do it. Revolutionary violence is the only way. . . .
>
> If you want to find us, this is where we are. In every tribe, commune, dormitory, farmhouse, barracks, and townhouse where kids are making love, smoking dope, and loading guns. . . . Within the next fourteen days we attack a symbol or institution of Amerikan injustice.

The choice of words in the last sentence was significant. Despite all the revolutionary bluster, Dohrn had signaled that the Weather Underground would henceforth attack symbols, not people. Bombs would be left in government buildings—courthouses, prisons, and police stations—timed to go off when no one was present.[57]

Over the next seven years, the Weather Underground became experts at blowing up toilets. Perhaps a dozen bombs were exploded in government buildings. No one was killed, though considerable destruction was caused. A huge outcry followed each bomb, but in truth the American Establishment was unaffected by the flea on its tail. The radical journalist Andrew Kopkind, who had once been impressed with Weatherman, quickly grew disenchanted. "It's not a revolution," he argued. "A bomb in Standard Oil's headquarters in Manhattan does as much material damage to Standard Oil as a tick does to a tiger. Universities have not ground to a halt. Draft boards have not shut down, the war in Indochina hardly has not ended. The resources of the corporations and the government that make public decisions and social policy are complete."[58]

In a decade of madness, the Weather Underground topped the lunacy charts. "It sounded like the Children's Crusade come back to life," wrote Stone, "a St. Vitus' dance of hysterical politics." The members' ability to influence others was seriously impeded by their obsession with purifying themselves. How does one explain a group so detached from reality and yet so certain of its righteousness? Kirkpatrick Sale, the chronicler of SDS, offered perhaps the best explanation:

> They tend to feel guilty about the comfortable, privileged, often very rich homes from which they come, especially when they try to take their message into the mangled, oppressed and very desperate homes of the poor. They feel guilty about what they regard as their own inescapable middle-class racism and that of the society that has showered its benefits on their parents. They feel guilty that they are, at least at the start, frightened of violence, and envy those, like the blacks and the working-class youths, who have confronted violence from infancy. They feel guilty that their brains, money, or pull has kept them safe on university campuses while others are sent to Vietnam. And they feel guilty that the society which has given them and their families so much, and which they have spent the better part of their adolescence trying to change, is obdurate in its basic inequities.

The fires of guilt were kept stoked by the war in Vietnam, which seemed to embody every pig evil. But then, in 1973, the last American troops came home. For the Weather Underground, the effect was like cutting off the supply of oxygen. With the war over, it was difficult to find reason to be angry. Rudd began to wonder at the point of it all. "What are we accomplishing?" he repeatedly asked his friends, who could not provide a credible answer. No longer a revolutionary organization, the group had become a ragtag collection of fugitive celebrities.[59]

One by one, they surrendered. The Weather Underground underwent an agonizingly slow death, punctuated occasionally by an explosion that made perfect sense to the bombers but seemed meaningless and quaint to everyone else. The Underground's eventual demise was both predictable and appropriate: the group eventually purified itself to death.

OLD BAILEY: ANOTHER OBSCENITY TRIAL

In Britain, the Sixties began with one obscenity trial and ended with another. In 1960, the jury at the Old Bailey had to decide whether *Lady Chatterley's Lover* was obscene. In 1971, the question was not so much whether *Oz* magazine was obscene, but whether it mattered.

Richard Neville started *Oz* in Australia in 1963, along with Richard Walsh and Martin Sharp. Exhausted by the persistent attention of censorious Australian authorities, he escaped to Britain in 1967. At first, he had no intention of starting a new magazine, but eventually he found himself pulled by an irresistible tide of nonconformity.

What distinguished *Oz* from the dozens of other underground magazines was its dazzling visual display, best enjoyed while tripping. *Oz* was not exclusively about sex, though sex played a huge part. It was instead a manual for life, offering advice about how to live unconventionally. It was, according to Neville, "the sounding board for people with new things to say and nowhere else to say them." Like the shark that has to keep swimming to stay alive, it had to shock repeatedly—a task that became ever more challenging. As Neville later reflected, much of what was in the magazine was simply ritualized conflict in the generational war: "What did *Oz* celebrate? . . . we knew what we were against, but what were we for? Being reared in the thrall of the stale, . . . [we] liked to think of ourselves as lovers of the new, but we defined the new only by tearing into the old."[60]

In the Sixties, obscenity was an expression of freedom. At issue was not the image but its intent; underground editors considered it perfectly acceptable to publish an utterly vile photo of a naked woman, as long as the purpose was to attack the Establishment rather than to arouse. The novelist Sara Maitland later reasoned: "Germaine Greer did not go around without her knickers on for hedonistic delight alone, nor did the *Oz* editorial people publish pictures of Rupert Bear with his cock out for pornographic motives. Libertarianism was of course fun . . . but part of the fun was the conviction that it was brave, important and socially useful, liberating at a global level." In the freedom war, *Oz* was well armed. The magazine was full of naked women (and very few naked men) in lewd poses. "People regarded us as pornographic but we were very serious about what we were doing and didn't regard ourselves as pornographic," Jim Anderson, one of the editors, remarked. "We were into sexual freedom . . . and if we wanted to publish a picture with sexual content, it would also have a point to make." Unfortunately, those who did not believe in the cause were immune to the message. Instead of political statements, they saw naked women.[61]

Despite the occasional police harassment, Neville and his colleagues managed to stay out of the courts until Issue 28 of May 1970, the "Schoolkids' Issue." According to Felix Dennis, the venture arose from the need to be revolutionary. "It was totally innocent." "Some of us are feeling old and boring," an ad in *Oz 26* announced. "We invite our readers who are under eighteen to come and edit the April issue." The schoolkids who responded were allowed to speak out on issues that concerned them, like pop music, drugs, sexual freedom, parental hypocrisy, schoolteachers, and exams. In truth, this meant an opportunity to put into print every puerile fantasy. The cover consisted of a montage of a nude woman, armed with a whip and dildo. While the same woman figures throughout, the repetition of images makes it look like a lesbian orgy. The image which caused the most controversy, however, was a comic strip by fifteen-year-old Vivian Berger. He took the head of Rupert Bear and inserted it in a strip drawn by Robert Crumb, an underground artist renowned for sexually explicit subjects. In this case, Rupert, with a disproportionately large erection, was shown raping an unconscious Honey Bunch K, a character in Crumb's *Big Ass Comics*.[62]

In July, police raided the magazine's offices. Three separate charges were brought. The first was that of obscenity, as outlined in the 1959 Obscene Publications Act, the same act tested in the Chatterley case. The second was a catch-all charge of sending indecent material through the post. Had this been the extent, the trial would have been relatively simple. *Oz* would probably have been found guilty and the editors slapped with a small fine. But Neville, Dennis, and Anderson were also charged with "conspir[ing] with certain other young persons to produce a magazine" which would "corrupt the morals of children and other young persons" and further-more was intended to "arouse and implant in the minds of those young people lustful and perverted desires."[63]

In the Chatterley trial the jury was asked to judge the merits of a work of literature. Since no one accused *Oz* of being literature, the issue in 1971 was more complex. The prosecution saw it as a simple matter of obscenity. The defendants, on the other hand, saw a civil rights case. Neville told the jury: "Because this 'underground' or 'alternative' press is a worldwide phenomenon and because it represents a voice of progress and change in our society, then it is not really only us who are on trial today . . . but all of you . . . and the right of all of you to freely discuss the issues which concern you."[64]

Just as the 1960 trial had focused on Constance Chatterley, the *Oz* court became fixated with Rupert Bear. For the British, the cartoon constituted a desecration of a national icon—equivalent to watching Snow White perform fellatio on Superman. Vivian Berger, who proved a formidable witness, insisted that his cartoon was not obscene, but was instead simply portraying obscenity—a distinction the jury did not understand. Explaining his motives to the defense counsel, John Mortimer, he confessed: "I subconsciously wanted to shock your generation, to portray us as a group of people who were different from you in moralistic attitudes." Shock, he suggested, had been achieved through irony. Rupert, the innocent, naïve, asexual bear, had been portrayed "doing what every normal human being does." Berger also insisted that the images were no different from those circulated by schoolboys at break time every day—a justification that shocked the presiding judge, Michael Argyll.[65]

The trial hinged on the issue of importance. The *Oz* editors insisted that not just the magazine but also its mission was important—that it served a useful social purpose. "So far from debauching and corrupting the morals of children and young persons," Neville told the jury, "*Oz* is part of a communications network which intends the very opposite. It sets out to enlighten and to elevate public morals." In his closing statement, he argued: "We felt it was of social value to find out what adolescents were complaining about, in the hope that when their complaints were published, someone might do something about them. . . . Even if some of the criticisms expressed in *Oz 28* are crude and silly, we believe it was of sociological and educational value that they should have been openly expressed." Trying to make a magazine which was, for the most part, anarchic fun into something ethically important took its toll. "I felt . . . trapped by my own vocalisation of the polarisation," Neville later wrote. "Polarised by the judge, exaggerating one's position, justifying every act as being of the most altruistic motives, when a lot of what happens in life is kind of accidental, random, selfish, a mixture of good and evil." In his own personal way, Neville was forced to make sense of the Sixties before a jury at the Old Bailey. It was not an easy task. "Being placed in the dock and forced to justify everything you ever did on high moral grounds made me feel a little uneasy by the time it was over."[66]

By highlighting importance, Neville walked into a trap. If the jury agreed that the magazine was important but also judged it obscene, he and his codefendants were in deep trouble. Taking up the issue, the prosecuting counsel, Brian Leary, offered a more elevated standard of judgment than that of mere obscenity. *Oz*, he argued, was not simply corrupting individual morals; it was corrupting society. He asked:

What good ever came out of *Oz 28*? What lesson is there for us to learn? Members of the jury, there is none, is there? Save that sex is a God to be worshipped for its own sake, culminating in fucking in the streets, even with minors. That doing one's own thing is an ideal to be looked up to—by young and old alike—no matter how selfish that ideal might be. That a police officer can be called a pig, that cannabis is harmless and that law against it is silly.

. . . We've been through the magazine from cover to cover a hundred times, and . . . within its pages there is not one word of tenderness. That's because *Oz* does not deal with love. It deals with sex—sex with a capital S."

At the time, Neville vehemently disagreed, as he was obliged to do. He argued that "*Oz* was trying to redefine love, to broaden it, extend it and revitalize it, so it could be a force of release and not one of entrapment." In retrospect, however, he decided that Leary was probably right: "[He] had made several telling points. One that struck home was the absence of tenderness in *Oz 28*. It was true. And strangely so, given that we once claimed that love was all you need."[67]

The case lasted six weeks—the longest obscenity trial in British history. Since the jury could not, in the end, distinguish between obscenity and freedom, the *Oz* editors were found guilty. The conspiracy charge was rejected, but majority verdicts were reached on the charges of obscenity and of sending indecent material by post. Britain's liberal establishment was outraged. Writing in the *Times*, Bernard Levin called it a national disgrace. "It served notice on the young that we will listen to them, but not hear; look at them, but not see; let them ask, but not answer." Eloquent as that assessment seems, it is unfair. While the trial started out as a callous assertion of authority by the old against the new, after six weeks it became something more. In retrospect, it seems more like a genuine attempt to come to terms with a decade of baffling change. After years of wandering in a surreal landscape of shifting standards, the British were desperately trying to put down stakes, consult their compass, and figure out their location. Part of that attempt was trying to define standards of decency, a much more complicated issue than obscenity. This was perhaps a futile quest, but an understandable one.[68]

That said, the sentences were undoubtedly vindictive. Argyll focused his hatred of nonconformity on three rather insignificant individuals for the simple reason that they happened to be in his courtroom. During the seven days he took to pass sentence, the defendants were refused bail and ordered to undergo "medical, social and psychiatric reports"—measures clearly designed to humiliate. On arrival at the prison, they had their long hair shorn, perhaps in the misguided belief that, like Samson, their strength would drain away. Virtually all of Britain assumed that Argyll would impose stiff fines, but no jail sentences. Instead, on August 5, 1971, he sentenced Neville to fifteen months, followed by deportation to Australia. Anderson got one year. Turning to Dennis, Argyll said: "Since you are the least intelligent of the three, I shall only sentence you to nine months." The *Daily Mirror*, no friend of the counterculture, was horrified. "OZ: OBSCENE! BUT WHY THE FEROCIOUS SENTENCES?" the headline shouted. Those who had not felt inclined to support Neville, Anderson, and Dennis on the obscenity issue now rallied to their side.[69]

The obscenity charge was quashed on appeal, but the charge of sending indecent material through the post was upheld. Small fines were levied. According to Geoffrey Robertson, the defense barrister, the obscenity convictions were reversed only after the lord chief justice, Lord Widgery, sent his clerk to Soho with £20 to buy the coarsest porn on the market. Widgery had no trouble deciding that *Oz* was tame in comparison.

Was *Oz* obscene? Clearly, *Oz* was a lot less depraved than scores of magazines and films freely available. But the jury had been asked to make an absolute decision, not a relative one. Because *Oz* did not claim to be pornography, it was judged according to higher standards of decency than would be applied to those magazines that clearly were. As Charles Shaar Murray wrote in retrospect: "This was a cultural war disguised as an obscenity trial: ordinary porn, which knows its place and reinforces rather than challenges the social order, rarely receives this kind of attention from the authorities. On the other hand, overtly radical work concerned with ideas becomes instantly vulnerable . . . to mass outbreaks of orchestrated indignation." In their defense, Neville, Anderson, and Dennis had repeatedly insisted that their magazine had a higher purpose than mere porn. In that argument, they were perhaps too convincing.[70]

Oz benefited enormously from the publicity gained at the trial, but as a result became what Neville never wanted. The pretense of social reform was dropped and the magazine became just another vehicle for advertisements. Increased profits fundamentally altered the obscenity issue. Stated simply, if two magazines both contain lewd pictures, the one that makes money is more likely to seem pornographic. Marsha Rowe, one of the office drudges, tried to make that point to Dennis when a post-trial issue contained a photo of a naked female straddling the US eagle. "It has no redeeming aesthetic nor any political allegorical point," she argued. "It is lewd, pornographic." Dennis either did not accept the logic or, more likely, no longer cared. He understood more than anyone that a watershed had been passed. For him, *Oz* had always been a business, not a barricade in the revolution. From the platform it provided, he eventually built a publishing empire worth £150 million, a rather effective rejoinder to Argyll's contempt.[71]

Because the *Oz* trial seemed to express the Old versus the New so perfectly, lines were easily drawn and nuances ignored. Strip away the libertarian rhetoric and one discovers a filthy, puerile magazine. At the time, it was difficult for liberals to ignore this apparently worthy cause: *Oz* became a shibboleth; something symbolic of a generational struggle that seemed crucially important. Nevertheless, some liberals felt uneasy about the cause they were expected to support. One potential defense witness explained her refusal to come to the aid of *Oz*: "I think in many ways that my character was partly shaped by Rupert Bear! My memories were being violated. The arrogant, male, aggressive style of drawing that appeared in the name of revolution worried me. It brought into symbolic shape areas of male antagonism to women that were completely covered up in the old socialist style of the movement. It awakened our antagonism to the way men had the arrogance to portray sexuality in *their* terms." A similar complaint was made by Marsha Rowe, whose experience with *Oz* inspired her to found the feminist magazine *Spare Rib*. "The underground press used sexobjectifying images which had developed from being fairly romantic to stridently sadistic," she declared. By 1971, she found it increasingly difficult to defend a magazine that regularly demeaned women. The issue was not obscenity but degradation. "I . . . was beginning to feel contradictions exploding inside my head."[72]

Oz was prosecuted at a time when it was already in terminal decline. "The 'alternative' society had . . . ended and this was its dying flourish," argued Geoffrey Robertson. "The 60s were over . . . and then suddenly this failing, fading magazine was put on centre stage, charged with corrupting a generation which was no longer bothering to read it." After a brief surge in popularity, the magazine went into liquidation in 1973. For the *Oz* staff, the demise was symbolically appropriate. The age of rebellion, when emotion mattered more than content, was drawing to a close. Readers had grown tired of magazines whose only purpose was to pillory the Establishment. Editors and writers, likewise, had exhausted themselves working within the strict confines of that genre. Rebellion for rebellion's sake had become boring. "Then it was goodbye, thank you very much," Sue Miles said of the final chapter in the *Oz* drama. "It was the end, and I wanted it to be the end." As for Richard Neville, he had no difficulty letting go. "I'd had enough of *Oz*. I was ready for it to go. I felt it had lost its innocence and daring. And all that anger generated by the trial fundamentally isn't my style. I was losing my sense of humour and the magazine was losing its sense of humour."[73]

The counterculture had changed, but so too had Neville. Rebellion by itself no longer appealed. The worship of excess had become facile or, worse, destructive. Years later, he recalled the whirl of emotions felt while writing one of his final editorials in *Oz*:

> With . . . heresy swirling in my head, I sat down with a joint on a Saturday night and wrote a state-of-the-nation address for *Oz*, state of the Woodstock nation: "The flower child that *Oz* urged readers to plant back in '67 has grown up into a Weatherwoman; for Timothy Leary, happiness has become a warm gun. Charles Manson soars to the top of the pops and everyone hip is making war and loving it."
>
> On and on it went; a litany of all my doubts. . . . How my best friends, sickened by the festering malaise of the Underground scene, were cutting their hair, changing their paisley patterns, losing themselves in the front stalls of Noel Coward revivals. While Leary might say that "World War III was being waged by short-haired robots," those who burnt you with bad dope, bounced their cheques, jumped your sureties, wrecked your crashpad . . . were not short-haired. On I raved: how the offices of *Rolling Stone* (visited on the way home from Sydney) were as icily functional as IBM and how its editor, Jann Wenner, was moved more by mammon than music; how Abbie Hoffman, briefly met at a recent soiree in Paris, tended to converse through his lawyer and was animated primarily by talk of

> book advances . . . ; how the legitimate new freedoms were being
> corrupted by selfishness, especially as the gonococcus germ hadn't
> heard of Women's Lib. In short, how we blithely declared World War
> III on our parents, while forgetting to look after our friends.

Rocking the Establishment had given way to making money. Those like Felix Dennis and Richard Branson who rode the counterculture like a bucking bronco eventually grew very rich. Those who vainly struggled to maintain hippie principles found only ignominy and poverty. As Neville reflected: "There have been times later in my life when I've been completely broke, standing in some dreadful bus shed in Melbourne, and said to myself, 'I should have kept it going and become Richard Branson.'"[74]

Germaine Greer, who often wrote for *Oz*, felt particularly well-placed to pronounce upon its flaws. "Instead of developing a political analysis of the state we live in, instead of undertaking the patient and unsparing job of education which must precede even a pre-revolutionary situation, *Oz* behaved as though the revolution had already happened." However apropos that criticism might be, it seems discordant coming from Greer, given her close involvement with the magazine. She has made a career of having her cake and eating it too, usually in front of admiring British television viewers. Her experience reveals rather starkly one lesson about the demise of *Oz*. Those who tried to use the media to further the countercultural revolution eventually found themselves used by the media. In time, the value of the counterculture was measured by its marketability. Somewhere along the road to revolution, Neville and his friends lost their way. Their ability to shock, when combined with their obvious intelligence, good looks, articulate manner, and engaging personalities, made them revolutionary celebrities. The liberal intelligentsia, headquartered at the BBC and the *Guardian*, was only too willing to give these obviously talented people a voice, since any program or features page that included them was bound to attract attention. To this day, Greer continues to milk that cow. But her experience, more than that of anyone else, raises a troubling question: How could the counterculture survive if it relied on the established culture to give it voice? Writing in the *New Statesman*, Neville's friend Angelo Quattrochi, remarked: "Poor misguided children of Marx and Coca Cola, you started making fun of society, but now you're making fun for it."[75]

EPITAPH: IT'S LIFE'S ILLUSIONS I RECALL

On August 25, 1992, Rosebud Abigail Denovo, armed with a machete, broke into the home of Chang-Lin Tien, chancellor of the University of California. The nineteen-year-old Denovo, a member of the People's Will Direct Action Committee, had come to execute Tien—enemy of the people. A police officer arrived just in time. She lunged at him, and he shot her dead.

On Denovo's body was a note: "We are willing to die for this land. Are you?" By "land," she meant People's Park, the sacred ground of Sixties throwbacks. Denovo's career as a terrorist began in the summer of 1991, in response to the university's decision to build volleyball courts in the park. At the time of her death she was on bail awaiting trial for possession of explosives, which police found at her home, along with a hit list of campus officials responsible for that decision. Her death caused 150 supporters to riot on Telegraph Avenue. Denovo, born in 1973, died in the Sixties.[1]

After Reagan won his little war in 1969, People's Park became Berkeley's ugliest and most important open space—informally dedicated to James Rector, the slain protester. Eventually, however, the communal spirit that had inspired the park—and which was supposed to change the world—dissipated in the "me" decade of the 1970s. Sybarites took over: it became a place for drug deals, loud music, and sex, the last of these not always consensual. Creating a better life gave way to reaching a better high.

In the Eighties, that old demon Reagan returned to haunt the park. Now president, his economic experiment created a tide of homeless people. Those in Berkeley camped out under the scrubby trees in People's Park. It was still a place for drugs, but those of despair, not decadence.

Heroin and crack replaced pot and LSD. For most people in Berkeley, the park seemed an embarrassing relic. For the sentimental, it remained a shrine.

In most cities, a generation is long enough for emotions to cool. Not so in Berkeley. In 1991, the city and the university decided to make something of the park. It would still be a park, but an improved one. When, however, workers started constructing volleyball courts, Berkeley radicals revolted, with histrionics on high. Volleyball, it seemed, was a rape of memory. Trouble erupted on August 3. A huge crowd surged down Telegraph Avenue, colliding with 200 police in full riot gear, armed with rubber bullets, stun guns, and truncheons. Helicopters whirred overhead; tear gas blew on the wind. Nostalgia was played out in real time.

The police won the battle, as the police always did. With the park cleared, construction began. Once finished, the courts became a surreal oasis of urban improvement in a desert of anger, poverty, and despair. Sheepish athletes occasionally made use of them, more to make a political point than to have fun. On the sidelines, Sixties sentimentalists shot withering glances and threw sand. Huge political significance was assigned to the simple question of whether or not to play volleyball in People's Park.

For Denovo, volleyball seemed a desecration—an evil so terrible it had to be crushed. She stood at the lunatic fringe of a Berkeley movement which continues to feed voraciously on the myths of the heavenly decade. Every September, new recruits are drawn from pimply-faced freshmen who now listen to "Maggie's Farm" on iPods. They share the ideals, if not the psychotic self-destructiveness, of Denovo. They keep on keepin' on, clinging to the tawdry symbols of an imaginary era of peace, love, and goodwill.

When history repeats itself, it does so in digital sound and color. In 1999, crowds gathered for a celebration to mark the thirtieth birthday of the park. On the surface it seemed that nothing had changed, except for the fact that the ponytails were gray and the pot, thanks to advances in plant husbandry, was a great deal stronger than when Grace Slick sang "White Rabbit." Predictably present was that group of exhibitionists who believe that protesting is best performed in the nude. Young activists, their tie-dyed shirts of recent vintage, sat cross-legged at the feet of venerated heroes who told tales and showed scars of 1969.

Eloquence had not improved. "Right on!" passed for profundity, while "Far out!" was still the hyperbole of choice. Lentils were fresh, but slogans stale. "Who are the cops or the UC, or anyone for that matter, to think anyone has a right to say they 'own' People's Park? Because, hey, the Indians were here first, right?" One speaker tried vainly to inject the present into the past by bringing up the war in Kosovo. "They shouldn't be dropping bombs on Yugoslavia, they should be dropping joints on them, man," he shouted. The crowd cheered this new version of a familiar refrain.[2]

To those gathered on that day in 1999, the Sixties is People's Park. For them, venerating the decade has meant turning it into dogma. Trapped within a cliché, they cannot accept the passage of time. Everything wonderful about that decade is contained in a few shabby acres of dirt. But what is the Sixties and what the park? To hippies old and new, venerating the past means resisting all forms of change. The radicals of old are conservatives now. Defending the park is their way of staying forever young. In the 1960s, those radicals wanted sincerely to improve their world and believed in the power of people to do so. Today, the dream is shabby artifact, something worshiped for itself rather than for what it might inspire.

If the park is seen instead as one point on a historical continuum, then a decidedly different Sixties emerges. Berkeley's decision to improve the park in 1991 was made after a lengthy democratic planning process which arose out of the 1960s campaign for participatory democracy. The decade popularized ideas about beautifying one's living space, protecting nature, and creating public leisure sites for everyone to enjoy. It also saw the beginnings of the health-consciousness movement—all that macrobiotic food, relaxation, yoga, and exercise. Perhaps, then, it is not entirely sacrilege that the people should play volleyball in People's Park.

The music was great, the drugs colorful, the dreams transcendent. Unfortunately that was not enough. The counterculture started from the assumption that changing the world begins with changing oneself. Metamorphosis is not, however, as easy as lighting a stick of incense. In any case, the soul is seldom a match for machines. In the Sixties, fantasy worlds were built on a flimsy understanding of how the real world works; in consequence, they had as much logic as a drawing by M. C. Escher. No wonder, then, that "Reality sucks" became a popular expression in the Seventies.

It was not enough just to imagine, as John Lennon once urged. Nor, it seems, was love all you needed. "It was important to explain to over-wrought eighteen-year-olds that the world crushes naive idealists," writes William McGill, chancellor of the University of California at San Diego, who witnessed a student setting fire to himself in protest against the Vietnam War. While McGill admits he did not remotely succeed in steering the young away from their quest for simplistic utopias, he still believes that "there was something undeniably beautiful about their crusade."[3]

McGill nevertheless objects to the nostalgia merchants who have turned the Sixties into a decade of glorious achievement. "There is a special problem for participants in any era of dramatic upheaval when they attempt to distil the significance of what they lived through. Temptation is strong to rewrite history in order to justify our own beliefs and actions. Memory can be very deceptive. Unerringly it seeks respectability for things done in ignorance and confusion. We all prefer to think of ourselves as moral agents rather than muddled actors in a theater of the absurd." The Sixties was an era of magnificent futility. What seemed profound to the actors in this drama often seemed absurd to those who watched them. Quite frequently, the sound and fury signified nothing.[4]

Rudi Dutschke invested hope in what he called the "long march through the institutions." The concept, an intentional homage to Mao's legendary march across China (itself a sordid myth), was loosely based on the ideas of the philosopher Ernst Bloch. According to the plan, radicals who had been forced into joining the Establishment for reasons of survival could still contribute to the revolution by undermining institutions from within. Dutschke had in mind an army of infiltrators slowly chipping away at every pillar holding up the Establishment.

Sixties romantics find it comforting to imagine that the long march is succeeding, albeit not quite as profoundly or quickly as Dutschke hoped. Yet the four decades since the end of the 1960s have actually demonstrated just how resilient institutions are to the leftists tunneling within. The individualism and freedom fostered by Sixties rebels became not a philosophy but a tool, used by disparate groups in idiosyncratic ways. Writing in the 1990s, Todd Gitlin bitterly observed: "Today pony-tailed ranchers rail against government regulation; antiabortionists claim the mantle of Martin Luther King, Jr.; antifeminists leave their children at home to travel the country giving speeches or blocking abortion clinics."[5]

Those of the Sixties generation who have risen to positions of prominence have not behaved distinctly differently from those who preceded them. Bill Clinton may have been a draft dodger, but he turned out to be a president quite capable of waging war. Tony Blair once played electric guitar, but otherwise he showed little harmony with the Sixties spirit. New Labour—a collection of earnest baby boomers—took Britain closer to the Orwellian nightmare than any government that preceded it. Likewise, the odious intolerance of right-wing parties in Holland is nowadays shouted by men and women who once supported Provo.

After the decade died, it rose again as religion. For quite a few people, the Sixties is neither memory nor myth, but faith. Religions do not require a foundation of logic—indeed, they defy logic. So it is with the religion of the Sixties. Believers in the gospel cling faithfully to a dream that ignores the laws of economics, politics, and human nature. They imagine into existence a world where everyone is rendered peaceful by the power of love and where greed, ambition, and duplicity are banished. Reality itself is suspended.

The believers worship a few martyred gods (Che, Lennon, Kennedy, King, Lumumba) and seek truth in the teachings of an assortment of sometimes competing prophets (Malcolm X, Leary, Hoffman, Hendrix, Dylan, Dutschke, Muhammad Ali, et al.). Their reliquary includes the incense, hash pipes, beads, buttons, tie-dyed shirts, and Day-Glo posters still sold at sacred sites in Berkeley, Greenwich Village, Soho, and Amsterdam. Their gospel is peppered with stock slogans from the Heavenly Decade: "All you need is love," "Make love not war," "Power to the people," "Turn on, tune in, drop out."

The power of the faith, and the equal and opposite zealotry of those who reject it, have impeded rational assessment of the decade. Quite simply, the Sixties has been invested with far too much uniqueness. For the faithful, it was a time of hope and promise, an example to us all. Thus, every glowing ember of that spirit is carefully nurtured, in the vain hope that it will someday flare again. On the other side, the Sixties is used as a morality tale, an example of what happens when freedom is allowed to run amok, and as a convenient scapegoat for all the ills that followed.

Books and documentaries devoted to the decade seldom mention Biafra, Jakarta, the Cultural Revolution, Curt Flood, Telstar, or the Six-Day War. In other words, the links to our times have been cut, allowing the decade to float like a balloon. Those who bemoan the betrayal of the

Sixties spirit are in effect arguing that the decade had no effect on our present, that it was a delightful interlude between the conformist Fifties and the self-indulgent Seventies. Yet this denies the law of historical continuity—the fact that everything develops from that which precedes it. No decade is unimportant; no period exists as anomaly. The Sixties was important, but not in ways that worshipers (or critics) of the myth like to admit. If the Sixties seems strange to us today, it is probably because we tend to look at the wrong things. By paying so much attention to what was happening on Maggie's Farm, we failed to notice the emergence of Maggie Thatcher.

The survival of the Sixties myth says something about the resilience of our spirit, if not about the reality of our world. The decade brought flowers, music, love, and good times. It also brought hatred, murder, greed, dangerous drugs, needless deaths, ethnic cleansing, neocolonialist exploitation, soundbite politics, sensationalism, a warped sense of equality, a bizarre notion of freedom, the decline of liberalism, and the end of innocence. Bearing all that in mind, the decade should seem neither unfamiliar nor all that special.

NOTES

BIBLIOGRAPHY

INDEX

NOTES

Secondary sources of quotations and other material used in the text are listed below by author name and, if necessary, a prominent word in the title to distinguish between multiple publications by the same author. Fuller citations are available in the bibliography. Many of the primary sources used in the book have been taken from the internet. Referencing these is problematic, since website addresses change frequently. Rather than providing a full web address which might prove out of date soon after publication of this book, I have simply noted that the source in question is taken from the internet. Readers wanting to locate the complete document can use a search engine to find it. References pertaining to online journals lack page numbers, as these are seldom available in online editions.

1. Preludes

1. Terkel, 446.
2. Ibid.
3. Ibid., 447.
4. Ibid., 447–448.
5. Ibid., 449.
6. Truman to Cavert, 11 August 1945; Truman Diary, 24 July 1945, Truman Library.
7. DeGroot, *Bomb,* 111; Truman, 87.
8. DeGroot, *Bomb,* 111.
9. Dylan, 29–30.
10. *Chesterton Tribune,* 1 December 2004, quoted in Terkel, 449.
11. Ibid.
12. Katz, 8; P. Levy, 15–16; *Atlantic Monthly,* August 1950.
13. Gitlin, 14; Halberstam, *Fifties,* 142; Sandbrook, *Never,* 116.
14. Halberstam, *Fifties,* 139; P. Levy, 34; Katz, 61–62, 122; Malvina Reynolds, "Little Boxes," *Ear to the Ground,* Audio CD, 2000.

15. Katz, 122; Friedan, 11.

16. Friedan, 11–13; Miller and Nowak, 92.

17. Sandbrook, *Never,* 388.

18. Katz, 25–26.

19. Terkel, 581.

20. Green, 49; Maitland, 210–211.

21. Potter, 83–84; Siegfried, 731; "Port Huron Statement," internet.

22. Hayden, *Reunion,* 14, 21; Maitland, 102–103, 165, 176.

23. Lucas, 255; Siegfried, 737.

24. Hayden, *Reunion,* 178.

25. Kerouac, 225; Siegfried, 737; Kennedy, 120.

26. Szatmary, 59; *Sunday Mail,* 24 May 1964; Booker, 15; Roth, 86; Kennedy, 124.

27. Cottle, 267; McAdam, 19.

2. Premonitions

1. *Transistorized,* PBS.org.

2. *Holiday,* June 1955.

3. *Consumer Reports,* April 1955.

4. Dolfsma, 424.

5. Halberstam, *Fifties,* 473; *Daily Mail,* 2 October 1963; Terkel, 582–583.

6. *The Times,* 2 April 1964; Booker, 236; Dolfsma, 426.

7. Katz, 92; *Daily Mail,* 4 and 5 September 1956; P. Levy, 26–27; Marqusee, 98.

8. Harvey, 266–267.

9. Steve Silberman, "How Beat Happened," internet.

10. Ginsberg, "Howl," internet.

11. Silberman.

12. Ibid.

13. *Esquire,* December 1958.

14. *New York Times Magazine,* 16 November 1952; Kerouac, 8.

15. Burns, 13.

16. Scrimshaw, 254.

17. Halberstam, *Fifties,* 605.

18. Greer, 48.

19. Weiner and Stillman, 100, 104; Maitland, 150–151; *American Experience,* segment entitled "The Pill: Shifts in Attitudes," PBS.org.

20. John Henrik Clarke, "The Passing of Patrice Lumumba," 1, internet.

21. Lumumba, Independence Day speech, 30 June 1960, internet.

22. Clarke, 1; Lumumba, Independence Day speech; Schwar and Shaloff, 495.

23. Clarke, 1; Marqusee, 116.

24. *US News and World Report,* 24 July 2000; Hargreaves, 181.

25. Bill Vann, "The Unquiet Death of Patrice Lumumba," internet; Gibbs, "Let Us Forget," 177; Schwar and Shaloff, 503.

26. Schwar and Shaloff, 617; Melvern, 152.
27. Vann.
28. Gibbs, "Misrepresenting," 456–457; Melvern, 151.
29. Patrice Lumumba to his wife, n.d. (December 1960), internet.
30. *Observer,* 6 November 1960; *Independent,* 18 March 2006; *The Times,* 21 October 1960; Levin, 281.
31. Levin, 284–285.
32. *Observer,* 6 November 1960; *Independent,* 18 March 2006.
33. Levin, 287–290.
34. *Observer,* 6 November 1960.
35. Sandbrook, *Never,* xii.
36. Kennedy Inaugural Address, internet.
37. Richard Goodwin, 98.
38. Sorenson, 99–100.
39. *New Statesman,* 27 January 1961; Steigerwald, 10.
40. P. Levy, 23–25.
41. Kennedy Inaugural Address.
42. Ibid.
43. Carter, 36; Kennedy Inaugural Address; Gromyko to Khrushchev, 3 August 1960, *Cold War International History Bulletin* (Fall 1994), 66.
44. Richard Goodwin, 116.

3. Hard Rain

1. David Sibeko, "The Sharpeville Massacre," 1976, internet.
2. Harold Macmillan, Winds of Change Speech, internet.
3. Sobukwe, quoted in Sibeko, "The Sharpeville Massacre."
4. Sobukwe press conference, 18 March 1960, internet.
5. Report of the Truth and Reconciliation Commission (TRC), Vol. 3, Chapter 6, para. 28, internet; Ambrose Reeves, "The Sharpeville Massacre: A Watershed in South Africa," 1966, internet.
6. "Sharpeville Feature," South African History Online; Sibeko, "The Sharpeville Massacre."
7. "Sharpeville Feature."
8. Reeves, "The Sharpeville Massacre."
9. "Sharpeville Feature"; Reeves, "The Sharpeville Massacre."
10. *On This Day,* 21 March 1960, bbc.co.uk; Reeves, "The Sharpeville Massacre."
11. TRC report, Vol. 3, Chapter 6, internet; Reeves, "The Sharpeville Massacre."
12. *On This Day.*
13. Reeves.
14. Ibid.
15. "A Program of Covert Action against the Castro Regime," 17 March 1960, National Security Archive (NSA).

16. Rusk, 449.
17. Aguilar, 220, 243, 245, 253.
18. Hunt interview, *The Cold War,* Episode 18, CNN.com.
19. CIA Information Report, 6 April 1961, NSA.
20. Kudryavtsev Diary, 14 April 1961, NSA; Gosse, 205.
21. Hunt interview.
22. "The Inspector General's Survey of the Cuban Operation," NSA.
23. Kennedy Speech, 20 April 1961, internet; *Time,* 28 March 1961.
24. "The Inspector General's Survey of the Cuban Operation," NSA.
25. Lansdale memorandum, 16 March 1962.
26. BBC News, 19 October 2000; *New York Times,* 19 November 1997; "Possible Actions to Provoke, Harass or Disrupt Cuba," 1 March 1962, NSA.
27. *Guardian,* 22 October 2005.
28. Trachtenburg, *History and Strategy,* 172.
29. Trachtenberg, "Berlin Crisis," 25, 31.
30. William Burr, "US Policy and the Berlin Crisis: An Overview," NSA, n.p.
31. Benina Gould, ed., "Living in the Question? The Berlin Nuclear Crisis Critical Oral History," 14–15, internet; Burr, n.p.
32. Gould, 18; *Khrushchev: The Man, His Manner, His Outlook, and His View of the US,* State Department PMK D/11, 25 May 1961, internet.
33. Gould, 21.
34. Burr, n.p.; Thompson to Rusk, 27 May 1961, NSA.
35. Gould, 15; Khrushchev, 454.
36. McNamara, 8.
37. Department of Defense News Release, 21 October 1961, NSA.
38. R. Reeves, 174–177; Memorandum of White House conference, 20 September 1961, NSA.
39. Lemnitzer, memo to Taylor, 6 September 1961, NSA; Hitchcock, 220.
40. Gould, 13–17; Burlatsky, 166–167; Khrushchev, 460.
41. Gould, 73.
42. Gustainis, 10.
43. Capps, 46.
44. Williams, 191.
45. Duiker, 126; Herring, *Pentagon Papers,* 57.
46. Williams, 195–196; Ball, 366.
47. Ball, 366.
48. Duiker, 146–147.
49. Truong Chinh, 116–117; Harrison, 145.
50. Chanoff and Toai, 61.
51. Harrison, 173; Race, 112.
52. MacDonald, 82; Lewy, 272.
53. Duncanson, 325; McMahon, 185.

54. Paterson, 243.

55. Schlesinger, 770.

56. Adamsky and Smirnov, 19.

57. Adamsky and Smirnov; Department of Defense Press Release, 21 October 1961, NSA.

58. *Financial Times,* 13 October 2001; CNN, "The Cold War," CNN.org.

59. "Address to the American People about the Cuban Missile Crisis," internet.

60. Rhodes, *Dark Sun,* 574.

61. Ibid., 565, 575; Blum, 87.

62. McNamara, 10; Blum, 88.

63. "Richard Rhodes on the Arms Race," *American Experience: The Race for the Superbomb,* pbs.org.

64. John Kennedy, "Address to the American People on the Nuclear Test Ban," 26 July 1963, internet.

65. Blight, 104.

4. All Gone to Look for America

1. Fayer, 100.

2. C. Carson, *Struggle,* 14; P. Levy, 41–42.

3. Williams, 153.

4. Fayer, 141.

5. Ibid., 106.

6. Ibid., 113.

7. Ibid.

8. Ibid., 109, 112–113.

9. M. L. King, "Letter from a Birmingham Jail," 16 April 1963, internet. The "distinguished jurist" he refers to is Supreme Court Justice Thurgood Marshall.

10. Steigerwald, 53.

11. P. Levy, 82.

12. Kennedy, Civil Rights Speech, 11 June 1963, internet.

13. Ibid.

14. White, *1964,* 206.

15. Schorr, 205.

16. Eisen and Steinberg, 89.

17. Mills, in *New Left Review,* Sept.–Oct. 1960; Savio, in *Humanity,* December 1964; P. Levy, 134.

18. Ross, 661; Jupp, 415; Marcuse, 1.

19. Hayden, 259.

20. Gitlin, 109.

21. Hayden, 73; Kurlansky, 86.

22. Miller, 329–330.

23. Gitlin, 102.
24. Viorst, *Fire*, 195; Miller, 332.
25. Gitlin, 102; Schneir, 30–31.
26. Kurlansky, 87.
27. P. Levy, 143.
28. Schneir, 29.
29. Young, *Dissent*, 361.
30. P. Levy, 142.
31. Lynd, 69; Marqusee, 165.
32. Marcuse, xii, 256; Lynd, 71; *New Left Review,* Sept.–Oct. 1960.
33. Brzezinski, in *New Republic,* 1 June 1968.
34. John Lewis, Speech in Commemoration of the 40th Anniversary of the March on Washington, 24 July 2003, internet.
35. Ibid.
36. Sitkoff, 160; Fayer, 161; Lewis speech.
37. Lewis speech; *New York Times,* 29 August 1963.
38. *I Have a Dream: The Rev. Dr. Martin Luther King, Jr., 1929–68,* audio recording (New York: ABC Records), n.d.; Harding, 123; Fayer, 167.
39. King, Dream speech, internet; Gentile, 250.
40. Fayer, 170; Albert and Hoffman, 240; Gitlin, 146; Malcolm X, "Message to the Grass Roots," internet.
41. King, Dream speech.
42. *Dialogue Magazine,* Spring 1964; King, Dream speech.
43. W. H. Lawson, "A Righteous Anger," unpublished M.Sc. thesis, Florida State University, 2005.
44. Kennedy, inaugural address, internet.
45. Berman, Personal recollection.
46. O'Donnell and Powers, 16; Charlton and Moncrieff, 81; Shapley, 262.
47. Williams, 187; Paterson, 249.
48. Rusk, 442.
49. Berman, 8, 19; Davidson, 302.
50. Herring, *Pentagon Papers,* 73–74, 79–81.
51. Newman, 422.
52. *Scotland on Sunday,* 14 November 1993.
53. Lawson, 246.

5. Call Out the Instigators

1. *New York Times,* 15 April 1964.
2. R. Carson, 2; *New York Times,* 22 July 1962.
3. *New York Times,* 22 July 1962, 15 April 1964.
4. Ibid., 15 April 1964; P. Levy, 53.
5. Patterson, 729.

6. Peter Coyote, interview with Etan Ben-Ami, 12 January 1989, Digger Archives, internet.

7. *Time*, 29 March 1999; Todd Gitlin, "Reassessing the Sixties," 5, Sunrise Dancer website.

8. Steigerwald, 220.

9. Fayer, 242.

10. Malcolm X, "Message to the Grass Roots," Nov. 1963, internet.

11. Blum, 254; Malcolm X, "Message to the Grass Roots"; Steigerwald, 221; Official website of Malcolm X, internet.

12. Malcolm X website.

13. Fayer, 244–245, 250, 254–255.

14. Marqusee, 70; Hauser, 105.

15. Malcolm X website; Fayer, 259–260; Steigerwald, 221.

16. Marqusee, 91, 138; Steigerwald, 221.

17. Malcolm X website; Marqusee, 138–139.

18. *Ramparts*, June 1967; Fayer, 262.

19. Fayer, 261; *Ramparts*, June 1967.

20. Weiner and Stillman, 43.

21. Mark Rudd, "How a Movie Changed My Life," internet.

22. *New Left Review*, Nov.–Dec. 1996.

23. Moreno, 122, 127.

24. Kurlansky, 159.

25. Ibid., 168.

26. Yevgeny Yevtushenko, "The Keys of the Comandante," *NACLA Magazine* (October 1971), nacla.org.

27. "The Greatest," Columbia Records, 1963; *Sports Illustrated*, 20 November 1965; Hauser, 78.

28. Riess, 395; *New York Times*, 27 February 1964.

29. Hauser, 83; Marqusee, 9.

30. Hauser, 82; *Ramparts*, June 1967; Riess, 394–345.

31. Marqusee, 78, 171.

32. Malcolm X, 414; Hauser, 65.

33. Marqusee, 80.

34. Ibid., 88.

35. *Ramparts*, June 1967; Hauser, 135; Marqusee, 142.

36. Marqusee, 84.

37. *Sports Illustrated*, 14 October 1965.

38. Hauser, 139–140.

39. Marqusee, 142.

40. Ibid., 162, 176.

41. Ibid., 175.

42. Ibid., 176.

43. Hauser, 154–155; Ali and Durham, 206.
44. Marqusee, 214–215.
45. Riess, 376–377.
46. Maitland, 37–38; Sandbrook, *White Heat,* 218–219.
47. Melissa Casburn, "A Concise History of the British Mod Movement," internet; Sandbrook, *White Heat,* 220.
48. Maitland, 192–193.
49. Weiner and Stillman, 18; *Washington Post,* 12 January 1969.
50. Booker, 275.
51. Weiner and Stillman, 104.
52. Sixties Fashion Exhibition, Victoria and Albert Museum.
53. Sandbrook, *White Heat,* 224.
54. *Guardian,* 10 October 1967; Maitland, 181–183.
55. Maitland, 39.
56. Maitland, 212; *Time,* 15 April 1966.

6. Universal Soldiers

1. Karnow, 411.
2. Ball, 379.
3. *New York Times,* 5 August 1964; Williams, 236–237.
4. Williams, 236–239; Baritz, 130; Herring, *Longest War,* 123.
5. Gardner, 139.
6. Duiker, 170–171.
7. Johnson, 125, 127; McMaster, 215–216.
8. Herring, *Pentagon Papers,* 114.
9. Jack Shulimson, "The Marine War: III MAF in Vietnam, 1965–1971," 1996 Vietnam Symposium, Vietnam Center, Texas Tech University, n.p., internet.
10. Williams, 243, 247; Kearns, 251–252; Steigerwald, 74–75.
11. VanDeMark, 51, 93; Taylor, 340–342; Schandler, 24; Herring, *Longest War,* 132.
12. Herring, *Pentagon Papers,* 123.
13. McMahon, 233; Herring, *Pentagon Papers,* 123; Williams, 251.
14. Johnson, 151–152; Kearns, 252–253; Halberstam, *Best and Brightest,* 643.
15. Johnson, 149; Emerson, 377.
16. Williams, 253; Gardner, 258.
17. James, 24–25.
18. Bregman, 106; Oren, 117, 125.
19. James, 26.
20. Bregman, 105; James, 35; Bowen, 70.
21. James, 32.
22. Ibid., 31–32.
23. Parker, 217; Amr Yossef, "The Six-Day War Revisited," internet.
24. Bowen, 73.

25. Ibid., 73, 92.
26. Ibid., 95.
27. Parker, 165; Bowen, 133.
28. Bowen, 324.
29. Ibid., 325.
30. Post, "Biafra," 27; Onwubu, 399.
31. Onwubu, 399.
32. Oguibe, 92.
33. Bamisaiye, 32; Oguibe, 86; *Sunday Times,* 12 May 1968.
34. Oguibe, 95.
35. Ibid.
36. Bamisaiye, 32.
37. *Life,* 12 July 1968.
38. Ponting, 231; BBC News, 3 January 2000.
39. Oguibe, 97.
40. Song Yongyi, "The Cultural Revolution and the War against Fascism," 2005, internet; *Epoch Times,* 23 December 2004.
41. Chang, 457–458.
42. Hsü, 831.
43. Hiniker, 292; Hsü, 833; van Ginneken, 62.
44. Schram, 616.
45. "Decision concerning the Great Proletarian Cultural Revolution," CCP, 8 August 1966, internet; Chang, 537–539; *Epoch Times,* 23 December 2004.
46. "Decision."
47. Wang Youqin, "The Past Is Not Another Country," internet.
48. Hoffman, 6, 14; *Epoch Times,* 23 December 2004.
49. Liang and Shapiro, 54.
50. "Decision"; Song Yongyi speech; Pye, 603.
51. Hsü, 848; Dittmer, 330.
52. Dittmer, 332.
53. ABC Online, 16 May 2006; Zhai Zhenhua, 150.
54. Song Yongyi speech.
55. Rossman, 25–26.
56. Sun-Childers, 245–246; Pu Ning, 255; Hiniker, 296.

7. And in the Streets . . .

1. Alan Fletcher, "Quadrophenia: The Story," internet.
2. Barnes, 8.
3. Melissa Casburn, "A Concise History of the British Mod Movement," internet.
4. "The Mods of 1960," 15 May 2002, bbc.co.uk.
5. Jamie Rave, "The Sawdust Caesars of 1964," 15 May 1997, internet.

6. Casburn.
7. Barnes, 15.
8. Rave, "The Sawdust Caesars."
9. *Independent,* 4 April 2004.
10. *Times,* 20 April 1992.
11. Cohen, 37; Barnes, 127.
12. *Times,* 19 May 1964; Cohen, 109.
13. *Times,* 20 April 1992; Rave; Cohen, 140; *Independent,* 04 April 2004.
14. Parliamentary Debates, 23 June 1964.
15. *Times,* 5 August 1964; *Independent,* 4 April 2004.
16. *Argus,* 24–25 September 2005; *Times,* 5 August 1964; Pearson, 75.
17. *Argus,* 24–25 September 2005.
18. *Los Angeles Times,* 11 August 2005.
19. McCone Commission Report, internet.
20. *Los Angeles Times,* 11 August 2005.
21. Ibid.
22. *Newsweek,* 30 August 1965.
23. Boskin, 3.
24. Lydon, 56.
25. McCone Report.
26. Ibid.
27. Ibid.
28. Ibid.; Brown, *Manchild,* vii–viii.
29. *Los Angeles Times,* 11 August 2005; Steigerwald, 211; Marqusee, 186.
30. McCone Report; *Washington Post,* 14 August 2005; *Newsweek,* 30 August 1965; Blum, 253.
31. *Newsweek,* 21 August 1967.
32. Telephone conversation, 18 August 1965, Johnson Presidential Library.
33. McCone Report.
34. Kerner Commission Report, internet.
35. Steigerwald, 199; Elaine Brown, "Until We're Free," Motown Records, 1973.
36. Steigerwald, 214; Kerner Commission Report.
37. Katope and Zolbrod, 32.
38. P. Levy, 131.
39. *Humanity,* December 1964; Katope and Zolbrod, 29.
40. Savio, Free Speech Movement address, 2 December 1964, internet; Kurlansky, 92.
41. Kurlansky, 180.
42. Stephen Smale, "Autobiographical Notes," Bancroft Library, Berkeley, 18; Rubin, *Growing,* 77.
43. Smale, 18; Morris Hirsch, interview with Gerard DeGroot, 6 September 1991.
44. *San Francisco Chronicle,* 23 May 1965.

45. Lucas, 218; Stephen Smale, interview with Gerard DeGroot, 1991.
46. Hirsch interview; *Life,* 10 December 1965.
47. *Daily Californian,* 17 November 1965; Vietnam Day Committee press release, 13 September 1965, Bancroft Library, Berkeley; Smale, 27; Rubin, *Do It!,* 38.
48. J. F. Coakley to Edmund G. Brown (copy), 1 Oct. 1965, Berkeley Chancellor Files.
49. *San Francisco Chronicle,* 15, 16, October 1965; *Oakland Tribune,* 16 October 1965. Rubin, *Do It!,* 40–41; *Life,* 10 December 1965.
50. *Sunday Examiner and Chronicle,* 3 April 1966; *San Francisco Examiner,* 26 October 1966.
51. Halstead, 59–60.
52. Vietnam Day Committee, *We Accuse,* 26.
53. Pas, "Bielievers," 8–11.
54. Teun Voeten, "Dutch Provos," *High Times,* January 1990.
55. Ibid.
56. Ibid.
57. Kennedy, 133.
58. Voeten.
59. Ibid.
60. Ibid.
61. Kennedy, 134.
62. Ibid., 135.
63. Ibid., 143.
64. Pas, "Bielievers," 8–11.
65. Jim Hougan, "Havamarawanna: A Floating Alternative Nursery," internet.
66. "Ordinary People Living Extraordinary Lives: The Civil Rights Movement in Mississippi," internet.
67. Johnson, Voting-rights speech, 15 March 1965, internet.
68. King, "Our God Is Marching On," internet.
69. Johnson, Civil Rights Address to Congress, 1968, internet.
70. Marqusee, 181.
71. Kurlansky, 7; Garrow, 557.

8. Sex, Drugs, and Rock 'n' Roll

1. Leary, 334.
2. Ibid., 324–327, 342–344.
3. Green, 177; Marwick, 311; Weiner and Stillman, 62; Katz, 221–222.
4. Lucas, 220.
5. Unger and Unger, 179.
6. Katz, 226; MacDonald, 15.
7. Green, 55; Lee and Shlain, 129.
8. *Sunday Times,* 20 August 2006; Stine, 131; Pollock, 28.

9. *Village Voice,* 15 June 1967; P. Levy, 45; Lee and Shlain, 229.

10. Green, 29–30, 434.

11. Neville, *Playpower,* 118.

12. Israelstam, 161; Neville, *Playpower,* 103; Weiner and Stillman, 61.

13. Partridge, 60; Lucas, 221; Lee and Shlain, 102.

14. Farrell, 208.

15. Neville, *Playpower,* 60.

16. Ibid., 62, 74; *Guardian,* 18 March 1993.

17. Collier and Horowitz, 86.

18. Green, 419.

19. Green, 423–424; Weiner and Stillman, 105.

20. Robin Morgan, "Goodbye to All That," internet.

21. Gershon Legman, *The Fake Revolt* (1967), 18–19, internet.

22. Maitland, 116; Green, 418; Crow, 62.

23. Green, 419–424; Allyn, 100; Weiner and Stillman, 97; *Guardian,* 18 March 1993.

24. *Sunday Times,* 20 August 2006; Pollock, 182.

25. Green, 424.

26. Ward Elliott, "Sexual Revolutions, Great and Small," Summer 1997, internet.

27. Katz, 423; Maitland, 214.

28. Maitland, 20.

29. Lydon, 9–10; Salisbury, 102.

30. *A Hard Day's Night* (DVD).

31. *Beatles Anthology,* 75; Sandbrook, *Never,* 465, 467.

32. Sandbrook, *Never,* 477; Quotable Sixties website; *Evening Standard,* 17 October 1963.

33. *Daily Mirror,* 7 February 1964.

34. Katz, 180; Sandbrook, *Never,* 676–677.

35. *The Times,* 27 December 1963; *Sunday Times,* 29 December 1963; Ingham, 20.

36. *Free Press* (Los Angeles), 3 September 1965; G. Marcus, 6.

37. Lydon, 15.

38. *Beatles Anthology* (cover); Lydon, 12; Ingham, 47.

39. Lydon, 19.

40. Ibid., 18; Salisbury, 101, 109.

41. Quotable Sixties website; MacDonald, 23.

42. Green, 81; *No Direction Home* (DVD).

43. Shelton, 301–302.

44. G. Marcus, 159, 161.

45. Dylan, 292–293.

46. Ibid., 34–35; Marqusee, 206.

47. G. Marcus, 18–19.

48. Ibid., 154; Lydon, 217.

49. Dylan, 82–83; "Bob Dylan and the White Picket Fence," *Catallaxy,* internet; G. Marcus, 54; Marqusee, 159.
50. Dylan, 115–116.
51. Marqusee, 147.
52. Dylan, 109, 114–116, 118, 120.
53. Shelton, 304; *60 Minutes,* 12 February 2004, CBS.
54. *Mojo,* July 1994.
55. Ibid.
56. Ibid.
57. *New York Times,* 19 August 1969.
58. *Mojo,* July 1994.
59. R. Jacobs, 22; A. Bennett, 66; P. Levy, 279–280; Katz, 284.
60. Michael Wadleigh (dir.), *Woodstock,* DVD.
61. Woodstock Festival Mailbag, internet.
62. Pollock, 202.

9. Everybody Get Together

1. Andrew, 76, 86, 149; *Time,* 10 February 1961.
2. Buckley, i; *The Nation,* 27 May 1961.
3. YAF, "The Sharon Statement," 11 September 1960, internet.
4. Ibid.
5. Hijiya, 206; Klatch, 85.
6. Andrew, 109.
7. Goldwater convention speech, 1964, internet.
8. Silverman, 273; Deleon, 524.
9. *Newsweek,* 30 September 1968; Troy and Greenburg, 5.
10. Braungart and Braungart, 307, 309; Andrew, 76, 86, 149.
11. *Oz,* July 1969.
12. Green, 12, 129.
13. *London Review of Books,* 6 July 2000; Green, 126, 257.
14. Neville, *Playpower,* 211–212; Green, 129, 258.
15. Green, 355.
16. Ibid., 187–189.
17. Neville, *Playpower,* 227; Green, 211–212.
18. Green, 111, 265.
19. Ibid., 130, 257–258.
20. Ibid., 434.
21. Neville, *Hippie,* 164; Maitland, 34; *Guardian,* 18 March 1993.
22. Farber, 192; Peter Coyote, interview with Etan Ben-Ami, 12 January 1989, Digger Archives, internet.
23. Davis, 150; Doyle, "Staging the Revolution," Digger Archives; Coyote interview.

24. Cavallo, 99; Coyote interview.
25. Cavallo, 120; Coyote interview; Coyote, 70.
26. Coyote interview.
27. Peter Berg, interview, Digger Archives, internet.
28. Digger Archives.
29. Digger Archives; Coyote, 90; Cavallo, 122.
30. Grogan, 278; Cavallo, 124.
31. Coyote interview.
32. Cavallo, 124.
33. Katz, 257; Pollock, 122; Coyote interview.
34. Cavallo, 98; Howard, 47; Anonymous, "The San Francisco Diggers Have Split," 18 April 1967, Digger Archives.
35. Coyote, "The Free Fall Chronicles," Digger Archives.
36. Coyote interview.
37. Lucas, 223; Weiner and Stillman, 23.
38. Schneir, 11; Lucas, 222–223.
39. Gitlin, 236.
40. Coyote interview.
41. Hoffman, 61–62; Neville, *Playpower,* 116.
42. Gitlin, 236–237; Doyle.
43. Neville, *Playpower,* 57; Gitlin, 234, 237, 322; Lee and Shlain, 206; Lucas, 224.
44. Doyle; *Village Voice,* 16 November 1967; Lucas, 224.
45. *Seed* (n.d., ca. March 1968), 8–9; Rubin, *Do It!,* 168.
46. Steigerwald, 145; Rubin, *Do It!,* 168; Lucas, 224.
47. Gitlin, 237.
48. Patterson, 660.
49. *The Movement,* August 1968; Blum, 265.
50. "Black Panther Party Platform," internet.
51. Kurlansky, 96.
52. Ibid., 113–114.
53. Steigerwald, 63; *New York Times,* 15 January 1970.
54. Newton and Blake, 148; *New York Times,* 3 May and 6 August 1967.
55. Jones, 257.
56. Kurlansky, 319.
57. *Berkeley Tribe,* 7 November 1969.
58. *Black Panther,* 7 June 1969; Staub, 57.
59. Salisbury, 253–254.
60. McCone Report, internet.
61. Steigerwald, 227; Ganz, n.p.
62. Ganz, n.p.; Drake, 87; Jensen, 167; Chavez, "Letter from Delano," internet.
63. Ganz, n.p.
64. Ibid.

65. Bagby, 77.
66. Chavez, "Letter from Delano."
67. Ibid.
68. UFW website, internet.
69. Steigerwald, 228.
70. *New York Times,* 24 April 1993.
71. "The Fight in the Fields," pbs.org; Steigerwald, 227.

10. Turn, Turn, Turn

1. Krepinevich, 191.
2. Karnow, 482.
3. Braestrup, 49–52.
4. Trewhitt, 235; Shapley, 444.
5. Gilbert and Head, 82; Werner and Huynh, 85.
6. Ford, 81.
7. Oberdorfer, 75; Gustainis, 43.
8. Oberdorfer, 231.
9. Duiker, 216.
10. Herring, *Longest,* 193; Gilbert and Head, 247.
11. Gilbert and Head, 43.
12. Oberdorfer, 241; Barrett, 113; P. Levy, 65; Kurlansky, 61.
13. Clifford, 613.
14. Werner and Huynh, 60; Capps, 133–134; Gilbert and Head, 84.
15. Gilbert and Head, 84.
16. Clio archives, internet.
17. Morgan, 62–63; *Washington Post,* 9 September 1968.
18. Neville, *Hippie,* 245.
19. Green, 412.
20. Friedan, 11, 27.
21. Green, 401, 408–409; *Oz,* Winter 1973; Robin Morgan, "Goodbye to All That," internet.
22. Herzog, 425; Green, 402; Maitland, 181–183.
23. Gitlin, 372; MacPherson, 467; Green, 407–408.
24. Kurlansky, 314; Green, 119, 369, 408.
25. MacPherson, 552; Allyn, 102; Gitlin, 372; Herzog, 419–420.
26. P. Levy, 204; Breines, "What's Love," 1119–1120; Small and Hoover, 179–180.
27. Taylor, 244; Brown, 362; *New York Times,* 17 November 1970.
28. *New Left Notes,* 30 June 1969; Sayres, 94.
29. Evans, 190–191.
30. Zolov, 77; MacPherson, 543.
31. Maitland, 181–183, 215; Herzog, 421.
32. Breines, "Review Essay," 504–505; Maitland, 126.

33. Maitland, 4.
34. E. Marcus, 199–200; Duberman, 161.
35. Duberman, 161.
36. Rutledge, 3.
37. *Daily News,* 28 June 1969; *Village Voice,* 3 July 1969.
38. *Village Voice,* 3 July 1969.
39. Salisbury, 83; E. Marcus, 201–202; *Village Voice,* 3 July 1969; Rutledge, 3.
40. P. Levy, 213; Salisbury, 83.
41. *Free Press* (Los Angeles), 8 September 1967; P. Levy, 215–216.
42. Green, 379; P. Levy, 213, 215.
43. Allyn, 156; Salisbury, 85–86.
44. Katz, 232–233; Perry, 171; Pollock, 120; Neville, *Playpower,* 29.
45. Pollock, 120–121; Wolf, 153, 157, 171.
46. Peter Coyote, interview with Etan Ben-Ami, 12 January 1989, Digger Archives, internet; Pollock, 120.
47. Gitlin, 219.
48. Salisbury, 228; Neville, *Playpower,* 30–31; Katz, 246.
49. Wolf, 172.
50. Katz, 246; Salisbury, 229.

11. Gone to Graveyards

1. Raines, 54.
2. Garrow, 612.
3. King, "Mountaintop Sermon," internet; Isserman and Kazin, 227; Boskin, 14.
4. Garrow, 375.
5. Katz, 259.
6. Resolution of the Communist Party of Czechoslovakia Central Committee Plenum, 5 January 1968, internet; Harvey, 265.
7. Hitchcock, 289; Ulc, 423; Harvey, 264.
8. Harvey, 266.
9. Stenographic Account of the Dresden Meeting between Dubček and Brezhnev, 23 March 1968, internet; Kurlansky, 125.
10. Weiner and Stillman, 49–50.
11. Blum, 290; Schneir, 25.
12. RFK speech, 22 October 1966, Robert Kennedy Papers, John F. Kennedy Library; Blum, 295.
13. Newfield, 186; Berman, 187.
14. Blum, 300; Gardner, 447; Williams, 272.
15. Williams, 275.
16. *George,* March 1998.

17. Johnson, 436.
18. Schneir, 77; McQuaid, 34.
19. Stein and Plimpton, 266.
20. *Los Angeles Times,* 4 June 1968.
21. Kurlansky, 262.
22. Schneir, 111.
23. Neville, *Hippie,* 110; Ching, 335.
24. Neville, *Hippie,* 116–117.
25. Schneir, 68–69; Kurlansky, 284.
26. Schneir, 114–115, 120–121, 149.
27. Blum, 310–311; Nixon, Acceptance Speech at the Republican National Convention, 8 August 1968, internet.
28. Gardner, 516.
29. Blum, 309; White, 441.
30. Zolov, 80.
31. Stevens, 220; Poniatowska, 128.
32. *New York Times,* 19 April 1968; Stevens, 203.
33. Ibid., 41. See also Gilbert, 217–219.
34. Stevens, 204, 214–215.
35. Kurlansky, 338.
36. Fink, 312.
37. Zolov, 28; Poniatowska, 82.

12. You Say You Want a Revolution?

1. Cornils, 108.
2. Mewes, 31.
3. Siegfried, 728, 742; Herzog, 442.
4. Mewes, 26.
5. Cornils, 103; Herzog, 425.
6. Schmidtke, 84.
7. Shell, 672.
8. Cornils, 105.
9. Neville, *Playpower,* 36–37; Shell, 674.
10. Siegfried, 742; Cornils, 107.
11. Merritt, 531.
12. Kurlansky, 154, 156.
13. *Globe and Mail,* 27 January 1971.
14. Columbia '68, internet.
15. Ibid.
16. *The Nation,* 13 April 1970; Garfinkle, 163.
17. Columbia '68, internet.

18. Kurlansky, 198.
19. Hayden, *Rebel,* 253.
20. R. Jacobs, 7; Collier and Horowitz, 72; Katz, 256; *New York Times Magazine,* 9 March 1969; Kurlansky, 208.
21. *Ramparts,* 15 June 1968; Witcover, 149; Schneir, 123.
22. Maitland, 111.
23. Delmas, 240.
24. Katsiaficas, 62.
25. Bourges, 28.
26. Neville, *Playpower,* 15.
27. Kurlansky, 218–219.
28. Maitland, 106–107.
29. Kurlansky, 221.
30. Fraser, 74; Kurlansky, 226; Maitland, 107–108.
31. Reader, 125.
32. Kurlansky, 225–226; Gordon, 45.
33. Gordon, 42; Wilson, 542; Quotable Sixties website.
34. Gordon, 45.
35. Ross, 665; Neville, *Hippie,* 111–112.
36. Maitland, 108–109; Gordon, 47–48; Bennett, *Catastrophist,* 103.
37. Katsiaficas, 66; Gordon, 48.
38. Kurlansky, 233.
39. Marwick, 618; Bourges, 78, 81; Gordon, 52; Kurlansky, 209.
40. *New Left Review,* May–June 1979.
41. Ross, 673.
42. Ibid., 674.
43. Green, 241.
44. Thomas, 282.
45. Siegfried, 727; Green, 255.
46. Crouch, 72–73.
47. Green, 26; Hobsbawm, 211.
48. Green, 56–57, 247–249.
49. Ali, 169; Maitland, 212.
50. Thomas, 288; *Observer,* 21 April 1968; Green, 241.
51. Ellis, 63.
52. Green, 246.
53. Jupp, 416; Green, 244.
54. Green, 240.
55. *The Sun,* 19 March 1968; Green, 243–244; Sandbrook, *White Heat,* 505–506.
56. *The Times,* 24 October 1968; Ellis, 66.
57. MacDonald, 237.
58. Ibid., 227.

59. *Manchester Guardian,* 18 March 1968; *The Times,* 24 and 28 October 1968.
60. Pink Floyd, "Time," *Dark Side of the Moon* (Audio CD, 1994).

13. Wilted Flowers

1. Algisi, 269; Pope John XXIII, Opening Speech to Second Vatican Council, 11 October 1962, internet.
2. Baker, 149.
3. Alting von Geusau, 9–10; *New Yorker,* 25 December 1965.
4. Hasler, 170, 283.
5. *Humanae Vitae,* internet.
6. Ibid.
7. Alting von Geusau, 8, 10; Viel, 47.
8. *Punch,* 14 August 1968; *New Scientist,* 1 August 1968; Alting von Geusau, 9–10; Baker, 145.
9. Westoff and Ryder, 6; John M. Swomley, "The Pope and the Pill," *Christian Social Action* (February 1998), internet.
10. *Daily Mirror,* 11 January 1969.
11. *The Dick Cavett Show,* 7 July 1969, internet.
12. *Sunday Times,* 9 September 2006.
13. Neville, *Hippie,* 222.
14. Green, 282, 310; *Daily Mirror,* 11 January 1969.
15. The Who, "My Generation," on the album *My Generation* (audio recording, 1965); Lydon, 81–82.
16. Maitland, 169; Miles, 297.
17. *Entertainment Weekly,* 21 July 2006; Green, 164; Katz, 367.
18. Peter Coyote, interview with Etan Ben-Ami, 12 January 1989, Digger Archives, internet.
19. Green, 434.
20. Scheer, 43.
21. Neville, *Playpower,* 51.
22. H. Jacobs, 242.
23. Scheer, 42.
24. Transcript of Reagan meeting with professors from the University of California, Berkeley, 21 May 1969, Hoover Institution Library.
25. H. Jacobs, 242; *Berkeley Barb,* 3–9 October 1969; Hirsch and Smale, interview with Gerard DeGroot, July 1991.
26. SDS press release, October 1965; Sevy, 196; Gustainis, 62.
27. Rubin, 38; Nisbet, 11; Kurlansky, 193; MacPherson, 457.
28. Kahn, 208–209.
29. MacPherson, 126; Gitlin, 262.
30. Steigerwald, 110; Garfinkle, 144; Lucas, 223.
31. Schreiber, 229.

32. Nisbet, 16.
33. Richard Nixon, "Silent Majority" speech, 24 November 1969; *San Francisco Chronicle,* 26 November 1969.
34. Brown, 41, 43; Schuman, 516.
35. *Washington Post,* 6 May 1970.
36. Salisbury, 199–200.
37. Ibid., 199, 202.
38. Wells, 425.
39. Michener, 413; Salisbury, 28–29.
40. Salisbury, 209–210.
41. *Berkeley Gazette,* 5 November 1965.
42. Maitland, 212.

14. Meet the New Boss

1. Central Intelligence Agency, "Research Study: Indonesia—The Coup that Backfired" (1968), 71, internet.
2. Scott, 253.
3. Pilger, 38.
4. Scott, 245; *The Times,* 8 August 1986.
5. Bunnell, 32, 44.
6. *The Nation,* 11 April 1981.
7. Sundhausen, 141.
8. Pilger, 26–27.
9. Brands, 803; *Independent,* 5 October 2005; Pilger, 33.
10. Pilger, 32–33.
11. Ibid., 34–35.
12. *Time,* 15 July 1966. Pilger, 28–29, 35.
13. Brands, 804; *New York Times,* 19 June 1966; Pilger, 35, 40–42.
14. Colby, 227; Brands, 806; *The Nation,* 11 April 1981; Szulc, 16; Pilger, 39.
15. Pilger, 26.
16. Dylan, 13–14.
17. Ibid., 5–6, 279.
18. Ibid., 27.
19. Whitburn, 461.
20. Anderson, 52; Lydon, 144; *Rolling Stone,* 23 August 1990.
21. *Oz,* October 1969; Terkel, 582–583.
22. Green, 223.
23. Bindas and Houston, 9, 14.
24. Denisoff and Levine, 117–122.
25. Green, 277; Sandbrook, *White Heat,* 207.
26. *Radio Times,* 16–22 September 2006.
27. Pollock, 140; *Radio Times,* 16–22 September 2006.

28. Vernon J. Christina, oral-interview transcript, Bancroft Library, 20–21.

29. P. Levy, 118.

30. Christina transcript, 20–21.

31. *San Francisco Chronicle*, 9 January 1966; *Bakersfield Californian*, 22 January 1966; Richard Kline, oral-interview transcript, Bancroft Library, 29.

32. Reagan speech, 4 January 1966, Reagan manuscripts, Hoover Institution Library; Stuart Spencer, oral-interview transcript, Bancroft Library, 30; News Release, 9 September 1966, Kline transcript, 29.

33. *Sacramento Bee*, 6 February and 6 November 1966.

34. *San Diego Union*, 17 June 1966.

35. Spencer transcript, 32; *Sacramento Bee*, 25 October 1966.

36. Spencer transcript, 31; *Los Angeles Times*, 7 January 1973.

37. Cow Palace Speech, 12 May 1966, Reagan manuscripts.

38. *Sacramento Bee*, 22 July, 23 August 1966.

39. *Sacramento Bee*, 9 August 1966; Reagan Speech, 2 April 1966; *San Diego Union*, 5 July 1966.

40. Donald Bradley, oral-interview transcript, 191; Caspar Weinberger, oral-interview transcript, 87–88, Bancroft Library.

41. *CBS Reports: "What about Ronald Reagan?"* 12 December 1967; Reagan press conferences, 17 December 1968, 8 January 1969, Reagan manuscripts; *Berkeley Daily Gazette*, 21 February 1969.

42. *Christian Science Monitor*, 9 July 1969.

43. Lyn Nofziger, oral-interview transcript, Bancroft Library, p. 18; *Sacramento Bee*, 16 June and 9 August 1966.

44. *Newsweek*, 22 June 1966.

45. Vecsey, 3.

46. Abrams, 65.

47. Flood entry, Baseball Reliquary website.

15. No Direction Home

1. Green, 318, 336; Neville, *Hippie*, 162–164.

2. Lydon, 173–174.

3. Ibid., 175.

4. Katz, 290; Lydon, 177; Gitlin, 406.

5. Salisbury, 229.

6. Lydon, 173.

7. *Rolling Stone*, 7 February 1970; *Entertainment Weekly*, 1 December 1995.

8. KTVU.com.

9. Salisbury, 230.

10. Police accident report, internet.

11. Edward Kennedy statement, 19 July 1969.

12. Damore, 80.

13. Ibid., viii.
14. Edward Kennedy, transcript of television speech, 25 July 1969, internet.
15. Swanson, 214.
16. Kennedy press statement, JFK Library, internet.
17. McDougall, 359.
18. *Newsweek,* 7 July 1969.
19. McCone Commission Report.
20. Migliore, 445.
21. *TV Guide,* 19 July 1969; Mailer, 70; *Washington Post,* 26 July 1969.
22. Walsh, 95.
23. *Houston Chronicle,* 19 July 1970.
24. Swanson, xii.
25. Statement by President Nixon on the Space Program, 7 March 1970, NASA History Office; Heppenheimer, "The Space Shuttle Decision," n.p, internet.
26. Heppenheimer, n.p.
27. See NASA History Office, Folder 6716, "Public Opinion 1967–69."
28. Cronkite interview, WAMU, Washington, D.C.; *New York Times,* 22 July 1974.
29. *Saturday Evening Post,* 11 April 1964, 18.
30. *New York Times,* 10 May 2002.
31. "How Does It Feel To Be Inside an Explosion?" by Sundance, quoted in H. Jacobs, 292.
32. R. Jacobs, 5; *The Weather Underground,* documentary.
33. R. Jacobs, 8.
34. "You Don't Need a Weatherman to Know Which Way the Wind Blows," internet.
35. Collier and Horowitz, 81.
36. Lader, 279.
37. *Hard Times,* 30 June 1969.
38. Collier and Horowitz, 81.
39. H. Jacobs, 254; Shin'ya Ono, "A Weatherman: You Do Need a Weatherman to Know Which Way the Wind Blows," *Leviathan* (December 1969), internet, n.p.; *I. F. Stone's Bi-Weekly,* 23 March 1970.
40. R. Jacobs, 43.
41. Ibid., 23.
42. "Everyone Talks about the Weather," internet.
43. Powers, *Diana,* 126; H. Jacobs, 202.
44. "Tales from the Underground," *Online Newshour,* 22 August 1996; Ono; R. Jacobs, 25.
45. *Fire,* 30 January 1970; H. Jacobs, 251–252.
46. *New Left Notes,* 23 August, 12 September 1969.
47. H. Jacobs, 85.
48. Ibid., 118.

49. Ono, "A Weatherman"; H. Jacobs, 128.
50. H. Jacobs, 125; *The Weather Underground; Hard Times*, 20 October 1969; Ono.
51. H. Jacobs, 174, 234–237.
52. R. Jacobs, 41; Sale, 628; Collier and Horowitz, 96.
53. *The Militant*, 16 January 1970; Collier and Horowitz, 96.
54. Collier and Horowitz, 75, 77, 87–88, 90.
55. Ibid., 47.
56. "Tales from the Underground," *Online Newshour*, 22 August 1996; Collier and Horowitz, 102.
57. Weatherman Underground, "Communiqué No. 1," internet.
58. *Hard Times*, 23 March 1970.
59. *I. F. Stone's Bi-Weekly*, 23 March 1970; *The Nation*, 13 April 1970; Collier and Horowitz, 108.
60. Transcript of *Oz* trial, 1971, internet; Neville, *Hippie*, 62.
61. Maitland, 13; Green, 383.
62. Green, 386; *Oz*, February 1970.
63. *The Guardian*, 2 August 2001.
64. Green, 392; transcript of *Oz* trial.
65. Transcript of *Oz* trial.
66. Ibid.; Green, 396–397.
67. Transcript of *Oz* trial; Neville, *Hippie*, 320.
68. Neville, *Hippie*, 343.
69. Transcript of *Oz* trial; *Daily Mirror*, 6 August 1971.
70. *The Guardian*, 13 November 1999, 2 August 2001.
71. Maitland, 163.
72. "The Rupert Bear Controversy," internet; Marsha Rowe, introduction to *Spare Rib Reader*, internet.
73. Green, 391, 397–398.
74. Neville, *Hippie*, 235–236; Green, 397–398.
75. Germaine Greer, "*Oz* Trial Post-Mortem," internet; Neville, *Hippie*, 196–197.

Epitaph

1. DeGroot, *Student Protest*, 3.
2. Kirstin Miller, "Chemystry Set," internet.
3. McGill, 225.
4. Ibid., 216–217.
5. Todd Gitlin, "Reassessing the Sixties," internet.

BIBLIOGRAPHY

Manuscript Collections

Berkeley Chancellor Files, University of California, Berkeley.
Dwight Eisenhower Papers, Eisenhower Library, Abilene, Kansas.
Lyndon Johnson Papers, Johnson Library, Austin, Texas.
John Kennedy Papers, Kennedy Library, Boston, Massachusetts.
Robert Kennedy Papers, Kennedy Library, Boston, Massachusetts.
NASA History Office, Washington, D.C.
National Security Agency (NSA), Washington, D.C.
Ronald Reagan Gubernatorial Papers, Hoover Institution, Stanford University.
Social Protest Project, Bancroft Library, University of California, Berkeley.
Harry Truman Papers, Truman Library, Independence, Missouri.

Books and Articles

Abrams, Roger. *Legal Bases: Baseball and the Law.* Philadelphia, 1998.
Adamsky, Viktor, and Yuri Smirnov. "Moscow's Biggest Bomb: The 50-Megaton Test of October 1961." *Cold War International History Project Bulletin* (Fall 1994).
Aguilar, Luis. *Operation ZAPATA: The "Ultrasensitive" Report and Testimony of the Board of Inquiry on the Bay of Pigs.* New York, 1981.
Algisi, Leone. *John XXIII: A Biography.* New York, 1963.
Ali, Muhammad, with Richard Durham. *The Greatest: My Own Story.* Chicago, 1976.
Ali, Tariq. *Street Fighting Years: An Autobiography of the Sixties.* London, 1987.
Allison, G., and P. Zelikow. *Essence of Decision: Explaining the Cuban Missile Crisis.* 2nd ed. New York, 1999.
Allyn, David. *Make Love, Not War: The Sexual Revolution—An Unfettered History.* New York, 2000.
Alting von Geusau, Leo. "International Reaction to the Encyclical *Humanae Vitae*." *Studies in Family Planning,* 1 (1970).

Anderson, David L., ed. *Shadow on the White House*. Lawrence, Kans., 1993.

Anderson, Terry. "American Popular Music and the War in Vietnam." *Peace and Change*, 11 (1986).

Andrew, John A. *The Other Side of the Sixties: Young Americans for Freedom and the Rise of Conservative Politics*. New Brunswick, N.J., 1997.

Auslander, H. Ben. "'If Ya Wanna End the War and Stuff, You Gotta Sing Loud': A Survey of Vietnam-Related Protest Music." *Journal of American Culture*, 4 (1981).

Bagby, Beth. "El Teatro Campesino Interviews with Luis Valdez." *Tulane Drama Review*, 11 (1967).

Baker, Jeffrey. "Science, Birth Control, and the Roman Catholic Church." *Bioscience*, 20 (February 1970).

Ball, George. *The Past Has Another Pattern*. New York, 1982.

Ball, Moya Ann. *Vietnam-on-the-Potomac*. New York, 1992.

Bamisaiye, Adepitan. "The Nigerian Civil War in the International Press." *Transition*, 44 (1974).

Baritz, Loren. *Backfire*. New York, 1985.

Barnes, Richard. *Mods!* London, 1989.

Barrett, David. *Uncertain Warriors*. Lawrence, Kans., 1993.

—— ed. *Lyndon B. Johnson's Vietnam Papers*. College Station, Tex., 1997.

Baskir, Lawrence, and William Strauss. *Chance and Circumstance*. New York, 1978.

Beatles. *The Beatles Anthology*. London, 2000.

Benjamin, Marina. *Rocket Dreams*. New York, 2003.

Bennett, Andy. *Remembering Woodstock*. Aldershot, U.K., 2004.

Bennett, Ronan. *The Catastrophist*. London, 1999.

Bergaust, Erik. *Wernher von Braun*. Washington, D.C., 1976.

Berger, Dan. *Outlaws in America*. Oakland, Calif., 1996.

Bergerud, Eric. *The Dynamics of Defeat*. Boulder, Colo., 1991.

—— *Red Thunder, Tropic Lightning*. New York, 1994.

Berkowitz, W. R. "The Impact of Anti-Vietnam Demonstrations upon National Public Opinion and Military Indicators." *Social Science Research*, 2 (1973).

Berman, Larry. *Planning a Tragedy*. New York, 1982.

—— *Lyndon Johnson's War*. New York, 1989.

Bethe, Hans. "Sakharov's H-Bomb." *Bulletin of the Atomic Scientists* (October 1990).

Bindas, Kenneth, and Craig Houston. "'Takin' Care of Business': Rock Music, Vietnam and the Protest Myth." *The Historian*, 52 (1989).

Blake, J. Herman. "Black Nationalism." *Annals of the Academy of Political and Social Science*, 382 (March 1969).

Blight, James G., and David A. Welch. *On the Brink: Americans and Soviets Re-Examine the Cuban Missile Crisis*. New York, 1989.

Bloom, Alexander, and Winni Breines. *Takin' It to the Streets: A Sixties Reader*. New York, 1995.

Blum, John. *Years of Discord*. New York, 1991.

Booker, Christopher. *The Neophiliacs.* London, 1970.

Boskin, Joseph. "The Revolt of the Urban Ghettoes, 1964–1967." *Annals of the Academy of Political and Social Science,* 382 (March 1969).

Bourges, Hervé, ed. *The French Student Revolt: The Leaders Speak.* Trans. B. R. Brewster. New York, 1968.

Bouvier, Leon. "Catholics and Contraception." *Journal of Marriage and Family,* 34 (August 1972).

Bowen, Jeremy. *Six Days.* London, 2004.

Boyer, Paul. *Fallout.* Columbus, Ohio, 1998.

Braestrup, Peter. *Big Story.* Novato, Calif., 1994.

Branch, Taylor. *Parting the Waters: America in the King Years, 1954–1963.* New York, 1988.

Brands, H. W. "The Limits of Manipulation: How the US Didn't Topple Sukarno." *Journal of American History,* 76 (1989).

Braungart, Margaret, and Richard Braungart. "The Effects of the 1960s Political Generation on Former Left- and Right-Wing Youth Activist Leaders." *Social Problems,* 38 (1991).

Bregman, Ahron. *A History of Israel.* London, 2003.

Breines, Wini. "Review Essay." *Feminist Studies,* 5 (1979).

—— "What's Love Got to Do with It? White Women, Black Women, and Feminists in the Movement Years." *Signs,* 27 (Summer 2002).

Brown, Claude. *Manchild in a Promised Land.* New York, 1965.

Brown, Elaine. *A Taste of Power: A Black Woman's Story.* New York, 1994.

Brown, L. Neville. "Student Protest in England." *American Journal of Comparative Law,* 17 (1969).

Brown, Sam. "The Politics of Peace." *Washington Monthly,* 2 (August 1970).

Buckley, William F., Jr. *God and Man at Yale: The Superstitions of "Academic Freedom."* Chicago, 1951.

Bunnell, Frederick. "American 'Low Posture' Policy toward Indonesia in the Months Leading Up to the 1965 'Coup.'" *Indonesia,* 50 (1990).

Burlatsky, Fyodor. *Khrushchev and the First Russian Spring: The Era of Khrushchev through the Eyes of His Advisor.* Trans. Daphne Skillen. New York, 1988.

Burns, Glen. *Great Poets Howl: A Study of Allen Ginsberg's Poetry, 1943–1955.* Frankfurt am Main, 1983.

Burrows, William. *This New Ocean.* New York, 1999.

Butler, Basil. *The Theology of Vatican II.* New York, 1967.

Capps, Walter. *The Vietnam Reader.* New York, 1991.

Carson, Clayborne. *In Struggle: SNCC and the Black Awakening of the 1960s.* Cambridge, Mass., 1981.

—— et al., eds. *The Eyes on the Prize Civil Rights Reader: Documents, Speeches, and Firsthand Accounts from the Black Freedom Struggle, 1954–1990.* New York, 1991.

Carson, Rachel. *Silent Spring.* Boston, 1962.

Carter, Burnham. "President Kennedy's Inaugural Address." *College Composition and Communication,* 14 (1963).

Carter, Dale. *The Final Frontier.* London, 1988.

Cavallo, Dominick. *A Fiction of the Past: The Sixties in American History.* New York, 1999.

Chaikin, Andrew. *A Man on the Moon.* New York, 1998.

Chang, Jung, and Jon Halliday. *Mao: The Unknown Story.* London, 2006.

Chanoff, David, and Doan Van Toai. *Vietnam: A Portrait of Its People at War.* London, 1996.

Charlton, Michael, and Anthony Moncrieff. *Many Reasons Why.* New York, 1978.

Cheng Yi. *Scarlet Memorial: Tales of Cannibalism in Modern China.* New York, 1996.

Ching, Barbara. "Groove Tube: The Revolution as It Was Televised." *American Quarterly,* 54 (2002).

Clifford, Clark. "A Vietnam Reappraisal: The Personal History of One Man's View and How It Evolved." *Foreign Affairs* (July 1969).

Cohen, Stanley. *Folk Devils and Moral Panics: The Creation of the Mods and Rockers.* London, 1972.

Colby, William. *Honorable Men: My Life in the CIA.* New York, 1978.

Collier, Peter, and David Horowitz. *Destructive Generation.* New York, 1990.

Cooper, David. *The Dialectics of Liberation.* Harmondsworth, U.K., 1968.

Cornils, Ingo. "Rudi Dutschke's Long March." In DeGroot, ed., *Student Protest.* London, 1998.

Cottle, Thomas. *Time's Children.* Boston, 1971.

Coyote, Peter. *Sleeping Where I Fall.* Washington, D.C., 1998.

Crouch, Colin. *The Student Revolt.* London, 1970.

Crow, Barbara. *Radical Feminism: A Documentary Reader.* New York, 2000.

Curtis, James. "Toward a Sociotechnological Interpretation of Popular Music in the Electronic Age." *Technology and Culture,* 25 (1984).

Damore, Leo. *Senatorial Privilege.* New York, 1988.

Davidson, Phillip. *Vietnam at War.* Oxford, 1988.

Davis, R. G. *The San Francisco Mime Troupe: The First Ten Years.* San Francisco, 1975.

Dean, Eric. "The Myth of the Troubled and Scorned Vietnam Veteran." *Journal of American Studies,* 26 (1992).

DeBenedetti, Charles. *An American Ordeal: The Antiwar Movement of the Vietnam Era.* Syracuse, N.Y., 1990.

Debray, Régis. *Revolution in the Revolution? Armed Struggle and Political Struggle in Latin America.* New York, 1967.

—— "A Modest Contribution to the Rites and Ceremonies of the Tenth Anniversary." *New Left Review* (May–June 1979).

DeGroot, Gerard, "The Limits of Moral Protest and Participatory Democracy: The Vietnam Day Committee." *Pacific Historical Review,* 44 (1995).

—— "Ronald Reagan and Student Unrest in California, 1966–1970." *Pacific Historical Review*, 65 (1996).

—— *The Bomb: A Life*. London, 2004.

——, ed. *Student Protest: The Sixties and After*. London, 1998.

Deleon, David. "The American as Anarchist: Social Criticism in the 1960s." *American Quarterly*, 25 (1973).

Delmas, Jean. "Military Power in France." In E. diNolfo, ed., *Power in Europe, II: Great Britain, France, Germany and the Origins of the EEC, 1952–72*. Berlin, 1992.

Denisoff, R. Serge, and Mark Levine. "The Popular Protest Song: The Case of 'Eve of Destruction.'" *Public Opinion Quarterly*, 35 (1971).

Diamond, Edwin. *The Rise and Fall of the Space Age*. New York, 1964.

—— "The Dark Side of the Moon Coverage." *Columbia Journalism Review* (Fall 1969).

Dickson, Paul. *Sputnik*. New York, 2001.

Dickstein, Morris. *Gates of Eden: American Culture in the Sixties*. New York, 1977.

Dittmer, Lowell. "Mao and the Politics of Revolutionary Mortality." *Asian Survey*, 27 (1987).

Divine, Robert. *The Johnson Years, Vol. 2: Vietnam, the Environment and Science*. Lawrence, Kans., 1987.

Dixon-Mueller, Ruth. *Population Policy and Women's Rights: Transforming Reproductive Choice*. Westport, Conn., 1993.

Dolfsma, Wilfred. "Consuming Pop Music / Constructing a Life World." *International Journal of Cultural Studies*, 7 (2004).

Drake, Susan. *Fields of Courage*. Santa Cruz, Calif., 1999.

Duberman, Martin. *Cures: A Gay Man's Odyssey*. New York, 1991.

Duiker, William. *Sacred War*. New York, 1995.

—— *The Communist Road to Power in Vietnam*. Boulder, Colo., 1981.

Duncanson, Dennis. *Government and Revolution in Vietnam*. New York, 1968.

Dylan, Bob. *Chronicles, Volume 1*. New York, 2004.

Ehrhart, William. *In the Shadow of Vietnam: Essays, 1977–1991*. Jefferson, N.C., 1977.

Eisen, Jonathan. *The Age of Rock*. New York, 1969.

—— and David Steinberg. "The Student Revolt against Liberalism." *Annals of the Academy of Political and Social Science*, 382 (March 1969).

Ellis, Sylvia. "'A Demonstration of British Good Sense?': British Student Protest during the Vietnam War." In DeGroot, ed., *Student Protest*. London, 1998.

Emerson, Gloria. *Winners and Losers*. New York, 1992.

Evans, Richard. *Feminists*. London, 1977.

Farber, David. *The Sixties: From Memory to History*. Durham, N.C., 1994.

Farrell, James. *The Spirit of the Sixties: The Making of Postwar Radicalism*. New York, 1999.

Fink, Carole, Philipp Gassert, and Detlef Junker, eds. *1968: The World Transformed*. Cambridge, 1998.

Flood, Curt. *The Way It Is.* New York, 1970.

Foot, Michael. *Dr Strangelove, I Presume.* London, 1999.

Ford, Ronnie. *Tet 1968: Understanding the Surprise.* London, 1995.

Fraser, Robert. *1968: A Student Generation in Revolt.* London, 1988.

Friedan, Betty. *The Feminine Mystique.* New York, 1963.

Ganz, Marshall. "The Power of Story in Social Movements." Paper presented at the annual meeting of the American Sociological Association, 2001.

Gardner, Lloyd. *Pay Any Price.* Chicago, 1995.

Garfinkle, Adam. *Telltale Hearts.* Basingstoke, U.K., 1995.

Garrow, David. *Bearing the Cross.* New York, 1986.

Gentile, Thomas. *March on Washington: August 28, 1963.* Washington, D.C., 1983.

Gibbs, David. "Let Us Forget Unpleasant Memories: The US State Department's Analysis of the Congo Crisis." *Journal of Modern African Studies,* 33 (1995).

—— "Misrepresenting the Congo Crisis." *African Affairs,* 95 (1996).

Gilbert, Marc Jason, and William Head, eds. *The Tet Offensive.* Westport, Conn., 1996.

Gitlin, Todd. *The Sixties: Years of Hope, Days of Rage.* New York, 1987.

Goodwin, Doris Kearns. *Lyndon Johnson and the American Dream.* New York, 1976.

Goodwin, Richard. *Remembering America: A Voice from the Sixties.* New York, 1989.

Gordon, Bertram. "The Eyes of the Marcher: Paris, May 1968—Theory and Its Consequences." In DeGroot, ed., *Student Protest.* London, 1998.

Gosse, Van. *Where the Boys Are: Cuba, Cold War America and the Making of a New Left.* London, 1993.

Gott, Richard. "Che Guevara and the Congo." *New Left Review* (November–December 1996).

Green, Jonathan. *Days in the Life.* London, 1988.

Greer, Germaine. *The Female Eunuch.* London, 1970.

Grogan, Emmett. *Ringolevio: A Life Played for Keeps.* New York, 1990.

Grossman, Andrew. *Neither Dead Nor Red.* New York, 2001.

Gunther, John. *Inside Russia Today.* New York, 1962.

Gurley Brown, Helen. *Sex and the Single Girl.* New York, 1962.

Gustainis, J. Justin. *American Rhetoric and the Vietnam War.* Westport, Conn., 1993.

Guttmann, Allen. "Protest against the War in Vietnam." *Annals of the Academy of Political and Social Science,* 382 (March 1969).

Halberstam, David. *The Making of a Quagmire.* New York, 1964.

—— *The Best and the Brightest.* New York, 1972.

Halstead, Fred. *Out Now.* New York, 1978.

Hampton, Henry, and Steve Fayer, with Sarah Flynn, eds. *Voices of Freedom: An Oral History of the Civil Rights Movement, from the 1950s through the 1980s.* New York, 1990.

Hargreaves, John. *Decolonization in Africa.* London, 1988.

Harrison, James. *The Endless War.* New York, 1989.

Harvey, Robert. *Comrades: The Rise and Fall of World Communism.* London, 2003.

Hasler, August. *How the Pope Became Infallible.* New York, 1979.

Hauser, Thomas. *Muhammad Ali: His Life and Times.* New York, 1991.

Hayden, Tom. *Reunion.* New York, 1988.

—— *Rebel: A Personal History of the 1960s.* Los Angeles, 2003.

Heineman, Kenneth. *Campus Wars.* New York, 1993.

Herring, George C. *America's Longest War.* New York, 1986.

—— *LBJ and Vietnam.* Austin, 1994.

—— ed. *The Pentagon Papers: Abridged Edition.* New York, 1993.

Herzog, Dagmar. "Pleasure, Sex, and Politics Belong Together: Post-Holocaust Memory and the Sexual Revolution in West Germany." *Critical Inquiry,* 24 (Winter 1998).

Heuser, Beatrice. *The Bomb: Nuclear Weapons in Their Historical, Strategic, and Ethical Context.* New York, 2000.

Hijiya, James. "The Conservative 1960s." *Journal of American Studies,* 37 (2003).

Hiniker, Paul. "The Cultural Revolution Revisited: Dissonance Reduction or Power Maximization." *China Quarterly,* 94 (1983).

Hinton, James. *Protests and Visions: Peace Politics in Twentieth-Century Britain.* London, 1989.

Hitchcock, William. *The Struggle for Europe.* London, 2003.

Ho Chi Minh. *Selected Writings.* Hanoi, 1973.

Hobsbawm, Eric. *Interesting Times: A Twentieth Century Life.* London, 2002.

Hoffman, Abbie. *Revolution for the Hell of It.* New York, 1968.

Holland, Max. "After Thirty Years: Making Sense of the Assassination." *Reviews in American History,* 22 (June 1994).

Holloway, David. *The Soviet Union and the Arms Race.* New Haven, 1984.

—— *Stalin and the Bomb.* New Haven, 1994.

—— "Soviet Nuclear History." *Cold War International History Project Bulletin* (Fall 1994).

Howard, John. "The Flowering of the Hippie Movement." *Annals of the American Academy of Political and Social Science,* 382 (March 1969).

Hsü, Immanuel. *The Rise of Modern China.* Oxford, 1976.

Hunt, Michael. *Lyndon Johnson's War.* New York, 1996.

Hunt, Richard. *Pacification.* Boulder, Colo., 1995.

—— and Richard Shultz, eds. *Lessons from an Unconventional War.* New York, 1982.

Huntington, Samuel. "Vietnam Reappraised." *International Security,* 6 (Summer 1981).

Ingham, Chris. *The Beatles.* London, 2003.

Israelstam, David. "Selected Bibliography in Marijuana and LSD-Type Drugs." *California Law Review,* 56 (January 1968).

Isserman, Maurice, and Michael Kazin. *America Divided: The Civil War of the 1960s.* New York, 2000.

Jacobs, Harold, ed. *Weatherman.* Berkeley, 1970.

Jacobs, Ron. *The Way the Wind Blew.* New York, 1997.

James, Laura. "Nasser and His Enemies: Foreign Policy Decision Making in Egypt on the Eve of the Six-Day War." *Middle East Review of International Affairs,* 9 (2005).

Jeffreys-Jones, Rhodri. *Peace Now!* New Haven, 1999.

Jennings, Anthony, ed. *Justice under Fire.* London, 1990.

Jensen, Richard, and John Hammerback. *The Words of Cesar Chavez.* College Station, Tex., 2002.

Jensen, Richard, et al. "Martyrs for a Just Cause: The Eulogies of Cesar Chavez." *Western Journal of Communication,* 67 (2003).

Johnson, Lyndon. *The Vantage Point.* New York, 1971.

Jones, Charles. *The Black Panther Party (Reconsidered).* Baltimore, 1998.

Jupp, James. "The Discontents of Youth." *Political Quarterly,* 40 (1969).

Kahn, Roger. *The Boys of Summer.* New York, 1972.

Kaiser, Charles. *1968 in America.* New York, 1988.

Kaplan, Fred. *The Wizards of Armageddon.* Stanford, 1983.

Karnow, Stanley. *Vietnam: A History.* Harmondsworth, U.K., 1993.

Katope, Christopher, and Paul Zolbrod. *Beyond Berkeley.* New York, 1966.

Katsiaficas, George. *The Imagination of the New Left.* New York, 1987.

Katz, Donald. *Home Fires.* New York, 1993.

Kauffman, James. *Selling Outer Space.* Tuscaloosa, Ala., 1994.

Keely, Charles. "Limits to Papal Power: Vatican Influence after *Humanae Vitae.*" *Population and Development Review,* 20 (1994).

Kennedy, James. *Nieuw Babylon in Aanbouw: Nederland in de jaren zestig* [Building New Babylon: The Netherlands in the Sixties]. Amsterdam, 1999.

Kerouac, Jack. *On the Road.* London, 1972.

Kerr, Jean. *Please Don't Eat the Daisies.* New York, 1957.

Khrushchev, N. S. *Khrushchev Remembers: The Last Testament.* New York, 1974.

Klatch, Rebecca. *A Generation Divided: The New Left, the New Right, and the 1960s.* Berkeley, 1999.

Klein, Michael, ed. *The Vietnam Era: Media and Popular Culture in the US and Vietnam.* London, 1990.

Kolko, Gabriel. *Confronting the Third World.* New York, 1988.

—— *Anatomy of a War.* New York, 1994.

Krepinevich, Andrew. *The Army and Vietnam.* Baltimore, 1986.

Kurlansky, Mark. *1968: The Year that Rocked the World.* London, 2004.

Kuzmiak, D. T. "The American Environmental Movement." *Geographical Journal,* 157 (1991).

Lader, Lawrence. *Power on the Left.* New York, 1979.

Launius, Roger, and Howard McCurdy, eds. *Spaceflight and the Myth of Presidential Leadership.* Urbana, Ill., 1997.

Lawson, Mark. *Idlewild.* London, 1995.

Leary, Timothy. "The Religious Experience: Its Production and Interpretation." *Psychedelic Review*, 1 (1963).

Lee, Martin A., and Bruce Shlain. *Acid Dreams: The Complete Social History of LSD, the CIA, the Sixties, and Beyond*. New York, 1992.

Lemarchand, René. "The CIA in Africa: How Central? How Intelligent?" *Journal of Modern African Studies*, 14 (1976).

Levin, Bernard. *The Pendulum Years*. London, 1989.

Levy, Jacques. *Cesar Chavez: Autobiography of La Causa*. New York, 1975.

Levy, Peter. *America in the Sixties: Left, Right and Center*. Westport, Conn., 1998.

Lewy, Guenter. *America in Vietnam*. Oxford, 1978.

Liang Heng, and Judith Shapiro. *After the Nightmare*. New York, 1986.

Logsdon, John. *The Decision to Go to the Moon*. Chicago, 1970.

Lomax, Michael. "'Curt Flood Stood Up for Us': The Quest to Break Down Racial Barriers and Structural Inequality in Major League Baseball." *Culture, Sport and Society*, 6 (2003).

Lucas, J. Anthony. *Don't Shoot—We Are Your Children*. New York, 1968.

Lunch, William, and Peter Sperlich. "American Public Opinion and the War in Vietnam." *Western Political Quarterly*, 32 (1979).

Lundberg, Ferdinand, and Marynia Farnham. *Modern Woman: The Lost Sex*. New York, 1947.

Lydon, Michael. *Flashbacks*. New York, 2003.

Lynd, Staughton. "The New Left." *Annals of the American Academy of Political and Social Science*, 382 (March 1969).

MacDonald, Peter G. *Giap: The Victor in Vietnam*. New York, 1993.

MacPherson, Myra. *Long Time Passing*. New York, 1984.

Mailer, Norman. *A Fire on the Moon*. New York, 1970.

Maitland, Sara. *Very Heaven: Looking Back at the 1960s*. London, 1998.

Marcus, Eric. *Making History: The Struggle for Gay and Lesbian Equal Rights, 1945–1990*. New York, 1992.

Marcus, Greil. *Like a Rolling Stone: Bob Dylan at the Crossroads*. New York, 2005.

Marcuse, Herbert. *One-Dimensional Man: Studies in the Ideology of Advanced Industrial Society*. New York, 1964.

Marqusee, Mike. *Redemption Song: Muhammad Ali and the Spirit of the Sixties*. London, 2005.

Mars, David. "The Federal Government and Protest." *Annals of the Academy of Political and Social Science*, 382 (March 1969).

May, Elaine Tyler. *Homeward Bound*. New York, 1988.

Mazrui, Ali. "Thoughts on Assassination in Africa." *Political Science Quarterly*, 83 (1968).

McAdam, Doug. *Freedom Summer*. Oxford, 1988.

McCurdy, Howard. *Space and the American Imagination*. Washington, D.C., 1997.

McDougall, Walter. *The Heavens and the Earth*. Baltimore, 1985.

McGill, William J. *The Year of the Monkey*. New York, 1982.

McMahon, Robert. *Major Problems in the History of the Vietnam War*. Lexington, Mass., 1990.

McMaster, Harold. *Dereliction of Duty*. New York, 1997.

McNamara, Robert. *Blundering into Disaster*. New York, 1986.

—— *In Retrospect*. New York, 1995.

McQuaid, Kim. *The Anxious Years: America in the Vietnam-Watergate Era*. New York, 1989.

Melvern, Linda. "Dispatching Lumumba." *New Left Review* (September–October 2001).

Menand, Louis. *American Studies*. New York, 2002.

Menashe, Louis, and Ronald Radosh. *Teach-Ins: USA*. New York, 1967.

Merritt, Richard. "The Student Protest Movement in West Berlin." *Comparative Politics*, 1 (1969).

Mewes, Horst. "The German New Left." *New German Critique*, 1 (1973).

Michener, James. *Kent State: What Happened and Why*. New York, 1971.

Migliore, Daniel. "Theological Table-Talk." *Theology Today* (January 1970).

Miles, Barry. *Hippie*. London, 2003.

Miller, James. *"Democracy Is in the Streets": From Port Huron to the Siege of Chicago*. New York, 1987.

Mitchell, Cleta. "The Rise of America's Two National Pastimes: Baseball and the Law." *Michigan Law Review*, 97 (1999).

Moïse, Edwin. *Tonkin Gulf and the Escalation of the Vietnam War*. Chapel Hill, N.C., 1996.

Moreno, José. "Che Guevara on Guerrilla Warfare: Doctrine, Practice and Evaluation." *Comparative Studies in Society and History*, 12 (1970).

Morgan, Robin. *Going Too Far: The Personal Chronicle of a Feminist*. New York, 1977.

Morris, John. "In the Wake of the 'Flood.'" *Law and Contemporary Problems*, 38 (1973).

Mumford, Lewis. *The City in History*. New York, 1961.

Neville, Richard. *Playpower*. London, 1971.

—— *Hippie Hippie Shake*. London, 1995.

Newfield, Jack. *Robert Kennedy: A Memoir*. New York, 1988.

Newman, John. *JFK and Vietnam*. New York, 1992.

Newton, Huey. *Revolutionary Suicide*. New York, 1995.

Nisbet, Robert. "Who Killed the Student Revolution?" *Encounter*, 32 (1970).

Nixon, Richard. *RN: The Memoirs of Richard Nixon*. New York, 1978.

Nwankwo, Arthur. *Nigeria: The Challenge of Biafra*. London, 1972.

Oberdorfer, Don. *Tet!* New York, 1984.

O'Donnell, Kenneth, and David Powers. *"Johnny, We Hardly Knew Ye."* Boston, 1970.

Oguibe, Olu. "Lessons from the Killing Fields." *Transition,* 77 (1998).

Onwubu, Chukwuemeka. "Ethnic Identity, Political Integration, and National Development: The Igbo Diaspora in Nigeria." *Journal of Modern African Studies,* 13 (1975).

Oren, Michael. *Six Days of War: June 1967 and the Making of the Modern Middle East.* London, 2003.

Parker, Richard, ed. *The Six-Day War: A Retrospective.* Miami, 1996.

Partridge, William. *The Hippie Ghetto: The Natural History of a Subculture.* New York, 1973.

Pas, Niek. "'Bielievers' in de Sixties: De Ontmaskerende Religiositeit van Provo" [Believers in the Sixties: Unmasking the Religiosity of Provo]. *Transparant,* 13 (2002).

—— "Political Art als Provotarisch Wapen: De Expressieve Politiek van Provo, 1965–1967" [Political Art as a Provo Weapon: The Expressive Politics of Provo]. *Spiegel Historiael,* 37 (2002).

——— *Imaazje! De Verbeelding van Provo, 1965–1967* [Imaazje! The Imagination of Provo, 1965–1967]. Amsterdam, 2003.

Paterson, Thomas. *Kennedy's Quest for Victory.* New York, 1989.

Patterson, James. *Grand Expectations: The United States, 1945–1974.* Oxford, 1996.

Pearson, Geoffrey. *Hooligan: A History of Respectable Fears.* London, 1983.

Pellegrino, Joseph, and Joshua Stoff. *Chariots for Apollo.* New York, 1999.

Perry, Charles. *The Haight-Ashbury: A History.* New York, 1984.

Peterson, Richard. "Why 1955? Explaining the Advent of Rock Music." *Popular Music,* 9 (1990).

Petras, James. "Che Guevara and Contemporary Revolutionary Movements." *Latin American Perspectives,* 25 (1998).

Pike, Douglas. *Viet Cong: The Organization and Techniques of the National Liberation Front of South Vietnam.* Cambridge, Mass., 1966.

—— *PAVN: People's Army of Vietnam.* Novato, Calif., 1986.

Pilger, John. *The New Rulers of the World.* London, 2003.

Podhoretz, Norman. "The Know-Nothing Bohemians." *Partisan Review,* 25 (Spring 1958).

Pollock, Bruce. *When the Music Mattered.* New York, 1983.

Poniatowska, Elena. *Massacre in Mexico.* Trans. Helen Lane. New York, 1975.

Ponting, Clive. *Breach of Promise: Labour in Power, 1964–1970.* London, 1989.

Post, Ken. "Is There a Case for Biafra?" *International Affairs,* 44 (January 1968).

—— *Revolution, Socialism and Nationalism in Viet Nam.* 3 vols. Aldershot, U.K., 1989.

Potter, David. *People of Plenty: Economic Abundance and the American Character.* Chicago, 1954.

Powers, Thomas. *Diana: The Making of a Terrorist.* New York, 1971.

—— *Vietnam: The War at Home.* Boston, 1984.

Pu Ning. *Flower Terror: Suffocating Stories of China.* Dumont, N.J., 1999.

Pye, Lucian. "Reassessing the Cultural Revolution." *China Quarterly,* 108 (1986).

Race, Jeffrey. *War Comes to Long An.* Berkeley, 1972.

Raines, Howell. *My Soul Is Rested: Movement Days in the Deep South Remembered.* New York, 1983.

Reader, Keith A., with Khursheed Wadia. *The May 1968 Events in France: Reproductions and Interpretations.* New York, 1993.

Reagan, Ronald. *An American Life.* New York, 1990.

Reeves, Richard. *President Kennedy: Profiles of Power.* New York, 1993.

Reeves, Thomas. *A Question of Character.* Rocklin, Calif., 1997.

Rhodes, Jane. "Fanning the Flames of Racial Discord: The National Press and the Black Panther Party." *Harvard International Journal of Press/Politics,* 4 (1999).

Rhodes, Richard. *The Making of the Atom Bomb.* London, 1986.

——— *Dark Sun: The Making of the Hydrogen Bomb.* New York, 1995.

Riess, Steven. *Major Problems in American Sport History.* Boston, 1997.

Rorabaugh, W. J. *Berkeley at War: The 1960s.* Oxford, 1989.

Ross, Kristin. "Establishing Consensus: May '68 in France as Seen from the 1980s." *Critical Inquiry,* 28 (2002).

Rossman, Michael. *New Age Blues.* New York, 1979.

Roth, Philip. *American Pastoral.* London, 1998.

Rubin, Jerry. *Do It!* New York, 1970.

——— *Growing (Up) at Thirty-Seven.* New York, 1976.

Rudd, Mark. "How a Movie Changed My Life." *Heartland Journal,* 51 (Summer 2005).

Rusk, Dean. *As I Saw It.* New York, 1990.

Rutledge, Leigh. *The Gay Decades: From Stonewall to the Present.* New York, 1992.

Sakharov, Andrei. *Memoirs.* New York, 1990.

Sale, Kirkpatrick. *SDS.* New York, 1973.

Salisbury, Harrison, ed. *The Eloquence of Protest.* Boston, 1972.

Sammons, Jeffrey. *Beyond the Ring: The Role of Boxing in American Society.* Chicago, 1988.

Sandbrook, Dominic. *Never Had It So Good.* London, 2005.

——— *White Heat.* London, 2006.

Saunders, Doris, ed. *The Day They Marched.* Chicago, 1963.

Sayres, Sohnya, et al., eds. *The '60s without Apology.* Minneapolis, 1984.

Schandler, Herbert. *The Unmaking of a President.* Princeton, 1977.

Scheer, Robert. "Who Ripped Off the Park?" *Ramparts,* 8 (August 1969).

Schefter, James. *The Race.* New York, 1999.

Schiffer, Michael. *The Portable Radio in American Life.* Tucson, Ariz., 1991.

——— "Cultural Imperatives and Product Development: The Case of the Shirt-Pocket Radio." *Technology and Culture,* 34 (1993).

Schlesinger, Arthur. *Robert Kennedy and His Times*. New York, 1979.

Schmidtke, Michael. "Cultural Revolution or Culture Shock? Student Radicalism and 1968 in Germany." *South Central Review*, 16 (Spring 2000).

Schneir, Walter, ed. *Telling It Like It Was: The Chicago Riots*. New York, 1969.

Schorr, Daniel. *Staying Tuned: A Life in Journalism*. New York, 1968.

Schram, Stuart. "The Limits of Cataclysmic Change: Reflections on the Place of the 'Great Proletarian Cultural Revolution' in the Political Development of the People's Republic of China." *China Quarterly*, 108 (1986).

Schreiber, E. M. "Opposition to the Vietnam War among American University Students and Faculty." *British Journal of Sociology*, 24 (1973).

—— "Antiwar Demonstrations and American Public Opinion on the War in Vietnam." *British Journal of Sociology*, 27 (1976).

Schuman, Howard. "Two Sources of Antiwar Sentiment in America." *American Journal of Sociology*, 78 (1972).

Schwar, Harriet, and Stanley Shaloff. *Foreign Relations of the United States, 1958–1960, Volume 14: Africa*. Washington, D.C., 1992.

Schwartz, Richard. *Cold War Culture*. New York, 1998.

Scott, Peter. "The United States and the Overthrow of Sukarno, 1965–1967." *Pacific Affairs*, 58 (1985).

Scremin, Glaucio. "Impact of Antitrust Laws on American Professional Team Sports." *Sport Journal*, 7 (2004).

Scrimshaw, Susan. "Women and the Pill: From Panacea to Catalyst." *Family Planning Perspectives*, 13 (1981).

Selvin, Joel. *Summer of Love*. New York, 1994.

Sevy, Grace, ed. *The American Experience in Vietnam*. Norman, Okla., 1989.

Shapley, Deborah. *Promise and Power*. Boston, 1993.

Sheehan, Neil. *A Bright Shining Lie*. London, 1990.

Shell, Kurt. "Extraparliamentary Opposition in Postwar Germany." *Comparative Politics*, 2 (July 1970).

Shelton, Robert. *No Direction Home: The Life and Music of Bob Dylan*. New York, 1986.

Shesol, Jeff. *Mutual Contempt: Lyndon Johnson, Robert Kennedy, and the Feud That Defined a Decade*. New York, 1997.

Sidey, Hugh. *John F. Kennedy, President*. New York, 1964.

Siegfried, Detlef. "'Don't Trust Anyone Older Than 30?' Voices of Conflict and Consensus between Generations in 1960s West Germany." *Journal of Contemporary History*, 40 (2005).

Silber, Irwin. "To Julian Beck, Judith Malina and the Living Theatre." *Drama Review*, 13 (1969).

Silverman, Henry. *American Radical Thought: The Libertarian Tradition*. Lexington, Mass., 1970.

Sinclair, Andrew. *Guevara*. London, 1970.

Sitkoff, Harvard. *The Struggle for Black Equality, 1954–80*. New York, 1981.

Sked, Alan, and Chris Cook. *Post-War Britain: A Political History*. Harmondsworth, U.K., 1979.

Small, Melvin. *Johnson, Nixon and the Doves*. New Brunswick, N.J., 1988.

—— and William Hoover. *Give Peace a Chance*. Syracuse, N.Y., 1992.

Song Yongyi. *Massacres during the Cultural Revolution*. Hong Kong, 2002.

Sorensen, Theodore. *'Let the Word Go Forth': The Speeches, Statements and Writings of John F. Kennedy, 1947–1963*. New York, 1991.

Staub, Michael. "Black Panthers, New Journalism, and the Rewriting of the Sixties." *Representations*, 57 (1997).

Steigerwald, David. *The Sixties and the End of Modern America*. New York, 1995.

Stein, Jean, and George Plimpton, eds. *American Journey: The Life and Times of Robert Kennedy*. New York, 1970.

Steinberg, Blema. *Shame and Humiliation*. Pittsburgh, 1996.

Stevens, Evelyn. *Protest and Response in Mexico*. Boston, 1974.

Stine, Peter. *The Sixties*. Detroit, 1995.

Sun-Childers, Jaia. *The White-Haired Girl: Bittersweet Adventures of a Little Red Soldier*. New York, 1996.

Sundhausen, Ulf. *The Road to Power: Indonesian Military Politics, 1945–1967*. Oxford, 1982.

Swanson, Glen E., ed. *"Before This Decade Is Out. . . .": Personal Reflections on the Apollo Program*. Washington, D.C., 1999.

Szatmary, David. *A Time to Rock*. New York, 1997.

Szulc, Tad. *The Illusion of Peace*. New York, 1978.

Taylor, A. J. P. *A Personal History*. London, 1983.

Taylor, Maxwell. *Swords and Plowshares*. New York, 1972.

Taylor, U. "The Historical Evolution of Black Feminist Theory and Praxis." *Journal of Black Studies*, 29 (1998).

Teodori, Massimo. *The New Left: A Documentary History*. New York, 1969.

Terkel, Studs. *The Good War*. London, 1985.

Thomas, Nick. "Challenging Myths of the 1960s: The Case of Student Protest in Britain." *Twentieth Century British History*, 13 (2002).

Thompson, Hunter. *Fear and Loathing in Las Vegas*. London, 1993.

Titus, A. Constandina. *Bombs in the Backyard*. Reno, Nev., 1986.

Trachtenburg, Mark. "The Berlin Crisis." Paper presented at West Point, 1988.

—— *History and Strategy*. New York, 1991.

Tran Van Don. *Our Endless War*. Novato, Calif., 1978.

Trewhitt, Henry. *McNamara*. New York, 1971.

Truman, Harry. *Years of Decision*. New York, 1955.

Truong Chinh. *Primer for Revolt*. New York, 1963.

Truong Nhu Tang. *A Vietcong Memoir*. San Diego, 1985.

Turner, Kathleen. *Lyndon Johnson's Dual War*. Chicago, 1985.

Ulc, Otto. "Political Participation in Czechoslovakia." *Journal of Politics,* 33 (1971).

Unger, Irwin, and Debi Unger, eds. *The Times Were a Changin': The Sixties Reader.* New York, 1998.

US Department of State. *The Foreign Relations of the United States.* Washington, D.C., various dates.

VanDeMark, Brian. *Into the Quagmire.* New York, 1991.

Van Ginneken, Jaap. *The Rise and Fall of Lin Piao.* London, 1976.

Vecsey, George. *Joy in Mudville.* New York, 1970.

Viel, Benjamin. "The Population Explosion in Latin America." *Proceedings of the Academy of Political Science,* 30 (1972).

Vietnam Day Committee. *We Accuse.* Berkeley, 1965.

Viorst, Milton. *Hustlers and Heroes.* New York, 1971.

—— *Fire in the Streets.* New York, 1979.

Vo Nguyen Giap. *The Military Art of People's War.* New York, 1970.

Vogelgesang, Sandy. *The Long Dark Night of the Soul: The American Intellectual Left and the Vietnam War.* New York, 1974.

Wajcman, Judy. "Delivered into Men's Hands? The Social Construction of Reproductive Technology." In Gita Sen and Rachel C. Snow, eds., *Power and Decision: The Social Control of Reproduction.* Boston: Harvard School of Public Health, Distributed by Harvard University Press, 1994.

Walsh, Patrick. *Echoes among the Stars.* Armonk, N.Y., 2000.

Warbey, William. *Ho Chi Minh.* London, 1972.

Washington, James, ed. *A Testament of Hope: The Essential Writings and Speeches of Martin Luther King, Jr.* New York, 1991.

Weiner, Rex, and Deanne Stillman. *Woodstock Census.* New York, 1979.

Weisbord, R. G. "Birth Control and the Black American: A Matter of Genocide?" *Demography,* 10 (1973).

Wells, Tom. *The War Within.* Berkeley, 1994.

Werner, Jayne, and Luu Doan Huynh, eds. *The Vietnam War: Vietnamese and American Perspectives.* Armonk, N.Y., 1993.

Westmoreland, William. *A Soldier Reports.* Garden City, N.Y., 1976.

Westoff, Charles, and Norman Ryder. "United States: The Papal Encyclical and Catholic Practice and Attitudes." *Studies in Family Planning,* 1 (1970).

Whitburn, Joel. *The Billboard Book of Top 40 Hits.* New York, 1987.

White, Theodore. *The Making of the President 1964.* New York, 1966.

—— *The Making of the President 1968.* New York, 1969.

Will, George. *Bunts.* New York, 1998.

Williams, Robert, and Philip Cantelon, eds. *The American Atom.* Philadelphia, 1984.

Williams, William, et al., eds. *America in Vietnam: A Documentary History.* New York, 1975.

Wills, Garry. *The Kennedy Imprisonment.* New York, 1982.

—— *Reagan's America.* New York, 1988.

Wilson, Frank. "The French Left and the Elections of 1968." *World Politics,* 21 (1969).

Windt, Theodore. *Presidents and Protesters.* Tuscaloosa, Ala., 1990.

Wirtz, James J. *The Tet Offensive: Intelligence Failure in War.* Ithaca, N.Y., 1991.

Witcover, Jules. *The Year the Dream Died.* New York, 1997.

Wolf, Leonard. *Voices from the Love Generation.* New York, 1968.

Wolfe, Tom. *The Right Stuff.* London, 1991.

Young, Alfred, ed. *Dissent: Explorations in the History of American Radicalism.* DeKalb, Ill., 1968.

Young, Marilyn. *The Vietnam Wars, 1945–1990.* New York, 1991.

Young, Nigel. *An Infantile Disorder? The Crisis and Decline of the New Left.* London, 1977.

Zaroulis, Nancy, and Gerald Sullivan. *Who Spoke Up?* New York, 1984.

Zhai Zhenhua. *Red Flower of China.* New York, 1992.

Zolov, Eric. "Protest and Counterculture in the 1968 Student Movement in Mexico." In DeGroot, ed., *Student Protest.* London, 1998.

Newspapers and Magazines

Air and Space

The Argus (Brighton, England)

Atlantic Monthly

Bakersfield Californian

Beat Scene (Coventry, England)

Berkeley Barb

Berkeley Gazette

Berkeley Tribe

Black Panther (Oakland, California)

Bulletin of the Atomic Scientists

Chesterton Tribune

Christian Science Monitor

Consumer Reports

Daily Californian

Daily Mail

Daily Mirror

Daily News

Dialogue Magazine

Entertainment Weekly

Epoch Times (New York)

Esquire

Evening Standard

Evening Star

Financial Times

Free Press (Los Angeles)

George

Globe and Mail

The Guardian

Hard Times

High Times

Holiday

Houston Chronicle

Humanity

I. F. Stone's Bi-Weekly

The Independent

International Herald Tribune

IT

Life

London Review of Books

Los Angeles Times

Manchester Guardian

The Militant

Mojo (London)

Montgomery Advertiser

The Movement

The Nation

New Left Notes

New Left Review

New Republic
New Statesman
Newsweek
New Yorker
New York Times
New York Times Magazine
Oakland Tribune
The Observer
Oz (London)
Radio Times
Ramparts
Rolling Stone
Sacramento Bee
San Diego Union
San Francisco Chronicle
San Francisco Examiner

Saturday Evening Post
Scholastic
Scotland on Sunday
The Seed (Chicago)
Sports Illustrated
The Sun
Sunday Examiner and Chronicle
Sunday Mail
Sunday Times
Time
The Times
TV Guide
US News and World Report
Village Voice
Washington Post

Videos and DVDs

Don't Look Back. Sony BMG, 2000.
Gimme Shelter. Criterion, 2000.
Hard Day's Night. Buena Vista Home Entertainment, 2002.
It Was Twenty Years Ago Today. Granada, 1987.
No Direction Home. Paramount Home Entertainment, 2005.
The Weather Underground. Free History Project, 2003.
When We Were Kings. Universal Pictures, 1996.

INDEX

PHOTOGRAPHIC CREDITS